D0535719

SHORT STORIES
for Students

Advisors

Jayne M. Burton is a teacher of secondary English and an adjunct professor for Northwest Vista College in San Antonio, TX.

Klaudia Janek is the school librarian at the International Academy in Bloomfield Hills, Michigan. She holds an MLIS degree from Wayne State University, a teaching degree from Rio Salado College, and a bachelor of arts degree in international relations from Saint Joseph's College. She is the IB Extended Essay Coordinator and NCA AdvancEd co-chair at her school. She is an IB workshop leader for International Baccalaureate North America, leading teacher training for IB school librarians and extended essay coordinators. She has been happy to serve the Michigan Association for Media in Education as a board member and past president at the regional level, advocating for libraries in Michigan schools.

Greg Bartley is an English teacher in Virginia. He holds an M.A.Ed. in English Education from Wake Forest University and a B.S. in Integrated Language Arts Education from Miami University.

Sarah Clancy teaches IB English at the International Academy in Bloomfield Hills, Michigan. She is a member of the National Council of Teachers of English and Michigan Speech Coaches, Inc. Sarah earned her undergraduate degree from Kalamazoo College and her Master's of Education from Florida Southern College. She coaches the high-ranking forensics team and is the staff adviser of the school newspaper, *Overachiever*.

Karen Dobson is a teen/adult librarian at Plymouth District Library in Plymouth, Michigan. She holds a Bachelor of Science degree from Oakland University and an MLIS from Wayne State University and has served on many committees through the Michigan Library Association.

Tom Shilts is the youth librarian at the Okemos branch of Capital Area District Library in Okemos, Michigan. He holds an MSLS degree from Clarion University of Pennsylvania and an MA in U.S. History from the University of North Dakota.

SHORT STORIES

for Students

Presenting Analysis, Context, and Criticism
on Commonly Studied Short Stories

VOLUME 43

Matthew Derda, Project Editor

Foreword by Thomas E. Barden

GALE
CENGAGE Learning·

Farmington Hills, Mich • San Francisco • New York • Waterville, Maine
Meriden, Conn • Mason, Ohio • Chicago

151.00

GALE
CENGAGE Learning®

Short Stories for Students, Volume 43

Project Editor: Matthew Derda

Rights Acquisition and Management: Moriam Aigoro

Composition: Evi Abou-El-Seoud

Manufacturing: Rhonda A. Dover

Imaging: John Watkins

Product Design: Pamela A. E. Galbreath, Jennifer Wahi

Digital Content Production: Edna Shy

Gale
27500 Drake Rd.
Farmington Hills, MI, 48331-3535

ISBN-13: 978-1-4103-1592-2

ISSN 1092-7735

This title is also available as an e-book.
ISBN-13: 978-1-4103-1594-6
Contact your Gale, a part of Cengage Learning sales representative for ordering information.

Printed in Mexico
1 2 3 4 5 6 7 20 19 18 17 16

✓

Table of Contents

Why Study Literature At All?

Short Stories for Students is designed to provide readers with information and discussion about a wide range of important contemporary and historical works of short fiction, and it does that job very well. However, I want to use this guest foreword to address a question that it does *not* take up. It is a fundamental question that is often ignored in high school and college English classes as well as research texts, and one that causes frustration among students at all levels, namely why study literature at all? Isn't it enough to read a story, enjoy it, and go about one's business? My answer (to be expected from a literary professional, I suppose) is no. It is not enough. It is a start; but it is not enough. Here's why.

First, literature is the only part of the educational curriculum that deals directly with the actual world of lived experience. The philosopher Edmund Husserl used the apt German term *die Lebenswelt*, "the living world," to denote this realm. All the other content areas of the modern American educational system avoid the subjective, present reality of everyday life. Science (both the natural and the social varieties) objectifies, the fine arts create and/or perform, history reconstructs. Only literary study persists in posing those questions we all asked before our schooling taught us to give up on them. Only literature gives credibility to personal perceptions, feelings, dreams, and the "stream of consciousness" that is our inner voice. Literature wonders about infinity, wonders why God permits evil, wonders what will happen to us after we die. Literature admits that we get our hearts broken, that people sometimes cheat and get away with it, that the world is a strange and probably incomprehensible place. Literature, in other words, takes on all the big and small issues of what it means to be human. So my first answer is that of the humanist we should read literature and study it and take it seriously because it enriches us as human beings. We develop our moral imagination, our capacity to sympathize with other people, and our ability to understand our existence through the experience of fiction.

My second answer is more practical. By studying literature we can learn how to explore and analyze texts. Fiction may be about *die Lebenswelt*, but it is a construct of words put together in a certain order by an artist using the medium of language. By examining and studying those constructions, we can learn about language as a medium. We can become more sophisticated about word associations and connotations, about the manipulation of symbols, and about style and atmosphere. We can grasp how ambiguous language is and how important context and texture is to meaning. In our first encounter with a work of literature, of course, we are not supposed to catch all of these things. We are spellbound, just as the writer wanted us to be. It is as serious students of the writer's art that we begin to see how the tricks are done.

Seeing the tricks, which is another way of saying "developing analytical and close reading skills," is important above and beyond its intrinsic literary educational value. These skills transfer to other fields and enhance critical thinking of any kind. Understanding how language is used to construct texts is powerful knowledge. It makes engineers better problem solvers, lawyers better advocates and courtroom practitioners, politicians better rhetoricians, marketing and advertising agents better sellers, and citizens more aware consumers as well as better participants in democracy. This last point is especially important, because rhetorical skill works both ways when we learn how language is manipulated in the making of texts the result is that we become less susceptible when language is used to manipulate us.

My third reason is related to the second. When we begin to see literature as created artifacts of language, we become more sensitive to good writing in general. We get a stronger sense of the importance of individual words, even the sounds of words and word combinations. We begin to understand Mark Twain's delicious proverb "The difference between the right word and the almost right word is the difference between lightning and a lightning bug." Getting beyond the "enjoyment only" stage of literature gets us closer to becoming makers of word art ourselves. I am not saying that studying fiction will turn every student into a Faulkner or a Shakespeare. But it will make us more adaptable and effective writers, even if our art form ends up being the office memo or the corporate annual report.

Studying short stories, then, can help students become better readers, better writers, and even better human beings. But I want to close with a warning. If your study and exploration of the craft, history, context, symbolism, or anything else about a story starts to rob it of the magic you felt when you first read it, it is time to stop. Take a break, study another subject, shoot some hoops, or go for a run. Love of reading is too important to be ruined by school. The early twentieth century writer Willa Cather, in her novel *My Antonia*, has her narrator Jack Burden tell a story that he and Antonia heard from two old Russian immigrants when they were teenagers. These immigrants, Pavel and Peter, told about an incident from their youth back in Russia that the narrator could recall in vivid detail thirty years later. It was a harrowing story of a wedding party starting home in sleds and being chased by starving wolves. Hundreds of wolves attacked the group's sleds one by one as they sped across the snow trying to reach their village. In a horrible revelation, the old Russians revealed that the groom eventually threw his own bride to the wolves to save himself. There was even a hint that one of the old immigrants might have been the groom mentioned in the story. Cather has her narrator conclude with his feelings about the story. "We did not tell Pavel's secret to anyone, but guarded it jealously as if the wolves of the Ukraine had gathered that night long ago, and the wedding party had been sacrificed, just to give us a painful and peculiar pleasure." That feeling, that painful and peculiar pleasure, is the most important thing about literature. Study and research should enhance that feeling and never be allowed to overwhelm it.

Thomas E. Barden
Professor of English and Director of
Graduate English Studies, The
University of Toledo

Introduction

Purpose of the Book

The purpose of *Short Stories for Students* (*SSfS*) is to provide readers with a guide to understanding, enjoying, and studying short stories by giving them easy access to information about the work. Part of Gale's "For Students" Literature line, *SSfS* is specifically designed to meet the curricular needs of high school and undergraduate college students and their teachers, as well as the interests of general readers and researchers considering specific short fiction. While each volume contains entries on "classic" stories frequently studied in classrooms, there are also entries containing hard-to-find information on contemporary stories, including works by multicultural, international, and women writers.

The information covered in each entry includes an introduction to the story and the story's author; a plot summary, to help readers unravel and understand the events in the work; descriptions of important characters, including explanation of a given character's role in the narrative as well as discussion about that character's relationship to other characters in the story; analysis of important themes in the story; and an explanation of important literary techniques and movements as they are demonstrated in the work.

In addition to this material, which helps the readers analyze the story itself, students are also provided with important information on the literary and historical background informing each work. This includes a historical context essay, a box comparing the time or place the story was written to modern Western culture, a critical overview essay, and excerpts from critical essays on the story or author. A unique feature of *SSfS* is a specially commissioned critical essay on each story, targeted toward the student reader.

To further help today's student in studying and enjoying each story, information on audiobooks and other media adaptations is provided (if available), as well as reading suggestions for works of fiction and nonfiction on similar themes and topics. Classroom aids include ideas for research papers and lists of critical and reference sources that provide additional material on the work.

Selection Criteria

The titles for each volume of *SSfS* were selected by surveying numerous sources on teaching literature and analyzing course curricula for various school districts. Some of the sources surveyed include: literature anthologies, *Reading Lists for College-Bound Students: The Books Most Recommended by America's Top Colleges*; *Teaching the Short Story: A Guide to Using Stories from around the World*, by the National Council of Teachers of English (NCTE); and "A Study of High School Literature Anthologies," conducted by Arthur Applebee at the Center for the Learning and Teaching of Literature and sponsored by the

National Endowment for the Arts and the Office of Educational Research and Improvement.

Input was also solicited from our advisory board, as well as educators from various areas. From these discussions, it was determined that each volume should have a mix of "classic" stories (those works commonly taught in literature classes) and contemporary stories for which information is often hard to find. Because of the interest in expanding the canon of literature, an emphasis was also placed on including works by international, multicultural, and women authors. Our advisory board members—educational professionals—helped pare down the list for each volume. Works not selected for the present volume were noted as possibilities for future volumes. As always, the editor welcomes suggestions for titles to be included in future volumes.

How Each Entry Is Organized

Each entry, or chapter, in *SSfS* focuses on one story. Each entry heading lists the title of the story, the author's name, and the date of the story's publication. The following elements are contained in each entry:

Introduction: a brief overview of the story which provides information about its first appearance, its literary standing, any controversies surrounding the work, and major conflicts or themes within the work.

Author Biography: this section includes basic facts about the author's life, and focuses on events and times in the author's life that may have inspired the story in question.

Plot Summary: a description of the events in the story. Lengthy summaries are broken down with subheads.

Characters: an alphabetical listing of the characters who appear in the story. Each character name is followed by a brief to an extensive description of the character's role in the story, as well as discussion of the character's actions, relationships, and possible motivation.

Characters are listed alphabetically by last name. If a character is unnamed—for instance, the narrator in "The Eatonville Anthology"—the character is listed as "The Narrator" and alphabetized as "Narrator." If a character's first name is the only one given, the name will appear alphabetically by that name.

Themes: a thorough overview of how the topics, themes, and issues are addressed within the story. Each theme discussed appears in a separate subhead.

Style: this section addresses important style elements of the story, such as setting, point of view, and narration; important literary devices used, such as imagery, foreshadowing, symbolism; and, if applicable, genres to which the work might have belonged, such as Gothicism or Romanticism. Literary terms are explained within the entry, but can also be found in the Glossary.

Historical Context: this section outlines the social, political, and cultural climate in which the author lived and the work was created. This section may include descriptions of related historical events, pertinent aspects of daily life in the culture, and the artistic and literary sensibilities of the time in which the work was written. If the story is historical in nature, information regarding the time in which the story is set is also included. Long sections are broken down with helpful subheads.

Critical Overview: this section provides background on the critical reputation of the author and the story, including bannings or any other public controversies surrounding the work. For older works, this section may include a history of how the story was first received and how perceptions of it may have changed over the years; for more recent works, direct quotes from early reviews may also be included.

Criticism: an essay commissioned by *SSfS* which specifically deals with the story and is written specifically for the student audience, as well as excerpts from previously published criticism on the work (if available).

Sources: an alphabetical list of critical material used in compiling the entry, with bibliographical information.

Further Reading: an alphabetical list of other critical sources which may prove useful for the student. Includes full bibliographical information and a brief annotation.

Suggested Search Terms: a list of search terms and phrases to jumpstart students' further information seeking. Terms include not just titles and author names but also terms and topics related to the historical and literary context of the works.

In addition, each entry contains the following highlighted sections, set apart from the main text as sidebars:

Media Adaptations: if available, a list of audiobooks and important film and television adaptations of the story, including source information. The list also includes stage adaptations, musical adaptations, etc.

Topics for Further Study: a list of potential study questions or research topics dealing with the story. This section includes questions related to other disciplines the student may be studying, such as American history, world history, science, math, government, business, geography, economics, psychology, etc.

Compare and Contrast: an "at-a-glance" comparison of the cultural and historical differences between the author's time and culture and late twentieth century or early twenty-first century Western culture. This box includes pertinent parallels between the major scientific, political, and cultural movements of the time or place the story was written, the time or place the story was set (if a historical work), and modern Western culture. Works written after 1990 may not have this box.

What Do I Read Next?: a list of works that might give a reader points of entry into a classic work (e.g., YA or multicultural titles) and/ or complement the featured story or serve as a contrast to it. This includes works by the same author and others, works from various genres, YA works, and works from various cultures and eras.

Other Features

SSfS includes "Why Study Literature At All?," a foreword by Thomas E. Barden, Professor of English and Director of Graduate English Studies at the University of Toledo. This essay provides a number of very fundamental reasons for studying literature and, therefore, reasons why a book such as *SSfS*, designed to facilitate the study of literature, is useful.

A Cumulative Author/Title Index lists the authors and titles covered in each volume of the *SSfS* series.

A Cumulative Nationality/Ethnicity Index breaks down the authors and titles covered in each volume of the *SSfS* series by nationality and ethnicity.

A Subject/Theme Index, specific to each volume, provides easy reference for users who may be studying a particular subject or theme rather than a single work. Significant subjects from events to broad themes are included.

Each entry may include illustrations, including photo of the author, stills from film adaptations (if available), maps, and/or photos of key historical events.

Citing Short Stories for Students

When writing papers, students who quote directly from any volume of *SSfS* may use the following general forms to document their source. These examples are based on MLA style; teachers may request that students adhere to a different style, thus, the following examples may be adapted as needed.

When citing text from *SSfS* that is not attributed to a particular author (for example, the Themes, Style, Historical Context sections, etc.), the following format may be used:

"How I Met My Husband." *Short Stories for Students*. Ed. Sara Constantakis. Vol. 36. Detroit: Gale, Cengage Learning, 2013. 73–95. Print.

When quoting the specially commissioned essay from *SSfS* (usually the first essay under the Criticism subhead), the following format may be used:

Dominic, Catherine. Critical Essay on "How I Met My Husband." *Short Stories for Students*. Ed. Sara Constantakis. Vol. 36. Detroit: Gale, Cengage Learning, 2013. 84–87. Print.

When quoting a journal or newspaper essay that is reprinted in a volume of *SSfS*, the following form may be used:

Ditsky, John. "The Figure in the Linoleum: The Fictions of Alice Munro." *Hollins Critic* 22.3 (1985): 1–10. Rpt. in *Short Stories for Students*. Vol. 36. Ed. Sara Constantakis. Detroit: Gale, Cengage Learning, 2013. 92–94. Print.

When quoting material from a book that is reprinted in a volume of *SSfS,* the following form may be used:

Cooke, John. "Alice Munro." *The Influence of Painting on Five Canadian Writers*. Lewiston, NY: Edwin Mellen Press, 1996. 69–85. Rpt. in *Short Stories for Students*. Vol. 36. Ed. Sara Constantakis. Detroit: Gale, Cengage Learning, 2013. 89–92. Print.

We Welcome Your Suggestions

The editorial staff of *Short Stories for Students* welcomes your comments and ideas. Readers who wish to suggest short stories to appear in future volumes, or who have other suggestions, are cordially invited to contact the editor. You may contact the editor via E-mail at: **ForStudentsEditors@cengage.com.** Or write to the editor at:

Editor, *Short Stories for Students*
Gale
27500 Drake Road
Farmington Hills, MI 48331-3535

Literary Chronology

1809: Nikolay Gogol is born on March 19 in Poltava, Russia.

1821: Fyodor Dostoyevsky is born on October 30 in Moscow, Russia.

1835: Nikolay Gogol's "The Diary of a Madman" is published in Russian in *Arabesques*. It is published in English in 1895 in *The Humor of Russia*.

1842: Ambrose Bierce is born on June 24 in Meigs County, Ohio.

1852: Nikolay Gogol dies on March 4 in Moscow, Russia.

1877: Fyodor Dostoyevsky's "Son smeshnogo cheloveka" is published in *Dnevnik pisatelya*. It is later published in English as "The Dream of a Ridiculous Man."

ca. 1880–1885: Anzia Yezierska is born in Plinsk, Poland.

1881: Fyodor Dostoyevsky dies of a lung hemorrhage on January 28 in St. Petersburg, Russia.

1882: Jessie Redmon Fauset is born on April 27 in Snow Hill Center, New Jersey.

1888: Katherine Mansfield is born on October 14, in Wellington, New Zealand.

1899: Jorge Luis Borges is born on August 24 in Buenos Aires, Argentina.

1907: Ambrose Bierce's "The Moonlit Road" is published in *Cosmopolitan*.

1912: Jessie Redmon Fauset's "Emmy" is published in part in the *Crisis*; the second part is published in 1913.

ca. 1913–1914: Ambrose Bierce disappears sometime after December 26, 1913, somewhere in northern Mexico.

1920: Anzia Yezierska's "The Fat of the Land" is published in *Hungry Hearts*.

1922: Katherine Mansfield's "The Fly" is published in *Nation*.

1923: Katherine Mansfield dies of a pulmonary hemorrhage on January 9, in Fontainebleau, France.

1927: Ruth Prawer Jhabvala is born on May 7 in Cologne, Germany.

1931: Alice Munro is born on July 31 in Wingham, Ontario.

1940: Frank Chin is born on February 25 in Berkeley, California.

1946: Tim O'Brien is born on October 1 in Austin, Minnesota.

1947: Jorge Luis Borges's "The Zahir" is published in Spanish as "El Zahir." It is published in English in 1962 in *Labyrinths: SelectedStoriesand Other Writings*.

1947: Patricia Henley is born in Terre Haute, Indiana.

1948: T. Coraghessan Boyle is born December 2 in Peekskill, New York.

1949: Jamaica Kincaid is born on May 25 in St. John's, Antigua.

1961: Jessie Redmon Fauset dies of heart failure on April 30 in Philadelphia, Pennsylvania.

1970: Anzia Yezierska dies of a stroke on November 21 in Ontario, California.

1975: Ruth Prawer Jhabvala is awarded the Booker Prize for *Heat and Dust*.

1978: Frank Chin's "Railroad Standard Time" is published in *City Lights Journal*.

1983: Jamaica Kincaid's "Blackness" is published in *At the Bottom of the River*.

1986: Jorge Luis Borges dies of liver cancer on June 14 in Geneva, Switzerland.

1988: T. Coraghessan Boyle's "Sinking House" is published in *Atlantic*.

1990: Patricia Henley's "The Secret of Cartwheels" is published in *Atlantic Monthly*.

1990: Tim O'Brien's "Sweetheart of Song Tra Bong" is published in *The Things They Carried*.

1993: Alice Munro's "Open Secrets" is published in *New Yorker*.

2003: Ruth Prawer Jhabvala's "Refuge in London" is published in *Zoetrope*.

2013: Ruth Prawer Jhabvala dies of complications from a pulmonary disorder on April 3 in New York, New York.

2013: Alice Munro is awarded the Nobel Prize in Literature for *The Stone Diaries*.

Acknowledgements

The editors wish to thank the copyright holders of the excerpted criticism included in this volume and the permissions managers of many book and magazine publishing companies for assisting us in securing reproduction rights. We are also grateful to the staffs of the Detroit Public Library, the Library of Congress, the University of Detroit Mercy Library, Wayne State University Purdy/Kresge Library Complex, and the University of Michigan Libraries for making their resources available to us. Following is a list of the copyright holders who have granted us permission to reproduce material in this volume of *SSfS*. Every effort has been made to trace copyright, but if omissions have been made, please let us know.

COPYRIGHTED EXCERPTS IN SSfS, VOLUME 43, WERE REPRODUCED FROM THE FOLLOWING PERIODICALS:

Booklist, 94. 22, August 1998. Copyright © 1998 American Library Association. Reproduced by permission.—*The Guardian*, October 27, 2000. http://guardian.co.uk. Copyright © 2000 *Guardian*. Reproduced by permission.—*Independent*, July 9, 2004, Copyright © 2004 Independent Publishing Ltd. Reproduced by permission.—*Journal of New Zealand Literature*, 2., 32, 11/2014. Copyright © 2014 *Journal of New Zealand Literature*.. Reproduced by permission.—*MELUS*, 24., 4, Winter 1999. Copyright © 1999 Oxford University Press. Reproduced by permission.—*Nation*, 8, 263, September 23, 1996. Copyright © 1996 *Nation*. Reproduced by permission.—*Publishers Weekly*, 8., 238, February 8, 1991. Copyright © 1991 *Publishers Weekly*.. Reproduced by permission.—*Publishers Weekly*, 241., 34, August 22, 1994. Copyright © 1994 *Publishers Weekly*.. Reproduced by permission.—*Publishers Weekly*, 245., 4, June 15, 1998. Copyright © 1998 *Publisher's Weekly*.. Reproduced by permission.—*Publishers Weekly*, 6., 246, February 8, 1999. Copyright © 1999 *Publishers Weekly*.. Reproduced by permission.—*Publishers Weekly*, 33., 247, August 14, 2000. Copyright © 2000 *Publishers Weekly*.. Reproduced by permission.—*Spectator*, July 8, 2006. Copyright © 2006 *Spectator*.. Reproduced by permission.—*Studies in Short Fiction*, 4., 3, Fall 1994. Copyright © 1994 Newberry College. Reproduced by permission.—*Studies in Short Fiction*, 2., 31, Spring 1994. Copyright © 1994 Newberry College. Reproduced by permission.

COPYRIGHTED EXCERPTS IN SSfS, VOLUME 43, WERE REPRODUCED FROM THE FOLLOWING BOOKS:

Alazraki, Jaime. From *Critical Essays on Jorge Luis Borges*. Gale/GK Hall, 1987. Copyright © Gale/Cengage Learning. Reproduced by permission.—Bateson, F.W.and B. Shahevitch. From *The Critical Response to Katherine Mansfield*. Santa Barbara, CA: Greenwood Press, 1996. Copyright © Greenwood Press. Reproduced by permission.—Braziel, Jana Evans.

From *Caribbean Genesis: Jamaica Kincaid and the Writing of New Worlds*. State University of New York Press. 2009 Copyright © 2009, State University of New York Press. Reproduced by permission.—Calloway, Licia Morrow. From *Black Family (Dys)Function in Novels*. Jessie Fauset, Nella Larsen and Fannie Hurst. Peter Lang International Academic Publishers, 2003. Copyright © Peter Lang International Academic Publishers. Reproduced by permission.—Daly, Saralyn R. From *Katherine Mansfield*. Twayne/ Gale. Copyright © Gale/Cengage Learning. Reproduced by permission.—Davidson, Cathy. From *Critical Essays on Ambrose Bierce*. GK Hall, 1982, 1-4. Copyright © G.K. Hall. Reproduced by permission.—Davidson, Cathy. From *The Experimental Fictions of Ambrose Bierce*. University of Nebraska Press, 1984. Copyright © University of Nebraska Press. Reproduced by permission.—Feuer, Robin. From *Dostoevsky's Unfinished Journey*. Yale University Press, 2007. Copyright © 2007, Yale University Press. Reproduced by permission.—Gleason, Paul. *Understanding T.C. Boyle*. University of South Carolina Press, 2009. Copyright © Uni-versity of South Carolina Press. Reproduced by permission.—Grenander, M.E. From *Ambrose Bierce*. Gale/Twayne, 1971. Copyright © Gale/ Cengage Learning. Reproduced by permission.— Herzog, Tobey C. From *Tim O'Brien*. Gale/ Twayne, 1997. Copyright © Gale/Cengage Learning. Reproduced by permission.—Lindberg-Seyersted, Brita. From *Black and Female: Essays on Writing by Black Women in the Diaspo-ra*. Scandinavian University Press, 1994. Copyright © 1994, Scandinavian University Press. Reproduced by permission.—Ling, Jinqi. From *Asian American Literature*. Oxford University Press, 1998. Copyright © Oxford University Press. Reproduced by permission.—Kaplan, Steven. From *Understanding Tim O'Brien*. University of South Carolina 1995. Copyright © University of South Carolina. Reproduced by permission.— Shapiro, Gavriel. From *Nikolai Gogol and the Baroque Cultural Heritage*. 1993. Copyright 1993 Penn-sylvania State University Press. Reproduced by permission.—Shoup, Barbara and Margaret-Love Denman. From *Novel Ideas: Contemporary Authors Share the Creative Process*. University of Georgia Press, 2009. Copyright © University of Georgia Press. Reproduced by permission.—Zeldin, Jesse. From *Nikolai Gogol's Quest for Beauty: An Exploration into His Works*. University Press of Kansas, 1978. Copyright © University Press of Kansas. Reproduced by permission.

Contributors

Bryan Aubrey: Aubrey holds a PhD in English. Entry on "The Fly." Original essay on "The Fly."

Rita M. Brown: Brown is an English professor. Entry on "Diary of a Madman." Original essay on "Diary of a Madman."

Jennifer Bussey: Bussey is an independent writer specializing in literature. Entry on "Sweetheart of the Song Tra Bong." Original essay on "Sweetheart of the Song Tra Bong."

Klay Dyer: Dyer is a freelance writer specializing in topics relating to literature, popular culture, and the relationship between creativity and technology. Entry on "Open Secrets." Original essay on "Open Secrets."

Kristen Sarlin Greenberg: Greenberg is a freelance writer and editor with a background in literature and philosophy. Entry on "The Fat of the Land." Original essay on "The Fat of the Land."

Michael Allen Holmes: Holmes is a writer with existential interests. Entries on "The Dream of a Ridiculous Man," "Emmy," and "Railroad Standard Time." Original essays on "The Dream of a Ridiculous Man," "Emmy," and "Railroad Standard Time."

David Kelly: Kelly is an instructor of creative writing and literature at a college in Illinois. Entries on "Refuge in London" and "Sinking House." Original essays on "Refuge in London" and "Sinking House."

Amy L. Miller: Miller is a graduate of the University of Cincinnati, and she currently resides in New Orleans, Louisiana. Entries on "Blackness" and "The Secret of Cartwheels." Original essays on "Blackness" and "The Secret of Cartwheels."

Michael J. O'Neal: O'Neal holds a PhD in English. Entry on "The Moonlit Road." Original essay on "The Moonlit Road."

Bradley Skeen: Skeen is a classicist. Entry on "The Zahir." Original essay on "The Zahir."

Blackness

JAMAICA KINCAID
1983

Jamaica Kincaid's short story "Blackness," from her 1983 collection *At the Bottom of the River*, uses ephemeral images of light and dark and a set of surreal characters to explore the meaning of blackness in the life of the narrator. In four dreamlike sections, Kincaid describes the narrator: a woman born of, made of, and surrounded by blackness; a victim of soldiers who shut out the light; a single mother to a confident, monstrous child; and a follower of the silent voice that shuts out the blackness for good. As beautiful as it is difficult to comprehend, "Blackness" resists easy interpretation, forcing readers to forge their own path through a tangle of metaphors, symbols, and fantasy. The text used for this essay is from *At the Bottom of the River*, Farrar, Straus, and Giroux, 2000.

AUTHOR BIOGRAPHY

Kincaid was born May 25, 1949, in St. John's, Antigua. Born Elaine Potter Richardson, Kincaid was raised primarily by her mother, Annie Drew, with whom she had a difficult relationship, and her stepfather, David Drew. Kincaid had little contact with her biological father, Frederick Potter. Kincaid learned to read at age three, but after the birth of her three half-brothers in 1958, 1959, and 1961, her mother insisted she focus on learning traditional housekeeping rather than

Jamaica Kincaid (© *Sueddeutsche Zeitung Photo | Alamy*)

pursuing an education. In school, Kincaid was a troublemaker who was forced to memorize passages from John Milton's *Paradise Lost* as punishment for her misbehavior.

In 1965, at the age of sixteen, in order to support her ailing stepfather, Kincaid moved to New York City to work as an au pair in the home of Michael Arlen, a *New Yorker* writer. She earned her high school diploma and attended community college, as well as studying photography. In 1973, in order to better represent her Caribbean background in her writing for various magazines, including *Art Direction*, *Ms.*, *Ingenue*, and *Village Voice*, she changed her name to Jamaica Kincaid. In 1976, she became a staff writer for the *New Yorker*, contributing to the "Talk of the Town" and penning a gardening column in which she reflected on her childhood in Antigua. She was married in 1979 to Allen Shawn, a professor at Bennington College in Vermont and son of the *New Yorker*'s longtime editor William Shawn, with whom she had two children.

Kincaid's short-story collection *At the Bottom of the River* was published in 1983, establishing Kincaid as an influential new author. Of the ten collected stories, only "Blackness" was previously unpublished, the rest having appeared in the *New*

Yorker. In 1984, *At the Bottom of the River* was awarded the Morton Dauwen Zabel Award from the American Academy of Arts and Letters and was short-listed for the PEN/Faulkner Award for Fiction.

In 1985, Kincaid published her first novel, *Annie John*, a Caribbean coming-of-age novel. In 1987, she returned to Antigua for the first time since leaving. The trip was disastrous in that it led to her informal banning from the island, but it marked a turning point in her writing, which took on a more direct tone. *A Small Place*, an antitourism essay published in 1988, recounts her reunification with the island. In 1990, Kincaid published *Lucy*, a novel based on her experiences as an au pair for the Arlen family, followed by *The Autobiography of My Mother* in 1996 and *My Brother*, a nonfiction account of her experience of her brother's death, in 1997. In 2001, she published *Talk Stories* and *My Garden Book*, two works of nonfiction, followed in 2005 by *Among the Flowers: A Walk in the Himalayas*. She published two additional novels: *Mr. Potter* (2002) and *See Now and Then* (2013). Her awards include two honorary doctorate degrees from Tufts University and Brandeis University, a Prix Femina Étranger, a Guggenheim Fellowship, a Lannan Literary Award for Fiction, and a Lila Wallace Reader's Digest Writers Award.

PLOT SUMMARY

"Blackness" begins with the unnamed narrator describing the softness of blackness as it falls. Though it is silent, blackness is deafening because there is no other sound. Blackness falls like soot from a candlewick. Black is visible in its invisibility because the narrator can see that she cannot see it. Blackness can fill any space: a room, a field, an island, even the narrator herself. Blackness brings her no joy, but she often finds herself happy while immersed in it. She cannot be separated from blackness, though she can observe it from the outside. Blackness is not air, earth, water, or food, yet the narrator breathes it, walks on it, and consumes it. It is not her blood, but it moves in her veins. The blackness enters the narrator, consuming her memories, erasing her form, until she joins a free-form, floating mass of matter. She no longer can speak her own name or identify herself as "I." She has no voice. Before, she was an individual, keeping abstraction at bay in favor an existence based on concrete fact. Once absorbed into the blackness, she becomes the chaos she wished to escape.

Her daily life contains moments of joy: looking up at the clear sky, a red ball tossed between the hands of a laughing child, and the beauty of the setting sun. The peace of this world is destroyed by the narrator's demanding nature. A voice asks if she can have her bread without the crust. A voice complains that she stopped liking bread without the crust long ago.

The narrator's heart is full to bursting with emotions, triggered by any random event in her life. Once, the narrator was frightened to notice a strange object, not recognizing at first that it was a part of her own foot. She was struck by the power of the moment in which she did not recognize herself, feeling as if she were separate. She compares the sensation to a shattered object—each of its fractured parts unaware of the others. Unsettled, the narrator held on to something familiar, her lantern, until the violent waves of her thoughts grew calm. The narrator questions her nature. She is most effective in isolation, as if she were the last member of a proud and ancient species, with its long history resting on her back. In isolation, the narrator pursues ideas as a miner hunts glittering gems. She wonders in what overlooked space she will discover her treasure. She describes the rocks of the cavern transformed into a beautiful meadow, adorned with a clear, running spring. The meadow is a mystery in its origin but is guaranteed to draw troubled souls to its peaceful atmosphere. She describes the heart, buried deep, feeling love, joy, pain, and desperation.

The narrator falls asleep with her head in her hands while sitting at a narrow table, dreaming of soldiers. Equipped with weapons but without ammunition, they wander without direction. They had fought in the field and grown weary of it. They walk toward the narrator's house, blocking the sun. Daylight is plunged into darkness, forever. The narrator cannot see the blooming flowers, the animals grazing in the pasture, the predators, the prey, or the smith as he works over his anvil. The soldiers move through the narrator's house in silence, destroying flowers with their fiery breath and marble columns with their bare hands. They leave the house in silence, their bodies still eclipsing the sunlight. The narrator stands at the window, watching them disappear into the distance.

The narrator watches her daughter rise from bed to examine herself in the mirror. Her body is straight and without scars. Her skin has no color. When she passes through a sunbeam, she is transparent. Her eyes are red rubies, burning like coal in the wind. At first she was too weak to chew, so the narrator chewed her food for her, like a mother bird. The narrator marvels at her child, whose head is thrown back in happiness as she sits in the cool shade.

Her daughter teases the hunchback boy without pity. When she sights him, she smiles cruelly in anticipation. Her teeth and fingers become sharp like fangs and claws. The hunchback boy avoids her, hiding among the trees. But the narrator's daughter has arms that can grow as long as she wants, seeking him out in the trees. She calls out his name. Though she speaks softly, the sound shatters the boy's eardrums. Now deaf, he has no sense of direction and no way to hear danger approaching. The girl has built a hut for the boy on the edge of a cliff, so that she can observe him as he resists the fate to which he knows he will one day succumb.

The narrator's daughter loves beauty and ancient history. She observes things from their humble beginnings, to their peak of power, to their quiet dwindling. She loves what is not accounted for, what has not been told in stories, and what has not been tended to with care. Yet she also loves that which has been carefully built, until its beauty outshines that which it was built to honor. On the shore, she watches the sea, the sea beneath the sea, and the sea beneath the sea beneath the sea. She hears the sounds within sounds. She feels the sudden chill of ghosts as they flit between atmospheres. Because she has observed how one physical existence feeds on another, she is beyond feeling sadness or spiritual emptiness.

The girl stands proud with one foot in dark and the other in light. Familiar with death, she rushes from one death to the next, unafraid. Though the narrator has brought her into a brief, dangerous existence that depends on chance, her daughter enjoys the passing time, though it is always the same and brings sadness along behind it.

The narrator hears the silent voice, standing opposite the blackness but not opposed to the blackness, because the silent voice has no impulse for contradiction. The narrator leaves her hatred behind in favor of love as she approaches the silent voice. She leaves behind her despair as she moves toward the voice with love. She stands inside the silent voice, which drapes itself over her. Inside the safety of the voice, even the narrator's memory of blackness disappears. She lives in a silence without borders, never ending. The fences of pastures fall, lions roam free, and the continents remained connected in Pangaea. The river flows free; the mountains do not shake and split. There is no mystery within the voice. It falls softly all around, encompassing everything in existence. Living inside the narrator is not an "I." She is at last at peace, because at last she is erased.

CHARACTERS

Child

The narrator's child is a young girl who has the powers of shape-shifting. Both fearsome and awe-inspiring to her mother, the child is cruel and beautiful. She has translucent and unscarred skin with red eyes like burning coals. Her mother chewed her food for her when her jaws were weak, like a mother bird and its young. The child loves to torture the hunchback boy, using her supernatural powers to hunt him. She moves between the land of the living and that of the dead without effort and has overcome human fear of the unknown. She loves history and beauty and does not resent her mother for bringing her into existence in a world "that is perilous and subject to the violence of chance."

Hunchback Boy

The narrator's child torments the hunchback boy, rendering him deaf with her voice and rooting him out of his hiding places with her long arms. She builds him a hut on the edge of a cliff, where she can "watch him day after day flatten himself against a fate of which he knows and yet cannot truly know until the moment it consumes him."

Narrator

The narrator is a woman who longs to be engulfed by nothingness. She has a daughter as well as a home, both of which bring her joy. She dreams of soldiers destroying her house and watches in awe as her daughter straddles the worlds of light and dark in equal measure. Unlike her daughter, the narrator's life is defined by the blackness. She spends her days meditating on it as well as on the silent voice that represents death: the only means of escape.

Soldiers

The soldiers appear in the narrator's dream, weary from battle and carrying weapons emptied of bullets. They walk aimlessly rather than march, blocking the sun as they make their way toward the narrator's house. Inside the house,

TOPICS FOR FURTHER STUDY

- Read Sharon G. Flake's young-adult novel *The Skin I'm In* (1998). In an essay, compare and contrast the novel with "Blackness," paying particular attention to the representation of race and gender in each of the works.

- After conducting online research on the postmodernist movement, choose a postmodern author who interests you. Construct a PowerPoint presentation about his or her life and work, including a brief biography, bibliography, and at least three quotations that exemplify the author's postmodernist style.

- Choose another story from *At the Bottom of the River* to read. Write an essay in which you explicate the story you have chosen, summarizing the plot and providing your own interpretation, followed by a comparison of the story's major elements (such as themes and style) to that of "Blackness."

- Write an essay in which you consider the various meanings of blackness given in "Blackness" and provide your theory to explain how they relate to the narrator. Is blackness a positive or negative aspect of her life? In what ways is blackness presented as both good and bad? Why do you think the narrator struggles with blackness so frequently while her daughter does not? Support your ideas with quotes from the story.

they pull down columns with their bare hands and kill fresh flowers on the dresser with their breath. When they leave, they continue to blot out the sun, walking silently into the horizon.

THEMES

Black Womanhood

In a short story of abstractions and complicated imagery, Kincaid makes clear that her narrator— the nameless "I"—is a black woman. The four

Kincaid's work often reflects her Antiguan heritage. (© loneroc / Shutterstock)

sections of the story are an exploration of black womanhood: the experience of blackness, the male gaze (in her dream of soldiers), the experience of motherhood, and the life-affirming, life-destroying silent voice (representing spirituality and death). For the narrator, blackness is a paradoxical experience. It is not her air, ground, water, food, or blood, yet symbolically she breathes it in with every breath, walks on it with every step (the soles of her feet, which she mentions again later), drinks it, eats it, and feels it flowing in her veins. She is inseparable from her blackness, yet she can observe it from an outside perspective. Blackness, in its role as the narrator's race, is an integral part of her experience of the world. Without it, she would not exist as she is in the story. Yet it is also so much a part of her that it does not necessitate constant acknowledgement. When, with a jolt, she realizes that the foreign object she had been looking at with fear is actually her foot, the narrator feels a surge of power. The narrator gains strength from her blackness, especially in its relation to the other blackness featured prominently in the story—that of the primordial darkness into which the universe was born. Her blackness and that of the universe are one and the same: a natural, ancient hue predating all else.

The terrible history of violence against the black race is depicted as well, through a symbol of colonialism in the form of the soldiers: silent males who enter the narrator's home without permission or explanation, leaving the foundations damaged. When they leave and the sun shines again, the narrator watches them until they appear as a spot on the horizon. The imagery brings to mind a ship far out at sea, a representation of the flight of the colonizers following independence. The colonizers vanish, but the damage they have caused is left to the narrator to fix. She accomplishes this reconstruction of self in part through her child, a girl untouched by marauding soldiers and thus uncontaminated by the crimes carried out against her mother's blackness.

Motherhood

The narrator's experience of motherhood is a source of wonder and joy in her life, as she contemplates the ease with which this younger self navigates life's most difficult questions. Unfazed by death, untroubled by the swift passage of time, the child is flexible like a young twig rather than being fixed to the spot like a tree trunk, like her mother. The narrator's joy as a mother is in observing as well as serving her child. She chews her food and carries her milk and, in return, is free to watch in fascination as her daughter bends the reality the narrator thought she knew into shapes that suit her preference. Her child travels farther into the unknown than the narrator dares, mistreats rather than feel the pain of mistreatment, and changes form where the narrator can, at most, step outside herself to observe from a different angle. The child is the next generation of the narrator: a more advanced and powerful form. Neither she nor her mother questions the natural order of their relationship, as mother yearns for the silent voice to take her from this world while daughter exhibits a mastery of it. By giving her resources to her young self, the narrator frees herself to enter the embrace of the silent voice, certain that her work of plunging into the dark in search of life's mysteries will be carried on by her daughter. Like the unrecognized part of her foot that frightens the narrator until she recognizes it as her own, her daughter is an awe-inspiring piece of herself who empowers the narrator through the audacity of her confident existence.

STYLE

Postmodernism

Postmodernism is a movement in literature, art, and music that began in the late twentieth century as a response to World War II, in particular the dropping of the atom bombs and the fragmented political, social, and physical landscape it left behind. Aspects of postmodernist fiction include self-referential or metafictional work, scattered narration, experimental structure and language, cross-disciplinary subjects, folklore, and satire or mistrust of established structures on any level, from the global industrial complex to the simplest sentence. "Blackness" is postmodern in its resistance to form (neither a short story nor a poem), its resistance to interpretation through the heavy use of symbols, and its incorporation of folklore through the religion Obeah. The difficulty of reading "Blackness" mimics the narrator's struggles in living blackness—a concept too complex to be expressed in preconceived forms and definitions.

Prose Poetry

The term *prose poetry* refers to the combination of elements of fiction (prose) and elements of poetry in a literary work to produce a hybrid form of writing. "Blackness" exemplifies prose poetry in that it preserves the format of a short story but reads like a poem. Sentence structure is loose, imagery is given greater importance than plot or character development, and figurative language dominates rather than dialogue. Because prose poetry occupies an imaginative space between the two forms, an interpretation of a work of prose poetry must approach from a combination of perspectives as well. For example, the characters in "Blackness" are an element of prose, but they are more symbolic than realistic—an element of poetry.

HISTORICAL CONTEXT

Colonialism

The effect of European colonialism in the Caribbean is a fundamental topic of Kincaid's work. In "Blackness," colonialism is most directly addressed in the weary soldiers who invade the narrator's house. Justin D. Edwards explains the symbolism of their actions in *Understanding Jamaica Kincaid*: "The protagonist's house can be read as symbolic of the Caribbean island itself—an island upon which the white army has marched and spread destruction." Europeans first came to the Caribbean in the fifteenth century, conquering the small islands through brute force and establishing their own colonies in place of the societies they had destroyed. The colonists brought their own European indentured servants as well as African slaves. After hundreds of years of oppression, slavery was abolished from the colonies in the early nineteenth century by the Dutch, British, French, and Spanish empires in turn, freeing hundreds of thousands of men, women, and children. As a result of generations of cultural exchange, twentieth-century Caribbean culture is Creole: a mix of African, European, and Asian traditions. However, colonial rule remained in place over the islands, exploiting the labor of the people and the rich natural resources for the benefit of wealthy nations an ocean away. Haiti was the first of the Caribbean islands to gain its independence, in 1804. Throughout the nineteenth and twentieth centuries, the other islands followed—with Kincaid's Antigua

COMPARE & CONTRAST

- **1983:** Like Kincaid, many Caribbean authors leave their island homes in search of opportunity elsewhere. Famous examples include Edwidge Danticat, V. S. Naipaul, and Kamau Brathwaite.

  Today: Reflecting a growing interest in Caribbean literature both at home and abroad, many of the island nations host annual literary festivals in addition to publishing literary magazines such as *Caribbean Writer, Caribbean Review of Books, BIM,* and *Kyk-Over-Al.*

- **1983:** With the publication of *At the Bottom of the River*, Kincaid becomes one of the most celebrated young authors in New York City.

  Today: Kincaid's body of work has established her place in the American literary canon—studied by students of literature,

  analyzed by academics, and lauded by critics for her powerfully original voice.

- **1983:** Antigua is officially disassociated from Britain, its former colonizer, in 1981 and established as a parliamentary democracy. A small percentage of the country's population is made up of the Carib and Arawak, peoples who are indigenous to the island. However, 90 percent of the country's population is black and made up of the descendants of Africans forcefully brought to the island through the European slave trade.

  Today: In 2013, at a meeting of the United Nations, Antiguan Prime Minister Baldwin Spencer called for reparations to be made for the years of slavery inflicted during Antigua's colonial past.

among the last to do so, in 1981, only two years prior to the publication of "Blackness." Kincaid explores the effects of racial oppression by the colonizing minority over the exploited majority in her short story, in which blackness covers the island, yet the narrator is vulnerable to the invading army. Years of colonial rule stunted the economic growth of the Caribbean nations, who—like the narrator of "Blackness"—must rebuild their damaged foundations following the colonizer's withdrawal from their home.

Obeah

Kincaid's mother and grandmother were practitioners of Obeah, a folk religion based on magic, spells, sorcery, and witchcraft. Practiced throughout the Caribbean, Obeah originated with African slaves brought to the West Indies to work the plantations. An amalgam of beliefs, Obeah features spells that can be harmful or beneficial, and a variety of methods can be used to counter malignant spells, such as

wearing protective sachets of herbs or taking mineral baths to ward off the Evil Eye. Obeah practitioners utilized the Christian symbols of the white colonizers of the Caribbean as a method of practicing their own religion while appearing to worship the Christianity of the slave masters.

One aspect of Obeah prominent in "Blackness" is the belief in *jablesses* and *soucriants*, bloodsucking shape-shifters who take the form of animals to hunt their prey. Kincaid, Lizabeth Paravisini-Gebert writes in *Jamaica Kincaid: A Critical Companion*, spent her childhood in fear of these creatures: while visiting her grandmother, "her contemplation of the Dominican landscape at twilight was often marred by her conviction that the deep shadows moving in the distant horizon were *jablesses* roaming in search of victims." The supernatural abilities of the narrator's daughter in "Blackness" match those of a *jablesse*, from her monstrous appearance and ability to shape-shift to her ability to travel between spiritual realms with ease.

The story portrays a complicated mother-daughter relationship, which is a common theme in Kincaid's work. (© *luminaimages / Shutterstock*)

CRITICAL OVERVIEW

"Blackness" is considered to be among the most difficult short stories within *At the Bottom of the River*, a collection known for its obscurity of both language and meaning. Edwards writes, "'Blackness' is one of the most challenging stories . . . because Kincaid uses the image of blackness to convey conflicting ideas: blackness . . . as an image of annihilation and erasure [and] also as an image of renewal and rebirth." Paravisini-Gerbert praises the story's lyricism and beauty: "'Blackness' is one of the most lyrical stories in *At the Bottom of the River*. The narrative . . . draws on the incantatory rhythms of prayers and the psalms for its poetic resonances." In "Alterrains of 'Blackness' in *At the Bottom of the River*," Jana Evans Braziel summarizes the reaction to the collection as a whole when *At the Bottom of the River* was first published: "The collection astounded critics with its breathtaking lyricism, fluid images, and innovative lines of poetic prose, even as it confounded critics and readers alike with its abstract language . . . and its recesses of metaphorical meaning."

Kincaid has been both praised and criticized for her writing style, which subverts expectations whether through the elusive prose poetry stories

of *At the Bottom of the River* or the unexpectedly harsh tone of her antitourism essay *A Small Place*. Harold Bloom defends Kincaid in his introduction to *Jamaica Kincaid*: "Kincaid transcends many critical accounts of her achievement to date. She is a stylist and a visionary, and imaginatively is essentially a fantasist." Aspects of her abilities as a fantasist are visible in "Blackness" in the characterization of the narrator's shape-shifting daughter. Of Kincaid's unique and potent narrative voice as a feminist, an Afro-Caribbean American, and a postmodernist, Giovanni Covi writes in "Jamaica Kincaid and the Resistance to Canons": "This combination is . . . not only disruptive of the institutional order, but also revolutionary in its continuous self-criticism and its rejection of all labels."

CRITICISM

Amy L. Miller
Miller is a graduate of the University of Cincinnati, and she currently resides in New Orleans, Louisiana. In the following essay, she explores Kincaid's masterful use of symbolism in "Blackness."

In Kincaid's "Blackness," a series of complex symbols serves to define the life of the narrator through her own experience (a black, female experience), rather than through borrowed terms from the white patriarchy. In the story's four sections, Kincaid reimagines blackness, colonialism, motherhood, and spirituality by throwing out preconceived definitions of the subjects and replacing them with her own symbolic vocabulary. If "Blackness" is difficult to understand, that is because the reader clings too fiercely to what is taught by the dominant culture. By resisting the Western tendency to understand life through binary opposites (good/bad, white/black, war/peace, and male/female, for example) a more nuanced understanding of the story is possible.

Hegemony refers to the influence of those in charge over the culture at large. In other words, those who rule control not only the people and what they can and cannot do but also the language and how things are perceived by society. Kincaid's experience of hegemonic power as an Antiguan and an American is, like most Western societies, that of white, male privilege. One only need look at American currency, which features white men almost exclusively, to deduce who

WHAT DO I READ NEXT?

- In Victoria Brown's young-adult novel *Minding Ben* (2011), sixteen-year-old Grace moves from Trinidad to New York City to become a live-in nanny. Caught between her desire to improve her life and the overwhelming needs of the family with whom she shares a crumbling house, Grace must navigate the treacherous pitfalls of life in the big city without sacrificing her dreams of a better life.

- Kincaid's nonfiction essay *A Small Place* (2000) is a ruthless condemnation of the tourist industry's control of Antigua and an accusation of the complacency of the Antiguan government in the exploitation of its people. Written in the second person, Kincaid forces "you," the hapless tourist, to confront the reality of your visit to the pretty Caribbean island: the underpaid, underprivileged hotel and resort workers; the corruption of the government; and the lack of educational opportunities for the Antiguans, whose lives are hidden from the tourist's view.

- *Men in the Sun and Other Palestinian Stories*, by Ghassan Kanafani (1999), is a collection of short stories illustrating Palestinian life—a life defined by conflict, displacement, and marginalization by the outside world. Translated from the Arabic by Hilary Kilpatrick, Kanafani's short stories focus on ordinary people who must make a new life after losing everything they called home.

- *Colonialism and Gender from Mary Wollstonecraft to Jamaica Kincaid*, by Moira Ferguson (1994), examines the relationship between colonialism and the oppression of women, a common theme in Kincaid's work. By surveying the work of women writers from the eighteenth century to today, Ferguson traces the evolving social and political ideologies surrounding feminism, slavery, and freedom in the Caribbean.

- *Texaco*, by Patrick Chamoiseau (1992), is a postmodern masterpiece about a Martinique shantytown named Texaco under the threat of destruction by an urban planner. Marie-Sophie Laborieux must convince the planner that her town is worth saving through a series of stories about its vivid history as a sanctuary for those who have nowhere else to go.

- Alice Walker's *The Color Purple* (1982) won both the Pulitzer Prize and the National Book Award for its heart-wrenching account of connections forged and broken between lovers, sisters, and friends. The position of African American women in the American South is explored through the story of Celie, a teenage bride who is beaten and raped first by her father and then by her husband before the arrival of lounge singer Shug Avery teaches Celie to love herself.

- *The Bluest Eye*, by Toni Morrison (1970), takes place in small-town Lorain, Ohio, where Pecola, a young girl who wishes for blue eyes, is tormented by the belief that her dark skin and eyes make her less valuable as a person. As she grows up during the Great Depression under the oppression of an abusive, unpredictable father, Pecola's downfall is witnessed by sisters Claudia and Freida but results from the brutal unfairness of society at large.

- *Wide Sargasso Sea*, by Jean Rhys (1966), is a prequel to Charlotte Bronte's *Jane Eyre*, exploring the life story of Mr. Rochester's mysterious wife. Set in Jamaica, *Wide Sargasso Sea* examines the sinister power of patriarchy as Creole heiress Antoinette Cosway's English husband takes away her name, her identity, her sanity, and her home.

- The postmodern tour de force *Mumbo Jumbo*, by Ishmael Reed (1972), satirizes racism in America through the story of the pandemic Jes Grew (jazz), which threatens the very foundations of the country, taking the population by storm. No one is spared by Reed's cutting wit as he exposes the damaging racial inequalities built into the structure of Western society.

> IN THE STORY'S FOUR SECTIONS, KINCAID REIMAGINES BLACKNESS, COLONIALISM, MOTHERHOOD, AND SPIRITUALITY BY THROWING OUT PRECONCEIVED DEFINITIONS OF THE SUBJECTS AND REPLACING THEM WITH HER OWN SYMBOLIC VOCABULARY."

created the rules. In the Caribbean, hundreds of years of oppression of African slaves under European colonizers is the basis for hegemonic power—a power Kincaid seeks to thwart in all her work as an author. Hegemonic power gives rise to hegemonic symbols: those symbols easily recognized and unwittingly taught simply by living within a culture. The example of a hegemonic symbol-pair most appropriate for a study of "Blackness" is that of black and white, or light and dark. What does it mean when someone is in a dark mood? How does a white knight act? What kind of luck does a black cat bring? In a western movie, who are the white hats and who are the black hats? What kind of person has a black heart? Why do brides traditionally wear white dresses? What does a raven symbolize as opposed to a dove? In Western culture, white and light are associated with goodness while dark and black are associated with evil. The fact that whiteness is so intrinsically valued in a hegemonic culture ruled by white men is not a coincidence. Rather, it is an example of how the subtleties of language can be used to perpetuate the degradation and abuse of a people. Edwards writes: "European languages have always defined blackness as something to fear, as something to overcome, and as something to dominate."

Kincaid, in opposition to the hegemony, creates her own symbols, her own meanings, and her own logic in "Blackness" in order to represent the experience of a black woman without relying on the language of white men. More than that, she seeks to destroy the basic structures of Western thought—rules of perspective, grammar, and style, in order to free her art from the rules of a society that does not reflect her perception of the world. Cove writes:

"The disruption of binary oppositions is devastating: everything is ambiguous, multiple, fragmented. . . . 'Blackness' disrupts the concept of identity as One." Kincaid gives blackness multiple definitions, some of them seemingly contradictory. She subverts the image of white male power through the dream of weary soldiers; blurs the boundaries between realities in the character of the narrator's daughter; and finally defies Western logic through her narrator's self-empowering embrace of her own destruction. "Blackness" is a rejection of all rules but those that come from within.

The story begins with blackness itself. Rather than rely on what society would teach of the frightful danger of blackness, Kincaid seeks out alternate experiences. Blackness, for example, can fall softly and silently, as in the moments just before sleep. Blackness can be lived through the experience of being black—both tangible and intangible but inseparable from one's identity. Blackness is also the voice from which the universe, the earth, and all life was born and where it will all return. Thus blackness shares with the narrator the identity of mother. Braziel writes: "'Blackness' refuses the division of subject and object, of self and others, of interiority and exteriority, of internal and external spaces; these spaces are interpenetrating, traversing one another." Blackness is not exclusively good, bad, or neutral but encompasses all. Like a gas, it spreads to fill any space, blanketing everything, but the narrator is not afraid of being "swallowed up in the blackness so that I am one with it."

In the first section both the narrator's blackness and the enormity of blackness as a concept are explored. In the second, blackness falls softly again, as the narrator begins to dream. The blackness the soldiers bring is frightful, an unnatural eclipse of the sun as they block it out during their invasion of the narrator's home. A symbolic rendering of the European invasion of the Caribbean, the soldiers are aimless but destructive. Even weary and without bullets, they seem unable to resist damaging another's property, as if violence were natural whether in wartime or not. Their brand of blackness robs the narrator of her sight as well as her happiness: "Night fell immediately and permanently. No longer could I see the blooming trefoils, their overpowering perfume a constant giddy delight to me." This is the hegemonic blackness, full of unspecific danger that blinds those who live their own blackness, like the narrator, to their value. Blinded thus, the narrator loses sight of her blooming flowers, grazing animals, wild hunters and prey, and the smith at his anvil, symbols of a functional, beautiful life. They destroy her fresh-cut flowers and marble columns: signs of her independence and success. When they leave with as little explanation for their intrusions as when they arrived, the narrator—her sight restored, watches them fade away with the resignation of the long victimized. She knows she will receive no apology, no offer of help, no recognition of her humanity, but, as a result, it is the soldiers, the colonizers, those in power, who seem inhuman.

The narrator's daughter emerges as a powerful antidote to the soldiers' abuses. Paravisini-Gebert writes, "The daughter is, unlike the narrator, self-affirming and beyond despair. She can always return to the light." Where the narrator is aware of the sight-stealing definitions of blackness, her daughter breaks free of even the definitions of a human. A shape-shifter, she bends time and space to her will. Having transcended skin tone, she is transparent—barely held together by the laws of physics as she morphs, travels between realms of life and death, and shrugs off the implications of passing time. She lives an ideal existence untouched by the hegemonic culture that troubles her mother. She takes the form of a *jablesse*, a bloodsucking creature from the Obeah religion of the Caribbean, and uses her powers to torture the hunchback boy in an inversion of her mother's victimization at the hands of the soldiers. Her mastery of life and death is absolute: "One foot in the dark, the other in the light. Moving from pool to pool, she absorbs each special sensation for and of itself. My child rushes from death to death." As a result of her extraordinary abilities to manipulate the world around her, she does not resent being born, much to the surprise of the narrator, who assumes her own resentment would be reflected in her child's attitude as well.

Braziel writes: "In the fourth section of 'Blackness,' Kincaid's lyricism is hymnlike, incantatory, and the narrator sings psalms of self and silence and self-erasure." If "Blackness" is read as the narrator's life story—from her birth both from and into blackness, to a male invasion of her home, to motherhood—then the final section describes the narrator's death in terms of a glorious spiritual release of selfhood. The blackness of

her experience in this world can be escaped only through absorption into the silent voice, where she both finds herself and lets herself fade away forever: "I stand inside the silent voice. The silent voice enfolds me. The silent voice enfolds me so completely that even in memory the blackness is erased." Time rewinds as she drifts deeper into the silent voice, arriving at the infinitely peaceful moment before the continents split, before the mountains split, and before humanity split into its ever-warring factions. Likewise, the separations in the narrator's mind—the divisions between known and unknown—are healed, fusing together even as they disappear. The narrator experiences her child's perception of an untamed, undivided world as an ecstatic discovery of self. But just as she grasps it, she is gone.

Kincaid's "Blackness" replaces the language of the colonizers with the language of the narrator's experience. Braziel writes, "Blackness is bodily and soulfully self and others; it is not metaphysical fact that leads nowhere but rather a spiritual and fantastical journey that soars everywhere." By releasing the narrative from binding hegemonic structures and definitions, Kincaid produces a work that dances as freely as the narrator's daughter atop the wreckage of such reductive and harmful binary symbol pairs as light and dark and black and white.

Source: Amy L. Miller, Critical Essay on "Blackness," in *Short Stories for Students*, Gale, Cengage Learning, 2016.

Jana Evans Braziel

In the following excerpt, Braziel explores the concept of blackness.

. . . Kincaid's short story "Blackness" probes blackness as both a postcolonial racialized identity category and a metaphysical definition. Kincaid's creative articulations of blackness draw on biblical motifs of darkness as a priori, uncreated substance: blackness, or darkness, precedes *ex nihilo* creation—or the divine force and dynamism of creation—that produces something (creatures, essences, elements) from nothing: it is precursive, before, outside of time even (if one accepts the Augustinian notion of space and time as created dimensions or the material parameters of the created world that are called into being alongside and in simultaneity with that world). Blackness, as darkness, gestures toward the infinite and the eternal, even as it may only be palpably experienced and visibly descried within the

The second section of the story uses an invading army as a metaphor for the concept of blackness. (©
akiyoko / Shutterstock)

parameter of space and time. Kincaid thus reverses the axiomatic, commonplace, or traditional metaphysical relations of black-white, blackness-whiteness, dark-light in which the former term—forgetful of the biblical order in Genesis—is subordinated to the latter, which has been historically valorized and privileged. Does darkness so war against light, and a priori essence mitigate against created substance, as evil with and against good? Kincaid seems to refuse this metaphysical mêlée, even as she acknowledges its historical encounters and even restages its performative battles.

Drawing on Antiguan folklore and obeah, Kincaid also explores blackness as metamorphic, transformative, and aleatory. The narrative voice alternates from being to nonbeing, from self to others, from subjects to objects: like blackness, the narrating I moves through these contradictory spaces, but remains bound and irreducible to none of them. Comprised of four fragmented sections, "Blackness" explores the alterrains of identity and being, loss of identity

and nonbeing, or "the small shafts that fall with desperation in between." "Blackness" swirls around two intertwined centers of gravity—blackness as identity and blackness as a metaphysical category. Although I refer to each narrative heartbeat separately, the two pulses "merge and separate, merge and separate" (to evoke Kincaid's words from another story in the collection, "My Mother"), propelling the reader through, at times synchronous—and at other moments, asynchronous—states. Through its metamorphic pulsations, "Blackness" is conceptualized as paradox—both negation and affirmation, genesis and apocalypse. Blackness vacillates across oppositional poles of being, nonbeing, and identity, masking truth with fiction and fiction with an alterreality. Kincaid's fictional alterterrains (or alterrains) open autobiography to alterity, or otherness, and to the powerfully deconstructive movements of alterbiography. As the story begins, a soft blackness "falls in silence"; at the end of the story, silence enfolds, and ultimately erases, the self, but this erasure also, paradoxically, affirms self, and she

THE BLACKNESS PRECEDES CREATION AND PERSISTS AFTER ANNIHILATION OF FORM, INDIVIDUATED EXISTENCE, AND CONTINGENT FORMS OF BEING: IT IS NECESSARY, A PRIORI, DIVINE."

reposes in the "silent voice" of blackness, not blackness itself.

Each of the four interwoven sections in the story "Blackness" are a reflection of blackness. The opening section is a contemplative passage exploring blackness sensately, lyrically, philosophically, and corporeally. Using synaesthesia—the fusion, even confusion, and overlay—of sensory experiences, Kincaid explores blackness as an ontological and subjective category. Multiple senses are explored here—aurality, touch, sight—and blackness pervades all experiences. In the second section blackness delves into subterfuge terrains, territories dreamed, and landscapes imagined. In sleep and dreams, on battlefields of window frames, the girl creates worlds of difference, of "hunter and prey," of brilliance and blindness. The third section, less directly self-reflexive than the first two sections, still swirls obliquely through self- and alterterrains as it moves from mother to daughter to mother to daughter and back again, straining the boundaries of self and other, subjects and objects, space and time. Self is defined and problematized, in alterrelation with mother, daughter, a "hunchback boy," and even through divine apotheosis. In the fourth section of "Blackness," Kincaid's lyricism is hymnlike, incantatory, and the narrator sings psalms of self and silence and self-erasure. The refrain, "Living in the silent voice, I am," blurs the boundaries of life and death, being and nonbeing, self and not-self. Moving through senses, elusive thoughts, and paradoxical states, "Blackness" defines and redefines its own contradictory terrains.

Recall Kincaid's words to Ippolita: "I have quite a few people running around in me who are not only Black." How might we interpret this idea in relation to "Blackness"? Kincaid evokes in this phrase both the strictures and

the open horizons of blackness as identity and as metaphysical category. And as Kincaid intimates to Allan Vorda in conversation: the parameters of identity and community as black are also universalized, resisted as marginal or marked differentially: "I come from a place where most of the people are black. Every important person in my life was a black person, or a person who was mostly black, or very deeply related to what we call a black person. So I just assume that is the norm and that it is other people who would need describing." These comments are related, it seems, to the author's creative literary refigurations of blackness in the short story. Blackness is both foundational and yet malleable.

"Blackness" begins with synaesthetic movement, fusing the senses of sight and touch: the color or the state of blackness is experienced through touch and through sound: "How soft is the blackness as it falls. It falls in silence and yet it is deafening, for no other sound except the blackness falling can be heard." Confounding "blackness" as a state of being (or nonbeing), Kincaid's opening lines express blackness *as* movement: "How soft is the blackness as it falls." Although blackness may traditionally, within Western frames, connote austerity or sterility, here blackness is soft. The blackness is not only synaesthetic, blurring sensory experiences; it is also paradoxic: "it falls in silence and yet it is deafening." Not only does the silence deafen; it eclipses all other sounds, even through its deafening silence. Building on this synaesthetic moving image, Kincaid writes, "The blackness falls like soot from a lamp with an untrimmed wick." Blackness falls, expiring "like soot" from flame, evoking ashes, dust, and death. Again, blackness is paradoxic: "[T]he blackness is visible and yet it is invisible, for I see that I cannot see it." Only in this line does blackness become visible, invisible, and only in this line, does blackness stand in relation to an I. Evoking Fanon's black epidermal visibility that creates black ontological invisibility (in *Black Skin, White Masks*), Kincaid writes, "[F]or I see that I cannot see it." Yet the blackness moves, expands, "fills up a small room, a large field, an island, my own being." Blackness is movement, force of nature, geopolitical transformation: it falls or fills; it falls as night falls over a "large field"; it expands, filling an "island" (or many islands within the Caribbean, as the Atlantic Slave Trade's violatory expanse filled American islands with African people). In this last line, though, blackness is more intimately connected with individual identity as it falls and fills "my own being." Still, the speaking I refuses the totalization of identity by blackness: "The blackness cannot be separated from me but often I can stand outside it." I and "blackness" are intimately linked, and although the blackness is inseparable from the I, the I is not inextricable from the blackness. I may "stand outside of it." As blackness moves, so the I moves, outside and even beyond.

Following a series of lines imbued with repetition and difference, lines that reiterate the syntactical pattern, "The blackness is not . . . , though I . . . ," Kincaid writes: "The blackness is not my blood, though it flows through my veins." The line rejects and critiques the nineteenth-century racialized sciences that theorized racial difference as biological, as genetic, as "in the blood," yet, she writes, "[blackness] flows through my veins." Blackness flows through I's veins, but not as blood; rather, it flows as being and nonbeing or as the annihilation of being, all the possible and variable meanings of blackness. I says, "The blackness enters my many-tiered spaces and soon the significant word and event recede and eventually vanish: in this way, I am annihilated and my form becomes formless and I am absorbed into a vastness of free-flowing matter." The body, as form of being, and its "many-tiered spaces" are penetrated by blackness, "and soon the significant word and event recede and eventually vanish." But what is the "significant word"? *Blackness*? And what is the "event"? the blackness as it "enters [her] many-tiered spaces"? And why do they "recede and eventually vanish"? The lines are ambiguous; still, Kincaid proceeds with precision and specificity: "*in this way*, I am annihilated and my form becomes formless" (emphasis added). As the "significant word" ("blackness"?) and the "event" ("blackness enters"?) "recede and eventually vanish," so "I [is] annihilated." A word, an event, a vanishing—of blackness, of I. A movement from being (blackness; I) to nonbeing (vanishing; annihilation) in which "form becomes formless." From being nonbeing; from form formlessness. Through this metamorphosis, the lyrical voice claims, "I am absorbed into a vastness of free-flowing matter." This act seems to reverse creation, yet it disavows *ex nihilo* creation, returning to that from whence it proceeded, "free-floating matter," raw materiality, blackness. This loss of form is not a loss of materiality, though, but a metamorphosis of being and incarnation and a transformative loss of individuality: "In the blackness, then, I have been erased. I can no longer say my own name. I can no longer point to myself and say 'I.' In the blackness my voice is silent." I is without identity, without being, and without voice. And yet, I speaks, and speaks of self, even if through the loss of self, and refers to "my own name," even as I never discloses it. Paradox. In blackness, self escapes self; I is erased; I eludes identitarian terms imposed by others and by society (recall Fanon's le Noir) and redefines self through annihilation, erasure, and even fusion with blackness in a cycle of identity, being, nonbeing, and above all, redefinition of these terms: "First, then, I have been my individual self, carefully banishing randomness from my existence, then I am swallowed up in the blackness so that I am one with it." The blackness precedes creation and persists after annihilation of form, individuated existence, and contingent forms of being: it is necessary, a priori, divine. And Kincaid's "blackness" manifests an apophatic gesturing toward what cannot be positively defined yet also an apotheosis. As an individual self, I banishes "randomness from my existence": I acts; I is discrete, separate, individual; I elects what shall constitute self and banishes "randomness." Then, blackness falls, fills, "enters my many-tiered spaces": I is "swallowed up in the blackness; I loses individuality, but I still exists, "one with" the blackness that has engulfed I. Kincaid seizes the language of neo-Platonic emanence and return in order to apotheosize blackness. Yet the lyrical voice of blackness also descends from ethereal heights to world-bound matter below. . . .

Source: Jana Evans Braziel, "Alterrains of 'Blackness' in *At the Bottom of the River*," in *Caribbean Genesis: Jamaica Kincaid and the Writing of New Worlds*, State University of New York Press, 2009, pp. 34–38.

Brita Lindberg-Seyersted

In the following excerpt, Lindberg-Seyersted characterizes Kincaid's work as autobiographical and postcolonial.

Antigua, this small Caribbean island—"nine miles wide by twelve miles long"—is the place where Jamaica Kincaid was born and which she left at an early age, but which affords setting, subject and value system for everything she has written so far. Columbus "discovered" and named the island, but it was the English who colonized it, brought slavery to its shores, and stayed on as rulers till the mid-twentieth century. Even after it achieved political independence in 1981, it

> AMONG THE MANY WOMEN NOW ADDING THEIR VOICES TO THE CHORUS, JAMAICA KINCAID IS ONE OF THE FOREMOST WITH HER INIMITABLE MONOLOGUES, UNFORGETTABLY INDIVIDUALIZED BY THEIR SHREWD HUMOR, THEIR DECEPTIVE SIMPLICITY AND UNFLINCHING HONESTY."

remained to some extent dependent on foreign powers, in particular economically, and influenced culturally by them. As part of the Caribbean world, Antigua typifies the post-colonial dilemma of what to do with the new freedom; what to preserve—if anything—of the colonial legacy; and how to decolonize the *mind*.

The postcolonial situation of a Caribbean island is by now a familiar concern in writings by men and women who have themselves experienced its many ambiguities and conflicts. With his autobiographical novel *In the Castle of My Skin* (1953) and the collection of essays *The Pleasures of Exile* (1960), Barbados-born George Lamming set an inspiring agenda for the life and work of many later writers. From a postcolonial position Jamaica Kincaid carries on the tradition with a highly individualized version of the complex of political and cultural colonialism that had driven many an artist into voluntary exile. Her special signature, which makes her work particularly rewarding to the reader, is to dramatize the colonial condition through certain striking scenes and objects, and to transform elements of a Bildungsroman into a symbolic contest between the colonial child and a representative of the mother culture. Another distinctive trait is her use of the English language which, as it is mediated through her narrator's voice, refrains from any "local color."

Like Lamming's work, Kincaid's writings are strongly autobiographical. In her stories of a young girl's fight for autonomy and identity the domestic-personal becomes the political. This is in line with her general method which is, as she has said in an interview, to "personalize" everything. This struggle, which is waged against the backdrop of an agonizing history of

slavery and colonialism, involves rebellion against various forms of oppression and domination. I shall focus on three forms of such rebellion: against cultural colonialism, against political colonialism, and against matriarchal domination. I see these various forms of rebellion as being epitomized in a few, quite specific episodes and objects which take on an emblematic meaning and mark Kincaid's stories as exemplary denunciations of colonial inequalities. I wish to argue that in all the facets of this struggle there is inherent an element of a specifically "postcolonial" ambiguity or tension which complicates the terms of the fight and raises doubts about what is victory and what is defeat, what is gain and what is loss.

Kincaid's writings date from the period when Antigua's colonial yoke was gradually being lifted, first by its joining associated groups of a few Caribbean islands, later when it achieved the status of an independent nation. The story she tells is largely set in the last phase of British rule, and the world she describes is the colonial one she knew as a child and adolescent. Kincaid left Antigua for America in 1965 at the age of sixteen; her characters Annie and Lucy leave, one for England, the other for the United States, at practically the same age as their creator. (The only piece where both subject and telling are postcolonial is her nonfiction essay *A Small Place* [1988] which is based on her observations during a return visit to the newly independent Antigua in the 1980s.)

Kincaid's three works of fiction—*At the Bottom of the River* (1983), *Annie John* (1985), and *Lucy* (1990)—tell a largely identical story of growing up. *Annie John* and *Lucy* are first-person narratives where we listen to the voice of a child who becomes a young woman. *Lucy* with its slightly wider scope of scene and outlook than *Annie John* contains a few more lines spoken by others than the daughter and her mother, the two protagonists-antagonists of the family drama which is at the center of these works. In *At the Bottom of the River* the author uses an experimental technique with a mixture of first-person narration of memories, dreams and visions, of fragments of an interior monologue, and of indirect and direct discourse. The complex and often puzzling nature of this book might lead one to perceive "a multiplicity of voices" in it, but what we hear is basically one voice, the daughter's. On a few occasions it is counterpointed by the mother's voice and once by the father's, but all the discourse is being passed through the sound box of the narrating self: it is *her* language we listen to.

I employ the term monologue for all three texts, for one thing because it is a handier one than "first-person narrative." More to the point, I find it useful for my purpose because it tallies with the way the narrator's voice dominates these texts, not just in tone and style, but also in perspective. Although there is a struggle going on between mother and daughter and we learn about the mother's position, any real debate is internalized in the daughter. No one else is allowed a role as an equal in this debate.

I thus regard the unnamed speaker of *At the Bottom of the River* and the eponymous narrators of *Annie John* and *Lucy* as the same person presented from partly different angles and at partly different periods in time, from early childhood to young adulthood. In all the books we find the same girl with her traumatic love for her mother, the respected matriarch; with the same rather neutral relationship to a gentle and responsible father (who nevertheless in the end will leave his widow penniless); and with her own "two-facedness," as she calls the split she has identified within herself—a split between an outside and an inside, between a false side and a true side (*Lucy*).

In *At the Bottom of the River* the bond between mother and daughter is the only important issue; in *Annie John* there are in addition other concerns, such as the issue of cultural imperialism. *Lucy* covers a scene peopled with another set of characters than the close-knit circle of the girl's family and friends, and although the relationship between mother and daughter is still there as a constant obbligato, there are other things that are as important to the young woman Lucy: as she is getting ready to enter a world larger than the one ruled by her mother, she faces white people's ignorance and self-centeredness and, again, cultural imperialism.

. . . The Caribbean writer's self-exile thus illustrates clearly the many ambiguities of the postcolonial condition. The domination of a foreign culture and that same culture's positive values create an acute division of loyalties. A Wordsworth would not necessarily be cut out for the part of oppressor, nor would a Charlotte Brontë inevitably step into the role of cultural heroine. The distribution of roles depends on the context and the kind and weight of "persuasion" applied: one was forced upon a defenseless young mind, the other was chosen voluntarily. But even a foreign culture imparted from above can turn out to be preferable in certain ways to a homegrown brand, as shown by Kincaid's bitterness at seeing the decline in her island's education and health care after independence. Derek Walcott has labeled any talk of Europe's "legacy" to the Caribbean world as "presumptuous," but he writes a great epic, *Omeros*, with echoes of a European classic. For the colonized there can be no ambiguity or ambivalence about the achievement of political independence as such, but hopes of an honest and efficient local government that sees to the welfare of those governed can all too quickly be dashed. And while the mother culture itself, with its African and Carib-Indian heritage, is something to honor and love, it can be restricting and hampering to growth.

Out of such conflicts and tensions has been created a unique situation for the Caribbean artist. From the varied culture of the Caribbean with roots in many parts of the world has arisen a literature of fruitful complexity. We witness a steadily growing output of poetry, drama and fiction written by men and women from the many "small places" that make up the West Indies; recently a Nobel Prize winner has emerged from their ranks. Among the many women now adding their voices to the chorus, Jamaica Kincaid is one of the foremost with her inimitable monologues, unforgettably individualized by their shrewd humor, their deceptive simplicity and unflinching honesty.

Source: Brita Lindberg-Seyersted, "Jamaica Kincaid's Postcolonial Monologues," in *Black and Female: Essays on Writing by Black Women in the Diaspora*, Scandinavian University Press, 1994, pp. 129–32, 146–47.

SOURCES

Bloom, Harold, Introduction to *Jamaica Kincaid*, Modern Critical Views, Chelsea House Publishers, 1998, pp. 1–2.

Braziel, Jana Evans, "Alterrains of 'Blackness' in *At the Bottom of the River*," in *Caribbean Genesis: Jamaica Kinkaid and the Writing of New Worlds*, State University of New York Press, 2009, pp. 21–40.

Burrows, Victoria, "*Lucy*: Jamaica Kincaid's Postcolonial Echo," in *Whiteness and Trauma: The Mother-Daughter Knot in the Fiction of Jean Rhys, Jamaica Kincaid, and Toni Morrison*, Palgrave MacMillan, 2014, pp. 72–85.

Covi, Giovanna, "Jamaica Kincaid and the Resistance to Canons," in *Jamaica Kincaid*, edited by Harold Bloom, Modern Critical Views, Chelsea House Publishers, 1998, pp. 3–12.

Edwards, Justin D., *Understanding Jamaica Kincaid*, University of Southern California, 2007, pp. 1–40.

Hunte, Sir Keith, "The Caribbean in Transition," New York Public Library website, 2011, http://exhibitions. nypl.org/africanaage/essay-caribbean-60-80.html (accessed August 8, 2015).

Kincaid, Jamaica, "Blackness," in *At the Bottom of the River*, Farrar, Straus, and Giroux, 1983, pp. 46–52.

Paravisini-Gebert, Lizabeth, *Jamaica Kincaid: A Critical Companion*, Greenwood Press, 1999, pp. 1–50, 72–74.

Timothy, Helen Pyne, "Adolescent Rebellion and Gender Relations in *At the Bottom of the River* and *Annie John*," in *Jamaica Kincaid*, edited by Harold Bloom, Modern Critical Views, Chelsea House Publishers, 1998, pp. 157–68.

Toney, Joyce, "The Contemporary Caribbean," New York Public Library website, 2011, http://exhibitions. nypl.org/africanaage/essay-caribbean-2000.html (accessed August 8, 2015).

155 scholastic essays on the author's essays, novels, and short stories.

Kincaid, Jamaica, *Lucy: A Novel*, Farrar, Straus, and Giroux, 1990.
    Kincaid's novel *Lucy* tells the story of a young girl from the West Indies who moves to New York City. Working as an au pair for a wealthy couple, Lucy witnesses the breakup of a marriage while coming to terms with the past she left behind.

Pratt, Geraldine, and Victoria Rosner, *The Global and the Intimate: Feminism in Our Time*, Columbia University Press, 2012
    This collection of sixteen essays approaches feminism from a variety of cultural and philosophical perspectives, illustrating the complexity of the issues at the heart of the subject. Written by prominent scholars, each essay examines the role of everyday life in such global feminist concerns as immigration, economics, and the popular culture's portrayal of gender.

FURTHER READING

Butler, Christopher, *Postmodernism: A Very Short Introduction*, Oxford University Press, 2003.
    Butler defines postmodernism in simple terms in this brief history of the movement, explaining the abstract concepts and difficult practices of postmodernist artists and authors in easily accessible terms.

Hester, Elizabeth J., *Jamaica Kincaid: A Bibliography of Dissertations and Theses*, CreateSpace Independent Publishing Platform, 2010.
    Hester's compendium of graduate- and doctorate-level work on Kincaid includes over

SUGGESTED SEARCH TERMS

Jamaica Kincaid

"Blackness" AND story AND Jamaica Kincaid

"Blackness" AND short story

At the Bottom of the River AND short-story collection

"Blackness" AND At the Bottom of the River

At the Bottom of the River AND Jamaica Kincaid

At the Bottom of the River AND 1983

"Blackness" AND Kincaid AND 1983

"Blackness" AND Kincaid AND motherhood

Diary of a Madman

NIKOLAY GOGOL

1835

Nikolay Vasilievich Gogol's "The Diary of a Madman" (1835) is perhaps his greatest short story. It represents the diary of a petty bureaucrat who rapidly descends into madness. Although the story is essentially satirical, the diarist Poprishchin's insanity is depicted with a command of the science of mental health as it existed in the 1830s and is one of the first recognizable descriptions of schizophrenia in literature. The story is surprisingly modern, having closer connections of theme and style to surrealism than to other Russian literature of the period. The presentation is also friendly to a generation who came of age in the Internet age, because the text is stitched together of mini-satires of many journalistic styles that were developed for the magazine format, which was new in the early nineteenth century, but continue to exist on websites and blogs. The story is available in *The Diary of a Madman, The Government Inspector, and Selected Stories*, translated by Ronald Wilks and published in 2005.

AUTHOR BIOGRAPHY

Gogol was born on his family's estate outside Poltava, Ukraine, on March 31, 1809. His mother was of Polish descent, and his father, who died when Gogol was fifteen, was Ukrainian. Although Gogol never wrote in Ukrainian dialect, he did use Ukrainian folk motifs in some instances and is fanatical re-drafter, copying out his works by hand over and over again before submitting them for publication. In 1836, Gogol published "The Nose," in which the nose of a civil servant detaches itself from its owner and soon becomes a higher-ranking civil servant. Because of themes like these, Gogol is often seen as a precursor of the surrealists.

Somewhat paradoxically, Gogol is known in Russian scholarship as the founder of the natural school, which includes writers he influenced, such as Ivan Turgenev and Fyodor Dostoyevsky. Gogol's 1835 novel, *Taras Bulba*, presents a romantic and nationalist view of Ukrainian history. Gogol principally thought of himself as a playwright (and seriously considered becoming an actor), and his most important dramatic work is *The Inspector* (sometimes *The Inspector General* or *The Government Inspector* in English), in which a rural town is torn apart by the rumor that a government inspector is coming. When they falsely come to believe that a minor bureaucrat who happens to be staying there overnight is the inspector, the various factions of the town outdo each other with bribes to make sure the corrupt power of government stays on their side. The censors wanted to suppress the play, but Tsar Nicholas I personally intervened to have it produced. Gogol's apparently unfinished novel *Dead Souls* (1842) was his last work.

In the 1840s, Gogol began to experience depression, a condition that intensified after Gogol returned from a pilgrimage to Jerusalem in 1848. He fell under the influence of the starets Matvey Konstantinovsky. (A starets is a monk believed to have uncommon spiritual powers; the most famous is Grigory Rasputin). The starets convinced Gogol that writing fiction is a form of lying and therefore a sin. Gogol burned a number of manuscripts at Konstantinovsky's direction, and among them may have been the second part of *Dead Souls*. Gogol was also induced to take up monastic ascetic practices, which may have contributed to his death. Gogol died in Moscow on March 4, 1852, of causes that have not been fully reconstructed; he may have starved himself to death.

Nikolai Gogol (Library of Congress)

often claimed as a Ukrainian author. Gogol attended a preparatory school but did not go on to university. In 1828, he moved to Saint Petersburg to find some sort of career and slowly established himself as a writer. He soon became connected to the literary circles in the capital and was befriended by the famous poet Alexander Pushkin. In 1834, his connections secured him an appointment as a history professor at Saint Petersburg University, but he was soon forced to resign when faced with the reality of his lack of technical knowledge in the field.

By 1835, Gogol had published four volumes of stories, essays, and plays, including *Arabesques* (1835), in which "Diary of a Madman" first appeared. In the story, Poprishchin, despite his pride in his style of writing, is a professional copier of documents. All copying of this kind was written out by hand in the 1830s; even typewriters did not exist. One can perhaps relate this to Gogol's own habits. As a writer, he was a

PLOT SUMMARY

"The Diary of a Mad Man" shows the progressive degeneration of a character into mental illness. The device is a vehicle for social satire.

MEDIA ADAPTATIONS

- In 1963, Richard Williams planned an animated film version of "The Diary of a Madman." The project was never completed, but it was meant to illustrate a narrator (Kenneth William) reading an abridged version of the story. The soundtrack was completed and is posted at https://www.youtube.com/watch?v=W6-xtJX5aJ8 and many other sites on the Internet.

- In 1994, David Holman wrote a stage adaptation of "The Diary of a Madman" that has been frequently performed throughout the English-speaking world; the text has never been published.

- In 2002, "The Diary of a Madman" was adapted on BBC Radio 4 as an episode of the program *Three Ivans, Two Aunts, and an Overcoat*, and is occasionally rebroadcast.

- The Living Pictures theater company in Wales has included a production of *Diary of a Madman* in its repertoire since 2011.

- In 2001, Jonathan Keren adapted "The Diary of a Mad Man" as an opera. It was professionally performed by the Gropius Ensemble in 2013, but it has not been commercially recorded.

The narrative is presented in the form of a series of diary entries, many very brief. The entries become progressively more disordered.

Poprishchin, the diarist, is a low-ranking civil servant. He works in a government office in Saint Petersburg, copying documents. The writing in his diary is rambling and confused but at the start is not disordered. On the day of the first entry, he oversleeps and is late for work (evidently he does not allow his servant, Mavra, to awaken him). He describes petty office politics, appealing to the director to ward off the criticism of the head of the department. He might have avoided the whole thing, but he needs to ask the office cashier (described in anti-Semitic terms) for an advance

on his salary. In other offices, bribery is rampant, but his is civilized.

While walking to work in the rain, Poprishchin spots a fellow civil servant and mentally criticizes him for stalking a girl for the purpose of looking at her ankles. This is not necessarily abnormal—Homer, the ancient poet, also praises the beauty of women's ankles. In both ancient Greece and nineteenth-century Russia, the ankles are one of the few parts of the body visible with the prevailing fashions in women's clothes.

Next Poprishchin sees the director's coach and the director's daughter, Sophie, getting out of it to go into a dress shop. Poprishchin stops to leer at her, overcome with desire. He becomes ashamed of his old and out-of-fashion coat. He notices that the girl's dog, Medji, also gets out of the carriage but does not go into the store and is left out in the street. Two other women walk past with another dog, Fidèle. Poprishchin hears the two dogs speak to each other in Russian, though mixing in a few barks. Medji gives the other dog a letter. Poprishchin is at first startled by this but then reminds himself that he has read several newspaper stories about animals that talk. Poprishchin mentions that he reads *The Little Bee* (a stand-in for the real *Northern Bee*, a reactionary newspaper), giving himself opportunity, by agreeing with the editorial stance of the paper, to praise those of higher social rank than he is and to vilify foreigners.

One day, the director's daughter visits the office and happens to ask Poprishchin where her father is. His mumbled response does not match the intensity of his complex fantasies. He falls on the floor picking up her handkerchief. That night he stalks her, waiting in the shadows outside her house, but he does not see her. The head of the office upbraids him for making a fool of himself over the director's daughter. Poprishchin fantasizes about taking revenge by achieving a higher social rank.

Every thought leads Poprishchin to the director's daughter—how her cosmetics must be arranged on her dresser, how her clothes are laid out on her bed. He recalls the letter exchanged between the two dogs. So he goes to Fidèle's house and barges in to steal Medji's letters to her from their hiding place in her basket, hoping they will contain gossip about her owner. Poprishchin reads extensively from the letters, which turn out to be satires of the kinds of articles that appear in middle-class magazines. Medji describes her mistress's romance with a guards officer named Teplov and then mentions Poprishchin himself, to say how ridiculous the director finds him and how Sophie can hardly keep from laughing whenever she sees him.

Poprishchin has read in magazines about peasants who turn out somehow to really be a count or a duke, so why cannot he, already a nobleman, turn out to secretly be a general? Then he would not be laughed at. He turns his attention to the succession crisis in Spain, where there is no clear heir to become the next ruler.

The entry headings change to fantastic dates (such as April 43rd, 2000), and Poprishchin declares that he is the king of Spain. He stops going to the office, and after three weeks someone comes and tells him he had better come in. So the next day he does, and the director comes and has him sign a paper, which he signs "Ferdinand VIII." Poprishchin goes to the director's house and barges into Sophie's bedroom, terrifying her and telling her that "happiness such as she had never imagined awaited her, and that we would be together, in spite of the hostile plot against us." He leaves, considering that the truth about women is that they are all in love with the devil.

Happening to see the tsar's carriage drive by in a procession, Poprishchin considers that all he needs is a royal robe to be presented at court. He cannot go to a tailor because they are all crooks (his judgment "most of them end up mending the roads" is a reference to the work typically done by convicts), so he cuts up his uniform to make a cloak.

A deputation from the Spanish government comes to take Poprishchin to Spain. The two-thousand-mile trip takes only half an hour by coach, but this does not surprise him because he is always reading about how much faster railroads are getting. It becomes apparent that where he has really been taken is to an insane asylum. As it becomes more obvious that he is being held against his will, Poprishchin comes to believe that he is in the hands of the Spanish Inquisition and that the man he first thinks is his chancellor (i.e., his doctor) is the grand inquisitor. The entries end with an appeal to a hallucinatory vision of his mother to save him.

CHARACTERS

Cashier

Poprishchin seeks out the cashier for an advance on his salary.

Civil Servant

The civil servant is a coworker whom Poprishchin encounters on his way to work one morning. Poprishchin disparages him for looking at a woman's ankles.

Director

The unnamed director is the head of the government office Poprishchin works in. He has a civil service rank equivalent to a general. He is the father of Sophie. Poprishchin is mostly too overwhelmed by the director's rank to say or do much in his presence but seems to devote time to thinking of new ways to grovel to him, beyond his regular practice of sharpening his quills. But something more than the obvious satire creeps into Poprishchin's sycophantic (fawningly flattering) praise:

> Our Director must be a very clever man: his study is full of shelves crammed with books. I read some of their titles: such erudition, such scholarship! Quite above the head of any ordinary civil servant. All in French or German. And you should look into his face and see the deep seriousness that gleams in his eyes! I have yet to hear him use *one* more word than is necessary.

It is far from impossible to imagine the French and German books are displayed in his office to impress visitors with his erudition but without his ever actually having read them. And the director's concision of language could just as well be an incommunicative gruffness. Poprishchin's vision, even before he goes mad, is distorted by his sycophancy.

Fidèle

Fidèle is the lapdog of one of Sophie's friends. In Poprishchin's delusion, the dogs not only speak to each other in Russian but also exchange letters. Fidèle means "loyal" in French—comparable to the stereotypical dog name Fido, which means "I am loyal" in Latin—indicating the Russian fashion for French culture.

Grand Inquisitor

The character called the grand inquisitor is Poprishchin's delusional screen for his psychiatrist.

Head of the Department

Poprishchin treats those in authority over him with a combination of sycophantic affection and hostility. In the case of the head of his department, hostility predominates because he reserves his praise and good opinion for the director, who is over both of them.

Mavra

Mavra is Poprishchin's servant. Although Poprishchin may seem too poor to have a servant, the gap in wealth between the emerging middle class and the peasantry was so great that even the poorest middle-class worker could afford a servant. Mavra is Finnish. In the 1830s, Finland was a province of the Russian Empire, and Mavra must be part of the influx of peasants into the growing industrial cities that characterized the emerging economy of the period.

Medji

Medji is Sophie's lapdog. Her character is part of Poprishchin's delusions and is conveyed through a series of letters she supposedly writes to her friend Fidèle and which Poprishchin steals and reads. The letters are for the most part a hodge-podge of popular magazine genres. They contain snippets of poetry but are mostly a satire of romance literature with the occasional platitude and aphorism thrown in. For instance, "I think that sharing thoughts, feelings and experiences with another person is one of the greatest blessings of this life" is a sentiment that would be at home on the blog site tumblr in the twenty-first century. Even a long digression on dog food captures a common topic of writing from the 1830s. Before the twentieth century, prepared commercial pet food did not exist, and pets were fed table scraps. There was a popular literature, particularly among those who kept sporting dogs, about what constituted an ideal diet for them, such as the amount of meat in relation to grain.

Aksenty Ivanovich Poprishchin

Poprishchin is the only character whose full name is given. In Russian names, the first name is a given name, and the last name is a family name. But the middle name is a patronymic, which is the person's father's name (in this case, Ivan), with a suffix indicating son of or daughter of. Whereas in many countries people are rarely addressed by their middle name, the custom in Russia is to address people by their given name combined with the patronymic or to use only the patronymic.

Poprishchin is a bureaucrat working in a government office in Saint Petersburg. His career has been a complete failure: in twenty years he had not received a single promotion. The story follows his progressive descent into madness. He is obsessed with Sophie, the daughter of his department director, who as a matter of class is completely unobtainable to him (one can see the first signs of madness in his fantasies of becoming a colonel or general, which would make her approachable). He can do nothing but stalk her and has a large and potentially dangerous fantasy life involving her. At one point, he has to caution himself against committing too much of this to the pages of his diary: "If only his daughter . . . scum that I am! Never mind, better say nothing about that." One of the most disturbing elements of the story is Poprishchin's detailed fantasy of spying on her in her bedroom:

> that's what I'd dearly love to see, her boudoir, with all those jars and little phials, and such flowers, you daren't even breathe on them. . . . One glance at that little stool where she puts her tiny foot when she steps out of bed, And then, over that tiny foot, she starts pulling on her snowy white stocking.

Poprishchin's actions as he follows Sophie around the city become so outrageous that the department head has to speak to him about it. Later, his invasion of her room is probably the cause of his commitment.

Poprishchin is obsessed with status. The director tells him, "Take a good look at yourself. *What* are you? Just nothing, an absolute *nobody*." He replies in his imagination because he does not dare to talk back to his superior:

> I'm a gentleman! I could get promotion if I wanted! I'm only forty-two, that's an age nowadays when one's career is only just beginning. Just you wait, my friend, until I'm a colonel, or even something higher. I'll acquire more status than *you*.

Although schizophrenia, which one may suppose Poprishchin has, is a brain disorder with a variety of physical causes, in Gogol's narrative one can see the source of Poprishchin's insanity. The disconnect between his status in the real world and the status he considers he is entitled to is so vast that he has to resort to fantasy to conceal the truth from himself. It is as if Gogol is saying that the cause of madness is this kind of fabulation made into a habit. The same obsession with status persists even as his thinking becomes more disordered. When he reads the letters written by the dog Medji, he sees his own lack of status exposed:

> He has a very peculiar name. All the time he sits sharpening quills. His hair looks just like hay. Papa always sends him on errands instead of one of the servants. . . . Sophie can't stop laughing when she looks at him.

He must be acutely aware of his own insignificance but at the same time hides it from his consciousness by his main mental effort. Naturally, he has to imagine himself as a king, to make up for the psychic distress he feels over his own powerlessness.

Poprishchin's first overt symptom of mental illness is hearing a conversation between Sophie's lapdog, Medji, and that of her dog friend, Fidèle. From there, the narrative becomes more fantastic. The reader has to do quite a bit of reading between the lines to figure out what is actually going on, for instance in seeing his final trip to Spain as Poprishchin's committal to an asylum. A more difficult example is Poprishchin's expedition into the apartment of Fidèle's owner to steal a bundle of letters from Medji out of the dog's basket. Many commentators take this episode as entirely delusion and the letters as products of Poprishchin's collapsing imagination. But it also seems possible to read the episode as his breaking into the house and stealing letters from Sophie to the other dog's owner, which he screens as being from her dog, perhaps so he can deny her low opinion of him.

The substance of Poprishchin's fantasies is drawn from magazine and newspaper articles. Even when he is still presented as fairly sane, his thoughts constantly refer to the world as he perceives it through reading magazines. His idea that a man's career can just be getting started in the modern world at age forty-two is just the subject for a magazine article (aimed, naturally, at an audience of men whose careers have stalled in middle age). As his hallucinations become more and more fantastic, he justifies them by comparing them to things he has read in magazines (which must therefore be true), for example, recalling stories about talking fish and cows after he begins to hear dogs talk. As his fantasies become more complex, they are more explicitly based on magazine material, from news articles about the succession crisis in Spain and other political news concerning France and England. Even Poprishchin's taste for the theater (which may seem his one redeeming quality) can be taken as reflecting magazine theater criticism.

Sophie

Sophie is the object of Poprishchin's morbid fantasies and the daughter of his office director. Just as Poprishchin looks on the men above him with alternating adoration and hatred, he views Sophie in two different lights. He first describes her as follows: "Her dress was white, like a swan. What magnificence! And when she looked at me it was like the sun shining, I swear it!" But after he breaks into her bedroom, he has a revelation:

> But how crafty women can be! Only then did it dawn on me what they are really like. So far, no one has ever discovered whom women are in love with. I was the first to solve this mystery: they are in love with the devil.

Poprishchin's conception of Sophie requires her to be good and evil at once.

Teplov

Teplov, an army officer, is Sophie's fiancé.

THEMES

Conspiracies

A conspiracy theory is a belief that has no basis in fact but that becomes widespread, particularly through circulation in print, and is widely accepted either by the population at large or by certain groups. The prototypical conspiracy theory is the blood libel, the belief, common in Europe during the Middle Ages that the matzo (unleavened bread) prepared by Jews for the celebration of Passover, was made with the blood of a Gentile child kidnapped and sacrificed by Jewish elders. This false belief was cited as justification for anti-Jewish massacres (pogroms) frequently committed by Christians during the Middle Ages and in Russia into the nineteenth century.

The following passage in "The Diary of a Madman" is generally taken as a reference to the moon hoax:

> I'm very annoyed by a strange event that's due to take place at seven o'clock tomorrow: the earth is going to land on the moon. An account of this has been written by the celebrated English chemist Wellington.

This hoax was a conspiracy theory propagated in a series of articles in the American newspaper *New York Sun* in 1835 that gained worldwide attention despite being immediately debunked. The idea, entirely fabricated to boost circulation, was that the astronomer Sir John Herschel had used a new telescope to observe life on the moon. Though it is generally forgotten, it was immensely influential at the time. Brigham Young even incorporated it into the doctrine of the Mormon Church.

TOPICS FOR FURTHER STUDY

- Lu Xun, considered among the most important modern Chinese authors, wrote his "Diary of a Madman" (1918; translated by William Lyle in *Diary of a Madman and Other Stories*, 1990) in part as an homage to Gogol's story. In this story, the people around the main character think he is going insane because he believes that tradition is becoming a form of cannibalism that is destroying Chinese civilization, which badly needs reform from without. Write a paper comparing the two stories.

- Many videos have been posted on YouTube and similar Internet sites of amateurs reading "The Diary of a Madman" or of scenes from theatrical productions (some of them by professional groups and representing filmed rehearsals or other works for their own reference, others by students or amateurs). Make a presentation to your class of excerpts from these readings, demonstrating variations in approach to adapting the story.

- Matt de La Peña's *I Will Save You* (2011) is a young-adult novel whose main character, with evidently few prospects in life, pursues a romance and has a mental illness, which is concealed from the reader in the early part of the text. The story is told in the form of diary entries and other types of text fragments. Write a paper comparing thematic and stylistic similarities between this work and "The Diary of a Madman."

- Many film and theater scripts, and even an opera libretto, have been produced to adapt "The Diary of a Madman" for the stage or film. Try you own hand at turning the story into a script.

Gogol referred to several other conspiracy theories in the story. The most prominent is that European politics was secretly orchestrated by a cabal of Freemasons. Another such theory, and one that seems peculiar to the hierarchical structure of Russian culture, is the story of the peasant who turns out to be a nobleman. One could probably hear this story repeated all the time without being able to find out any definite details. Another conspiracy mentioned in the story that seems strangely modern concerns a barber who "wants to spread Mahommedanism throughout the world. And I've already heard tell that most of the people in France are now practicing the faith." This kind of reading has instilled a conspiratorial mind-set in Poprishchin, revealed in his hopes for the stolen canine letters: "Now at last I would find out every little detail of what had been going on . . . who was mainly behind it—and finally I would get to the bottom of everything."

The production and dissemination of conspiracy theories accelerated with the introduction of the Internet. Two of the most famous to emerge in the twenty-first century were that the 9/11 terrorist attacks were staged by the US government, the Israeli intelligence service Mossad, or both and that Barack Obama is not a US citizen (often combined with the detail that he is an agent of an anti-American Islamic conspiracy). In 2015, the common conspiracy theories were that millions of foreign Muslims were being hidden in national parks in America and that the military exercise code-named Jade Helm was cover for an impending coup d'état. That Poprishchin's belief in the truth of such conspiracies is presented as evidence of his madness is part of Gogol's critique of contemporary culture.

Bureaucracy

One of the subjects of Gogol's satire is the Russian civil service. This subject is often taken as an attack on the Russian government itself, since the topic could hardly be broached directly when the same government has a tight rein of censorship on everything published in the country. Gogol lampooned the incompetence and venal corruption of the officials. As in any bureaucracy, these factors must have been all too obvious to people who had to deal with a civil service office, though the real situation would naturally be more complex. This subject is also addressed in Akira Kurosawa's film *Ikiru*.

Because bureaucracies are composed of human beings, the members of such an institution will inevitably try to rise through the organization's hierarchy on the basis of human relations rather than merit (a prime cause of bureaucratic incompetence). One aspect of this is the sycophancy, or

The story is told in the form of Poprishchin's diary entries. *(© neelsky / Shutterstock)*

sucking up, shown by junior to superior bureaucrats. Sloan Wilson, the author of *The Man in the Gray Flannel Suit*, recalled a classic example to David Halberstam in an interview for Halberstam's study *The Fifties*. Wilson had been a promising young junior executive, the kind that senior executives surrounded themselves with. On one occasion, he was part of group of senior executives and their young assistants when they came in out of the rain. When he quickly found he was the only junior holding only his own hat, he suddenly realized that he had lost a competition between the younger men to take and hold the hats of their superiors. It showed him how insane his situation was. A similar activity that was notorious in the Russian civil service was the junior men's sharpening quills for their seniors, an obsessive pastime of Poprishchin, though in his case it does no good.

STYLE

Short Story

A short story is defined as a work of fiction generally between three thousand and ten thousand words long (though those numbers are not absolute). The short story is a characteristically modern format, although certain older works would meet the technical definition. The second-century Greek writer Lucian of Samosata, for example, wrote many works that could be considered short stories, such as *The True History* or *The Dialogues of the Courtesans*. During the Renaissance, the transcription of traditional storytelling reintroduced short fiction into literature in such works as Boccaccio's *Decameron* (and numerous imitators) and especially in fairy tale collections. The earliest fairy tales were *The Facetious Nights of Straparola* (1550–1555), from Italy, and the best known were the nineteenth-century collection by the brothers Grimm, from Germany. *Märchen*, the German word for "fairy tale," means "little story."

The short story became a major literary genre around 1820. For the first time, there was an abundance of short stories, and new authors made their reputations writing them, including Washington Irving, Edgar Allan Poe, and E. T. A. Hoffmann. Gogol, best known for his short stories—including "The Diary of a Madman," "The Nose," and "The Overcoat,"—belongs to this group. Why did this happen just at this time? The rise to prominence of the short story was not an aesthetic development and properly speaking is not part of the history of literature. Rather, around 1820, the cost of printing was dramatically reduced by mechanization and a new and larger middle class was emerging out of the industrial economy. These factors led to the creation of the magazine, a monthly, or in some cases, weekly, publication that contained a miscellany of reading material meant to attract an audience to the advertising that made publishing it profitable. The length of the short story was established by the commercial format of the magazine, which demanded works that middle-class readers could digest in a single sitting, such as after dinner or on a Saturday morning. "The Diary of a Madman" is particularly interesting in regard to the commercial origins of the modern short story, because it largely consists of satires of the genres of literature regularly printed in the early magazines.

Epistolary Literature

Epistolary literature is work that takes the form of pseudo-documents, such as a fabricated series of letters or, in the case of "The Diary of a Madman," a diary. The technique allows the creation of verisimilitude, because there are letters and diaries that one can read, often with a semiliterary form themselves. Not much disbelief has to be suspended to accept a diary that happens to convey a more tightly constructed narrative than usual. The epistolary form also relates to the origins of fiction. Whereas in the twenty-first century, fiction is the premiere form of literature, to the extent that nothing seems more natural and expected than making up stories that relate events that never happened to characters who never existed, this was not always the case.

Writing began as a form of record keeping, such as keeping track of how many cattle in a herd a certain investor owned. Prose emerged to record important events, especially the acts of rulers. The records of divination, such as early forms of astrology, are actually among the oldest writings. Although such records were manipulated with fabrication for the purposes of propaganda, the concept was that they related true events. As government administrations became better organized, especially in the first millennium BCE, they produced a variety of documents, including letters, which were stored in archives.

Greek culture took over the practice of record keeping, along with writing itself, from the Near East. In the classical period, the beginnings of higher education were aimed at teaching future bureaucrats how to write letters and other documents. The letters composed as classwork, especially exemplars composed by teachers, were necessarily hypothetical or fictional, such as writing a letter to persuade a king to send food in a time of famine). By the fourth century, this practice had become so ingrained that some educated bureaucrats began to write letters as a form of literary expression, dealing with entirely fictive topics. This kind of exercise soon produced full-blown fiction in the modern sense, represented by the Greek novels produced in the Roman Empire, such as the *Aethiopica* of Heliodorus and the better known *Metamorphoses*, also called *The Golden Ass*, of Apuleius, which was written in Latin.

The epistolary, or in this case documentary, conceit of "The Diary of a Madman" is straightforward and suited to Gogol's purpose. The text is presented in a series of diary entries showing the progressive mental decline of the diarist. The entries become more and more disordered as the insanity worsens. This is signaled in the entry headings of the diary. They begin with ordinary dates, such as October 3rd. But as the thinking of the writer becomes more evidently disordered, the headings become strange, such as dates in the far future and impossible days, such as April 43rd, 2000, which was nearly 170 years in the future when the story was written. The dates then proceed to made-up months, such as Martober, and "No date. The day didn't have one." The final heading is gibberish: "Da 34 te Mth eary February [written upside down] 349."

HISTORICAL CONTEXT

Carlism

In 1833, Ferdinand VII of Spain died, leaving an infant daughter to succeed him on the Spanish throne as Isabella II with her mother, Maria Cristina, as regent. Spanish law had been changed in 1830 to allow this succession, but a serious opposition developed that wanted to elevate the heir under the traditional legal arrangement, Isabella's uncle Carlos. This faction accordingly became known as the Carlists. Spain was racked by civil war between supporters of the two claimants for the next forty years, until the legislature deposed Isabella and invited a relative of the king of Italy to become king; thereafter the Carlists developed into an ordinary political party.

The wars and the Carlist movement took on a nationalist dimension, finding support in the Basque region and Catalonia, both areas with separatist ambitions. The Carlists also became politically reactionary, opposing liberal reform. They were eventually subsumed into the Falange, the fascist party of Franco, in the 1930s. The initial secession crisis was highly topical in 1833 and was much in the newspapers. This is the reason it becomes fixed in Poprishchin's mind that he is the rightful heir—his whole mental life is composed of magazine and newspaper articles.

In the final section, Gogol refers to other current events relevant to the deposition of monarchies when he wrote the story. He mentions the resistance to monarchy coming from the Prince de Polignac, a French politician responsible for the revolt against the Bourbon dynasty in 1830. Though he was in prison for treason, de Polignac published his memoirs in 1832. Gogol also refers to the dey of Algiers, the monarch of Algeria who was deposed by the French in 1830.

COMPARE
&
CONTRAST

- **1830s:** Dogs are generally fed table scraps.

  Today: A multibillion dollar multinational industry exists to manufacture specially formulated dog foods.

- **1830s:** Magazines are a new and pervasive influence on middle-class culture.

  Today: Print magazines are waning, but many of the literary forms established in nineteenth-century magazines continue in formats delivered by the Internet.

- **1830s:** All publications in Russia must be passed by a board of censorship that has the explicitly defined task of protecting the interests of the Russian government and upholding the traditions of Russian cultural institutions like the church.

  Today: The Internet and other communication media in Russia are tightly censored in the interests of high-ranking politicians and business owners by means such as unofficial police harassment and the misapplication of laws originally passed to protect the interests of children.

The Russian Civil Service

In the seventeenth century, the Russian tsar Peter the Great, after a disastrous military defeat by Sweden, realized how backward many institutions in Russia were compared with those in western Europe. He famously toured the west, both openly and in disguise, to ascertain how conditions in Russia could be improved, and he set out to systematically modernize his country. The best-known step he took was to force Russian noblemen to adopt Western clothing and hairstyles, such as shaving their long beards. He compelled them with a special tax on beards. He also compelled all noblemen to serve in the army, figuring that this duty would offset their privileges. Later, this requirement was modified so that noblemen, as they acquired technical educations, could serve either in the army or in the newly created civil service.

Controlled by the autocratic power of the tsar, the civil service considerably increased the government's reach into the affairs of its citizens. One example of this was the board of censorship, which all of Gogol's writings had to pass through before publication. The board deleted several passages (since restored) of "The Diary of a Madman" perceived as critical of the government and some deemed anti-Semitic. It is because of this historical link between the nobility and the civil service that Poprishchin is constantly spouting off about his noble status. His ancestors probably were noblemen, but any lands they owned were long since lost to him. The civil service had a precise table of ranks that corresponded directly to the military ranks of the army and had military-style uniforms, though they did not routinely wear them to the office. For all of his dreams of becoming a colonel or general, Poprishchin is a collegiate registrar, the lowest rank in the civil service. His work consists of copying documents by hand so that the different copies can be placed in various document depositories. In the twenty-first century, this task would be done electronically.

CRITICAL OVERVIEW

Vsevolod Setchkarev, in *Gogol: His Life and Works*, established a biographical framework for approaching "The Diary of a Madman." He presented the often repeated, but poorly documented, story that Gogol turned to the story after hearing, and even taking notes on, someone discoursing on the inexorable, logical progression of madness once it takes hold of a person. Setchkarev also pointed to the obvious influence of E. T. A. Hoffmann on Gogol's fantastic narrative. Setchkarev offers a pop psychology

Poprishchin is a lowly civil servant during the conservative reign of Nicholas I, when corruption was rampant. (© KOSMOPHOXA / *Shutterstock*)

explanation of Poprishchin's madness: "The development of the mental disturbance into delusions of grandeur as a consequence of an inferiority complex resulting from an unhappy love affair is described with realistic detail and considerable empathy." Setchkarev was conscious of the story's relation to contemporary journalistic writing but discounted this point in favor of a philosophical aesthetic dualism:

> Is this not what we do in this devil-directed world? Where is the fixed point by which truth and illusion can be distinguished? Even when complete nonsense is related, the style of a factual report is brilliantly maintained.

Mikhail Weiskopf, in "The Bird Troika and the Chariot of the Soul: Plato and Gogol," offered an ambitious reading of "The Diary of a Madman" as a gnostic satire of Plato's *Timaeus*. The textual evidence Weiskopf cited in support of this interpretation was an anti-Semitic slur that

rabbis wash only once a week (cut from the story by government censors), implying that the entire cosmic architecture of gnosticism arose from the practice of measuring time in weeks. Weiskopf saw in the story a version of the gnostic myth of the savior in which the savior's (Poprishchin's) true character is revealed in his new identity as the king of Spain. Weiskopf read Poprishchin's final appeal to his mother to save him as a return to Sophia (the embodiment of holy wisdom) or other feminine heavenly entity (he made no connection to the name of the director's daughter, Sophie).

Another interpretation of the ending of "The Diary of a Madman" may have been offered by Terry Gilliam in the film *Brazil* (1985). The main character seems to effect a beatific escape from a totalitarian regime, but then it is revealed that he has gone mad and entered a state of catatonia under torture.

Anne Lounsbery, in the monograph *Thin Culture, High Art*, treated Gogol in a postmodern manner. She tore the text apart to see what it is made from, as Poprishchin himself claims critics do to plays. Her basic observation was that Poprishchin has no identity and must desperately try to construct one. When the office manager calls him a nothing, according to Lounsbery, "the insult embodies Poprishchin's own repressed knowledge of his utter insignificance in a society that takes both rank and the outward signs of rank just as seriously as he takes them." He must respond with his detailed fantasies that his own rank will somehow, or someday, be discovered:

> Poprishchin's diary is the written record of a subjectivity composed entirely from the detritus and flux of print culture, with its emphasis on novelties (fashions, gossip, "news") that are in reality the same endlessly repeated and recycled fragments.

Lounsbery found mini-satires in Gogol's text of numerous popular genres: the detective story, the human-interest story, the editorial style, the story of romantic intrigue, travel writing, and official pronouncements. Moreover, she writes of Poprishchin, "the crazier he becomes, the more frequently and freely his writing seems to adapt the conventions of journalism." Style becomes, in an emerging capitalist economy, a personal brand. Poprishchin is obsessed with style, and he thinks that behind a style is always a person, and a person of some importance. One way to read his madness is as an attempt as an author to create himself, to create a new reality in which he has a different identity.

CRITICISM

Rita M. Brown

Brown is an English professor. In the following essay, she examines "The Diary of a Mad Man" within the framework of the history of mental illness.

The complex of ideas and institutions that make up mental illness and psychiatry seems like an ordinary part of modern life. People can be identified as having mental illness and can be treated by psychiatrists, the same way victims of cancer or diabetes can be identified and treated by other kinds of physicians. These are facts to be accepted like any other part of modern life, without any special consideration. But the modern Western culture that seems so much to be taken for granted is the result of a series of historical processes, and there is nothing simple about its existence. Mental illness, like anything else, has a history. Gogol's story "The Diary of a Madman" documents an early stage in the codevelopment of insanity and psychiatry as modern institutions.

Michel Foucault was a French philosopher and historian who was originally trained as a psychiatrist. His large body of work on cultural history is among the most influential historical writing of the twentieth century. He imported the approach of structuralist anthropology into history, allowing him to follow the larger trends of cultural development across disciplines and institutions. Three times in the 1950s, he attempted to write a history, not of mental illness but of the cultural reception of mental illness, finally producing his *History of Madness* in 1961.

Foucault began his history in the Middle Ages, but it is worth noting as relevant background that the Old Testament is unequivocal that madness, like any other illness, is a punishment for sin. The New Testament interprets mental illness as a test of faith and specifies that what would be called mental illness in the twenty-first century was frequently caused by possession by a fallen spirit. The Catholic Church claimed to be able to drive out such spirits through the ritual of exorcism, which before the eighteenth century was the only form of treatment applied to mental illness in Europe.

Foucault was critical of the attempt to model the science of human behavior on the physical sciences and did not have much faith in writing an actual history of mental illness, because it would be difficult, for example, to assess centuries-old cases in modern medical terms. Foucault was not interested in how it was that certain people became mentally ill (though he never denied that mental illness had a real existence) but wanted to discern how certain people came to be treated as mentally ill.

Foucault's structural approach to the history of mental illness and its treatment allowed him to connect his subject to the larger history of civilization and society. For Foucault, the history of mental illness was part of the history of the development of the modern state and modern class structures. As state control of society expanded, as capitalism and bourgeois culture demonized the poor in the seventeenth century, it was generally seen as desirable to clear the streets of beggars by removing them to institutions where they would be provided for in exchange for labor. This swept up together the lame, prostitutes, the mentally ill, and many other classes, often into institutions that had been founded centuries before to house lepers (leprosy was one of the first diseases eradicated in Europe).

The profession of psychiatry emerged not from the medical field but from the keepers of the asylums—a word that originally meant a place of refuge. Asylums usually descended from institutions under monastic control and inherited many features of monastic life: asceticism, work, morality, obedience, and supervision. Whereas people with mental illness were confined in earlier periods, often by their families, in the late eighteenth century, legal commitment procedures were introduced and mental illness was integrated into the emerging social system of modernity: the asylum became an organ of state power. It also became a source of capitalist exploitation, because the people in the asylums were routinely put to work, their labor benefiting the asylum owners.

WHAT DO I READ NEXT?

- *Norwegian Wood* (1987; translated by Jay Rubin, 2000), by Haruki Murakami, is a Japanese novel telling the story of a young man's overwhelming but ultimately hopeless love for a college classmate who is eventually committed to an insane asylum.

- Edgar Allan Poe was an American contemporary of Gogol and a pioneer of the short story. He often dealt with the same fantastic subject matter and produced satires of the new magazine genres. Poe's stories are out of copyright and are frequently reprinted; almost all can be found on the Internet. Stories of Poe's most relevant to "The Diary of a Madman" are "William Wilson," "The Unparalleled Adventure of One Hans Pfaall" (both reprinted in Poe's 1840 collection *Tales of the Grotesque and Arabesque*), "The Tell-Tale Heart" (1843), and "The Balloon Hoax" (1844).

- Sloan Wilson's *The Man in the Gray Flannel Suit* (1955) is a novel about a young executive's realization that the petty office politics that consume his life is a meaningless round of sycophancy; he withdraws from it before it destroys his personal life.

- Francesca Zappia's *Made You Up* (2015) is a young-adult novel about the main character's mental illness.

- *Girl, Interrupted* is a 1993 memoir by Susanna Kaysen describing her institutionalization after a suicide attempt as a teenager. James Mangold adapted the book into a film in 1999.

- Among the many insane things Poprishchin reads are fantastic stories such as "It's said that in England a fish swam to the surface and

said two words in such a strange language the professors have been racking their brains for three years now to discover what it was." Sensational stories have always been fabricated in newspapers and magazines to generate circulation. For many years, a tabloid called *Weekly World News* was famous for publishing nothing else. On the Internet, similar stories, among other enticements to visit a web page, are called clickbait. In the early twentieth century, Charles Fort devoted himself to collecting and republishing such stories. He seems to have sincerely believed that all such stories were true and constituted evidence of an alternative reality that science suppressed (a conspiracy theory). The first of many such volumes Fort published was *The Book of the Damned* (1919).

- *Dead Souls* (1842) is often considered Gogol's masterpiece. The novel concerns a low-level bureaucrat dismissed for corruption. He goes to a rural village and starts buying up dead souls—deeds on peasants who have died but on whom the owner owes taxes until the next official census (serfdom in Russia of the period was much like slavery in the American South). He intends to conduct a swindle using the ownership papers as collateral for a bank loan. The title has a secondary meaning referring to the spiritual condition of the novel's characters. The novel ends abruptly, but given Gogol's originality this may be as he intended. It may also be that the second half of the novel was among the manuscripts Gogol burned in a fit of religious mania a few days before his death.

Once an institution to treat mental illness was established, it naturally attracted patients. H. C. Erik Midelfort, in delivering an important historical corrective to Foucault's rather freewheeling philosophical analysis, pointed out that between 1800 and 1850 in the United States, France, and Great Britain (where statistics are available, unlike in Russia), the rate of commitment increased from approximately three persons per hundred thousand to nearly twenty (a number that would increase tenfold over the following century, with the greatest rate of institutionalization of the mentally ill in the 1950s and 1960s). This, however, validated Foucault's thesis that the growth of the mental health industry had to be viewed in terms of expanding social control by governmental and capitalistic institutions. It is certainly not the case that more people were experiencing mental illness; rather, the asylums as institutions were becoming more powerful.

In "The Diary of a Madman," Gogol provided a highly informative description of the nineteenth-century asylum system and psychiatry, though much of it was disguised behind the delusional interpretation that Poprishchin puts on it. Although various contemporaries of Gogol tell quite different stories about the origin of "The Diary of a Mad Man," it is in any case true that much of the material in the story came from a series of articles on the new asylums in the *Northern Bee*, a reactionary literary journal published in Saint Petersburg. One such article concerned the special propensity of civil servants to go mad. Poprishchin's fantasies about noses seem also to come from this source. More generally, however, the satirical purpose of the story is revealed from the details of the fantasies that define Poprishchin's madness. They are all drawn from the new magazine literature that was emerging at the time, with snippets of international news, poetry, and fiction for young women all mixed together. Although Gogol's own literary success depended on the new magazines, he seems to be satirizing the new genre as more than a little mad.

Gogol presented a detailed and, one must suppose, accurate view of life in a Russian asylum in the 1830s, derived from reporting on the subject, though one must be careful in untangling reports obscured by Poprishchin's madness. In the 1830s, the standard of psychiatric care was still in large part derived from the Christian models of mental illness. Therapy consisted of pointing out the patient's guilt in refusing to work or in generally refusing to conform. It established the standard of behavior that was expected and punished patients who did not live up to that standard. One can see that this form of treatment and the penal theories that underlay the incarceration of criminals descended from a common monastic ancestor. More enlightened asylums mixed traditions of Hippocratic medicine into their treatments, using

diet, exercise, and a healthful climate and surroundings as part of the treatment. This does not seem to be the case in Poprishchin's asylum.

When Poprishchin returns to work after a three-week hiatus, the document the director gives him to sign, and which he signs as Ferdinand VIII, is probably his commitment papers (though a good question is how his signature could be valid if he is mentally unsound). Poprishchin had already invaded the director's home and been stalking his daughter, providing a motive for the commitment. The Spanish deputation that takes him to Spain a few days later is clearly the ambulance taking him to the asylum. (The delay occurs because the commitment papers had to work their way through the correct bureaucratic channels.) The first thing he notices in his palace in Spain is that everyone has shaved heads. He rationalizes that this must be the Spanish fashion among courtiers and soldiers, but he is really seeing the inmates of the asylum, whose heads have been shaved as a measure against lice (most of the staff would also have shaved their heads for the same reason). Even in the twenty-first century, stereotypical depictions of people with mental illness, especially in Great Britain, show them with shaved heads.

One of the grandees of the court of Spain—an asylum attendant—throws Poprishchin into a cell and tells him, "Sit there, and if you call yourself King Ferdinand once more, I'll thrash that nonsense out of you." When Poprishchin refuses to obey, he is severely beaten. This was an actual form of psychiatric treatment. The idea was that the patient was simply willfully refusing to conform to the consensus reality that everyone else agreed to and like a petulant child could be persuaded to do so by punishment. Another treatment Poprishchin undergoes is to be doused with cold water. This was viewed as a sort of shock treatment that would snap the patient back to reality. Poprishchin eventually concludes that he has fallen into the hands of the Spanish Inquisition and that his psychiatrist is the grand inquisitor. Actually, the Inquisition, though famous for burning heretics, committed many more people to long-term imprisonment with the idea that through study and instruction they could be brought back into the fold of orthodox belief, an important institutional ancestor of the asylum.

Gogol's story is amusing and often seems lighthearted. But the humor, as great humor

Poprishchin first glimpses Sophie as she steps out of a carriage. (© *Viacheslav Lopatin | Shutterstock*)

almost always does, conceals a more serious critique of society. It is obvious, without Gogol's having to say so clearly enough to antagonize the censors, that the government Poprishchin is part of is hopelessly corrupt and ineffective. It is equally obvious that a psychiatric treatment system that may be mistaken for the Spanish Inquisition, even by a madman, is deeply flawed.

Source: Rita M. Brown, Critical Essay on "Diary of a Madman," in *Short Stories for Students*, Gale, Cengage Learning, 2016.

Gavriel Shapiro

In the following excerpt, Shapiro examines Gogol's use of anaphora and epiphora.

. . . Anaphora, the repetition of a word or a phrase at the beginning of successive lines, can be found at least as early as the Bible: "Give them according to their deeds, and according to the wickedness of their endeavours: give them after the work of their hands" (Psalms 28:4). We frequently come across anaphora in the literature of antiquity, when the rhetoricians asserted that the figure should be employed "for the sake of force

and emphasis," as Quintilian summed up in his *Institutio Oratoria* (9, 3:30). A century earlier Virgil employed "here" for this purpose in his *Eclogues*: "Here are cold springs, Lycoris, here soft meadows, here woodland; here, with thee, time alone would wear me away" (10:42–44). In the Middle Ages, Dante, who took Virgil as his guide not only in his imaginary infernal journey but also in his literary undertakings, inscribed over the gates of Hell: "THROUGH ME THE WAY INTO THE WOEFUL CITY, / THROUGH ME THE WAY TO THE ETERNAL PAIN, / THROUGH ME THE WAY AMONG THE LOST PEOPLE" (III, 1–3).

. . . Epiphora, the counterpart of anaphora, involves the repetition of a word or a phrase at the ends of successive lines. Quintilian described this in his *Institutio Oratoria*, quoting a passage from Cicero's *Pro Milone* (22:59): "Who demanded them? Appius. Who produced them? Appius." Further on, Quintilian indicated that this passage, containing both the anaphora "who" and the epiphora "Appius," illustrates the device known as *complexion*. In the following passage from Cicero's *Philippics*,

> GOGOL EMPLOYED BOTH ANAPHORA AND EPIPHORA THROUGHOUT HIS CAREER. HE USED THEM FOR EMPHASIS, ALONG THE LINES PROPOUNDED BY QUINTILIAN AND FOLLOWED BY MEDIEVAL AND BAROQUE WRITERS."

we find another epiphora: "Men have been brought back from exile by a dead man; citizenship has been given, not only to individuals, but to whole tribes and provinces by a dead man; by boundless exemptions revenues have been done away with by a dead man" (1, 10:24). Like anaphora, epiphora is employed for emphasis: repetition of a word or phrase, whether at the beginning or end of successive lines, in itself arrests the reader's attention.

. . . All the examples of Gogol's use of anaphora given so far, despite their appearance in passages with differing tonalities, were used by the narrator, even though at times, as in *Hanz Kuechelgarten*, they conveyed the character's thoughts. The use of anaphora by the character himself is a different matter. We find this in the "Diary of a Madman," a rare instance of first-person narrative in Gogol's oeuvre. This type of narrative penetrates deeper into the character's inner world, and an emphatic literary device like anaphora contributes greatly to this effect. The protagonist and narrator of this tale, Poprishchin, suffers from his inferior status, which does not correspond to his pride in his nobility and to his high ambitions, a discrepancy that ultimately drives him to madness. Poprishchin's predicament is exacerbated by his infatuation with the director's daughter. In one of the entries in his diary Poprishchin shows his longing for this world of the director and his daughter, a world in which he does not belong and to which he has no access:

> I should like to know what he [the director] thinks most about. What is going on in that head? I should like to get a close view of the life of these gentlemen, of all these *équivoques* and court ways. How they go on and what they do in their circle—that's what I should like to find out! . . . I should like to look into the drawing room, of which one only sees the

open door and another room beyond it. Ah, what sumptuous furniture! What mirrors and china! I long to have a look in there, into the part of the house where her Excellency is, that's where I should like to go!

Having no access to the inner chambers of the director's house, Poprishchin attempts to overcome this obstacle in his imagination. We watch his imaginary wandering about the director's house, going from the study, the only room he is allowed into, to the drawing room, then to a room the name of which he does not know, and finally to the most desirable of them all—the boudoir of the director's daughter. The use of the phrase "I should like to" as anaphora, and at times also as epiphora, highlights the intensity of Poprishchin's aspirations. Another epiphora, also conducive to the reader's entering into the protagonist's innermost feelings, appears later on in this narrative. Very distressed by the prospect of the director's daughter's marriage to a court chamberlain, Poprishchin ponders his own low rank of titular councilor, which appears to him as the only obstacle on his way to happiness: "Why am I a titular councilor and on what grounds am I a titular councilor? Perhaps I am not a titular councilor at all? Perhaps I am a count or a general, and only somehow appear to be a titular councilor? . . . I should like to know why I am a titular councilor. Why precisely a titular councilor?." The emphatic repetition of "titular councilor" underscores Poprishchin's obsession with rank, which he views as the source of his misery, and helps to lay the psychological ground for the "resolution" of this obsession in the character's leap into *mania grandiosa*.

The epiphora device is much in evidence in Gogol's works, both early and late. In a passage of lyrical tonality in "A May Night," a tale of the *Evenings* cycle, Gogol used the sixfold epiphora "night" to highlight the beauty of that time in his native Ukraine: "Do you know the Ukrainian night? Aie, you do not know the Ukrainian night! . . . Heavenly night! Enchanting night! . . . Divine night! Enchanting night!."

We find the epiphora "virtuous man," in combination with the anaphora "because," employed sarcastically in *Dead Souls*. Explaining his reasons for taking Chichikov as the protagonist of the *poéma*, the narrator, whose voice in this passage sounds especially close to Gogol's, expresses his resentment at the exploitation of the virtuous man as a literary character, which by Gogol's time could set a reader's teeth on edge:

"Because it is time at last to give the poor virtuous man a rest . . . because they make a hypocritical use of the virtuous man; because they do not respect the virtuous man."

In Gogol's letter to the poet Nikolai Iazykov (September 27, 1841), there is a passage with three repetitions of the phrase "then you do not love me":

> And if, when we bid farewell to each other, a spark of my soul's strength does not pass from my hand into your soul at our handshake, then you do not love me. And if sometime ennui overcomes you and, remembering me, you do not have enough power to overcome it, then you do not love me; and if a momentary ailment makes you heavier and your spirit bows low, then you do not love me.

This passage, like "The Rule of Living in the World" cited earlier, is very indicative of Gogol's frame of mind in the 1840s, when he came to believe in his prophetic powers. The letter is pervaded with the tone of a preacher certain of his gift of foresight—"For never has the voice that flies out of my soul deceived me"—and his unique role in the destiny of his friends—"From now on, your gaze should be brightly and cheerfully raised upward—our meeting occurred for that reason." In this frame of mind Gogol used the epiphora "then you do not love me" to assist his ailing friend to overcome his despondency, which, as we may recall, Gogol viewed as a terrible sin eventually leading to spiritual death.

Gogol employed both anaphora and epiphora throughout his career. He used them for emphasis, along the lines propounded by Quintilian and followed by medieval and Baroque writers. Gogol employed these figures with remarkable diversity in his poetry and prose, fiction and correspondence, in passages with differing tonalities—lyrical, satirical, or moralizing. In addition Gogol used both anaphora and epiphora in the first-person narrative "Diary of a Madman" to highlight important features of Poprishchin's character, contributing to our better understanding of this miserable man's inner world and our knowledge of his most cherished dreams, which, remaining unrealized, drove him to insanity. . . .

Source: Gavriel Shapiro, "Figurative Language: Anaphora and Epiphora," in *Nikolai Gogol and the Baroque Cultural Heritage*, Pennsylvania State University Press, 1993, pp. 184, 186, 191–93.

Jesse Zeldin

In the following excerpt, Zeldin explains how Gogol's works explore different levels of reality.

. . . When we turn to "The Diary of a Madman," on the surface we seem to have a straightforward, comparatively modern portrayal of schizophrenia, the degeneration of a poor downtrodden clerk who thinks that he hears two dogs talking to each other. Later, he reads what he takes to be letters—composed by Lord knows who—between them, and he finally imagines himself to be the king of Spain. He is a little man who has been crushed by a cruel, unfeeling world, one of the "insulted and injured," who has been driven out of his mind by the pressures of the Russian milieu. The account of the treatment accorded Poprishchin (whose name is only mentioned one time, towards the end of the story) in the madhouse, coupled with his pathetic appeals to his mother, might well be taken as an attack on a system that refuses to give people a chance—a kind of Russian *Oliver Twist* without a happy ending. Technically, Gogol accomplished a feat by telling the story in the first person, so that the impact, from the point of view just outlined, is all the greater. For once, it can be claimed at the same time, Gogol was not being typical, because what are depicted are the particular processes of one mind. Considered on this level, "The Diary of a Madman" is certainly more successful than Dostoevsky's more famous *The Double*.

No such story, however, can escape being involved in the problem of reality; it could be said that the schizoid has simply chosen a different reality from that of the rest of us. The curious thing here is that Gogol gives no reason categorically to state, no matter what our inclinations may be, that the dogs did *not* talk to each other and that they did *not* exchange letters; the assumption that they did not is simply based on the audience's different perception of what is real. Are those genuinely the wanderings of a sick mind, as the reader automatically assumes and as Gogol's title indicates, or, once again, is reality not quite so simple as the reader would like to think? Is it not possible, rather, that reality, while "objective," is not material? The device of narration in the first person here assumes additional significance, since it is the *narrator's* reality that we are involved in, the *narrator's* point of view that the reader must accept—and it is the point of view, the reality, of a man who is completely alone, in a state of

> POPRISHCHIN IS MEANT TO BE LAUGHED AT, NOT WITH. THE LAUGHTER IS MEANT TO PUT A DISTANCE BETWEEN READER AND CHARACTER, NOT TO ENLIST SYMPATHY. NOT ONLY IS POPRISHCHIN'S WORLD WRONG; *HE* IS WRONG."

utter separation. The frightening thing is that once we grant Poprishchin's premise that things are not what they seem to be, that no one sees the truth about him, and that he lives in truth, whereas everyone else lives in falsity, then everything makes sense—the absurdity, the grotesqueness that so many critics have commented upon, disappears. If the madman is one who has lost touch with reality, then we have a right to ask what reality is. And this question is precisely the one that is posed for us here.

This does not mean that for Gogol reality is relative. Perhaps neither of Poprishchin's worlds—either that of his office or that of his madness—is the real one; perhaps everything in the story, in short, is mad. The officials, without exception, are more interested in their positions and ranks than in what they are. It is on the basis, indeed, of position and rank that one man speaks to another. One might go so far as to say that this emphasis on rank is what teaches Poprishchin to become the king of Spain. He is, after all, officially only a titular councillor, the equivalent of a captain, ninth on the Table of Ranks. This defines him, as the others' ranks define them. It is like being defined by a piece of clothing or a hairdo or a particular kind of moustache (Gogol often, in fact, uses inanimate objects to define his characters). But what does this definition have to do, Poprishchin asks, with what a person is in reality: "I have many times wanted to discover why all these differences occur. Why am I a titular councillor and on what grounds am I a titular councillor? Perhaps I am some count or general, and only seem to be a titular councillor? Perhaps I myself don't know who I am."

The last sentence is of particular significance—does anyone, even granted that all the characters are seen through Poprishchin's eyes, know who he is? As he says, "Give me a fashionably cut coat, and let me tie on a necktie like yours—and then you wouldn't hold a candle to me. No income—that's the trouble." And later: "Everything that's best in the social world is gotten either by court chamberlains or by generals. You find some poor treasure, you think you've got it in your hand—a court chamberlain or a general snatches it away from you.... I'd like to become a general myself.... I'd like to be a general only to see how they would try to get around me and do all their court tricks and *équivoques* and then say to them: I spit on you both." When reading the dog's letter, he makes a comment that applies to his entire world: "How can anyone fill a letter with such foolishness! Give me a man! I want to see a man. I ask for food to nourish and pleasure my soul, and instead these bagatelles." But no one knows, nor cares, even about himself, much less about Poprishchin. No one is a man.

Poprishchin's fault, for which he is called mad, is his attempt to find a personality, to become somebody. And he is the only one who makes such an attempt. He suffers, as his colleagues do, from what most Western readers would regard as a normal and legitimate desire: he wants to be regarded, to be noticed, to be paid attention to; his complaint is the same as that of Dostoevsky's Devushkin in *Poor Folk* and of Golyadkin in *The Double*, not to mention the line of buffoons that Dostoevsky trailed behind those two. Once Poprishchin decides that he is king of Spain, he is aware that people have a different attitude towards him; now they pay attention. He may be tormented, but at least he is there, which is more than can be said of anyone else. He is there, that is, except for one brief moment at the very end of the story when, tormented in the madhouse, he cries out: "They do not heed me, do not see me, do not listen to me. Why do they torment me? What do they want of poor me? What can I give them? I have nothing." Then, calling upon his mother, he laments, "Press your poor orphan to your breast! There is no place in the world for him! He is persecuted! Mother, pity your sick child!" There is indeed no place in this world, or in any world, for him. Poprishchin seems to have an intimation of the truth, but no more than that; he is as much isolated at the end as he was at the beginning. The king of Spain is as egocentric as Poprishchin's colleagues in the office. Value remains on this false level. From this point of view, there is no serious difference between Poprishchin mad and Poprishchin sane; both of his worlds and both of his "states of soul" are denials of reality—one as empty and meaningless as the other—so that his "thereness" turns out not to exist after all. The point is that while Poprishchin may have a mind that is susceptible to such terms as sanity and madness, it is his soul that is lost; and for one moment at the end of the story he knows it, as surely as did Chartkov, the philosopher, and Petro.

One of the strangest things about "The Diary of a Madman" is the humor with which Gogol treats his central character. This is not the good humor or the jocularity of some of the Little Russian tales; on the contrary, Poprishchin is meant to be laughed at, not with. The laughter is meant to put a distance between reader and character, not to enlist sympathy. Not only is Poprishchin's world wrong; *he* is wrong. His and his world's falsity is being unmasked, as a warning to the reader; and from this point of view the story is relentless. Like all Gogol's humorous tales, this is a horror story—not because we are witnesses of the crushing of the "little man" (after all, Poprishchin's ambitions are only to be superior to others, as he thinks they are superior to him; to crush as he is crushed), but because we are witnesses of the loss of humanity by those who do not see the truth—we are witnesses of the void. As Poprishchin himself says, he has nothing to give. This statement is a far more profound one than Poprishchin realizes.

We know that whatever reality we choose in "The Diary of a Madman," it will be false, for they are all vulgar and, thus, ugly. Nowhere do we find Gogol's touchstone of beauty and harmony, and nowhere do we find reconciliation. The office that Poprishchin works in is a jangle of discordant elements, each isolating itself: things everywhere are struggling with things. It is marked by separation rather than by unity, even though nobody really cares who he is. Only Poprishchin for a moment realizes the loss, as he says, as much of himself as of others: "Give me a man! I want to see a man. I ask for food to nourish and pleasure my soul, and instead these bagatelles." This might well be the complaint of Gogol himself. This is not only a tedious world, but an insane one, outside the asylum's walls as well as inside them. The one thing we can be certain of is that it is not in this insanity that the truth will be found.

It would appear that this interpretation would lead to a condemnation of the central character as well as of the milieu he inhabits; it would seem that Gogol has gone Swift one better.

I do not think that this was Gogol's intention, for condemnation without an alternative is meaningless. The difficulty was that the beauty that Gogol had already implied in his essays and stories as being the reality transcending and capable of transfiguring material appearance had not yet been actualized in human affairs and thus was incapable of being depicted. Even Gogol had to recognize that his later attempts to do so in *Selected Passages* and in the destroyed portion of *Dead Souls* were failures. But those were endeavors undertaken in desperation. At this stage the only immediate material for the pen of an artist—or at any rate, of an artist like Gogol—was the false, in the belief that the exposure of the false would lead at least to a realization of its opposite. His teaching vocation was to be accomplished through the unmasking of the void. In this sense, Gogol's great talent—and a most unusual one it was—consisted in the portrayal of meaninglessness rather than of meaning, not because Gogol despaired and thought the world absurd, but because truth, like Plato's Good and Dante's God, was ineffable, even though real. Poprishchin, after all, was meant to be laughed at, not to be pitied, because of what Gogol regarded as a false sensibility. I would suggest that Gogol was here confronting the reader with problems that the reader did not previously know existed, problems of the ordinary and everyday that the reader has always taken for granted—"Things are not what they seem" is over and over again his point. What is real and who is sane, if anybody is, in "The Diary of a Madman"? If we are men like Poprishchin's colleagues, the answer is plain—Poprishchin is the one who has lost touch with reality. Few readers, if any, will willingly identify with them, however—they are obviously far too shallow, too petty, too vulgar for us to do so; we know that their perception of reality is false, that they do not have souls. Does that mean that we must identify with Poprishchin, the "victim"? The same objection arises; otherwise there would be no reason for our laughter. Where, then, does reality lie? Or is it all false, and are we?

The point is doubly emphasized by the upset in time when Poprishchin discovers that he is king of Spain. Before that, the dates of the entries in the diary all make perfectly good "sense," running from October 3 to December 8 (and including, in this "normal" sequence, the episodes of the talking and letter-writing dogs). Then time begins to disappear—from "2,000

A.D., April 43"; through "Martober 86 between day and night"; "no day—the day had no date"; and so on, and so forth; to utter temporal gibberish for the last entry, which is "February" written upside down and backwards. This last entry, interestingly enough, is what returns us to lucidity, with Poprishchin's call to his mother. The very notion of the stability of time has been called into question, while a reality transcending time has been indicated. Time, in short, is irrelevant, so that it is not only Poprishchin's world that is disturbed, but our own. We too, despite our laughter, are involved in the problem. Indeed, Gogol the teacher is telling us that it *is* our problem . . . .

Source: Jesse Zeldin, "Petersburg," in *Nikolai Gogol's Quest for Beauty: An Exploration into His Works*, Regents Press of Kansas, 1978, pp. 43–48.

SOURCES

Carcraft, James, *The Revolution of Peter the Great*, Harvard University Press, 2003, pp. 54–74.

Foucault, Michel, *History of Madness*, translated by Jonathan Murphy and Jean Khalfa, Routledge, 2006, 463–510.

Gogol, Nikolay, "The Diary of a Madman," in *The Diary of a Madman, The Government Inspector, and Selected Stories*, translated by Ronald Wilks, 2005, pp. 174–96.

Halberstam, David, *The Fifties*, Random House, 1993, p. 555.

Lounsbery, Anne, *Thin Culture, High Art: Gogol, Hawthorne, and Authorship in Nineteenth-Century Russia and America*, Harvard University Press, 2007, pp. 210–16.

Midelfort, H. C. Erik, "Madness and Civilization in Early Modern Europe: A Reappraisal of Michel Foucault," in *After the Reformation*, edited by Barbara Malament, University of Pennsylvania Press, 1980, pp. 247–65.

Setchkarev, Vsevolod, *Gogol: His Life and Works*, translated by Robert Kramer, New York University Press, 1965, pp. 37, 133–35.

Weiskopf, Mikhail, "The Bird Troika and the Chariot of the Soul: Plato and Gogol," in *Essays on Gogol: Logos and the Russian Word*, edited by Susanne Fusso and Priscilla Meyer, Northwestern University Press, 1992, pp. 126–42.

FURTHER READING

Gabriele, Alberto, *Reading Popular Culture in Victorian Print: Belgravia and Sensationalism*, Palgrave Macmillan, 2009.
    Gabriele focuses on the impact of the new magazine format on nineteenth-century intellectual and cultural life through a detailed analysis of the history of a single magazine, *Belgravia*, which in the 1860s was one the most popular in the world, thanks to its strategy of sensationalism.

Gogol, Nikolai, *Taras Bulba*, translated by Peter Constantine, Modern Library, 2003.
    Based on elements of Ukrainian legend, Gogol's first novel tells the story of a medieval Cossack revolt against Poland in the straightforward form of an adventure novel.

Hoffmann, E. T. A., *The Life and Opinions of the Tomcat Murr*, translated by Anthea Bell, Penguin, 1999.
    This 1821 novel is an obvious and much cited source for "The Diary of a Madman." The premise of the story is that Hoffmann has completed a scholarly biography of a well-known but fictitious orchestral conductor and leaves the sheets of manuscript stacked on his desk while he goes on a long summer holiday. When he returns, he has a servant box up the manuscript and send it to the publisher. The editor, suspecting that no one will ever read the book, also does not bother to read it but sends it on to the typesetter. When Hoffmann receives his copies of the book, he sees that there is another text interwoven with his own on alternating pages. While Hoffmann was away, his cat (whose name in cat language is Murr) wrote his autobiography on the backs of Hoffmann's pages.

Nabokov, Vladimir, *Nikolai Gogol*, New Directions, 1961.
    Although it contains no more than a passing mention of "The Diary of a Madman," Nabokov's study is the most important critical treatment of Gogol.

SUGGESTED SEARCH TERMS

Nikolay Gogol

"Diary of a Madman" AND Gogol

natural school

surrealism

mental illness

madness

schizophrenia

conspiracy theory

The Dream of a Ridiculous Man

FYODOR DOSTOYEVSKY

1877

Russian writer Fyodor Dostoyevsky's multiple masterpiece novels have received so much attention that his short fiction often gets overlooked, but "The Dream of a Ridiculous Man" ("Son smeshnogo cheloveka"), the last story published in his lifetime, is a classic of first-person emotional and philosophical drama and fantasy. By the mid-1870s, Dostoyevsky had published several of his greatest works, including *Crime and Punishment* (1866), *The Idiot* (1868), and *The Devils* (1872). His ideological perspective had long before been shaped by his imprisonment for subversion, for participating in a liberal literary group. After four years of hard labor and four more in exile as a soldier, Dostoyevsky returned to a more conservative viewpoint. Politically, he was inclined to support the czar (the ruler) and to criticize the liberal reformers and revolutionaries of the day, who too often only brought about violence and disorder. Believing in the importance of the soul's salvation above all else, he favored what were effectively religious solutions to the problems of humankind, such as the promotion of universal love.

Such a promotion is a significant part of what is fully titled "The Dream of a Ridiculous Man: A Fantastic Story." It is narrated by a man who has recently fallen into despair and suicidal thoughts. However, a brief but crucial occurrence gives him pause, and the dream of the title proves a revelation—for him, if no one else. The story was first published in Dostoyevsky's short-lived Russian monthly *Diary of a Writer* (or *A Writer's*

Fyodor Dostoyevsky (© *RIA Novosti / Alamy*)

Diary) in April 1877. It can be found in *The Best Short Stories of Fyodor Dostoevsky* (2001), translated by David Magarshack; in *From Karamzin to Bunin: An Anthology of Russian Short Stories* (1969), translated by Olga Shartse; and online at Fiction: The EServer Collection, translated by Constance Garnett, among other books and websites.

AUTHOR BIOGRAPHY

Fyodor Mikhailovich Dostoyevsky was born on October 30, 1821, the second of seven children of a former army surgeon employed in a Moscow hospital for the poor and a woman whose father was a merchant. They had a degree of nobility, owning an estate with serfs (peasants who had few rights), but a middle-class level of status and prosperity. As led by the devout father, the family were highly observant Orthodox Christians; they were also isolated, following a routine of religious readings, mathematical instruction, and regular walks, and the siblings developed close relationships with each other in the absence of more ordinary friendships. Dostoyevsky, prone to becoming emotionally overinvested in casual friendships, would find social relationships difficult as an adolescent and an adult.

With his brother Mikhail, who was a year older, Dostoyevsky at age twelve was sent to boarding school in Moscow in order to fulfill his father's expectation that he become an army engineer. However, he focused on literature, with which he was already infatuated. By the age of seventeen, he had read not only Russia's own Aleksandr Pushkin and Nikolai Gogol but all of the works of the English playwright William Shakespeare, most of the works of French novelists Honoré de Balzac and Victor Hugo, and the German novel *Faust*, by Johann Wolfgang von Goethe, among other works. He would prove especially fond of the German writer Friedrich Schiller. Not long after his sickly mother's death in 1837, Dostoyevsky entered the military academy in St. Petersburg in 1838. There, he was perceived as an odd character who was not inclined to enjoy the careless pursuits that his peers favored. He performed his duties with diligence, but he was withdrawn in his manner, was clumsy and awkward in military gear, and often spent his free time simply walking about lost in thought. He did, nonetheless, form a few meaningful friendships, such as with a pensive and openhearted older boy.

In June 1839 Dostoyevsky received a shock—one that likely contributed to the onset of the epilepsy he would endure throughout his later life—upon learning that his father had been murdered. The father had become cruel to his estate's serfs and lecherous with their wives, and a dozen or so of the serfs, who were never convicted, took brutal revenge. Completing his academy education in 1843, Dostoyevsky entered the Engineering Corps. As a first literary venture—also financially necessary—he translated Balzac's *Eugénie Grandet* in 1844. He soon left the corps to focus on writing. When he completed his first novel, *Poor Folk*, in May 1845, he literally met with overnight success: he gave it to a friend, who along with a young poet read the entire manuscript during the night, and the poet then brought it to the era's leading literary critic, Vissarion Belinsky. Upon reading the work for himself, Belinsky summoned Dostoyevsky and, as quoted by William J. Leatherbarrow in *Fedor Dostoevsky*, quite remarkably told him,

> "Truth has been revealed and proclaimed to you as an artist. . . . It has been apportioned to you as a gift. Value your gift and be faithful to it, and you will become a great writer."

The highly anticipated work was published in January 1846, and Dostoevsky was greatly applauded. But his social uncertainty manifested itself in arrogance and anxiety, and he quickly lost stature. His next few works, less grounded in ordinary people and more artistically and psychologically oriented, failed to impress Belinsky, who believed literature needed high contemporary social value. Meanwhile, Dostoyevsky became involved in several intellectual circles, including a relatively harmless one, a more politically subversive one, and one full of relatively idle dreamers like himself who would be manipulated by an intended revolutionary. After reading aloud at one gathering a liberal letter written by Belinsky to the conservative Gogol, objecting to the state of society under Czar Nicholas I, Dostoyevsky was among those arrested by the czar's forces on April 23, 1849. They were in fact sentenced to death, and before the eyes of Dostoyevsky and the others, who were next, three were lined up for the firing squad. Just in time, a messenger arrived commuting their sentences to hard labor in Siberia followed by exile in military service. During their sentence, one of the condemned men lost his sanity, and the onset of Dostoyevsky's epilepsy was accelerated.

After four years of laboring intensely and living side by side with common criminals, Dostoyevsky was released to military service. Befriending a prosecutor, he regained the right to publish in 1856 and soon published two short novels. After returning to St. Petersburg in 1859, Dostoyevsky found among the young intellectuals not the idealism he knew but a materialist agenda that he found distasteful. He had come to align his perspective not only with the Orthodox faith but with the common people, and thus believed that restoring people's faith was more important than violently revolutionizing society. Over the ensuing years, Dostoyevsky wrote, traveled, was inspired by art, and gambled indiscriminately. His wife died of consumption in 1864, followed shortly by Mikhail, leaving Dostoyevsky to support the family with his writing. He remarried, to his young stenographer, in 1867, which helped restore balance to his life. He wrote some of the greatest works in world literature through the 1870s—his short story "The Dream of a Ridiculous Man" was published in his *Diary of a Writer* in 1877—and worked up until his death from a lung hemorrhage on January 28, 1881.

PLOT SUMMARY

I

"The Dream of a Ridiculous Man" begins with the narrator and protagonist describing the lowly position he holds in society, being generally

MEDIA ADAPTATIONS

- An audio version of "The Dream of a Ridiculous Man" was produced by LibriVox in 2013, as read by Mike Pelton for the Dostoyevsky collection *Short Stories*, and is available at the LibriVox website.

considered ridiculous, even insane. He still loves the people but is sad because they do not know the truth that he knows. The narrator has practically always known—at the latest since age seven—that he is ridiculous. The worst part is that others do not realize that he is aware of his ridiculousness, and out of pride, he refuses to reveal his awareness to anyone. As he grew up, he became more and more convinced of his defining fault, which led him into a state of pure indifference toward the world; his mind went so far as to imagine that nothing at all really exists.

Coming home on what seems the most dismal evening of his life—rainy and foggy, with the memory of a social embarrassment fresh in his mind—the man happens to see a single star through a break in the clouds, and he is inspired to decide that this will be the night that he kills himself. He has been considering doing as much since two months ago, when he purchased, with what little money he had, a revolver. It has been sitting loaded in a drawer ever since. As he regards the sky, a girl grabs his elbow. She is trembling with both chill and fright and mumbling about her mother—as if, the narrator realizes, her mother is dying and needs help. Trying to coldly walk away, the narrator grows angry as the girl follows him, and at last he yells at her. She runs away, to a man who has appeared across the street. The narrator returns home, sits in his armchair, takes up the pistol, and resolves anew to shoot himself—except he will not, because of the girl.

II

The narrator explains that he realized, upon being confronted by the girl, that he felt compassion for her in spite of himself. This angered him, because he thought he ought to be feeling perfectly indifferent toward everyone in the hours leading up to his erasure from the world—which is, in a sense, the world's erasure. The question of whether or not he ought to care about the morality of his response to the girl in such a scenario plagues his mind, until, with noise from the neighboring army captain's apartment having dwindled to an occasional murmur, he falls asleep in his armchair and dreams. In narrating, he ponders the strangeness of dreams and how his own has earned him more ridicule—and yet has also revolutionized his appreciation for life.

III

The protagonist's dream matches reality at first. Finding himself in his armchair, he takes up his revolver and shoots himself in the heart (though in real life he had resolved to do so in his right temple). Everything fades to blackness, and he lies motionless, but is still conscious of what goes on around him. He hears the voices of his landlady and the captain, then he is placed in a coffin and carried out, and at last he finds himself buried. As drops of water start tapping his eyelid once every minute, he feels a pang of indignity, indeed pain, in his heart. Calling upon whatever deity is responsible for his situation, he affirms that however much he might be tortured with the absurdity of life in death, his silent contempt is greater.

Thereupon, after a minute of assured anticipation, the narrator finds himself swept up out of the coffin and grave and whisked out into space by some grand being. Proudly quiet at first as they speed across unknown distances, the narrator at last gives in to the impulse to ask a question—whether a star he sees is Sirius. The being replies that the star is, instead, the same one he saw on his way home. Unwilling to be humiliated in any way in this afterlife, the man utters a comment that implicitly acknowledges the being's divinity, his own fear of the being, and his understanding of the being's contempt for him. The being responds, without speaking, by communicating that the man is being taken on an important journey.

Having traveled interstellar distances, they at last come upon a star that the man recognizes as the earth's sun—that is, a repetition of it, if such a thing is possible. They approach a planet identical to the earth, and the narrator declares that he cannot accept any world other than his

own, where suffering is a part of love. The protagonist then finds himself left in a celebratory, paradise-like atmosphere on a Greek coast, among a nature and a people overflowing with love—which the people soon shower upon him, as if intent to alleviate all his suffering. He has been left on an earth before the Fall. (In Christian belief, humans were created in a state of innocence; the moment when they disobeyed God and introduced sin into the world is known as the Fall of Man.)

IV

Getting to know the children of the sun, as he calls them, the protagonist becomes familiar with their personalities and their society. What they lack in scientific knowledge they make up for with simple love, bestowed and shared innocently and universally. He wonders about how they fail to arouse negative emotions even in a person like him. In the evening, they sing songs of praise for the natural world and for each other. He is astounded by the "sensation of the fullness of life" that the children of the sun exude.

People now, the narrator says, scoff at the notion that he could have experienced such a clear dream, and he even concedes that he may have created some of the details around the mere experience of that sensation. This only makes people laugh at him all the more. And yet, he remains unsure over whether it was a dream, because what happened next rings with such truth: he corrupted the sun children.

V

Though he is not quite sure how it happens, the narrator gathers that the core of a simple, amiable lie led to the people's embracing the idea of lying, and then self-gratification, leading to jealousy, discord, and division into factions with varying codes of morality. (The dream, the narrator notes, somehow encompasses thousands of years.) Different peoples seek their own truths, languages, and laws; punishments are created, and the idyllic happiness they once enjoyed is completely forgotten. In fact, even if they still believed such a happiness were possible, they would not want it. People nurse their own separate personalities and levels of strength, leading to the existence of slaves and saints and wars and religions. Knowing that he has brought about this corruption, the protagonist begs for his crucifixion but is denied it. Sorrowful and angst-ridden, the narrator awakes.

He is in his room at about six in the morning, with the entire house unusually silent. Jumping up in amazement and seeing his gun, the narrator pushes it away and feels a rapturous appreciation for life and for truth. He feels inspired to preach the truth he now knows. This, indeed, is what he has been doing, despite those who laugh at him. He may at times seem confused, but only because what he learned of the experience of universal love is impossible to reduce to verbal explanation. Regardless of who may scoff, the protagonist will go on preaching love for one's neighbor, a creed that could fix the world in hardly any time at all. As an afterthought or very brief epilogue, the protagonist affirms that he did find the girl—and that he shall go on.

CHARACTERS

Army Captain
The man on the other side of the protagonist's wall at home has six coarse visitors with whom he drinks, plays loud games, and fights. He sometimes begs for change on the street. Their ruckus is a constant backdrop that frightens and upsets the other boarders but never bothers the indifferent protagonist.

Being
In the protagonist's dream, some essential individual or force, referred to only as a "being"—one with a humanlike face—is summoned by the protagonist's insolent challenge to whoever is responsible for his absurd postmortem circumstances. The being collects the man from his grave and carries him off to a distant planet, which proves to be an alternate version of the earth. The being apparently intends for the human to learn something from his experience.

Children of the Sun
The people whom the protagonist finds on the alternate earth in his dream are a humankind that has never fallen from grace, as Adam and Eve did. Their hearts are pure, their innocence is complete, and their love flows freely among each other as well as into the heart of the protagonist during his visit. But in time his presence corrupts them, and over the centuries they experience a flawed and wicked history not unlike that of real-life humankind's.

Engineer
Before encountering the little girl, the protagonist was visiting an engineer's home. The engineer and two others were having a heated discussion about some controversial matter, leading the protagonist—who could not believe they could actually care about the matter—to declare their interest false. They only saw through to his own indifference and laughed at him.

Little Girl
A desperately cold and frightened little girl tugs at the protagonist's elbow on the street and, despite his hostility, pleadingly follows him. After he shouts at her, she runs to another person—but the protagonist cannot forget her.

Narrator
From beginning to the end, "The Dream of a Ridiculous Man" closely follows the experiences and mental processes of the title character, who in narrating the story forthrightly relates the course of his life up to this point, with a focus on recent events. In particular, he means to tell about what happened the night when he headed home intending to kill himself, had a profound experience with a pitiful girl on the street, and ended up falling asleep and dreaming a dream that turned his life around. The image of the narrator in the reader's mind is likely an uncertain one, given the utter lack of physical description of his person. He declares that he has "always cut a ridiculous figure," but how this statement should be applied to his character is entirely unclear. It might refer to a physical defect, or a misaligned posture, or a homely countenance, or perhaps none of these; the narrator's so-called ridiculousness might rather lie in his personality, or his self-presentation, or his conversational manner. Regardless, the point is that, through interactions with people from his youth on through his adulthood, he has been continually confronted with the fact of his ridiculousness—or rather, with people's perceptions of his ridiculousness, which they have presumably communicated through look, word, and gesture as well as outright laughter. It is this compromised sense of his self-worth that leads the narrator on his fantastic existential journey, from suicidal loner to moral questioner to utopian dreamer.

Wife of an Army Officer
At the protagonist's house of lodging in St. Petersburg, there is a woman referred to as the wife of an army officer. She has three children,

and they all fall ill, apparently at least in part from the constant tension of living with the terrifying army captain.

THEMES

Isolation

While it is not quite possible to identify how the protagonist of Dostoyevsky's story is ridiculous, one can easily analyze the consequences of that quality—or rather that *perceived* quality, since the trait is not truly a part of the narrator, but rather of the others who make him into an object of ridicule. That is to say, a person cannot be "ridiculous" in isolation; he can only be so if there are others to ridicule him. And yet isolation is precisely what ridicule results in, as the person subjected to derisive laughter, for whatever reason, naturally turns away from those doing the laughing, minimizing contact and trying to disregard their derogatory perceptions. The person in time may even turn away from those merely suspected to hold derogatory perceptions.

As communities and societies have increasingly come to realize in the twenty-first century, the isolation caused by ridicule is a hazard to mental health. Studies and surveys of the news reveal that peer harassment, which is greatly enabled by the simultaneous interactive access and emotional distance of technology and social media, has led to suicides at alarmingly young ages. Human beings are social creatures; they have succeeded in propagating themselves not merely through physical evolutionary advantages but through communication and cooperation. It is true that modern society can allow an individual to function in almost perfect independence, practically speaking. One can live alone, shop alone, cook alone, learn alone, work alone, and spend all one's free time alone, if one wishes to—or is obliged to, as in the case of Dostoyevsky's narrator, who likely cannot bear the ridicule he experiences, though he claims to be accustomed to it. But the isolation of the person entails the isolation of the mind, and more critically of the emotional self, and without any social support, it can be hard to find meaning in life.

Suicide

The narrator actually does not directly attribute his suicidal state of mind to the ridicule he has experienced. Rather, he describes his experience

TOPICS FOR FURTHER STUDY

- Write a story in which the narrator faces some difficulty in life, has a fantastic dream, and emerges in a more or less improved psychological position.

- Read either Aleksandr Pushkin's story "The Queen of Spades" or Edgar Allan Poe's story "A Tale of the Ragged Mountains" and write an essay in which you draw insightful comparisons and contrasts between the story you chose and "The Dream of a Ridiculous Man." Conclude by explaining which story you find more effective and why.

- Select and read one of the stories from the young-adult collection *Geektastic: Stories from the Nerd Herd* (2009), edited by Holly Black and Cecil Castelucci. Then imagine a (terribly anachronistic) conversation—why not an online chat?—between a character from your chosen story and Dostoyevsky's ridiculous man, in which each both seeks and offers advice about life as a disregarded person.

- Create a single artwork, using whatever medium you choose (drawing, painting, music, animation, and so forth), that represents the essence of "The Dream of a Ridiculous Man." The dream may lend itself well to images, but a challenge will be how to depict, suggest, or connote the idea of the narrator's ridiculousness. Be prepared to explain what the parts of your artwork represent.

- Using an Internet search engine, trace the most notable philosophical concepts and standpoints in "The Dream of a Ridiculous Man" to major philosophers, especially those who first or most famously formulated those positions. Then create a PowerPoint presentation or website that takes excerpts from the story and links them to the philosophers you identify, providing pictures and summaries of their ideas.

of ridicule and how, for some unknown reason, he became more and more conscious of his ridiculousness, and yet also more "composed" as time passed. Meanwhile, he relates, "the conviction . . . was gaining upon me that nothing in the whole world *made any difference*." This is, in essence, *nihilism*, a long-considered philosophical standpoint that nothing matters. One way to justify nihilism is to take a cosmological viewpoint: at some point, thousands or millions or billions of years in the future, the earth will be gone, and likely humanity as well; thus, why should anything matter? Of course, this ignores the rights and feelings of the individual completely.

This narrator's nihilism, accordingly, seems directly attributable to his isolation. With no positive feedback about his existence from other human beings, the narrator has no tangible grounds for affirming that what *he* does or what happens in *his* life makes a difference. His manner of employment goes unstated, but it is not hard to imagine him toiling away at some thankless bureaucratic task like copying files in the civil service. If a person comes to feel that his or her own life makes no difference, the emotional belief in the worth of life disappears, and a natural conclusion is that there is no worth to anyone's life, or indeed to anything. If a person's emotional investment in life is deadened by constant negative feedback, it can shut down—at least such is the case in the nihilist. There are many ways in which such a person's emotional investment in life can be revived—a moment of unexpected laughter, a kind word in passing, even a productive conversational relationship with a professional counselor. As this story shows, one highly significant means of emotional revival is forced moral engagement with the world.

Compassion

The narrator has become—or at least he declares that he has become—perfectly indifferent toward the world, having not the slightest care for whether or not anything even exists. This is a manifestation of depression or despair, and in fact the inertia of indifference is so strong that, though he motivates himself to purchase a revolver, the narrator seems unable to motivate himself to actually do the deed. All human beings, indeed all living creatures, have an instinct for self-preservation, and this may be what is kicking in without the narrator's quite realizing it. Paradoxically, while his indifference is what has led him to want to kill himself, it is also what holds him back. He relates, "I was so utterly indifferent to everything that I was

anxious to wait for the moment when I would not be so indifferent and then kill myself. Why—I don't know." It is as if he is waiting for a spark in order for there to be a spark to extinguish—but deep down he must know that the spark could start a fire, and indeed he must instinctively desire as much.

That spark seems to arrive in the image of the star, which leads the narrator to declare the sealing of his own fate, but the true spark comes in the form of a moment of compassion—and not on the part of another toward him, but from him toward another, a creature even more pathetic and pitiful than himself, a small girl whose own mother, the fount of her existence, is likely on the verge of dying. The narrator imagines that he should be able to ignore the girl's pleas while retaining perfect indifference—and yet he does not. He feels compassion and pity toward her. He realizes, finally, that indeed he remains a human being, and as long as he remains one, he will feel whatever a human will naturally feel, including compassion for a poor young girl in distress. This spark does not at once light a fire, but its glow does keep the narrator pondering what it might mean until he falls asleep—and the spark flares up into the dream.

Dreams

The narrator's dream is no ordinary dream, yet he is careful to point out the significance of dreams in general, as visions perhaps influenced by the mind but, as he sees it, fundamentally produced by the heart. And no matter what happens in a dream, the mind seems to accept it—as if the heart is using the dream to pass some vision or truth along to the mind. This, at least, seems to be precisely the case with the narrator's dream. Having just had the momentous experience of feeling unmistakable compassion for a girl whom he actually wanted to care nothing about, the narrator has the workings of the heart fresh in his mind (so to speak). This compassion, then, combined with his not-yet-resolved suicidal outlook, produces perhaps the most fantastic dream anyone could ever have—or could never have; the piece is subtitled "A Fantastic Story," after all. But Dostoyevsky himself is said to have indeed had dreams, likely in simpler form, of such an ideal society.

On the one hand, the narrator's dream is, as those who ridicule him see it, only a dream, and should not be taken seriously. It may be easy to disregard what happens in someone else's dream,

As the story begins, the narrator is roaming through St. Petersburg. (© *Eugene Sergeev / Shutterstock*)

but, as the narrator relates, when one actually undergoes a profoundly moving experience in one's dream, it may be impossible to ignore. The experience is an experience whether real or imagined, and if the experience rings with truth, as the narrator's does, the truth is the truth regardless. Of course, whether or not there is any one truth for all humanity remains unknown, but it is truth for the narrator, and knowing it as he knows it, he is compelled to try to share it with the world.

Love

The truth that the narrator stumbles upon is the supreme importance of love. Even a mere moment of compassion like what he felt toward the shivering girl is, at bottom, a manifestation of love. If a world could be filled with such compassion, with such love—well, one would have exactly the world that the narrator dreams about. This world is one with love, and there is no hatred, no jealousy, no resentment, no cruelty. Humans can dream, and have dreamed, of such a world, but whether it could ever be reality is an open question. According to Christian dogma, as the story points out, such a world did exist, in the Garden of Eden before humankind's fall. In

reality, such a society is more difficult to figure, which helps explain why, despite his wholly benevolent intentions, the narrator is only ridiculed all the more for preaching the truth he has perceived. Whether or not the establishment of a world of universal love is practical, it makes for an excellent, indeed a perfect ideal, and it is certainly worth preaching about.

STYLE

Diary

"The Dream of a Ridiculous Man" is representative of styles that Dostoyevsky used in a number of other novels and stories, combining certain perspectives, elements, and approaches. To begin with, the story is, in effect, a diary, a first-person record understood to be written by the narrator as a record of his experiences. (This is fitting, since the story appeared in what was generally a nonfiction outlet for Dostoyevsky, his *Diary of a Writer* periodical.) Such narration is especially effective for a story of isolation, to begin with because the first-person format (in which the narrator is a character who refers to himself as

"I") allows the protagonist to share the experience of his isolation more acutely than does third-person narration (in which characters are all referred to as "he" or "she"). The reader can get inside the protagonist's head either way, but isolation is very much a subjective experience, taking place in and having an impact on one's thought processes, and only through a character's direct reporting can the full subjective experience of isolation be related. The fact of the protagonist's writing serves to lessen his isolation—it gives him someone, even if only an unknown reader, to share his experiences with, thus perhaps offering some consolation. And yet of course, the writer by nature works in isolation; thus, writing might be seen to both lessen and perpetuate the ache of solitude.

Often in first-person narration there are open questions about whether the narrator is reporting experiences accurately or not. In a few instances here, one might conceive that the narrator cannot quite be relied upon. His experience of ridicule, for example, may be too sensitive a topic to be related with full accuracy, and the extent to which he really did not sleep at night would be open for debate. But his conviction that he has resolved to preach the truth, the truth of love, suggests that he himself can only be truthful—and indeed he confesses having intended to leave out the part of his dream where he corrupted the sun children, but his sense of truthfulness would not allow him. Critics generally treat the narrator as reliable, even if his dream was perhaps not exactly a dream.

Fantasy

As the subtitle declares, this story is a fantastic one. In fact, it is well grounded enough in reality that, by modern standards it makes for a fairly tame "fantasy." But Dostoyevsky has undeniably indulged in a narrative extravagance in this story, and thus the genre characterization in the subtitle helps prepare the reader to indulge in the extravagance along with him. That extravagance, of course, is the protagonist's dream, which somehow encompasses thousands of years and generations' worth of societal discord and evolution and philosophical development. (The narrator's apparent claim that he never sleeps can only really be taken as an exaggeration.) And yet still, the story itself need not be considered a fantasy; the narrator leaves room for the idea that although he did not actually have the exact dream that he relates, with all the manifold details of how the children of the sun lived and loved, but rather he

had a sensation in his dream—perhaps just a brief spell in such a society—and his subconscious or even conscious mind invented the details around it. Thus, while it is hard to imagine a person having the dream he had in its entirety, it is not hard to imagine the dream at least going from the acted-out suicide to travel through darkness and space to an alternate earth of loving people—again, with all the utopian details filled in later by the protagonist. Considered this way, the story is both fantastic and realistic, and indeed the term *fantastic realism* has been put forth to describe it.

Philosophy

Dostoyevsky is at the pinnacle of philosophical fiction, as culminating in the section of *The Brothers Karamazov* extracted as "The Grand Inquisitor." This portion of the novel imagines Christ returning to earth during the persecution of the Spanish Inquisition and visiting the man responsible for carrying out murder supposedly in Christ's name. In "The Dream of a Ridiculous Man," while the story's ultimate aim, on the surface, is to posit and support the idea of a world in which everybody loves one another, Dostoyevsky takes up a number of philosophical questions along the way. Is there meaning in existence? Can the fact of "existence" even be proved at all? What are the limits of human indifference, compassion, and shame? Is humankind innately good, evil, both, or neither? Could negative emotions be eliminated? Is suffering necessary in order for there to be love? Is a human society characterized by universal love desirable? Is it possible? Most of these questions are addressed in the story, but it would be hard to argue that any of them get resolved; perhaps they are irresolvable. But the story does illustrate that such questions can be significant in the life of the individual person, and not always in standardized ways. That is, as far as philosophical consideration goes, the end may be less important than the means. The questions may never be answered, but they can sharpen the sense of one's own existence in the world and play a significant role in shaping how a person—such as the narrator—lives or dies.

HISTORICAL CONTEXT

Dostoyevsky and the Czars

The Romanov family ruled the Russian Empire for three centuries, until the 1917 revolutions.

COMPARE
&
CONTRAST

- **1870s:** The Russian Empire is under the autocratic rule of the czar; that is, the ruler has absolute power. Socialist ideas, which are thought to better balance out material prosperity among all citizens, are suppressed, and in response, some of those with socialist convictions become terrorists or revolutionaries.

  Today: After three-quarters of a century of Communist government in the Soviet Union ended around 1990, Russia embraced capitalism. However, with foreign relations complicated by economic uncertainty as well as revolutionary and terrorist activity, in Russia and in the neighboring republics formerly under Soviet rule, the government has veered from democracy back toward autocracy.

- **1870s:** In the era before famed psychologists Sigmund Freud (1856–1939) and Carl Jung (1875–1961) scientifically analyze and schematize the working of dreams, they remain a fantastic and mysterious aspect of life open to new and changing interpretations.

  Today: While some are inclined to follow Freudian and Jungian frameworks and assign specific symbolic value to objects and actions in dreams, there are other, less famous schemes of understanding as well. Many regard dreams as fantasies of the mind and heart whose meanings might be imagined or intuited but are ultimately unknowable.

- **1870s:** Because of the masterful, nuanced explorations of psychology, spirituality, and morality in his novels, Dostoyevsky is favored by Czar Alexander II, who has eight children altogether, with regard to his sons' education.

  Today: President Vladimir Putin has two adult daughters from his first marriage, which ended in 2013, as well as a young son and a daughter with a former gymnast and parliament member, but he shrouds their lives in secrecy. Putin himself has expressed a preference for outdoorsy, adventurous, manly tales by the likes of Jack London and Ernest Hemingway. He also recommends nature writer Mikhail Prishvin's short stories.

Dostoyevsky came to their attention when the author, already celebrated for *Poor Folk*, was in his late twenties. In 1849, orders from Nicholas I led to the arrest of Dostoyevsky and twenty others who were part of the intellectual circle of Mikhail Petrashevsky, whom Leatherbarrow calls "an eccentric scholar-socialist." The times were precarious ones, as popular revolutions swept through Europe in 1848—most notably in France, to which Russia was culturally attached and where many Russian literary and political emigrants ended up. These events made Nicholas exceedingly wary, even angry, and with his secret police highly active, political dissenters could gather only in private and at their own risk. The Petrashevskyites favored utopian socialism, which Dostoyevsky found potentially in agreement with his Christian ideals. "The Dream of a

Ridiculous Man" is recognized as emerging in part from the author's youthful idealism.

The political scene changed dramatically in 1855, when, following Nicholas's death in the course of Russia's humiliating defeat in the Crimean War, his son Alexander II became czar. Russia's defeat was largely attributed to the persisting medieval nature of its society, revolving around estate holders and their slave-like serfs. Alexander recognized that reforms were needed to modernize the economy and the political order, but he did not go so far as to imagine abolishing the czarist autocracy. Alexander quickly pardoned the Petrashevskyites, opening the door for Dostoyevsky's return to St. Petersburg in 1859, and his most famous accomplishment was the emancipation of the serfs through imperial decree, in the face of active opposition

The narrator is sent to a utopia that seems to be a Greek island. (© *leoks / Shutterstock*)

especially from estate holders, in 1861. At the time, there were some fifty-three million serfs, accounting for 90 percent of Russia's population. And yet the decree did not improve serfs' circumstances as much as they would have liked—very similar to how the slaves freed in America several years later were resigned to sharecropping arrangements that plantation owners were easily able to manipulate.

As for Dostoyevsky, even if the reforms were not liberal enough for many, he quite devotedly aligned himself with the monarchy's interests, looking up to the czar as the moral patriarch Russia's common people needed. This ensured Dostoyevsky's ability to publish, and it also led to his gaining in 1873 the post of editor of St. Petersburg's *Citizen*, a semiofficial periodical whose director of operations, Prince Meshchersky, fiercely opposed liberal reforms. In *Romanov Riches: Russian Writers and Artists under the Tsars*, Solomon Volkov quotes Meshchersky as saying that Dostoyevsky's

> soul burned with fiery loyalty to the Russian Tsar. . . . I had never seen or met such a total and focused conservative. . . . The apostle of truth in everything, major and trifling, Dostoevsky was as strict as an ascetic and as fanatical as a neophyte in his conservatism.

Dostoevsky's 1872 novel *The Devils*—also translated as *The Possessed* and *Demons*—was inspired in part by the attempted assassination of Alexander II in 1866 by Dmitri Karakozov, a student from a secret revolutionary group whose bullet grazed Alexander's military cap.

Dostoyevsky was appalled at the attempt. *The Possessed* portrays revolutionaries like Karakozov as, per the title, people with ultimately evil motivations and methods. By the later 1870s, Alexander II's son Sergei and nephew Konstantin—who would become a well-regarded poet under his initials K.R.—were schooling themselves on Dostoyevsky's literature, including *The Devils* and *Crime and Punishment*. In 1878, Dostoyevsky was even called upon by the tutor of the czar's sons, speaking on behalf of Alexander himself, to further the sons' education, intellectual as well as moral, through conversation. From then on Dostoyevsky was welcomed at the Winter Palace on a number of occasions. Konstantin wrote a few interesting notes on the famous and fairly aged author in his diary. His first impression, cited by Volkov, was mixed: "This is a sickly looking man, with a thin, long beard and extremely sad and thoughtful expression on his pale face. He speaks very well, as if reading a prepared text." Konstantin later wrote, "I love Dostoevsky for his pure, childlike heart, for his profound faith and observant mind." After the author's death, Alexander II informed Dostoyevsky's widow, Anna Grigorevna, that the imperial offices would support her and her children with a pension of two thousand rubles per year. Anna later stated that if her husband had not died suddenly as he did in January 1881, news of the assassination of Alexander II by a nihilist terrorist's bomb on March 1, 1881, would have killed him.

CRITICAL OVERVIEW

Although Dostoyevsky's matchless novels are so critically consuming that his stories are often left by the wayside, translator David Magarshack makes their value clear:

> It is in Dostoevsky's smaller works that we find the highest expression of his creative power and the profundity of his thought. In these smaller works we find reflected as in a convex mirror the whole immensity of Dostoevsky's world, concentrated with gem-like brilliance and startling clarity.

Magarshack cites the famed Russian critic Belinsky as locating Dostoyevsky's genius in two qualities above all: "his amazing truthfulness in the description of life" and "his masterly delineation of character and the social condition of his heroes."

Critics have found much to admire and much to discuss in "The Dream of a Ridiculous Man," which is referred to under various translated titles—"The Dream of a Comic Man," "A Funny Man's Dream," and others. Russian critic Leonid Grossman wrote that with each of his final two stories (the next to last being "A Gentle Creature"), Dostoyevsky

> created a tragic short story of extraordinary power and undeniable truth, and rose to new heights of narrative skill. His lyricism and philosophy of life found forceful expression in two short and perfectly fashioned stories that attained the conciseness and profundity of Pushkin's work.

(As a point of literary reference, Pushkin is considered Russia's equivalent of Shakespeare.) Grossman characterizes "The Dream" as a "highly original" story in which "the motifs and imagery of Dostoevsky's earlier work are developed with maximum economy—the Golden Age, the beautiful man, the question of the possibility of arranging 'universal happiness,' the facts of unbearable human suffering, especially of children." Mikhail Bakhtin, in *Problems of Dostoevsky's Poetics*, similarly observed, "The themes of 'The Dream' are almost an encyclopedia of all of Dostoevsky's leading themes." Bakhtin declares that the reader of the story is "struck by the work's extreme universalism and at the same time by its extreme terseness and its amazing artistic and philosophical laconicism. . . . Dostoevsky's extraordinary ability . . . to artistically *see and feel an idea* is very clearly manifested here."

Considering the story's ultimate message, critics have taken various approaches, with the most noted differences of opinion relating to whether the story is seen as promoting or discrediting the narrator's utopian vision. Vladimir Seduro, in *Dostoyevski in Russian Literary Criticism, 1846–1956*, reports that Grossman, for one, found the story to be "a satire on utopian socialism"; on the other hand, Seduro reports that A. S. Dolinin regarded the story as "a tribute by Dostoyevski to his youthful visions of a well-ordered world based on social justice" and that O. V. Tsekhnovitser likewise considered it one more piece of evidence of "the vitality of his belief in socialism."

James Michael Holquist, in "The Either/Or of Duels and Dreams: *A Gentle Creature* and *Dream of a Ridiculous Man*," bases an argument on the contentions that the narrator is intentionally seeking and affirming his own isolation and that he is trying to promote sameness among others. N. N. Shneidman, in *Dostoevsky and Suicide*, leans on the biographical fallacy—attributing the character's views to the author—in trying to decode what the story says about suicide and the human desire for the sublime. In *Dostoevsky: Child and Man in His Works*, William Woodin Rowe contemplates whether the narrator might be considered utterly unreliable, such that either the dream or perhaps the entire story never happened.

Two of the most in-depth studies of the story have been published in the twenty-first century. Robin Feuer Miller, in *Dostoevsky's Unfinished Journey*, considers an array of possible textual inspirations—above all Charles Dickens's *A Christmas Carol*—and critical approaches to the story. Ksana Blank, in her volume *Dostoevsky's Dialectics and the Problem of Sin*, draws on the two distinct Russian words for types of truth—*pravda* and *istina*—to consider how the narrator's dream serves to unify certain dichotomies, or contradictions. She concludes that while the story poses an "objection to socialists" through the figurative crashing and burning of the dreamed utopia, "nevertheless, the story's overall message is positive. It suggests that the darkness is not all-encompassing, that a star in the nocturnal sky may show the way out for those walking in darkness."

CRITICISM

Michael Allen Holmes

Holmes is a writer with existential interests. In the following essay, he considers how the philosophy in

WHAT
DO I READ
NEXT?

- An array of other tales by Dostoyevsky have connections with "The Dream of a Ridiculous Man." "A Gentle Creature" (1876) revolves around the idea of suicide. "The Landlady" (1847) and "White Nights" (1848) both deal with the shortcomings of the dreaming idealist. *A Raw Youth* (1875) features a very similar utopian dream. And *Notes from the Underground* (1864) also concerns the possibility of a golden age and the fate of humankind.

- Dostoyevsky identified Nikolai Gogol (1809–1852) as a supreme influence on him, especially in light of his appreciation for, as Magarshack cites, "the divine spark in man." *The Collected Tales of Nikolai Gogol* (1998), translated by Richard Pevear and Larissa Volokhonsky, includes his most famous tale of the impoverished human spirit, "The Overcoat."

- Although Leo Tolstoy (1828–1910) is often cited along with Dostoyevsky as one of Russia's two greatest literary masters, Tolstoy was somewhat critical of Dostoyevsky's style and works, and vice versa. Tolstoy's short fiction is collected in *The Death of Ivan Ilyich and Other Stories* (2015), translated by Nicolas Pasternak Slater.

- The poet who first brought Dostoyevsky's *Poor Folk* to the famed critic Belinsky was Nikolai Nekrasov, who had a more progressive outlook than Dostoyevsky but would remain his friend for life. Dostoyevsky read a speech at Nekrasov's 1877 funeral. Nekrasov provides a fascinating ethnographic study of the city so central to Dostoyevsky's life in *Petersburg: The Physiology of a City*. A 2009 edition is translated by Thomas Gaiton Marullo from the 1845 original.

- One of the non-Russian authors Dostoyevsky favored was the German playwright and essayist Friedrich Schiller. Schiller produced a small body of short fiction—generally dealing with human nature and morality—that is available along with scholarly commentary in *Schiller's Literary Prose Works: New Translations and Critical Essays* (2008), edited by Jeffrey L. High.

- Bakhtin has proposed that Dostoyevsky may have been familiar with French author Cyrano de Bergerac's *Histoire comique des états et empires de la Lune* (1647–1650), a philosophic-fantastic novella in which an earthly paradise is imagined on a different planetary body—namely, the moon—and the narrator is considered a corrupting influence.

- Leigh Bardugo has embarked on a young-adult fantasy series set in Ravka, an alternate czarist Russia. The first book in the series is *Shadow and Bone* (2012), introducing two orphans, Alina and Mal, who are conscripted into the army but end up in a borderland where Alina's magical powers emerge.

"The Dream of a Ridiculous Man" reflects several world traditions and thus reinforces a conception of religion as universal.

The leading point of discussion in critical considerations of the last short story Fyodor Dostoyevsky published, "The Dream of a Ridiculous Man," has been the value of the utopian or Eden-like world that the narrator encounters in his dream. There is evidence for finding either that the loving society is intended as a genuine ideal or that it is not only impractical but impossible and in the end a harmful delusion. Typically critics have considered the society of the narrator's dream in a Christian light, which is of course encouraged by the narrator himself, who declares, "Oh, at the first glance at their faces I at once understood all, all! It was an earth unstained by the Fall." This definitively refers to the biblical fall of humankind brought about when Adam and Eve are lured by the serpent to taste of the forbidden fruit in the Garden of Eden.

THE IMPORTANCE OF THE VISION, IN THE END—JUST AS THE IMPORTANCE OF ANY RELIGION LIES IN HOW IT BENEFITS THE PRACTITIONER—IS THE INSPIRATION THAT THE VISION PROVIDES THE NARRATOR: THE INSPIRATION TO GO ON LIVING."

Humankind ever since, in the Christian view, has been stained with original sin, as well as with continuing sin, for which Christ offers redemption through belief in Him and in God. Aside from this in-text reference, Dostoyevsky was outspokenly religious in his political, literary, and humanitarian perspectives as an Orthodox Christian. It is interesting, then, that the story makes no reference to any figure designated "God," which suggests two possibilities. The first is that the narrator should be understood as an atheist—a state of nonbelief to which Dostoyevsky objected as lacking any moral foundation—and that his godlessness is his major flaw, even after his discovery of the truth. The second is that Dostoevsky specifically intended to present a utopian fantasy to be recognized not as specifically Christian, but as universal. A consideration of the story's universal religious qualities supports the notion that the dreamer's vision of utopia should be seen in a positive light.

The first aspect of the story that bears a stamp of religious universality is the very ridiculousness of the narrator, which he announces in the opening sentence. He then proceeds in the second sentence directly to the fact that he is considered by some a madman. Whether he is or not, the reader at once realizes that the narrator is an exceedingly unusual individual, someone whose particular uniqueness has made him an object of ridicule. Dostoyevsky himself had experience with being considered unique, especially at the military academy he attended and in which he was undeniably out of place. William J. Leatherbarrow, in *Fedor Dostoevsky*, cites a contemporary as writing, about Dostoyevsky,

At that time [Dostoyevsky] was very thin, the color of his face was a sort of pale grey, his hair was light and sparse, his eyes sunken, but with a penetrating, profound expression. . . . He stood out distinctly from all his other, more or less frivolous, comrades.

No matter how he may have been treated at the time, the modern-day reader will readily identify Dostoyevsky as a potential target for ridicule, simply for being so different. But such difference often signals an extraordinary quality of person, with sensibilities so acute as to perhaps befit a prophetic figure. It is easy to imagine individuals like the Buddha (a meditative person who rejected pleasurable indulgences), Chuang-tzu (an apparently absentminded irrationalist), and Jesus of Nazareth (an all-loving pacifist) as being laughed at by some for their differences, their actions, and the views they held. As Leatherbarrow relates, the awkward young Dostoyevsky would prove to be a phenomenal individual who, in speaking at Pushkin's funeral, "held out the hope that the qualities embodied in the Russian people might lead the world to true brotherhood"; in the end, he was indeed "hailed as a prophet."

In the story, the narrator's isolation, which is effectively a consequence of his ridiculousness, can also be seen as a prelude to an experience of spiritual transcendence. Seclusion in a monastery represents the classic image of the Christian saint, but there are monks and nuns in most major religious traditions, including Buddhism, along with other sorts of ascetics and mystics who use their isolation to better commune with the spirit of the divine. In his tract *The Varieties of Religious Experience* (1902), William James presents numerous narratives written by people about their experiences of transcendence or enlightenment, and what they nearly all have in common is isolation. Only in the absence of the formulaic thought processes and pressures brought about by human interaction, apparently, can a person reach a higher consciousness. American transcendentalists like Ralph Waldo Emerson and Henry David Thoreau similarly give detailed accounts of what solitude, especially in the wilderness, can bring about in the individual's consciousness.

Despite the positive possibilities it represents, however, the narrator's isolation cannot be seen as having immediate positive consequences. The onset of his nihilism is generally understood as a dark turn in the story, and indeed, this nihilism, this indifference toward everything, seems to be precisely what brings about the narrator's suicidal thoughts. And yet there can be a religious value to such nihilism, as shown above all in the beliefs of Buddhism. As a doctrine, Buddhism holds that suffering in humankind is caused by the emotions, both the positive and the negative—since there cannot be one kind without the other—and that one ideal goal is to empty oneself of one's passions. The notion of emptiness is taken philosophically further as a way of grasping the interconnectedness of everything, the identity of everything altogether as a universal whole. Thich Nhat Hanh, in *Zen Keys*, cites a brief dialogue in which the question "Lord, why is the world called empty?" is answered with "It is because in the world a separate self and things possessing a separate self do not exist." That is, all is one. As cited in *The Essential Mystics*, edited by Andrew Harvey, the Dalai Lama takes the notion a step further: "To say that phenomena are 'empty' means that we have taken their inherent existence as an object to refute and that it is the absence of such substantiality that constitutes emptiness." In other words, "the emptiness of the inherent existence of the object is that which has never really existed at all." This may be getting too metaphysical for most minds to grasp, but one can at least recognize that these formulations are quite similar to the ridiculous man's conceptions with regard to "whether the world existed or whether nothing existed anywhere at all." He goes on to report, "I began to be acutely conscious that *nothing existed in my own lifetime.*" To some, these are indeed the ravings of a lunatic—surely it is self-evident that the world and the wonderer both exist—but many serious philosophers have taken up the subject of proving existence, and in fact, the narrator's pondering seems to bring some benefit. He proceeds:

> Later on I came to the conclusion that there had not been anything even in the past, but that for some reason it had merely seemed to have been. Little by little I became convinced that there would be nothing in the future, either. It was then that I suddenly ceased to be angry with people and almost stopped noticing them.

This last remark may seem disconnected from what led up to it, but it is not. The narrator's nihilism has led to a conviction of nonexistence, that is, of universal emptiness, and in fact

this conviction serves to *empty* out the narrator's negative emotions—just as the notion of emptiness is intended to in Buddhist thought. What follows for the narrator is specifically encouraged by the Zen tradition, the cessation of conscious thought. He writes, "I had nothing to think about—I had stopped thinking about anything at the time: it made no difference to me." Although, again, the thoughts have negative connotations here, in other circumstances this might be a stage of mind on the way to genuine enlightenment. *Nirvana*, after all, means "extinguishment"—in a sense, the fading of everything into nothing.

Soon, the narrator does have a highly enlightening experience, his fantastic dream. His account suggests that he has a growing premonition about what will be encountered as the divine being carries him along. Approaching a planet uncannily like the earth he knows, the narrator feels compelled to profess his devotion to his earth, and to the people on it, however flawed they may be. Emphasizing the flaws, he asks the being, "Is it the same earth as ours? Just the same poor, unhappy, but dear, dear earth, and beloved for ever and ever?" At the nearer sight of the planet, the narrator has a deeper instinctive idea of what he will find there, in the form of "a strange feeling of some great and sacred jealousy"—over an earth and a humanity more perfect than his own. He is led to specifically wonder, "Is there suffering on this new earth? On our earth we can truly love only with suffering and through suffering! We know not how to love otherwise . . . I want suffering in order to love." This thought could be expanded into a philosophical consideration of whether evil is necessary for there to be good, but more to the point here, the narrator seems to believe that there is some specific value in suffering, in pain. This speaks not only to the idea of the Christian martyr, sacrificing life as a demonstration of the perfection of faith, and specifically to Jesus's suffering on the cross, but also especially to Buddhism.

Eugen Herrigel writes in *The Method of Zen*, "The Buddhist starts from the assumption that life is suffering." As Thich Nhat Hanh explains in more depth in *The Heart of the Buddha's Teaching*, suffering is the central phenomenon in each of the Four Noble Truths, which "are the cream of the Buddha's teaching." The first truth is the fact that "we all suffer to some extent," the second is that suffering arises from some particular origin, the third is that suffering can be made to cease by eliminating the origin, and the fourth truth is that there is a path that can be followed—the Noble Eightfold Path—to eliminate the suffering. Notably, the fourth truth, suggesting that the individual's suffering can be eliminated, does not mean to suggest that *all* suffering can be permanently eliminated; this would negate the first truth. Thus, the Four Noble Truths suggest themselves as an acknowledgment that humanity is not, and cannot be, perfect. On the other hand, the idea of a Pure Land is held up in doctrinal Buddhism much as Heaven is in Christianity, suggesting a place of perfection where the pure of soul will go in the afterlife.

To return to the ridiculous man's utopia—which is not suggested to be an afterlife exactly, though the man is brought there after killing himself in his dream—the perfection of the society is imagined not as divinely created (heavenly) and thus perfect by definition, but rather as a natural condition of humanity before its corruption. The story makes no reference to the creation of these people, or who might have created them, or how they came into existence at all, but merely describes their society as persisting in a state of perfect childlike innocence. As long as one has been exposed to the innocence of children, it is possible to imagine such a society, as fantastic as Dostoyevsky's conception may be. As some observers have pointed out, there is nothing practical about it; it cannot be understood as a *realistic* possibility for humanity. And yet it also does not suggest itself as a specific *religious* possibility. Altogether, this perfect society is imagined without reference to creation, or a god, or any end times, or any theology whatsoever. There is only nature, with which the people commune so readily—and the people are even named the children of the sun. One tradition in which lore of such a society can also be found is the Taoist tradition, in writings attributed to Chuang-tzu, one of the foundational Taoist philosophers. Where Taoism revolves around the Way and Virtue, the people of the perfectly innocent society are characterized not by love but by virtue—with love being a natural component of virtue. As recorded in *The Book of Chuang Tzu*,

> In this time of perfect Virtue, people live side by side with the birds and beasts, sharing the world in common with all life. No one knows of distinctions such as nobles and the peasantry!

Totally without wisdom but with virtue that does not disappear; totally without desire they are known as truly simple.

This characterization has a great deal in common with the ridiculous man's dream society.

In time, the story arrives at what the narrator has learned in the course of his dream travel: that humanity's deepest truth is the importance of love, of unbounded, generously bestowed love like that he found among the children of the sun. Respect for other creatures, which is the essence of love, is inherent in the governing Virtue of Taoism. Buddhism, while identifying suffering as a root of difficulty, affirms the role of compassion in overcoming difficulty, of feeling compassion for all other living creatures and respecting them as such. Of course, the narrator's formulation that "the main thing is to love your neighbour as yourself" is taken not from Buddhism or Taoism but Christianity—from Christ's famous Sermon on the Mount. That it speaks to all three traditions, as well as other religious traditions revolving around the spirit of brotherhood in a community, ideally among all humans, is fine evidence of the universality of Dostoyevsky's utopian vision. The importance of the vision, in the end—just as the importance of any religion lies in how it benefits the practitioner—is the inspiration that the vision provides the narrator: the inspiration to go on living. He affirms it in the story's final stirring phrases: "And I shall go on! I shall go on!" In the end, the ridiculous man's dream must be judged not for the societal possibility it represents—or fails to represent, if the dream is an impossible one, as the narrator himself suggests—but for the way that the dream sustains the man himself. Both Dostoyevsky and his ridiculous man would likely cheer on a universal message about religion and truth offered by the Hindu saint Ramakrishna, quoted in *The Essential Mystics*, who identified Krishna with Jesus and Allah, and indeed all gods with each other: "Truth is one; only It is called by different names. All people are seeking the same Truth."

Source: Michael Allen Holmes, Critical Essay on "The Dream of a Ridiculous Man," in *Short Stories for Students*, Gale, Cengage Learning, 2016.

Robin Feuer Miller

In the following excerpt, Miller compares Dostoyevsky's ridiculous man with Charles Dickens's Ebenezer Scrooge.

Early on, the narrator turns the little girl away, but by the close of the story he finds her again.
(© BestPhotoStudio / Shutterstock)

. . . On a gloomy, urban winter evening, a lonely and isolated man walks home through the dark city. Its few lights serve not to cheer but to highlight the surrounding gloom. Having turned his back on humanity, in part by rejecting the request of a poor child abroad at night, he prepares to sleep. He is preoccupied with himself, and himself alone. What ensues may or may not be a dream. He undergoes both a vision and a visitation. An unearthly being (or series of beings) takes him on a spiritually uncanny journey, for it is a journey to the familiar, to what he already knows. At some point during the course of the vision be believes he has died. As the dream time passes, he watches himself move from relative innocence to corruption. He watches his fall with helpless despair. He betrays those he had loved. Suddenly he awakens and finds it has all been a dream. Delirious with happiness, he helps a child and actively revels in his own ridiculousness (and impenetrable goodwill) in the eyes of the world.

This paragraph summarizes "The Dream." It also summarizes a work by a writer Dostoevsky knew well, "A Christmas Carol" by Charles Dickens. "The Dream" may be read as a kind of meta-Christmas story, in which the main character undergoes his conversion in the course of a single night and becomes a man of goodwill. Both main characters move from indifference to love, to a struggle toward life itself and away from theories of life, to an acceptance, even a joyous one, of futility, of process over product, of the endlessly unfinished over the perfectly realized. "A Christmas Carol" is, if you will, a story in a major key. "The Dream" transposes the same elements into a minor key and provides the reader with a resolving cadence whose resolutions have proved to be ambiguous. Holquist has argued that although "The Dream" seems to relate a typical Dostoevskian conversion, it does not, for it is instead a thrice-told tale of the narrator's "megalomania and solipsism." This reading, while persuasive, does not fully take into account the ending of the story and the ridiculous man's conscious effort to dissociate himself from solipsism. As he observes, "I have beheld it—the Truth [*istina*]—it is not as though I had invented it with my mind, but I have beheld it, beheld it." The ridiculous man has experienced both a vision of paradise and a conversion.

It might seem strange to link together two stories whose emotional thrust is so different. However one chooses to read "The Dream," it remains a baffling, provocative, and ultimately unsettling text. "A Christmas Carol," by contrast, leaves readers awash in a pleasant sea of sentiment. Even as they know that the happy ending is in honor of the Christmas season and that it would be far more prudent to expect, in the real world, that Tiny Tim's chair would indeed be vacant by the next Christmas, readers find themselves willing to believe Tiny Tim saved, to accept Scrooge's conversion as authentic, and to rejoice with him in his purchase of a large turkey for the Cratchits. The end of "The Dream," on the other hand, does not ask readers either to draw upon their capacity for sentimentality nor does it call upon them to rejoice. Nevertheless, the striking structural and thematic correspondences between these two stories deserve a closer look.

The tradition of the Christmas story, brought to perfection by Dickens, embodies a curious welding together of despair and optimism. The ground-work of grim reality is covered, for a

> SCROOGE, THE MISER WHO CARED ONLY FOR FINANCIAL GAIN, AND THE RIDICULOUS MAN, THE METAPHYSICAL MISER WHO CARED ONLY FOR HIMSELF, EACH ADOPT A SIMILAR CODE BY THE END; EACH STORY ARGUES FOR THE VALUE OF PERSONAL GOODNESS AND CHARITY, EVEN IN THE FACE OF DEFEAT."

moment, by a fragile growth of hope and charity. The author of a Christmas story seeks readers' complicity in setting aside their sense of the way things really are; he asks readers to yield to an optimism that both he and they know is foolish. Dickens invites his readers to become happy and ridiculous with Scrooge: "Some people laughed to see the alteration in him, but he let them laugh, and little heeded them; for he was wise enough to know that nothing ever happened on this globe, for good, at which some people did not have their fill of laughter at the outset. . . . His own heart laughed: and that was quite enough for him."

Dostoevsky, on the one hand, asks us to celebrate with the ridiculous man the fact that he has awoken transformed from his dream and has found the little girl, but Dostoevsky also asks us to experience the chilling, unsettling effect of the ridiculous man's exhilaration: "I love all who laugh at me more than all the rest. Why that is so, I don't know and I cannot explain, but let it be so . . . I don't want and I cannot believe that evil is the normal condition among men. And yet they all only laugh at this very faith of mine." He acknowledges his own muddlement, embraces it, and admits that his Edenic dream has been just that: "Even if, even if paradise on earth never comes true and never will be (that, at any rate, I can see very well!) . . . I shall go on preaching." He asks us to see the whole process of hope and failure and still to hope. In effect, Dickens is asking the same of his readers in a less abrasive way. But the ridiculous man embodies that human willingness to show oneself as vulnerable and illogical in order to express hope in the power of some higher good. (It is no surprise that the others call him a "holy fool" [*yurodivyi*].)

Although by the ends of their stories Scrooge and the ridiculous man actively embrace their ridiculousness in the eyes of the world, initially each is a character who lives according to a plan or doctrine. At the outset, each one believes that his life is a rational reaction to his milieu. By the end, each has abandoned reason and cares only for the dictates of the heart. This progression follows a similar course in each story. Both "A Christmas Carol" and "The Dream" contain five parts. In Stave 1 of "A Christmas Carol," Scrooge several times refuses requests for Christmas charity and turns away a beggar child who has come to sing at his door. He is indifferent to all around him: "No warmth could warm, no wintry weather chill him." At the beginning he asserts, "If I could work my will, every idiot who goes about with 'Merry Christmas' on his lips should be boiled with his own pudding, and buried with a stake of holly through his heart." He lives according to a political and economic doctrine of rational, miserly indifference: the prisons, the Union workhouses, and the Poor Law should take care of those who suffer. Those who would rather not submit to such institutionalized charity had better die "and decrease the surplus population."

Scrooge's comic but impenetrable isolation from his fellow man is echoed much more somberly by the ridiculous man. In Part 1 he describes how he arrived at the conviction that "nothing in the whole world made any difference." His philosophical indifference leads him to solipsism: "I suddenly felt that it would make no difference to me whether the world existed. . . . I began to be acutely conscious and to feel with my whole being that nothing existed in my own lifetime." The ridiculous man expresses philosophically and tragically what Scrooge does in practice and comically. Each man, in the course of his nighttime vision, clashes head-on with his cherished doctrines and ideas and comes to a rejection of them based upon the emotions of the heart.

As Scrooge walks home from work through London, the fog and darkness thicken. The murkiness is lit by the "flaring links" the people carry and by a fire some workers have started. The light illuminates "ragged men and boys"; the lamps of the shop windows briefly make "pale faces ruddy." Dickens here uses the effect of light in the typical gothic way: to deepen rather than to alleviate gloom and poverty. Likewise, while walking home, the ridiculous man gazes first upon a gaslight that "oppressed the heart so much just because it shed a light upon it all." He glances up from the gaslight and sees a little star amid the fathomless dark patches of the night sky. Once again Dostoevsky has deepened and rendered metaphysical an element that Dickens has used affectively. The light amid the darkness in Dostoevsky's story sets up a complex pattern of correspondences (of the Swedenborgian or Baudelairean variety suggested by Milosz) that ultimately serves to connect the ridiculous man's despair, the rejection and the ultimate rediscovery of the little girl, and his Edenic vision.

The presence of another darkness, the darkness of death, illumines the first part of each story as well. "A Christmas Carol" begins: "Marley was dead: to begin with." Marley is Scrooge's partner and alter ego, initially indistinguishable from him in every respect. But at the end of Stave 1, Marley's ghost has appeared to Scrooge, who, though he wishes to dismiss the ghost rationally as "an undigested bit of beef, a blot of mustard, a crumb of cheese, a fragment of underdone potato," cannot do so. His assertion that "There's more of gravy than of grave about you" falls flat, though, for he believes in the ghostly vision. Marley warns Scrooge that he will be visited by three spirits and urges him to embrace the doctrine of personal charity, of "Christian spirit working kindly in its little sphere."

Death appears in Part 1 of "The Dream" in the form of the ridiculous man's plan to commit suicide that night. After his dream suicide, he questions God with a hostility not unlike Scrooge's to Marley, although it is, of course, purged of all comicality. The ridiculous man has deliberately turned away from the consideration of any personal charity, and yet it is his instinctive, unconscious bond with the little girl that will save him: "And I should of course have shot myself, had it not been for the little girl." In the opening section of each story the specter of death has, in fact, foreshadowed the redemption of an indifferent man.

Scrooge and the ridiculous man both slide imperceptibly into sleep and believe throughout that they are awake. Each continues, both during and after his visionary experience, to be uncertain whether or not it was a dream. While Scrooge awaits the first spirit after Marley's ghost departs, he cannot decide whether he is dreaming: "Every time he resolved within himself, after mature inquiry, that it was all a dream, his mind flew back

again, like a strong spring released, to its first position, and presented the same problem to be worked all through, 'Was it a dream or not?'." The ridiculous man also falls asleep "without being aware of it at all." Although he reports to us after the fact, he does describe his uncanny awareness during his dream that it is indeed a dream. After his "death," the dark and unknown being flies with him to that bright little star, and the ridiculous man describes the dreamlike quality of this flight: "I cannot remember how long we were flying, nor can I give you an idea of the time; it all happened as it always does happen in dreams when you leap over space and time and the laws of nature and reason, and only pause at the points during which your heart is lost in reverie."

The first time the ridiculous man speaks at length about dreams, he tells us how he sometimes dreams about his brother, who, though he has been dead for five years, "takes a keen interest in my affairs." Although the ridiculous man knows, even during the dream, that his brother is dead, he nevertheless "is here beside me, doing his best to help me." Although the autobiographical references to Dostoevsky's own beloved dead brother are unmistakable, this passage could also call to mind Marley's appearance to the dreaming Scrooge. Marley, although he has been dead for seven years, takes a keen interest in Scrooge's affairs and tries to help him. Moreover, he laments in words that seem to foreshadow the ridiculous man himself, "Why did I walk through crowds of fellow-beings with my eyes turned down, and never raise them to that blessed Star which led the Wise Men to a poor abode?" If we allow ourselves to connect the ridiculous man to Scrooge and, in this instance, to Marley, we can see a biblical (and Christmas) resonance to the bright star that leads the ridiculous man (read "wise man") to that poor abode (read "poor child") and to salvation. At any rate, as he tells his tale, the ridiculous man repeatedly asks himself if it was a dream: "What does it matter whether it was a dream or not?" "What if it was only a dream? . . . Perhaps it was no dream at all!." By the end, he wholly rejects the need to separate dreams from everyday life: "What is a dream? And what about our life? Is that not a dream too?"

Both Scrooge's and the ridiculous man's conversions may be described as a shifting of the locus of their being from the head to the heart: hence Scrooge's tears and the ridiculous man's deliberate shifting of the aim of his gun from his head to his heart. It is fitting, then, that each of them at the end should have lost his former capacity for reasoned discourse. Each awakens from his dream with a face bathed in tears. Scrooge awakens and laughs for joy: "I don't know how long I've been among the Spirits. I don't know anything. I'm quite a baby. Never mind, I don't care. Hallo! Whoop! Hallo here!" The ridiculous man's joy is, predictably, a more sober intoxication, but it, like Scrooge's, renders his language emotive rather than logical: "Rapture, boundless rapture welled through my entire being. Yes, life and preaching [*propoved*] . . . After my dream I lost the knack of putting things into words." The paradoxical notion of a preacher who knows he has lost the knack for words renders his life, rather than his words about that life, a living symbol of faith as opposed to reason.

Scrooge and the ridiculous man each make a fantastic journey in the company of a mysterious being. The Spirits Scrooge sees—the Ghosts of Christmas Past, Present, and Future—fill him with ever greater fear and dread, but each shows for Scrooge a solemn, if not affectionate, concern. His visit to his own childhood constitutes a journey to a personal Golden Age. The ridiculous man, too, quickly realizes that his unearthly guide cares for him: "He did not answer me, but I suddenly felt I was not despised, that no one was laughing at me or even pitying me, and that our journey had a purpose, an unknown and mysterious purpose that concerned only me." Scrooge's journey is to the stages of his own life, and thus also concerns him alone.

Scrooge learns by the end, however, that the fates of others are connected to him. Although the ridiculous man does not journey to his own past, he too is led to what he already somehow knows—to the past of all humanity—yet does not know. He travels to a planet that is an exact copy of our earth, to one of the islands of the Greek archipelago. His dream, moreover, has been prefigured and shaped by his thoughts just before going to sleep and is a dramatic recasting of them. After rejecting the little girl, he had returned home and unconsciously transformed his shabby deed into an intellectual proposition. He had asked himself to imagine that if he had once lived on the moon or Mars and had committed a disgraceful deed there, would he afterward, on earth, have felt that such a deed made no difference?

Scrooge's cranky comments about the surplus population, also uttered just before going to sleep,

likewise come back, quite literally, to haunt him. He begs the Ghost of Christmas Present to tell him if Tiny Tim will live: "Say he will be spared." The Ghost replies that, unless the shadows of the future intervene, Tiny Tim will die and adds, "If he be like to die, he had better do it, and decrease the surplus population." Later Scrooge sees the starving children, Want and Ignorance, hiding under the cloak of the Ghost of Christmas Present and cries out in sorrow, "Have they no refuge or resource?" The Spirit responds, "Are there no prisons? Are there no workhouses?" *The seeds that engender each character's conversion lie encased in the husks of those very doctrines that had led him astray.*

The best clue to the uneasy relationship between perversion ("Nothing makes any difference"; "It's a matter of reducing the surplus population") and conversion ("I'll keep on preaching even if they laugh at me"; "Please let the crippled child live") comes from the ridiculous man. "Dreams," he writes, "seem not to be induced by reason but by desire, not by the head but by the heart." If so (and Freud would back him up), *when* does the actual moment of the conversion experience occur for Scrooge and for the ridiculous man? When they each lament, during the course of the dream, the plight of the suffering child? When they each find a new mode of being in ridiculousness? When they awaken from their dreams with tears and joy? Or, does conversion occur at the point when the dream begins? For the very fact of the dream expresses, from its first moment, the desire of the dreamer for conversion. Or, does conversion occur with the first birth of that desire, which is merely enacted in the dream? When does potential desire become spiritual reawakening? How does this kind of transformation occur? Scrooge, the miser who cared only for financial gain, and the ridiculous man, the metaphysical miser who cared only for himself, each adopt a similar code by the end; each story argues for the value of personal goodness and charity, even in the face of defeat. . . .

Source: Robin Feuer Miller, "Unsealing the Generic Envelope and Deciphering 'The Dream of a Ridiculous Man,'" in *Dostoevsky's Unfinished Journey*, Yale University Press, 2007, pp. 115–22.

SOURCES

Bakhtin, Mikhail, *Problems of Dostoevsky's Poetics*, translated by R. W. Rotsel, Ardis, 1973, pp. 122–28.

Blank, Ksana, *Dostoevsky's Dialectics and the Problem of Sin*, Northwestern University Press, 2010, pp. 105–10.

Chuang-tzu, *The Book of Chuang Tzu*, translated by Martin Palmer, Elizabeth Breuilly, Chang Wai Ming, and Jay Ramsay, Arkana, 1996, p. 73.

Dostoyevsky, Fyodor, *The Best Short Stories of Dostoevsky*, translated by David Magarshack, Modern Library, 1992, pp. 297–322.

Grossman, Leonid, *Dostoevsky: A Biography*, translated by Mary Mackler, Bobbs-Merrill, 1975, pp. 527–28, 536–37.

Harvey, Andrew, ed., *The Essential Mystics: The Soul's Journey into Truth*, Castle Books, 1996, pp. 53, 80.

Herrigel, Eugen, *The Method of Zen*, edited by Hermann Tausend, translated by R. F. C. Hull, Vintage Books, 1974, p. 15.

Holquist, James Michael, "The Either/Or of Duels and Dreams: *A Gentle Creature* and *Dream of a Ridiculous Man*," in *Critical Essays on Dostoevsky*, edited by Robin Feuer Miller, G. K. Hall, 1986, pp. 170–76.

Jackson, Robert Louis, *Dialogues with Dostoevsky: The Overwhelming Questions*, Stanford University Press, 1993, pp. 130, 156.

Leatherbarrow, William J., *Fedor Dostoevsky*, Twayne's World Authors Series No. 636, Twayne Publishers, 1981, pp. 13–31.

Magarshack, David, trans., Introduction to *The Best Short Stories of Dostoevsky*, Modern Library, 2001, pp. vii–xxiii.

Matthews, Owen, "Kremlin Family Secrets," in *Newsweek*, August 29, 2014, http://www.newsweek.com/2014/08/29/top-secret-family-life-vladimir-putin-265425.html (accessed August 5, 2015).

Miller, Robin Feuer, *Dostoevsky's Unfinished Journey*, Yale University Press, 2007, pp. 105, 148.

Nhat Hanh, Thich, *The Heart of the Buddha's Teaching: Transforming Suffering into Peace, Joy and Liberation; The Four Noble Truths, The Noble Eightfold Path, and Other Basic Buddhist Teachings*, Broadway Books, 1998, p. 9.

———, *Zen Keys*, Doubleday, 1995, p. 105.

"Putin's New Kid with Russian Gymnast," in *Page Six*, January 28, 2013, http://pagesix.com/2013/01/28/putins-new-kid-with-russian-gymnast/ (accessed August 5, 2015).

Rowe, William Woodin, *Dostoevsky: Child and Man in His Works*, New York University Press, 1968, pp. 96–97.

Seduro, Vladimir, *Dostoyevski in Russian Literary Criticism, 1846–1956*, Columbia University Press, 1957, pp. 187–88, 243.

Shneidman, N. N., *Dostoevsky and Suicide*, Mosaic Press, 1984, pp. 95–97.

"Vladimir Putin's Reading List," in *New Yorker*, May 24, 2011, http://www.newyorker.com/books/page-turner/vladimir-putins-reading-list (accessed August 5, 2015).

Volkov, Solomon, *Romanov Riches: Russian Writers and Artists under the Tsars*, translated by Antonina W. Bouis, Alfred A. Knopf, 2001, pp. 193–208.

Wood, Alan, *The Romanov Empire, 1613–1917: Autocracy and Opposition*, Hodder Arnold, 2007, pp. 219, 251–61.

Yarmolinsky, Avrahm, *Dostoevsky: Works and Days*, Funk & Wagnalls, 1971, pp. 357–59.

Zernov, Nicolas, *Three Russian Prophets: Khomiakov, Dostoevsky, Soloviev*, S.C.M. Press, 1944, pp. 97–109.

FURTHER READING

Fleming, Candace, *The Family Romanov: Murder, Rebellion, and the Fall of Imperial Russia*, Schwartz & Wade, 2014.

> In this young-adult title, Fleming recounts the dramatic and fascinating history of one of the longest-lived dynasties in world history, while also relating what life was like for common peasants through the Romanovs' reign.

King, Martin Luther, Jr., *A Call to Conscience: The Landmark Speeches of Dr. Martin Luther King, Jr.*, Grand Central Publishing, 2002.

> This volume presents the most memorable speeches by King, one of the foremost advocates of love and brotherhood in world history. It includes his famous speech "I Have a Dream," as well as "I've Been to the Mountaintop."

More, Thomas, *Utopia*, edited by Edward Surtz, Yale University Press, 1964.

> Originally published in 1516, More's short novel considers an ideal society in the utmost social, political, and philosophic detail and is the origin of the term *utopia*, coined by More from the Greek for "no place."

Pushkin, Alexander, *Complete Prose Fiction*, translated by Paul Debreczeny, Stanford University Press, 1983.

> While the most famous story by Pushkin (1799–1837) is "The Queen of Spades," which is included in this volume, all of the stories written during his relatively short life speak to his genius.

SUGGESTED SEARCH TERMS

Fyodor Dostoyevsky OR Dostoevsky

"The Dream of a Ridiculous Man"

Dostoyevsky AND short stories

Dostoyevsky AND dreams

Dostoyevsky AND suicide

Dostoyevsky AND Alexander II

utopia AND fiction

Christianity AND paradise OR golden age

dreams AND literature OR science

universal love

Emmy

JESSIE REDMON FAUSET

1912

1913

"Emmy," a story about life and love for two African Americans in the technically integrated North of over one hundred years ago, was written by Jessie Redmon Fauset, a pivotal figure in the Harlem Renaissance. A flourishing of African American art, especially literature, in the 1920s, the Harlem Renaissance saw such writers as Claude McKay, Countee Cullen, and Langston Hughes rise to nationwide fame. Fauset wrote four novels herself during this period, but she is better known for discovering those very authors and others in her role as literary editor of the *Crisis*. As the organ of the National Association for the Advancement of Colored People (NAACP), which was founded in 1909, the *Crisis*, founded in 1910, was largely independent under the creative direction of W. E. B. Du Bois.

While Fauset would be employed by the *Crisis* as of 1919, the proactively minded magazine was earlier host to her first known story published in wide circulation, "Emmy," written when she was teaching secondary school in Washington, DC. The story concerns a self-assured young African American woman, Emmy, and her bosom friend Archie, who has lighter skin and is somewhat less assured—not without reason. First published in the *Crisis* in two installments in December 1912 and January 1913, the story can be found in *The "Crisis" Reader: Stories, Poetry, and Essays from the N.A.A.C.P.'s "Crisis" Magazine* (1999) as well as in *Short Fiction by Black Women, 1900–1920* (1991) and *Anthology of the American Short Story* (2008).

Archie loses his job when he tells his boss about his mixed racial background. *(© BelleMedia / Shutterstock)*

AUTHOR BIOGRAPHY

Jessie Redmona Fauset—she would later use Redmon, her father's name—was born on April 27, 1882, in Snow Hill Center, New Jersey, to an African Methodist Episcopal (AME) Church minister and his wife, with six other children (most of whom died young). After Fauset's mother died, her father remarried, adding three step-siblings and later three half siblings to her family. The biographical record on Fauset's early years is sparse. Some scholars have jumped to the conclusion that, based on inscriptions in a family Bible—as well as on the bourgeois setting of much of her fiction—Fauset's family was among the black community's well-to-do old Philadelphians. Her father's status as an AME minister in the region of the church's greatest influence, around its headquarters in Philadelphia, did lend the family cultural prestige, and politics and intellectual matters were actively discussed, but memoirs left by one of Faucet's half brothers indicates that—after the father lost hold of property that he did not have the time to manage—the family had little more than the collection-plate income to live off of.

The Philadelphia schools abolished black-designated schools in 1881, meaning that students could attend whichever eligible school they chose. Fauset thus happened to spend most of her school years in racial isolation, generally as the only African American girl in her classes. She had close white friends through grade school, but when she reached the high-achieving ranks of the Philadelphia High School for Girls, her long-time friends disregarded her because of her skin color. Fauset nonetheless excelled academically, and in light of her achievements her father was invited to give the invocation at the graduation ceremony. Fauset was inclined to proceed to Bryn Mawr College, but as letters would later publicly reveal, the college's officials were afraid that Fauset's presence would provoke a regrettable number of southern students to withdraw. Instead, interested parties helped land Fauset a scholarship to attend Cornell University, where she was possibly the first female African American student—the only one in her class, alongside several dozen male African Americans. She again excelled, especially in the study of languages, including Latin, French, and German. She would graduate in 1905 as possibly the nation's first black woman elected to Phi Beta Kappa.

It was through a Cornell professor that Fauset first got in touch with Du Bois, in part to express her appreciation for his landmark 1903 study *The Souls of Black Folk*. Du Bois helped Fauset get a summer teaching internship at Fisk University, in Nashville, Tennessee, in 1904, an experience that she appreciated for introducing her to a different segment of the nation's African American population. After graduating, Fauset taught in Baltimore before settling in the M Street High School, later renamed Dunbar High School, in Washington, DC, for fourteen years. As of 1916, the school had 1,149 students, forty-eight teachers, and a modern, well-equipped campus and was considered the nation's elite black school—indeed, the *Crisis*, as cited in Carolyn Wedin Sylvander's *Jessie Redmon Fauset, Black American Writer*, labeled it "The Greatest Negro High School in the World." It was during her time as a teacher in Washington, DC, that Fauset wrote and published "Emmy" in the *Crisis*, in 1912 and 1913.

Having long been in touch with Du Bois, Fauset was communicating with other leading figures in the NAACP and the *Crisis*'s management within a few years of their inception. Through the 1910s she contributed not only fiction but also poetry, journalistic and philosophic essays, and book reviews. Du Bois made a point of singling Fauset's fiction out in his editorial commentaries, and in 1918, when she took leave from her teaching position, he put her under contract as a writer. Concluding that, with the advancement of African American achievement in literature and the arts being one of his major goals, the publication would benefit from a literary editor, Du Bois assigned Fauset to that position in October 1919, at which time she moved to New York. In 1919 Fauset also concluded the classwork for her master of arts degree from the University of Pennsylvania.

With her name and role appearing just below Du Bois's on the *Crisis* masthead, Fauset engaged in a variety of duties beyond the selection and shepherding to print of fiction and poetry, including full management of the magazine during Du Bois's occasional absences. But it was as literary editor that she gained renown,

and it is no coincidence that the Harlem Renaissance is often dated to 1921, not long after she assumed her role at the *Crisis*. Fauset identified and encouraged the most promising writers, first seeing them into print, and Du Bois and other boldfaced names within the NAACP, especially association secretary Walter White, used their contacts to help writers such as Hughes, Jean Toomer, and Gwendolyn Bennett gain book contracts. Fauset has thus been characterized—with a term some feminist-minded commentators balk at—as the midwife of the Harlem Renaissance.

Fauset's own novels came out during and through the end of the Harlem Renaissance. Her first, *There Is Confusion* (1924), sold briskly and was well reviewed from New York to London. The imprint Boni and Liveright's publicity campaign, which accorded book and author alike as much attention as was given any white writer, was recognized as marking a new era in African American literature. Fauset left the *Crisis* in 1926, perhaps partly for time to write, partly to relieve the pressures of working under the exacting Du Bois. She proceeded to teach high school French in New York City for seventeen years, meanwhile publishing her other novels. Her second and most critically admired, *Plum Bun*, came out in 1929, while her fourth and final novel, *Comedy, American Style*, was issued in 1933. Fauset married Herbert Harris in 1929, and for a while they lived in Harlem. They moved to Montclair, New Jersey, in the early 1940s, and after her husband's death in 1958, Fauset moved in with a stepbrother in Philadelphia. She died of heart failure there on April 30, 1961.

PLOT SUMMARY

I

In class at school, the eleven-year-old protagonist of "Emmy" recites what her class has learned about the world's five races. Afterward, Miss Wenzel asks which race is hers and at once regrets it—until Emmy, after pondering whether her brown color makes her "Malay," gives the expected answer "Negro." Later, Mary Holborn suggests that Emmy ought to mind being colored; walking her home, Archie confirms Emmy's belief that she should not mind—though he finds his own light African American skin problematic. Reaching Emmy's house just before it starts raining, the children forget the issue while playing a game with their peas at dinner.

II

Miss Wenzel takes Emmy aside the next day to try to subtly communicate that Emmy will not be entitled to everything that white people have, but the girl's self-assurance is already firm. Later, talking to Hannah, Miss Wenzel expresses chagrin over failing to cut Emmy down a notch; Hannah thinks she never should have tried. Miss Wenzel gives Emmy a trinket with a quote from Robert Louis Stevenson, suggesting she ought to have low expectations in life (that is, because she is black), but Emmy seems to take it as a reasonable lesson in humility, which is actually intended for some man (since the quote uses the male third person).

III

Emmy goes along needing to concern herself little with race until one day, years later, when she refuses to let Elise Carter copy test answers, Elise insinuates that Emmy will not be invited to a club event because she is black. At this, Emmy at once realizes she does not want to go anyway.

She later explains the occurrence to Archie, who envies the directness of her experience. He recounts a period when he worked at a camp (of some kind) as a waiter until, defending a black cook against racist comments, his own race was revealed and—being in a more visible position than the cook—he was fired. Nonetheless, over the last seven years Archie has met with good fortune in life and work. Most recently, a man without prejudice who appreciated Archie's abilities, Robert Fallon, connected him with a firm run by Nicholas Fields in Philadelphia. Fallon instructed Archie not to disclose his race, and he was hired. Emmy is disappointed to hear that Archie is denying his racial identity. Getting emotional, Archie gradually asks Emmy to marry him; she hesitates, but he convinces her.

IV

While Archie, now twenty-one, works in Philadelphia, Emmy, still in Plainville, basks in the affection in his letters. One letter relates how he coincidentally met up with (and seemed to admire) the lighter-skinned Maude Higgins, and they were seen by Archie's boss's son, a potential disaster. Since Archie and Maude are both light-skinned, however, neither's race was realized. The story disconcerts Emmy.

When work will not let Archie return to Plainville in September as planned, he persuades Emmy and her mother to visit for a week in October. Archie and Emmy enjoy city life, although Archie has to cover up a distressing incident: they are refused admission to the floor seats at the theater because of Emmy's skin color, and, ignoring the suggestion of balcony seats, Archie leads Emmy outside in a huff. He ends up taking her to a musical performance at the Academy, which they enjoy. At night's end, she remains unaware of what happened at the theater, while he remains irritated—but is uplifted by a kiss from her.

V

Taking a last tour of Philadelphia, Archie and Emmy are seen together from a distance by Mr. Fields. When Archie literally bumps into his boss at work, Mr. Fields ribs him about lavishing money on a colored woman (suggesting the relationship is little more than a paid arrangement). Archie is angered but fails to defend Emmy, which he later deeply regrets.

Another day, Mr. Fields summons Archie to say that since his son, Peter, is not interested in running the business, he wants Archie to do so instead. He further instructs Archie to move to his neighborhood and perhaps get married; Archie reports his engagement, which Mr. Fields celebrates—and assumes aloud that it is, of course, not to the colored woman he was dallying with.

VI

Archie is buoyant walking home until he realizes that Emmy cannot possibly move in with him so close to Mr. Fields's home, since her race would be discovered. Despite previously pressing for her to marry him by Christmas, instead of the following October, Archie now plans to tell Emmy that they will have to wait a couple of years. He dispatches a note to tell her that he will visit for a few hours on Sunday afternoon with an important question to ask. Emmy assumes he will be asking her once more to marry him sooner, and she decides to relent.

When Archie arrives and begins talking business, Emmy is startled; when she asks why they should have to wait two years to marry after all, he explains logically, without expressing his own regrets. Deeply offended, she announces that she was never serious about the relationship, which she is now through with. In disbelief he pleads with her, but she stonewalls him, and he departs.

VII

Beside himself, Archie is angst ridden for ten days, with Emmy answering none of his daily letters. Finally, calling in sick to avoid work, Archie composes a letter he is sure she will have to answer. He is gazing at her photograph when Mr. Fields surprises him with a tap on the shoulder, takes hold of the photo, recognizes the black woman from before, and disparages her. Now fiery with indignity, Archie affirms that Emmy is his betrothed, which leads Mr. Fields to curse Archie out for being a deceptive Negro. Archie accepts his firing and pushes Mr. Fields out the door. He eventually finds another job but, having revealed his race to the boss, must keep his race secret from his coworkers while working for unequal pay.

VIII

Emmy is despairing in solitude when Thanksgiving comes. Her mother suggests that she is making a mistake, at which Emmy imagines that her mother cannot understand her position. Her mother then relates how, owing to a misunderstanding—Emmy's father, Emile, witnessed Mrs. Carrel being kissed by her white father without knowing who he was—she and her husband had a fight and broke up. Mrs. Carrel left France with Emmy and Céleste for America. Two years later she and Emile reconciled by letter; but on his way from France via New York to his family in Pennsylvania, he was killed in a wreck. Emmy's mother finishes the tale in tears.

IX

Still gloomy, Emmy for once finds herself imagining how nice it would be to be white. Her mother goes to New York for the days before Christmas, and in the meantime Emmy tries to pull herself together—while fondly remembering last Christmas with Archie. Hearing a coach on Christmas Eve and thinking her mother has returned, she walks right into Archie's embrace. He reports that he has been fired for defending Emmy, which she admires. He thinks he will have to go to the Philippines, where Emmy is willing to go along with him. A special delivery message arrives—a telegram from Peter Fields, sent along by Archie's landlord, telling him to return to the firm and accept their apologies. Grateful to be able to stay in America, Archie

asks once more when Emmy can marry him, and she suggests Christmas Day.

CHARACTERS

Emile Carrel

Emmy never knew her father, a West Indian man whom Mrs. Carrel met in France. Emile proved as hot-tempered as Mrs. Carrel proved stubborn when they fought over her having kissed a white man; Emile failed to learn at the time that the man was her father. He struck her, they split up, and he stayed in France while she left for America. After a couple of years, he sent his wife a letter expressing his contrition and desire to reunite. Tragically, he was killed in a wreck (presumably a train wreck) on the journey, not long before reaching Plainville.

Emilie "Emmy" Carrel

With her name being the title, Emmy is nominally the main protagonist but generally shares center stage with Archie. Emmy's sense of self is so strong—and she has met with little enough discrimination in Plainville, Pennsylvania—that through most of her life she feels no compulsion to regret her skin color, even when white people try to make her regret it. She is intelligent, polite, and composed, with bronze skin and curly but not kinky hair. Her mother's income allows Emmy to remain at home, relatively idle, after finishing school. Having always looked up to Archie, she comes to feel affection for him when he expresses his affection for her, though she remains demure in a dignified feminine way; even in resolving to give in to Archie's anticipated entreaty to marry him come Christmas, she plans to deny him two or three times first. Emmy's pride is deeply wounded when Archie appears to care more about his job than about marrying her, and after a falling out and much loneliness, she finally comes to regret her skin color. Swayed by her mother's tale of squandered love, Emmy welcomes Archie's embrace on Christmas Eve and is at last prepared to do whatever it takes to be with him.

Mrs. Carrel

Emmy's mother is an intelligent woman who speaks French fluently and earns good money as a translator. Her daughter is so well adjusted that her input hardly seems needed through the bulk of the story; however, when Emmy is languishing in isolation that her pride has brought about, Mrs. Carrel finally tells the story of her own ill-fated romance to encourage her daughter to take action to secure her happiness and avoid a lifetime of regret.

Elise Carter

With an attitude similar to Mary Holborn's but more malicious, Elise tries to punish Emmy when she refuses to help in a cheating scheme by denying her an invitation to an afternoon "club spread"—presumably a country club luncheon. Apparently Emmy is invited in the end anyway, demonstrating that, within their social circle, Emmy's integrity outweighs Elise's racist vengefulness.

Céleste

Céleste is a French, presumably white maid who has worked for Mrs. Carrel ever since before Mrs. Carrel and Emile split up.

Robert Fallon

Fallon is the man who, believing it to be ridiculous that a man as talented as Archie should be held back because of his black blood, arranges for his employment with Nicholas Fields's firm in Philadelphia—under the condition that Archie keep his race a secret, which Fallon believes is a perfectly justified course of action.

Archie Ferrers

Archie is as much a focus of the story as Emmy, with the plot revolving around his experiences at the Philadelphia engineering firm he joins. He has only ever been fond of Emmy, two years his junior, and he orients his life toward becoming successful enough to make her his wife. This seems to necessarily entail denying his African American heritage, though Emmy finds that doing so compromises his integrity. Matters come to a head when it seems that Archie cannot both advance his career and marry his wife at the same time. In the end, he speaks up on Emmy's behalf and gets himself fired, but he is rewarded when Peter Fields invites him back to the firm.

Nicholas Fields

Fields has old-fashioned values as far as work is concerned—a man who works hard earns his respect—and unfortunately also as far as race is concerned. Having favored Archie ever since hiring him, Mr. Fields wants to groom Archie to replace him in running the firm. When his racially charged comments about Emmy incite Archie to at last declare himself African American, Mr. Fields despises him for the deception—and for his race—and fires him. Mr. Fields's son, however, it seems, persuades him to reconsider.

Peter Fields

The son of Mr. Fields is content to earn money perhaps through some sort of estate management—the "filthy social settlement business"—rather than through the sort of daily effort his father admires. Peter's work ethic may be lacking, but his racial ethics are not: the telegram inviting Archie back to the firm comes from him, suggesting that Peter learned of his father's rash dismissal of their star employee and managed to convince him that Archie's race should not be a factor in the matter of his employment.

Maude Higgins

Maude is an African American as light-skinned as Archie. When they run into each other in Philadelphia and then are seen by Peter Fields, Archie fears for his job until he realizes that Maude passes as white.

Mary Holborn

Emmy's young classmate is the first one to plant in Emmy's mind the notion that she should regret having dark skin. Mary cannot understand how Emmy can be as decent as any white person despite her brown skin.

Mr. Pechegru

Mrs. Carrel's father was a white man who helped her mother, a New Orleans slave, escape to Haiti. It seems he got Mrs. Carrel's mother pregnant before sending her on to France, where Mrs. Carrel was born. Mr. Pechegru had not seen his daughter for ten years—since the mother's death—when he visited and was seen by Emile kissing Mrs. Carrel. He is the one who first helped Mrs. Carrel get translation work.

Hannah Wenzel

Hannah, who seems to be Miss Wenzel's sensible sister, does not understand why Miss Wenzel feels compelled to reduce the young Emmy's confidence, pride, and expectations in life. Hopefully, Hannah suggests, Emmy will never need to face the discrimination Miss Wenzel is supposedly preparing her for; either way, she can deal with such discrimination when it comes.

Miss Wenzel

The eleven-year-old Emmy's teacher has an utterly misguided—indeed, racist—sense that Emmy needs "to have some of the wind taken out of her sails" in order to prepare her for future prejudice; in reality, this is a thinly disguised rationale for Miss Wenzel's acting on her own prejudice.

THEMES

Race Relations

In "Emmy," as in most of her fiction, Fauset puts race relations front and center. It is simple enough to create a story in which there are conflicts between people of different races, but Fauset complicates matters by including an African American character, Archie, whose skin color is light enough that he can pass as white—specifically, without prompting, people tend to imagine him to be of Spanish extraction. This presumption itself is the beginning of the prejudice: Archie is a highly educated, accomplished, ambitious, and in every way respectable young man, and this, Fauset suggests, is part of why people tend to imagine him not to be African American. Their preconceptions of the character of black people are so strong that they will jump to conclusions in order to preserve those preconceptions. A similar preconception emerges in the consciousness of little Mary Holborn, who, even when face to face with the undeniably bronzed brown skin color of Emmy, finds it hard to believe that she *is* African American because of the quality of her person. Such prejudices often derived from the public's absorption of years of racist rhetoric and public belittlement of black people, including in the North. Emmy provides the evidence of an *Atlantic Monthly* writer propagating racist conceptions of all African American peasants as "fierce," "base," and "silly." Emmy at once recognizes that the writer clearly has not met the sorts of people to whom she is applying a broad-stroked, blanket characterization—a stereotype.

Between individuals and the media, Emmy and Archie are left to navigate their way through a world—decades before the civil rights movement would usher in laws to begin to establish racial equality—in which such prejudices are the norm. Interestingly, Emmy, who has the darker skin, has a much easier time of it. Her skin color leaves her harboring no doubts about her racial identity, and with no doubts, she is able to

TOPICS FOR FURTHER STUDY

- Familiarize yourself with the moral frameworks established by Lawrence Kohlberg and Carol Gilligan. Then write two modest reflection papers, one drawing on Kohlberg to defend Archie's decision to accept his promotion and delay his marriage and one drawing on Gilligan to criticize Archie's decision.

- Read the Marita Bonner story "Nothing New," which can also be found in *The "Crisis" Reader* as well as in *Frye Street & Environs: The Collected Works of Marita Bonner* (1987). The story concerns a young man who must choose between an angry response to racism and a levelheaded one. Write an essay in which you analyze this story with a focus on sentimentality versus rationality, drawing comparisons with "Emmy" where appropriate.

- Select one of the works in young-adult author Walter Dean Myers's collection *145th Street: Short Stories* (2000)—preferably one featuring some romantic intrigue. Then write an essay in which you consider the differences in courtship between Myers's contemporary story and Fauset's "Emmy," also commenting on other differences that reflect changing times.

- Write a research paper, assemble a PowerPoint presentation, or create a website that relates the history of African Americans in Philadelphia, being sure to discuss the black community's "old Philadelphians" and the African Methodist Episcopal Church.

develop her natural abilities and reflect the high quality of her upbringing through her integrity and composure. Of course, being a woman at a time when women were restricted from many of the professional fields men aspired to, Emmy is left to confront fewer venues in which her race is an issue. Archie, on the other hand, is seeking to make his way in a white-collar professional world not just dominated by generally racist white men, but indeed run by them. His experiences with Nicholas Fields and after getting fired by him demonstrate that, knowing Archie to be African American, owners and managers simply will not employ him. They may be doing this because they truly believe, as Mr. Fields seems to, that he is inferior simply because of his race—this is racism—or because they fear that his presence would cause upheaval among coworkers or customers, as the camp manager and Archie's last employer seem to. These employers' practical concerns are less easy to classify as racism, but either way, the refusal to employ Archie amounts to acting on prejudice, in a prejudiced way, which is discrimination.

Fauset's story, especially in showing the experiences of Archie—who is sometimes perceptibly black, sometimes perceptibly white—illustrates how the life of an African American in the days before civil rights was much like taking the life of a white man and inserting obstacles, even entire walls, in certain paths he might otherwise want to take—indeed practically all the paths leading to socioeconomic uplift. Success for Fauset's African Americans seems to come only when a benevolent white character—who by virtue of his race holds the keys to all the doors, if not hammers for all the walls—steps in to enable that success, as Mr. Pechegru does for Mrs. Carrel and as Robert Fallon does for Archie. Fauset makes clear that this has nothing to do with the African American characters' abilities and everything to do with the prejudiced society in which they live.

Morality

In light of the prejudice the African American characters face, the reader would not be surprised to find them doing whatever it takes to get along, even bending or breaking their personal moral codes. One result of Emmy's fairly impeccable upbringing, unblemished by the sort of discrimination that would have upset her sense of the world's moral balance, is that her own moral code has nothing to do with race. As a child she never develops different sets of rules for dealing with people of different races, and so when such a matter as Elise Carter's request for help cheating comes along, Emmy never imagines that, because Elise is white and has a social advantage, she ought to help her cheat; to the contrary, Emmy knows that cheating is wrong, and she simply will not do it. Moreover, as soon as it becomes apparent that Elise is willing to act on racist conceptions, Emmy wants nothing to do with her; she is

unwilling to compromise her moral code—to *capitulate*, as Stevenson's credo has it—for the sake of retaining a friendship.

Moral codes become a more pressing issue when Emmy has Archie's experiences to consider. Archie has already learned from experience that if people of influence or authority know he is African American, he is placed at a disadvantage. As a practical concern, then, he becomes open to the idea of staying quiet about his race—which is not the same as lying—simply not to disadvantage himself. Indeed, when he admits his race at the camp, the manager calls him "the blankest kind of a blank fool" for not having stayed quiet. Robert Fallon expresses a similar opinion, saying Archie should feel no obligation to reveal his race to employers. In fact, as Fallon frames it, even if Archie were to directly lie about his race, this would be morally defensible, because he is up against an immoral system, the prejudiced white capitalist business world. Still, Emmy has a concern: not that Archie is being dishonest with others but that he is being dishonest with himself, that he is effectively disavowing his race. He is pretending that he is not African American and thus slighting the African American race, herself included. This concern is at the heart of the clash of perspectives that brings about both the story's climactic conflict and its resolution. It is bad enough that Archie is willing to disavow his own race, but when he goes so far as to disavow Emmy's race as well, to forestall their marriage in order to hide her away from his employer, he has crossed a line—a line of honor.

Honor

Emmy has a great deal of pride, and not in a negative sense but in the sense that she has a strong sense of morality, and her sense of honor depends upon her not compromising that morality. She finds Archie's denial of his race for practical purposes dishonorable, but when he dishonors her as well, he goes too far. Archie learns something from the experience. He eventually recognizes that he has failed Emmy. The narration does not quite state as much, but the evidence is that, when Mr. Fields speaks ill of Emmy one last time, Archie does not allow the stain on her honor, the public slander of her name, to stand. He defends her, and thus he loses the job. However, in acting out of a sense of honor, he has boosted his karma, so to speak. Most important, Emmy gains new respect for him by virtue of his defending her honor. Also, professionally, he has opened

Emmy';s mother reluctantly reveals the truth about her family history. (© Monkey Business Images / Shutterstock)

the door to a racially open relationship with Mr. Fields and his son; when they, too, decide to act honorably—perhaps as inspired by Archie's own acting honorably—Archie gets back not only his beloved but also his livelihood.

STYLE

Bourgeois Fiction

Fauset has sometimes been characterized, and not favorably, as a writer of bourgeois fiction, that is, fiction dealing with the middle (not the lower) classes and their relatively comfortable middle-class concerns. In "Emmy," for example, the characters are not hungry, or traumatized, or truly desperate, or caught up in any life-or-death intrigue; rather, they are concerned with their jobs, they are in love, and they have everyday problems—for African Americans in the 1910s—to deal with. Sylvander,

discussing the value of Fauset's longer fiction in the *Dictionary of Literary Biography*, is inclined to state: "Though her novels are rife with romantic and entertaining plots, largely revolving around the black middle class, she is nevertheless thorough in confronting race and sex stereotyping." Indeed, "Emmy" may be both a romantic and an entertaining story, but its thematic value is immediately apparent.

Still, a few aspects of the story's plot perhaps reflect a desire on the author's part to amplify the drama, as if for the sake of the (bourgeois) romance, even at the expense of realism. This was, after all, Fauset's first published story, in which a few points of evident narrative deliberation or weakness are to be expected. One such point comes when Mr. Fields taps Archie on the shoulder while he is looking at Emmy's photograph; it is possible but, as distracted as Archie may be, odd to imagine that Mr. Fields might have somehow entered Archie's apartment either without knocking or without Archie's having heard him make the slightest noise. It also seems unlikely that Emmy, at the age of nineteen, would not have any idea about her father's origins or identity. In both cases, the plot seems mildly contrived for the sake of drama; when this happens, the result is often considered melodrama—a mainstay of bourgeois-type fiction. In "Emmy," upon closer examination, such plot elements as these may not be as smooth as one ideally expects in a polished piece of fiction, but the engaged reader is unlikely to take issue with them in a first reading, and it would be unjust to suggest that they compromise the high moral as well as literary quality of the story.

African American Literature

Fauset's story was published in 1912 and 1913 as part of one of the opening waves of what would evolve into the tidal surge of major African American literature called the Harlem Renaissance. "Emmy" was first published in the *Crisis*, the magazine issued by the NAACP. Readers of the *Crisis* were invested in the social lives of African Americans, were politically aware, and were interested in being informed and involved. They would read stories in the *Crisis* not merely for escape or entertainment but also to be that much more enlightened about the society in which they lived. Thus, as evidenced by the content of "Emmy," Fauset's fictional sensibility was quite aptly attuned to the *Crisis*'s audience. This helps explain why Du Bois made a point of singling out Fauset's fiction for readers' notice and eventually tapped her to become literary editor. In "Emmy," she makes a point of forthrightly addressing issues of prime interest to African Americans—discrimination, racism, employment, passing, and, of course, love—with the story's dialogue, especially between Emmy and Archie, constituting a forum in which those issues are discussed and with the plot reflecting hypothetical resolution to the sorts of situations being dramatically presented.

HISTORICAL CONTEXT

The NAACP, the Crisis, and the Harlem Renaissance

The NAACP came into existence at a time when Reconstruction was failing African Americans, and some believed that the most prominent black voices were not doing enough to help the race's cause. Specifically, the country's primary black weekly, the *New York Age*, was in the hands of allies of Booker T. Washington, who took a conciliatory stance toward blacks' assimilation into white culture—he effectively believed that blacks should be patient and grateful for whatever white culture extended to them, regardless of the persistence of injustice. It was actually proactively minded white figures, including Mary White Ovington, a descendant of abolitionists, who first issued the call for the creation of an organization to address continued lynchings and to secure the rights promised all citizens in the Thirteenth through Fifteenth Amendments. Of the sixty or so people who signed their names to this call, only seven, including William Edward Burghardt Du Bois, then an Atlanta University professor, and Ida B. Wells-Barnett, were African Americans; among the new organization's executives, Du Bois, director of publications and research, was the only one.

Du Bois at once pushed for the creation of an organ that would allow the NAACP and its allies to counter the views expressed in the *New York Age* as well as in white publications. As expressed by Sondra Kathryn Wilson in her introduction to *The "Crisis" Reader*, only through such an organ could the NAACP "break the stubborn stereotype that had misrepresented and malformed implicitly every external view of African-American life." Sylvander, citing in her book an article titled "Negro Character as Seen by White Authors," is more specific about the stereotype—or rather stereotypes—that readers had gleaned from white literature: "the contented slave, the wretched freeman, the comic, the brute, the tragic mulatto, the local color Negro, and the exotic primitive."

First published in November 1910, the *Crisis* was immediately successful, if not immediately profitable, as Du Bois relates in his 1951 essay "Editing the *Crisis*." He attributes this success in part to "some blazing editorials which continually got us into hot water with friends and foes" as well as to the magazine's running pictures of African American citizens, sometimes in color. As Du Bois points out, it was the rule among many white publications to publish photographs of colored people only if they were criminals, which, of course, contributed to persistent stereotypes. The *Crisis* had a circulation of nine thousand copies in 1911, its first full year; by 1916 it had become self-sufficient, with subscriptions paying for the entire publishing operation; and by 1918 its circulation was seventy-five thousand copies. A journalistic revelation about the US military's discriminatory attitude toward its own African American soldiers accounted for a jump in circulation to one hundred thousand in 1919, but through the early 1920s circulation dropped down again by two-thirds. Du Bois notes that the readership was known to largely be the black proletariat, or low-income workers, leaving advertisers wary, while the radical nature of some of the published material turned away certain white supporters.

Despite the literary and journalistic efforts of Fauset and others through the *Crisis*, even in the mid-1920s, once the Harlem Renaissance was in swing, Du Bois would contend that white audiences were uninterested in literature that failed to fulfill their stereotypes. He remarked, as cited by Sylvander, "The more truthfully we write about ourselves, the more limited our market becomes. . . . When we cease to be exotic, we do not sell well." Fauset was among those particularly challenged by such narrow-mindedness on the part of white readers, as communicated to her by editors of her novels. As Sylvander records, in light of the characteristic bourgeois setting of her fiction, one publisher stated in rejecting her first novel, "White readers just don't expect Negroes to be like this." Another, in rejecting her third novel, stated, in Fauset's paraphrasing, "There ain't no such colored people as these, . . . who speak decent English, are self-supporting and have a few ideals."

COMPARE & CONTRAST

- **1910s:** Since national media are by and large controlled by white interests in the age of segregation, publications focusing on issues in black communities generally have only local circulation. Of the three major African American–centered publications— *Crisis, Opportunity*, and the *New York Age*— two are the organs of civil rights groups.

  Today: With desegregation eventually bringing the disappearance of both visible and invisible barriers to black ownership of media, African American publications, especially magazines, have proliferated, with *Black Collegian* and *Ebony* as well as the online magazine *Harlem World* being among those giving priority to political matters.

- **1910s:** W. E. B. Du Bois is recognized as the leading African American intellectual. Holding a doctorate in history from Harvard University, Du Bois has taught at Atlanta University, has published several groundbreaking sociological studies, has founded the temporary Niagara movement in 1905, and has been a leading figure in the establishment of the NAACP and the publication of the *Crisis*.

  Today: Henry Louis Gates Jr. is recognized as the leading African American intellectual.

Holding a doctorate from the University of Cambridge, Gates has taught at Harvard, published over a dozen books, created over a dozen documentary films, was among the first year's winners of the MacArthur Foundation "genius grants," and has long served as director of the W. E. B. Du Bois Institute for African and African American Research, now called the Hutchins Center.

- **1910s:** As Fauset's story "Emmy" suggests, people of intermediate coloring between black and white skin are generally assumed to be either mulattoes—that is, part black and part white—or foreigners. As of 1900, twenty-six states, including the entire South, have antimiscegenation laws, forbidding marriage between members of different races.

  Today: Following the landmark 1967 Supreme Court decision *Loving v. Virginia*, all antimiscegenation statutes in the United States were overturned. Multiracial children are increasingly common wherever different races are intermixed, especially cities, and those with skin of intermediate hues between white and black may well have a mixture of ethnic ancestry.

Fauset's role in the Harlem Renaissance, which is sometimes roughly dated from 1921 to 1931, is unquestioned. As Sharon L. Jones remarks in her essay "Reclaiming a Legacy," Fauset "was one of the most significant individuals in regard to shaping the direction of the Harlem Renaissance." She was the first to recognize the talent of such soon-to-be phenomenal authors as Jean Toomer, best known for the mixture of poetry, prose, and drama in *Cane* (1923); Countee Cullen, whose first volume of poetry was *Color* (1925); Claude McKay, whose novel *Home to Harlem* (1928)

was a best seller; and, above all, Langston Hughes, whose poem "The Negro Speaks of Rivers" (1920) was enough to lead Fauset to declare him a seminal talent. Hughes would prove to be a prolific author of poetry, essays, short stories, novels, memoirs, plays, and even children's books. Speaking of children's literature, one of Fauset's less heralded roles as a spark in the Harlem Renaissance was as editor and primary writer of the material in the *Brownies' Book*, a children's monthly published throughout 1920 and 1921. Sylvander, in the *Dictionary of Literary Biography*, quotes a

Emmy's brown skin means she cannot pass for white like Archie. (© *And-One / Shutterstock*)

writer as affirming that Fauset "saw daily the need for children and young people to have insight into their past and hope and pride in their future."

CRITICAL OVERVIEW

Fauset's critical reputation revolves around her four novels, since she published a share of short fiction but never put together her own collection. In *Jessie Redmon Fauset, Black American Writer* (1981), Sylvander surveys contemporary reviews of Fauset's various novels. Those for her debut, *There Is Confusion*, "were generally quite favorable." In *Opportunity*, the organ of the National Urban League—which played a role parallel to that of the *Crisis* in bringing African American writers to national attention—Fred DeArmond, Sylvander cites, praised Fauset for declining to color her text with colloquial dialect "and other

thought-to-be-indispensable earmarks of race literature." Across the Atlantic, the *Times Literary Supplement* called the novel an "able and unusual study" that would enlighten English readers with "apt allusions to circumstances of negro life." And Sylvander further notes that a *Literary Digest International Book Review* writer was especially impressed, declaring that Fauset

> neither demands nor makes any sentimental concessions. She possesses the critical insight and resolute detachment of the novelist, and her picture of the society which her novel surveys is achieved with art as impersonal as that of Mrs. Wharton. Her novel is neither propaganda nor apology but art.

Fauset's ensuing novels met with mixtures of praise extended and withheld. With *Plum Bun*, character psychology and development were admired, but some reviewers found the plot too sentimental or melodramatic. *The Chinaberry Tree*, her third novel, was found to be intellectually engaging, but some lamented that, in treating a segment of African American society living like middle- to upper-class whites, Fauset seemed to avoid black culture altogether. Her final novel, *Comedy: American Style*, was generally considered less impressive than her earlier novels.

Beyond initial reviews, the prevailing white male critical establishment in the decades that followed generally panned Fauset for what were perceived as failures of intention and style. Robert A. Bone, writing in 1958, offered a cursory and imperceptive take on her novels, which he judged "uniformly sophomoric, trivial, and dull." He considers *There Is Confusion* "burdened" by an overabundance of characters, calls *Plum Bun* a "typical" passing novel, and seems too ill-informed to offer any insight into her later novels. Hugh M. Gloster, writing in 1965, was more favorable. He affirms that *There Is Confusion* is "the trail-blazer among works in which Miss Fauset illustrates that bourgeois Negroes are interesting subjects for literary treatment"; he also credits it, as have others, with being "the first nationally recognized novel by an American colored woman" (though Pauline Hopkins, for one, wrote several novels—apparently not nationally recognized ones—two decades earlier). Gloster concludes more broadly that "Fauset's description of the lives and difficulties of Philadelphia's colored elite is one of the major achievements of American Negro fiction."

Fauset's reputation would be more fully restored when, following the successes of the civil rights movement and the first waves of feminism, female and nonwhite critics, among others, explained away the misconceptions of earlier critics like Bone and demonstrated the aptness of her style and thematic approaches. Among those who have sought to redeem Fauset's reputation is Jacquelyn Y. McLendon, who notes in the volume *Feminist Writers*,

> Critics not only misread her novels but also passed along misinformation about her life in a foundationless conflation of the author and her sentiments with her characters and theirs, missing the political and subversive aspects of her work, especially in her treatment of black women.

In his essay "A Sardonic Unconventional Jessie Fauset: The Double Structure and Double Vision of Her Novels," Joseph J. Feeney declares that there is

> far more to Jessie Fauset than melodrama, romance, conventionality, and middle-class material. . . . A deep pain and anger affect both the form and content of her novels. They are not at all as conventional as they have appeared.

Sylvander has gone the farthest in restoring Fauset's reputation. In her 1981 volume, she formulates that Fauset "sensitively and unobtrusively examined the difficulties and the achievements of an understudied group in her portrayal of Black women." In the *Dictionary of Literary Biography*, Sylvander declares that "Fauset's influence on black art in the period of the Harlem Renaissance was extensive." She posits that "Fauset's strength may lie in her unobtrusive presentation of alternatives for defining the black American woman: more exploratory than dogmatic, more searching than protesting." Sylvander concludes that Fauset's fiction "reflects the growth of a struggling, self-made, sophisticated, widely read and deliberate literary artist, whose thematic concerns and formal experiments are worth critical investigation."

CRITICISM

Michael Allen Holmes

Holmes is a writer with existential interests. In the following essay, he considers the balance that "Emmy" strikes between rationality and sentimentality.

Those inclined to criticize the fiction of Fauset have typically done so on the grounds that it is too

> MAGICAL KISSES, ONE MIGHT ARGUE, ARE THE STUFF OF SENTIMENTAL ROMANCE."

bourgeois, too romantic, too melodramatic, too sentimental. Carolyn Wedin Sylvander, in the *Dictionary of Literary Biography*, quotes one scholar dramatically claiming that her "vapidly genteel lace-curtain romances" fail to rise "above the stuffy, tiny-minded circulating-library norm." Even Joseph J. Feeney, whose project in a 1979 *CLA Journal* essay is to help recuperate Fauset's reputation, feels obliged to concede, "It cannot be denied that there is conventionality and sentimentality in her books. . . . She wrote romance and melodrama and occasionally manipulated probability." The short story "Emmy," like Fauset's novels, might conceivably be criticized as sentimental, given the outsized role that the romance between Emmy and Archie plays in the progress of the drama, not to mention the happy ending. Of course, as far as the ending goes, an unhappy one would have represented the suggestion that hopes for African Americans such as these are dim—that owing to the strictures imposed by white American society, such a romance cannot survive. The positive-minded Fauset certainly would not have wished to convey such a suggestion. Considering the value of popular appreciation for the story among African Americans and others reading the *Crisis*, then, the happy ending is far more suitable. Meanwhile, sentiment turns out to be an especially interesting facet of the story, because the two main characters happen to be highly rational people, and their sentiments do not just make for an emotionally satisfying read but play an integral role in the story's resolution.

The rationality of both Emmy and Archie is demonstrated foremost in their conversations, in which they try to reach rational understandings of their complex, race-inflected experiences. The nature of the functioning of Emmy's mind is explicitly stated in the narration, at the point when she calls Miss Wenzel out with regard to what the teacher is trying to discreetly—that is, insidiously—communicate to Emmy: "'Then because I'm brown,' she had said, 'I'm not as good as you.' Emmy was at all times severely

WHAT DO I READ NEXT?

- Fauset's literary talent is generally recognized as having reached fullest fruition with her second novel, *Plum Bun* (1929). With a title taken from a nursery rhyme, *Plum Bun* focuses on the relationships and revelations of race in the lives of two sisters, one with darker skin and one with lighter skin.

- Nella Larsen is recognized as the other most significant female African American novelist from the Harlem Renaissance. Her second novel, *Passing* (1929), not unlike Fauset's second novel, explores the differences in the lives of two mixed-race sisters, one of whom embraces her African American identity, and the other of whom passes as white.

- A male author who made a point of exploring stories of passing was Charles Waddell Chesnutt. Some of his shorter works were included in *The Wife of His Youth and Other Stories of the Color Line* (1899), while a modern edition is *The Short Fiction of Charles W. Chesnutt* (1974).

- Perhaps best known for the lyricism and insight of his poetry and essays, Langston Hughes also wrote several collections of biographies for young adults. *Famous American Negroes* (1954), *Famous American Negro Music Makers* (1955), and *Famous Negro*

Heroes of America (1958) can all be found in *The Collected Works of Langston Hughes*, Vol. 12, *Works for Children and Young Adults: Biographies* (2001).

- Writer James Weldon Johnson became a leader of the NAACP under the title of field secretary in 1916. Among his best-known works is his novel *The Autobiography of an Ex-Colored Man* (1912), about an African American who decides to live his life passing as white.

- Walter White served as secretary of the NAACP and published a number of books beginning in the mid-1920s. Like Fauset, White includes treatment of black members of the bourgeoisie in *The Fire in the Flint* (1924), which follows the post–World War I experiences of a Europe-educated black doctor in Central City, Georgia.

- A novel by a fairly well-known white American that includes confusion of racial identity as a plot element is Mark Twain's *Pudd'nhead Wilson* (1893–1894). Set in Missouri during slavery times, the novel relates what happens when a woman switches her light-skinned African American baby with a white baby at birth.

logical." This throws off Miss Wenzel, who clearly did not expect the young student to so readily grasp what she was trying to be subtle about. The scene aptly illustrates how an adolescent confronted with racist attitudes either naturally is or soon becomes highly attuned to nuances of communication—word choice, facial expressions, tones of voice, body language— because people so frequently try to disguise their true sentiments when interacting with them. Emmy's logicality is a veritable weapon in her personal fight against racism, both in decoding and defending against racism, and so naturally,

being immersed in white society, she comes to rely on a logical frame of mind.

Archie similarly favors rational thought, as illustrated, for example, when the thirteen-year-old boy admires the work of a spider, exclaiming, "Gee, if I could swing a bridge across the pond as easy as that!" He then shows a vested interest in the toy railroad at Emmy's house because "when one is trying to work out how a bridge must be built over a lop-sided ravine, such things are by no means to be despised." Unsurprisingly for a boy with such a frame of mind, already engaging with very practical construction scenarios, Archie becomes an engineer—a bridge designer or structural engineer, if these episodes are reckoned to prefigure his future. Interestingly, both of these practical concerns—the spiderweb and the railroad—tug at the young Archie's attention when he and Emmy are dwelling on the very complex problem of racial identification, a problem with highly sentimental implications, as related to feelings rooted in pride, morality, and honor. Archie's mind gravitates toward the strictly practical concerns of bridge building as if precisely to escape the more serious and sentimental concerns that have surfaced in their lives. The contest of skill between Archie and Emmy while eating their peas amounts to a similar escape into a strictly unsentimental, or strictly rational, concern: how to methodically manipulate one's peas with a fork in the deftest possible manner. This is certainly more of a kinesthetic contest than an intellectual one, but either way, concerns of sentiment are absent.

The dichotomy between sentimentality and rationality flares into a major concern when Archie, returning to Plainville for a couple of weeks, reports to Emmy that he has procured an excellent job in Philadelphia, but has had to deny his race in order to do so. This dialogue highlights the importance of sentiment in human interactions, even when those interactions are rooted in rationality. After he explains the scenario, Emmy protests at his behavior, such that he goes on "a little pleadingly." He has adopted a tone intended to acknowledge his moral deference to Emmy's stance, that it is wrong to disavow one's race; he knows that his position is subordinate to hers and therefore must "plead" in order to have his transgression be validated. When Archie expresses his hope that Emmy is not now "changed toward" him—has not been affected to such an extent that her perception and summary judgment of him have changed—Emmy "gravely" informs him, "I'm not changed, . . . only somehow it makes me *feel* that you're different. I can't quite look up to you as I used" (emphasis added). Emmy's shifting attitude toward Archie is founded in her morality, and morality might be characterized as a primarily rational concern: certain behaviors are right, certain behaviors are wrong, and a code (like the Ten Commandments) can be drawn up to distinguish in a rational manner between right and wrong. And yet *feeling* plays an undeniable role in morality, given that, in complex situations, where the most proper ethical course often cannot be easily analyzed, people are left to do what *feels*

right. In this sense, sentiment cannot be seen as merely a hallmark of inadequately intelligent fiction; rather, it is an essential part of intelligent fiction, at least if that fiction pretends to have any bearing on living humanity, because human beings do not operate in isolation from sentiment; to the contrary, sentiment often, perhaps usually, plays a governing role in determining what people do.

As Emmy and Archie's pivotal conversation continues, with Archie gradually relating his desire to marry Emmy, the exhibition of sentiment continues. Seeing that Emmy is "inflexible" in her moral resolve, which runs counter to what he has done, Archie speaks "miserably" over his concern that she does not even respect him anymore; "he was very humble." Here Archie's sentimental display helps Emmy realize how important her opinion of him is—as important as anything in his life. As she realizes how much Archie feels for her, Emmy "faltered"; Archie, then, "gaining courage"—since Emmy is no longer standing quite so firmly against him—at last boldly declares his love. This ongoing sentimental drama should not be taken as suggesting that rationality has been placed by the wayside (though it often does in matters of romance). In fact, Emmy goes so far as to say, in her hesitation, "I couldn't really tell anything about my feelings anyway"—as if she remains so predominantly rational that she cannot even get in touch with her sentimental side. The two proceed to go painstakingly over "reasons why he had always loved Emmy; reasons why she couldn't be sure just yet; reasons why, if she were sure, she couldn't say yes." Emmy is still not letting a sentimental perspective win out.

The final day of Archie's stay brings about the resolution of the tension hovering between the two in a markedly sentimental way. In asking about marriage once more, Archie "was so grave and serious that she really became frightened." When she yet demurs, Archie speaks "harshly, his face set and miserable," then "proudly" concludes that he will not take maybe for an answer—will desert her altogether. She proceeds to regard him "pitifully" and to speak "tremulously," and the scene culminates in Archie's getting down on his knees, Emmy's crying, and their uniting. With the buildup of emotional descriptors, a detractor might suggest that such a scene as this is *too* sentimentally dramatic. It is worth observing that Fauset has declined to overplay the romance where she most easily could have:

Emmy's final assent goes unspoken, and their kiss goes undescribed. And there is great significance in the fact that Emmy is left to sing "rapturously" after Archie's departure: her rational nature has finally been overcome; she has opened herself to and acted on sentiment, and it brings about probably the greatest joy she has yet experienced in her young life, the joy of love.

The importance of love in a person's life is soon emphasized, when Archie is left fuming because Emmy's skin color has been used as a reason to deny them the theater seats for which he had already bought tickets. Again, sentiment is a crucial part of the scene: the descriptions reveal that racism is not just rationally unfair but is something that profoundly affects a person's emotional self, whether one wants it to or not. Archie, upon learning the racist news from the theater usher, grasps his beloved's arm tightly enough to hurt her, turns pale, and explains away the matter while "trying to keep his voice steady." Only through a sentimentally invested description of such an interaction can a white reader in a white-majority society even begin to understand what the experience of racism is like. Notably, the tension of the theater interaction is at last dispelled only when Emmy kisses Archie at the end of the night. Magical kisses, one might argue, are the stuff of sentimental romance, and yet love truly does often have the power to invigorate a downtrodden person, to inspire one to persist in the face of life's difficulties, knowing a loved one is there for support.

The importance of both sentiment and rationality are demonstrated throughout the remaining scenes. When Mr. Fields speaks ill of Emmy, Archie must decide whether to bow to his sentimental response and speak up in Emmy's honor, or to take the rationally wiser option of remaining quiet, to ensure that he keep his job. That Archie feels he makes the wrong choice in making the rational one is suggested when he afterward "tasted the depths of self-abasement . . . , alternately reviling and defending himself"—the reviling being sentimental, the defending being rational. When Archie is soon offered a major chance for career advancement, he feels "lucky" but, realizing the dilemma with regard to his marriage, is left to rationally figure how to preserve both the career opportunity and the relationship. His solution, the two-year delay of his marriage, seems reasonable enough, but his mistake comes when he communicates the situation to Emmy

and completely leaves out his own sentiments regarding the proposed delay. Although she is properly taken aback at the mention of it, "even then he might have saved the situation by telling her first of his own cruel disappointment, . . . but he only floundered on." Emmy's response, appropriately enough—Archie has favored the rational at the expense of *her* sentiments—is to completely withdraw her emotional investment, leaving her "quite cool now." This withdrawal, as it happens, proves to be Emmy's mistake—or at least her mother suggests as much in pointing out how foolish it would be to throw away the love of a lifetime for the sake of one indignity. Both Archie and Emmy, then, are seen to err in failing to pay heed to their sentiments, and their situation deteriorates accordingly.

From this point on, the two protagonists succeed in gradually recovering their sentimental sensibility. Archie, sufficiently offended when Mr. Fields speaks ill of Emmy once more, finally acts on his sentimental reaction, expressing just how he feels about Mr. Fields's comments by threatening physical harm should he continue to injure Emmy's honor. As for Emmy, her outlook is revolutionized when her usually composed mother explains her own sentimental mistake years ago and concludes her tale in an uncharacteristic display: "Her mother in tears! To Emmy it was as though the world lay in ruins about her feet." Both Archie and Emmy thus return to acting on sentiment—which was what brought them together in the first place—and now all that remains is for their lives to come together once more. Given how he feels, Archie cannot simply forget Emmy, and when he at last returns, Emmy shows a loving interest that leaves no room for misunderstanding. Their reunion is fitting, Archie's being granted his old job is an apt reward for his display of integrity, and as the story sentimentally demonstrates, sometimes—in the best of times, perhaps—in romance, as in reality, love does not just find a way but leads the way.

Source: Michael Allen Holmes, Critical Essay on "Emmy," in *Short Stories for Students*, Gale, Cengage Learning, 2016.

Licia Morrow Calloway

In the following excerpt, Calloway explains that Fauset rejects the literary convention of a light-skinned heroine.

. . . As many scholars have observed, mixed racial ancestry had a very definite impact

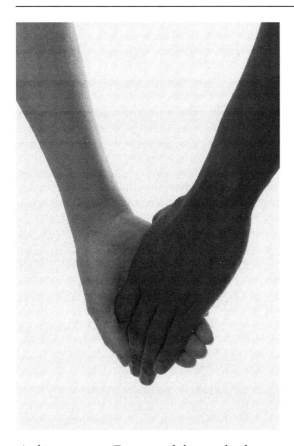

Archie returns to Emmy, and the couple plans to marry very soon. (© *Dmitri Mikitenko / Shutterstock*)

on class status and social standing in the black community. Willard Gatewood points out that not "all mulattoes belonged to the upper class. Color alone, without proper family credentials, education, or evidences of good breeding and respectability" was insufficient to merit "a passport to the upper stratum of black society." However, as Kevin Kelley Gaines notes, miscegenation produced "African Americans with access to wealth, education, and power, and many of the race's leaders during Reconstruction had emerged from the social advantages that accrued to whiteness." Whereas Fauset's novels certainly encode these historical observations of the collusion of color and class and how they operate to structure social relations in the black community, she displays resistance to the invariably fair-skinned heroine and the reification of color discrimination within the race.

In a radical and daring departure from established literary convention, Fauset takes great pains not to replicate the "fair mulatta" heroine type

widely popularized through Harriet Beecher Stowe's *Uncle Tom's Cabin*, and made standard by Hopkins, Harper, Chesnutt, and other turn-of-the-century African-American novelists. As critic Claudia Tate contends, "Without a doubt the ideology of Western beauty had conditioned readers—black and white alike—to expect fair heroines and to bestow sympathy on the basis of the purity of character, aligned to the purity of Caucasoid comeliness." Fauset's first novel boldly resists this audience expectation; the reader is reminded insistently throughout the text of *There Is Confusion* that the principal character, Joanna Marshall, is brown-skinned and scorns the use of artificial methods to straighten her hair. Fauset then divests the traditional pale heroine of her supposedly intrinsic quasi-perfection by encumbering the representative lighter-skinned women in the novel with quintessentially anti-heroic baggage: they are women whose suitors are less than ardent, who get mired in the shameful business of obsessive social climbing, who possess such unenviable qualities as questionable judgment, superficial values, skin color prejudice, working class poverty, retrogressive domestic servility, and a plebeian work ethic. By contrast, the undeniably brown Joanna is the beneficiary of beauty which requires no cosmetic enhancement, above-average intelligence, artistic talent, healthy ambition, good breeding, solid family values, and natural refinement, all in addition to the requisite unimpeachable virtue. In this way, Fauset both expands the boundaries of acceptable, sympathetic black female characters and reverses the image of the black feminine ideal by severing the "natural" link between desirable attributes and near-white skin tones.

Like her mentor W. E. B. Du Bois, who mused, "Now can there be any question but that as colors bronze, mahogany, coffee and gold are far lovelier than pink, gray, and marble?" Fauset emerged as a strong advocate for the appreciation of the spectrum of skin hues visible in the black community. In her effort to configure a set of culturally autonomous maternal standards, Fauset first and foremost labored to promote and validate images of black femininity which defied the Eurocentric formula for what is aesthetically pleasing. Laurentine Strange of *The Chinaberry Tree* is "a beautiful deep gold" mulatta, while the "maidenly prettiness" of her cousin Melissa Paul shines through "her clear light brown skin, her carefully treated reddish hair, her surprising green eyes, her thin supple figure." Angela Murray of

> SINCE SURVIVING DEGRADATION WAS PERCEIVED AS SUSPECT, RATHER THAN A REMARKABLE DISPLAY OF RESILIENCE UNDER EXTREMELY ADVERSE CIRCUMSTANCES, TURN-OF-THE-CENTURY BLACK AUTHORS SET OUT TO REFORM THE LITERARY IMAGE OF BLACK WOMEN WHO CONCEIVE CHILDREN WITH WHITE MEN."

Plum Bun, with her "creamy complexion and her soft cloudy, chestnut hair," can pass for white effortlessly, but her type of beauty "pales" in comparison to that of her darker little sister, Virginia, who is distinguished by "the rose and gold of her smooth skin. Her eyes were bright and dancing. Her hair, black, alive and curling, ended in a thick velvety straightness like cut plush." The visible contrast between Angela and Virginia complicates the issue of racial identity and its connection to appearance. The Murray sisters share an identical genetic ancestry, even though they look as if they belong to different races. For social entitlement to be based solely upon the arbitrary distribution of melanin content and hair texture, Fauset demonstrates, is fundamentally unsound.

In the other of Fauset's novels that deals substantively with the phenomenon of passing, *Comedy: American Style*, she similarly uses a woman capable of being taken for white to remark upon the beauty of the browner women of the race. When the exclusive prep school Teresa Gary is attending as a "white" female alerts the student body that a black girl, Alicia Barrett, has been accepted for the following term, it causes quite an uproar on the small campus. In an effort to relieve their apprehensions about having a "colored" classmate, Teresa informs the other girls, "Why, when I was in the graded schools, the prettiest and the most popular girl there was a dark, brown girl; not black, you know, but brown, like—like a young chestnut. Her skin was just as thin. You could see the red under it." Teresa is describing her childhood playmate Marise Davies, who later becomes a critically acclaimed dancer on Broadway, as does *Confusion*'s Joanna Marshall.

The characterization of Joanna as a "rosy brown vision" with "thick crinkling hair" challenges the claim that Fauset devoted her literary talents to the fetishization of Anglo-Saxon facial features, pale skins, and silky tresses. Furthermore, it debunks the corollary allegation that she depicted such characteristics as the inevitable genetic property of the black privileged classes. Fauset's effort to fashion admirable darker-skinned black heroines continues a legacy of increasingly resistant portrayals of black femininity by her most significant literary predecessors. Literary critic Hazel Carby has pointed out how, irrespective of the hue of their skins, early black female characters unilaterally become excluded from the "cult of true womanhood" which provided the model criteria governing feminine behavior in the nineteenth century:

> Measured against the sentimental heroines of domestic novels, the black woman repeatedly failed the test of true womanhood because she survived her institutionalized rape, whereas the true heroine would rather die than be sexually abused. Comparison between these figurations of black versus white womanhood also encouraged readers to conclude that the slave woman must be less sensitive and spiritually inferior.

Since surviving degradation was perceived as suspect, rather than a remarkable display of resilience under extremely adverse circumstances, turn-of-the-century black authors set out to reform the literary image of black women who conceive children with white men.

Marie, the mother of Iola Leroy in Frances E. W. Harper's 1892 novel of the same name, is actually the lawfully wedded wife of the father of her children; although she had been his slave, Marie was as fair as any white woman, and her three children never suspected their African ancestry. In Pauline Hopkins's *Contending Forces* (1900), Sappho Clark, born Mabelle Beaubean, is abducted and raped at fourteen by her own uncle, her father's white half-brother. Her uncle deposits her in a brothel, where her father eventually finds her and brings her home. When Mr. Beaubean threatens legal action against his rich, well-connected brother, mob violence is the response. With the exception of the pregnant Mabelle, who is rescued by a family friend and conveyed to the safety of a convent, the entire Beaubean family is brutally murdered. To protect herself, and effactually perform a figurative suicide upon her true identity, Mabelle adopts the name

Sappho Clark. Sappho's shame about her past, her illegitimate son, and the sordid circumstances of his conception, are each interrogated through a variety of avenues in the novel, and Sappho's journey to reclaim her child is a moment of epiphany that exonerates her of any culpability in her ordeal, celebrates her strength to overcome her victimization, and demonstrates that love supersedes the violation of conventional morality. As Hazel Carby argues, in order to fit herself for marriage, Sappho Clark had to achieve a reconciliation with her child in order to come to terms with what she had endured as Mabelle Beaubean. "'Mother-love' was present in the text as a process of purification, a spiritual revival that could purge the circumstances of birth and that prepared Sappho for the future." Sappho, along with Hopkins's audience, learns that maternal devotion transcends the socially dictated demands of the "true woman" ideal regarding feminine delicacy.

Charles Chesnutt engages the same issue of the black woman's difficulty in conforming to social convention in his novel *The Marrow of Tradition* (1901). Towards the end of the narrative Chesnutt engineers the discovery of the certificate documenting the legal marriage of Samuel Merkell, a white man, to Julia Brown, his former housemaid. The marriage, which is Julia's firm precondition for continuing to reside in the Merkell home after the death of her former mistress, proves the legitimacy of their daughter, Janet. Janet has long been repudiated by her white half-sister Olivia Merkell Carteret, who is married to their town's most virulent white supremacist, but it is Olivia who finds the marriage certificate long after both her father and his black second wife are dead. The marriage has been kept secret from even the reader; Chesnutt exploits the "traditional" assumption that Julia is Sam Merkell's willing concubine not only by revealing that they had been married but by ensuring that Julia's virtue is unquestioned. Accompanying his will, Merkell leaves a letter addressed to his lawyer which explains in detail why the marriage had never been openly acknowledged: "It was her own proposition that nothing be said of this marriage. If any shame should fall on her, it would fall lightly, for it would be undeserved." Chesnutt's wry plot twist remarks not only upon this particular relationship, for he does not present Julia as an anomalous black woman. Instead, he seems to suggest that moral condemnation is rarely, if ever, justified because we can never be certain we have all

of the pertinent information necessary to make an accurate judgment. Chesnutt's larger message notwithstanding, Julia's bold dismissal of the weight of public opinion is meant to be indicative of true virtue, which does not demand social recognition but remains a private covenant between an individual and God. . . .

Source: Licia Morrow Calloway, "Revising the Victorian Maternal Ideal in Jessie Fauset's *There Is Confusion:* Revisiting the Tragic Mulatto," in *Black Family (Dys)-Function in Novels by Jessie Fauset, Nella Larsen, & Fannie Hurst*, Peter Lang, 2003, pp. 52–56.

SOURCES

Bone, Robert A., *The Negro Novel in America*, Yale University Press, 1958, pp. 101–102.

Du Bois, W. E. B., "Editing the *Crisis*," in *The "Crisis" Reader: Stories, Poetry, and Essays from the N.A.A.C.P.'s "Crisis" Magazine*, edited by Sondra Kathryn Wilson, Modern Library, 1999, pp. xxvii–xxxii.

Fauset, Jessie, "Emmy," in *The "Crisis" Reader: Stories, Poetry, and Essays from the N.A.A.C.P.'s "Crisis" Magazine*, edited by Sondra Kathryn Wilson, Modern Library, 1999, pp. 51–78.

Feeney, Joseph J., "A Sardonic Unconventional Jessie Fauset: The Double Structure and Double Vision of Her Novels," in *CLA Journal*, Vol. 22, No. 4, June 1979, pp. 365–82.

Gloster, Hugh M., *Negro Voices in American Fiction*, Russell & Russell, 1965, pp. 131–39.

"Henry Louis Gates, Jr.," Hutchins Center website, http://hutchinscenter.fas.harvard.edu/dubois/henry-louis-gates-jr (accessed July 30, 2015).

Jones, Sharon L., "Reclaiming a Legacy: The Dialectic of Race, Class, and Gender in Jessie Fauset, Zora Neale Hurston, and Dorothy West," in *Hecate*, Vol. 24, No. 1, May 1998, pp. 155–64.

McLendon, Jacquelyn Y., "Jessie Redmon Fauset: Overview," in *Feminist Writers*, edited by Pamela Kester-Shelton, St. James Press, 1996.

"NAACP: 100 Years of History," NAACP website, http://www.naacp.org/pages/naacp-history (accessed July 30, 2015).

Posner, Richard A., "The Race against Race," in *New Republic*, January 29, 2010, http://www.newrepublic.com/book/review/the-race-against-race (accessed July 30, 2015).

Sylvander, Carolyn Wedin, "Jessie Redmon Fauset," in *Dictionary of Literary Biography*, Vol. 51, *Afro-American Writers from the Harlem Renaissance to 1940*, edited by Trudier Harris, Gale Research, 1987, pp. 76–86.

————, *Jessie Redmon Fauset, Black American Writer*, Whitston Publishing, 1981, pp. iii–iv, 1–94, 131–32.

"W. E. B. Du Bois," PBS website, http://www.pbs.org/wnet/jimcrow/stories_people_dubois.html (accessed July 30, 2015).

Wilson, Sondra Kathryn, ed., Introduction to *The "Crisis" Reader: Stories, Poetry, and Essays from the N.A.A.C.P.'s "Crisis" Magazine*, Modern Library, 1999, pp. xix–xxvi.

FURTHER READING

Hopkins, Pauline, *Contending Forces: A Romance Illustrative of Negro Life North and South*, Southern Illinois University Press, 1978.

> First published in 1899, a dozen years before the appearance of Fauset's first story, Hopkins's self-designated romantic novel is an important precursor to Fauset's body of work. This edition includes an afterword by noted poet Gwendolyn Brooks.

Hughes, Langston, *The Big Sea*, Knopf, 1940.

> This autobiographical volume of Hughes's covers the time when he was discovered by Fauset, whose encouragement and warmth helped him through the overwhelming experience of being introduced to the leading African American political and literary figures of the era—one of which he was destined to be.

Stribling, T. S., *Birthright*, Century, 1922.

> Also available in a 1987 reprint edition, Stribling's novel is largely forgotten today but served as inspiration—or rather, motivation—

for Fauset at the beginning of her literary career. Stribling, a white author, sought to depict the experiences of a mulatto protagonist, and Fauset at once realized that she could do life in the African American community far better justice.

Wall, Cheryl A., *Women of the Harlem Renaissance*, Indiana University Press, 1995.

> Wall's focuses on the three most famous women to have emerged from the Harlem Renaissance, including Fauset, Larsen, and Zora Neale Hurston, whose most significant volumes were published beginning in the mid-1930s.

SUGGESTED SEARCH TERMS

Jessie Redmon Fauset AND Emmy

Fauset AND the Crisis

Fauset AND Harlem Renaissance

Harlem Renaissance AND short fiction

Harlem Renaissance AND black magazines OR newspapers

Philadelphia AND black fiction

Fauset AND W. E. B. Du Bois

Fauset AND Langston Hughes

Fauset AND Countee Cullen

Fauset AND Claude McKay

The Fat of the Land

ANZIA YEZIERSKA

1920

Anzia Yezierska came to America from Poland when she was fifteen years old and settled with her family on New York's Lower East Side. Her work reflects her experiences growing up in a Jewish immigrant neighborhood in the early twentieth century, capturing particularly well the rhythms of language used by her community.

In Yezierska's story "The Fat of the Land," which first appeared in the collection *Hungry Hearts* (1920), a Jewish immigrant ages from a frazzled young mother struggling to feed her six children to an elderly woman supported in luxury by her now-prosperous family. In spite of her material comfort, the woman is unhappy because she is isolated from her neighbors in the poor immigrant tenement where she raised her children. "The Fat of the Land" is available online from Project Gutenberg and in numerous short-story collections.

AUTHOR BIOGRAPHY

Yezierska was born in Plinsk, Poland, a town near Warsaw. Her birth date is uncertain— somewhere between 1880 and 1885—perhaps because she genuinely did not know or perhaps because, according to her daughter, she claimed in interviews to be younger than she was to hide that she started writing relatively late in life. Yezierska was the youngest of a large family with nine or ten children. Her oldest brother,

Anzia Yezierska (© NY Daily News Archive / Getty Images)

Meyer, left home and went to America first. At Ellis Island, he was given the name Max Mayer, so when the rest of the family followed him, they also took that surname. Yezierska, about fifteen years old at the time, was rechristened Harriet. She was called Hattie until she was in her late twenties and reclaimed her birth name.

Yezierska's father was extremely pious. He spent his days studying the Torah and the Talmud (Jewish religious texts), while her mother worked menial jobs to support the family. Although Yezierska's brothers were encouraged to pursue their educations, Yezierska had only a few years of formal schooling before starting work. She worked as a maid, as a laundress, or in sweatshops by day and took classes in English at night. Against her father's wishes, she falsified a high school diploma and applied to Columbia University's Teachers College. She earned a scholarship and studied literature and

philosophy. After graduating in 1905, she worked as a teacher for several years.

In 1910, Yezierska married lawyer Jacob Gordon, but she applied for an annulment the very next day. She married teacher Arnold Levitas in 1911, and the couple had a daughter, Louise, the following year. The marriage was not a happy one; Yezierska moved out with Louise several times before divorcing Levitas in 1916. Because she feared she would not be able to support her daughter, Yezierska sent her to live with her father. Though she visited Louise often, the relationship between mother and daughter was strained.

Yezierska began writing seriously around 1913. Her career was encouraged by writer and philosopher John Dewey, one of her teachers at Columbia. Dewey was much older than Yezierska, and their relationship was partly romantic and partly that of mentor and protégé. Her first story was published in 1915: "The Free Vacation

House." This story also appears in Yezierska's first book, *Hungry Hearts* (1920), which includes "The Fat of the Land." The stories, like most of Yezierska's work, reflect her experiences growing up in the immigrant communities of New York's Lower East Side.

Hungry Hearts received positive attention from the press and was noticed by Samuel Goldwyn, who used the stories as a basis for a 1922 silent film. Yezierska's novel *Salome of the Tenements* (1923) was also adapted into a movie, and Yezierska was hired by Goldwyn's studio to write screenplays. Hollywood did not suit her, however. She returned to New York and wrote more short stories and novels. *Bread Givers* (1925) is considered by many to be Yezierska's best, most polished work. After *All I Could Never Be*, a fictionalized account of her relationship with Dewey, appeared in 1932, Yezierska did not publish anything until her autobiography, *Red Ribbon on a White Horse*, came out in 1950.

In the last two decades of her life, Yezierska wrote book reviews for the *New York Times* and occasionally gave lectures. She moved to California to be near her daughter in 1966. Though she was nearly blind by this point, she still continued to write with the help of assistants hired by her daughter to transcribe. On November 21, 1970, Yezierska died of a stroke in a nursing home in Ontario, California.

PLOT SUMMARY

Hanneh Breineh calls across the air shaft to her neighbor, Mrs. Pelz, asking to borrow her boiler so that she can do laundry. She complains that a repairman did not properly fix her own boiler. Hanneh Breineh ties her baby, Sammy, into his highchair, gives him a pacifier, and leaves him there to go to Mrs. Pelz's apartment to get the boiler. The two women discuss another neighbor, Mrs. Melker, who has come up in the world from scrounging to feed her family to buying fifty pounds of chicken for her daughter's wedding. Mrs. Pelz and Hanneh Breineh bemoan the contrast between the lives of those like Mrs. Melker— or even their own lives back in Poland—with their own current hardscrabble lives.

Sammy screams because his wiggling has knocked the highchair over. Hanneh Breineh dashes back to her apartment and picks him up, crying out in worry and hugging him. Mrs.

MEDIA ADAPTATIONS

- The collection *Hungry Hearts*, which includes "The Fat of the Land," was adapted into a silent film in 1922. E. Mason Hopper directed the film, and Rosa Rosanova, E. Alyn Warren, Bryant Washburn, and Helen Ferguson starred. The film was recently restored by the National Center for Jewish Film and given a new musical score.

Pelz calmly examines the baby and finds that he is unharmed except for a lump on his forehead. She offers a folk remedy for reducing the swelling and ties a red string around his neck, believing it will prevent further mishap.

Later in the day, Hanneh Breineh brings Sammy to Mrs. Pelz's kitchen. As she begins to peel potatoes for dinner, Hanneh Breineh complains about her difficult life raising six children. She speaks resentfully of having to tend Sammy instead of being able to go out and earn money to improve the family's situation. When she goes so far as to suggest it would be better if one of her children died rather than live to be a drain on her, Mrs. Pelz scolds her and suggests she will be glad for her large family when the children grow old enough to earn money themselves. Mrs. Pelz gives Hanneh Breineh some gefilte fish on a piece of bread, hoping that something to eat will make her less hopeless and grumpy. Hanneh Breineh relishes the food.

While Hanneh Breineh is out looking for bargain prices on food, her children come home from school and bicker over what little there is to eat in the kitchen. When Hanneh Breineh returns with her shopping basket, the children devour the bread and fish she has brought from the market. Hanneh Breineh realizes that Benny did not come home with his brothers and sisters.

Hanneh Breineh goes to the school to look for him, but when Benny's kindergarten teacher says he never came to school that morning, Hanneh Breineh panics. She sees Mrs. Pelz at a fruit cart and begs her and other passersby to help. Bemoaning the loss of Benny, whom she calls her favorite child, she works herself up, threatening suicide and finally fainting. When she comes to, a policeman is bringing Benny home. Now that he is found, Hanneh Breineh no longer sings his praises; she slaps him and claims he has always caused her trouble. Mrs. Pelz pulls Benny away from Hanneh Breineh to prevent a beating. Hanneh Breineh gives Benny some food, but he is too upset to eat.

A break in the text indicates a jump forward in time. Mrs. Pelz is visiting Hanneh Breineh, who now lives in a brownstone house instead of the apartment with the narrow air shaft. As she climbs the steps and rings the doorbell, Mrs. Pelz notes how nice Hanneh Breineh's new home is and becomes afraid that she will not be recognized or might not be allowed in by the servant. However, Hanneh Breineh is thrilled to see her former neighbor, invites her into the kitchen, and makes her something to eat.

Hanneh Breineh fondly remembers the time when they lived near each other and complains that her children, now grown, do not consider her feelings. Mrs. Pelz exclaims that everyone envies the success of Hanneh Breineh's children and the way they take care of her. Hanneh Breineh explains that her husband passed away and his insurance money enabled her to open a small grocery store and better support her children. This small start led to big success for her children.

Her son Abe married well and now owns his own factory. Mrs. Pelz hopes that Abe might give her husband a job. Hanneh Breineh's daughter, Fanny, has a hat shop and trains poor girls to learn the millinery trade. Benny wrote a play, which was produced on Broadway, and Sammy, the baby of the family, is the quarterback on his college football team. Jake is a landlord in charge of renting "the swellest apartment-houses on Riverside Drive."

In spite of her children's success, Hanneh Breineh is not happy. The family wealth means she lives comfortably, but she misses the close feeling of community from the old neighborhood, and she feels that her children are embarrassed by her Old World ways. She even feels that the servant judges her for not acting like a fine, proper "American lady."

Hanneh Breineh's children gather for a dinner celebrating Benny's new play, which is such

a success the president is supposed to come see it that evening. Benny brags about how much his royalties from the play will earn him. Fanny has used Benny's newfound fame to impress wealthy customers, and she expresses romantic interest in the leading man of the cast.

Hanneh Breineh feels left out of her family's banter, and she is hurt that she has not been invited to go with them to see the play that evening. She leaves the dining room in tears. Benny intended his mother to accompany them, but Fanny is too embarrassed by what she sees as her mother's crassness to bring her to a fancy theater box. They can hear Hanneh Breineh scolding the servant in the kitchen, and Fanny complains that she will need to scramble to replace the maid if she quits because of Hanneh Breineh's sharp tongue.

Jake moves Fanny and his mother to one of his apartments, where there is a "dining service," which means they no longer need a servant. Hanneh Breineh dislikes eating with the other tenants because she does not have proper table manners, leading Fanny to scold her. In a fit of rebellion, Hanneh Breineh returns to the old neighborhood to buy goods at the market. She enjoys haggling over the price of fish, though she can easily afford to pay. When she returns home, however, the doorman does not allow her to take her basket with her on the elevator because the building rules require deliveries to come through the back door.

Fanny arrives with Mrs. Van Suyden, one of the wealthy customers she wants to impress. Embarrassed by her mother's actions and by Mrs. Van Suyden's pity, Fanny becomes angry and reproaches her mother. Hanneh Breineh yells back at her daughter, saying that everything the children do for her is meaningless if not done with love. Hanneh Breineh storms out and goes to see Mrs. Pelz.

Hanneh Breineh arrives at Mr. and Mrs. Pelz's humble home in a feathered hat and fur coat. Hanneh Breineh complains about her children's treatment and about eating in fancy restaurants. Mrs. Pelz points out Hanneh Breineh's fine clothes, saying that she is "sinning before God" to whine when she has such an easy life now. However, Hanneh Breineh will not listen. She continues, explaining that her children are "strangers" and are ashamed of her.

Mrs. Pelz agrees to let Hanneh Breineh spend the night. Mr. Pelz sleeps on a few chairs, leaving his space in the bed for Hanneh Breineh. The wretched conditions of the Pelz's home make it impossible for Hanneh Breineh to sleep: the hair mattress is lumpy, there are mice in the walls, and she is cold, even with her coat over her.

In the morning, Hanneh Breineh gives Mrs. Pelz some money before leaving to roam the neighborhood streets. She does not want to return to the apartment house where she lives with Fanny. After wandering for most of the day, she finally goes home. Standing by the door in the rain, she laughs, but she feels only bitterness that her desire to grow rich on the "fat of the land" has brought her so much unhappiness.

CHARACTERS

Mrs. Melker

Mrs. Melker does not appear in the story. She is one of the people in the old neighborhood. Mrs. Pelz and Hanneh Breineh discuss how Mrs. Melker used to struggle financially but now buys grand food for her daughter's wedding.

Mr. Pelz

Mr. Pelz appears only briefly in the story. When Hanneh Breineh flees her comfortable apartment and goes back to the old neighborhood, she stays with Mr. and Mrs. Pelz in their chilly, mouse-infested home. Mrs. Pelz hopes that her husband might get a good job at Abe's factory.

Mrs. Pelz

Mrs. Pelz is Hanneh Breineh's neighbor in the old neighborhood. In contrast to Hanneh Breineh's emotional ups and down, Mrs. Pelz is very level-headed. When the children are young, she encourages Hanneh Breineh to look forward to the future, when her children will be able to earn money and take care of her. Once the family is successful, Mrs. Pelz also reminds Hanneh Breineh she should be grateful for what she has.

Abe Safron

Abe is one of Hanneh Breineh's children. When he grows up, he marries a rich girl, which enables him to start a business and become a success. He owns a shirtwaist factory, and Mrs. Pelz hopes he might give her husband a job.

Benny Safron

Benny is Hanneh Breineh's second-youngest child. In the early part of the story, Benny does not come home from school with his siblings, causing

Hanneh Breineh to panic. As an adult, Benny becomes a successful Broadway playwright. He is kinder to his mother than his sister, Fanny.

Fanny Safron

Fanny is Hanneh Breineh's daughter. She owns a millinery shop and hopes to rise in society. Though she shows kindness to the poor girls who work in her shop and "even pays them sometimes while they learn the trade," she is not very kind to her mother, whose low-class speech, manners, and habits embarrass Fanny.

Hanneh Breineh Safron

Hanneh Breineh is the protagonist of "The Fat of the Land." At the start of the story, she is a harried mother, trying to keep her six children fed on her husband's meager salary. Though she complains about her brood bitterly, even saying she wishes they would die to save her the struggle of caring for them, when she believes them lost or injured, she panics. She relies on her neighbor, Mrs. Pelz, for practical matters like borrowing laundry equipment as well as for emotional support.

In the second half of the story, we see Hanneh Breineh as an older woman, once her children have grown. They have all become successful adults, and they support her in a very comfortable lifestyle, but Hanneh Breineh is unhappy. She feels too much distance between herself and her children, who she believes are ashamed of her, and she misses the sense of community in the old neighborhood. At the story's close, Hanneh Breineh feels she does not belong in her new life because she will never become a fine "American lady," but when she tries to return to her old neighborhood, she realizes she cannot go back because she has grown used to a higher standard of living.

Jake Safron

Jake is one of Hanneh Breineh's children. Hanneh Breineh tells Mrs. Pelz that Jake has become a successful landlord.

Sammy Safron

Sammy is Hanneh Breineh's sixth and youngest child. When he is a baby, she ties him in his highchair and becomes hysterical when he falls, fearing he is hurt or killed. By the end of the story, Sam is in college, where he plays on the football team.

Mrs. Van Suyden

Mrs. Van Suyden is one of Fanny's wealthy customers. Fanny wants to impress her by

TOPICS FOR FURTHER STUDY

- Using traditional print and online sources, research the experience of immigrants in New York in the 1910s and 1920s to learn what life was like for people living in the tenements and ghettos and working in the sweatshops. Using a program like PowerPoint, create a presentation to share with your class, explaining what you have discovered.

- Imagine what Hanneh Breineh would say in a letter to friends and family left behind in Poland. She has become disillusioned with the American dream. Would she tell her friends to stay in the old country? Or would she encourage them to come to America in spite of her unhappiness? Write at least one letter from Hanneh Breineh when she still lives in the old neighborhood, when her children are little, and one written when she is living in the apartment with Fanny and feels trapped in her more prosperous new life.

- Read the Paule Marshall's young-adult novel *Brown Girl, Brownstones* (1959), which focuses on a family from Barbados living in Brooklyn during the Great Depression up to World War II. As you read, think about how Marshall portrays the Barbadian immigrant community compared with Yezierska's depiction of the Jewish immigrant community on the Lower East Side in "The Fat of the Land." Do you think the communities appear different to the protagonists because Selina is a very young woman and Hanneh Breineh is a grown married woman with children? Do you think the portrayals of immigrant community are different because the stories were written in different periods? How does each author present the central mother-daughter relationship in her story? Write an essay comparing the two works that analyzes all of these issues.

- Hanneh Breineh clearly believes she has every right to assume her children will care for her once they are successful in their own careers. Do you think parents have the right to expect their children to support them financially in their later years as well as give them respectful treatment? Do the sacrifices of a parent who immigrated to another country justify this expectation more than for other parents? With a group of classmates, stage a debate about this issue, with half of the group supporting the idea that the parents have a right to expect some caretaking from their children and half of the group arguing that parents owe their children support and help without anything in return.

---

inviting her to the theater to meet her playwright brother. When Hanneh Breineh is arguing with the apartment building doorman, Fanny arrives with Mrs. Van Suyden and is embarrassed by her mother's behavior.

THEMES

Immigrant Life

The element most praised in Yezierska's work is her realistic portrayal of the Jewish immigrant community. In "The Fat of the Land," the little details of the setting and the day-to-day things in the characters' lives contribute to this realism. Yezierska notes the narrow air shaft outside Hanneh Breineh's tenement window and describes Mrs. Pelz's superstitious remedies. She also shows her characters chatting and complaining with neighbors and borrowing household items, evidencing the spirit of community that supports the neighborhood. In addition, Yezierska shows the financial struggles of her characters: in trying to feed her children, Hanneh Breineh "had to trudge from shop to shop in search of the usual bargain, and spent nearly an hour to save two cents."

Hanneh Breineh is frazzled from caring for her children and keeping house. (© *Everett Collection / Shutterstock*)

Yezierska also shows the unfortunate emotional effects of the immigrants' hardships. Because of her background and her meager education, Hanneh Breineh often feels herself to be inferior to those around her—even to her own children. When Hanneh Breineh is catching up with Mrs. Pelz and hears the servant returning to the brownstone, she rushes her guest out of the kitchen, fearing that if the maid "sees I eat on the kitchen table, she will look on me like the dirt under her feet." Similarly, Hanneh Breineh hates eating in the public dining room of the building where she shares an apartment with Fanny: "No matter how hard she tried to learn polite table manners," Hanneh Breineh worries that her fellows diners are "staring at her." Also, while they eat, Fanny is constantly rebuking "her for eating with the wrong fork or guzzling the soup or staining the cloth." These emotional insights, coupled with the everyday details, add up to a comprehensive portrait of the Lower East Side

New York immigrant community in which Yezierska herself grew up.

American Dream

The American dream is a common theme in immigrant literature, but rather than portraying the American dream as a wonderful ideal, Yezierska shows it as an unattainable fantasy. Early in the story, at least some of the immigrant characters have hope of attaining success for themselves and their families. When Hanneh Breineh complains loudly about her life, with six children and little money to support them, Mrs. Pelz tries to encourage her. "Wait only till your children get old enough to go to the shop and earn money," Mrs. Pelz says. "You will live on the fat of the land, when they begin to bring you in the wages each week."

Though it is Mrs. Pelz who has faith in the American dream, it is Hanneh Breineh who seems to achieve it. Yezierska carefully lists the accomplishments of each of Hanneh Breineh's children. Even though what the children have achieved is impressive enough to make any parent proud, Hanneh Breineh is not happy. She feels stifled by her new lifestyle uptown, "where each lives in his own house, nobody cares if the person next door is dying or going crazy from loneliness. It ain't anything like we used to have" back in the old Lower East Side neighborhood. Because she has servants to do the housework, she has nothing to do. "The lonely idleness of Riverside Drive stunned all her senses and arrested all her thoughts. It gave her that choked sense of being cut off from air, from life, from everything warm and human." The very work that she used to complain about—cooking, cleaning, and hunting for bargains—is what she misses about her old life.

By giving Hanneh Breineh precisely what she thought she wanted but showing how it makes her miserable, Yezierska seems to suggest that chasing the American dream is, for many, an empty goal. Somewhere along the way to material wealth, Hanneh Breineh's children lost touch with what was good about their early life in America, such as a sense of community and close family ties.

STYLE

Dialect

Yezierska is often praised by critics for her use of dialect. Having grown up in the Jewish immigrant community of New York's Lower East Side, Yezierska was intimately familiar with the speech patterns of her neighbors and managed to capture them in the dialogue of her stories. The way the immigrants speak is influenced by their mother tongue and sometimes does not reflect textbook English grammar. For example, when Hanneh Breineh is feeling put upon by the countless chores of housekeeping and child rearing, she seems to resent Mrs. Pelz's holiday cleaning. Her accusatory question shows the unusual syntax of a nonnative speaker: "What are you tearing up the world with your cleaning?" Yezierska also adds to the atmosphere of the story and makes it clear that her characters are Jewish by including Yiddish words like "Gewalt!" and "Oi weh!" (both exclamations of surprise or complaint) and "mezummen" (money). Using the unique

vocabulary and the particular rhythms of speech of the immigrant community contributes to the realism of Yezierska's stories.

Point of View

"The Fat of the Land" is told with a third-person narrative, which means the narrator is not directly involved in the action of the story and refers to the characters in the third person; that is, as *he, she,* or *they.* The story is told mostly from Hanneh Breineh's point of view, which makes sense because the story revolves around her. Occasionally, however, Yezierska shifts to another character's point of view to offer insight into the situation that Hanneh Breineh would not be able to offer. For example, when coming to visit Hanneh Breineh in her upscale brownstone home, Mrs. Pelz notes the details of the house, which Hanneh Breineh herself would not notice because they have become familiar to her: "Even the outside smells riches and plenty," Mrs. Pelz marvels. "Such curtains! And shades on all windows like by millionaires."

Another perspective shift occurs when Hanneh Breineh is arguing with the building doorman about taking her market basket into the elevator. When Fanny appears with Mrs. Van Suyden in tow, the narrative changes to Fanny's point of view, allowing the reader to experience the progression of Fanny's emotions. From Hanneh Breineh's perspective, the reader would see that Fanny is angry, but from Fanny's own point of view, Yezierska is able to go into further depth, explaining that not only her mother's behavior but also Mrs. Van Suyden's pity are distressing her. Allowing the narrative to change between different characters' points of view allows Yezierska more freedom than sticking with only one character's perspective.

HISTORICAL CONTEXT

Jewish Immigrants in the 1920s

In the "Great Wave" of immigration that lasted from the 1880s into the 1920s, many of those arriving on America's shores were Jews from Romania, Austria-Hungary, and the Russian empire. These Eastern European Jews differed from other groups of immigrants in several ways. A higher number of these immigrants settled permanently in America; only 7 percent returned to their homelands, as opposed to approximately 30

COMPARE & CONTRAST

- **1920s:** In 1876, the American Working Men's Party's proposed a ban on employment of children under age fourteen. In 1881, the American Federation of Labor proposed a similar ban. However, major reform to national child labor laws did not occur in the United States until 1904, when the National Child Labor Committee was formed. Even as late as 1924, a constitutional amendment to regulate child labor fails because not enough states ratify it.

  Today: In 1938, the federal Fair Labor Standards Act takes effect. The act sets strict regulations about the employment of children regarding hours of work, working conditions, and minimum age. The laws as of 2015 do not allow any child to work during school hours, and the minimum employment age is fourteen.

- **1920s:** The "Great Wave" of immigration that began in the 1880s continues into the 1920s. An average of six hundred thousand people come to America per year, most of them from Europe. America's industrial economy is on the rise, and many immigrants find work in factories.

  Today: In reaction to the vast numbers of immigrants arriving in the United States, federal quotas were instated in the mid-1920s that limited immigration to approximately two hundred thousand people per year. These regulations stayed in effect until the mid-1960s, when Congress set up new

quotas that were based on world population. This resulted in an increase in diversity of the American immigrant population. The new system was an attempt to be fair in terms of race and ethnicity rather than favoring immigrants from Europe. Today, federal laws maintain an immigration rate lower than that in the early part of the twentieth century. The first decade of the twenty-first century sees an increase of over 30 percent in the foreign-born population, and the immigration population is far more diverse, coming from all over the world rather than the vast majority coming from Europe. Many Americans feel that immigration laws are outdated. Some push for new legislation that would help undocumented immigrants become naturalized, hoping that these new citizens would boost the economy by being legally employed, paying taxes, and contributing to Social Security.

- **1920s:** After decades of protest, lobbying, and civil disobedience by suffragists, Congress passes the Nineteenth Amendment to the US Constitution on June 4, 1919. The amendment is ratified on August 18, 1920, giving American women the right to vote.

  Today: In every presidential election since 1980, women vote in higher numbers than men. In the 2012 election, less than 60 percent of men voted compared with almost 64 percent of women. The difference was even greater among unmarried men and women.

---

percent of all immigrants. Additionally, 44 percent of Eastern European Jewish immigrants were women, which is a much higher number than for other groups, in which single men came to the United States looking for work. The importance of these two statistics is that these immigrants tended to stay in the states to raise their families. By 1920, when Yezierska published "The Fat of the Land," women of Eastern

European Jewish heritage and their children born in the United States outnumbered their Central European counterparts five to one.

This is significant because most of the Jews coming from Eastern Europe were not peasants like the vast majority of the immigrant population. Most of them came from towns and cities rather than farms and consequently settled in

Hanneh complains about her family and ties her baby into his highchair but becomes protective when her children are injured or in danger.
(© Gelpi JM / Shutterstock)

large urban centers. The 1920 US Census shows that it was the first year that more Americans lived in the city than in the country. Though it was only by a small margin—51 percent of the population in cities versus 49 percent in rural areas—the census showed the impact of the increased industrialization of America's economy, which worked to the advantage of Eastern European Jewish immigrants because of their backgrounds.

Many male Jewish immigrants were peddlers or experienced tradesmen and therefore were better able to find success in America than the unskilled laborers that made up most of the immigrant population. Families that made their living through trade in the old country continued to do so, and many were accustomed to the idea that women would work alongside men to support the family, helping to run the family shop. Many Jewish immigrant women worked in sweatshops in the garment and textile industry, which fell into a decline in the 1920s. Many also continued to work in the family business if their husbands were skilled tradesmen, like tailors or shoemakers. There were also a small number of very traditional households in which the fathers, like Yezierska's own, passed all their time in religious study, leaving their wives to support the family.

Though many women and even young girls worked just as hard as their parents to keep their families fed, in America there were more educational opportunities. Some girls became teachers or entered other professionals, though marriage and children was still the norm for most Jewish immigrants. After marriage women were not expected to work outside the home, except perhaps in the family-run business.

CRITICAL OVERVIEW

Yezierska's work has garnered mixed critical reviews over the years. The initial reaction to *Hungry Hearts* was mostly positive, and the good press caught the attention of movie mogul Samuel Goldwyn, which led to both that collection and *Salome of the Tenements* being adapted into films. However, the biting social commentary in *Arrogant Beggar* (1927) caused an uproar among critics by exposing some of the hypocritical practices of charity organizations and revealing the class tension between the more established German American Jewish community and the more recent Jewish immigrants from Eastern Europe and Russia. Yezierska's popular success faded in the 1930s and 1940s, but critical interest increased again when her 1950 autobiography was published.

In Sara R. Horowitz's profile of Yezierska for the Jewish Women's Archive, she points out how "Yezierska pays particular attention to the hardships of poverty for women saddled with child care and crowded conditions, and utterly financially dependent on husbands," which has made her interesting to feminist critics. A. O. Scott, writing in *Nation*, praises in particular Yezierska's 1925 novel *Bread Givers*, pointing out that it "has found a place on course syllabuses in women's writing, ethnic literature and Jewish studies, and in many high school English courses. She holds an important place in the literature of immigrant experience." Werner Sollors agrees in an article on *Salome of the Tenements*, explaining that Yezierska has "become an important figure for American Jewish literary history and for feminist recastings of the canon." This strength was also noted in a *Publishers Weekly* review of *Arrogant Beggar*, which explained that the novel's "social commentary about Jewish class and ethnic tensions still rings true. Fast-paced, the book brings to life the teeming activity of the Lower East Side with both passion and careful attention to detail."

Horowitz mentions that Yezierska was sometimes called the "Cinderella of the sweatshops," but her realistic portrayals were not always well received. Though she saw herself "as giving voice to her people," according to Horowitz, she was sometimes rejected by "the American mainstream as 'too Jewish,'" but "within the Jewish community her writing was offensive to both immigrant and Americanized Jews who felt mocked and exposed."

Critics focus on Yezierska's style of writing as both the best and worst thing about her stories. As Carole Stone writes in *Journal of the Short Story in English*, Yezierska masterfully captures immigrant speech:

> Yezierska's Eastern European immigrant voice, with its Yiddish women's component, forges a new American identity while maintaining a Jewish identity. . . . She used the Yiddish-English dialect to enhance her depiction of her characters' ghetto life.

However, Stone points out, Yezierska's "voice contains a vibrant, heightened, high-pitched emotionalism and euphoria, candor and openness," that is, in part, a product of her time. The highly emotional tone of Yezierska's dialogue can seem, according to *Publishers Weekly*, to a modern ear, "dated and sometimes melodramatic."

CRITICISM

Kristen Sarlin Greenberg

Greenberg is a freelance writer and editor with a background in literature and philosophy. In the following essay, she examines Hanneh Breineh's complicated relationship with her children in Yezierska's "The Fat of the Land."

In her 1920 short story "The Fat of the Land," Yezierska portrays an unusual relationship between parent and children, one that reflects the common immigrant struggle to blend what was good about the traditions of the old country with the unfamiliar ways of America. The story focuses on Hanneh Breineh, a Jewish immigrant on New York's Lower East Side, as she struggles to keep her six children fed on her husband's small salary. Though she is fiercely protective of her brood, she also resents them as a burden. Determined to pursue the American dream, Hanneh Breineh does not give up and eventually raises her children to financial success. Rather than being happy

> HANNEH BREINEH'S RELATIONSHIP WITH HER CHILDREN IS LIKE ONE BIG FINANCIAL TRANSACTION: SHE MADE SACRIFICES TO COME TO AMERICA AND MAKE A BETTER LIFE FOR HER CHILDREN AND EXPECTS THOSE SACRIFICES TO BE REPAID."

when the family grows wealthy, however, Hanneh Breineh grows bitter and angry, prompting readers to wonder about her seemingly contradictory behavior.

Hanneh Breineh's behavior seems to be inconsistent throughout the entire story. Early on, this inconsistency is illustrated best by her reactions to her children. She resents the children's needs yet loves them and worries for them. Hanneh Breineh becomes hysterical when she believes her children's safely is threatened. When baby Sammy falls out of his high chair, she dashes to him and picks him up in a panic. "Run for a doctor!" she tells her neighbor Mrs. Pelz. "He's killed! He's killed! My only child! My precious lamb!" Only a little while later the same day, however, Hanneh Breineh complains to Mrs. Pelz about Sammy, calling him a "bloodsucker" and asking "Could anybody keep that brat clean?" When the baby becomes frightened at her angry tone, she orders him to "Shut up!"

A similar pattern occurs when Benny does not come home from school with his siblings. Hanneh Breineh goes to Benny's kindergarten teacher to ask about him and "shrieked" in anguish when told that he never came to school that morning. "Woe is me! Where is my child?" Hanneh Breineh cries. Out in the street, she accosts Mrs. Pelz, begging her and the other neighbors for help: "I'll go crazy out of my head! Get me my child, or I'll take poison before your eyes!" Once Benny has been safely found, however, Hanneh Breineh's emotions take a violent turn in the opposite direction She "sprang toward him, slapping his cheeks, boxing his ears, before the neighbors could rescue him from her" and claims, "I didn't have yet a minute's peace from that child since he was born." Any parent

WHAT DO I READ NEXT?

- Many critics look at Yezierska's novel *Bread Givers* (1925) as her best, most polished work. Like "The Fat of the Land," *Bread Givers* shows Yezierska's knack for capturing the unique speech patterns of the immigrant community. The novel also contains many autobiographical elements: Sara, the protagonist, lives in a Lower East Side tenement with her mother and siblings, who struggle to make ends meet while her father studies the Torah. Conflict arises between the father's traditional ways and the daughter's very American desire for independence.

- Newbery Award–winning author Katherine Paterson portrays a complicated mother-daughter relationship in her young-adult novel *Jacob Have I Loved* (1980). The story focuses on Sara Louise Bradshaw as she finds her own path, different from the one her mother has chosen, and struggles out from under her twin sister's shadow.

- Americans were shocked by the photographs in Jacob Riis's *How the Other Half Lives*, in which he documented the terrible living conditions in the tenements of New York City. The work was originally published in 1890, but there is a 2009 edition available.

- Immigrants' disillusionment with the American dream features prominently in Pietro di Donato's *Christ in Concrete* (1939), which focuses on the struggles of an Italian American family during the 1920s and the Depression after the father is killed in a work-site accident.

- Although it was published in 1918, only two years before "The Fat of Land," Willa Cather's *My Ántonia* is a very different immigrant story. It centers on Bohemian immigrant Ántonia Shimerda, a willful pioneer woman on the plains of Nebraska.

- Modern immigrant life comes under the lens in Karolina Waclawiak's *How to Get into the Twin Palms* (2012). Rather than striving to hold on to her Polish heritage or blend in with mainstream culture in America, protagonist Anya decides to make herself over to pass as Russian and gain entry to an exclusive nightclub. Though the novel has a humorous side, Waclawiak portrays the sometimes intense loneliness of the immigrant experience.

---

whose child has gone temporarily missing can understand the simultaneous urges to give a hug to celebrate a safe return and to punish the child for wandering off, but Hanneh Breineh's reactions are extreme enough to be puzzling.

Some of Hanneh Breineh's seemingly contradictory behavior may be because she feels somewhat helpless and out of place in America. Yezierska gives clues that Hanneh Breineh does not understand the way things work in America. For example, she regrets that she was not given "a chance to go to school and learn the language" and cannot learn proper table manners "no matter how hard she tried."

Also, although she scrimps and pinches every penny, she cannot make ends meet on her husband's meager salary. Some of Hanneh Breineh's complaints about her children result from the fear and stress of struggling to provide for them. She relates to Mrs. Pelz "the fights I got by each meal. Maybe I gave Abe a bigger piece of bread than Fanny. Maybe Fanny got a little more soup in her plate than Jake." If Hanneh Breineh could afford plentiful food for her family, the childish squabbling would likely not irritate her so much. Because "eating is dearer than diamonds," there is not enough to go around, and every argument only reminds

Hanneh Breineh of that fact. Mrs. Pelz points out that one day, the children will help on the road to the American dream: "Wait only till your children get old enough to go to the shop and earn money," Mrs. Pelz says. "You will live on the fat of the land, when they begin to bring you in the wages each week."

If Hanneh Breineh's unhappiness and inconsistent behavior were caused only by feelings of helplessness and the struggles of being poor, it follows that once these stresses are gone, she should be content. However, once her children become successful and support her in a luxurious lifestyle, she seems even more unhappy than when she was a harried young mother. Hanneh Breineh feels isolated in her fancy brownstone home because she is cut off from the old neighborhood and her old ways. She explains to Mrs. Pelz that "uptown here, where each lives in his own house, nobody cares if the person next door is dying or going crazy from loneliness. It ain't anything like we used to have it in Delancey Street."

Hanneh Breineh also feels distant from her own children. They are embarrassed by her and by the fact that she has not assimilated into mainstream American culture. She knows that they "want to make me over for an American lady." Her grown children show her time and time again that they are scornful of and embarrassed by her low-class, old-world way of doing things. When Hanneh Breineh makes latkes (fried potato pancakes) especially because Benny liked them as a child, Fanny says that making such traditional foods will make people "think we were still in the push-cart district." Though Benny pats his mother's arm and says, "Stop your nagging, sis, and let ma alone," he also subtly criticizes her cooking: "My stomach is bomb-proof." He also jokes that the bad food will not hurt him because "I'm home only once a month," highlighting the fact that he visits his mother infrequently. When the conversation turns to how much money Benny is earning from his play, Hanneh Breineh does not understand about royalties and receipts, and Abe explains that Benny is going to earn enough "to buy up all your fish-markets in Delancey Street." The constant joking is to Hanneh Breineh "like a knife-thrust in her heart." She is hurt that instead of being able to share her children's lives she feels "shut out from their successes."

Hanneh Breineh's sons say many hurtful things, but much of the disrespect she receives comes from Fanny. Benny is willing to have his mother come to see his play, but Fanny does not pass along the invitation, more worried about what Mrs. Van Suyden will think than about her mother's feelings. Fanny resents her brothers for leaving her with the biggest burden when it comes to taking care of their mother and rails at them:

> I've borne the shame of mother while you bought her off with a present and a treat here and there. God knows how hard I tried to civilize her so as not to have to blush with shame when I take her anywhere.

Fanny objects to her mother's lingering interest in finding a bargain at the fish market and cooking for herself, but what really bothers Fanny is their poor roots and the worry that her mother will "spill the beans that we come from Delancey Street the minute we introduce her anywhere." Thus the discussion returns to the issue of money. Just as her children's bickering over food reminded Hanneh Breineh of her financial difficulties, her behavior also reminds Fanny of the family's humble beginnings in America.

In a way, Hanneh Breineh's relationship with her children is like one big financial transaction: she made sacrifices to come to America and make a better life for her children and expects those sacrifices to be repaid. By concentrating on material success, she has taught her children that financial wealth is what is most important in life, so they pay her back with material comforts and never think of offering anything else. They all seem to think that gaining wealth is the entirety of the American dream, and in those terms the family does indeed achieve success.

When considering the American dream in the ideal sense, however, "The Fat of the Land" shows a failure. Achieving the American dream is supposed to make a person happy and fulfilled, but by the end of the story, Hanneh Breineh is weeping. She repeats "the fat of the land," as if she finally understands her mistake: she has concentrated on the wrong goals. To continue the financial metaphor, Hanneh Breineh gets a return on her investment but in like kind. She focused only on providing for the physical needs of her children and never nurtured them emotionally beyond screaming panic when they were in danger. Therefore, they

Even with her furs and fine home, Hanneh is not happy at the close of the story. (© *Kiselev Andrey Valerevich | Shutterstock*)

pay her back with the same treatment when she is older, making sure she lives in comfort but giving her little respect or affection. Because Hanneh Breineh did not invest love into her children's lives, she receives none in return.

Source: Kristen Sarlin Greenberg, Critical Essay on "The Fat of the Land," in *Short Stories for Students*, Gale, Cengage Learning, 2016.

A. O. Scott

In the following review, Scott praises Yezierska's novel Salome of the Tenements.

If someone were to update Flaubert's *Dictionary of Received Ideas*, the entry for "radical novel" might read something like: "Great Depression; Socialist Realism; proletarian fiction characterized by slavish devotion to ideological orthodoxy at the expense of creative vision; justly forgotten." The words "radical novel" call to mind the thirties and a dreary literary scene beset, as Alfred Kazin re-called a decade later, by "dozens of cheaply tendentious political novels" plotted not along the contours of human experience but according to the iron laws of "Stalinist

cosmogony." Terms like "Socialist Realism," "proletarian fiction" and "strike novel," central to the political and aesthetic debates of the Depression years, survived in the cold war era as terms of abuse. The most recent *Columbia Literary History of the United States*, which represents liberal received wisdom in its current, pluralist manifestation, notes that "[the] thirties are not usually thought of as years of unusual creativeness, and few literary masterpieces composed during the decade can be attributed to New Deal influences," thus illustrating how the logic of anti-Communism has entangled literary judgment with ideological prejudice. Even the reputations of authors whose work has survived to represent the thirties—John Steinbeck, John Dos Passos, James T. Farrell, Clifford Odets—suffer from the suspicion that their engagement with social and political questions compromised their artistic achievements.

The bias against overt (or at least overtly left-wing) politics in literature is not limited to writing associated with the Depression. The mighty Dreiser, whose best work is as close as

SHE HOLDS AN IMPORTANT PLACE IN THE LITERATURE OF IMMIGRANT EXPERIENCE, IN WHICH SOME OF THE MOST DISTINCTIVE VOICES— GRACE PALEY, AMY TAN, EDWIDGE DANTICAT— BELONG TO WOMEN."

we may ever come to Tolstoy, occupies at best the second tier of the national canon; and Harriet Beecher Stowe, author of perhaps the most politically consequential novel in history, has only recently, and grudgingly, been readmitted to the pantheon. As these examples suggest, the radical impulse in American writing is deep and longstanding, and can scarcely be quarantined within a single period or style. The radical American novel may not be an oxymoron but a redundancy.

The recent revival of interest in the literature of the left has brought new perspectives to debates about both the politics of American literature and the literature of American political and social movements. The Feminist Press has reprinted books like Agnes Smedley's *Daughter of Earth* and Josephine Herbst's *Rope of Gold* (part of a trilogy, the other two parts of which Illinois plans to include in this series); smaller independent houses like Black Sparrow and Thunder's Mouth have brought out work by John Fante, Nelson Algren and others; and scholars like Alan Wald, Barbara Foley, Cary Nelson and Paula Rabinowitz have examined the lost traditions of radical writing and how they got lost in the first place. "The Radical Novel Reconsidered," a new series from the University of Illinois under Wald's general editorship, promises to extend this work in some surprising directions. The paperback volumes are handsomely presented; their colorful covers and solid typefaces evoke the golden age of American book design, when the novels first appeared. The introductions, by scholars whose learning is matched by their devotion to the material, are thorough and accessible, and take care to link the work of long-forgotten authors with the political and cultural concerns of the present. This is an ambitious project. If it finds

the audience it deserves in and beyond the classroom, it should substantially alter our understanding of twentieth-century American literary history.

The selections are not limited to the thirties, or to works that follow the conventions of Socialist Realism. Future titles will move on to the fifties and early sixties, and embrace such disparate genres as the war novel, the thriller and perhaps even science fiction. But the series does not ignore the importance of the strike novel, the novel of production or the other modes of realism that were indisputably central to the literature of the Depression and the New Deal. Indeed, the novel in the first batch of reprints that most closely conforms to the conventions of proletarian fiction is also the most interesting.

Grace Lumpkin's *To Make My Bread* (1932) deals with the Communist-organized textile strikes in Gastonia, North Carolina, in 1929. Lumpkin was a well-born white Southerner active in Communist intellectual circles in New York in the twenties and thirties. After the war she became a Christian anti-Communist crusader, following the lead of her friend Whittaker Chambers in denouncing her former comrades.

To Make My Bread's success as a novel is in no small part enabled by its clear engagement with a Marxian understanding of historical change. This novel covers much of the same thematic terrain as *The Grapes of Wrath*, but with less literary pretension and more historical insight. In simple, unsentimental prose, Lumpkin tells the story of the McClures, a family that lives by hunting, farming and moonshining on a remote Appalachian mountain. When a timber company drives them off their land, they descend into the textile mills. This dislocation is not the loss of a pre-industrial Eden: On the mountain, the McClures live autonomously but at the level of subsistence, and they gladly trade freedom and scarcity for the luxuries—sturdy houses, free schools and steady wages—that industrialization offers. Only gradually do they discover the cruelty at the heart of their new life, and the means to resist it.

To Make My Bread, in addition to being a novel of Southern childhood somewhat in the manner of Marjorie Rawlings's *The Yearling*, is also a novel about class formation, Taylorization and alienated labor. These words, quaint as they may sound, are not simply theoretical abstractions: Properly understood, they denote real experiences of self, time and society, the relations between people and the conditions in which they live. These are matters of profound literary interest, matters that cry out to be embodied in narrative. To be sure, Lumpkin's narrative is in places flawed, in others forced; but this novel is an honest, clear-eyed and coherent attempt to make sense of the enormities of social change as they manifest themselves in the lives of individuals.

If *To Make My Bread* might help redeem Socialist Realism from undeserved opprobrium, Myra Page's *Moscow Yankee* (1935) might help explain how radical writing got such a bad name in the first place. *Moscow Yankee* tells the story of an unemployed Detroit autoworker who travels to the Soviet Union in the days of the first Five Year Plan and is changed into a New Soviet Man (complete with a New Soviet Girlfriend, who takes the place of the two-timing petit-bourgeois commodity fetishist he left back in the U.S.A.). While Page's blithe approval of all things Soviet appalls (those kulaks apparently had it coming), the real disaster is her choice of a slangy, hard-boiled stream-of-consciousness style peppered with "Christ"'s, "Jeez"'s and passages like:

> A fellow ought to feel a girl needs, depends on him. Looks up to him sorta. This one was too smart. Too sure of herself Not a Smart-Alec, though, had to hand her that. Can't get sore at her. Fact is, admit it, you lousy sucker. She's got the goods.

Barbara Foley's superbly argued (if somewhat doctrinaire) introduction convinced me that *Moscow Yankee* is of historical interest, depicting as it does "the project of socialist construction" and the powerful hold the Soviet experiment exercised over the imaginations of some American intellectuals. But because of Page's allegiance to another failed experiment—the "documentary" style pioneered by John Dos Passos in *Manhattan Transfer* and the U.S.A. trilogy—*Moscow Yankee* is apt to remain a literary curiosity.

The prose style of Anzia Yezierska's *Salome of the Tenements* (1923) is also curious—it is rare these days to find the pure extravagance of melodrama in serious novels, and modern readers may squirm at outbursts like:

> I am a Russian Jewess, a flame—a longing. A soul consumed with hunger for heights beyond reach. I am the ache of unvoiced dreams, the clamor of suppressed desires. I am the unlived lives of generations stifled in Siberian prisons. I am the urge of ages for the free, the beautiful that never yet was on land or sea.

It is worth remembering, however, that Salome was made into a silent movie; the outsized, almost parodic theatricality of its scenes and speeches calls to mind the speeded-up, stylized gestures and emphatic intertitles of that medium. Unlike *Moscow Yankee*, whose attempt to capture the idiom of "the people" reeks of intellectual condescension and literary self-consciousness, Salome unabashedly embraces the conventions of popular entertainment; it's a bodice-ripper with a social conscience.

Based in part on Yezierska's own affair with John Dewey, and in part on the celebrated marriage of labor organizer Rose Pastor to millionaire philanthropist Graham Stokes, Salome chronicles the romance of Sonya Vrunsky (the fiery Jewess above) and John Manning, a rich do-gooder who represents "the austere perfections of the Anglo-Saxon race." Sonya's story combines social protest with social climbing: It offers both a biting critique of the liberal paternalism of the Progressive era and a utopian vision of assimilation and upward mobility. In the end Sonya forsakes Manning for the good-hearted dress designer Jacques Hollins (ne Jake Solomon), and becomes a kind of haute couture social worker, bringing Park Avenue fashions to the huddled masses of the Lower East Side.

Yezierska is one of the better-known writers in the series. Her 1925 novel *Bread Givers* has found a place on course syllabuses in women's writing, ethnic literature and Jewish studies, and in many high school English courses. She holds an important place in the literature of immigrant experience, in which some of the most distinctive voices— Grace Paley, Amy Tan, Edwidge Danticat— belong to women. Although John Sanford (ne Shapiro) is virtually unknown, *The People From Heaven* (1943) resonates with more familiar works even as it alters the context in which we read them. *The People From Heaven* belongs with Edgar Lee Masters's *Spoon River Anthology* and Sherwood Anderson's *Winesburg, Ohio*, meditations on place that seek to distill the essence of the American character. It also belongs to a tradition of Modernist works—including William Carlos Williams's *In the American Grain*, Jean Toomer's *Cane*, Hart Crane's *The Bridge*, Faulkner's *Absalom, Absalom!*—that defy conventions of genre in their attempts to reimagine American origins. Like these books, *The People From Heaven* is a strange hybrid. Its central story is about a small-town white shopkeeper's rape of an itinerant black woman, and her public vengeance. This story is intercut with wry vignettes that comment on life in post-Depression New York State, and with verse passages tracing violence and dispossession from Columbus to the Civil War. While the links between the book's divergent parts are not always clear, and the blank verse is not exactly Milton, *The People From Heaven* is a compelling experiment in bending the parameters of literary form to accommodate the brutal facts of history.

"The Radical Novel Reconsidered," in sum, invites reconsideration of more than the individual works in the series. Our understanding of the gangster novels and films of the thirties and forties is sure to be altered by Ira Wolfert's *Tucker's People* (filmed by Abraham Polonsky as *Force of Evil*, a pungent, talky 1948 noir starring John Garfield), which suggests that monopoly capitalism is just organized crime carried out by other means. Our sense of the literature of race is likely to be challenged both by Sanford's novel, which is by a Jewish man and has a black woman named America Smith as its heroine, and by the reappearance of the work of Willard Motley, a celebrated black novelist of the late forties whose protagonists are almost exclusively working-class Poles, Italians and Jews. And the category of Southern literature will have to be expanded to include not only Grace Lumpkin but also Alfred Maund, another white Southern Marxist, whose The Big Boxcar adopts the story-telling methods of *The Canterbury Tales* to expose the cruelties of American racism.

At the same time, the novels in this series clearly belong to what can only be called, in the best sense of words grown somewhat suspect, a native tradition. To rediscover these books is to rediscover American writing in the twentieth century, with all its energy and its eclecticism, its failed experiments and its neglected possibilities, its naive optimism and its oppressive sense of the past.

Make room on your shelves.

Source: A. O. Scott, Review of *Salome of the Tenements*, in *Nation*, Vol. 263, No. 8, September 23, 1996, p. 30.

SOURCES

"Anzia Yezierska (1881?–1970)," in *Heath Anthology of American Literature*, 5th ed., edited by Paul Lauter, Cengage Learning, http://college.cengage.com/english/lauter/heath/4e/students/author_pages/modern/yezierska_an.html (accessed September 6, 2015).

Austerlitz, Saul, "Anzia Yezierska," in *My Jewish Learning*, http://www.myjewishlearning.com/article/anzia-yezierska/ (accessed September 6, 2015).

Bryan, Dan, "The Great (Farm) Depression of the 1920s," American History USA website, March 6, 2012, http://www.americanhistoryusa.com/great-farm-depression-1920s/ (accessed September 7, 2015).

———, "Working and Voting: Women in the 1920s," American History USA website, March 6, 2012, http://www.americanhistoryusa.com/working-voting-women-1920s/ (accessed September 7, 2015).

"Child Labor in U.S. History," Child Labor Education Project website, https://www.continuetolearn.uiowa.edu/laborctr/child_labor/about/us_history.html (accessed September 7, 2015).

"The Facts on Immigration Today," Center for American Progress website, October 23, 2014, https://www.americanprogress.org/issues/immigration/report/2014/10/23/59040/the-facts-on-immigration-today-3/ (accessed November 9, 2015).

Horowitz, Sara R., "Anzia Yezierska," Jewish Women's Archive Encyclopedia website, http://jwa.org/encyclopedia/article/yezierska-anzia (accessed September 6, 2015).

Hyman, Paula E., "Eastern European Immigrants in the United States," Jewish Women's Archive Encyclopedia website, http://jwa.org/encyclopedia/article/eastern-european-immigrants-in-united-states (accessed September 7, 2015).

"Jews in America: American Jewish Women," Jewish Virtual Library website, https://www.jewishvirtuallibrary.org/jsource/US-Israel/ajwomen.html (accessed September 7, 2015).

"19th Amendment to the US Constitution: Women's Right to Vote," National Archives website, http://www.archives.gov/historical-docs/document.html?doc=13&title.raw=19th+Amendment+to+the+U.S.+Constitution:+Women%27s+Right+to+Vote (accessed September 7, 2015).

Rampell, Catherine, "Why Women Are Far More Likely to Vote Than Men," in *Washington Post*, July 17, 2014, https://www.washingtonpost.com/opinions/catherine-rampell-why-women-are-far-more-likely-to-vote-then-men/2014/07/17/b4658192-0de8-11e4-8c9a-923ecc0c7d23_story.html (accessed September 7, 2015).

Review of *Arrogant Beggar*, in *Publishers Weekly*, March 18, 1996, p. 63.

Rose, Or N., "Heaven and Hell in Jewish Tradition," in *My Jewish Learning*, http://www.myjewishlearning.com/article/heaven-and-hell-in-jewish-tradition/3/ (accessed September 7, 2015).

Scott, A. O., Review of *Salome of the Tenements*, in *Nation*, Vol. 263, No. 8, September 23, 1996, p. 30.

Sollors, Werner, "*Salome of the Tenements*," in *Journal of American Ethnic History*, Vol. 17, No. 4, 1998, p. 98.

Stone, Carole, "Immigrant Jewish Identity and the Female Voice: Anzia Yezierska and Grace Paley," in *Journal of the Short Story in English*, Vol. 32, Spring 1999, http://jsse.revues.org/171 (accessed September 7, 2015).

"U.S. Federal Child Labor Law," Child Labor Education Project website, https://www.continuetolearn.uiowa.edu/laborctr/child_labor/about/us_laws.html (accessed September 7, 2015).

"U.S. Immigration History," United States Immigration Policy: Environmental Impact Statement, http://www.immigrationeis.org/about-ieis/us-immigration-history (accessed September 7, 2015).

Yezierska, Anzia, "The Fat of the Land," in *Hungry Hearts*, Grosset & Dunlap, 1920, pp. 178–223.

FURTHER READING

Farish, Terry, *The Good Braider*, Skyscape, 2012.
Seventeen-year-old Viola and her mother make a harrowing journey to escape civil war in South Sudan and come to her uncle's home in Portland, Maine. Viola starts school and wants to embrace American culture, which causes conflict with her mother, who clings to familiar ways from home. The brutality of Viola's experiences while escaping her war-torn homeland makes the story more appropriate for older students, but the honesty of emotion in this critically acclaimed novel makes it a valuable addition to American immigrant literature.

Hopkinson, Deborah, *Shutting Out the Sky: Life in the Tenements of New York 1880–1924*, Orchard Books, 2003.
Hopkinson provides a broad history of immigrant communities around the turn of the twentieth century, bringing statistics and facts to life by including the personal stories of five individuals.

Lahiri, Jhumpa, *The Namesake*, Houghton Mifflin Harcourt, 2003.
Lahiri masterfully captures the odd mixture of freedom and difficulty of the immigrant experience with this family saga. Ashoke and Ashima Ganguli emigrate from India to New York and make a home for themselves. Their struggle to integrate their background and their new American lives is reflected in the inner conflict of their son, Gogol, who also copes with the burden of his parents' expectations.

Yezierska, Anzia, *Red Ribbon on a White Horse*, Persea, 2004.
This volume is a modern edition of Yezierska's autobiography, which recounts her journey from sweatshop worker to Hollywood success to forgotten author. When it was originally published in 1950, the book revived interest in her fiction, which had fallen out of favor.

SUGGESTED SEARCH TERMS

New York AND tenement

Anzia Yezierska AND Hollywood

Anzia Yezierska AND social causes

Anzia Yezierska AND Hungry Hearts

Anzia Yezierska AND "The Fat of the Land"

Anzia Yezierska AND immigrant literature

Anzia Yezierska AND Jewish American writer

immigrant life AND New York AND child labor

Jewish communities AND New York AND Lower East Side

The Fly

KATHERINE MANSFIELD
1922

"The Fly" is a story by New Zealand short-story writer Katherine Mansfield. It was first published in March 1922, in the *Nation*. One of the last stories that Mansfield completed before her death, it was included in her short-story collection *The Dove's Nest and Other Stories* in 1923. "The Fly" has long been one of Mansfield's most highly regarded stories. It is about two men who both lost their sons in World War I but are dealing with their loss in different ways. The central figure, named only as "the boss," entertains his old friend, the enfeebled Mr. Woodifield, at his office. Mr. Woodifield mentions the military cemetery in Belgium, where both the dead men are buried. Being reminded of his son is deeply upsetting for the boss, who, after his friend leaves, toys with a fly that is struggling to escape an ink pot and slowly and deliberately kills it. Death, cruelty, grief, and helplessness are among the themes of the story, which has given rise to a number of different interpretations.

AUTHOR BIOGRAPHY

One of the most admired of short-story writers of the early twentieth century, Mansfield was born as Kathleen Mansfield Beauchamp on October 14, 1888, in Wellington, New Zealand. She was the third daughter of six children born to Harold Beauchamp, a businessman and banker, and

Katherine Mansfield (© *World History Archive / Alamy*)

in 1910 and 1911. Her health was poor; she had rheumatic fever and then pleurisy during those years. In 1911, she published her first book, *In a German Pension*, consisting of sketches based on her time in the sanatorium. During the 1910s, she published stories in magazines on a regular basis. She met D. H. Lawrence in 1913 and Virginia Woolf three years later. In 1917, she was diagnosed with tuberculosis. During World War I, Mansfield spent time living in France, returning to London in April 1918, where she was divorced by her husband. Mansfield remarried within four days, to a long-established friend, John Middleton Murry, a prominent editor and literary critic. Mansfield then contributed book reviews and stories to the *Athenaeum*, a journal edited by Murry. In 1920, *Bliss and Other Stories* was published, and *The Garden Party and Other Stories* followed in 1922. In February 1922, she wrote "The Fly," which was published in the *Nation*.

Mansfield's health had by then deteriorated; after the failure of radium treatments, in October she entered the Gurdjieff Institute at Fontainebleau, France, to study the teachings of George Gurdjieff. She died of a pulmonary hemorrhage there on January 9, 1923. Two collections, *The Dove's Nest and Other Stories* and *Something Childish and Other Stories* (1924) were published posthumously. (The latter was published in the United States as *The Little Girl and Other Stories*.) Mansfield's *Poems* (1923) and *The Journal of Katherine Mansfield* (1927) were also published after her death.

PLOT SUMMARY

A few years after the end of World War I, Mr. Woodifield visits a man identified only as the boss, in the latter's office in the city, probably London, although it is unnamed. Woodifield is old and feeble and has had a stroke, but his family allows him to visit the city on Tuesdays. He sits, smoking a cigar and admiring the office, which pleases the boss, because he has recently had the office spruced up with new furniture and carpeting and electric heating. Above the boss's table is a photograph of a young man in uniform.

The boss serves Woodifield whiskey. Woodifield is delighted because his family at home will not let him drink whiskey. The boss says it will do him good. After Woodifield has drunk some of the whiskey, he remembers something he wanted

Annie Burnell (Dyer) Beauchamp. Mansfield was educated in Wellington, and at the private school she attended from 1899 to 1903, she wrote most of the school's magazine and also served as editor. In 1903, the family visited England, and the three oldest daughters were enrolled in Queen's College, a small school in London. Mansfield remained there until 1906 and published some sketches in the college magazine, which she also edited. In 1906, the family returned to New Zealand. In 1907, four of Mansfield's stories were published in a magazine in Melbourne, Australia, and the following year she returned to London.

In 1909, she married George Bowden, whom she had known for only three weeks; she left him the same day and within a week had joined her friend Garnet Trowell in Glasgow. She became pregnant by him. Her mother placed her in a sanatorium in Germany, but she suffered a miscarriage in June. Returning to London, Mansfield continued to write, publishing stories in *New Age*

MEDIA ADAPTATIONS

- An audio recording of "The Fly," read by Bart Wolffe, was released by Saland Publishing in 2013. It is available from YouTube, at the following URL: https://www.youtube.com/watch?v = 6gCCwLQVSwo.

to tell the boss. He says that his daughters visited Belgium the previous week and saw the grave of his son, Reggie, and they also saw the grave of the boss's son, which was nearby. (Both young men were killed in World War I.) Woodifield asks if the boss has seen it, and the boss replies that he has not. Woodifield then comments about how annoyed he was to hear that his daughters were charged too much for a pot of jam at the hotel. He felt they were being exploited by the Belgians. The boss agrees with him, but he seems distracted and not really listening.

Woodifield leaves. The boss tells Macey, his office messenger, that he does not wish to see anybody for half an hour. He slumps in his chair and covers his face with his hands. It had been a shock for him when Woodifield mentioned his son's grave, even though it is six years since he died. He has experienced much grief over his loss and wept often. He had been grooming his only son to take over his business eventually, and the boy had worked in the office for a year before the war began. The news of his son's death had devastated him. Now, six years later, it still seems like yesterday that it happened. He gets up and looks at the photograph of his son over his table.

The boss then notices that a fly has fallen into his ink pot and is struggling to get out, but it keeps falling back in. The boss picks up a pen and scoops the fly out of the ink pot and lays it down on a piece of blotting paper. The fly cleans the ink from its wings and face and is ready to fly off, but the boss dips his pen in the ink pot and deliberately drops a blob of ink on the fly. The fly begins the same process of

cleaning itself. The boss admires the courage of the fly, but just as it finishes cleaning itself again, he drops another blob of ink on it. The fly tries again to clean itself, but it is weakened. Determined to kill it, once more the boss drops a blob of ink on the fly, and the fly dies. The boss lifts the dead fly on his paper knife and throws it into the trash can. Having done so, however, he feels bad. He calls for Macey and tells him to bring him some fresh blotting paper. The boss then tries to remember what he had been thinking about before, but he is unable to recall.

CHARACTERS

The Boss

The boss is five years older than Mr. Woodifield, so he is likely around retirement age. However, he appears to be in good health and shows no signs of relinquishing the helm of his own company or losing his zest for life. He likes to be in control of things and up to date on what is happening in the business world (as suggested by the copy of the *Financial Times* that he has in the office). He likes to show off the new furniture in his office, and having old Woodifield there to admire it gives him a deep feeling of satisfaction. The boss seems to set much store by these material accoutrements of life. It seems he feels a little superior to his old friend, and his robustness contrasts with the other man's feebleness. The boss treats the other man kindly, however, and with some warmth.

Like Woodifield, the boss lost a son in World War I. However, unlike his old friend, he does not seem to have recovered from his grief, even though that is not at first apparent from his cheery, positive manner. The loss of his only son was at the time a devastating blow for him; he had been training the young man to eventually take over the running of his company, and the news of his son's death robbed his life of meaning and purpose. He keeps a portrait of his son in uniform above his desk. For years he would weep whenever he thought of him. When Woodifield mentions that his daughters visited their brother's grave in Belgium and while they were there also saw the grave of the boss's son, the boss's grief is reawakened, although this is not apparent until after Woodifield leaves. Perhaps because of the depths of his grief, the boss has never managed to visit his son's grave. He looks at the photograph of his son, but he does not recognize the stern expression on the young man's face. It is not as he remembers him. After Woodifield leaves, the boss notices the fly struggling in the ink pot and deliberately kills it, in a long-drawn-out way, as if he is motivated by some cruel instinct that even he does not understand.

The boss is therefore again contrasted sharply with Woodifield. The latter has apparently processed his grief and got over it, and he seems reasonably mentally healthy while physically frail. The boss is the opposite; while physically robust and active, his mind, at some deep level, is still troubled by the death of his son, for which he can find no meaning. In the past, he was able to weep about it, but he cannot do so now. For some reason, no tears come. His killing of the fly perhaps is unconsciously an acting out of the senselessness and cruelty of the soldier's death, or it could be that the boss is envisioning his own death, which he finds difficult to accept.

Macey

Macey is a gray-haired old man who works as a messenger at the boss's office. His manner toward the boss is very subservient. He has obviously become used to being ordered around, and he knows his place.

Mr. Woodifield

Mr. Woodifield is a feeble old man who has retired from his job and lives with his wife and daughters. He is not in good health, having suffered a stroke. He shuffles around and is forgetful and is compared to a baby in a pram. He speaks with a piping, childish voice. His family looks after him well, however, and every Tuesday they allow him to go to the city, where presumably he used to work, to visit his old friends. He is five years younger than the boss, who appears to be an old friend, not a former boss. Woodifield lost his son, Reggie, in World War I but seems to have gotten over the loss. His daughters have recently visited Reggie's grave at a military cemetery in Belgium. The only comments old Woodifield makes to the boss about their visit is how well the cemetery is being cared for, like a garden, with flowers on all the graves, and the fact that he is indignant about how much his daughters were charged at the hotel for a pot of jam.

TOPICS FOR FURTHER STUDY

- In "The Fly," the boss was dealt a devastating blow when his son was killed in World War I, and six years later the loss still troubles him. Read *The Grieving Teen: A Guide for Teenagers and Their Friends* (2000), by Helen Fitzgerald, or consult a website that deals with the same issue. Give a short class presentation in which you discuss the various stages of grief and then lead a discussion in which members of the class share their personal experiences of grief and recovery.

- Write a short story with a symbolic element involving a bird, animal, or insect. As in "The Fly," use a flashback that reveals something about the past that has had a major impact on the main character and still affects him or her in the present.

- Read another story by Katherine Mansfield and write an essay in which you compare and contrast it to "The Fly."

- Go to http://www.easel.ly/ and create an infographic for the life and work of Katherine Mansfield. Try to show the most important facts in a way that is easy to read and visually pleasing.

THEMES

Death

The unwelcome specter of death permeates the story. The two young men who died in World War I are evoked, as is the military cemetery in Belgium. The boss has held in his mind an image of his son "lying unchanged, unblemished in his uniform, asleep for ever," which is a euphemistic way of looking at the stark reality of death. The fear of death, the inability to process what happened to his son, lies behind the busy, assertive activity of the boss. It is the dark shadow he does not care to look at too closely.

Death is clearly hinted at in the description of Woodifield, who, the narrator says, like all

Both the boss and Woodifield lost their sons in World War I. *(© Grisha Bruev / Shutterstock)*

men clings to his "last pleasures" (in this case, visiting his friends in the city) "as the tree clings to its last leaves." Seeing how frail Mr. Woodifield is, the boss thinks "he's on his last pins." Indeed, old Woodifield is kept "boxed up" in the house every day but Tuesday; a coffin-like image that also suggests death. Death is the inevitable destination toward which all life moves.

Death as presented in the story is cruel, because for the two young soldiers it comes before its natural time, and it is a cruel thing for fathers to have to mourn the deaths of their sons rather than the other way around. Death is cruel also for the fly, because the insect is subject to the capricious will of a stronger force, even a sadistic one, which it is powerless to resist for long and which offers it no mercy.

Helplessness

If everyone is at the mercy of fate, some seem more helpless than others. The story begins with a portrait of old Mr. Woodifield, who is enfeebled following his stroke. His hands tremble, and his voice is weak. He sits in a large armchair in the boss's office and peers up at his friend "as a baby peers

out of its pram." His wife and daughters control his life now and tell him when he is allowed to go out to the city. They help get him dressed for the occasion. It is as if he is in his second childhood. When the boss offers him some whiskey, he confesses that his family does not allow him to drink at home, "And he looked as though he was going to cry" (like a baby or small child). The boss has just told him, tellingly, that the whiskey is good and "wouldn't hurt a child."

The helplessness theme is picked up again, somewhat unexpectedly, after Woodifield leaves. The boss seems to be a man who prides himself on being in control, on continuing to move forward in life—he does not think of retiring and spends money on new office furniture. He especially seems to like being in control of others, not only Macey, his subservient employee, but also his son, whose course in life was likely mapped out for him by a dominant father whether he liked it or not. However, the boss unexpectedly finds himself helpless in the face of the uncomfortable feelings that seize hold of him following Woodifield's comment that his daughters had seen the grave of his, the boss's, son. It was a "terrible shock" to him and "was exactly as though the earth had opened and he had seen the boy lying there with Woodifield's girls staring down at him."

After Woodifield leaves, the boss covers his face with his hands. He is helpless in the face of this newly awakened grief, which he does not know how to deal with. He no longer has the ability to weep about it, but the feelings he does have (the nature of which are unstated) are not those he wishes to have. He toys with and eventually kills the fly just as a means of distraction from his troubled thoughts. At that point, it is the fly's turn to be helpless in the face of cruel circumstances, even though it puts up a good fight against the inevitable. However, the boss's actions succeed only in making him feel worse; he feels wretched and is even frightened, which is just another manifestation of a state of helplessness as a result of experiencing feelings one cannot control or understand (and also, possibly, because of his realization, through the hopeless struggles of the fly, of the inevitability of death). The boss is saved only by his own forgetfulness. After he has told Macey to bring him some fresh blotting paper, he tries to remember what he was thinking about, but he cannot. However, since he was unable adequately to process the feelings he had on recalling his son's death, those feelings are likely to return at some future time to torment him. In that respect, then, he remains helpless; the only uncertainty being when, not if, such feelings will reoccur.

STYLE

Narrative Technique

The story is told by an omniscient third-person narrator. This means that the narrator refers to the characters in the third person as "he" and can divulge their thoughts and feelings to the reader. Such a narrator knows everything that is going on in the present as well as all the significant events from the past. The latter is important for "The Fly," as a significant part of it consists of a flashback to the past. A flashback is when the flow of the narrative in the present is interrupted by a return to something that happened in the past that has a bearing on the present. In this case, it is the information supplied about how the boss reacted to his son's death six years earlier and why it affected him the way it did. However, there is one small exception to the omniscience of the narrator. He presents the boss's dead son entirely through the memories and impressions of the boss; what the son actually may have thought or felt remains unstated. This could be important to the interpretation of the story, since it creates the possibility that the son might have been somewhat different from how the boss remembers him or thought of him during his life.

Metaphor

The fly might be seen metaphorically, although it is not essential to do so in order to understand the story. A metaphor is a description of one thing in terms of another. The fly could be a metaphor for human life, in which case humans are shown struggling bravely to hang on to their lives and flourish even when faced with tremendous obstacles that will ultimately defeat them. Seen in this light, there could be a biographical element in the story. At the time she wrote it, Mansfield was very sick, and she would die within a year. Perhaps the fly represents, in some sense, her own struggle to live and to be creative in her work, despite repeated setbacks. The fly could also represent collective human life, an entire society that is subject to an arbitrary fate that it does not understand, all the while being a victim of malevolent forces that manipulate and destroy it. It is conceivable there is an allusion here to the slaughter of World War I. This might involve a metaphorical interpretation of the boss, too. Perhaps he is more than just an old man who cruelly kills a fly. Perhaps the boss metaphorically represents capitalism and its role in plunging the world into a cruel and monstrously destructive war. Another possibility is that since Mansfield sympathized with feminist ideals and frequently presented women as victims, perhaps the boss might be the entire patriarchal system that oppresses women.

HISTORICAL CONTEXT

World War I

In June 1914, Archduke Franz Ferdinand, who was heir to the throne of the Austro-Hungarian Empire, was assassinated in Sarajevo, Serbia. The following month, Austria-Hungary declared war on Serbia, and Russia entered the conflict in support of its Serbian ally. Within a few weeks, because of the complicated web of treaty obligations, virtually the whole of Europe was at war,

COMPARE & CONTRAST

- **1910s:** The British Empire has nearly 8.9 million men in military service during the course of World War I. Of that figure, over 900,000 were killed and 2.1 million wounded. Nearly 36 percent of all members of the armed forces are casualties. France suffers even more grievously, with 1.36 million dead, 4.3 million wounded, and 73.3 percent casualties as a percentage of total forces. In total, 65 million members of the armed forces of all the countries involved die in World War I, and 21.2 million are wounded.

  1920s: World War I and the devastating carnage that it wrought is still fresh in the minds of millions of people. It seems to many as if almost an entire generation of young men has been wiped out.

  Today: Hundreds of commemorations of World War I take place across the world, beginning in 2014, the one hundredth anniversary of the start of the conflict, and are scheduled to continue to 2018, one hundred years after the end of the war.

- **1910s:** Mansfield starts to publish her short stories. Other notable short stories of the decade in English literature include E. M. Forster's *The Celestial Omnibus and Other Stories* in 1911, which contains the well-known story "The Road from Colonus," and James Joyce's collection of stories, *Dubliners*, in 1914, which contains "Araby."

  1920s: In addition to the many stories by Mansfield that are published in the early years of the decade, D. H. Lawrence's collection of stories *England, My England* is published in 1922. Virginia Woolf's *Monday or Tuesday* (1921) is her first short-story collection. It contains eight stories, including the "The Mark on the Wall," first published in 1917, which is often cited as an example of the stream-of-consciousness technique.

  Today: The short story continues to flourish in British literature in such collections as *Ten Stories about Smoking* (2011), by Stuart Evers; *The Beautiful Indifference* (2011), by Sarah Hall; *The Rental Heart and Other Fairy Tales* (2014), by Kirsty Logan; and *The Stone Thrower* (2013), by Adam Marek.

- **1910s:** The Edwardian era in English literature, named after King Edward VII, who reigned from 1901 to 1910, continues up to 1914. Prominent British writers of the period include E. M. Forster, John Galsworthy, and P. G. Wodehouse.

  1920s: Modernism is the dominant literary mode in British, European, and American literature. New literary techniques and ideas emerge in response to the enormous cultural changes of the period.

  Today: Contemporary literature is often referred to as postmodern. Postmodernism refers to the notion that objective reality cannot be determined; all reality is subjective, relative to time, place, and culture, and such conditions as class, race, and gender.

---

with Austria-Hungary, Germany, and Italy (known as the Central powers) pitted against Britain, France, and Russia (the Triple Entente, or Allied forces). Britain declared war on Germany in August after Germany invaded neutral Belgium.

Mansfield was living in London when the war broke out. Out in the streets, she and her friend John Middleton Murry observed the strong emotions that the crowds of people were expressing at the news that war had been declared. She and Murry watched a regiment depart for the conflict, but neither of them had strong views for or against the war.

In battles in August and September 1914, British and French forces engaged the Germans at the Battle of Mons in Belgium and then the

Battle of the Marne in France and succeeded in stopping the German advance. In the fall of 1914, Mansfield was at Charing Cross railway station to watch the wounded soldiers returning, and she also wrote a piece that appeared in a Wellington, New Zealand, newspaper about the plight of the Belgian refugees who were arriving in London, having fled the conflict. She even decided at one point that she wanted to become a newspaper reporter near the war zone, but nothing came of that idea. In October 1915, her brother, Leslie Beauchamp, who had enlisted in the army the previous year, was killed in France when a faulty hand grenade blew up in his hand.

It was soon clear that the war would be a long drawn-out one, contrary to what both sides had been expecting in 1914. Trenches were dug on the western front to prevent enemy advancement. Battles fought from the trenches resulted in huge casualties and were often virtual stalemates, with only a few hundred yards gained on either side. One of the deadliest battles was the Battle of Verdun, in northeastern France, which began in February 1916. In a few months, casualties numbered over three hundred thousand on each side. In July, to relieve the pressure on Verdun, the British and French armies initiated the Battle of the Somme. On the first day of battle, nearly twenty thousand British soldiers were killed and close to forty thousand injured as they advanced under heavy machine gun fire by the Germans. When the battle ended in November, the Allies had advanced only five miles. Total casualties on all sides were about 1,265,000.

In 1917, Russia withdrew from the war following a domestic revolution, leaving Germany in a stronger position. But the United States declared war on Germany in April, bringing fresh troops, supplies, and financial assistance to the allies. In 1918, Germany began an offensive on the western front, but an allied counter-offensive freed much of France and Belgium from German control. In November 1918, with Germany defeated, an armistice was signed.

Modernism

Mansfield wrote during the period when the dominant literary movement was modernism. Modernism had its roots in the late nineteenth century and became more firmly established after World War I. Modernist writers broke with previous literary traditions of the romantic, Victorian, and Edwardian eras. They experimented with new literary forms and styles and also questioned many of the basic assumptions that had formed a part of Western culture for centuries. In part this was due to the devastation of World War I. Many believed that Western civilization had failed, and there was a loss of belief in established systems of thought. Previous notions of stability and order no longer provided meaning in life or appeared to reflect an objective truth. As Mansfield wrote in a letter dated November 1919 (as quoted by Antony Alpers in *The Life of Katherine Mansfield*), "I feel in the *profoundest* sense that nothing can ever be the same—that, as artists . . . we have to take it into account and find new expressions, new moulds, for our new thoughts and feelings." Modernism was therefore marked by experimentation. During a time of cultural instability people were searching for fresh approaches to understanding life. Pessimism about the human condition was common, in contrast to the Victorian belief in progress.

James Joyce's novel *Ulysses* (1922) is a famous modernist work, as is Marcel Proust's novel sequence *Remembrance of Things Past* (1913–1927) and Virginia Woolf's novels *Mrs. Dalloway* (1925) and *To the Lighthouse* (1927). Joyce and Woolf rejected traditional narrative structure in favor of a stream-of-consciousness technique that presented the unfiltered flow of a character's thoughts. British novelist Dorothy Richardson is also considered a pioneer of the stream-of-consciousness technique, in her thirteen novels collectively known as *Pilgrimage* (1915–1938).

Modernism was central to Mansfield's work. "Through her critical writings as well as her brilliant innovations in fiction, she influenced, reflected, and conveyed modernist aesthetic principles," writes Sydney Janet Kaplan, in *Katherine Mansfield and the Origins of Modernist Fiction*. Mansfield's modernist innovations in the genre included, according to Kaplan, the "'plotless'" story, the incorporation of the 'stream of consciousness' into the content of fiction, and the emphasis on the psychological 'moment.'" Her use of these techniques "preceded Virginia Woolf's use of them, and they have been absorbed and assimilated—often unconsciously—by writers and readers of the short story." Kate Fullbrook, in *Katherine Mansfield*, concurs with the notion that the structure of Mansfield's fiction resembled the direction modernism was taking; Mansfield moved "away

The boss finds a fly in his ink and pulls it out.
(© natu / Shutterstock)

from plot as the organising principle in her writing," and her work reflected the "modernist view of the discovery of meaning and of the self—brief, unpredictable, discontinuous, tied in no orderly way to rational or sequential experience."

CRITICAL OVERVIEW

"The Fly" has been much commented upon, from a variety of perspectives, and it is generally held in high regard by literary critics. As James Gindin explains in his entry on Mansfield in *Dictionary of Literary Biography*,

> The story . . . has been read as a metaphor of the torture of the younger generation by the war, as a figurative tableau of capitalistic exploitation of struggling life, as an emblem of Mansfield's vigorous and successful father who long outlived both his only son and his artist daughter, or as an echo of a Chekhov story in which a poor office clerk tortures a cockroach in futile rebellion against his boss.

Antony Alpers, in *The Life of Katherine Mansfield*, comments that the story is a "little masterpiece of symbolic attention to what the war had meant." Alpers also notes that "the helpless insect . . . had been one of Katherine Mansfield's favorite images for years."

Gillian Boddy, in "From Notebook Draft to Published Story: 'Late Spring' / 'This Flower,'" sees a biographical element in the story:

> Desperately ill, weak, worn out by massive doses of radiation therapy, disillusioned by the war and by her own relationships, Mansfield composed a tale that is surely the final indictment of so much that she despised. Perhaps it is she who is the fly, too exhausted to struggle any longer, finally crushed by an implacable, omnipotent fate.

For Sydney Janet Kaplan, in *Katherine Mansfield and the Origins of Modernist Fiction*, the story is an example of Mansfield's feminism. It "demonstrates how power corrupts, how patriarchal dominance victimizes." The victim "is small and powerless" and dies because of the man's "refusal to relinquish control." Mansfield makes it clear, Kaplan further comments:

> The man is wrong, no matter how much he has suffered. Nothing justifies his mistreatment of the "other" (and certainly, "other" here brings with it a full realization of how the man has projected his own vulnerability into another creature).

Saralyn R. Daly, in *Katherine Mansfield*, offers the view that the boss is a bully, as is seen in his domineering behavior toward Macey and Woodifield. He likely bullied his son as well. He enjoys seeing weakness in others "but fears [it] in himself." In his tormenting of the fly, he is like an immature boy: "In his good health he is no more manly than old Woodifield, but he is far more disturbing."

In *Katherine Mansfield and Her Confessional Stories*, C. A. Hankin argues that the story is "a profound psychological portrait" of the principal character, the boss. The story reveals "the confused emotional state of an aging man who secretly fears death but cannot bring himself to accept, or even admit, that he too must die." He is a "self-deceiver" in that respect. Hankin also regards the boss as being based on Mansfield's father and the boss's dead son as resembling Mansfield's brother, Leslie, who in 1922, when the story was written, had been dead six years, just as the boss's son has been.

CRITICISM

Bryan Aubrey

Aubrey holds a PhD in English. In the following essay, he analyzes "The Fly" in both its realistic and symbolic contexts.

Interpretations of Mansfield's "The Fly" may differ, but there is no doubt that it is a profoundly pessimistic story that ends in an act of wanton cruelty that disturbs even the individual who perpetrates it. The darker turn the story will take is not apparent from the way it begins; it rests on a fissure that suddenly opens up in what has been up to that point the stable, even benevolent psyche of the character known only as the boss.

Almost from the beginning, the boss is contrasted with the other main character, old Woodifield. Woodifield seems by far to be the weaker man in terms of his hold on life. He is old and infirm, likened frequently to a child or baby. The boss, although he is five years older than Woodifield, is the man in charge (as his name implies). Woodifield sits in a large armchair "staring almost greedily at the boss," as if he wants to lap up the life energy that the latter clearly has in abundance as he "rolled in his office chair, stout, rosy . . . and still going strong, still at the helm." It seems to make Woodifield feel better simply to be in the older man's presence. The boss is, it seems, in his element. He loves to be in his newly refurnished office, receiving the admiration of his old friend. It gives him a feeling of "deep, solid satisfaction." Pleased at the fact that old Woodifield is looking up to him and making him feel good, the boss can feel generous, and he offers Woodifield some choice whiskey from a locked cupboard under his desk. But then Woodifield tells the boss of the visit his daughters made to the war graves in Belgium, where they saw not only the grave of their brother but also that of the boss's son. Woodifield, who seems to have long ago accepted the loss of his son, has not the remotest idea that his mention of the boss's dead son has hit a raw nerve in the older man. The boss says almost nothing that would reveal the sudden jolt in his feelings. After Woodifield is gone, however, he is faced with a personal crisis that a few minutes earlier he could not have envisaged happening. It is as if an abyss has opened up in his psyche, paralyzing it, putting him in a kind of limbo, a strangely barren but also confusing psychic space. He is caught between the death of old feelings—complete with the comfortable ritual he

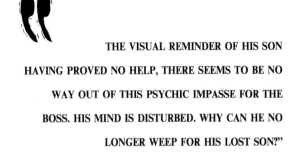

THE VISUAL REMINDER OF HIS SON HAVING PROVED NO HELP, THERE SEEMS TO BE NO WAY OUT OF THIS PSYCHIC IMPASSE FOR THE BOSS. HIS MIND IS DISTURBED. WHY CAN HE NO LONGER WEEP FOR HIS LOST SON?"

developed around them—and the birth of something new, which he has yet to even dimly fathom.

After Woodifield leaves, for a "long moment" the boss stands still, "staring at nothing." It is as if he is in a moment of suspended time. Then he goes back to his desk, ready to weep for the loss of his son. The death happened six years earlier, and weeping is how he has always handled his feelings about it. He has managed to convince himself that this would always be so; even the passage of time would not ease his grief, and he expects to weep again now. After all, the memory of his son is still vivid to him and his death "might have happened yesterday." Then something strange happens that puzzles and disturbs him. He is unable to weep, and he thinks that something must be wrong with him. Why can he not react as he has always done to his loss? All he knows is that "he wasn't feeling as he wanted to feel." It seems as if he does not know what he is feeling or if he is feeling anything at all in this situation. He looks at the photograph of his son that hangs on the wall but acknowledges to himself that he has never liked this photograph much; the young man looks too stern, and that is not how the boss remembers him: "The boy had never looked like that." Critics have speculated about this aspect of the story, suggesting that perhaps the boss has had too rosy a view of the boy. J. F. Kobler, in *Katherine Mansfield: A Study of the Short Fiction*, offers the view that the boss in his "memory of his son may be seriously distorting the way things really were." Indeed, the boss's description of the son does make him seem almost too good to be true: he had taken to the business like a duck to water; everyone at the firm loved him; and he was always "just his bright natural self, with the right word for everybody." This does not match the stern-faced boy in the photograph.

WHAT DO I READ NEXT?

- "An Indiscreet Journey" is the only story by Mansfield set during World War I. It was published in *Something Childish and Other Stories* (1924) and was based on Mansfield's own experience. An Englishwoman takes a risky, illicit train journey in France to meet her lover, who is a corporal in the French army. The train is full of soldiers, and she sees more soldiers as she looks out the window, as well as military cemeteries, but the war seems unreal to her. The corporal must evade the police in order to meet her, and the final scene shows them in a café, the war still in the background.

- There is nothing quite like a collection of letters to reveal the life and personality of a historical figure, and *Katherine Mansfield: Selected Letters* (1989), edited by Vincent O'Sullivan, is no exception. It contains letters over a period of more than twenty years, from Mansfield's adolescence to shortly before her death. Recipients include family, friends, and acquaintances.

- *The War to End All Wars: World War I* (2013), by Russell Freedman, is an account of World War I for young readers. Freedman clearly explains the complex causes of the war. He describes the battles, with their huge casualties, as well as the military leaders and military technology employed. He also shows the legacy of the war, how it ended American isolationism and indirectly led to the rise of Nazi Germany in the 1930s and World War II. The book includes many archival photographs.

- "The Fly" is a poem by English romantic poet William Blake, from his *Songs of Innocence and of Experience* (1794). The speaker says he has just killed a fly and then seems to regret his actions, likening himself to the fly,

since each is subject to the fickle hand of fate that can end life in an instant. The poem is available in any edition of Blake's work, including the 1992 Dover Thrift edition of *Songs of Innocence and of Experience*.

- Alice Hoffman's young-adult novel *Green Angel* (2003), like "The Fly," is about how a character copes with loss. Fifteen-year-old Green loses her entire family in a disaster and must work out a way to survive and deal with the devastating blow. It is not an easy path for her, but eventually she finds her way.

- *The Penguin Book of First World War Stories* (2007), edited by Barbara Korte and Ann-Marie Einhaus, includes stories by British writers, written at the time of the war and in the 1920s, as well as stories from a more modern perspective. Authors include Richard Aldington, W. Somerset Maugham, Joseph Conrad, John Galsworthy, D. H. Lawrence, Robert Graves, Muriel Spark, and Julian Barnes, in addition to Mansfield. The book includes maps, a guide to places on the western front, a glossary, a list of military abbreviations, and suggestions for further reading.

- *The Letters* (2002), is a young-adult novel by Kazumi Yumoto, set in Japan. Chiaki Hoshino, a twenty-five-year-old young woman, looks back on her life in flashbacks, including the time her father died. An older woman named Mrs. Yanagi befriends her and helps her cope, suggesting that she write letters to her dead father and that she, Mrs. Yanagi, would take the letters to the girl's father when she died. The cultural background is Japanese, but the theme of how to grieve and how to go on living transcends any particular culture.

Be that as it may, the point here is that the boss is no longer in control of the situation, in terms of knowing and getting what he wants and

needs. This is a serious issue for a man who seems to have based much of his life, as a successful businessman, on his ability to be in control and get people to do what he wants them to do. The visual reminder of his son having proved no help, there seems to be no way out of this psychic impasse for the boss. His mind is disturbed. Why can he no longer weep for his lost son? In *Katherine Mansfield*, Rhoda B. Nathan suggests that the boss "is incapable of weeping for his dead son because the boy had disobeyed him and joined the army." What follows, as the boss torments and kills the fly, is a "a realistic portrait of a man whose rage must be relieved because his sorrow goes unpurged." Such a view must be approached with caution. Nothing in the story suggests that the boy had disobeyed his father in this way, and it seems likely that what the boss feels at this moment is not rage but frustration and confusion. The sight of the struggling fly is just a convenient distraction for him. He behaves cruelly toward it because of his own disturbed state of mind at this point. It momentarily takes his mind off his present predicament.

It is hard to give a satisfactory explanation at the realistic level for how the boss's frustration at his inability to weep for his son leads to his behavior toward the fly. It seems that at this point the significance of the story moves firmly from the literal to the metaphoric level. The fly, it seems, is not just a fly, and the boss is something more than an unhappy man who is taking out his frustrations on a helpless insect.

A number of critics have pointed out that imagery of insects, birds, and animals occurs frequently in Mansfield's work. She uses comparisons between people and insects to reveal "disagreeable emotions," according to Julia van Gunsteren in *Katherine Mansfield and Literary Impressionism*. Gunsteren continues,

> The animal images . . . encompass the whole range of human emotions and feelings. Disappointment and pessimism are revealed: the helpless insect, the preying spider, the cunning snake, the escaping rabbit, they all represent a cruel or suffering aspect of mankind.

An example of this can be found in Mansfield's story "At the Bay," which she completed in September 1921. Jonathan Trout, an office clerk who is dissatisfied with the drab monotony of his life, says,

> I'm like an insect that's flown into a room of its own accord. I dash against the walls, dash against the windows, flop against the ceiling, do everything on God's earth, in fact, except fly out again.

Five months later, in February 1922, just a few days before she began writing "The Fly," Mansfield was in very poor health and wrote in her journal that her life was "rather like being a beetle shut in a book, so shackled that one can do nothing but lie down." During those few days, she wrote comments such as "Felt ill all day. . . . I feel more ill now than ever, so it seems" and "Another hellish day." It was in this depleted, pessimistic, and rather helpless frame of mind that she wrote "The Fly," and she confessed in a letter to William Gerhardi in June that she had "*hated* writing it." It does not seem unreasonable to suppose that the fly in the story, in its struggle against hopeless odds and the cruel fate it meets, is in some sense Mansfield herself. The struggling fly, which fights so hard against its unseen tormentor, also likely has a symbolic reach beyond just one individual. Given Mansfield's feminism, the fly may well be seen as representing how women are kept down and crushed by men in the patriarchal society in which she lived. In such a reading, the boss would be much more than just one man; he would symbolize an entire social, political, and economic system that oppresses women. Even more than that, the fly may embody the fate of all human beings, men and women alike. Kate Fullbrook, in *Katherine Mansfield*, writes that in Mansfield's late fiction, the "dominant impression" is the "'sunlessness' of women's lives, and perhaps all lives." This fiction is, Fullbrook continues,

> the fiction of catastrophe, with varieties of deprivation, unhappiness and despair in control of human consciousness which Katherine Mansfield is constantly pushing to the breaking-point. The most important impulses behind the writing are emotions of anger and pity, and in her late work Katherine Mansfield at times abandoned the emotional cynicism of modernism to compose stories which are pure outcry.

"The Fly," with its cruel and pointless outcome, would certainly qualify as an example of that "pure outcry." It is a savage verdict on the human predicament that puts in mind the despairing words of Gloucester in Shakespeare's tragedy, *King Lear*: "As flies to wanton boys are we to th' Gods; / They kill us for their sport" (act 4, scene 1, lines 36–37). Although there are no gods, either benign or malevolent, in Mansfield's fictional world, "The Fly" demonstrates nonetheless that that world is as little designed to promote human happiness as the chaotic world Shakespeare depicts in *King Lear*.

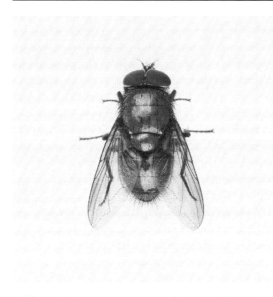

Although the man seems to cheer the fly on, he drips ink onto it until it dies. (© *irin-k | Shutterstock*)

Source: Bryan Aubrey, Critical Essay on "The Fly," in *Short Stories for Students*, Gale, Cengage Learning, 2016.

Aimee Gasston

In the following excerpt, Gasston compares Mansfield's short stories with those of Virginia Woolf.

. . . The short fiction of both Woolf and Katherine Mansfield ran in vigorous opposition to such a record of discontent, although the subject-object relation they depicted was often complicated. The hand as described by the partygoer is a convincing model for the material focus of much of their experimental short fiction; sitting at the border between subject and object, the hand undergoes sensory experience before transcribing that experience from a liminal hinterland. Jean-Paul Sartre's *Nausea* (1938), a work perceptibly influenced by modernist literature as well as contemporaneous thinkers such as Heidegger, the protagonist Roquentin's first experience of nascent existential nausea or angst occurs in his hand: "I felt in my hand a cold object which attracted my attention by means of a sort of personality. I opened my hand and looked: I was simply holding the doorknob." Shortly after this scene, a pebble asserts itself against Roquentin's hand (despite his outrage that "objects ought not to touch since they are not alive"), which he describes as a "sweet disgust" passing from the pebble to his hands; "a sort of nausea of

the hands." The short fictions of Mansfield and Woolf prefigure these moments of crisis and are similarly concerned with relaying those encounters brought about by the experience of an "everyday existence haunted by matter." By revising and unsettling categories of subject and object, their short fiction suggests a democratised worldview and works to undo the unchallenged hegemony of the subject.

As innovators of stream-of-consciousness narration, Mansfield and Woolf are still primarily considered articulators of subjective inferiority, but the ways in which this is enabled by an engagement with the external world and ordinary objects is only beginning to be fully recognised. As commentators such as Jessica Feldman have observed, this material fascination was not isolated: "modernist writers brought dead objects back to life: railroad timetables, cracked teacups, golden bowls, heather-mixture stockings, Connemara cloth, vaseline and orangeflowers." Yet the emphasis is far more sharply drawn in the short fiction of Mansfield and Woolf, where objects loom large in the truncated story form and "material objects seem a condition of narratability," often projecting an unsettling presence or agency which articulates the uneasy subject/object relationship. Lorna Sage even went as far as describing Mansfield's stories as "intensely crafted and evocative objects-on-the-page."

Both Mansfield and Woolf displayed a material sensibility that was unusually highly attuned. In her notebooks, Mansfield attempts to explain a sense of epiphany by noting that "this sensitiveness [. . .] has never anything to do with present people but is nearly always connected with 'things'." Elsewhere, she writes that she would "be quite content to live here, in a furnished room, and watch," implying a preference for the object world over that of the subject. In a letter of October 1918 to Roger Fry in response to praise of her story "The Mark on the Wall," Woolf would comment: "I'm not sure that a perverted plastic sense doesn't somehow work itself out in words for me," highlighting the reiterative material bent of her literary output. In their short fiction, objects refuse to stay still and be quiet. In Mansfield's "Prelude," Linda Burnell's wallpaper famously "come[s] alive" beneath her fingertips; "[t]hings had a habit of coming alive like that," it is explained, "[n]ot only large substantial things like furniture but curtains and the patterns of stuff and the

> A LONG WAY FROM THE HEMISPHERE OF HER BIRTH, FROM HER HUSBAND AND FROM HER FRIENDS (BAR HER DEDICATED YET UNFATHOMABLY INFURIATING COMPANION, IDA BAKER), MANSFIELD CLEARLY FELT DISPLACEMENT KEENLY, YET SHE APPEARS TO HAVE COUNTERBALANCED THIS TO SOME EXTENT THROUGH A RICH AND CONCENTRATED MATERIAL ENGAGEMENT."

fringes of quilts and cushions." In Woolf's unpublished piece "Nurse Lugton's Curtain," the pattern being stitched on the curtain stirs; as the nurse begins to snore, "all the animals began to prance" and "the blue stuff turned to blue air; the trees waved; you could hear the water of the lake breaking; and see the people moving over the bridge and waving their hands out of the window" (*HH*). And of course Miss Brill's fur necklet cries when put away in its box.

In the concluding part of his book *The Bases of Modern Science* (1928), Mansfield's sometime friend W. N. Sullivan asserts that "science, by its very nature, can tell us nothing about phenomena but their structure"; it is this gap left by science which Mansfield's and Woolfs short fiction fills. As Woolf put it in her 1927 review of Mansfield's journal: "writing, the mere expression of things adequately and sensitively, is not enough"—it must also be "founded upon something unexpressed; and this something must be solid and entire" (*Journal* 257). Capturing the ineffable quality of the ineluctably material was something that could only be achieved by literary, not scientific, experiment.

If "in the end, at its moment of ending, every narrative is stilled in a kind of objecthood," then perhaps the plastic proclivity of these authors' short fiction can be partially explained by the frequency of endings which somehow crystallise these fictions into decidedly phenomenal entities. They are also objects which ought not to touch since they are not alive, but do—again and again. This essay aims to explore these authors' depictions of an everyday (subjective) existence haunted by (object) matter—their exploration

and narration of what Bill Brown calls "an interaction at once physical and psychological, at once intimate and alienating"—and to probe their captivating and disturbing texts with cautious but grateful fingers.

A TOUCH OF FAIRY?

In November 1919, in a characteristically graceful yet pointed letter to her husband John Middleton Murry, Mansfield wrote:

> How I envy Virginia; no wonder she can write. There is always in her writing a calm freedom of expression as though she were at peace— her roof over her—her own possessions round her—and her man somewhere within call.

Here, Mansfield equates the security afforded by personal possessions with that provided by shelter or a lover. Her jealousy appears to have sprung directly from perceived lack, with the statement following rich and lively description of all the "lovely [yet unaffordable] things" for sale in the San Remo antique shops, as well as Mansfield's reflection on her marriage, which straddled international borders and failed to offer her all she had anticipated.

A long way from the hemisphere of her birth, from her husband and from her friends (bar her dedicated yet unfathomably infuriating companion, Ida Baker), Mansfield clearly felt displacement keenly, yet she appears to have counterbalanced this to some extent through a rich and concentrated material engagement. The Katherine Mansfield Birthplace Society's diverse collection of personal ephemera attests to their significance to the author, as do her letters, in which these objects play cameo parts with frequency. These possessions were often sentimentalised, becoming like "old and trusted friends in a nomadic existence," sometimes also signifying distant or departed loved ones. In her memoirs, Ida Baker recalls how "wherever she was, Katherine made and kept her 'home' as beautiful and as expressive as possible," explaining that "however poor and sparse her possessions," Katherine's sense of "order and form always imparted a feeling of space and beauty." Elsewhere in the memoirs, Baker describes Mansfield's talent for making a "room come alive" by rearranging its components, stating how "things needed her presence," thus highlighting the interdependency between subject and object which would also permeate her fiction. Objects become animated in Mansfield's presence with a startling frequency; in her journal she ponders whether chinaware sat upon a writing table "may or may not have shaken itself awake for just one hundredth of a second out of hundreds of years of sleep" (*Journal*). Elsewhere, she records at Pordand Villas, Hampstead: "My room really has for me a touch of fairy. Is there anything better than my room? Anything outside?" (*Journal*). Kitty, protagonist of the unfinished piece "Confidences," similarly exclaims with delight at her friend's home which always gives one "the feeling it's so alive" (*Fiction 2*), as if the domestic arena itself were imbued with transformative powers.

Woolf also displayed a keen sensitivity to domestic objects and their harmony of arrangement; on viewing a Bloomsbury flat she expresses her distaste on being "shown into a beautiful room" which was "disfigured horribly with velvet curtains, gigantic purple cushions, & the usual swarm of gilt & lemon coloured objects" (*Diary 1*) and finds Ottoline Morrell's Garsington Manor claustrophobic with "too many nick nacks for real beauty, too many scents, & silks" (*Diary 1*). When Woolf and her sister, Vanessa Bell, move from their parental home at Hyde Park Gate, she wrote of the way in which familial artefacts were rejuvenated by the bright spaces of Gordon Square: "Things one had never seen in the darkness there [at Hyde Park Gate]—Watts pictures, Dutch cabinets, blue china—shone for the first time in the drawing room at Gordon Square." In 1918, she writes to Vanessa of the "exquisite pleasure" her painting has given her on hanging it at home ("so cool, so harmonious, so exquisitely tinted") which leads her "to conceive the room as a whole, in relation to [Bell's] picture" and commence a frantic hunt for a suitable covering for the yellow chair which disrupts the concord of the scene (*Letters VW 2*). And, in 1919, Woolf records her delight at being given a green glass jar by the chemist, long coveted because "glass is the best of all decorations, holding the light and changing it" (*Diary 1*). Although in Woolfs autobiographical writings the animism of objects is arguably less pronounced than in Mansfield's (or the short fiction of either), there is the similar sense of the importance of the non-subject world, of its capacity to resonate and reverberate, to influence the subject rather than be dominated by it.

As Jean Baudrillard has observed, "human beings and objects are indeed bound together in a collusion in which the objects take on a certain density, an emotional value—what might

be a presence." He locates this density in the "complex structure of interiority" brought about by the domestic, where objects serve as "boundary" markers of the symbolic configuration known as home "with anthropomorphism" curiously rendering them "household gods." If these objects signify the boundary of the confluence between the subject and object worlds, they do not do so with a sense of authoritative distinction. Instead, they function as markers of liminality, rather like the short fictions of Mansfield and Woolf which ruminate on the stilling of the subject by death, and the vivification of the insensate. The domestic environment then not only bestows objects with an unusually affective potency; it also enables and lubricates the slippage between the realms of human and material that these stories exploit. . . .

Source: Aimee Gasston, "Phenomenology Begins at Home: The Presence of Things in the Short Fiction of Katherine Mansfield and Virginia Woolf," in *Journal of New Zealand Literature*, Vol. 32, No. 2, November 2014, p. 31.

F. W. Bateson and B. Shahevitch

In the following excerpt, Bateson and Shahevitch provide an in-depth analysis of "The Fly," including Mansfield's careful use of language.

"The Fly" is probably the shortest *good* short story in modern English. Its two thousand words therefore permit, indeed encourage, the kind of close analysis that has been so successful in our time with lyric poetry but that is impossibly cumbrous or misleadingly incomplete when applied to the novel or the *conte*. The object of this exercise is to demonstrate that, granted the difference of *genres*, exactly the same critical procedure is in order for realistic fiction as for a poem. "The Fly" was written in February 1922 and was included later that year in *The Garden Party and Other Stories*.

"The Fly" assumes in its readers a readiness to accept and respond to two parallel series of symbolic conventions: (i) those constituting the English language as it was spoken and written in the first quarter of the twentieth century, (ii) those constituting the realistic narrative in prose of the same period. That this story is written in modern English is immediately apparent, and the initial display of irrelevant descriptive detail is an equally clear signal to the critical reader that the narrative *genre* to be employed here is realism. Why *Woodifield*

> THE TEST OF THE GOOD SHORT STORY IS THEREFORE THE DEGREE OF THE READER'S SURPRISE WHEN HE DISCOVERS IN HIMSELF THE JUDGEMENTS THAT HAVE BEEN FORCED UPON HIM. BUT THE SURPRISE HAS ALSO TO BE FOLLOWED BY CONVICTION."

(dozens of other surnames would have done just as well)? Why a *green* armchair (rather than light brown, purple, dark brown, etc.)? Why the cut back to the City on *Tuesdays* (rather than Mondays, Wednesdays, Thursdays or Fridays)?

That the critical reader does not in fact ask such questions is because of his familiarity already with the realistic formula. The particular suspension of disbelief that realism demands is an acquiescence in the author's limited omniscience provided his external setting "looks" historically authentic. The reader must be able to say, "On the evidence provided, which seems adequate, this series of events could have taken place in real life as I know it."

It follows that to look for allegorical symbols in "The Fly" is to accuse Katherine Mansfield of a breach of her chosen convention. Specifically "The Fly" is not a beast-fable, like Blake's poem with the same title in "Songs of Experience." In this story the confrontation of the boss with the fly is only subjectively anthropomorphic. It is the boss who attributes human courage—and the human necessity to suffer pain under torture—to the fly. The boss's corrupt imagination has blown this up into the semblance of a human being, but objectively, as the reader knows, the fly is just an ordinary house-fly. Some earlier critics of "The Fly" have gone astray by ignoring the story's technical limitations, and various abstract 'themes' have been read into it, like "time," "cruelty" and "life." Middleton Murry's own comment— "the profound and ineradicable impression made upon her by the War . . . found perfect utterance in the last year of her life in the story 'The Fly'"—may have encouraged such misinterpretations. It is certainly tempting to relate the story to Katherine Mansfield's tuberculosis and to her dislike of her father, who was a New Zealand banker. But such elements are of the nature of "sources." No doubt without them the story could not have been begun, but they are not *inside* the story. The realistic convention is resistant both to abstractions and to strict autobiography. The story must appear to tell itself; it must be the sort of concrete human situation that might have happened just so. And once the reader begins to detect the intrusion of abstract concepts or moral attitudes, such as the hatred of war, or alternatively of obviously autobiographical episodes, his confidence in the writer's omniscience will be weakened. An unnecessary strain is being put on the realistic suspension of disbelief.

The irrelevance of allegorical interpretations in this case can be clarified by contrasting the proverb, an even shorter narrative *genre*, with the realistic short story. The concrete details in a proverb are all functional. Nobody wants to know what kind of stone it is that gathers no moss, or that is thrown by the inhabitants of glasshouses. The exact size, colour, weight and shape of the respective stones are irrelevant, because a proverb demands immediate implicit conceptualisation ("Restlessness is unprofitable," "Guilty parties should not accuse others of guilt"); it is in fact allegory in capsule form. But in a realistic short story the particularity is a large part of the meaning. Suppress Mr. Woodifield's name, the colour of the armchair, the day of the week allotted to his City visits, and the convention collapses. They are indispensable signals from author to reader; they also assume a common interest and confidence in the concrete detail of the phenomenal world. (We are on Dr. Johnson's side against Berkeley in the matter of the stone.)

But "The Fly" is something more than narrative imbedded in slice-of-life realism. Some sort of general statement about modern life is implicit in it. How has Katherine Mansfield managed to evade the limitations of the realistic convention? How can a value-judgement emerge at all from what appears to be a temporal sequence of particularities? These are the essential questions the critic must ask.

One answer, an important critical one, is that the medium of a narrative sequence is language, and that it is always possible to exploit the generality inherent in both vocabulary and grammar so that a value-judgement emerges. This is just what Katherine Mansfield does, but discreetly, tactfully. A simple linguistic device is to use descriptive epithets to hint at a generalisation. Thus at the beginning of "The Fly" the boss is "stout" and "rosy." In combination with the "snug" office to which Woodifield pays a tribute twice in the first two paragraphs, the epithets produce an impression of luxuriant good health, of self-indulgence perhaps, though at this stage in the story the indulgence is not apparently censured in any overt way. Later, in the mounting tension of the passage when the boss, having sent Woodifield on his way, returns to the office, he treads with "firm heavy steps." These, especially in contrast to Woodifield's "shuffling footsteps," loom rather ominously. The boss who "plumps" down in the spring-chair is no longer merely stout, he has become "fat." Still later, when he suddenly "has an idea" and plunges his pen into the ink, before we quite know what he is up to we get a premonition of it as he leans his "thick" wrist on the blotting paper. The harmless stout and rosy figure has turned out to be physically coarse, even brutal.

Similarly we get an inkling of the boss's character from the colouring of the verbs long before we are introduced to the decisive situation. When he is still "stout and rosy," he "rolls" in his chair. Soon he "flips" his *Financial Times*—a slightly arrogant gesture. By this time he is "planted" there, "in full view of that frail old figure," and the adjective qualifying his satisfaction is "solid." Later on we suddenly see him "swooping" across for two tumblers ("Coming down with the rush of a bird of prey . . . making a sudden attack," *Oxford Dictionary*).

The adjectives and verbs serve to "place" Woodifield too, who never speaks but "pipes" (three times) or "quavers." He does not look, he "peers." The wife and girls keep him "boxed up" in his home. On Tuesdays, he did not dress but *was* "dressed and brushed" and then "allowed" to go to town—all images reinforcing the simile in which he is originally introduced, that of a baby in a pram.

But the crucial linguistic device in "The Fly" is the protagonist's anonymity. He is always referred to as "the boss," twenty-five times to be precise, or approximately once every eighty words. The word is etymologically an Americanism (adopted from the Dutch *baas*-master in the beginning of the nineteenth century), which passed into British English about the middle of

that century and had certainly lost all its foreignness by 1922. The dictionary meaning then as now is "a master, a business manager, anyone who has a right to give orders." The word has still an unpleasantly vulgar connotation, which is perhaps heightened by its use in U.S. political jargon, where "boss" means the "dictator of a party organisation." Used with a capital it turns into a particular, not a general, word, in fact, from a common noun into a proper noun, thus making the connotation depend on what we know of the person so named. Thus "Boss" may often have a kindly ring. But in "The Fly" Katherine Mansfield persists in spelling the word with a minuscule, that is, as a common noun, at the same time refusing to alternate it with any synonym or other appellation. She even refuses to let us know what the boss's actual name is. "Mr. Woodifield," "Gertrude," "Woodifield," "Macey," but the hero's names (and his son's) are resolutely excluded. Katherine Mansfield cannot, of course, altogether prevent the process by which a common noun becomes a proper noun, but she does her best to keep in the reader's mind the more general significance of the word. Each time we read it, the general somewhat repugnant idea of the term is again imprinted in our consciousness, even after it has almost become a proper name. The boss, clear-cut individual as he is in the realistic narrative, is *nominally* an allegorical figure simply by virtue of the word's insistent repetition.

The other linguistic device deserves notice. This is Katherine Mansfield's habit here of allowing direct description to merge into reported speech. Here are a few examples: "His talk was over; it was time for him to be off. But he did not want to go. Since he had retired. . . ." Up to this point the description is in straightforward narrative prose, but in "since his . . . stroke" the short break which the three dots denote—so expressive of the reluctance of a sick man to call his complaint by its frightening real name—turns author's statement into semi-direct speech. The reluctance is now Woodifield's, not the narrator's.

A few lines later an inversion occurs. "Though what he did there, the wife and girls couldn't imagine" may still be taken as objective statement with emphasis causing the object-clause to be put first. But the following clause, "Make a nuisance of himself they supposed" has the full effect of direct speech. Again the object-clause is given first, but the main clause does not seem to be the author speaking; it is as if between concealed quotation marks, a comment really spoken in the first person instead of the apparent third person.

A little later the boss's "he explained, as he had explained for the past—how many?—weeks" seems to be another bit of direct speech that is masquerading as narrative statement. In a story within the realistic convention the author is supposed to know all about how often one of the characters did this or that. The slight uncertainty here, the momentary ignorance—perhaps only half genuine—belongs to everyday speech. The boss, not the author, is speaking.

Again in "How on earth could he have slaved, denied himself, kept going all those years without the promise, for ever before him, of the boy's stepping into his shoes and carrying on where he left off?" the complete sentence in the form of a question is not introduced by any main clause, nor is it in quotation marks. But can it in fact be anything but a question asked by the boss himself?

This mixing of direct statement with indirect or concealed dialogue is used all through the story—by interpolating exclamation in otherwise regular narrative, by putting complete sentences in the form of questions not introduced by main clauses yet impossible to be taken otherwise than as questions asked by the characters, by breaks in the line, and by inversions of a colloquial nature. The result is that we have very little regular narrative. Instead, in a frame of thin lines of this quasi-narrative, which could almost be spoken by a chorus, we have the effect of drama. In this setting the repeated recurrence of the two words "the boss" has the impersonality of a stage-direction, a datum, as it were, outside the narrative. It reiterates so as to become an alternative title to the story: "The Fly [Boss]: a Short Story."

The point at which a linguistic device, either of vocabulary ("the boss") or syntax (the indirect speech), becomes a rhetorical figure should not be detectable in realistic fiction. The reader has suspended his disbelief on condition that the naturalistic particularities are maintained, as they certainly are in "The Fly." What could be more reassuringly particular than the story's penultimate sentence? "He took out his handkerchief and passed it inside his collar." But in some of the devices here analysed language has unquestionably become rhetoric. The repetition of *any* phrase or construction will give it, if repeated often enough, a new semantic dimension. A similar process occurs if some parallelism establishes itself between the separate episodes in a narrative or drama. Gradually an unstated generality superimposes itself on the sequence of particulars. A narrative pattern emerges.

The most memorable episode in "The Fly" begins when the boss, having completed the rescue operations from the inkpot, conceives his "idea." This is the story's *peripeteia*, the point of dramatic reversal in the reader's attitude to the protagonist. We began with a distinct liking for him. Woodifield was expected by his family to make a nuisance of himself to his old friends on the Tuesday excursions into the City; and in general, from the specimen provided us of his conversational powers, their gloomy anticipations seem likely to be fulfilled. But the boss's reaction is different. The boss is genuinely delighted to see Woodifield, and he produces his best whisky to entertain him, "feeling kindly," as the narrator (apparently it *is* the narrator) informs us. At this early point in "The Fly" the tone is light and almost comic: the bars in the electric heater are compared to sausages, and Woodifield couldn't have been more surprised, when the whisky bottle appears, "if the boss had produced a rabbit." This boss—in spite of his descriptive label—cannot be taken very tragically because of the disarming atmosphere of cordiality in which we make his acquaintance. Moreover his son has been killed in the war (of 1914–18), and we are naturally sorry for him. It is true some disturbing elements in the boss's character already contradict the generally good impression he creates. Some of the pleasure he takes in Woodifield's company seems to derive from the contrast he cannot help drawing between his own excellent health and the younger man's frail condition. And the ritual of immediately available tears in his son's memory, if pathetic, is also distasteful. But these reservations—the list could be extended—do not affect our general liking for him and sympathy with him until he turns his experimental attention on to the fly.

As the three blobs of ink fall the reader's attitude changes from considerable sympathy to total antipathy. The admiration the boss professes to feel for the fly's determination is no doubt real, but it does not prevent him from proceeding with his appalling "idea." The horrifying thing is that this admiration makes the experiment all the more entrancing for him. As flies to wanton boys are we to the gods, they kill us for their sport. If the victim did not show some spirit, the gods would lose half their sport. (A half-consciousness of Gloucester's dictum is no doubt expected in the reader.)

In the light we now possess of the boss's other nature we can see how ambiguous the boss's earlier words and actions were. From this moment therefore the story takes on a two-way pattern. It is read as mere "story," so that we can discover what comes next, but with each step forward a mental step is also taken back into earlier more or less parallel episodes, and so we correct our first impressions in the light of the new information. A dual element reveals itself at this point in the boss's relations with both Woodifield and his son. The tenderness with the one or admiration for the other is not to be denied, but it is a sadistic tenderness, unconscious of course, but almost that of an executioner for his victim. Woodifield was not allowed whisky at home, and the boss must have known that drinking it might precipitate a second stroke. But the "generous finger" is enthusiastically provided. The son was no doubt genuinely loved and mourned, but the son's death provided the boss with a splendid opportunity to demonstrate his superiority to other bereaved parents, like the Woodifields. *His* tears were Niobean; hence the shock of aggrieved disappointment when they finally dry up.

A second *peripeteia* presents itself, there, at the fly's death. The grinding and frightening feeling of wretchedness is not what either the boss or the reader had expected. This emotional reversal in the boss creates a new reversal in the reader's attitude to him. Had the boss perhaps glimpsed, briefly and startlingly, the abyss of moral nihilism into which he had unconsciously descended? Katherine Mansfield leaves the question unanswered, almost unasked, and the answer proposed by a recent American critic does not convince ("he thought his grasp on his last pleasure was gone"—the pleasure of his office routine). But the framework of parallel episodes that has built itself up in the reader's mind forces us to half-formulate some ghost of a conceptual conclusion. What *had* the boss been thinking about before the fly entered his life? "For the life of him he could not remember." And so the reader dismisses him, finally, with some contempt. Early in the story we had quite liked the

boss, then we had discovered that we detested him, and now we can merely despise him. The boss's final gesture with the handkerchief, which he passes inside his stiff collar to cool and dry the hot sticky skin, "places" him with superb economy and precision. The intensity of the battle the mighty boss has waged with the minute fly has left him physically exhausted, mere weak brutal oblivious flesh.

In terms of plot, then, though there is dramatic progress (shifts in the reader's sympathies, a mounting intensity, a transition from the near-comic to the near-tragic), there is also dramatic repetition. The episodes combine similitude with dissimilitude in a kind of extended metaphor. If the Woodifield episode is called Act I, the re-enactment of the son's death Act II, and the murder of the fly Act III, then the parallelism works out as follows:

(i) in each of the three acts the boss holds the centre of the stage, and the three subsidiary characters' dramatic function is to throw light on him as the protagonist;

(ii) in Act I Woodifield's feebleness illumines the boss's image of himself as a man of affairs, in Act II it is the boss's image of himself as father that is illumined, in Act III the image is of the boss as animal-lover;

(iii) in each act the boss's image of his own altruism is found to be contradicted by his actions;

(iv) the cumulative effect of the parallelisms is to superimpose on the boss's image of himself in Act I the self-images of Acts II and III, but the image of the hospitable man of the world is blurred by that of the proud heart-broken father and the cheerer-on of flies in difficulties (the images do not cohere);

(v) contrasting with this blur is the clear-cut outline that emerges from the superimpositions of the essential boss as he really is all the time—an ordinary decent human being irretrievably demoralised by the power that corrupts.

A final critical corollary remains to be drawn. Katherine Mansfield's realism has begun with a tactful introduction of the story's setting. The reader, encouraged by the apparent authenticity of the details, tends unconsciously to identify himself with the *dramatis personae*, as though they were being presented by living actors in a West End theatre. They—that is, Katherine Mansfield's accounts of her characters—accept identification. Under the make-up and the costume a living heart is beating, but it is the actor's heart—in the case of a realistic short story, the reader's heart—not the *persona*'s. The authenticity is confirmed, re-created, guaranteed, by the reader. But the judgement that he passes on these impersonations of his, who are technically the characters of the story, is the author's contribution, not the reader's, because the reader is not aware that a moral attitude is gradually forming itself within his consciousness. The test of the good short story is therefore the degree of the reader's surprise when he discovers in himself the judgements that have been forced upon him. But the surprise has also to be followed by conviction. This is what the particular words and the particular word-orders *must* mean; this is what the significance of the dramatic episodes in their sequence of parallelisms *must* add up to.

It will be remembered that Dr. Johnson's discussion of poetic wit proposed a similar criterion: a good poem is "at once natural and new," because what it is saying, "though not obvious, . . . is acknowledged to be just."

Source: F. W. Bateson and B. Shahevitch, "Katherine Mansfield's 'The Fly': A Critical Exercise," in *The Critical Response to Katherine Mansfield*, edited by Jan Pilditch, Greenwood Press, 1996, pp. 82–88.

Saralyn R. Daly

In the following excerpt, Daly analyzes Mansfield's style in her late short stories.

It remains to describe the final artistry of Katherine Mansfield in terms of three stories which display her technique brought to a fine finish and her attitudes expressed at their greatest depth. In the late months of 1920, while exploring the theme of isolation, she wrote "The Stranger" and "The Daughters of the Late Colonel." "The Fly," her next-to-last completed story, was composed in February 22, while she underwent drastic treatment for tuberculosis.

These three episodes of discovery embody the typical Mansfield work. The subject in each is people who suffer some emotional loss. In each instance the characters are affected by a physical death, but it becomes clear that this death is not central in the author's mind; she delineates, instead, spiritual death in her main characters, death of which none of them is completely aware. All of these stories are, in Mansfield's phrase, "a cry against corruption"—specifically against failure of the spirit.

The action is typically slight: a man visits with a friend, then kills a fly; a man meets his wife's ship, takes her to a hotel, and is disheartened by

> THE BOY, MACEY, WOODIFIELD, THE FLY, AND DEATH ARE STAGES IN A LIFE SEQUENCE IN WHICH THE BOSS HAS TOO MANY POSITIONS. HIS POSITION AS PRIME MOVER HE ENJOYS; HIS IDENTITY WITH ALL OF THOSE WHO MOVE TOWARD DEATH HE PREFERS TO FORGET."

her account of a shipboard experience; two women try vaguely to organize their affairs after the death of their father. The most complicated structure, that of "The Daughters of the Late Colonel," surrounds the least action. The other two are brief incidents, largely chronological in order, though in "The Stranger" Janey tells briefly of the death of the young man and in "The Fly" Woodifield remembers his daughters' trip to Belgium and the boss recalls briefly his son's participation in the business. Both these stories open on highly particularized scenes and are immediately focused in the consciousness of the protagonist, after which the narrator has little access to any other awareness. "The Daughters of the Late Colonel" is a virtuoso piece in the use of multipersonal viewpoint.

Since the tone of the narrator is that of the interior monologues, it is difficult to locate a purely narrative segment in any of the stories. The treatment is dramatic, with summary and generalization avoided by the author. The reader must infer from the gestures and the speech of the characters what their natures are and what Mansfield means to convey. She builds her stories toward such moments of discovery. John Hammond states and the colonel's daughters intimate what they have realized, but the boss can reach no conclusion. In each case, the implicit revelation is greater for the reader than for the characters. The dramatic effect is increased by this irony of a more accurate knowledge in the audience, a knowledge, however, which the author does not define. This approach represents the mature Mansfield, practicing her ideal of objective narrative, devoid of the author's intrusive voice.

. . . With neither compassion nor humor, "The Fly" emerges as Mansfield's starkest view, her bitterest and almost her final cry against corruption. At its most obvious level, the events of the story are slight. The boss enjoys the admiring visit of an enfeebled old friend until the deaths of their sons are recalled. Alone, unable to summon the self-pity he has mistaken for grief, he diverts himself by tormenting to death a fly, but he is further depressed by this activity. He is clearly sadomasochist. The satisfactory docility of the remembered son, coupled with his guilt in looking at the boy's picture, leads one to suspect that his treatment of the fly reflects similar though less extreme behavior toward his son. He no doubt bullied the boy as he now bullies Macey and Woodifield. But the feeling persists that there must be more than the immediately perceived meaning in this much-explicated story.

Mansfield's notebooks, letters, and short stories are sprinkled, from 1918 on, with images of flies. It might be merely a visual description of a baby, as in "The Voyage"; of little boys dressed in black; or an account of her own illness, as in the letters of 1918 and 1919. She had felt herself to be like a fly "dropped into the milk-jug & fished out again . . . still too milky and drowned to start cleaning up yet" (*Letters*), and she had imaged Jonathan Trout, who felt himself a victim of unknown forces, as an insect that could have been a fly (Berkman, 194). It is not unlikely, then, that her own position in a losing conflict with ill health, destiny, an insensitive father, and even, since the fly struggles in the ink, the battle to meet short story deadlines are reflected at the biographical level in the story.

But if biographical readings are often dubious, how much more so for a writer who avowedly projects her being, for the literary moment, into every person or beast she describes. The meaning of the story may be more deeply plumbed within the fictional frame.

The likeness between old Mr. Woodifield and the boss goes beyond their mutual loss of sons in the war. Neither has been to Belgium to visit the graves; both have apparently suffered deeply from grief; but most significantly, both, when the thought of these deaths crosses their minds, quickly forget. It is not just doddering old Woodifield who cannot remember that he intended to mention his daughters' visit to their sons' graves, but the final sentence of the story emphasizes a similar lapse on the part of the robustly healthy boss: "*For the life of him* he could not remember" (my italics). There is multiple meaning here: not remembering seems to the boss to support his own vitality, but to restore the life of his son, he would not be able to remember, because he does not really wish to have that "stern-looking" young soldier take over the business and mastery that he himself possesses with such pleasure. He also does not wish to come, as has his near-double Woodifield, under the tutelage of his junior.

The condition of Woodifield, which the boss enjoys in others but fears in himself, is clearly defined from the beginning, when he is compared to a baby in a pram. His voice is a weak piping. Others govern his behavior and even dress him. But if he is a baby, the boss is little more: in the imagery of Mansfield, he "rolled in his office chair, stout, rosy, five years older." He is a boy, a greedy boy, whose new office furniture suggests treacle and sausages. And like a boy, he torments the fly. In his good health he is no more manly than old Woodifield, but he is far more disturbing.

Through such a portrait of what Mansfield had called in 1919 "the Boss Omnipotent" she flung her final defiance in his teeth. From the beginning her stories had asked, "What is it all for?" and the answer had only been "how *stupid*." She was without belief in any superior force governing the affairs of men, but her protest here is made clear in anthropomorphic terms. The force, she would say, that creates and then destroys is materialistic, gross, motiveless. There is no transcendence, no glimmer of the ideal in the process of bloom and decay. But worse, there is immaturity, lack of depth, in the cruel, destructive pattern.

The hope implicit in flowering intensifies the desolation of destruction. All the relationships of the story demonstrate this point. The boss has treated his son as he treated the fly, alternately assisting and encouraging, then crushing. In the rearing of boys such behavior is typically called "making a man of him," but the portrait of the man challenges the boss, so his grief at the loss is false. His treatment of Woodifield and Macey splits the two aspects of the bully's behavior or the pattern of life. To Woodifield the boss is benevolent, giving him a taste of whiskey. Macey he has bullied until the old office worker is reduced to subhuman behavior, a doglike personality. "Look sharp" are the boss's words to both Macey and the fly.

But the feelings of the boss are involved in his behavior. He enjoys the visit of the enfeebled old man and the slavish nervousness of Macey. His empathy with the fly connects him symbolically with these men. The fly "cowed" is Macey; "timid and weak," it is Woodifield. Past grief has carried the boss through these stages, compelling him to stand in relation to the forces of life as the fly stands to himself. The author has placed him in a cyclic progression, the meaning of which he unconsciously senses. The boy, Macey, Woodifield, the fly, and death are stages in a life sequence in which the boss has too many positions. His position as prime mover he enjoys; his identity with all of those who move toward death he prefers to forget. A frightening reminder of his low degree is the "grinding feeling of wretchedness" which occurs when he kills the fly. It is an unwitting enactment of his own position. He destroys, but he is destroyed. On one level it is a statement about the sadomasochist; on another, a last description of the incomprehensible life pattern which feeds on its own destruction. . . .

Source: Saralyn R. Daly, "'Will There Be a Ripple . . . ?'" in *Katherine Mansfield*, Twayne, 1994, pp. 94–95, 101–103.

SOURCES

Alpers, Antony, *The Life of Katherine Mansfield*, Viking Press, 1980, pp. 258, 356–57.

"Battle of the Somme," BBC History website, http://www.bbc.co.uk/history/worldwars/wwone/battle_somme.shtml (accessed August 18, 2015).

Boddy, Gillian, "From Notebook Draft to Published Story: 'Late Spring' / 'This Flower,'" in *Critical Essays on Katherine Mansfield*, edited by Rhoda B. Nathan, G. K. Hall, 1993, pp. 101–112.

Daly, Saralyn R., *Katherine Mansfield*, rev. ed., Twayne, 1994, p. 102.

Fullbrook, Kate, *Katherine Mansfield*, Indiana University Press, 1986, pp. 33, 126.

Gindin, James, "Katherine Mansfield," in *Dictionary of Literary Biography*, Vol. 162, *British Short-Fiction Writers, 1915–1945*, edited by John Headley Rogers, Gale Research, 1996.

Gunsteren, Julia van, *Katherine Mansfield and Literary Impressionism*, Rodopi, 1990, p. 162.

Hankin, C. A., *Katherine Mansfield and Her Confessional Stories*, St. Martin's Press, 1983, pp. 243–44.

Kaplan, Sydney Janet, *Katherine Mansfield and the Origins of Modernist Fiction*, Cornell University Press, 1991, pp. 1, 3, 189–90.

Kobler, J. F., *Katherine Mansfield: A Study of the Short Fiction*, Twayne, 1990, p. 60.

Mansfield, Katherine, "At the Bay," in *Selected Stories*, Oxford University Press, 1985, p. 229.

———, "The Fly," in *Selected Stories*, Oxford University Press, 1985, pp. 353–58.

Murry, John Middleton, ed., *The Journals of Katherine Mansfield*, McGraw-Hill, 1964, pp. 234–35.

———, *The Letters of Katherine Mansfield*, Vol. 2, Knopf, 1929, p. 473.

Nathan, Rhoda B., *Katherine Mansfield*, Continuum, 1988, p. 101.

Shakespeare, William, *King Lear*, Methuen, 1972, p. 140.

"WWI Casualty and Death Tables," PBS.org, https://www.pbs.org/greatwar/resources/casdeath_pop.html (accessed August 11, 2015).

FURTHER READING

Butler, Christopher, *Modernism: A Very Short Introduction*, Oxford University Press, 2010.

As its title states, this is a concise introduction to one of the most significant movements in twentieth-century art and literature. Butler explains what the movement was, how it began, and how its legacy permeated the twentieth century and continued into the twenty-first.

Hankin, Cherry A., ed., *Letters between Katherine Mansfield and John Middleton Murry*, New Amsterdam Books, 1998.

This is a collection of three hundred letters exchanged between Mansfield and Murry during their eleven-year relationship, from January 1912 to January 1923.

Mounic, Anne, *Ah, What Is It?—That I Heard: Katherine Mansfield's Wings of Wonder*, Rodopi, 2014.

In separate chapters, Mounic examines Mansfield's fiction in a number of different contexts, including her links with other writers such as Marcel Proust, D. H. Lawrence, Virginia Woolf, and Dorothy Richardson; themes such as metamorphosis and a sense of wonder; and places such as Paris.

New, W. H., *Reading Mansfield and Metaphors of Form*, McGill-Queen's University Press, 1999.

Among the issues addressed in this scholarly book are Mansfield's relation to imperialism, gender, and textuality. New also examines Mansfield's revisions of her stories, including "The Fly."

Tomalin, Claire, *Katherine Mansfield: A Secret Life*, Viking, 1987.

> Using letters not available to previous biographers, Tomalin takes a fresh look at Mansfield's relationships with the central figures in her life. She is more skeptical of John Middleton Murry's account of events than earlier biographers and also suggests that Mansfield's friendship with D. H. Lawrence was more important to her than has generally been thought.

Wilson, Janet, Gerri Kimber, and Susan Reid, eds., *Katherine Mansfield and Literary Modernism*, Bloomsbury Academic, 2011.

> This is a collection of sixteen scholarly essays on all aspects of Mansfield's work that cements her place as a central figure in modernism.

SUGGESTED SEARCH TERMS

Katherine Mansfield

"The Fly" AND Mansfield

World War I AND literature

modernism

modernism AND short story

short stories AND Mansfield

John Middleton Murry AND Mansfield

Katherine Mansfield AND Virginia Woolf

The Moonlit Road

AMBROSE BIERCE

1907

"The Moonlit Road" is a short story published in January 1907 by American author Ambrose Bierce. The tale, a ghost story, first appeared in *Cosmopolitan*, a prominent family magazine that published the work of such accomplished writers as Theodore Dreiser, Rudyard Kipling, Annie Besant, Jack London, and Edith Wharton and where H. G. Wells's *The War of the Worlds* first appeared. In April 1910 Bierce's story was included in *Can Such Things Be?*, a collection of tales that made up the third volume of his *Collected Works*. Potential confusion can arise because in 1893 he had published a considerably different collection of stories under the same title, and that book was reissued in 1903. For the 1910 edition, Bierce eliminated nineteen stories from the earlier collection and added twenty-eight from other sources, among them "The Moonlit Road."

By the late nineteenth and early twentieth centuries, Bierce was widely known as a newspaper journalist and editorialist, a satirist, and a writer of short stories. Many of these short stories are set in the American Civil War and draw on Bierce's experience as a Union soldier. Many others, including "The Moonlit Road," were based on themes of death, horror, ghosts, and spiritualism. Written in three parts, each narrated in a different voice, "The Moonlit Road" examines a macabre murder and the effort of the spirit of the murdered woman to make contact with her surviving loved ones in death.

Ambrose Bierce (© *Mary Evans Picture Library* / *Alamy*)

"The Moonlit Road" is widely available in print and on the Internet. It is included in *Ambrose Bierce: The Devil's Dictionary, Tales, & Memoirs*, edited by S. T. Joshi (Library of America, 2011). Online the story is available from *The Literature Network* at http://www.online-literature.com/bierce/2012/.

AUTHOR BIOGRAPHY

Ambrose Gwinnett Bierce was born on June 24, 1842, in a backwoods settlement along Horse Cave Creek in Meigs County, a county in southeastern Ohio across the Ohio River from West Virginia. He was the youngest of ten surviving children born to Marcus Aurelius and Laura Sherwood Bierce; oddly, the names of all ten children began with the letter *A*. Four years later the family moved to Indiana, where he eventually received some schooling, but he always maintained that he owed his education to his family's library and his father's love of literature—this despite the fact that he thought of his parents as backward and crude. In 1847 he left home and moved to Warsaw, Indiana, to work for an abolitionist newspaper, the *Northern Indianan*. After a stint at the Kentucky Military Institute, Bierce returned to Indiana, working at odd jobs in Elkhart until the outbreak of the Civil War, when he enlisted in the Ninth Indiana Infantry Regiment. During the course of the war he rose to the rank of lieutenant and saw action in a number of major battles, including the Battle of Shiloh. In 1864 he was seriously wounded, and in early 1865 he resigned from the Union army for medical reasons.

In 1866 Bierce was a member of an expedition that traveled from Omaha, Nebraska, to San Francisco on an inspection tour of military posts. He remained in San Francisco, where he began to write for the periodical press. His first published work was a poem, "Basilica," which appeared in the *Californian*. He contributed work to the *San Francisco News Letter*, of which he became editor in 1868, and over the next three and a half years he wrote 173 "Town Crier" columns for the paper. In 1871 he published his first short story, "The Haunted Valley" (in Bret Harte's magazine, *Overland Monthly*), and on Christmas Day of that year he married Mary Ellen ("Mollie") Day; he separated from her in 1889, and they divorced in 1904. He resigned from his position at the *News Letter*, and from 1872 to 1875 he lived in England, where he wrote for magazines in London. During these years he published three books: *The Fiend's Delight* (1872), *Nuggets and Dust Panned Out in California* (1872), and *Cobwebs from an Empty Skull* (1874).

After returning to the United States, Bierce became editor of the San Francisco *Argonaut*, but he left that position in 1879 to embark on a brief, unsuccessful mining venture in the Dakota Territory. Back in San Francisco he edited the *Wasp* for five years before joining the staff of William Randolph Hearst's *San Francisco Examiner* in 1887 as chief editorial writer. Hearst, known for muckraking journalism, turned Bierce loose to write sharp, satiric attacks on corruption and folly. In 1892 he published *Tales of Soldiers and Civilians*, a collection of short stories that included what some readers might consider his finest story, "An Occurrence at Owl Creek Bridge." In 1893 he relocated to Washington, DC, where he continued to write for newspapers and magazines, including the *Examiner* and the *New York Journal*; that year, too, he published the first edition of *Can Such Things Be?* Among the many short stories he wrote was "The Moonlit Road," which first appeared in 1907 in Hearst's *Cosmopolitan* (the ancestor publication of the modern-day fashion magazine often referred to as "Cosmo"). He cemented his reputation as a satirist—his friends called him "Bitter Bierce"—with *The Devil's Dictionary*, first published in 1906 as *The Cynic's Word Book*, a collection of acerbically ironic definitions. From 1909 to 1912 his twelve-volume *Collected Works* were published; the collection includes 1,164 individual works, less than a third of his published output.

In 1913 Bierce went on a tour of Civil War battlefields. He continued his trip with visits to Texas and New Orleans before crossing into northern Mexico, where Pancho Villa was leading the Mexican Revolution. On December 26 he wrote a letter from Chihuahua, Mexico, to a friend, indicating that he would be leaving for an unknown destination the following day. He was never heard from again, no remains or belongings were ever found, and his fate remains unknown, although it has been conjectured that he somehow fell victim to the revolution in Mexico.

PLOT SUMMARY

I: *Statement of Joel Hetman, Jr.*

"The Moonlit Road" is divided into three numbered parts. Part I is narrated by Joel Hetman, Jr., the son of Joel and Julia Hetman. The younger Joel is looking back on the night when he learned of the murder of his mother. At the time he was nineteen years old and a student at Yale. He was summoned by telegram to his country home a few miles from Nashville, Tennessee. When he arrived at the railroad station in Nashville, a relative informed him that his mother had been murdered, but it was unknown why and by whom.

Joel then narrates the circumstances as he understands them. His father had gone to Nashville on business. His intention was to return the following afternoon, but the business was never accomplished, so he returned early, arriving just before dawn. Not wanting to disturb the servants, he went to the back of the house to gain entry. As he came around the corner of the house, he heard the sound of a door being closed, then saw the figure of a man disappearing into the trees. Initially, he thought that someone was having a secret tryst with a servant. He entered the house, then went upstairs to his wife's room. As he stepped into the dark room, he fell over the body of his wife, who had been strangled. The killer was never found.

Joel abandoned his studies to remain with his dejected father, who turned nervous and apprehensive. One night several months later, Joel and his father were walking home from Nashville. It was nighttime, but there was a full moon. As they approached the house, the father suddenly stopped and in great agitation indicated that he saw something. As he stared fixedly at what he saw, he backed away. His son turned his eyes to a light that suddenly came from an upper window of the house. When he turned back, his father was gone. Young Joel never learned of his father's fate.

II: *Statement of Caspar Grattan*

The second part is narrated by a man who calls himself Caspar Grattan but who adopted the name some twenty years earlier and has no knowledge of who he was before that; he describes himself now as an old man. He indicates that tomorrow he will be dead, perhaps suggesting an intention to commit suicide, a suggestion bolstered by his reference to the document he is writing, which can be regarded as a suicide note. He has a vague recollection of having once been known by a number, suggesting that he was once either imprisoned or held in an insane asylum. His awareness of himself began when he found himself walking in a forest, then asking for help at a farmhouse. He knows that he once lived near a large city, that he was a prosperous farmer, and that he was married to a woman he loved but distrusted. Determined to test his wife's fidelity, he told her that he would be absent until the following afternoon, but he returned early and entered the house, having earlier tampered with the locks so that the door would appear to be locked but not actually fasten. As he approached the door, he saw a man steal away in the darkness. In a blind, jealous rage, he entered the house, ascended the stairs, and stumbled across his wife cowering in the darkened room. He then strangled her to death.

Caspar says that he sees all of this as in a dream that plays over and over in his consciousness. He has another dream, which takes place in the shadows of a moonlit road. He becomes aware of another presence, a gleam of white garments, and the figure of a woman confronting him, his wife. Her eyes are fixed on him, but not in reproach or menace. He retreats from the apparition. At the end of his statement, Caspar indicates that he lives a life of punishment but that today the term of that punishment expires.

III: Statement of the Late Julia Hetman, through the Medium Bayrolles

The third and final part of the story is narrated by the spirit of Julia Hetman through a medium, Bayrolles, who is able to make contact with the dead. She describes the night of her murder. She had retired to bed, but she awoke with a sense of peril. Her husband, Joel, was away from home. As the terror grew on her, she turned on the lamp by her bed, but the light provided no relief from the horrors she felt. She extinguished the lamp, but she lay awake for hours until she heard footfalls. After the footfalls turned away, Julia rose from her bed and went to the door to call for help. As the footfalls returned rapidly, Julia retreated to a corner of the room. The door opened, and the intruder strangled her to death. Now, as a spirit, Julia haunts the house and grounds, trying to make contact with her husband and son. She tells of a moonlit night, when she searched for them at the house and on the grounds around it. She left the lawn and was on the road when she heard the voice of her husband and that of her son nearby. The elder man's eyes were fixed on her, and Julia felt not terror but love. She moved toward him, smiling and offering endearments, but he went pale and, looking like a hunted animal, backed away and fled. Julia's narration closes with her lament that she has never been able to impart a sense of her presence to her son.

CHARACTERS

Bayrolles

Bayrolles is the name of the medium through whom Julia Hetman narrates the story of her murder and its aftermath in part III of "The Moonlit Road."

Caspar Grattan

Caspar Grattan is the name adopted by the wretched figure who narrates part II of "The Moonlit Road." He indicates that he adopted the name some twenty years earlier and that he has few memories of a time before that, although he is much older. He may have been imprisoned or possibly confined to an insane asylum. He insists that this is the last day of his life, although whether he plans to commit suicide or whether he will be executed is not made clear. He tells a story of having tested the fidelity of his wife by absenting himself from their home, then returning sooner than he said he would. He arrived at his home in time to see a figure furtively leaving. He entered the house, located his wife in the bedroom, and strangled her to death. As his story unfolds, the reader comes to understand that "Caspar Grattan" is in actuality Joel Hetman, Sr., who lost his sanity and identity after seeing the apparition of his murdered wife and who likely is the one who murdered her, though it is possible that the reader is to understand that he had no conscious memory of doing so.

Joel Hetman, Jr.

Joel Hetman, Jr., narrates part I of "The Moonlit Road." Years earlier, he was a nineteen-year-old student at Yale when he was summoned to his country home outside Nashville, Tennessee. When he arrives, he learns that his mother has been brutally murdered in the home, although it is not know why or by whom. In the version of events that the younger Joel tells, his father entered the bedchamber and fell over the body of his wife, already dead. Joel drops out of Yale and remains at home with his devastated father. On a moonlit night some months later, the two men are walking down the road near their home when the father suddenly sees an apparition. Joel never sees his father again.

Joel Hetman, Sr.

Joel Hetman, Sr., is described as a well-to-do gentleman who, with his family, occupies a large country home near Nashville, Tennessee. In the first part of the story, his son narrates his understanding of the events surrounding his father's arrival at home to find the body of his murdered wife, and of the moonlit night when the elder Joel sees an apparition of his murdered wife. The son turns away when his attention is drawn by a light from an upper window of the house; when he turns back, his father is gone, never to be heard from again. As the reader reads the statement of Caspar Grattan in part II, it becomes apparent that Caspar is, in fact, Joel Hetman, Sr., telling his story many years later.

Julia Hetman

Julia Hetman, the wife of Joel Hetman, Sr., and the mother of Joel Junior, is murdered in her bedroom in the family's house outside Nashville, Tennessee. Her spirit is the narrator of part III of "The Moonlit Road"; her statement is delivered through a medium named Bayrolles. She describes her fear and apprehension as she lay in bed on the night of her murder. She listened to footsteps coming up the stairs; the steps left and then returned. She cowered in a corner of the room, but her killer entered and strangled her. Much of Julia's narration is taken up with her description of her life in the spirit realm. In particular, she tells of wanting to make contact with her husband and son and offer them comfort. On the night Joel Senior disappeared, the apparition he saw on the "moonlit road" was that of his wife. Julia laments that she has never been able to make contact with her son.

THEMES

Spirits

"The Moonlit Road" depends for its effects on spirits and spiritualism—the belief that the dead might be able to communicate with the living, which forms the premise of the story. In part I, the younger Joel Hetman is walking with his father down the "moonlit road" near their house when suddenly the father becomes deeply agitated. It is clear that he has seen an apparition that has caused him great fear; as the story unfolds, the reader learns that the apparition is that of his wife, who haunts the house and grounds trying to make contact with her husband and son. In part II, the figure who goes by the name Caspar Grattan writes of a dreamlike experience in which he saw an apparition of his murdered wife. Part III develops the spiritualist theme most fully, for the narration of Julia Hetman, the murdered wife and mother, is communicated through a spirit medium named Bayrolles. In this portion of the story Julia talks about her "life" in the "Valley of the Shadow," where she is forced to "lurk in its desolate places, peering from brambles and thickets" at the world's "mad, malign inhabitants." Julia's purpose in haunting the family's country home is to make contact with her husband and son and "to speak words that should restore the broken bonds between the living and the dead" and to offer them comfort.

Guilt

The statement made by Caspar Grattan is that of a man who is either mentally unbalanced or who has undergone some kind of traumatic experience. While it is initially unclear who precisely Grattan is, the story he tells tracks closely with what readers know, or think they know, about the murder of Julia Hetman, who seems to have been murdered by her husband. If, in fact, Grattan is Joel Hetman, Sr., his statement is an expression of a corrosive feeling of guilt for his actions. That guilt manifests itself in a number of ways. In part I, the son indicates that his father grew nervous and apprehensive in the weeks and months after the murder: "At any small surprise of the senses he would start visibly and sometimes turn pale, then relapse into a melancholy apathy deeper than before. I suppose he was what is called a 'nervous wreck.'" Still in part I, the father sees an apparition that, it will later become clear, is that of his murdered wife. In response, he turns rigid and pale. When his son turns away, he disappears, never to be heard from by the son again, apparently having fled in fear and guilt. In part II, the character who calls himself Caspar Grattan is consumed by guilt over the crime he believes he committed: "Nor shall I recount further incidents of the life that is now to end—a life of wandering, always and everywhere haunted by an overmastering sense of crime in punishment of wrong and of terror in punishment of crime."

Love

Perhaps the principal irony of "The Moonlit Road" is that Julia Hetman does not know who murdered her (perhaps leaving open the question of whether the deed was committed by another man, whom, according to the son, his father said he saw that night and whom Caspar Grattan claims he saw). Throughout much of her narration in part III, Julia laments her inability to convey her love to her husband and son, whom she wishes to comfort. At one point she says:

> We know this well, we who have passed into
> the Realm of Terror, who skulk in eternal
> dusk among the scenes of our former lives,
> invisible even to ourselves and one another,

TOPICS FOR FURTHER STUDY

- Investigate the history of the spiritualist movement in the late nineteenth and early twentieth centuries. What did spiritualists believe? Who were the major figures in the movement? What hoaxes were perpetrated? To what extent did the interest in spiritualism make the reading public more receptive to ghost stories? Present the results of your findings in an oral report for your classmates.

- Read "Afterward," a ghost story published in 1910 by Bierce's American contemporary, Edith Wharton (*Edith Wharton: Collected Stories: 1891–1910*, edited by Maureen Howard, Library of America, 2001). In a written report, explain how the two authors use the theme of ghostly apparitions for differing purposes.

- Investigate the history of gothic literature in British and American literature. What is gothic literature, and why is the word *gothic* used to refer to it? What is the relationship between gothic literature and the ghost story? Who were prominent writers of gothic literature, particularly in the United States? What are the conventions of gothic literature? Present the results of your findings in a chart, and share it with your classmates on a social networking site.

- Violet Kupersmith is the American author of *The Frangipani Hotel* (2014), a collection of contemporary tales, most with supernatural elements, based on traditional Vietnamese folktales. Read one or more stories in the collection, perhaps the title story, "The Frangipani Hotel," and prepare an oral report for your classmates that explores how a culture like that of the Vietnamese can employ ghosts and spiritualism for unique purposes.

- In addition to writing short stories (and some poetry), Bierce employed his pen to write acid-tongued newspaper editorials opposing greed and corruption for his boss, William Randolph Hearst. One of his prime targets were the corporate magnates who built the transcontinental railroad (the "Railrogues") and then tried to back out of paying back the government loans that financed the project. Among them was Leland Stanford, the founder of California's Stanford University, whom Bierce referred to in print as "$tealand Landford" or "£eland $tanford." Conduct research on Bierce's role in opposing the Railrogues and write an editorial in what you might think of as Bierce's voice about the issue (or another, similar issue).

- Bierce was the author of *The Devil's Dictionary*, which provides short, trenchant, satirical definitions of words and concepts. Send one or more tweets to your classmates providing your own satirical definitions of something from contemporary American culture. Here are some suggestions: fast food, bottled water, reality TV, presidential debates, werewolves, nostalgia, dating websites, the Internet, tattoos, rap music, country music, beauty pageants.

- *The Ghost Files* by Apryl Baker (Limitless Publishing, 2013) is a ghost story featuring a teenage girl who sees ghosts, including that of her dead foster sister. Read the novel and write your own short story in which the protagonist, Mattie Hathaway, encounters the ghost of Ambrose Bierce and solves the lingering mystery of his disappearance.

- If you have artistic talent, prepare a series of illustrations for a graphic version of "The Moonlit Road." Post them on a website and invite your classmates to comment.

yet hiding forlorn in lonely places; yearning for speech with our loved ones, yet dumb, and as fearful of them as they of us. Sometimes the disability is removed, the law suspended: by the deathless power of love or hate we break the spell.

Julia tells her version of the story through a medium. (© *Photographee.eu / Shutterstock*)

Later, when she appears to her husband on the moonlit road and she knows that he sees her, she feels a sense of exhilaration. She refers again to the "law" and asserts that "Love had conquered Law!"

STYLE

Point of View

The chief stylistic element of "The Moonlit Road" is its use of point of view. The story is told in three parts, each part narrated in the first person by one of the principals. In the first part, Joel Hetman, Jr., narrates the story surrounding the murder of his mother. However, what he knows of the murder, or thinks he knows, is limited to what his father told him. Accordingly, he is able to provide only an incomplete version of the events. Further, he has no knowledge of the fate of his father, who disappeared on the night the apparition of Julia appeared on the moonlit road.

Part II is also narrated from a limited perspective. The words are a statement about his life that "Caspar Grattan" is writing, but again, he is an unreliable narrator, for his guilt, along with the appearance of his wife's ghost, has robbed him of his identity, and he can describe the relevant events only vaguely and without certainty.

Part III is narrated by Julia Hetman; her narration is not offered directly but through the agency of a spiritualist medium, Bayrolles. The reader is not given any reason to trust Bayrolles, and Julia's perspective, like that of her son and husband, is limited. She exists only in a nighttime shadow world of isolation. She is haunted by her memories, but although she describes her murder, she does not know who killed her, for she did not see him. No special knowledge about her death is provided to her in the afterlife. Thus, if the reader assumes that her husband is, in fact, her killer, her longing to make contact with him and comfort him is highly ironic. As Martin Griffin points out in his article on "The Moonlit Road" for the *Ambrose Bierce Project Journal*, "The Moonlit Road' is a ghost story, or perhaps a gothic tale of extreme and morbidly unreliable states of mind." It is also

COMPARE & CONTRAST

- **1907:** Although spiritualism and the belief that one can commune with the ghosts of the dead is beginning to wane in popularity, spiritualism maintains a large following.

  Today: Spiritualism in numerous forms is practiced by many proponents of the New Age movement.

- **1907:** Hereward Carrington publishes *The Physical Phenomena of Spiritualism*, which exposes the tricks used by fraudulent mediums in slate writing, table turning, trumpet mediumship, materializations, sealed-letter reading, and spirit photography.

  Today: In 2009, writing in the *Skeptical Inquirer*, Karen Stollznow described spiritualism thus: "It is religion without a rule book. There is no unified theology, no universally defining characteristics nor collective history. There is no doctrine. The holy book of spiritualism is whatever self-help book is currently on the *New York Times* Best Seller list."

- **1907:** Ghost stories and folktales about ghostly apparitions and haunted places are widely popular in American culture, particularly in the American West.

  Today: Tales of the supernatural and bizarre feature not only traditional ghosts but also vampires and zombies, as attested by the widespread popularity of the *Twilight Saga* novels and movies (vampires) and *The Walking Dead* TV series (zombies).

---

a text that plays with the ostensible rationality of the first-person voice, while gradually revealing a non-rational psychic landscape of uncertainty and delusion. The doubts and implications are not resolved but rather, in an ironic authorial maneuver, bequeathed to the reader, to see if he or she can make any sense of them.

Setting

"The Moonlit Road" draws on the conventions of gothic literature: a supernatural subject matter; the uncanny, in the Freudian sense of something being familiar and alien at the same time; an isolated setting, usually a house with secret passages or rooms; images of darkness and shadows; repressed secrets; and such motifs as punishment and retribution, despair, terror, and the lingering impact of past events on the present. In terms of setting, it is the images of darkness and shadows that predominate. The story begins in a daytime, rational world, as Joel Hetman, Jr., narrates what he thinks he knows about the murder of his mother. Quickly, though, the story turns to a nighttime world of terror: Joel Senior claims to have seen the indistinct figure of a man in the darkness. He opened the bedroom door and stepped into the "black darkness." Later, as the son walks down the road with his father, he observes black shadows interrupted by gleams of "ghostly white." In his narration, Caspar Grattan, too, refers to the "black darkness" and the "darkness of the hall" in the house where the murder occurred. Later, however, he refers to the "gleam of white garments" that appears on the moonlit road. These images, taken together, create a gothic setting that reinforces the supernatural, alien, uncanny subject matter of the story.

HISTORICAL CONTEXT

For much of American history, the West—that is, the vast region of the continent west of the Mississippi River—was as much an idea as it was a place. For most Americans, the West was an enormous tabula rasa, or blank tablet, on which they could project their own desires, their ideals, and, in particular, a mythology. Lacking a

As the father and son walk along the moonlit road, the father turns pale and runs away. (© *Balazs Kovacs Images / Shutterstock*)

history of its own (at least from the perspective of white settlers, though American Indians might disagree), the region became a place of adventure, excitement, and especially mystery in the American imagination. Further, the process of settling the American West was one fraught with danger, disease, hunger, privation, and often violence. Forts were built, then abandoned. Towns sprang up overnight and suddenly turned into ghost towns as people picked up and moved on—or died out. Parties of settlers disappeared on the prairies or in the mountains and deserts, never to be heard from again. Battlefields offered mute testimony to bloody conflicts between settlers and Indians, and most Americans "remember the Alamo," which continues to play a role in the mythology of American coalescence.

This atmosphere of mystery and the unknown fostered a fervent interest in ghosts and ghost stories in the American West, all based on the belief that such an untamed and largely unpopulated region must be populated by specters and phantoms. Tales of the supernatural and the uncanny came to surround such places as Camp Floyd and Fort Douglas in Utah; Fort Riley, Fort Scott, Fort Leavenworth, and Fort Dodge in Kansas; Fort Brown and Fort Phantom in Texas; Fort Laramie in Wyoming; and Drum Barracks and

Alcatraz in California—the kinds of places Bierce would have inspected in the post–Civil War military tour that led him to California. In California alone, there are more than one hundred ghost towns, and hundreds more existed in Texas, Arizona, New Mexico, Nevada, Utah, Colorado, Wyoming, Montana, and other states. Numerous sites in and around San Francisco, among them hotels and historic mansions, have long been regarded as haunted.

The Old West has provided a rich tradition of legends and ghost stories, such as those about Black Jack Ketchum; the Buffalo Ranch and the ghosts of the Cripple Creek mining district, both in Colorado; the ghost of Armbruster Pike in Nevada; the haunting of the Bullock Hotel in South Dakota; the Weeping Woman of the Southwest; the phantoms of the Vallecito Stage Station in California . . . a list of these legends and tales of ghosts and hauntings could go on and on. Interest in the supernatural and the eerie was fed in part by the large number of "dime novels" in the United States—inexpensive and highly sensationalized tales of Western adventure—and, in Britain, by "penny dreadfuls"—so called because they cost a penny and were thought to inspire dread through tales of crime and supernatural beings.

It was in this literary climate that Bierce wrote and published his ghost stories and tales of the supernatural, including "The Moonlit Road" and the other stories in *Can Such Things Be?* Further, he took advantage of the growth of the spiritualist movement, which was waning slightly by 1907 but still enjoyed popularity. Spiritualism comprises a set of quasi-religious beliefs that say, in essence, that it is possible for living persons to contact the spirits of the dead and vice versa—a theme that is depicted in "The Moonlit Road." Spiritualism emerged in the 1850s and became widely popular in the decades that followed. Professional mediums—like Bayrolles in "The Moonlit Road"—offered spirit photography, spirit lectures on social issues, and séances in which the dead spoke to the living in a variety of ways (for example, levitating trumpets, sealed slates, knocking), although much—some would say all—of this activity was fraudulent. This interest in spiritualism intersected with the emergent field of psychology—Sigmund Freud had published his seminal work *The Interpretation of Dreams* in 1899—to produce a new, more modern sensibility in literature, one that broke with traditional forms to explore the unconscious mind, to depict humankind's darkest instincts and fears, and to plumb the inexplicability of human experience.

CRITICAL OVERVIEW

For more than a century, Bierce has been regarded as an important practitioner of the short-story form. Writing for *Bookman* in 1911, Frederic Taber Cooper, in "Ambrose Bierce: An Appraisal," remarked:

> It is as a writer of short stories that Mr. Bierce's future fame rests upon a firm foundation. It is not too much to say that within his own chosen field—the grim, uncompromising horror story, whether actual or supernatural—he stands among American writers second only to Edgar Allan Poe.

Cooper added: "It is in his supernatural stories that Mr. Bierce shows even more forcefully his wizardry of word and phrase, his almost magnetic power to make the absurd, the grotesque, the impossible, carry an overwhelming conviction."

When *Can This Thing Be?*, volume 3 of his *Collected Works*, which contains "The Moonlit Road," was published, a reviewer for the London *Athenaeum* wrote: "We could ask for a happier choice of theme, but hardly for a more impeccable execution." The reviewer went on to conclude: "Even the wildest themes have underlying them some sort of metaphysical notion or conjecture."

Robert L. Gale, however, in *An Ambrose Bierce Companion*, pointed out with regard to the publication of *Collected Works*: "This collection, especially the *edition de luxe*, was derisively and, at times, witlessly reviewed, owing to the countless enemies Bierce had managed to make in the literary establishment over the decades." Gale noted, for example, that prominent American critic H. L. Mencken called the *Collected Works* "a depressing assemblage of worn-out and fly-blown stuff." One anonymous reviewer called the elegantly printed volumes "pure piffle in plush pants."

Among more recent critics, Stuart C. Woodruff, in *The Short Stories of Ambrose Bierce*, places Bierce and "The Moonlit Road" in the context of the literature of the American West at roughly the turn of the twentieth century. Referring to the "great popularity, among California readers, of ghosts and the supernatural," Woodruff wrote: "While an author's choice of subject is rarely an entirely conscious one, Bierce's ghost stories represent, in part at least, a deliberate attempt to find a wider audience and a better financial return from his fiction."

Cathy N. Davidson, in *The Experimental Fictions of Ambrose Bierce*, expressed admiration for Bierce's supernatural tales in general and "The Moonlit Road" in particular:

> "The Moonlit Road" is also a work in which the comic mode of presentation and the tragic facts of the discourse which make that mode possible go oddly together. . . . Like numerous twentieth-century writers, Bierce breaks the old rules of decorum. More accurately, he redefines them, suggesting that it is perhaps more appropriate to laugh, with black humor, at the tragic follies of humanity than to suggest that, with sentimentalism, the consequences of such follies can somehow be washed away by cathartic tears.

Other critics have focused on Bierce's craftsmanship. Richard Saunders, for example, in *Ambrose Bierce: The Making of a Misanthrope*, wrote: "It was Bierce's uncompromising honesty in portraying the world as he saw it that puts him above most other writers. His tragic and unflattering view of human existence is, if nothing else, his own unique vision." Saunders continued:

> Bierce had been brave enough to say what he thought about the human condition in his newspaper work, and he felt he owed the same courtesy to the readers of his fiction. The convincingly terrifying visions put before us in *Can Such Things Be?* are all the more remarkable when you consider their lack of conventional character development, sparse descriptions and economy of line. He creates his own isolated vacuum of fear and terror, and the reader is dropped into it and left to fend for himself.

In her book *Ambrose Bierce*, M. E. Grenander enthused:

> Bierce, at his best, was a consummate craftsman. The key to his technique is that it compresses much in narrow compass. He was master of a fluid and limpid prose, often intentionally ambivalent, in which exactly the right words are chosen to convey precise shades of meaning. Bierce's style is stark and stripped, without excess verbiage but freighted with vast implications. Since it usually operates at more than one level, it poses a continual challenge and may trap the unwary.

CRITICISM

Michael J. O'Neal

O'Neal holds a PhD in English. In the following essay, he examines "The Moonlit Road" as a story about the unreliability of memory.

That "The Moonlit Road" is a good old-fashioned ghost story is undeniable. In part I, the elder Joel Hetman sees the apparition of his murdered wife on the "moonlit road" outside his home near Nashville. Through his narrator, the younger Joel, Bierce sets the scene in expert (and highly alliterative) fashion:

> The full moon was about three hours above the eastern horizon; the entire countryside had the solemn stillness of a summer night; our footfalls and the ceaseless song of the katydids were the only sound aloof. Black shadows of bordering trees lay athwart the road, which, in the short reaches between, gleamed a ghostly white.

Suddenly, the father sees an apparition and reacts in predictable fashion: "Presently he began to retire backward, step by step, never

> ONE WAY OF READING "THE MOONLIT ROAD" IS TO SEE IT AS AN EXPLORATION OF THE EFFECTS OF THE ABSENCE OF ANY OBJECTIVELY VERIFIABLE TRUTH. TESTIMONY IS SUSPECT. IDENTITY IS FLUID. MOTIVES ARE UNCLEAR. COMMUNICATION FAILS."

for an instant removing his eyes from what he saw, or thought he saw."

So far, the story employs the conventions of gothic literature, a style of fiction that originated in the late eighteenth and early nineteenth centuries and that features an atmosphere of gloom and horror, with mysterious, macabre, and violent incidents—such as the nighttime murder of Julia Hetman. The gothic is a literature of the irrational and the inexplicable, a literature of madness and desperation, a theme that is carried out in "The Moonlit Road" through the narration of Caspar Grattan, whose madness borne of guilt and fear is apparent, and through the narration of Julia, executed through the agency of a medium who claims to open a portal allowing the dead to communicate with the living.

But "The Moonlit Road" is more than just an eerie ghost story whose intent is to elicit from the reader the frisson of fear. More fundamentally, the story explores the issue of memory and the relationship of memory to a person's identity and reliability. It comments on this theme in large part through its narrative technique. The story is narrated in three parts. Each part has a different first-person narrator, and each of the three narrators details the events surrounding the murder of Julia Hetman. Each, then, provides a differing version of the events, forcing the reader to integrate the three accounts into a coherent sequence of events—or at least try to do so. The first part is narrated by Joel Hetman, Jr., the son of Joel Senior and his murdered wife, Julia. At the time of his mother's death, Joel is a nineteen-year-old student at Yale. He is summoned back to the family home outside Nashville to learn that his mother has been murdered. He seems to function as a framing narrator who provides what at first seems to be an

WHAT DO I READ NEXT?

- Bierce's most famous short story, "An Occurrence at Owl Creek Bridge" (1890), is based on his experiences during the Civil War. It tells the story of a man who—apparently—escapes the hangman's noose at the hands of Union soldiers. The story has been adapted for film numerous times and formed an episode of Rod Serling's TV series *The Twilight Zone*.

- "The Moonlit Road" inspired a story by Japanese writer Ryunosuke Akutagawa entitled "Yabu no naka" ("In a Grove" or "In a Bamboo Grove"). This story, in turn, provided the basis for Akira Kurosawa's classic film *Rashomon*, made in 1950. The story is available in *Rashomon and Seventeen Other Stories* (Penguin, 2009).

- One of Bierce's contemporaries was Henry James, the author of ten ghost stories, collected in *Ghost Stories of Henry James* (Wordsworth Editions, 2008). Among them is his famous novella, the disturbing psychological story *The Turn of the Screw* (1898).

- In 1907, the year in which "The Moonlit Road" was first published, Algernon Blackwood, regarded as one of the foremost writers of ghost stories in Britain, published *The Listener, and Other Stories*, available in an edition from Books for Libraries Press (1971).

- In 1899, African American author Charles W. Chesnutt published *The Conjure Woman*, seven tales dealing with racial issues in the American South after the Civil War. The stories, narrated for a white northern couple by Uncle Julius McAdoo, are derived from African American folktales and include numerous supernatural occurrences built around the voodoo conjuring tradition.

- Roald Dahl selected fourteen ghost stories for *Roald Dahl's Book of Ghost Stories* (1984), a volume for young adults. Included are tales by such storytellers as E. F. Benson, Sheridan Le Fanu, Edith Wharton, and Rosemary Timperley.

- Sir Arthur Conan Doyle is best known for his highly logical character Sherlock Holmes, yet Doyle wrote numerous books about spiritualism, the most famous of which is *The History of Spiritualism*, first published in 1926.

- Readers interested in the history of spiritualism and mediumship might start with Christopher M. Moreman's three-volume *The Spiritualist Movement: Speaking with the Dead in America and around the World* (2013).

- Ransom Riggs's *Miss Peregrine's Home for Peculiar Children* (2013) combines text and eerie photographs in a young-adult ghost novel (though one that adults enjoy) featuring a sixteen-year-old boy who, after a family tragedy, encounters potentially dangerous ghosts in the crumbling ruins of Miss Peregrine's Home for Peculiar Children on the coast of Wales. The book is also available as a graphic novel.

---

authoritative view of the events surrounding his mother's murder. The key word, however, is "seems," for it must be remembered that the reader is learning of the events at two removes. Joel narrates his understanding of events, but his version is based on the version provided to him by his father, who, it will become apparent, may have his own reasons for misleading his son. Thus, while young Joel appears to be a reliable narrator, outlining events in a candid voice the reader can trust, in fact he is a very unreliable narrator, basing his recollection of what happened on the faulty account of his father. This lack of reliability is further suggested by the opening sentence of his account: "I am the most unfortunate of men." He then comments: "In the stress of privation and the need of effort I might sometimes forget the somber secret ever baffling the conjecture that it compels." These statements betray a tendency on Joel's part to pity himself. From an emotional standpoint, he seems to have never found a way to come to terms with the loss of his parents, and this lingering shock may be regarded as distorting his narration.

The concept of the unreliable narrator comes into full force in part II, the narration of "Caspar Grattan." From the beginning of his narration, the reader senses that "Caspar" is not in command of his faculties. He indicates his intention to commit suicide (or, possibly, his expectation that he will be executed) when he says that tomorrow he will be "a senseless shape of clay." The reader further learns that the figure who calls himself "Caspar Grattan" lacks any firm sense of identity: "The name has served my small need for more than twenty years of a life of unknown length. True, I gave it to myself, but lacking another I had the right. In this world one must have a name; it prevents confusion, even when it does not establish identity." He goes on to note an incident when two men in uniform indicate that he looks like number "767." The suggestion is that Caspar may have been identified by a number as an inmate either in a prison or in an insane asylum, which would serve to impeach his testimony.

Caspar goes on to note that his intention in the document he is writing is to provide a "record of broken and apparently unrelated memories," some of which he describes as having the "character of crimson dreams with interspaces blank and black—witch-fires glowing still and red in a great desolation." Throughout his narration, Caspar emphasizes his lack of clarity: "I see nothing clearly; it comes out of a cloud." "I *seem* once to have lived near a great city" (italics added). Referring to his son, he says: "He is at all times a vague figure, never clearly drawn, frequently altogether out of the picture." With regard to the man he saw leaving the house on the night of his wife's murder, he says: "I sprang after him, but he had vanished without even the bad luck of identification. Sometimes now I cannot even persuade myself that it was a human being."

The reader's sense of Caspar's unreliability is further supported when he becomes unhinged in describing the night he saw the apparition: "Before this awful apparition I retreat in terror—a terror that is upon me as I write. I can no longer rightly shape the words. See! they—" The net effect of Caspar's fevered narration is to create a picture that differs markedly from that of Joel Hetman, Jr., in part I.

The reader then arrives at part III and the narration of Julia Hetman, the murdered woman. The first complication is that her narration comes to the reader through the agency of a medium, Bayrolles. A reader might be justified in thinking that Bierce wants us to distrust the very foundations of the account, for no framing narrative establishes the credibility of Bayrolles. Moreover, the reader once again encounters a narrative that may or may not be accurate. Julia says, for example, that she has "passed into the Realm of Terror." She is among those who "skulk in eternal dusk among the scenes of our former lives, invisible even to ourselves and one another, yet hiding forlorn in lonely places." The sense that Julia occupies a gray world that provides her with no answers, no insight, is underscored by her reference to her "stammering intelligence." She goes on: "O God! what a thing it is to be a ghost, cowering and shivering in an altered world, a prey to apprehension and despair!" Julia's terror and apprehension in the spirit realm are little different from those she experienced on the night of her death. Taken as a whole, her statement can be read as the pitiful disclosures of a soul wandering through eternity, one who has learned to her chagrin that the afterlife is little more than an alienated version of this life. Given Julia's emotional state, the reader has reason to distrust the accuracy of her memories as well as those of her husband and her son.

What, then, does the story add up to? One way of reading "The Moonlit Road" is to see it as an exploration of the effects of the absence of any objectively verifiable truth. Testimony is suspect. Identity is fluid. Motives are unclear. Communication fails. The result is that the story is about the suffering humans undergo when they want to believe that rational explanations for things exist, even if they have to invoke nonrational or supernatural agencies to provide them—only to discover that even the supernatural world fails to provide clarity.

The father says that he caught a glimpse of his wife's ghost on the moonlit road. (© *Lario Tus* | *Shutterstock*)

Bierce was very much a religious sceptic. He called himself an atheist, making clear that his atheism was not a denial of the existence of God but an admission that no one can know whether there is a God. In *The Devil's Dictionary* he defined religion as "a daughter of Hope and Fear, explaining to Ignorance the nature of the Unknowable." "The Moonlit Road" is an exercise in the unknowable and an exercise in the futility of efforts to find anything more than illusory light in a world of darkness and despair.

Source: Michael J. O'Neal, Critical Essay on "The Moonlit Road," in *Short Stories for Students*, Gale, Cengage Learning, 2016.

Cathy N. Davidson

In the following excerpt, Davidson analyzes the structure of "The Moonlit Road."

. . . A still more extended example of separate stories within the story is "The Moonlit Road," which has three distinct subtexts, not two implied ones. The "Statement of Joel Hetman, Jr." is followed by the "Statement of Caspar Grattan" (actually Joel Hetman, Sr., father

of the preceding Joel, but now passing under an assumed name), and then comes the "Statement of the Late Julia Hetman, through the Medium Bayrolles."

These three dubious and self-serving accounts of a murder and its aftermath are variously interconnected but cannot be fitted together to tell the whole story. Instead, they present different cosmologies abstracted from three different interpretations of two separate events. The two events, the facts of the case, can be rearranged in their chronological order and summarized as follows. First, Joel Hetman, Sr. (later to be Caspar Grattan), leaves town ostensibly on a business trip but actually to test the fidelity of his wife. Stealthily returning home before dawn and a day before he was due, the suspicious husband witnesses, he thinks, an absconding lover. Enraged at her infidelity, he kills the wife, whom he finds cowering in a corner of their bedroom. The second event then takes place when Joel, Jr., a student at Yale, comes home from school to help and comfort his bereaved father. A "few months" after Julia's death, as father and son walk down a moonlit road, the

> **TRACING THAT CIRCLE, WE HAVE ALSO PERUSED ONE OF THE MORE UNUSUAL FAMILY PORTRAITS IN ALL SHORT FICTION. THIS ODD THREE-SOME—ONE SURVIVING, ONE DYING, AND ONE DEAD—ARE CONJOINED AS A REPRESENTATIVE GROUPING, THE ESSENTIAL FAMILY, SOCIETY IN MINIATURE."**

father again sees a perturbing visitor who might not be there. He is struck to terror by a presence that the son cannot perceive. The latter, momentarily distracted by a light suddenly visible from the house, turns briefly away, and the father is gone when the son, moments later, looks for him again. That loss, like the mother's murder, remains for the son an unsolvable mystery. The three accounts of these two mysteries constitute an unmitigatedly somber comedy of errors in which the different products of fact, fantasy, and fiction confirm only the defectiveness of human (and even superhuman) vision and communication.

The first narration is provided by the surviving son, who knows nothing definite of either tragedy other than the fact that each occurred. But all he knows is all he needs to know. His inability to resolve either mystery keeps them both ever in mind. He can therefore lament, as he does in the first sentence of his "Statement," the enduring sorrows that render him "the most unfortunate of men." His relative material wealth only adds to his misfortune, for it gives him the leisure to savor more fully his emotional suffering. As he early points out, had my "advantages . . . been denied me . . . [in] the stress of privation and the need of effort I might sometimes forget the somber secret ever baffling the conjecture that it compels." Such self-indulgent self-pity does not inspire the reader's confidence. Yet the son, it should be noted, is the one character who could well be cast as the objective observer capable of solving the double mystery that his parents perpetrate on one another. Some of the evidence whereby he could have done so is clearly present in his account. For example, he notes his father's "jealous and exacting devotion."

The son also reports to the coroner the father's unlikely explanation for his unlikely backdoor, early morning, unexpected return and the fortuitous view of a fleeing man who can fortuitously be blamed for the murdered wife. Later the son observes the fitful and apprehensive nature of his newly bereaved father who would "start visibly and sometimes turn pale" for no apparent reason at all.

Instead of attempting to explain (or choosing to overlook) these minor mysteries that surround the major ones, the son revels in them all. He does so for several reasons. First, he is the son. We can hardly expect him to be objective. But equally important, the son chooses not to make any attempt at objectivity other than dwelling on the objective details. He can declaim about "those terrible finger-marks upon the dead woman's throat—dear God that I might forget them!" despite the fact that he never saw them. Limiting himself to the known facts and trying to work out any clarifying probabilities would spoil his fun. Following the sensible course just described would also force him to define his limited role in the action and to admit how little he actually has observed. He was not there when his mother died; he was not looking when his father disappeared. All he can do is dwell on his cherished inability to resolve the mystery that, years later, he still mourns.

The son's account is succeeded by his father's, which also early strikes a few dubious notes. The "Statement of Caspar Grattan" begins by announcing an intention to commit suicide but soon passes on to other, more interesting matters. The writer imagines some discoverer of his dead body asking of the inert remains, "Who was he?" He even decides to respond in the present to the hypothetical query that he will not hear subsequently: "In this writing I supply the only answer that I am able to make—Caspar Grattan. Surely that should be enough." Yet Grattan goes on at considerable length, giving us both more than and less than enough. We also soon find out that Caspar Grattan is a name he assumed, over twenty years ago, after some tragic event ostensibly wiped the slate of his consciousness so clean that he had seemingly sprung full-grown into the world at that point. Indeed, Grattan sees himself as born as an adult: "One does not remember one's birth—one has to be told. But with me it was different; life came to me full-handed and dowered me with all my faculties and powers." Any "stammering intima-tions that may be memories and may be dreams" refer, he would insist, not to him but to some "previous existence." Here, however, he is less than candid, for he can recount quite clearly what it is that he cannot remember.

Joel Hetman, Sr., alias Caspar Grattan, first tries to avoid those intimations by empha-sizing, very much in the manner of the son, the sorrows of what we might term his Grattanian disguise, what he terms "this *via dolorosa*—this epic of suffering with episodes of sin." Writing his suicide note, he pictures himself at the brink or "eternity" looking back to trace the course of the footprints that have brought him to where he presently stands. Only "twenty years of footprints" are "fairly distinct":

> They lead through poverty and pain, devious and
>   unsure, as
> of one staggering beneath a burden—
> Remote, unfriended, melancholy, slow.
> Ah, the poet's prophecy of Me—how admirable,
>   how
> dreadfully admirable!

Here too we see the self-serving posing that ran through the son's narrative. Who could desire that this heavily burdened man should be more heavily burdened? Yet we also have hints that give Grattan's pose away, the first hint being the very way the character overdra-matizes himself. The reader should observe how inappropriately Grattan proclaims his life to be a *via dolorosa* and the appropriate subject of the poet's art. The internal contradictions of the strained religious and literary allusions (we even get a stirring affirmation of spiritual invincibil-ity from W. H. Henley's "Invictus" incorpo-rated into the rambling goodbye of the man who intends to sink forthwith his own ship) merely reflect a more basic contradiction. This man of imagined sorrows and nebulous grief has conducted a twenty-year charade of suffer-ing in an attempt to hide from himself the real thing. It does not work: as indicated, first, by the forthcoming suicide; as indicated, finally, by the memories that he cannot elude.

He pretends that he does not remember partly because he retrospectively recognizes that he did not see. Later in the "Statement of Caspar Grattan," we learn how Julia Hetman actually died. "Crazed with jealousy and rage, blind and bestial with all the elemental passions of insulted manhood . . . there in the darkness, without a word of accusation or reproach, I

strangled her till she died!" He also pretends that he does not remember partly because later he *did* see what he had done. His "murdered wife" appeared to him with "death in the face" and "marks upon the throat." The two memo-ries are ever present, and he himself notes the appropriateness of the present tense he employs in describing them: "The eyes are fixed on mine with an infinite gravity which is not reproach, nor hate, nor menace, nor anything less terrible than recognition." The only escape is suicide, and on that note his note concludes: "'To Hell for life'—that is a foolish penalty: the culprit chooses the duration of his punishment. To-day my term expires."

Wrong again. As the testimony of his dead wife indicates, death does not resolve the delu-sions of life. It only perpetuates them. "The sum of what we knew at death is the measure of what we know afterwards of all that went before." Julia Hetman, in death, demonstrates the premise that she here voices. She still does not know, for example, that it was her husband who killed her, and so blames "some blind and mindless malevolence." As she was in dying, so is she in death: "O God! what a thing it is to be a ghost, cowering and shivering in an altered world, a prey to apprehension and despair." That state, however, is not simply a continua-tion of her last human emotions. Ghosts fear the living, she explains, as much as the living dread the ghostly visitations of the dead.

That balancing of antipathies brings her to the crux of her recital of her own trials and tribulations, an account that is, surprisingly, more coherent than the two comparable stories provided by her living survivors. Since she did not know that her husband was the blind "mon-ster of the night," she had tried to call to him to save her. Held by love, she remains spectrally present after her death and would continually draw near the husband only to encounter "the terrible eyes of the living, frightening me by the glances that I sought from the purpose that I held." In short, existence is not organized any more advantageously for the dead than for the living. It is not then surprising that what prom-ised to be Julia Hetman's first success as a ghost turns out to be a devastating postmortem failure that strangely parallels her last mortal defeat and her husband's greatest moral failure too. She approaches the husband, who, accompanied by the son, walks in the moonlit road. Since she shines brightest in the moonlight, she hopes that he can at last see her and comprehend her benign intentions instead of starting in fear (as described in the son's narration) whenever he senses her presence. "Love" would "conquer Law": she could "restore the broken bonds between the living and the dead." It does not quite work out that way. The husband knows how those bonds were broken, how lawlessness defeated love. She "moved forward," she reports, "smiling and consciously beautiful." He saw, as already noted, death upon her face, and on her throat the marks of his fingers. He flees like "a hunted animal" leaving her "doubly desolate." Yet she applies that phrasing, at the end of her account, to the son, whom it fits also. The father recounted the way in which he mistakenly removed the mother; the mother has now told how she mistakenly removed the father; and we are left, at the end of the third story, exactly where we were at the beginning, with the suffering son.

Tracing that circle, we have also perused one of the more unusual family portraits in all short fiction. This odd three-some—one surviving, one dying, and one dead—are conjoined as a representative grouping, the essential family, society in miniature. They are what they are through the illusions and delusions that they all worked out together. The living possess a few additional illusions, particularly the hope of a release from the burden of consciousness through the escape of death. The dead know better. As Julia Hetman observes of the dead: "We still dwell in the Valley of the Shadow, lurk in its desolate places, peering from brambles and thickets at its mad, malign inhabitants. How should we have new knowledge of that fading past?" They are all—all the living and all the dead—"mad malign inhabitants" of "the Valley of the Shadow." How could any of them know the whole truth or speak it clearly, even the woman who has shed some of the illusions of life? A grimly comic work, "The Moonlit Road" is one of Bierce's darkest portrayals of human existence—and beyond.

"The Moonlit Road" is also a work in which the comic mode of presentation and the tragic facts of the discourse which make that mode possible go oddly together (and much more oddly in Bierce's time than in ours). As was noted, each character is unintentionally self-revealed through what we might term the humor of his or her recitation. The son is

characterized and made comic by excessive self-pity; the husband by excessive self-justification; the wife by excessive self-romanticizing. Each knows little of the other two, whom each claims to love and presumably knows best, so they can all act at comic cross-purposes. Yet the consequences of those acts and the subjects of the text as a whole are murder, grief, loss, suffering, death—hardly appropriate objects for the reader's amusement. Like numerous twentieth-century writers, Bierce breaks the old rules of decorum. More accurately, he redefines them, suggesting that it is perhaps more appropriate to laugh, with black humor, at the tragic follies of humanity than to suggest that, with sentimentalism, the consequences of such follies can somehow be washed away by cathartic tears. . . .

Source: Cathy N. Davidson, "Perception as Conflict and Confusion," in *The Experimental Fictions of Ambrose Bierce*, University of Nebraska Press, 1984, pp. 88–94.

Cathy N. Davidson

In the following excerpt, Davidson looks at the lack of critical attention paid to Bierce's work.

How many times, and covering a period of how many years, must one's unexplainable obscurity be pointed out to constitute fame? Not knowing, I am almost disposed to consider myself the most famous of authors. I have pretty nearly ceased to be "discovered," but my notoriety as an obscurian may be said to be worldwide and apparently everlasting.— Bierce in a letter to George Sterling

Ambrose Bierce is certainly the most *rediscovered* writer in American literary history. As his letter to George Sterling attests, Bierce himself was well aware of his "notorious obscurity." As the letter, however, does not make clear, Bierce at least partly insured that his reputation would be, in the term of a 1909 reviewer, "underground." For example, Bierce refused to publish his short stories in national magazines that customarily edited contributions to conform to the popular stylistic and sentimental standards of the time, standards that Bierce rightly despised. When an editor of *Metropolitan Magazine* approached him on the matter, the inimitable Ambrose replied: "I know how to write a story . . . for magazine readers for whom literature is too good, but I will not do so so long as stealing is more honorable and interesting." Instead of seeking a national audience Bierce preferred to publish

BIERCE CAN SEEM TO BE AN HISTORICAL
MISFIT. HE CAN ALSO OFFEND MORE
FORMALISTICALLY-ORIENTED CRITICS SUCH AS THE
NEO-ARISTOTELIANS OR THE NEW CRITICS."

his stories in brief collections of limited editions that were often produced by small California presses run mostly by friends who did not insist upon the extensive editing required by many major Eastern-based publishing companies. Furthermore, those stories that were printed by the big houses (Putnam, for example, published *In the Midst of Life—Tales of Soldiers and Civilians* in 1898) were not widely reviewed partly because the work had already appeared earlier elsewhere and partly because Bierce himself was a caustic reviewer who had offended many of the other established reviewers of his day. Neither would Bierce take the standard route to literary prominence and produce novels: "I'll die first!" he insisted. And he did.

Bierce's attitude toward his obscurity was characteristically defiant: "My independence is my wealth; it is my literature." Yet it would be grossly inaccurate to maintain that Bierce really was, in Wilson Follett's phrase, "America's neglected satirist." On the contrary, this "neglected satirist" was one of America's best known—and, by his targets, most hated—newspaper columnists during the 1890s. His vituperative attacks on fellow journalists, on novelists (most notably "Miss Nancy" Howells and "Miss Nancy" James), and on self-serving businessmen and politicians enlivened such newspapers as the San Francisco *Examiner* and the New York *Journal*. His columns were widely read and highly praised by those who did not elicit his eagle-eyed—and eagle-clawed—attention.

Today, of course, Bierce is best known as a short story writer, and Bierce himself seems to have taken somewhat less pride in his journalism than in his other literary endeavors. The twelve volume *Collected Works*, published between 1909 and 1912 and supervised by the author himself, includes relatively little of his estimated four million words of journalistic writing. Disorganized,

inaccurate, incomplete, the *Collected Works* is a collection of undated selections, a scholar's nightmare that has not at all served to preserve Bierce's reputation as a journalist. So it is not surprising that most commentary on Bierce written in the decades since his peculiar "passing" should focus on his fiction. His journalism simply is not accessible to a large audience, although collections such as *The Ambrose Bierce Satanic Reader*, edited by E. J. Hopkins, and Lawrence I. Berkove's recent *Skepticism and Dissent* do give the general reader a sampling of Bierce at his journalistic best.

But if the focus of Bierce criticism is on the fiction, it must be emphasized that such attention has taken an unusual form. We see various literary critics who, at odd intervals and in different generations, "rediscover" the same "lost" writer. As early as 1928 Wilson Follett could note that "nearly all" of the criticism of Bierce begins with the "conviction that in the general purport of Bierce there is something far greater than has yet got itself recognized in American literary history of the official sort." In his fine introduction to a 1957 edition of *The Devil's Dictionary*, Carey McWilliams sounds much the same note when he comments on Bierce's current "rediscovery after long intervals of neglect," a neglect "that continues to the present time." Still more recently, Jeffrey F. Thomas observes that "writers of dissertations on Ambrose Bierce and his works often proclaim their desire to call critical attention to an unjustly neglected artist." Even a cursory survey of the essays in the present collection can affirm one's sense that Bierce criticism does not so much "evolve" as play at "lost and found." Something is clearly wrong here if for nearly seventy-five years the standard essay on Bierce must begin by attempting to reclaim him—again—from critical obscurity.

One can hypothesize that Bierce has enjoyed or endured such a checkered history precisely because his own writing is a mixed bag. Bierce himself delighted in opposing the reigning assumptions of his day. He regularly played the devil's advocate and violated many of the accepted rules of life and art in late nineteenth-century America, the Gilded Age in which he incongruously flourished. And since he broke the rules of his time, he often does not fit our contemporary retrospective categories. The historical critic, for example, might have a difficult time placing Bierce amongst his fellow realists. Bierce, it will be remembered, defined "realism" as "the art of depicting nature as it is seen by toads." Only an *expanded* definition of realism accommodates Bierce's idiosyncratic writing. Thus Howard Bahr, in his fine essay, "Ambrose Bierce and Literary Realism," carefully redefines realism to include the subconscious and inexplicable realms that more traditional realists ignored. As Bahr notes, Bierce himself redefined the reigning literary mode and thought of himself as a *true* realist, a realist who knew that the full measure of reality could not be taken by inchworms.

Neither can Bierce be called a naturalist—at least not without qualification. As such stories as "The Coup de Grâce" and "Chickamauga" amply attest, Bierce's sense of human suffering is certainly as keen as Theodore Dreiser's or Jack London's. Yet Bierce would never fully absolve humans of the responsibility for their own misfortunes by the naturalist's ploy of blaming the environment or "crass Casualty." Nor does Bierce take human mortality with the naturalist's deadly seriousness. As M. E. Grenander shows in "Bierce's Turn of the Screw: Tales of Ironical Terror," Bierce's perspective is generally cosmic, and from that perspective human failings—war, superstition, religion, science—seem paltry, comical. Naturalists are rarely as funny—or as wise—as Bierce.

Nor is Bierce's humor always in good taste (a term he would despise). In some senses he was a black humorist before his time. For example, the story "An Imperfect Conflagration" begins with the memorable line: "Early one June morning in 1872 I murdered my father—an act which made a deep impression on me at the time." The unnamed narrator of the same tale later experiences a certain regret:

> That afternoon I went to the chief of police, told him what I had done and asked his advice. It would be very painful to me if the facts became publicly known. My conduct would be generally condemned; the newspapers would bring it up against me if ever I should run for office. The chief saw the force of these considerations; he was himself an assassin of wide experience.

A reflective patricide operates in a world as absurd as he himself is. Such tales do not represent the forms of humor we commonly associate with the late nineteenth-century and the tall tale tellers or local colorists, writers such as Joel Chandler Harris or Bret Harte.

Bierce can seem to be an historical misfit. He can also offend more formalistically-oriented critics such as the neo-Aristotelians or the New Critics. Intentionally, and blithely, violating the concept of "unity of action" or effect; preferring, it seems, the inappropriate to the fitting; disrupting linear plot lines to give a disjointed rendering of a tale, Bierce does not fit the categories of those who prefer that art be orderly. If, for example, Cleanth Brooks and Robert Penn Warren represent New Criticism at its finest, or at least its most consistent, we can easily see how Bierce's fiction eludes these critics' categories. Brooks and Warren, in their discussion of "An Occurrence at Owl Creek Bridge," discover, despite ample evidence to the contrary, only an action tale with a trick ending. So they dismiss the whole story as if Bierce were some inept O. Henry. As F. J. Logan points out in his essay on this same story, these critics did not read the story with the attention to detail that the New Critic is supposed to prize. They should have discovered that, as Logan puts it, "the ending is in the beginning and throughout." The story is all of a piece but the piece is more complicated than their terms will admit.

Bierce has eluded standard critical categories, but he certainly has not eluded a popular audience. Presently his fiction is available in several editions and virtually every anthology of short fiction intended for classroom use includes a Bierce story or two. But despite the many attempts that have been made to elevate him into the "canon" of major American writers, he still is not generally accorded that status. As already suggested, one reason for the exclusion is the fact that Bierce's fiction does not fit readily into standard critical categories. Another might be that his corpus, as a fiction writer, amounts to less than one hundred stories, not a substantial hook upon which to hang the designation of "major" writer. Bierce is, and may well remain, a "major minor" or "minor major" writer—which means that he will undoubtedly continue to enjoy a wide popular appeal and will also be the subject of many more essays which attempt at the outset to oust him from his half-respectable niche into the full light of acceptability—an elevation which the

FUNDAMENTALLY, THIS EFFECT OF IRONICAL TERROR DEPENDS ON A FIRM GRASP OF THE CONNECTION AMONG INTELLECTUAL, EMOTIONAL, AND SENSORY FACTORS IN THE HUMAN PERSONALITY. IN BIERCE'S TALES OF IRONICAL TERROR, A CHARACTER'S REACTION TO GIVEN CIRCUMSTANCES INVOLVES ALL THREE OF THESE FACTORS."

man himself would have abhorred. The reader versed in Bierce will recall that that master of aphorisms defined "famous" as "conspicuously miserable." . . .

Source: Cathy N. Davidson, "Introduction," in *Critical Essays on Ambrose Bierce*, G. K. Hall, 1982, pp. 1–4.

M. E. Grenander

In the following excerpt, Grenander gives an overview of Bierce's horror stories.

. . . Most of Bierce's mimetic tales of passion are those of ironical terror (including "An Occurrence at Owl Creek Bridge," "Chickamauga," "One of the Missing," "One Officer, One Man," and "The Man and the Snake"). In these stories, Bierce combined irony with terror in a specific way. In any terror tale, the emotional effect is basically an intense degree of fear. To this fear, Bierce adds, in these tales, an ironic twist, which rests primarily on a certain kind of relationship between plot and character, so that the reader feels an intense fear coupled with a bitter realization that it is cruelly inappropriate.

Fundamentally, this effect of ironical terror depends on a firm grasp of the connection among intellectual, emotional, and sensory factors in the human personality. In Bierce's tales of ironical terror, a character's reaction to given circumstances involves all three of these factors. First, he has an intellectual awareness of a dangerous situation—typically one which he believes threatens his life or his honor. Second, this knowledge arouses in him an emotion of fear, it deepens to terror, and frequently thence to madness. Third,

this emotional involvement results in a particular kind of physical reaction—usually a tremendous heightening and acceleration of sensory perceptions, the latter often indicated by a slowing-up of subjective time.

Obviously the base of this psychology is the intellectual awareness of danger. Bierce, however, makes the intellectual awareness on which the whole psychology of his protagonist's terror rests a wrong one; hence all the emotional and sensory reactions which follow are erroneous, and the reader's perception of this gruesome inappropriateness to the real situation is what gives their peculiar distillation of horror to these tales.

Since the situation in terror stories must arouse fear, it must either be dangerous or be thought dangerous. Bierce's best tales of ironical terror can be divided into two groups: those in which the actual situation is harmful, with the protagonist conceiving it to be harmless and reacting accordingly; and those in which the actual situation is harmless, with the protagonist conceiving it to be harmful and reacting accordingly. In either of these groups, the reader may share the protagonist's misconception, not discovering the truth until the end of the story; or he may realize all along that the protagonist is wrong. What the reader's grasp of events will be is controlled by the narration.

In the first category are such stories as "An Occurrence at Owl Creek Bridge" and "Chickamauga." In "Owl Creek Bridge," Peyton Farquhar, a captured guerrilla on the point of being hanged, undergoes sensations at first "unaccompanied by thought. The intellectual part of his nature was already effaced; he had power only to feel." Suddenly, however, "the power of thought was restored; he knew that the rope had broken and he had fallen into the stream. . . . His brain was as energetic as his arms and legs; he thought with the rapidity of lightning." He thinks (wrongly) that he has made a miraculous last-minute escape from being hanged.

The lost child in "Chickamauga," whose mother has been killed and whose home has been destroyed in battle, believes that the group of maimed and bleeding soldiers he comes upon is "a merry spectacle," one reminding him "of the painted clown whom he had seen last summer in the circus." He fails to recognize his home when he sees its blazing ruins, and he also thinks them a pleasing sight.

Thus in both stories the protagonist thinks himself safe in what is really a harmful situation. Accompanying his intellectual misunderstanding are emotional reactions which are painfully *mal à propos*. Farquhar eagerly makes his way homeward (he thinks), joyfully anticipating a reunion with his wife. The boy in "Chickamauga" has a gay time playing with the pitiful specimens he comes upon, "heedless . . . of the dramatic contrast between his laughter and their own ghastly gravity." He even tries to ride pig-a-back on one of the crawling and broken soldiers, and he dances with glee about the flaming embers of his home.

In both stories the protagonist also has unusual physical reactions. Farquhar's senses are preternaturally acute: "Something in the awful disturbance of his organic system had so exalted and refined them that they made record of things never before perceived." He feels each ripple of water on his face; he sees the veining of individual leaves in the forest on the river bank, the insects on them, and the prismatic colors of the dew in the grass. He even sees through the rifle sights the eye of the man on the bridge who is firing at him. And he hears "the humming of the gnats. . . ; the beating of the dragon-flies' wings, the strokes of the water-spiders' legs," the rush of a fish's body. Accompanying these perceptions is the slowing of time; the interval between his falling and suffocating is "ages," and the ticking of his watch is so strong and sharp it "hurt[s] his ear like the thrust of a knife."

The "Chickamauga" boy, on the other hand, has senses which are subnormally dull. He is a deaf-mute, which accounts for his sleeping through the battle: "all unheard by him were the roar of the musketry, the shock of the cannon." When he recognizes the torn and mangled body of his dead mother, and a belated understanding bursts upon him, he can express himself only by "a series of inarticulate and indescribable cries—something between the chattering of an ape and the gobbling of a turkey—a startling, soulless, unholy sound, the language of a devil."

In "An Occurrence at Owl Creek Bridge," the reader, unless he be extremely acute, does not realize the true state of affairs until the end of the story, although, as Lawrence Berkove

points out in a perceptive analysis, the narrator gives some clues which the reader can subsequently find. In "Chickamauga," the reader is constantly aware of the true situation and of the irony of the boy's reaction to it.

In the second group of stories—represented by "One of the Missing," "The Man and the Snake," and "One Officer, One Man"—the technique of ironic terror is reversed. A basically harmless (or at least, not very harmful) situation is misinterpreted as an extremely perilous one. The protagonist has not only all the emotional reactions which would be appropriate to terrible danger but also (as in the stories of the first group) unusual physical sensations; and the story concludes with his death.

Jerome Searing, a scout in "One of the Missing," recovers consciousness to find himself lying trapped in a wrecked shanty; he faces the muzzle of his own rifle, pointed directly at his forehead. Convinced that the gun is still loaded and set on a hair-trigger, as it was before he was knocked senseless, he believes that it will go off if he makes the slightest move.

In "One Officer, One Man," Captain Graffenreid, under fire for the first time in a minor engagement, not only misinterprets his situation but his own character. Thinking himself a courageous man, "his spirit was buoyant, his faculties were riotous. He was in a state of mental exaltation." But after the shooting starts, "his conception of war" undergoes "a profound change. . . . The fire of battle was not now burning very brightly in this warrior's soul. From inaction had come introspection. He sought rather to analyze his feelings than distinguish himself by courage and devotion. The result was profoundly disappointing." In his change from ignorance to knowledge of his own character, he realizes his cowardice; but he still thinks he is in a dangerous battle.

Harker Brayton in "The Man and the Snake" is the guest of a distinguished herpetologist who keeps his collection of serpents at home. One evening, when Brayton is sitting in his room reading, he glimpses a snake under the bed. He thinks the reptile is trying to hypnotize him with its malevolent glare. At first he is "more keenly conscious of the incongruous nature of the situation than affected by its perils; it was revolting, but absurd." He thinks of calling the servant, but it occurs to him "that the act might subject him to the suspicion of fear, which he certainly did not feel." Then he considers the offensive qualities of the snake: "These thoughts shaped themselves with greater or less definition in Brayton's mind and begot action. The process is what we call consideration and decision. It is thus that we are wise and unwise." But, when he over-estimates his own powers of emotional resistance, he makes a fatal mistake: "I am not so great a coward as to fear to seem to myself afraid."

In all these cases, the protagonist reacts emotionally to what he thinks is a situation of extreme jeopardy. Jerome Searing is a brave man; and, as he creeps forward on his scouting expedition, his pulse is "as regular, his nerves . . . as steady as if he were trying to trap a sparrow." When he sees the rifle pointed at his head and remembers he has left it cocked, he is "affected with a feeling of uneasiness. But that was as far as possible from fear." Gradually, however, he becomes conscious of a dull ache in his forehead; when he opens his eyes, it goes away; when he closes them, it comes back. He grows more and more terrified. As he stares at the gun barrel, the pain in his forehead deepens; he lapses into unconsciousness and delirium: "Jerome Searing, the man of courage, the formidable enemy, the strong, resolute warrior, was as pale as a ghost. His jaw was fallen; his eyes protruded; he trembled in every fibre; a cold sweat bathed his entire body; he screamed with fear. He was not insane—he was terrified."

Captain Graffenreid, as he hears his men laughing at his cowardice, burns with "a fever of shame" and "the whole range of his sensibilities" is affected. "The strain upon his nervous organization was insupportable." Agitation also grips Brayton, though he is a reasonable man. The snake's horrible power over his imagination increases his fear; and he, too, finally screams with terror.

In these stories, as in those of the first group, the protagonists react with unusual physical sensations. Searing "had not before observed how light and feathery" the tops of the distant trees were, "nor how darkly blue the sky was, even among their branches, where they somewhat paled it with their green. . . . He heard the singing of birds, the strange metallic note of the meadow lark." Time slows, space contracts, and he becomes nothing but a bundle of sensations: "No thoughts of home, of wife and children, of country, of glory. The whole record of

memory was effaced. The world had passed away—not a vestige remained. Here in this confusion of timbers and boards is the sole universe. Here is immortality in time—each pain an everlasting life. The throbs tick off eternities."

Captain Graffenreid, in his state of terror, grows "hot and cold by turns," pants like a dog, and forgets to breathe "until reminded by vertigo." Harker Brayton is also affected physically; when he means to retreat, he finds that he is unaccountably walking slowly forward. "The secret of human action is an open one: something contracts our muscles. Does it matter if we give to the preparatory molecular changes the name of will?" His face takes on "an ashy pallor," he drops his chair and groans: "He heard, somewhere, the continuous throbbing of a great drum, with desultory bursts of far music, inconceivably sweet, like the tones of an aeolian harp. . . . The music ceased; rather, it became by insensible degrees the distant roll of a retreating thunder-storm. A landscape, glittering with sun and rain, stretched before him, arched with a vivid rainbow framing in its giant curve a hundred visible cities." The landscape seems to rise up and vanish; he has fallen on the floor. His face white and bloody, his eyes strained wide, his mouth dripping with flakes of froth, he wriggles toward the snake in convulsive movements.

All three men die of their fright: Brayton and Searing, from sheer panic; Graffenreid, a suicide because he can no longer tolerate the disorganization of his nervous system. But all their terror and pain were needless—Searing's rifle had already been discharged; Graffenreid's battle was a mere skirmish; Brayton's snake was only a stuffed one with shoe-button eyes. In these stories, as in "Chickamauga" and in "An Occurrence at Owl Creek Bridge," Bierce has given the terror tale an ironic turn of the screw. . . .

Source: M. E. Grenander, "Mimetic Tales of Passion," in *Ambrose Bierce*, Twayne, 1971, pp. 93–99.

SOURCES

"Ambrose Bierce," in *Merriam-Webster's Encyclopedia of Literature*, Merriam-Webster, 1995, p. 138.

Bierce, Ambrose, "The Moonlit Road," in *Ambrose Bierce: The Devil's Dictionary, Tales, & Memoirs,* edited by S. T. Joshi, Library of America, 2011, pp. 239–47.

———, "Religion," in *Collected Works*, Vol. 7, *The Devil's Dictionary*, Neale Publishing, 1911, p. 283.

Cooper, Frederic Taber, "Ambrose Bierce: An Appraisal," in *Critical Essays on Ambrose Bierce*, edited by Cathy N. Davidson, G. K. Hall, 1982, pp. 35, 37; originally published in *Bookman*, Vol. 33, July 1911, pp. 471–80.

Davidson, Cathy N., *The Experimental Fictions of Ambrose Bierce: Structuring the Ineffable*, University of Nebraska Press, 1984, p. 94.

Day, Leon, *My Hunt for Ambrose Bierce*, August 8, 2007, http://donswaim.com/bierce.leon.day-6.html (accessed August 7, 2015).

Gale, Robert L., *An Ambrose Bierce Companion*, Greenwood, 2001, p. 55.

Grenander, M. E., *Ambrose Bierce*, Twayne Publishers, 1971, p. 79.

Griffin, Martin, "The Moonlit Road," in *Ambrose Bierce Project Journal*, Vol. 2, No. 1, Fall 2006, http://www.ambrosebierce.org/journal2griffin.html (accessed August 9, 2015).

"History of Modern Spiritualism," BBC, October 28, 2009, http://www.bbc.co.uk/religion/religions/spiritualism/history/history.shtml (accessed August 11, 2015).

History of the Spiritualist Movement," Church of the Living Spirit website, http://www.churchofthelivingspirit.com (accessed August 8, 2015).

Joshi, S. T., ed., "Chronology," in *Ambrose Bierce: The Devil's Dictionary, Tales, & Memoirs*, Library of America, 2011, pp. 841–50.

"Old West Legends: Ghost Stories from the Old West," Legends of America website, http://www.legendsofamerica.com/we-ghoststories.html (accessed August 13, 2015).

Review of *Can Such Things Be?*, in *Athenaeum*, No. 4311, June 11, 1910, p. 702.

Richards, Rand, ed., *Haunted San Francisco: Ghost Stories from the City's Past*, Heritage House Publishers, 2004.

Robinson, B. A., "New Age Spirituality," 2011, Religious Tolerance: Ontario Consultants on Religious Tolerance website, http://www.religioustolerance.org/newage.htm (accessed August 8, 2015).

Saunders, Richard, *Ambrose Bierce: The Making of a Misanthrope*, Chronicle Books, 1985, pp. 68–69.

Stollznow, Karen, "New Age Spiritualism: I Still Haven't Found What I'm Looking For," in *Skeptical Inquirer*, October 12, 2009, http://www.csicop.org/specialarticles/show/new_age_spiritualism_i_still_havent_found_what_im_looking_for (accessed August 12, 2015).

Sword, Helen, *Ghostwriting Modernism*, Cornell University Press, 2012, p. 2.

Woodruff, Stuart C., *The Short Stories of Ambrose Bierce: A Study in Polarity*, University Pittsburgh Press, 1964, p. 123.

FURTHER READING

Dalby, Richard, ed., *The Mammoth Book of Victorian and Edwardian Ghost Stories*, Carroll & Graf, 1995.

This volume is part of a series of "mammoth" volumes of ghost stories. It contains not only "The Moonlit Road" but also ghost stories by such other major nineteenth- and early-twentieth-century writers as Charles Dickens, Sheridan Le Fanu, Henry James, and Bram Stoker, along with such lesser-known figures as Rhoda Broughton, Amelia B. Edwards, and Lettice Galbraith. Other volumes in the series include *The Mammoth Book of Ghost Stories*, *The Mammoth Book of Haunted House Stories*, and *The Mammoth Book of 20th-Century Ghost Stories*.

Gale, Robert L., ed., *An Ambrose Bierce Companion*, Greenwood, 2001.

This volume includes an opening essay that presents an overview of Bierce's contributions to literature and journalism. A chronology summarizes the key events in his life. Most of the book consists of alphabetically arranged entries on Bierce's major works and characters and on historical persons and writers who figured prominently in his life and career.

Joshi, S. T., and David E. Schultz, eds., *A Much Misunderstood Man: Selected Letters of Ambrose Bierce*, Ohio State University Press, 2003.

Bierce remains widely known as a cynic whose acerbic writings skewered numerous victims, but this selection of letters tries to reveal another side of his personality. Among the letters are those that reveal his reactions to the untimely deaths of his two sons, his care for his daughter, his interest in the writers who lionized him, and flirtatious letters he often wrote to female correspondents.

Morris, Roy, Jr., *Ambrose Bierce: Alone in Bad Company*, Crown, 1996.

In this biography of the author, Morris draws parallels between Bierce's dark vision and his unhappy life. Morris notes that Bierce suffered a lonely and unhappy childhood in Indiana. These feelings intensified during the Civil War. The book goes on to trace Bierce's career as a newspaperman and his troubled relationships with others, including his wife.

St. Pierre, Brian, ed., *The Devil's Advocate: An Ambrose Bierce Reader*, Chronicle Books, 1987.

Readers interested in a sampling of Bierce's work in different genres will find this volume valuable. It includes the complete text of *The Devil's Dictionary* and *Write it Right*. Also included are Civil War stories, tales of the supernatural, and some of Bierce's essays.

SUGGESTED SEARCH TERMS

Ambrose Bierce

Ambrose Bierce AND Collected Works

Ambrose Bierce AND "The Moonlit Road"

Can Such Things Be? AND Bierce

Cosmopolitan magazine AND Bierce

ghost stories

gothic literature

spiritualism

Western American literature

William Randolph Hearst

Open Secrets

ALICE ANN MUNRO

1993

Originally published in the *New Yorker* magazine in February 1993 before lending its name to the collection *Open Secrets* (1994), Alice Munro's story "Open Secrets" continues her long and acclaimed tradition of subtle, multilayered, and open-ended narratives. Exploring a small town's reaction to the disappearance of a new girl, Heather Bell, during an annual overnight hike to a local waterfall, the story reveals the dark underbelly of a town riddled with rumor, gossip, and a long-established power structure. Townspeople are judged heavily by where they are born, who their relatives are, and what decisions they have made.

Alice Munro is widely recognized as one of the finest story writers of her generation. She has been celebrated with the 2013 Nobel Prize in Literature and the 2009 Man Booker International Prize, and she has won every major literary award in Canada at least once. Both a stamp and a coin have been issued in her honor.

AUTHOR BIOGRAPHY

Alice Ann Munro (born Alice Ann Laidlaw) was born on July 10, 1931, in Wingham, Ontario, Canada, to Annie Clarke and Robert Eric Laidlaw. Her mother was a teacher, and her father was a fox and mink farmer who later turned to poultry farming. Alice studied English and journalism for

Alice Munro (© *ZUMA Press, Inc. | Alamy*)

two years at the University of Western Ontario before heading west to Vancouver in 1951 with her new husband, James Munro. The couple eventually relocated to Victoria, on Vancouver Island, where they opened Munro's Books. The couple had three daughters (Sheila, born in 1953; Jenny, 1957; and Andrea, 1966) before divorcing in 1972. Munro returned to Ontario, where she married cartographer Gerald Fremlin in 1976; he passed away in 2013.

Munro's first collection of stories, *Dance of the Happy Shades* (1968), launched her career strongly, winning the Governor General's Award. This initial success was followed by two series of interlinked stories: *Lives of Girls and Women* (1971) and *Who Do You Think You Are?* (1978); the latter was published in the United States under the title *The Beggar Maid: Stories of Flo and Rose*. The 1980s saw Munro establish a pattern of publishing first versions of her stories in such magazines as the *New Yorker, Atlantic Monthly, Grand Street, Harper's Magazine*, and *Paris Review* before collecting them in book form. The story "Open Secrets," for instance, appeared in the *New Yorker* magazine

before appearing as the title story of her collection *Open Secrets* (1994). Later collections include *Hateship, Friendship, Courtship, Loveship, Marriage* (2001), *The View from Castle Rock* (2006), and *Too Much Happiness* (2009). Her stories have been translated into more than a dozen languages.

Munro's career has been marked by an impressive collection of prestigious awards. She was the recipient of the 2013 Nobel Prize in Literature and the 2009 Man Booker International Prize. She is also a three-time winner of Canada's Governor General's Award (1968, 1978, and 1986), a two-time winner of the Giller Prize (1998 and 2004), and winner of the Man Booker International Prize (2009) and the 2004 Rogers Writer's Trust Fiction Prize. Related honors include recognition as a Foreign Honorary Member of the American Academy of Arts and Letters (1992) and Knight of the Order of Arts and Letters (2014). She has also had both a silver coin (2014) and a postage stamp (2015) issued in honor of her Nobel Prize.

PLOT SUMMARY

Set in the small town of Carstairs, Ontario, in 1965, the story begins with a short poem that sets the scene as seven girls, chaperoned by Miss Johnstone, head off on an annual overnight camping trip to a local river falls as part of the Canadian Girls in Training (CGIT) program. It then shifts to the memories of Frances Wall, who recounts an incident during the hike, at a farmhouse, when several of the girls sprayed each other with hoses. The story is remembered now as an example of the particularly bad behavior of one of the girls, Heather Bell. Frances goes on to emphasize that however much people might want to believe they know what happened that day, stories and facts tell different versions. Frances in turn tells her cousin and employer Maureen Stephens about the events of that day, including much speculation about what happened to Heather.

The story shifts to a description of the Falls on the Peregrine River, which was the goal of the overnight hike, as well as the place from which Heather disappeared. Six other girls have also made the trip. The story moves fluidly back and forth in time, from the twenty-four-hour period following Heather's disappearance to a brief history of the CGIT hike, which has been going on for decades, though with fewer girls each year.

Maureen's story becomes the next layer of "Open Secrets." She is her husband's second wife. They live in a house along with Frances, who is their maid. The relationship between the two women is strained, as Frances is known to be an incessant, malicious gossip, which makes Maureen uncomfortable.

Shifting from Maureen to Mary Johnstone, the story continues creating a history of a small town that is deeply judgmental and full of storytelling, innuendo, and rumor-mongering. It is a town, as the title of the story suggests, that contains many secrets, both real and imagined. As Maureen's husband describes it, the town is full of "gossip, rumor, [and] the cold-hearted thrill of catastrophe."

The story returns to the morning of the hike, which traditionally began before breakfast and included a first stop at a favorite place for locals known as the Rock. It is at this first stop that Heather Bell realizes she has forgotten her sweater and, with Miss Johnstone's permission, heads back to get it. When she does not return

MEDIA ADAPTATIONS

- The collection *Open Secrets* was released as an audiobook by the Canadian National Institute for the Blind in 2004. Read by Sandra Scott, it is available in CD format with a running time of eight hours and fifty-seven minutes.

and is not found at the camp, Miss Johnstone launches only a superficial search, believing that Heather is simply up to mischief. Even when Heather does not reappear, Miss Johnstone does not allow the girls to search extensively or sound an alarm with the townspeople. Only when Mr. Trowell delivers ice cream to the camp does the story of Heather's disappearance comes to light, which involves the town in the search.

The conversation and remembering are cut short when Maureen's husband calls her, and the story shifts to a recounting of the couple's story and of his placement in the town's social life. Maureen slips back in time, recalling her adventures as part of the CGIT hike from twenty years earlier. She remembers the games of Truth or Dare, and the noisy evening spent with the other girls on the trip. When Maureen goes to the post office later that afternoon to mail her husband's correspondence, she hears two stories that might or might not relate to Heather's disappearance: the story of a girl who was seen getting into a car just outside of town and the story of some people cleaning up a family grave who reported hearing a scream in the middle of the afternoon. Stories accumulate around the disappearance: a man carrying a knife or gun had abducted her. She met a stranger or friend at a predetermined place and time.

The next morning, when Frances and Maureen are getting breakfast prepared for the household, Marian Slater and her husband arrive. He is a younger man she had married only a few years earlier. They have come to Mr. Stephens, a retired lawyer, to talk about Heather's disappearance.

Marian tells a story about an incident that had happened a few days before, while her husband was tending their cows while she lay down after taking some painkillers for a recent minor surgery. She was awakened by the family dog barking at something in their yard. Stepping outside, she saw the dog welcoming Mr. Siddicup, a town eccentric who was known to walk across private property without caring. His behavior, readers are told, had rapidly deteriorated after a battle with cancer and the death of his wife. He is known in the town as a man of questionable hygiene and an equally questionable grasp on sanity. In Mrs. Slater's story, he was more agitated than usual; he tried to communicate something of importance to her but failed, unable to get words out from his damaged throat.

Trying to communicate with actions rather than words, he drew water from the yard's pump, then threw himself under it as though replicating a waterfall. He then pointed in the general direction of the bush and river. Thinking that he wanted a cup to drink water, Marian went into her kitchen, returning with a cup and some graham crackers. By this time, though, Mr. Siddicup had disappeared from the yard. Later, Marian remembered that Miss Johnstone had stopped by with the girls on the previous Saturday morning, and that the girls had cooled off with their hose and behaved rambunctiously. Connecting the girls with the sudden, erratic appearance of Mr. Siddicup, Marian and her husband have come to the lawyer to get his advice on what to do next. He tells them to take their information to the police.

As she listens to Marian's story, Maureen thinks of the many reasons that the townspeople found Mr. Siddicup an unsettling presence, most notably his collection of clothes: "Women's clothes, underwear—old frayed slips and brassières and worn-out underpants and nubbly stockings, hanging from the backs of chairs or from a line above the heater, or just in a heap on the table." And while Maureen approaches this knowledge with reason and logic, she knows, too, that the clothes "were there week after week." Suspicions surround him: "Did he leave them lying around to suggest things? Did he put them on himself next to his skin? Was he a pervert?"

When Marian and her husband leave the house, heading in the direction of the police station but never going into it, Maureen sits quietly with her husband and reflects. She thinks, too, about her own past and her relationship with her husband, which had become absent of physical intimacy following a miscarriage early in their marriage. When he calls her to his bedroom following Marian's visit, Maureen is hopeful for some physical contact, but she is taken aback by the fact that his sexual appetite had returned with new levels of aggression and control that made her feel dirty and feeble. She describes the sex as a "rampage," and puts it out of her mind when she turns to the kitchen.

Working in the kitchen, Maureen thinks back again to the CGIT hike she had taken, and of the story that Miss Johnstone had delivered as part of the overnight adventure. Miss Johnstone had recounted how Jesus had visited her when she was battling polio and inspired her to not give in to the disease. She then talked with the girls on the hike about how vices, including sex, could ruin a life. Maureen contemplates how her own life is not one of her own choosing or making, and how it, too, hides secrets both benign and sadistic.

The story concludes with a series of realizations, confessions, and admissions. The first is that Heather Bell will never be found, and her mystery will go unsolved. The second is that the town's belief that Mr. Siddicup had something to do with Heather's disappearance has grown exponentially, especially when he is eventually committed to a mental health facility nearby. The third is that Miss Johnstone continues to explain her actions on that fateful day, until she is told that the story of Heather Bell is no longer worth retelling.

Finally, Maureen admits to herself that she is passing time waiting for her husband to die so that she can move on with her life with a more gentle man in a house that is open to new discoveries and new joys.

CHARACTERS

Heather Bell

Heather Bell, a new girl in town, disappears mysteriously during the annual CGIT overnight hike to the Falls at Peregrine River. Although she is the subject of many stories and rumors, little is known about her other than the fact that she disappears on a Saturday morning and that her story will never be finished.

Ginny Bos

Ginny Bos is one of the girls who takes part in the overnight hike to the Falls on Peregrine River during which Heather Bell disappears. Known by the town as a "double-jointed monkey" who loves swimming and horsing around, she lives next door to the chaperone, Miss Johnstone. She is mentioned only briefly in the story.

Lucille Chambers

Lucille Chambers is one of the girls who takes part in the overnight hike to the Falls on Peregrine River during which Heather Bell disappears. She a minister's daughter and is mentioned only briefly in the story.

Mary Johnstone

Miss Johnstone is the leader and chaperone of the annual overnight hike to the falls. Now in her sixties, she had been leading the hike of the CGIT for many years. Having survived polio at the age thirteen or fourteen, she is described as having "short legs, a short, thick body, crooked shoulders, and a slightly twisted neck, which kept her big head a little tilted to one side." A bookkeeper by training, she spends her spare time working with girls from the town, whom she attempts to keep pure through her stories about religion and chastity. Even after the disappearance of Heather Bell has passed from the headlines, she continues to try to justify her actions on the day to all who will listen.

Robin Sands

Robin Sands is one of the girls who takes part in the overnight hike to the Falls on Peregrine River during which Heather Bell disappears. She is a doctor's daughter and is mentioned only briefly in the story.

Mr. Siddicup

Mr. Siddicup first appears in Marian Slater's story. At one time, he worked as a piano tuner; he was then "a dignified, sarcastic little Englishman, with a pleasant wife." Having survived an operation on his throat that left him unable to talk, "just make wheezing and growling noises," he had gone into a spiral of deterioration following the death of his wife. Once a decent man, he is now "a morose and rather disgusting old urchin" with "dirty whiskers, dribbles on his clothes, a sour smoky smell, and a look in his eyes of constant suspicion, sometimes of loathing." Antisocial in the extreme, he just walks the roads around the town. Later he is sent to a local asylum, leaving behind a swirling mass of gossip about his imagined role in Heather Bell's disappearance.

Marian Slater (née Hubbert)

Marian Slater visits Mr. Stephens, a lawyer, one morning. She is a local farmer who also makes made-to-measure corsets, who is rumored to have secured her new husband via an advertisement. After an encounter with an agitated Mr. Siddicup in the days following Heather Bell's disappearance, she comes with her husband to see Mr. Stephens for advice on how to share the information that she has. A victim of the malicious gossip that defines the town, she does not treat Mr. Siddicup with the same disdain that the rest of the townspeople do.

Mr. Theo Slater

Mr. Theo Slater is the younger husband of Mrs. Slater, who finds him through a newspaper ad following the death of her parents. An outsider to the town, he is seen as an oddity and tolerated only because of his wife's status, however limited, as a member of one of the town's longest family lines.

Gordon Stephens

Gordon Stephens is Mr. Stephens's son from his first marriage. He teaches at a military college and returns home often with his wife and children.

Helena Stephens

Helena Stephens is Mr. Stephens's daughter from his first marriage. She is single, rarely returns home to visit, and tends to be argumentative when she does.

Maureen Stephens (née Coulter)

Maureen is the second wife of the former lawyer of the town, who is established as a pinnacle of reason and power. With no children of her own, she is still seen as a country girl who benefited from a lucky marriage, given that her family had been labeled as "country" (or being of a country lineage, with its implication of lower social status) within the town hierarchy many generations ago. She is a tall, healthy woman with "rosy skin and auburn hair." Her husband's nickname for her is Jewel, but she does not feel like one under his oppressive control of the household and sadistic control of her body. She finds herself drawn into the speculation of the town surrounding Heather Bell's death, which leads her to reflect upon the realities of her own life and how she has been affected by those around her. She ends the story admitting to herself that she is actually only passing time until her husband dies, at which point she can carry her secrets into a new relationship in a new town.

Mr. Stephens

Mr. Stephens is Maureen's husband. He is sixty-nine years old, and he had suffered a stroke two years before the events of the story. Now retired, he was once the town's most respected lawyer, and he is still known as Lawyer Stephens. He is known around town as a man of few words and high principles. He holds considerable power in the town, and, as Maureen acknowledges, he knows when to use this power and when to hold it back. He is also an emotionless man "who detested tears above all things," but he finds pleasure in the physical domination of his wife.

Mary Kaye Trevelyan

Mary Kaye is one of the girls on the overnight hike, who recounts a version of Heather's behavior during the hose incident. She is the granddaughter of Frances Wall and is mentioned only briefly in the story.

Betsy Trowell

Betsy Trowell is one of the girls on the overnight hike to the Falls during which Heather Bell disappears. Betsy and her sister Eva are known throughout the town as the country girls who are part of the CGIT hike. She is mentioned only briefly in the story.

Eva Trowell

Eva Trowell is one of the girls on the overnight hike to the Falls during which Heather Bell disappears. She is mentioned only briefly in the story.

Frances Wall

Frances is Maureen's cousin, though she is nearly a generation older. She lives in Maureen's house as the maid. She is described as "a dumpling sort of woman with gray hair like brambles all over her head, and a plain, impudent face" who is known for her "mean remarks, and wild, uncharitable, confident speculations."

Mr. Trowell

Mr. Trowell (the name is spelled both as Trowell and Trowel in the story) is the father of Betsy and Eva and the first person from the town on the scene following Heather's disappearance, although his presence is inadvertent. He comes to deliver ice cream, only to discover a girl has gone missing from the group.

THEMES

Female-Male Relations

As she does in many of her stories, in "Open Secrets" Munro explores how ideas of femininity and femaleness collide with ideas of masculinity and male power. The women of the story relate to men in a narrow range of ways. Miss Johnstone, for instance, has never married, and she chooses to see men through the prism of her religious faith, which positions them as either saviors (Jesus) or more commonly as threats to female virtue and honor. Others, like Frances Wall, tend to see men as the epitome of dignity (Lawyer Stephens) or perverts (Mr. Siddicup) even though there is evidence to the contrary in each case.

The relations between men and women within marriage are equally complicated in "Open Secrets." Although she spends her days caring for her husband in his failing health, Maureen is subjected to emotional and physical abuse from him. In a more subtle diminishing of power, Marian Slater's husband remains unnamed and referred to only as "he" by both his wife and the rest of the town. Brought into the town, so the story goes, in response to an advertisement, he is a newcomer who will never achieve even the status worthy of a formal name.

Rumor

Rumors and gossip abound in this story. Rumors may or may not be true, but they circulate quickly among people and often cause distress or real damage to the people who are their subjects. As Maureen comes to understand soon after the disappearance of Heather Bell, once rumors are fabricated, they cannot be undone. More unsettling is the fact, as she learns through her conversation with Frances Wall, that rumors can be spread without any connection to reality, and that they can very quickly lead to unfair judgment of an individual.

The town in "Open Secrets" seems to thrive on unsupported stories and "the coldhearted thrill of catastrophe." From Frances's tendency to make "wild, uncharitable, confident speculations" to Maureen's own thoughts about Mr. Siddicup, the town's reality is shaped by the

TOPICS FOR FURTHER STUDY

- Ted Solotaroff writes in the *Nation* that "one of Munro's strengths, as well as a source of her appeal, is that she is so firmly rooted" in what he calls "an older feminist sensibility." Express your agreement or disagreement with this statement in a well-structured and carefully detailed blog post. What do you think Solotaroff means by "an older feminist sensibility," for instance, and where do you find examples of it in "Open Secrets"? Hint: Margaret Walters's *Feminism: A Very Short Introduction* (2005) is a wonderfully quick read that will shed light on what Solotaroff means by an older (or first-wave) feminism and a more contemporary (or second-wave) feminism. Upload your post to a blog and allow your classmates to comment on it.

- "Open Secrets" develops a clear sense of place (the geography of the town) and of the connections between people, and between people and specific locations. On a poster-size piece of paper, create a map of the town and its surrounding area from the evidence provided in the story.

- Andre Dubus III, in a review in *America*, suggests that one of the defining characteristics of Munro's stories is the recognition that "the only constant is change and within that lies mystery upon mystery." Another writer about whom this can be said is the southern Gothic writer Flannery O'Connor. Read O'Connor's "The Comforts of Home"

(suitable for young-adult readers) and write an essay in which you compare and contrast the sense of mystery that exists in each story.

- In many ways, "Open Secrets" is reminiscent of David Lynch's cult classic *Twin Peaks*, a short-lived (1990–1991) television series that followed an idiosyncratic FBI agent who investigates the murder of a young woman in the secretive and equally idiosyncratic town of Twin Peaks. An important part of the atmosphere that Lynch created for the series was his use of music and songs (most notably the voice of Julee Cruise). Imagine that you have been asked to create a soundtrack for a short film based on "Open Secrets." Create a playlist of songs, old or new, that you would use for each section of the story. Include with your playlist a written statement about your overall vision of the soundscape you are hoping to create, explaining how each song contributes to the overall effect.

- John Green's young-adult novel *Paper Towns* (2009) presents a mystery much like that of "Open Secrets," in which Margo, the childhood friend of protagonist Quentin Jacobsen, suddenly disappears. Read Green's novel and write a thoughtful, well-structured essay in which you compare the two works as detective stories. What elements do they have in common, and how does each author use these elements to create a sense of mystery?

---

stories people tell. Power resides with those people who have the most access to the secrets of the town, like Mr. Stephens, and who master the intricacies of holding and sharing that information to their advantage.

Social Class

As in all Munro stories, social class places a central role in "Open Secrets." The story explores the inner workings of a town that defines itself strongly by a sense of social order that is passed

down from generation to generation as an unspoken code. Individuals are defined by where they are born or by where their families originate, by the status of their parents or grandparents, or by stories that take hold of their lives. Marian Slater, for instance, must bear the social burden of being a farmer who, so the story in the town goes, had to advertise in order to find a husband following the death of her parents. Similarly, the girls who accompany Miss Johnstone on the hike to the Falls are catalogued according to social status:

Heather is playful when the girls are spraying each other with the hose in Marian and Theo's yard.
(© Pukhov Konstantin | Shutterstock)

the Trowell sisters are labeled country and therefore of a lower social status, because farmers are seen as less wealthy and less educated. Robin Sands is the doctor's daughter, Lucille Chambers is the minister's daughter—both of a higher social status because their fathers' occupations require education—and so on.

Social class is so woven into the town's fabric that upward social mobility (the chance to improve one's standing over time) is almost impossible. When Maureen marries Mr. Stephens, for instance, she does not find her status to be elevated, although she is now a lawyer's wife. Rather, she is haunted by the belief that she secured a lucky marriage and by the fact that her family, the Coulters, would always be seen as "country. No more, no less." Even Heather Bell, the girl ostensibly at the center of the story, is defined within a clearly delineated range by the townspeople. She is variously the new girl, the girl who disappeared, and the girl whose single mother has very questionable morals. At no point does the town move beyond these easy

markers of status to understand the real people or the real lives that exist beyond the labels.

STYLE

Complex Characters

Part of Munro's skill is her ability to develop layered characters who often appear one way to the outside world while carrying deep scars or memories into their personal and emotional lives. As Maureen acknowledges in the closing sentence of the story, the glimpses of the lives involved in this story are like "looking into an open secret, something not startling until you think of trying to tell it."

Munro's characters are complex, multidimensional people living in small towns that are defined, inevitably it seems, by almost petrified social hierarchies and deep channels of rumor and gossip. They move in this world cautiously, alternating (as in Maureen's case) between external and internal worlds, and between telling

COMPARE
&
CONTRAST

- **1993:** The disappearance of Heather Bell spreads quickly within the town, but much more slowly when it reaches the town limits. As Marian Slater notes, there is a gap of days between Saturday's disappearance and her awareness of the events of the day. Once the story begins to spread, it does so slowly through word of mouth and the traditional print media (the newspaper).

  Today: The six remaining girls on the CGIT hike would not have to wait for Mr. Trowell's ice-cream truck to get the news of Heather's disappearance out to the world. Instead, they would have been tweeting, texting, and e-mailing the details almost instantaneously. Heather's picture would have been circulated widely via social media, and the likelihood of her disappearance going unexplained would diminish significantly.

- **1993:** Munro's town in "Open Secrets" is either void of people of color and other nationalities or is unwilling to acknowledge that these people exist as part of the fabric of the town. The one exception is Mr. Siddicup, whose slippage into madness is connected clearly with his position as the town's Englishman. It is a familiar strategy in Munro's writing to mark outsiders by nationalities other than Canadian- or more specifically Ontario-born.

  Today: Given that Canada is a deeply multi-cultural country from coast to coast, it is highly unlikely that this representation would be seen as likely or realistic. According to Citizenship and Immigration Canada, the country has welcomed more than five million immigrants since the 1980s. About 1.3 million people were admitted in the 1980s, with the 1990s increasing to more than 200,000 individuals annually. In 2014, for instance, this number topped 260,400 people. In the decade between 1991 and 2000 in which "Open Secrets" is set, about 2.2 million immigrants were admitted to Canada.

- **1993:** Marian Slater's reputation in Munro's town is damaged irrevocably by the rumored decision to advertise for a husband in a newspaper.

  Today: The decision to advertise for a partner would be more usual today than in 1993, although she would likely use one of the many online sites dedicated to her search rather than a newspaper.

---

stories and having stories told about them. In response to these constantly shifting positions, these are characters that live in a constant state of uncertainty, never sure what is real and what is story, and always aware that any moment of certainty can vanish in an instance.

Denouement

A French word meaning "unknotting," *denouement* refers to the point of resolution of the conflict or plot complexities that have accumulated throughout a story. An exceptional moment in any Munro story, including "Open Secrets," is her characteristic style of denouement, which is never a point of closure but always a point of opening outwards. No conclusion is provided,

only more questions: What did happen to Heather Bell? What is the tragic story behind the eccentric Mr. Siddicup? Why is Miss Johnstone so determined to prove her innocence surrounding the events of that day? And what does the future hold for Maureen, as she waits for her husband to die and a new chapter of her life to begin, free from his emotionless control and abuse?

HISTORICAL CONTEXT

Canadian Demographics

Canada changed dramatically during the 1990s, both in terms of its long-established population

When Theo and Marian speak to the judge, there are hints of both accusation and confession.
(© Andrey_Popov / Shutterstock)

mix and in its settlement pattern. After 1851, population growth in Canada was defined by three distinct demographic patterns. From 1851 to 1900, the population grew slowly by a few million, with a high fertility rate offset by a high infant mortality level and with relatively balanced growth in cities and in the traditional rural small towns scattered across the country. Then, in the first half of the twentieth century, despite the two world wars, the population growth rate generally accelerated, notably because of the settlement of western Canada and by a strong surge in immigration. From 1946 through to the late 1990s, the country's population surged from 12.3 million to 32.6 million.

Although readers never get a sense of this dramatic increase in population from Munro's stories, which are often set in the 1960s or early 1970s, there is a significance to be realized by understanding this context. Munro creates communities that have been isolated (or that have isolated themselves) from the influx of new people, new cultures, and new ideas that were defining the country at this time. She creates

communities that are closed and inward-looking, both of which are qualities that allow for rumor, small-town politics, and narrow-mindedness to fuel the moral and physical decay that inform a story like "Open Secrets."

The Development of the Canadian Short Story

Appearing initially in the *New Yorker* magazine in 1993, "Open Secrets" was recognized almost immediately as an important addition to what had already been established as a vibrant and powerful generation of story writing in Canada. The 1990s are generally seen as a time of balanced paradoxes, when Canadian writers continued to tell powerful stories but did so with an expanding sophistication of style and technique. Regionalism was still influential, with such writers as Carol Shields (associated with Winnipeg, Manitoba), Alistair McLeod (Cape Breton, Nova Scotia), Mordecai Richler (Montreal, Quebec), and Guy Vanderhaeghe (the Canadian prairies) joining Alice Munro (small-town Ontario) as Canadian writers who consciously focused on Canadian voices and Canadian geographies in their writing.

Increased attention to story writers fed into a rebirth of the story form during this period as well. Hundreds of collections came to market in the 1980s, and anthologies with multiple authors appeared regularly, in part to feed the growing interest in Canadian literature in high schools, colleges, and universities. Traditional themes such as the complexities of love, the struggle of individuals within a community, and the power of evil, while still present in Canadian stories, were joined by more direct questions about what it means to be Canadian, how to understand the expansive and dangerous geography of that country, and how language shapes the reality in which we live. A modernist perspective still predominated and produced a focus on realistic characters, well-structured linear plots, and firm resolutions, but many writers, Munro included, began to explore postmodern techniques that often saw time and space bend freely within a story as questions and uncertainties added texture.

CRITICAL OVERVIEW

Part of the collection *Open Secrets*, which the *Library Journal* voted as one of the best books of 1994, the story of the same name marks a departure for Alice Munro in many ways. As Wendy Lesser explains in her review in *New Republic*, this story, and the book as a whole, is a venture "into new terrain: the terrain of the fantastical, the psychologically introverted, the purely suppositional." It is also a collection in which the literary point of view "has become vagrant, anonymous, almost impersonal."

Tracy Ware, a long-time reviewer of Munro's writing, similarly comments in *Studies in Short Fiction* that the collection is an indicator that "Munro has become more adventurous"; compared with her earlier stories, these "are much longer, with more elaborate plots, often ranging over several decades, and containing abrupt shifts in point of view."

Michiko Kakutani, writing in the *New York Times*, sees this as a collection in which Munro is in "consummate control of her craft" in which "often startling developments never come across as mere plot twists or gratuitous displays of authorial invention." Considered collectively,

the stories come together "to give the reader a sense of a world, a world of waiting, loneliness and unfinished gestures." Although these stories feel "somewhat more detached than earlier Munro collections," Munro's "generous gifts of sympathy and insight . . . remain undiminished, and she uses those gifts in these pages to create slim, quick-paced narratives that magically unfurl into dense, novel-like examinations of people's entire lives."

Praise for the collection was almost universal. Josephine Humphreys, also writing for the *New York Times*, argues that Munro's skill comes because she "dares to teach, and by the hardest, best method: without giving answers." This collection "dazzles with its faith in language and in life." Branko Gorjup in *World Literature Today* writes:

> *Open Secrets* is Munro's finest achievement yet. It offers an accurate image of a journeying psyche as it registers all the unexpected shifts caused by destiny's whimsical manipulation. Every stone that is overturned along the road will reveal another life, a life of secrets.

Writing in *Nation*, Ted Solotaroff looks to position Munro "as the mother figure of Canadian fiction," calling her "a Katherine Anne Porter brought up to date" or a female equivalent of Raymond Carver. Her skill, he argues, is her ability to "create unexpected individuals rather than walking tropes," capturing "the difficulties of life rather than of art." But whereas Carver is a minimalist, Munro is what Solotaroff calls "a maximalist," who "uses her glass to explore, bit by magnified bit, the narrative configuration of a life . . . and to take in as much as possible of its ground." In doing so, he comments, Munro achieves great impact "from her subtle creation of patterns that enable seemingly disparate elements of her story to talk to each other." Ann Hulbert of the *New York Review of Books* takes a similarly broad approach, suggesting that Munro "is the latest and best proof that a provincial literary imagination can be the most expansive kind of imagination there is."

Those reviews focused on the title story itself were somewhat mixed. A fan of the collection, Lesser is less than impressed with the story "Open Secrets" as an individual unit of writing.

> Unfortunately, the story that lends its name to the collection falls below its author's usual standards. . . . This is not a bad story, but it is like a pale evocation of all the usual Munro elements: the nearly witchlike unmarried woman; the rural

setting; the innocently malicious gossip of small-town life; the dark secrecy of families; the unauthoritative perspective.

In contrast, Andre Dubus III in *America* praises the story for its "deeper metaphorical implication" and for the fact that "Munro never forces any of her characters to make a larger point; she seems to respect them and the inherent complexity of their story far too much for that."

CRITICISM

Klay Dyer

Dyer is a freelance writer specializing in topics relating to literature, popular culture, and the relationship between creativity and technology. In the following essay, he explores how Alice Munro's "Open Secrets" is a story that simultaneously positions a reader as detective and frustrates all hopes of answering the question "What happened to Heather Bell?"

Alice Munro is fascinated with vanishing, both literal and metaphorical: the vanishing of people (as in the case of Heather Bell), of truth (into the morass of rumor and gossip), and of the basic structures of a connected, caring community (as is seen in the town's treatment of Mr. Siddicup). There is always, too, a connection between vanishing and geography in a Munro story, as happens in "Open Secrets" when Heather Bell disappears during a seemingly benign overnight hike to a local waterfall.

As Munro emphasizes, vanishing necessarily involves a terrain that has within it the potential for things that are new, unexpected, and uncertain. Vanishing does not, and cannot, take place in a place or world of stability or certainty, and such worlds rarely (if ever) exist in Munro's stories. In some cases, these instabilities are expressed through characters who live in adjacent worlds that are connected to the actual world of the story but function as a kind of distorted reflection of its norms and values. In other instances, the uncertainties and possibilities lead to conflicting inner landscapes of her characters, the kind of emotional and psychological charting of a real life that shapes a character.

As Jane Urquhart notes, one of the great skills of Munro as a writer is that she is "capable of entering hidden, sometimes practically invisible spaces of her characters' . . . inner lives and obsessions." Munro, like every great mystery

> FACT AND TRUTH ARE IMMEDIATELY AT ODDS IN 'OPEN SECRETS,' LEAVING READERS STUMBLING TO MAKE SENSE OF A VANISHING THAT LEAVES NO BODY, NO TRACE, AND NO CLUES TO BE DISCOVERED."

writer before her, "hands us the tools, not only to examine her characters but also to look at the world through their eyes—no matter how strange or how dark the vision may be." One of her key strategies is "the presentation of various versions" of the same event." This multiplicity of perspectives "serves to slightly disorient the reader" and makes the act of reading into the act of playing detective, in a world in which the verb "to vanish" resonates profoundly.

In "Open Secrets," the most obvious mystery facing Maureen and readers alike focuses on the vanishing of a new girl in town, Heather Bell. Appropriately she disappears en route to a place that is "nothing like the waterfalls you see pictures of," which is the first clue that the place of this story is unlike any other. This is not a place where a waterfall is really a waterfall, and, as readers come to sense, the facts are not always harbingers of a full truth. As Frances is quick to point out early in the story, however much of the story of Heather's being "some poor innocent" might appeal to some people in the town, "the facts are dead different." Fact and truth are immediately at odds in "Open Secrets," leaving readers stumbling to make sense of a vanishing that leaves no body, no trace, and no clues to be discovered. As Ildikó de Papp Carrington notes in an analytical essay in *Studies in Short Fiction*, a "reader must not only search the text for clues to the mystery, but also recognize and eliminate the false clues and red herrings" (misleading information) that build up. Reading this story is akin to searching through underbrush for evidence, but in "this text the underbrush is the thorny tangle woven by the many kinds of language and its interpretations and deliberate misinterpretations."

Appropriately, Munro begins the story with Maureen weaving her way through a series of

WHAT
DO I READ
NEXT?

- *Alice Munro's Best: A Selection of Stories* (2008) is a powerful representation of her body of work across the years. Read individually, these stories are exemplars of technique and control; read together, they unfold patterns and mysteries that draw a reader into a new world of glimpses and secrets.

- Anton Chekhov's *The Lady with the Dog and Other Stories* (1899) provides a sense of why Munro is often compared to this classic Russian storyteller, who lived from 1860 to 1904. Both use language in subtle, multifaceted ways while exploring seemingly usual moments through a slightly angled lens.

- Munro often cites Carson McCullers, Flannery O'Connor, and Eudora Welty as early influences. *The Heart Is a Lonely Hunter*, written by McCullers in 1940, remains one of the best examples of her trademark style and openness to exploring the darkness that lingers below the surface of American society.

- *Dubliners* (1914), by Irish writer James Joyce, is an important collection of short stories that explore middle-class struggles and values during times of great change and uncertainty. These stories were instrumental in establishing the Joycean epiphany—a realization or recognition of something important, sparked by a seemingly ordinary stimulus—as an important literary technique.

- Canada has produced an abundance of internationally acclaimed short-story writers: Margaret Atwood, Margaret Laurence, and Mavis Gallant, to name but a few. The late Alistair MacLeod, however, would be at or near the top of every list, and his *As Birds Bring Forth the Sun and Other Stories* (1986) is a masterful collection rich with stories that overlay character, setting, and theme as few writers can. This collection is ideal for young-adult readers.

- African Canadian storyteller M. G. Vassanji's *The Gunny Sack* (1989) takes many of the themes familiar to readers of Munro and transports them to Tanzania. The novel is emotionally charged and impeccably executed.

- W. H. New's *Land Sliding: Imagining Space, Presence, and Power in Canadian Writing* (1997) is very readable and profound look at Canadian writing, including some works by Munro, as they relate to the ever-present cultural focus on land, weather, and adapting to the harsh conditions of northern geographies.

- Margaret Peterson Haddix's The Missing is a series of young-adult novels that explores the mysterious lives of children who are transported from other times and places to this world. The first book, *Found*, was published in 2008 and explores the adventures of thirteen-year-old Jonah as he discovers that he is one of many adopted children who have, in fact, been brought to this world by baby-smuggling time travelers.

---

questions that spin off from one single, relatively simple one: What happened to Heather Bell? Interestingly, she attempts to answer this question by using two unique but equally unreliable sources of information: her cousin Frances, and her own memories of the CGIT hike that she took part in more than twenty years earlier.

Listening to Frances, Maureen recognizes early in the story that there are deep (and deeply unsettling) layers to the story that took place in the days leading up to Heather's vanishing. Most obviously, Frances is introduced as a witness of dubious reliability. Known for her "wild, uncharitable, confident speculations," she is a classic Munro figure. She is the conjurer of rumors and the purveyor of gossip who, in trademark Munro grammar, is at once "confident" and speculative, an apparent contradiction. This questionable relationship is underscored linguistically (through Munro's choice of words) in a clause like this one: "and Frances said that Mary Kaye said Heather Bell had been the worst one." The more Frances speaks, the more convoluted truth and story both become, moving two degrees away from an original source (Mary Kaye) whose own interpretations of Heather's behavior is subjective and tainted by memory (as indicated by "had been").

One of the central difficulties facing Munro's readers is that of harmonizing inventiveness and reality, which is often made even more complicated by the alliance between inventiveness and power. As Humphreys notes, "people are continually telling and hearing stories—sometimes more than one at a time—in confessions, letters, rumors, ballads, conversations, newspapers" throughout this story. Although Maureen repeatedly serves as a kind of balance for the speculations gathering around her, noting that at least one of Frances's theories is "pretty far-fetched," she is not immune to the inventiveness that overwhelms the truth of Heather's vanishing. Among her issues as a potential source of reliable information is the unsettled nature of two key aspects of her own evidence: the structure of her stories and their reliance on memory.

Like other great story writers, noticeably James Joyce and Anton Chekhov, Munro erases any firm boundary between time, experience, and understanding. Maureen's memories are examples of this, appearing as a series of deferrals or misdirections that compile into a series of embedded narratives that layer past and present while drawing connections (albeit tenuous) between past and present. The past represents to Maureen a kind of stability, a sense of comfort that comes from knowing that Miss Johnstone has never changed (and will never change) the routine of the CGIT hike, from the evening sermon on her visitation from Jesus to the schedule of events along the route, which includes stopping at a place known as the Rock.

But the comfort that Maureen takes in her memories of the hike has already been undermined by the reader's knowledge that Miss Johnstone, in fact, changed the routine and moreover that this change contributed directly to Heather's vanishing. As was the traditional pattern for the day, Miss Johnstone leads the girls to the Rock before breakfast "as she always did." As she does so, the girls are forced to scramble over a path that "hardly deserved

to be called one" given the prominence of "rotted tree trunks" and ferns so high the girls have to "wade through them." Halfway through this wilderness journey, Heather announces that she has forgotten her sweater and would have to head back to get it.

This moment is a pivotal one in the story, for it is made clear that "in the old days Miss Johnstone would probably have said no. Get a move on and you'll warm up without it, she would have said." But because of the waning popularity of the CGIT hikes, which Miss Johnstone "blamed on television, working mothers, [and] laxity in the home," Miss Johnstone says yes. She does specify that Heather is to hurry up, but she breaks the usual routine and allows one of the girls to leave her sight and her supervision. Later, when Heather fails to reappear, Miss Johnstone shows herself wholly incapable of managing this breaking of routine. She attempts to lure Heather back to camp, certain that the young girl is lurking mischievously nearby. When her misguided attempts fail, she compounds her mistake by returning to her tradition of a "Sunday-morning-of-the-hike sermon, without any qualms or worries." She continues to lecture although Heather does not appear, delaying the mobilization of the townspeople in the search for the missing girl.

To the reader, then, Maureen's misrememberings appear as units of a story that are displaced from the chronology only to reemerge when Maureen is capable of releasing it, clarifying its possibilities in a significant new way. These are moments the story begins to fracture, exposing hidden memories that have been sealed away, sometimes on their own and at other times within a cluster of memories of past experiences.

Maureen's memories, which include the story of her husband's sexual idiosyncrasies that border on abuse, begin to eclipse the supposedly key story of Heather's vanishing. The deeper readers venture into "Open Secrets," the more there emerges a sense that this is a town in which alternative lives impinge on the edges of the main story line, until Heather's story is eclipsed by the story of the town.

As its title suggests, "Open Secrets" continues in Munro's tradition of exploring the inescapability of gaps and complexities in any story, especially those that are defined by a mystery or lingering question. In the end, as Urquhart

Maureen seems to forget whatever she learned about the secret, but years later, while cooking, she has a flash of memory. (© *Anna Alekseenko | Shutterstock*)

comments, readers of such a story as "Open Secrets" come to the profound and potentially unsettling realization that "two conflicting truths . . . can often ride unquestioned side by side without one being in the shadow of the other, and we come to understand that what is perceived as reality is a kind of reality in itself."

Source: Klay Dyer, Critical Essay on "Open Secrets," in *Short Stories for Students*, Gale, Cengage Learning, 2016.

Ildikó de Papp Carrington

In the following excerpt, Carrington examines the recurring theme of communication difficulties in Munro's work.

Alice Munro has written several stories about the difficulties of characters who must interpret another person's unintelligible speech. The earliest of these stories are "The Peace of Utrecht" and "Winter Wind," autobiographical narratives about Anne Chamney Laidlaw, Munro's mother, whose speech was distorted by Parkinson's disease. In these stories the afflicted character's daughters must interpret her frantic

and frustrated efforts to communicate. In a later story, "Mrs. Cross and Mrs. Kidd," Mrs. Cross interprets for a newspaper editor whose stroke has made him aphasic. Now, in the title story of her latest collection, *Open Secrets*, Munro doubles these difficulties by creating two characters who require interpretation: Mr. Siddicup, a completely speechless old widower whose throat cancer has necessitated a laryngectomy, and Alvin Stephens, an elderly lawyer whose stroke has reduced him to short, slurred phrases. Their physical obstacles to speech, however, are only the two most obvious references to language in this story.

Throughout *Open Secrets*, as in many earlier Munro stories, language is repeatedly foregrounded. These references to language can be classified into three major categories: spoken language, written language, and body language. The references to spoken language include the comparison of human sounds to animal sounds; the subspeech of Mr. Siddicup, the truncated syllables of Lawyer Stephens, and the childishly simple speech of another character, along with

> " THIS PARALLEL BETWEEN MUNRO'S AND STEINBECK'S CHARACTERS GRADUALLY TRANSFORMS BOTH GEORGE AND LENNIE INTO TWO ADDITIONAL INTERPRETERS OF MUNRO'S MYSTERY: BY ANALOGY, THEY REVEAL NOT ONLY THE SIGNIFICANCE OF MAUREEN'S HALLUCINATION BUT ALSO THE REASON FOR HER UNWILLINGNESS TO COMMUNICATE ITS MEANING."

the "translations" of the interpreters who talk for them; language characterized by its tone, for example, its wild confidence; language labeled by its sexual content, such as talking "dirty" or "plain talk" about sexual "urges"; the imaginary metaphorical language of Jesus, who appears to a "crazy" character; and, most significantly, the silence of characters who, either of their own volition or under another's orders, keep their mouths shut. Second, in addition to these references to spoken language, there are also several to written language: to a crude ballad-like poem; to a hymn, which is scurrilously parodied; to letters and legal documents; and, through allusions, to John Steinbeck's *Of Mice and Men*. Finally, there are different kinds of nonverbal expression or body language, ranging from unconsciously revealing bodily movements and facial expressions to miming, acting, and the symbolic acting out of the language of touch on both a realistic and a hallucinatory level.

This recurring emphasis on different types of language structures Munro's plot about an unsolved mystery: Heather Bell, a teenage girl, disappears from an annual supervised overnight hike to a waterfall. Mr. Siddicup may have witnessed Heather's fate, and Maureen Stephens, the lawyer's wife and the story's protagonist, experiences a hallucination that seems to reveal one open secret, the identity of the man involved in Heather's disappearance. But the girl is never found, and the mystery is never solved. Because it is not, the reader—along with Munro's characters—is forced into the role of a detective. Just

as in Munro's earlier stories—for example, "Something I've Been Meaning to Tell You," "Fits," "Oranges and Apples," and "A Wilderness Station"—the reader must not only search the text for clues to the mystery, but also recognize and eliminate the false clues or red herrings. Even when her plots do not involve a mystery, Munro "takes us skilfully, with numerous shifty dodges, through the underbrush of the text" (Rooke 25). In this text the underbrush is the thorny tangle woven by the many kinds of language and its interpretations and deliberate misinterpretations. As the reader tries to follow the dodging author and her characters through this underbrush, Munro's thematic insistence on the issue of language allies the reader with Maureen, her chief interpreter. In *Narcissistic Narrative: The Metafictional Paradox*, Linda Hutcheon describes metafiction as "bringing the formal language issue into the foreground, into the thematized content itself," and emphasizes the close connection in metafiction between detective plots and language.

Detective plots . . . function as self-reflective paradigms, making the act of reading into one of active "production," of imagining, interpreting, decoding, ordering, in short of constructing the literary universe through the fictive referents of the words. Reader and writer both share the process of fiction-making in language. (original emphasis)

But ironically, in this story the writer's language is finally silence: the meaning of what Mr. Siddicup witnesses and Maureen hallucinates remains unspoken. Revealing the mystery's paradoxical "open secret" would be translating the nonverbal language of touch into spoken language, and such verbalization would be talking dirty. Therefore, to reconstruct the crime and solve the mystery, the reader must talk dirty for Munro and her characters.

Munro begins her story by introducing two thematically linked elements: the use of different kinds of language to interpret what has happened and to conceal secret, "dirty" meanings under innocuous surfaces. By starting her story with the first stanza of a crude, anonymous ballad composed about Heather's disappearance, Munro describes "the annual hike of the . . . Canadian Girls in Training," always led by the elderly, thick-bodied Miss Mary Johnstone. For a generation Mary has begun the hike by having the girls sing a hymn:

For the Beauty of the Earth, For the Beauty of the Skies, For the Love that from our birth Over and around us lies—.

But "under the hymn words" the girls "hum, . . . cautiously but determinedly," a nasty parody about "Johnstone's bum,/Waddling down the County Road."

Further stanzas of the ballad later comment self-reflexively on the mystery plot in which the ballad is embedded. Like the story, the ballad is an attempt to solve the mystery by classifying various possibilities of what might have happened to Heather. Was she murdered? Picked up by a strange man in a car? Picked up by a man whom she knew and had arranged to meet? Attempting to answer these questions, Maureen begins with two sources of information, her own memories and her cousin Frances. Maureen vividly remembers her adolescent participation in the hikes to the waterfall—instead of looking at the famous view, she used to look for discarded condoms—and in the hikers' gleeful use of "rude language." Besides secretly parodying the hymn, Maureen and her friends also used to play "midnight . . . games of Truth or Dare," demanding answers to such questions as "How many peekers have you seen and whose were they?" In addition to remembering all this, Maureen listens to the "mean remarks, and wild, uncharitable, confident speculations" of her "impudent" cousin Frances, who works for her. Frances describes how on Saturday morning, on their way to the falls, the hot hikers visited the Slater farm and cooled off by spraying themselves with Theo Slater's hose. According to one of the other hikers, Frances says, "Heather Bell had been the worst one, the boldest, getting hold of the hose and shooting water on the rest of them in all the bad places." In the context of the rude verbal language of these references to condoms and "peckers," the phrase "bad places" suggests rude body language: Heather's horseplay with Theo's hose seems sexually symbolic. Later Marian Slater, Theo's wife, tells Maureen that one of the girls turned cartwheels and that he "had to practically wrestle the hose away from [the girls], and give them a few squirts of water to make them behave." Thus described, Theo's active participation intensifies the possibility of hidden phallic connotations in the "wild" horseplay. Is it only a childish summer game, or, as the tone of Frances's speculation implies, are the girls and Theo unconsciously acting out another secretly dirty parody of the hymn? If one of the ballad's speculations is right and

Heather was picked up by a man in a car, the "Love that . . . around us lies" can have more than one meaning.

The interpreters of the story's meanings are both within and without the text. The intratextual interpreters are the two wives, Maureen Stephens and Marian Slater. Maureen interprets for her husband, the stroke victim, and after Mr. Siddicup also visits the Slater farm on Sunday to try to deliver a wildly urgent but unintelligible message, Marian interprets his speechless miming for the Stephenses. But when she does so, Marian talks not only for Mr. Siddicup but also for her husband, a janitor at the nearby atomic energy station, who accompanies her to the Stephens home. Theo, Maureen immediately realizes, is "not very bright." When he is not cowed into helplessly bewildered silence by his "bossy" wife's unspoken commands, he speaks like a small child who has been carefully coached to be polite. He says "please and thank you as often as possible"; he suppresses giggles when Marian is offered sugar in her coffee, for he seems to consider the word lumps a double-entendre; and he sits with "both hands on the table, fingers spread, pressed down, pulling at the cloth." Through Maureen's immediately suspicious observation of the Slaters' behavior, Munro introduces the interpreters outside the text of her story. Her allusions to Steinbeck's *Of Mice and Men* make the Slaters' relationship parallel the relationship between Steinbeck's two itinerant ranch hands, George Milton and the retarded Lennie Small. Lennie, like Theo, "ain't bright," so whenever Lennie is questioned, George "scowl[s] meaningfully at" him to keep him quiet. Because George always speaks for Lennie, who "look[s] helplessly to [him] for instruction," their behavior when they arrive at the ranch arouses the suspicion of Curley, the ranch owner's son, just as the Slaters' behavior arouses Maureen's. This parallel between Munro's and Steinbeck's characters gradually transforms both George and Lennie into two additional interpreters of Munro's mystery: by analogy, they reveal not only the significance of Maureen's hallucination but also the reason for her unwillingness to communicate its meaning.

Maureen's professional and personal qualifications to be her husband's interpreter and the chief detective in the mystery plot are carefully defined. They are her intelligence and dependability, "qualities her husband . . . value[d]" when he hired her to be his legal secretary and, after the death of his first wife, married her. Because Maureen could "draw up documents and write letters on her own," Stephens called her "the Jewel." After his stroke, Maureen significantly extends her use of language: she not only writes but also speaks for her husband. "His speech was sometimes slurred, so she had to stay around and interpret for people who did not know him well." In this capacity she listens and observes when the Slaters come to ask Lawyer Stephens's advice about the strange visit from Mr. Siddicup on the day of Heather's disappearance.

Mr. Siddicup, an English widower who, unlike Stephens, has not remarried, has no wife to interpret the "wheezing and growling noises" to which his laryngectomy has reduced him. Grief-stricken by his wife's sudden death, he has rapidly "deteriorated from a decent old man into a morose and rather disgusting old urchin" who behaves very strangely. Sometimes drivers on the road "spot him standing still" in "ditch[es], mostly hidden in tall weeds and grass . . . ." Visitors to his home also see something disturbing. They wonder what he does with the permanent piles of his wife's old underwear and stockings, "lying around" the house: "Did he put them on . . ., next to his skin? Was he a pervert?" When Marian tells the Stephenses about his equally strange visit to her farm, she becomes his interpreter, and she "show[s] them just what Mr. Siddicup had done" in reply to her questions. Over and over again, she tells them that she asked him, "What are you trying to tell me?"

But is her interpretation of what he was trying to tell her true? Her veracity is made questionable in several ways. First, when the Slaters arrive on Tuesday morning, Maureen observes that Marian is obviously dressed up for her errand to the lawyer. Instead of her usual slacks, Marian is wearing a heavy suit, gloves, a brown feather hat, and such "a quantity of makeup" that, although Maureen has known her for years, at first she has difficulty in recognizing her. This difficulty suggests that Marian's outfit and cosmetics might be analogous to an actress's costume and stage makeup, put on for the authoritative performance of a dramatic role. Maureen silently concludes that the "determined" Marian "present[s] herself as if she had absolute fights. She ha[s] to be taken account of." Next, Maureen also notices that while Marian "lurche[s] and crouche[s] and bang[s] her hands to her head" to act out what

Mr. Siddicup did in her farm yard, she is simultaneously "watching" Theo to make sure that he plays his assigned role. Even though he is visibly agitated, "a nerve jumping in one cheek," he keeps "his deferential eyes on her by an effort of will," as "her look" commands him, "Hold on. Be still." . . .

Source: Ildikó de Papp Carrington, "Talking Dirty: Alice Munro's "Open Secrets" and John Steinbeck's *Of Mice and Men*," in *Studies in Short Fiction*, Vol. 31, No. 4, Fall 1994, p. 595.

SOURCES

Carrington, Ildikó de Papp, "Talking Dirty: Alice Munro's 'Open Secrets' and John Steinbeck's *Of Mice and Men*," in *Studies in Short Fiction*, Vol. 31, No. 4, Fall 1994, pp. 595–606.

"Citizenship and Immigration: Research and Statistics," Government of Canada website, http://www.cic.gc.ca/english/resources/statistics/ (accessed November 16, 2015).

Dubus, Andre, III, Review of *Open Secrets*, in *America*, Vol. 173, No. 1, July 1995, pp. 27–28.

Gorjup, Branko, Review of *Open Secrets*, in *World Literature Today*, Vol. 69, No. 2. Spring 1995, p. 363.

Hulbert, Ann, "Writer Without Borders," in *New York Review of Books*, Vol. 42, No. 21, December 22, 1994, pp. 59–60.

Humphreys, Josephine, "Mysteries Near at Hand," in *New York Times*, September 11, 1994, https://www.nytimes.com/books/98/11/01/specials/munro-secrets.html (accessed August 31, 2015).

Kakutani, Michiko, "Love, Found and Lost, Amid Sharp Turns of Fate," in *New York Times*, September 6, 1994, http://www.nytimes.com/1994/09/06/books/munro-secrets.html (accessed August 31, 2015).

Lesser, Wendy, "The Munro Doctrine," in *New Republic*, Vol. 211, No. 18, October 31, 1994, pp. 51–53.

Levene, Mark, "'It Was about Vanishing': A Glimpse of Alice Munro's Stories," in *University of Toronto Quarterly*, Vol. 68, No. 4, Fall 1989, pp. 841–60.

Munro, Alice, "Open Secrets," in *Open Secrets*, Penguin Canada, 2007, pp. 108–34.

Solotaroff, Ted, "Life Stories," in *Nation*, Vol. 259, No. 18, November 28, 1994, pp. 665–68.

Urquhart, Jane, Introduction to *Open Secrets*, by Alice Munro, Penguin Canada, 2007, pp. ix–x.

Ware, Tracy, Review of *Open Secrets*, in *Studies in Short Fiction*, Vol. 33, No. 1, Winter 1996, pp. 123–24.

FURTHER READING

Carscallen, James, *The Other Country: Patterns in the Writing of Alice Munro*, ECW Press, 1993.

In a book that ranges freely over Munro's various collections, Carscallen focuses on a biblical typology in order to explore the characters and geographies that define her writing. Although it is at times dense and even cluttered with detail, this book does trigger a rethinking of many of the subtleties of the body of Munro's work.

Heble, Ajay, *The Tumble of Reason: Alice Munro's Discourse of Absence*, University of Toronto Press, 1994.

Although *Open Secrets* is not included in this discussion, this remains a valuable and elegantly written discussion of Munro's first six collections of short fiction. Heble is a careful reader who elegantly explains Munro's growing thematic interest in the absences, incongruities, and legend making that collide in the lives of her characters. This book is one of the major contributions to critical interest in Munro's writing.

Howells, Coral Ann, *Alice Munro*, Manchester University Press, 1998.

Part of the Contemporary Writers series, this chronological study is a thorough and readable overview of Munro's early life and early stories. It establishes some solid groundwork from which to understand the patterns that come to shape a Munro story.

Munro, Sheila, *Lives of Mothers & Daughters: Growing Up with Alice Munro*, Union Square Press, 2001.

Written by Munro's eldest daughter, also a writer, this book is an unusual and deeply intimate memoir that reflects on a life growing up with a mother of international literary reputation. Tracing her mother's personal journey allows Sheila to tell her own story of becoming a writer while trying at once to respect and stay clear of her mother's footsteps.

Thacker, Robert, *Alice Munro: Writing Her Lives*, McClelland and Stewart, 2005.

The definitive literary biography of Munro, this book is the story of Munro's life and of her rise to international prominence as the builder of some of her generation's finest stories. Intricately detailed and easy to read, this book is essential for any fan of Munro's writing.

SUGGESTED SEARCH TERMS

Alice Munro

Open Secrets AND story

Open Secrets AND Munro

Canada AND short story

short story AND disappearance

short story AND small town

short story AND gossip

short story AND secrets

Railroad Standard Time

FRANK CHIN

1978

"Railroad Standard Time" is a short story by Frank Chin (Frank Chew Chin Jr.), an American author of Chinese descent, that provides a portrait of a young writer reminiscing and reflecting on his life on the West Coast and his cultural heritage. Chin has been one of the most polarizing figures in Asian American literature. His accomplishments speak for themselves. He became the first Chinese American playwright to have work staged off-Broadway. *The Chickencoop Chinaman* was produced in 1972 and *The Year of the Dragon* in 1974. Chin helped bring neglected Chinese and Japanese American writers to light in coediting *Aiiieeeee! An Anthology of Asian-American Writers* (1974), the first major anthology of its kind, and in co-organizing the first conferences for Asian American writers. He turned Asian American literature in a new direction by giving prominence to a consciousness that—rather than being formulaically both traditional and modern, pulled to both old and new—was outspokenly antithetic to Americanized Chinese culture.

Chin's passionate engagement with literature earned him detractors. He was critical, sometimes in derogatory ways, of such highly respected writers as Maxine Hong Kingston and Amy Tan. Some readers were put off by the aggressively masculine effect of some of his stories.

First published in *City Lights Journal* in 1978, "Railroad Standard Time" appears in Chin's debut short-story collection, *The Chinaman*

Chin discusses the phenomenon of Chinatowns, where people cling to traditions from their homelands.
(© Misunseo | Shutterstock)

Pacific & Frisco R.R. Co. (1988), which won an American Book Award from the Before Columbus Foundation. It also appears in *Growing Up Ethnic in America: Contemporary Fiction about Learning to Be American* (1999) and *Bold Words: A Century of Asian American Writing* (2001). Although "Railroad Standard Time" contains little more than juvenile, objectifying descriptions of a fondly remembered music teacher, other stories in Chin's collections contain explicit and graphic sexual material.

AUTHOR BIOGRAPHY

Chin was born on February 25, 1940, in Berkeley, California. From birth on, he was thrust into a complicated relationship with culture: his father, a Chinese immigrant, broke his word to Chin's future grandmother, who had helped set him up in a butcher shop, by impregnating her teenage daughter, a fourth-generation Chinese American. The father then took pains to conceal Chin's

birth from the grandmother. In the words of Frank Abe in a *Bloomsbury Review* profile, Chin "was raised by a retired white couple in a tar-paper shanty on an abandoned gold mining site in the Motherlode country of California, taking on Wild West affectations and tastes." The temporary foster parents were Jack and Beatrice Conroy, a former acrobat and a former actress. As the scholar Calvin McMillin details in his introduction to *The Confessions of a Number One Son*, Chin painted in essays and interviews

> an idyllic portrait of his time with the Conroys—filled with vibrant memories of playing out in the great outdoors, hearing the sounds of the railroad sing him to sleep, and watching cowboys move herds of cattle through their property every spring.

Chin was also fond of listening to *The Shadow* and *The Lone Ranger* on the radio—and liked to imagine that, behind his black mask, the Lone Ranger was actually Chinese. When Chin and his family moved back to San Francisco's Chinatown, a local labor organizer gave Chin the nickname the Chinatown Cowboy.

Chin attended the University of California (UC), Berkeley, beginning in 1958. At Berkeley, he contributed regularly to the campus humor magazine, the *California Pelican*, eventually becoming associate editor and then editor. As he told Abe, he enjoyed the chance to write lightly and prolifically, to make the act of writing as natural as the act of speaking, and he never felt writer's block. Chin left Berkeley in 1961 for the Iowa Writers' Workshop but found the subtle racism on the part of instructors disheartening. He returned to California two years after leaving for Iowa, to finish his bachelor's degree at UC Santa Barbara. Around this time, he spent a couple of years as a railroad clerk in Oakland and then became a brakeman on the Southern Pacific Railroad, for which his grandfather had been a steward. Chin proudly claimed to have been the first Chinese American to work as a brakeman, near the top of the train crew hierarchy, on that line. In 1966, he took a job as writer and story editor for King Broadcasting, out of Seattle, where he remained until 1969, when he became a lecturer at UC Davis. He also taught creative writing at UC Berkeley.

Chin's play *The Chickencoop Chinaman* won an East-West Players playwriting contest, but ultimately the actors were too intimidated to stage it because it dealt so forthrightly with Asian American self-contempt. Chin soon formed the Asian American Theater Workshop in San Francisco, which attracted other cutting-edge literary and dramatic talents. After the production of his first two plays in New York in the early 1970s, Chin enjoyed a transient lifestyle along the Interstate 5 corridor between California and Washington for the rest of the decade. During that time, he published a number of short stories and worked on but abandoned several novels. In 1980, he moved to Los Angeles to join the East-West Players. In time, Chin forsook the theater, finding that in such collaborative, performative settings, those interested in fame won out over those interested in truth.

Chin's short-story collection *The Chinaman Pacific & Frisco R.R. Co.*, which includes "Railroad Standard Time," was published in 1988 and received an American Book Award in 1989. Chin received the Lannan Literary Award for Fiction in 1992 and an American Book Award for Lifetime Achievement in 2000. His first novel published was *Donald Duk* (1991), which became a classic in Asian American studies. An activist streak was evident in Chin's participation in the reclamation of Japanese American literature and history after the devastation of the community during World War II internment. In 2002, he published his extensively researched volume *Born in the USA: A Story of Japanese America, 1889–1947*. This book was followed by a variety of works, including another novel, plays, essays, and even the text to comic books bringing Chinese fairy tales to life. He has two children, Elizabeth and Gabriel, from his first marriage and as of 2015 lived in Los Angeles with his third wife and their son, Sam.

PLOT SUMMARY

"Railroad Standard Time" begins with the narrator, who is never named, being given his grandfather's Elgin-brand railroad watch by his mother. His grandmother has just died—the day before, apparently. This scene occurs when the narrator is about thirteen years old, but the depth of insight and verbal maturity of the narration make clear that within the context of the story, the narrator is reflecting on the experience. They are in the kitchen, which to the narrator seems flooded with Chinese culture, as if the domestic sanctuary above all other places is insulated from the outer Anglo-American world. (The thematic conjunction of railroad paraphernalia and people of Chinese descent strongly suggests that the American West is the setting, which the story's details gradually confirm.) The mother is speaking in Chinese. She has been up all night hosting family members mourning her mother. Having put the watch on the table, the mother stares at it and ignores calls from the other rooms until the narrator picks it up.

As the narrator regards the watch, his mother relates that it is the best one from the grandfather's collection. When the narrator asks what his grandfather's name was, his mother lapses into English and trails off giggling, as if the Chinese name eludes her, while shuffling around trying to sit in chairs that are not currently in the kitchen; she seems to be exhausted. She concludes that the watch is no good, without apparent reason (though the son has narrated that his mother's slipping into English dramatically cheapens the watch).

MEDIA ADAPTATIONS

- An audiocassette version of *The Chinaman Pacific & Frisco R.R. Co.* was issued in 1994 by Stone Arbor Corporation.

Even though the watch is not up to modern standards, the narrator treasures it and uses it while working as a brakeman on the Southern Pacific railroad. He also wears it to his courthouse wedding, which takes place during his time working as a news writer in Seattle and on his twenty-seventh birthday. On a Saturday soon after that birthday, he arrives home to find his wife and two children being driven away by his wife's new love, his daughter repeatedly calling out "goodbye Daddy." The narrator passively endures the experience, but the trauma affects him; he adopts a negative attitude and acts out in violence from time to time.

The narrator abruptly refers to disliking the Chinatown novel he has written, in which a mother dies, now that his own mother is dead. He speaks ill of several other authors' Chinatown books, which he considers culturally cheap and thus denigrating. His own book is heavy with passages about traditional Chinese food. He hates it, after his mother's death, but does not disown it. He reminisces about how youths like him learned English by watching cartoons at movie houses. Many of them remain genuinely grateful to certain cartoon characters.

The narrator changes his movie habits when he has to read to his newly paralyzed father once a week. Now favoring live-action films, the narrator returns home one day to read spooky Edgar Allan Poe stories in the voice of the actor Peter Lorre. This scene offers an implicit contrast to the narrator's ensuing mention of how old men in the Chinatown books always signify traditional culture and ceremonies, which for the narrator call to mind kowtowing—kneeling and touching the ground with the forehead in a show of respect—not only to elders but also to the chicken being offered to the dead. Having never met his grandfather, the narrator can only imagine his toughness and resourcefulness. The narrator used to contemplate passing the watch to his own son, but he no longer does.

The narrator is driving south along Interstate 5, also old Highway 99, from Seattle toward San Francisco for his mother's funeral. Instead of having the traditional white food for the funeral, the family will likely be going to a Chinese restaurant. Crossing the Carquinez Bridge, in the San Francisco Bay Area, the narrator finds the smooth quality of the ride disrupted by the bridge's bumpy steel grating. It is dusk; he has been driving for sixteen hours, listening to country-and-western music during the night. He first learned of such music, along with the national anthem, from a music teacher in school, who happened to have an ample bosom. This led the boys in the class to gawk and to persuade the teacher to sing chest-heaving opera music. As for old-fashioned country music, the narrator finds that it spurs him to leave town whenever the time comes. His arrival in his home region is marked by agitated and discordant feelings and by the drive past Oakland's diminished Chinatown, where the road runs parallel to the railroad tracks.

CHARACTERS

Barbara

The narrator's wife looks strikingly beautiful, even divine, while driving away in a station wagon with her new love behind the wheel and her and the narrator's children in the backseat. The description suggests that the departure of his family comes as a shock to the narrator.

Father

The narrator's father becomes paralyzed, and the narrator reads to him once a week.

Grandfather

Having worked as a steward—on the railroad, one gathers—the narrator's grandfather becomes a collector of railroad watches. The narrator never knows him, because he dies too young, but he likes to imagine that despite his subservient job, the grandfather was tough, perhaps even a cunning thief. His best watch is passed from his wife to his grandchild.

Grandmother

The grandmother's death is what leads to the mother's giving the grandfather's watch to the narrator. Otherwise, nothing substantial is said about her.

Aurora Morales

Aurora Morales is the large-breasted music teacher from the narrator's school days. The narrator provides little beyond an objectifying portrait of her bust, but it is at least clear that she invests the fullness of her spirit in her singing.

Mother

The reader meets the narrator's mother at a singular time, the day after the death of her own mother. That she has been up all night stoically serving other grieving family members suggests emotional resilience and a firmness of spirit. Yet by the time she is through with the ritual of giving her son her father's railroad watch, exhaustion seems to set in, as she lapses into English and woozily dances around looking for someplace to rest her weary body. The mother's death spurs the narrator's drive from Seattle to San Francisco and is perhaps what sparks the reminiscence of the mother's passing along the watch in the story's beginning.

Narrator

The narrator is a Chinese American man from San Francisco now living in Seattle and making his living as a writer. He is a novelist, apparently with his days as a news writer behind him. The key event in the narrator's life as far as this story is concerned is the day his mother gives him his grandfather's best railroad watch. The watch becomes a symbol of the narrator's Chinese heritage (for both himself and the reader), one that he carries through some momentous events in his life, which he enumerates with little detail. The most significant are his marriage in a courthouse on his day off and, later, his wife's departure from his life, with their children in tow. This event is far more significant, in terms of his personality and character, than the bestowal of the watch, though he quickly shifts away from the topic after reporting its negative effects on him. In the course of the story, the narrator shows great depth of consciousness in considering the implications of his Chinese heritage on his ongoing, imperfect life.

Narrator's Son

The narrator does not have the chance to say good-bye to his son because the boy is sleeping in the car when his mother and the children drive away for good.

Sarah

The reader's only glimpse of the narrator's daughter comes when she is being driven away by her mother's new love and bids good-bye to her father several times.

THEMES

Chinese Culture

A complicated relationship between a young Chinese American man—he calls himself a Chinaman—and his cultural heritage is on display in "Railroad Standard Time." It is difficult, perhaps impossible, to accurately define that relationship because there are so many contrasting, interwoven layers to it. Early on, the narrator establishes a sense of irony when he refers to his extended family as "Chinamen from the royalty of pure-talking China-born Chinese, old, mourning, and belching in the other rooms." The unnecessary repetition of the root word *China* suggests that the emphasis on Chinese purity is overblown: the family members seem far more ordinary than royal. The narrator seems to be mocking his heritage. Yet before the end of the paragraph, the narrator relates the profound effect that being immersed in his mother's Chinese words has on him. She fairly casts a spell over her son, lending her bestowal of the watch an air of traditional ritual, and this seems important to the narrator.

When it comes to funeral rites, however, the narrator makes a caricature of the ritual act of kowtowing by referring to it as scrambling down and bonking one's head on the floor for the sake of a dead chicken. One may surmise that, like his mother, he would prefer that the mourners at his funeral forgo the traditional home-cooked white food in favor of a simple visit to a restaurant, especially since "nobody had these dinners at home anymore." This would only be half-correct, as he reports, "I wouldn't mind people having dinner at my place after my funeral, but no white food." This seems to position him halfway between tradition and modernity.

TOPICS FOR FURTHER STUDY

- Write a first-person short story in which the context is a long car ride somewhere for an important occasion, such as a funeral, that spurs reminiscences about times past. Try to heighten the story's interest by including internal conflict or uncertainty.

- Read one of the short stories in *Aiiieeeee! An Anthology of Asian-American Writers* (1974), edited by Chin, Jeffery Paul Chan, Lawson Inada, and Shawn Wong, and write an essay analyzing its plot, themes, and style, making comparisons with "Railroad Standard Time" where fitting.

- Read *April and the Dragon Lady* (1994), a young-adult novel by Lensey Namioka, in which April Chen finds herself at a cultural crossroads as she finishes high school. Write an essay in which you compare and contrast the attitudes of April and the narrator of "Railroad Standard Time." Ponder which character seems more adapted, which more assimilated, which more fulfilled, and which happier, among other possible comparisons.

- Using at least one print and one online source, research the historical treatment of women in Chinese society. Write a paper detailing what you learn—be sure to cover the topics of foot binding and the abandonment of infant girls—and close by weighing in on Chin's opinions of Chinese American women authors' works. Might what Chin perceives as their disloyalty to Chinese traditions be philosophically justified?

- Research the history of Chinese railroad workers in the nineteenth century and create a website that includes original text, pictures, maps, and links to bring the Chinese workers' story to life. Alternatively, research and prepare a website on the history of San Francisco's Chinatown.

Yet again, he may be averse to white food because of what the color white in Anglo America has come to signify for him.

Language and Languages

A major component of the narrator's engagement with traditional Chinese culture is the language. This is most evident in his interactions with his mother as she passes along her father's railroad watch. Her speaking Chinese is veritably magical, as she "conjured the meaning of what she was saying in the shape of old memories come to call. Words I'd never heard before set me at play in familiar scenes new to me, and ancient." The narrator reveals a profound engagement with the mere sound of his mother's voice. Here they are in America, where the greater world speaks strictly English, meaning that the Chinese language itself takes on a specialized connotation, that of family and community history. It is worth noting that Mandarin Chinese is a prescriptively inflective language, meaning that syllables and words are delivered with a specific tone or lilt to properly convey the meaning. A single-syllable word can have four different meanings if spoken with four different inflections. To an English speaker, this may seem to give a person less freedom to impart one's own inflections on whatever one wants to say—to say it how one wants to say it. This may be the case, but prescriptive inflections also place greater emphasis on the language as a tradition, in that even the pronunciation of words is accomplished in a traditional, even ritual manner. Any given word uttered with its particular inflection can take on the aura of a mantra, spoken with half-conscious deliberation, as if to accomplish a mystical effect.

Such an effect is precisely what the narrator reports feeling while listening to his mother. This makes all the more dramatic the mother's lapse into English, "faintly from another world," when she cannot identify her own father's Chinese name. The nuanced characterization of the mother's state of mind, through her words and actions, suggests that perhaps the name's pronunciation or inflection is so completely foreign to the English tongue—which she probably speaks primarily in her daily life (otherwise she would not slip into English at all)—that her mouth has kinesthetically forgotten how to produce the sound of the name. Notably, with this slip of the tongue from Chinese to English, the mother goes from casting a genuine spell to "mumbling . . . in strange English, like an Indian medicine man in a movie." Her magic has been reduced to a mere theatrical trick.

Time

Another component of the narrator's engagement with his heritage is time, as signaled by the importance of the grandfather's railroad watch in the story, in his life, and in his consciousness. From the beginning, the narrator embraces the watch despite its supposed shortcomings. His mother alludes to its being no good (without seeming to explain why), and it is not up to modern standards for professional railroad use. But the narrator appreciates its being gold and warm to the touch—not unlike a treasured memory, figuratively speaking. It is as if, even in living out what seems to be an irreverent Chinese American's life, he yearns for and is reaching back into the past, "timing today's happenings with a nineteenth-century escapement." An escapement is a particular part of a watch's mechanism that draws from the power source to govern the movement of the gears, but the word effectively connotes the sense of escape, back into the past, that the narrator at least partly desires in his modern life.

Twice in the story the narrator speaks of bringing his grandmother or grandfather along with him on whatever ride he is taking at the time, as if he wishes that they, and more to the point their old-fashioned sensibilities, could be there with him. The persistent ambivalence in the narrator's relationship with his cultural heritage is reflected in the potential fate of the watch: he once envisioned passing it along to his son, but with his son gone—being raised by white parents and presumably estranged from his birth father—the narrator has ceased to feel an impulse to do this. It is as if time itself, along with his cultural heritage, will stop with him. Neither the watch nor a sense of Chinese culture will be passed along to his absent son. Still, during the ride back to San Francisco for his mother's funeral, the protagonist relates, "The watch ticked against my heart and pounded my chest as I went too fast over bumps in the night." As long as he lives, at least, he cannot escape his fixture in time and the sometimes jarring significance of his Chinese heritage.

Art and Life

Beyond the story's focus on the narrator's relations to his cultural heritage and his family lies the theme of the conjunction of art and life. The narrator eventually reveals that he is not just the implied writer of this story but is a former journalist and novelist. He also reveals that he has

Traditional Chinese culture clashes with American mainstream culture, such as Western movies and Charlie Chaplin. (© *Popperfoto* / *Getty Images*)

come to question his artistic engagement with his heritage as embodied in that Chinese American literary cliché of clichés (as he sees it), Chinatown. Every Chinese American writer, it seems, has his or her respective Chinatown memoir or semiautobiographical novel, filled with references to food, family, and precious traditions. The narrator derogatorily refers to such literature as "books scribbled up by a sad legion of snobby autobiographical Chinatown saps all on their own . . . hardworking people who sweat out the exact same Chinatown book." Clearly the narrator takes issue with the degree of artistry, or lack thereof, in evidence in such creatively tepid books. He says that writers, himself included, only fake art in writing them.

There are several other references in the story to interactions between the way people live and forms of art—in particular, popular forms like film and music. Although some of the story's lines are laced with irony, the narrator seems genuine when he reports how much youths like him appreciated even cartoon characters for helping them learn the English language, as if Mighty Mouse and Woody Woodpecker were not imaginary entertainers but effectively real teachers. As for the country music, it seems to neatly align with the narrator's mood as he goes from town to town. It is as if, even if the music is figuratively "run through Clorox and Simonized"—bleached and waxed—as far as artistry is concerned, it successfully embodies the roaming spirit of the West. Whether the narrator will ultimately ally himself with his Chinese heritage and the traditions that stem from it or focus on appreciating, even if ironically, what American culture has to offer—or do both—it seems that art will be the nexus of this balance, as suggested by the very creation of this story.

STYLE

Semiautobiographical Fiction

The stories in Chin's debut collection are widely recognized as at least semiautobiographical if not fully autobiographical. Almost all of the important details of "Railroad Standard Time" match elements of Chin's biography. One reviewer, Douglas Sun of the *Los Angeles Times*, went so far as to suggest that the overlap of details compromises the story. He states that this story and the one that follows it in the collection "read like meandering stream-of-consciousness memoirs and are self-indulgent enough to make them the weakest of the bunch." His comments spoke to the potential weaknesses of a story based on a portion of one's life. In portraying real life with all its untidiness, the story may lack the sort of dramatic arc one expects to find in a good piece of fiction. It may not give the reader the feeling of having gained anything or having been taken somewhere. Sun finds that ethnicity-inflected semiautobiographical fiction in particular "tends to reach inward, instead of outward toward the universal significance that . . . marks literature in its highest form."

For all the legitimacy of Sun's argument, one should not overlook the value of Chin's story. If an author intently depicts a character whose experiences are universal, the character may simply seem superficial. To the contrary, in writing precisely from his unique individual perspective, Chin is free to pull thoughts and emotions from his own most profound depths to produce a story that rings true because there is nothing false about it. This should not detract from the degree of creativity that Chin shows in his choice of words, verbal patterns, and ordering of his thoughts. Notably, the journal in which "Railroad Standard Time" was first published, *City Lights Journal*, was issued by the imprint that ushered the Beat generation to fame, including twentieth-century America's grand master of autobiographical fiction, Jack Kerouac.

Postmodernism

Chin's storytelling has hallmarks of the movement in which the most innovative literature of the later twentieth century has been classified, postmodernism. In the early twentieth century, the credo of modernist writers was to make things new. They used narrative ingenuity—stream-of-consciousness narration, alternating narrators, unreliable narrators, lack of chronology, and other disruptions—to better delve inside the experiences of fictional characters. Postmodernism took this credo a step or two further, often reconstructing what modernism had deconstructed in ambiguous or paradoxical ways. Thus, for example, whereas flashbacks and flash-forwards became more common with modernism, the temporal state of "Railroad Standard Time" is fluid, taking place somewhere between the narrator's experiences as a youth, his drive to Seattle, and the time when he wrote the poem. It is often difficult to identify whether the sense of a narrative comment should be applied to the narrator as actor, as reminiscer, or as writer. The result is a free-floating consciousness that wafts among all three of these periods of the author's life and makes the story, in a way, more four dimensional, the fourth dimension being time.

Another postmodern trait of Chin's story is the extended rumination on the quality of Chinese American writing. In one long paragraph, the author both loathes and treasures his own Chinatown novel. He belittles his compatriots for writing Chinatown drivel, but he practically basks—again, if ironically, another hallmark of postmodernism—in the Chinatown glow of his own experiences with food. In the end, in a classically postmodern way, Chin's story refuses to provide neat narrative closure. As the last sentence indicates, the author's irritation seems to

COMPARE & CONTRAST

- **1970s:** For the first time, an Asian American play—Chin's *The Chickencoop Chinaman* (1972)—is staged in New York City; an Asian American anthology—*Aiiieeeee!* (1974), edited by Chin, Chan, Inada, and Wong—is published; and an Asian American writers conference (1975) takes place, organized by Chin and his associates.

  Today: As a genre and an area of study, Asian American literature flourishes in numerous anthologies and histories and in university departments nationwide. Also gaining in prominence are Asian American actors (Lucy Liu), comedians (Margaret Cho), and professional athletes (Jeremy Lin).

- **1970s:** In 1976, Maxine Hong Kingston wins what is arguably the most highly esteemed award thus far among Asian American writers when *The Woman Warrior*

  receives the National Book Critics Circle Award for Nonfiction.

  Today: Although no Asian American writer has been awarded the Pulitzer Prize for Fiction as of 2015, the National Book Award—next in the hierarchy of American honors—is awarded to Ha Jin in 1999 for his novel *Waiting*, which is set in the fictional Muji City, China. Jin was born in China and came to the United States during his university years.

- **1970s:** It is not out of the ordinary to find someone who uses a pocket watch, although wristwatches are far more popular.

  Today: Even though huge numbers of people carry cell phones, which include a clock feature, wristwatches are common for convenience and as jewelry. It is uncommon to find someone still using a pocket watch.

have built up without any release. It leaves the reader with plenty to think about in both reading and recalling the story.

HISTORICAL CONTEXT

Chinese American Culture and Literature

"Railroad Standard Time" revolves around the narrator's personal engagement with broader Chinese American culture, which is readily understood to represent Chin's own engagement with the culture. Such a connection between protagonist and author should not be made for any given work of fiction with a first-person narrator—this is the biographical fallacy—but the details of the unnamed protagonist's life match those of Chin's so comprehensively that the connection affirms itself here. Moreover, Chin's statements in

interviews and essays precisely accord with the attitude of the protagonist. That attitude is ultimately a confrontational one, as he alternately mocks, praises, questions, honors, rejects, and embraces his ethnic community.

Although the biographical connection should not be taken too seriously, a particular aspect of Chin's life worth considering in relation to his protagonist is his having spent the first six years of his life living with, and absorbing the culture of, a white couple. Experiences from the earliest years of a person's life are highly influential, indeed formative, as far as personality and worldview are concerned. If one applies this biographical fact to the protagonist's attitude, it is easy to see why, for example, he seems both fond and dismissive of country music, just as he is both fond and dismissive of Chinese culture.

Returning to the story proper, what especially emerges as a point of confrontation is the

The parallel rails of the train tracks reflect the parallels the narrator sees in his own life. (© Kevin_Hsieh / Shutterstock)

protagonist's perception of literature by other Chinese Americans, particularly the generations before him. In the early 1970s, Chin began contentiously referring to individuals of Chinese descent whose Christianity enabled their assimilation into US society as Chinese Americans, but he used the term *Chinaman*, which by then was considered derogatory, to refer to those who remained loyal to Chinese tradition and ideals. In "Railroad Standard Time," the protagonist cites Pardee Lowe's *Father and Glorious Descendant* (1943), Jade Snow Wong's *Fifth Chinese Daughter* (1950), and Virginia Chin-lan Lee's *The House That Tai Ming Built* (1963) as all inspiring his hatred for being cookie-cutter, Christianized versions of Chinese American stories. Chin, in real life, was also dismissive of the successful writers Maxine Hong Kingston and Amy Tan, particularly for the ways in which they seem to compromise Chinese tradition and cater to stereotypes for the sake of appeasing white readers.

Chin clarified his objections to such authors as Lowe, Wong, Kingston, and Tan

most notably in his long polemical essay "Come All Ye Asian American Writers of the Real and the Fake," included in *The Big Aiiieeeee!*, and in his *Bloomsbury Review* interview with Frank Abe, both in 1991. Speaking with Abe, Chin detailed the Christianized stereotype of traditional Chinese culture that settled into the mainstream consciousness largely owing to the depictions found in the earliest Chinese American literature, which was almost exclusively written by Christians. Chin tells Abe the accepted stereotype was

> that Chinese culture is passive . . . submissive . . . physically cowardly in comparison to the West. That it consists of smart, sometimes brilliant yellow men, who are unoriginal, unassertive, not aggressive, and sexually despicable. . . . That Chinese and Japanese culture are so misogynistic they don't deserve to survive.

These comments speak to why Chin has primarily taken issue with Chinese American authors who emphasize misogyny or disempower male characters. In his 1991 essay, Chin disparagingly summarizes Lowe's autobiography and its anti-Chinese message as follows:

> A young Chinese American Christian . . . badgers his tongman father into converting to Christianity, and the story closes with his acceptance by whites in the form of his marriage to a white woman.

This quotation refers to the tongs, or Chinese fraternal societies. Chin wrote that Americans perceived the tongs as gangs and "the symbol of all Chinese heathen evil"—a symbol that Lowe amplified in his book. In the essay, Chin found that Wong, in her memoir,

> sharpens the misogynistic edge of the Christian stereotype by closing her book with a recollection of her father, an ordained Christian minister and sewing contractor, apologizing to her for all the Chinese ill treatment and humiliation of women.

Chin similarly faults Kingston for supporting the legend of Chinese misogyny. He tells Abe, "She says the written Chinese character for 'woman' and 'slave' is the same word. Well, she's nuts." He sees Tan as unjustly making the kitchen god, a traditional figure whose story is a love story, "into his wife's oppressor. She has to twist the story to make her point." Chin also faulted the successful playwright David Henry Hwang for an aspect of his play *F.O.B.* (the title being the acronym for fresh off the boat, an epithet used among immigrants for the most recently arrived). In that play, as Chin tells Abe, "Kwan Kung, the god of writers and fighters, gets down on his hands and knees and begs for white acceptance. Kwan Kung would *never* do that."

Chin, in parallel with the unnamed protagonist of "Railroad Standard Time," found much to be aggrieved about in the works of certain Chinese Americans, owing to the ways they are seen to misrepresent and turn their backs on Chinese culture. It hardly seems fair to judge writers for the content of autobiographical books; one cannot be expected to deny or falsify one's own life story. Yet Chin contended that such works were selectively published by savvy agents and editors who well knew what mainstream—that is, white—audiences would be likely to favor: the glorification of their own society and the subordination of the Chinese. In truth, the cumulative effect of these publications on broader American perceptions is the source of Chin's objections.

CRITICAL OVERVIEW

The critical response to *The Chinaman Pacific & Frisco R.R. Co.*, as to virtually all of Chin's work, has been mixed. Ellen Lesser wrote a highly favorable review for the *New England Review and Bread Loaf Quarterly*. She states, "With a ranting effusiveness, a dark poetry, an agile, furious sliding between the tracks of realism and visionary reality, playwright Chin jolts us into his new world." Lesser uses the title of the opening story to suggest the postmodern temporal quality of all the stories:

> For the most part, Chin's idiosyncratic version of "Railroad Standard Time" moves too quickly, too crazily, to be contained by a conventional narrative. Even when a story tracks a specific event, it splices in other times, other layers of experience.

Praising the author's "breathless, irreverent breed of story," Lesser concludes:

> Chin's rapid-fire language and imagery, his shifting realities, sometimes make for slippery travelling, but it's worth holding on by a strap, or the seat of your pants. This angry, funny, sexy, deeply moving romp through one man's Chinatown is about as far as you could journey from the arid rigors of recent minimalist fiction.

In *World Literature Today*, Robert Murray Davis calls Chin's collection "another skirmish in his long campaign" against "what he calls 'Ornamental Orientalia,' the sentimentalization and reduction of Asian culture to satisfy white preconceptions." Davis concludes of the collection, "The pace and energy can be breathtaking and confusing, but the ride on this line can be exciting."

Douglas Sun, in the *Los Angeles Times*, provided an especially insightful review. He finds that Chin's two overarching literary virtues are "considerable skill as a storyteller" and "a wicked sense of humor that runs a provocative gamut from jangled whimsy to scathing satire." Still, Sun observes, "Chin's rhetoric is often sharp and funny, but he also rides the high horse of racial bitterness for more than it's worth." In terms of style, Sun comments that Chin's temporal shifts and his intermingling of memory and experience represent "an absorbingly dense reflection of the way in which past, present and future come to bear upon each other in the mind." Drawing on Northrop Frye's conception that the best literature is universal, Sun acknowledged that ethnocentric fiction like Chin's is less able to achieve universality. Nonetheless, "it should at least show a human dimension that will move us and provoke us." According to Sun, Chin's collection "achieves such transcendence often enough to make it worthwhile fiction."

Tani E. Barlow in the *San Francisco Review of Books* acknowledged the quality of the humor in *The Chinaman Pacific & Frisco R.R. Co.* and the challenging historical context Chin faced. But she laments, "None of the above, however, lets Frank Chin off the hook for his inexorably adenoidal sexual politics." Barlow was put off by the collection's afterword—a bald parody of *The Woman Warrior*—which she deems "a sexually vituperative *ad hominem* attack on Maxine Kingston." In the absence of that piece, she would "have found reading his other work more tolerable."

In their entry on Chin in a *Dictionary of Literary Biography* volume on American western writers, Keith Lawrence and John Dye characterize "Railroad Standard Time" as "the tale of a recently orphaned young man looking for spiritual strength." Addressing Chin's controversial role within Asian American literature, Lawrence and Dye state, "As the original Chinatown Cowboy, Chin . . . seems to enjoy his self-assigned gunslinger role, his self-imposed charge to ferret out from Asian American literary ranks those he refers to as 'traitors.'" Summarizing Chin's campaign of "masculine empowerment" in the face of "white values" that are seen to subjugate Chinese Americans, men in particular, Lawrence and Dye conclude, "Unquestionably, these are quirky, aggressive, controversial, and even offensive arguments, but they remain potent points of debate, influencing and polarizing new generations of Asian American writers and goading the collective conscience of America."

CRITICISM

Michael Allen Holmes

Holmes is a writer with existential interests. In the following essay, he considers the issue of the narrator's likability in "Railroad Standard Time."

The reader of "Railroad Standard Time" is likely to finish with a slight, or even a great, personal dislike of the narrator-protagonist, perhaps concluding that he is not likable in general. The narrator himself reports, after the breakup of his family, that he won't be likable

> THERE CAN BE LITTLE DOUBT THAT CHIN, ALONGSIDE HIS PROTAGONIST, HAS LEGITIMATE CAUSE FOR RESENTMENT OF CERTAIN PARTIES AND IS NOW OUT TO UNDERMINE PEOPLE'S PRECONCEIVED NOTIONS."

anymore. He may be justified in his resentment of his ex-wife and the white man who drove his children away from him, but it is hard to connect this resentment to the story's evidence of his unlikability. He attacks the Chinese American authors who preceded him, practically invalidating their lives in condemning their autobiographical books. When he drives over a bridge, he makes gratuitous reference to parts of his body in a way that is likely to leave the reader saying, "Okay, I didn't need to know that." Worst of all, his description of Aurora Morales, a former music teacher, can only be properly classified as misogynistic. Under these considerations, it is clear that the protagonist is indeed not likable—at least not to everyone. The question that remains is whether his unlikability is in any way justified in the context of the story.

The unfortunate characterization of Mrs. Morales, which can be expected to appeal to few beyond the ranks of hormonal male adolescents, demands further attention. The protagonist introduces the music teacher by making offensive use of a metonym to reduce her identity to a sexualized part of her body. Not she but her chest—implicitly, the only part that matters—is said to be singing. The narrator tosses out a careless figurative description, saying she cups her hands as if to catch saliva dripping from her mouth. This description, clearly not literal, contributes to the image in the reader's mind and as such infantilizes her, or at least takes away her dignity. The protagonist conveys the sense that he is proud that he and other boys liked to con her into singing opera for them, which is a way of saying that they deceived her to objectify her, without regard for her sentiments or state of mind. The deception alone (it is not used to attain a

WHAT DO I READ NEXT?

- Chin's most highly regarded work of fiction is *Donald Duk* (1991), which recounts the difficult upbringing of a Chinese American boy who must cope with all of the usual challenges implied by his racial difference and with a name that further makes him a target for negative attention.

- Regardless of what Chin has expressed or contended, the place of Maxine Hong Kingston's memoir *The Woman Warrior* (1975) in the canon of modern Chinese American literature—and in broader Asian American and all ethnic American literature—is secure. The book is nostalgic, poetic, philosophic, and visionary.

- Whether or not her novels should be seen to cater to popular preconceptions of Chinese mentalities and traditions, Amy Tan has drawn positive attention to Chinese American literature and has left open an avenue for critics like Chin to share in and benefit from that attention. Her best-known work is *The Joy Luck Club* (1989), which concerns four immigrant families in San Francisco and is structured around the Chinese tile game of mah-jongg.

- Not unlike Chin, who met with difficulty finding publishers, in part because his stories did not cater to marketable stereotypes, Monfoon Leong was unable to publish the collection of short stories he wrote during the 1950s. His collection *Number One Son* was published posthumously, at his family's expense, in 1975.

- One of the most highly regarded modern Korean American writers is Chang-rae Lee, whose breakout novel *Native Speaker* (1995) won the PEN/Hemingway Award. Like the narrator of "Railroad Standard Time," the main character, Henry Park, who works as a spy, is coping with the absence of his child and the departure of his white wife, but Park's attitude is constructive, not destructive, and a reunion is possible.

- Chang-rae Lee and Chin have both been compared with Ralph Ellison, whose novel *Invisible Man* (1952) is a phenomenal classic of the African American experience in the shadow of white-majority racism and discrimination.

- Although Jack Kerouac is best known for the jazz-inflected automotive travels depicted in *On the Road* (1957), among the pieces in his nonfiction collection *Lonesome Traveler* (1960) is "The Railroad Earth," which begins in San Francisco and revolves around his time working on Southern Pacific trains.

- Laurence Yep is a Chinese American author who was born in San Francisco and has won the Laura Ingalls Wilder Medal for lifetime contributions to youth literature. His middle-grade novel *Child of the Owl* (1977) focuses on a twelve-year-old girl who learns about her Chinese heritage when she is sent to live with her grandmother in San Francisco's Chinatown.

- Chin would probably question whether Kay Honeyman has the credentials to write a novel focusing on Chinese culture and its attitude toward girls. She is a white American who, with her husband, adopted a boy and a girl from China. Her novel *The Fire Horse Girl* (2013) features a Chinese girl whose zodiac sign makes her far too independent for her family's liking. Her resourcefulness comes in handy when she travels to America.

virtuous aim) should be a source of shame, not pride. If the boys truly did fool her, she may well have eventually realized that their only goal was to, in effect, visually assault her; she may well have felt taken advantage of, violated. All in all, the description of Mrs. Morales and the narrator's attitude toward her are, in a word, tasteless.

To get to the root of Chin's—or his protagonist's—attitude toward women, and perhaps more important his conception of his own masculinity, the history of the Chinese in western America merits in-depth consideration. The aspect of this history that Chin highlights with the titles of both the story, "Railroad Standard Time," and the collection, *The China-man Pacific & Frisco R.R. Co.*, along with the most significant object in the story, the grandfather's watch, is the Chinese contribution to the building of the railroads. In *Nothing Like It in the World: The Men Who Built the Transcontinental Railroad, 1863–1869*, Stephen E. Ambrose identified the point when the ambitious engineers of the construction of the Central Pacific railway turned to Chinese laborers to fill out their desired crew totals. In 1865, recent silver strikes in Nevada were constantly luring away the adventurers who made it out to California, where railway work was highly taxing: the crews had to fill gullies, erect bridges, and use powder to blow open tunnels to lay rails over and through the Sierra Nevada.

The man in charge of hiring the crews for the Southern Pacific line in California, James Harvey Strobridge, was reluctant to deal with the Chinese at first, not only because they were so foreign but also because the perception, as Ambrose reports, was that "they averaged 120 pounds in weight, and only a few were taller than four feet ten inches." Yet a report of a hardworking crew of twenty Chinese elsewhere—along with mention that their culture had erected the Great Wall—swayed his mind. At the time, Chinese workers were discriminated against both in social relations and by law. They paid an abundance of special taxes, including a school tax, and yet could not be citizens, vote, testify in court, or send their children to school. The Chinese were, in effect, as Ambrose relates, perceived as an infestation: "The politicians cursed them, vied with one another about who hated the Chinese the most, declared them to be the dregs, said they worried about the terrible habits the Chinese brought with them." Specifically called into question—and this circles back to some of Chin's issues—was the masculinity of the Chinese. In Ambrose's words:

> White men despised the Chinese even as they used them. They constantly compared the Chinese to another subordinate group, white women. The Chinese were small, with delicate hands and hairless faces and long, braided hair. One editor called them "half-made men."

With newspaper editors, the white men controlling the presses, being among those holding such attitudes, it is no wonder that racist conceptions blanketed western American culture. The irony in all this was that, as Strobridge quickly discovered, the Chinese hired by the Central Pacific Railroad were model workers. Although California banned Chinese immigration, ineffectively, in 1858, by 1868 such news outlets as *Lippincott's Monthly Magazine* were ready to acknowledge the contributions and humanity of Chinese Americans. As quoted by Ambrose, an unidentified *Lippincott's* writer observes that the Chinese

> toiled without ceasing. . . . He may have less muscle, but by his untiring persistence he accomplished more work than the Caucasian. . . . [They] quickly got the "hang" of whatever you set them at, and soon display a remarkable adroitness.

Lee Chew, a Chinese immigrant who progressed from houseboy to railroad worker to laundry owner, concludes in a 1903 article for *Independent* magazine (cited by Ambrose) that the Chinese

> were persecuted not for their vices but for their virtues. No one would hire an Irishman, German, Englishman or Italian when he could get a Chinese, because our countrymen are so much more honest, industrious, steady, sober and painstaking.

Chinese workers proved especially valuable when drawing on knowledge of how their ancestors built fortresses in the gorges of the Yangtze River. They devised a system of pulleys and baskets to accomplish what seemed like the impossible task of carving ledges out of a steeply graded cliff side using black powder—a Chinese invention. The *Lippincott's* article concluded by declaring the need for a federal bureau to support the Chinese, not unlike the Freedmen's Bureau for previously enslaved African Americans.

The history of Chinese work on the railroads in the nineteenth century demonstrates both Chinese capabilities and the roots of white condescension and discrimination. As Lawrence and Dye note, Chin's fictional protagonists are "the literal and spiritual descendants of the Chinese American laborers," yet typically they are "alienated from Chin's ideal of Chinese American masculinity." Thus, the grandfather of the protagonist of

"Railroad Standard Time" was not one of the hardy laborers—he came too late for that—but was only a member of what the narrator calls the kiss-ass steward service. The narrator likes to imagine him as tough, someone who "had a few laughs and ran off with his pockets full of engraved watches"—in other words, both a warrior and a trickster. But this envisioning of the grandfather's identity feels forced, and the protagonist, one imagines, must know it.

Meanwhile, the protagonist feels less of a man when his wife leaves him for another man. The experience would be difficult enough strictly from a romantic perspective, and many a man has been driven to anger, and, pathetically but tragically, even violence, by romantic rivalry. The protagonist, to the contrary—whether because of philosophical pacifism, or stoicism, or perhaps a subconscious urge to spitefully fulfill the stereotypical role prescribed for him—only remains "still and expressionless as some good Chink." What must be even more difficult for the protagonist is the removal of his children from his life. The action of the scene of his wife and children's departure is highly underplayed, being compressed into just two sentences of text. Nonetheless, the daughter's "waving, shouting through an open window, 'Goodbye Daddy', over and over," as if saying good-bye forever, is an emotionally devastating scene. The psychological impact of this episode cannot be understated. The reader can hardly blame the protagonist for becoming a sore loser, someone who throws a punch if he feels like it and who refuses to be polite, to care about being obnoxious. He states of his evolved (or devolved) persona, "I'll be more than quiet, embarrassed. I won't be likable anymore." That is, he will never again be that stereotypical "good Chink."

At this point, the narrator's unlikability must be recognized not simply as an intentional reaction to an unpleasant occurrence but as a deeply rooted response to emotional trauma. The experience of losing his children in such a way would fairly turn a man inside-out—would reverse his conceptions of what to feel and how to respond to people, which is just what the protagonist's description suggests. Perhaps he lays part of the blame for his wife's departure on his culture—for fostering an individual who, in the eyes of the white woman he married, could not escape the stereotypes that, even in the 1970s, pervaded American culture. Thus, the protagonist may reject the autobiographical

books of Lowe, Wong, and Lee largely for the same reason he rejects his own book: because it emphasizes a sentimental period of his life that he faults for entrenching him within the broader cultural stereotype of Chinese Americans. He makes clear that he takes issue with the authors' Christianity. Chin explained himself in his discussion with Abe for the *Bloomsbury Review*. His comments implicitly link the idea of having his children taken away to the deleterious impact of Christianity:

> We're talking about the enemy that destroyed my culture, my civilization, my history. The history of Chinese America, the history of Chinatown, is not written in Chinese names. It is written in the names of the Chinese missionaries who wrote the Chinese out of history. These people might have had good intentions, but they destroyed us in the name of their god. Not in the name of *our good*, but in the name of *their god*. And to a large degree they've succeeded.

This helps contextualize Chin's objections to the propagation of Chinese American stories written by Christian authors, whose lives reflect the very subjugation Chin rails against.

There can be little doubt that Chin, alongside his protagonist, has legitimate cause for resentment of certain parties and is now out to undermine people's preconceived notions. That is, preconceived in accord with pervading stereotypes and selective literary representations—about Chinese culture and individuals. He is out to explode such notions, as he suggests with striking imagery in the closing paragraphs of his story. When he states regarding himself, "The fat man's coming home on a sneaky breeze," this is likely not a literal description of himself (otherwise no physical description appears) but is a reference to the nickname of the atomic bomb that was dropped on Nagasaki, Japan, to put an end to World War II. This is reinforced by his ensuing characterization of himself as "a bomber, flying my mother's car into the unknown charted by the stars and the radio." The protagonist is, as he later specifies, unsettled, ill at ease; he is practically ready to blow. It is unfortunate that he closes the story by dwelling on an objectifying description of his music teacher, but perhaps this should be taken as a sign of how much he is overflowing with bile, such that in the wake of his wife's departure—which likely compromises his ability to feel love at all, especially toward

The narrator's mother keeps a railroad watch on the kitchen table. (© PAUL ATKINSON | Shutterstock)

any given white woman—he cannot help but release some of his pent-up anger through indulgence in an objectifying attitude toward a woman.

The story closes with the key image of the protagonist's route running parallel to the local railroads. In the end, the so-called railroad standard time by which the protagonist functions, the time ticked off by the hands of his outdated pocket watch—which, he reports, "ticked against my heart and pounded my chest as I went too fast over bumps in the night"— represents not only the attitudes and traditions of bygone eras but also the entire history of Chinese Americans as embodied in the experience of the railroad. This experience was marked by racist disregard, dislike, and discrimination. And as outdated as such attitudes were by the time Chin was writing in late 1970s, he still had to face them, ticking away the days and years of his life just as the clock he cannot let go of ticks away the seconds.

Source: Michael Allen Holmes, Critical Essay on "Railroad Standard Time," in *Short Stories for Students*, Gale, Cengage Learning, 2016.

Susan B. Richardson
In the following excerpt, Richardson asserts that some of Chin's common techniques, such as his inclusion of many pop culture references, are not always effective.

Frank Chin's *Donald Duk* is a spirited novel of education whose comic protagonist makes a welcome addition to the roster of American literary boy heroes. The novel entertains readers with its coming-of-age account of twelve-year-old Donald carping and spluttering his way to new understanding—about himself, about his community, about his place in American society. Yet beyond any entertainment value, the author clearly intends his novel to have a serious didactic purpose. Stories, according to Chin, are essential to an education that would "create informed, morally conscious citizens"; he claims that Chinese legends and stories are a "valuable tool" for reminding Chinese-Americans of their heritage and a "necessity" for bringing understanding to white Americans about the history and culture of others. The novel exemplifies his claim; *Donald Duk*'s comic strip bildungsroman becomes a novel of education for readers as well—especially for white readers. The lessons that drive the novel are explicit and unambiguous. *Donald Duk* presents the heroic dimensions of Chinese-American history even as it exposes the invidious popular stereotypes, the prejudices, and the injustices that characterize that history. The unrelenting indictment of the status of Chinese-Americans and their treatment in American society, in the past and now, becomes an argument for social correction—a call for change dictated by respect for all and fair play as promised by American democracy.

The cultural issues explored by *Donald Duk* are not new to Frank Chin's work—Chin's role as a spokesman for Chinese America is well established. The legal and social forces that have victimized Chinese-Americans (e.g. racist U.S. exclusion laws, the nineteenth century exploitation of Chinese laborers, the distortion of classic Chinese philosophy and literature, the erasure of Chinese-American history, the emasculating stereotypes of Chinese in the American media) inform Chin's work from his earliest essays and plays to his 1994 novel, *Gunga Din Highway*.

Curiously, however, in spite of *Donald Duk*'s clear didactic purpose, Chin's narrative choices undermine the effectiveness of his argument to persuade and transform his readers. Various

" EVEN IN THE CASE OF THEIR COMPLETE IGNORANCE ABOUT CHINESE-AMERICAN CULTURE, UNINFORMED WHITE OUTSIDERS ARE SPARED EMBARRASSMENT SINCE BASIC INSTRUCTION IS APPROPRIATE FOR A TWELVE-YEAR-OLD LIKE DONALD. THIS STRUCTURE, THEN, IS ONE OF A NUMBER OF CHIN'S TECHNIQUES TO EASE READERS INTO THE UNFAMILIAR TERRAIN OF CHINESE CULTURE."

formal features, such as his cartoon format and the use of characters as surrogate-learners, serve to distance readers from the text and from the characters. Chin's insistence upon presenting unfamiliar ethnic material as familiar and "normal" blunts an outsider reader's encounter with Chinese-American experience and reduces the possibility of reproducing for the-reader a multicultural experience. Also, Chin's repeated use of analogy between Chinese-American and mainstream cultures in order to foster white acceptance of Chinese America establishes a false homogeneity between the two cultures. These narrative strategies that simplify and homogenize also distort experience and mitigate against genuine understanding of the "other." Beyond these problems with form, moreover, the argument itself is compromised by its particularity. Even as the novel calls for the erasure of race-based prejudice and injustice, it leaves intact discrimination based on other categories such as gender or class. Voices emerge from the text that complicate the novel's seemingly simple message and that call into question the integrity of its underlying principles. The discussion of the lessons of *Donald Duk* which follows will focus first on the effectiveness of certain of Chin's narrative techniques in delivering the novel's lessons and then will consider the implications of the contending subtextual voices for the novel's didactic impact.

The style and spirit of *Donald Duk* are uncharacteristic of much of Chin's earlier work. The adversarial anger and bitterness of, for example, *The Chickencoop Chinaman* or "Come

All Ye Asian American Writers of the Real and the Fake" here give way to wry humor, comic scenes of burlesque, and dialogue peppered with broad punning and the slangy, insult-laden bantering of young siblings. Although elsewhere Chin's outrage and combativeness propel him virtually to declare war on his (non-Chinese) audience—he has testified that "writing theater is like making war" (qtd. in McDonald xix), that stories are cultural weaponry, and that storytelling is a tactic to defend oneself "against all forms of oppression and exploitation" ("Uncle Frank's Fakebook of Fairy Tales")—in this novel, Chin becomes uncharacteristically solicitous of outsiders in his audience. That is, in *Donald Duk* he exchanges the role of adversary for that of teacher. Instead of a jeremiad, the novel becomes a primer with a series of lessons about Chinese-American culture.

These lessons are presumably directed at Donald although I believe that Chin's real target is his audience. Donald personifies the self-hating Chinese-American who embraces white majority attitudes as his own, including the debasement of Chinese-Americans, and the novel provides a melange of teacher figures to rectify this misguidedness. Donald's primary teacher is his father, the wise and powerful King Duk who takes pride in his name and heritage, but numerous other figures (significantly all male) provide him instruction, from Uncle Donald, the wise elder, to Crawdad Man, the teller of old Chinese stories, and Victor Lee, a Vietnam veteran.

The steady flow of explanation and advice from these many and various teachers is activated by Donald's constant refrain of "What does it mean?", a didactic structuring that places the reader in the position of onlooker. While the lessons apply to readers as well as to Donald, the audience is not addressed directly or aggressively (in the way, for example, that the audience is challenged by *The Chickencoop Chinaman*); here the arsenal of "cultural weaponry" is sheathed in the interest of the reader's comfort. Even in the case of their complete ignorance about Chinese-American culture, uninformed white outsiders are spared embarrassment since basic instruction is appropriate for a twelve-year-old like Donald. This structure, then, is one of a number of Chin's techniques to ease readers into the unfamiliar terrain of Chinese culture. The comfort gained by readers has a cost, however:

a reduced potential for emotional commitment or cross-cultural understanding.

The novel's cartoon form also works to ease the reading (and sugar-coat the lessons) of *Donald Duk*. The title itself heralds the novel's identification with Disney—an identification which suggests that Donald Duk is as American and as non-threatening as Donald Duck and deserves as much attention and valorization as his namesake. The cartoon-like young protagonist expresses appropriately uncomplicated thoughts in appropriately simple syntax. Furthermore, the flattening of experience characteristic of comic books makes reading the narrative quick and effortless. The novel's progression of events is linear for, in spite of the double-layered setting of Donald's dreamworld and San Francisco's Chinatown, a single protagonist and the same lessons operate in both realms. In addition, with the exception of Donald, the novel's characters are one-dimensional, static and—in some cases—parodic. Even Donald's character lacks complexity; the novel charts the change in his understanding and attitudes, yet—in part because of the lack of space in so short a work—the effect of the change upon his character is limited. Finally, as in a cartoon, Donald Duk exhibits a Disney-like clarity about values and morals. The novel explores issues in a humorous, non-threatening, and engaging way in which there is no ambiguity about right and wrong. Issues and behavior are clearly marked as bad or good. These features create an economy of form that allows Chin to foreground his didactic agenda; again, however, the form discourages the reader's commitment to the story or characters.

Along with Donald, Chin creates some auxiliary learner/characters who function as another important "easing" strategy. The primary example is Donald's best (white) friend, Arnold Azalea, who serves as a kind of alter ego for white readers. When Arnold is invited to spend Chinese New Year's in Chinatown with the Duk family, the family members incessantly give Arnold explanations about Chinese customs—often at length and sometimes more than once—to ensure the comfort of their uninformed guest. Arnold asks questions on behalf of the audience, and the answers he receives function in such a way as to inform the audience as well and to preclude their confusion about cultural or linguistic matters. For example, as soon as Arnold hears a Chinese term such as lay see, someone is quick to translate "lucky money in New Year's red envelopes";

when the red envelopes are distributed, Arnold receives detailed instruction as to their purpose and the protocol for behavior. Explanations to Arnold are sometimes so detailed, in fact, that the author has Donald react with embarrassment for the condescension Arnold might feel—perhaps to deflect any suspicion of condescension by the author toward his readers.

Chin introduces a second white male initiate whose presence signals the broad application of the novel's lessons. Arnold's father is characterized, even caricatured, as a rich and successful California businessman. We learn only a few facts about the Azalea family—Arnold attends an exclusive private school, his parents take expensive vacations to Hawaii, the Azaleas support Arnold's friendship with Donald—but these are sufficient to Mr. Azalea's narrative function as an adult character who takes instruction from King Duk and Uncle Donald about the meaning of things. Readers thereby understand that the novel's lessons are not only for children, but pertain even to rich, successful, white men. Although he makes a limited appearance in the narrative, Arnold's father serves the important function of validating the narrative's message for adults in the audience.

Chin never leaves his readers puzzled about the meaning of the many Chinese phrases that flavor the narrative. In general, terms are translated directly as they occur, and definitions are repeated at several places. The term may be explicitly explained to a character: "The mandate of heaven. Tien ming. 'What's that?' Donald asks. . . . 'The Chinese say, Kingdoms rise and fall. Nations come and go,' Dad says." Or the synonym may appear in apposition, as in "bok gwai, the white monsters." On the rare occasion when Chin omits explanation, the context makes the meaning abundantly clear. For example, Goong hay fot choy (Happy New Year) is not defined when it first occurs during the New Year celebration, but it is unmistakably a greeting. (In case readers should miss its meaning, King Duk defines it later for Arnold.) Only with a few terms that are used continuously, like lay see [lucky money] or sifu [respected teacher], does Chin leave the reader to negotiate meaning without a (repeated) definition. Unless the reader is excessively absentminded, then, there are no instances when a Chinese term is ambiguous.

Another rhetorical technique designed to make the strange familiar in the world of Donald

Duk is Chin's extensive use of comparison and the juxtaposition of elements from classical Chinese and American pop cultures. Beginning with the obvious identification of the hero and his family with Walt Disney characters, Chinese figures, stories, and places are regularly presented in conjunction with a mainstream American counterpart. Throughout the novel, Chinese-somethings are cited: the Chinese Fred Astaire, the Chinese Betty Crocker, the Chinese Frank Sinatra, and so on. Uncle Donald explains the Water Margin of classic Chinese legend in terms of Robin Hood: "The Water Margin was a place like [Sherwood Forest]," and "One of those 108 Chinese Robin Hoods is a hood name of Lee Kuey." Uncle Donald suggests that the band of 108 Chinese outlaws is all very much like Robin Hood, Little John and the rest of Robin Hood's Merry Men. When the Crawdad Man tells "a famous fairy tale" called The Candlewick Fairy, his listeners wonder if it is a "real" story. Crawdad Man authenticates it by comparing it to a Euro-American tale: "It's the real Chinese story, like 'Goldilocks and the Three Bears.' Everybody knows it." The reader's ignorance is thus excused with the implication that erasing such ignorance requires very little effort.

Through their constant reference to old-time movies and Hollywood stars, including Donald's self-identification with Fred Astaire, the novel's characters ally themselves with "typical" mainstream Americans and thereby claim the same popular culture (a legitimate claim, of course, since it is also theirs). By presenting themselves as "not strange," the characters are able to dilute the strangeness of their ethnic customs and allusions. Almost invariably throughout the novel, the references to classical Chinese characters (Kwan Kung, Soong Gong, Lee Kuey, Ngawk Fay), to Chinese culture (Confucian thought, the Mandate of Heaven), to ethnic customs (New Year's firecrackers, dragons, tai chi, Cantonese opera), or to events in Chinese-American history (laying railroad track in the High Sierras, detention at Angel Island) occur in tandem with names dropping from the popculture world of American television and Hollywood: Ginger Rogers, Shirley Temple, Frank Sinatra, and so on.

Again, this technique carries some risk. Chin uses a similar approach in his 1992 collection of Asian fairy tales, a project designed to introduce Asian American children to their Asian heritage and to make Asian tales palatable through a kind of homogenization: "Here," Chin writes, "you'll find we try to use the fairy tales and myths of the west, the stories you're familiar with, to take the mystery and fear of fatal exotic Orientalia out of the stories [of] the immigrants" (*Fakebook*). Shirley Geoklin Lim reminds us that "juxtaposing ancient Chinese images and contemporary American cultural graffitti, when the Chinese allusions are unreconstructed, can only lead to uncomprehending rejection. . . ." ("Reconstructing" 56). Lim's way to achieve comprehension is to place responsibility for reconstruction upon the "untrained reader." But when Chin chooses instead to aid readers' comprehension by simplifying material and removing "the mystery and fear," much of the original flavor and meaning of the Chinese folk material—in the fairy tale translations or in *Donald Duk*—must be lost . . .

Source: Susan B. Richardson, "The Lessons of *Donald Duk*," in *MELUS*, Vol. 24, No. 4, Winter 1999, p. 57.

Jinqi Ling

In the following excerpt, Ling describes some of the controversy Chin has stirred with his strong opinions about his fellow Asian American writers.

. . . The publication of Maxine Hong Kingston's autobiography *The Woman Warrior* in 1976 was a landmark phenomenon in postwar American literary history: the book self-consciously injected a dissenting Asian American feminist perspective into the largely male-dominated Asian American literary discourse; it enjoyed immediate commercial success with mainstream publishers and widespread institutional recognition; and, because of the book's ambivalent relationships with both the evolving Asian American social movement of the 1970s and a seemingly accommodating yet suspiciously "expansive" literary establishment capable of mis-appropriating the autobiography ideologically, it generated vigorous, uncompromising debates within Asian American communities with regard to the nature and social function of their literary practices in contemporary America. Frank Chin, it is well known, has advanced perhaps the harshest critique of *The Woman Warrior*. In his various comments on Kingston's autobiography, Chin suggests that the book achieved its success mainly through the author's "selling out" of Asian American interests, either by misrepresenting Chinese culture as inherently "anti-individualistic" and

> THE OVERTLY OPPOSITIONAL LITERATURE PRODUCED BY CHINESE AMERICAN MALE WRITERS SUCH AS CHIN IN THE EARLY 1970S STRATEGICALLY RAISED ASIAN AMERICA'S ANGRY VOICE PUBLICLY, A DEVELOPMENT OF ASIAN AMERICAN CULTURAL IDENTITY CONGRUENT WITH AND PARTLY SHAPED BY THE BLACK PROTEST AND COUNTERCULTURE MOVEMENTS OF THE ERA."

thus morally inferior, or by caricaturing Chinese American males as "cruel" and "misogynistic" sexual perverts (e.g., 1985, 110, 130; Chan et al. 1991, 9, 27, 28). Numerous counterarguments have been made since the early 1980s that challenge Chin's critique of Kingston's book, his implicit attempt to impose a single standard on the polyphony of Asian American literary expression, and his insensitivity to the social and cultural inequalities suffered by Asian American women both historically and in their contemporary experience (e.g., Sledge 1980, 70; Sau-ling Wong 1988, 23–25; Cheung 1990; Kim 1990b, 75–80; Lim 1993, 576–78). Despite these and other efforts to direct attention to the historical specificity of Kingston's autobiography, the controversy has shown little sign of abating. For example, Chin has recently reaffirmed with undiminished seriousness his commitment to reviving a masculinist Asian American heroic ideal, as well as his lack of sympathy for critical efforts to address gender inequality through both community activities and academic criticism (Chan et al. 1991, 7–8). At the same time, some Asian American feminist critics continue their impassioned exchange with Chin, mostly in reaction to the obviously simplistic aspects of his position, with the aid of analytical tools available from posthumanist discourses of the late 1980s and 1990s.

The hardening of Chin's stance toward *The Woman Warrior* is, without a doubt, an unfortunate turn of events. But the context of Chin's solidification of his attitude merits some critical attention for the simple reason that there is a difference between Chin's angry endorsement of ethnic essentialism and Asian masculine ideals through rhetoric, and the actual fulfillment of his declared goals in a material sense. In making such a distinction, however, I do not intend to sever the relationship between Chin's aversion to *The Woman Warrior* and the entrenched patriarchal thinking and practice in American society in general and in Asian American communities in particular. Nor do I wish to downplay the consequences of Chin's continued refusal to acknowledge the impact of women's contribution to the development of Asian American literary discourse from the 1940s to the present. On the contrary, as I have argued elsewhere, Chin's contestatory invocation of an Asian American masculine ideal as a corrective to the historical "emasculation" of Asian men in America is useful only when such a critique is capable of revealing how race, gender, class, and national identities are entwined in the construction of Asian men's sexuality in American culture and of self-consciously accepting its inevitable dissolution into more self-reflexive counter-hegemonic positions (1997, 318–19).

What I wish to suggest beyond the general agreement on the limitations of Chin's approach is that the hardening of his position has also been affected by a gradual shift of critical attention in the debate from the social and cultural forces that surround the feminist position in *The Woman Warrior* to Chin's uncompromising self. Such a shift clearly reflects Asian American critics' recognition of the overwhelming success of *The Woman Warrior* as a firmly established ethnic/feminist literary text in the American canon, a fact that makes Chin's polemical approach to the autobiography stand out even more negatively. But at the same time, this shift is accompanied by two problematic tendencies among Chin's critics after the autobiography's canonization both by the literary establishment and by the ethnic community: the first is to view the established analytical frameworks for reading the feminist message in *The Woman Warrior* as somehow definitive and the second is to reproduce discursively gained initial insights about the debate despite new developments that point toward the need to rethink the book's intertextual significance. As I suggested in the foregoing chapters of this book, Chin's suppression of Asian American women's voices is undeniable, but it is neither wholly intentional nor successful, and his unidimensional critique of racism and his narrow definition of Asian American identity in the 1970s promoted an oppositional consciousness that dialectically facilitated Asian American women's efforts to voice their concerns in their own terms. Such critical appropriations and revisions of Chin's oppositional strategy by Asian American women indicate that new social formations have taken place. If we recognise the substantive progress that has subsequently been made both in Asian American social life and in its academic discourses, then we should also agree that insistence on using some of the obviously thoughtlessly articulated aspects of *Aiiieeeee!*'s and *The Big Aiiieeeee!*'s positions as the only point of reference to advance new arguments about gender becomes inadequate in itself. For such an approach continually elides the immediate political contexts of the publication and reception of *The Woman Warrior*, including those of Chin's and his critics' engagement with one another; it makes Asian American critical practice less demanding by reproducing only the familiar and the predictable; and it turns the Asian American critical gaze away from sites where emerging problematics in ethnic critical practice demand new and creative answers.

In the analysis that follows, I examine some of the ideological complexities that have been neglected in prior analyses of the reception of *The Woman Warrior* through a recontextualization of the debate. My contention is that the controversy does not have to be seen as a purely negative turn of events. As a terrain where vital issues concerning Asian American subject formation were contested and negotiated, it has also served as a necessary precondition for renewed transformative articulations in Asian American literary creation and criticism.

Most discussions of the debate have so far focused on the limitations of Chin's view that the literary establishment's misappropriation and adoption of *The Woman Warrior* for its own purposes reflect nothing but the motivated urge for assimilation on the part of Kingston. It is equally problematic, I would add, to regard Asian American male writers' and critics' negative responses to the autobiography's canonization as merely sexist reactions against Asian American women's artistic freedom or as manifestations of an implicit male desire to maintain control over women. Rather, these varying responses need to be viewed as illustrations of how the articulation of Chinese American

women's oppression is caught up with that of Chinese American men's, and how the reception of *The Woman Warrior* reflects both the epistemological and the ontological difficulties posed for a woman writer of color, whose ability to speak—and whose chance to be heard—was severely limited by given racial, gender, and class power structures. Chin's negativity toward *The Woman Warrior*, as critics point out, arises partly from his failure to see the entanglement of the socioeconomic oppression of Asian men in America with their own cultural oppression in terms of sexism (Cheung 1990, 234–36; Kim 1990b, 75–79). When Asian American women seek to expose anti-female prejudices in their own ethnic community, he and others not illogically feel "betrayed" by attacks that appeared to line up with the majority culture's positions. As is also well known, from the mid-1950s until the publication of *The Woman Warrior* in 1976, most writings by Chinese American women did not feature explicit critiques of racism and sexism in American society. The overtly oppositional literature produced by Chinese American male writers such as Chin in the early 1970s strategically raised Asian America's angry voice publicly, a development of Asian American cultural identity congruent with and partly shaped by the black protest and counterculture movements of the era. If this emergent Asian American sensibility was at a fledgling or, in the words of the editors of *Aiiieeeee!*, "delicate" stage (Chin et al. 1974, ix), it was also little informed by Asian American women's urgent social demand for gender equality. With the publication of *The Woman Warrior*. Kingston virtually started a revolution within a revolution. Shortly after the formation of a narrowly defined counterhegemonic Asian American literary discourse represented by Chin and other editors of *Aiiieeeee!*. Kingston's Chinese American feminist discourse defiantly branched out from the largely community-based Asian American literary revival and drew support from the mainstream feminist movement. This formative moment created a context ripe for perceived betrayal. More important, it revealed the complex internal and external constraints on these almost simultaneously emergent, unavoidably conflictual, yet ideologically interdependent discourses within a restrictive cross-cultural space of self-representation.

As a product of this historical moment, Kingston's articulation of oppressed Chinese American women's voices in their male-dominated community could scarcely have been free from reactive impulses, and it was understandably done without full control over how it might intersect with the social construction of gender and sexual politics at a time when the social history of Chinese American women's oppression was largely ignored. In an era in which practitioners of a male-oriented Asian American literary discourse saw it as a newborn vehicle for cultural identity and worked hard to cultivate a sense of ethnic pride and solidarity, a previously submerged Chinese American feminist discourse challenged the sexism in Asian American communities in striving to make its voice heard and to subvert established gender hierarchies. In fact, Kingston was quite sensitive to the cultured risk and the multivalent nature of her injection of a Chinese American woman's voice into a discourse characterized by a male ethos. Immediately after the publication of *The Woman Warrior*, for example, she recognized that her hook "was one of only heroines. Men are minor characters. It seems an unbalanced view of the world" (quoted in Taylor 1976, B1). On another occasion, Kingston reflected that although she intended to write about women's and men's experiences as an "interlocking story," because of her fear that the men's story was "anti-female and would undercut the feminist viewpoint," she decided to write about women's issues "separately" in *The Woman Warrior*—her "selfish book" (quoted in Kim 1982, 207–8). Kingston's concerns here obviously were not unique to her own position of enunciation but would be shared by other women writers of color in an era when women's claim on the ethnic community's interests, as Elaine Kim persuasively argues, became inseparable from their claim on female self and subjectivity and when women's interpretation of their own experiences as women could hardly be made without simultaneously "airing the 'dirty laundry'" (1990b, 78, 81). . . .

Source: Jinqi Ling, "Maxine Hong Kingston's Remapping of Asian American Historical Imagination in *China Men*," in *Narrating Nationalisms: Ideology and Form in Asian American Literature*, Oxford University Press, 1998, pp. 112–16.

Publishers Weekly

In the following review, an anonymous reviewer faults Chin's essays for being "bitterly accusatory rather than rational."

Whether he is writing about a trip to Cuba he took as a student during the 1960s, his visits with the inhabitants of the Chinatowns along the California-Baja California border, interviews with a white police officer in San Diego who has succeeded in reducing tensions between Cambodian and Laotian youth gangs there or his experiences at a writers' conference in Singapore, Chin tends to portray everyone, and everything, in this collection of six essays, in terms of race, ethnicity and cultural stereotypes. Chin heaps scorn not only on whites (Anglos) but also on Asians in Singapore city whose culture he disdains), and especially on Chinese American writers whom Chin accuses of having sold out to white American culture and values. Waving about classic texts, in particular Sun Tzu's *The Art of War*, he denigrates those who like Maxine Hong Kingston and Amy Tan. "They like the idea of falsifying Chinese culture in the name of art and Westernization. They are admitted and joyous white supremacists." Throughout, Chin, who prefers to be referred to as a Chinaman rather than a Chinese-American, makes references to being someone without "a sense of home." The problems of the ethnically displaced and the merits of cultural diversity versus assimilation are important issues. The tone of Chin's arguments against the desirability and possibility of assimilation is emotional rather than intellectual, bitterly accusatory rather than rational. Unfortunately that will probably limit his book to preachifying to the converted.

Source: Review of *Bulletproof Buddhists and Other Essays*, in *Publishers Weekly*, Vol. 245, No. 24, June 15, 1998, p. 50.

Publishers Weekly

In the following review, an anonymous reviewer describes Chin's Gunga Din Highway *as an "always interesting read."*

Ancient and contemporary myths of China and America propel this provocative, multilayered tale of a willful Chinese American's 50-year odyssey from black sheep to reluctant head of the family. Ulysses Kwan, son of actor Longman Kwan—famous for his roles as Charlie Chan's Number Four Son and as "the Chinaman Who Dies" in numerous war films—never accepts his lot in the family or in the San Francisco Bay Chinese community. Nor does he respect the life's work of his ambitious, self-absorbed father. Through the sweeping changes of four decades, from the 1950s to the present, Ulysses, in a kaleidoscope of roles, from artist to revolutionary, from railroadman to writer, confronts various societal presumptions. Chin's forceful, often vitriolic narrative alternates among the points of view of Longman Kwan, of Ulysses's two child-hood blood-brothers, and of Ulysses himself. Juxtaposing Hollywood mythology with Chinese legend, Chin (*Donald Duk*) writes with penetrating insight into the power and persistence of ethnic stereotypes—implicating fellow Chinese American authors and artists in the process. The multiplicity of Chin's narrative agenda does occasion some flaws, however; initially convincing characterizations and plot elements weaken as Chin molds them into targets for ideological or satiric fusillades. Nevertheless, Chin's strong prose, angry wit, intelligence and even arrogance make this a vital, always interesting read.

Source: Review of *Gunga Din Highway*, in *Publishers Weekly*, Vol. 241, No. 34, August 22, 1994, p. 41.

Publishers Weekly

In the following excerpt, an anonymous reviewer calls Chin's novel Donald Duk *"charming."*

. . . Frank Chin, author of the trade paperback original *Donald Duk*, coming from Coffee House Press in March, has for two decades waged a veritable one-man war against the stereotype of the "exotic oriental." Chin started as an angry young man in the late 1950s and stayed that way, through various incarnations.

Earliest was Chin the playwright, author of *The Chickencoop Chinaman* and *The Year of the Dragon*, which attracted quite a lot of attention when they were staged off-Broadway in the early 1970s. Next came a very pronounced war of words against Maxine Hong Kingston, David Henry Hwang and several other authors, whom he accused of perpetuating stereotypes and bending traditional culture to satisfy their needs. (The character of Whittman Ah Sing in Kingston's *Tripmaster Monkey* [Knopf] is supposedly modeled on Chin.) In his current life—despite an undampened ardor for the literary attack—Chin's fiction has started to garner an audience once again.

Coffee House publisher Allan Kornblum first heard about Chin's work through a former employee. "Frank had been turned down by an agent as not being sufficiently 'commercial,' but when I read his stories, I was enthralled with the writing." A collection, *The Chinaman Pacific & Frisco R.R. Co.*, was published in 1988, and Kornblum says, "in small press terms, it has done well."

For *Donald Duk*, Coffee House is really putting itself on the line, printing an "unprecedented"

first run of 7500 copies, and organizing its second-ever author tour.

The story, set in contemporary San Francisco, focuses on 12-year-old Donald Duk and his family—mother Daisy, father King, sisters Venus and Penny—and his white friend Arnold Azalea. The novel takes place amidst Chinese New Year festivities—particularly painful for Donald, since he hates everything Chinese. We see and hear and feel Donald's embarrassment over his family and culture—the kind of feelings 12-year-olds of every persuasion have been known to harbor from time to time.

Eventually, of course, Donald begins to come to terms with his heritage. Kornblum found himself "falling in love with the story. The book is charming, even if the reputation of its author is bristly!"

Chin displayed some of those bristles in conversation with *PW*, arguing with an intense racial passion. "I want people to recognize the stereo-types they have created. Many Asian Americans are detached from their history and end up loathing themselves. But white people don't demand the submission many of us think they do—after all, here's a story in which the only 'real' white racist is Donald Duk. I feel people are just as open to real information about Asian Americans as they are to the fake."

If these fictional offerings are anything to go by, a lot more "real" information about Asian Americans will be coming our way soon, and a lot more attention might just be paid to it. But as Gish Jen says, "What we don't want is to be lumped together, ghettoized. I hope that 25 years from now, we'll achieve the kind of standing that Jewish American writers have—that is, we'll just be judged as writers."

Source: "Spring's Five Fictional Encounters of the Chinese American Kind," in *Publishers Weekly*, Vol. 238, No. 8, February 8, 1991, p. 25.

SOURCES

Abe, Frank, "Frank Chin: His Own Voice," in *Bloomsbury Review*, Vol. 2, No. 6, September 1991, pp. 3–4.

Ambrose, Stephen E., *Nothing Like It in the World: The Men Who Built the Transcontinental Railroad, 1863–1869*, Simon & Schuster, 2000, pp. 149–57.

Barlow, Tani E., Review of *The Chinaman Pacific & Frisco R.R. Co.*, in *San Francisco Review of Books*, Vol. 13, No. 4, Spring 1989, pp. 9–11.

Chin, Frank, "Come All Ye Asian American Writers of the Real and the Fake," in *The Big Aiiieeeee! An Anthology of Chinese American and Japanese American Literature*, edited by Jeffery Paul Chan, Frank Chin, Lawson Fusao Inada, and Shawn Wong, Meridian, 1991, pp. 22–26.

———, "Railroad Standard Time," in *The Chinaman Pacific & Frisco R.R. Co.*, Coffee House Press, 1988, pp. 1–7.

Davis, Robert Murray, Review of *The Chinaman Pacific & Frisco R.R. Co.*, in *World Literature Today*, Vol. 63, No. 3, Summer 1989, pp. 487–88.

Goshert, John Charles, "Frank (Chew), (Jr.) Chin," in *Asian American Writers*, edited by Deborah L. Madsen, *Dictionary of Literary Biography*, Vol. 312, Thomson Gale, 2005, pp. 44–57.

Lawrence, Keith, and John Dye, "Frank (Chew), (Jr.) Chin," in *Twentieth-Century American Western Writers: First Series*, edited by Richard H. Cracroft, *Dictionary of Literary Biography*, Vol. 206, The Gale Group, 1999, pp. 42–50.

Lesser, Ellen, Review of *The Chinaman Pacific & Frisco R.R. Co.*, in *New England Review and Bread Loaf Quarterly*, Vol. 12, No. 1, Fall 1989, pp. 98–108.

McMillin, Calvin, ed., Introduction to *The Confessions of a Number One Son: The Great Chinese American Novel*, by Frank Chin, University of Hawai'i Press, 2015, p. 11.

Sun, Douglas, Review of *The Chinaman Pacific & Frisco R.R. Co.*, in *Los Angeles Times*, January 1, 1989.

FURTHER READING

Hwang, David Henry, *Trying to Find Chinatown: The Selected Plays*, Theatre Communications Group, 2000.
Like Chin, Hwang made a name for himself writing for the theater, but unlike Chin, he stuck with the genre. His 1988 play *M. Butterfly*—inspired by the Puccini opera *Madama Butterfly*—was a Broadway success, a masterly consideration of ethnic stereotypes and gender roles. This collection includes eight plays that speak to some of Chin's concerns about his Chinese American homeland.

White, Richard, *Railroaded: The Transcontinentals and the Making of Modern America*, W. W. Norton, 2011.
This is a five-hundred-page history of the significance of the railroad construction in which the Chinese played no small part. Readers of Chin's fiction may be most interested in chapter 7, section 3, "Contract Labor and the Chinese."

Yin, Xiao-huang, *Chinese American Literature since the 1850s*, University of Illinois Press, 2000.
Yin's comprehensive history includes an excellent dissection of Chin's arguably misguided criticism of Chinese American women authors in the section in chapter 7 titled "Kwan Kung versus Fa Mulan: The War of Words between Chin and Kingston."

Yung, Judy, and the Chinese Historical Society of America, *San Francisco's Chinatown*, Images of America, Arcadia Publishing, 2006.
Among the many histories treating San Francisco's historic Chinatown, Yung's, part of the encyclopedic Images of America series, tells the district's story primarily through photographs and descriptive captions.

SUGGESTED SEARCH TERMS

Frank Chin AND "Railroad Standard Time"

Frank Chin AND plays

Frank Chin AND fiction

Frank Chin AND Asian American literature

Chinese American literature

Chinatown AND American literature

Chinese AND transcontinental railroads

Chinese AND masculinity

Chinese AND misogyny

Frank Chin AND Maxine Hong Kingston

Refuge in London

RUTH PRAWER JHABVALA
2003

"Refuge in London," by Ruth Prawer Jhabvala, is the story of a sixteen-year-old girl growing up in a boardinghouse in London in the years after World War II, when the city was flooded with refugees from war-torn parts of Europe. The house is filled with exotic characters, but she focuses on two: Kohl, a once-famous artist in Germany who toils in obscurity to create drawings and paintings that he does not sell, and Marta, his wife, who has her own room in the house, where she openly entertains other men. The love-hate relationship between the two pulls the young narrator in. Marta takes her out to restaurants and parties with the rich men who court her, while Kohl, silent and contemplative, has her sit for him as he creates sketches that will one day be collected in the great museums of the world. "Refuge in London" was originally published in the Winter 2003 edition of *Zoetrope* and is available in *The O. Henry Prize Stories 2005*, edited and with an introduction by Laura Furman.

AUTHOR BIOGRAPHY

Jhabvala was born on May 7, 1927, in Cologne, Germany. In 1939, as the Nazi Party was on the rise, she moved with her family to London. After the war, her father, who found that family members left behind died in Hitler's concentration

Ruth Prawer Jhabvala (© *Ron Galella | Getty*)

camps, committed suicide. Jhabvala attended Hendon County School in Barnet, London, and then Queen Mary and Westfield College, at the University of London, taking her master of arts degree in literature in 1951. Upon graduation, she married C. S. H. Jhabvala, an Indian architect, and in 1951 they moved to New Delhi. In India she began publishing short stories and novels about the culture clash between England and its former colony.

In the 1960s, Jhabvala began writing screenplays. She also began a long working relationship with James Ivory and Ismail Merchant, who collaborated with her in bringing her novel *The Householder* to the screen in 1962. It was the first collaboration of Merchant and Ivory, who wrote, directed, and produced twenty-three films with Jhabvala over the next three decades. The team dominated the Academy Awards in the 1980s and 1990s. In 1984, they began to focus their films on adaptations of period novels. Jhabvala won the

Best Adapted Screenplay Oscar for her adaptation of E. M. Forster's *A Room with a View* (1985) and *Howards End* (1992). She was nominated for her adaptation of Kazuo Ishiguro's 1985 novel *The Remains of the Day*.

Jhabvala was also recognized for her fiction. She won the Booker Prize, Britain's highest literary prize, for her 1975 novel *Heat and Dust*, for which she wrote the screen adaptation in 1983, once again working with Merchant and Ivory. She won the O. Henry Prize in 2005 for "Refuge in London," which was first published in 2003. She continued writing fiction, publishing a total of twelve novels and several well-regarded short-story collections. In 1998 she was made a Commander of the Order of the British Empire for her service to literature, even though she had been living in New York since the 1970s and held dual citizenship. Jhabvala died in Manhattan on April 3, 2013, at the age of eighty-five.

PLOT SUMMARY

"Refuge in London" begins with the narrator, who is never given a name in the story, describing the circumstances under which she has come to live in London. Her aunt, whom she refers to as La Plume, persuaded her parents to send her to England when the girl was two years old, in the early 1930s, promising her parents that they would be reunited someday. She never sees her parents again. She is sixteen years old at the time of the story.

In the boardinghouse for refugees that her aunt manages, the two of them live in the basement. On the other floors, some people stay for a while, and some leave quickly. For example, a man named Dr. Levicus is mentioned briefly in the beginning of the story but never comes up again. A woman named Miss Wundt lives there for a short time, but La Plume makes her leave because of her active sex life. She is mentioned later in the story but never actually appears.

Gustav Mann is a lodger who comes from Germany. He is a big, hearty man who jokes and flirts with the women. A married couple, the Kohls, are the focus of the story. Kohl is a man in his fifties, a painter who was slightly famous in Germany before the rise of Adolph Hitler. His wife, Marta, is much younger than he is. They have separate rooms on the top floor of the house. His room is his studio, a workplace where he does his painting. Marta uses her room, which is decorated in high fashion, to entertain male visitors. Kohl accepts Marta's infidelity, though begrudgingly. He is particularly angry when Mann, one of Marta's lovers, tries to act friendly toward him.

Because he cannot afford models, Kohl has people in the house sit for his sketches. He is particularly fond of the narrator and has her sit often. She thinks that he is a boring old man, but she does not have many friends. She is impressed with his dedication to his work and with the joy he finds in it. The narrator has trouble telling whether Kohl is interested in her as an artistic subject or romantically. He asks her to walk with him to the nearby park sometimes, taking her arm as they walk, and he sits on the bench beside her, reciting the poetry of the French writer Charles Baudelaire. She likes to see him happy, as he is on their walks in the park together, but she often makes excuses to get out of spending time with him because he is so old and strange. She would rather spend time with Marta and her friends, who eat at nice restaurants and constantly have fun.

The more time the narrator spends with Kohl, the more other people become suspicious of their relationship. Her aunt interrupts their portrait sittings and later tells the narrator about a similar situation she had when she was about the narrator's age. She and the narrator's mother began spending time at the home of an opera singer, but they decided that they did not understand the people in that crowd and went on to marry more conventional men. Marta, too, makes excuses to interrupt their sittings. Usually she does not give any explanation for bursting into the room, though one time she says that she is there to invite Kohl to her birthday party, which leads to a long, significant scene in the story.

Birthdays are causes for big celebrations in the boardinghouse, and Marta, who is used to being the center of attention, wants her birthday celebration to be a major event. Although most of the house's parties are held in the basement, which has the house's only big room, Marta arranges the party to spread between her room and Kohl's studio. All of her guests are men, and there are so many of them that they line the stairway, drinking liquor acquired by guests who are too wealthy to live in a house like this one.

Marta notices during the party that Kohl is absent, and she sends the narrator out to find him. The narrator knows just where to go: the bench in the park. Kohl is there with a present under his arm, wrapped in paper he has decorated himself. He carefully unwraps the gift to show it to the narrator. It is a sketch of Marta when he first knew her, when she was about the narrator's current age, dated 1931. She is not the same person now, fifteen years later, Kohl declares.

When they try to leave the park, they find the gate locked. The narrator climbs the fence and then has Kohl pass Marta's present to her. As he scales the fence himself, though, he tears the seat of his pants. They walk back to the house with the narrator behind Kohl, shielding him so that no one passing can see the tear.

At the house, they enter the basement, where La Plume has Kohl give her his pants to sew them. He sits at the table to hide the fact that he is pantsless. Mann comes in, sees the wrapped present, and starts to leave with it, to take it to Marta, but Kohl puts his hand on it and, though he is much smaller and older than Mann, stares him down.

Marta calls Kohl upstairs just as the repair of his pants is finished. She is delighted to see the gift and grabs it immediately, tearing at the paper to open it. After looking at the sketch for a moment, she expresses approval—not of Kohl's artwork but of the way she used to look. They talk lightheartedly about their early relationship, about who first showed interest in whom, until the partiers spoil the moment.

One of Marta's admirers, who is referred to only as the lawyer, comments on the picture and on Kohl's interest in young women. With this intrusion into their moment of gift giving and receiving, Marta invites Kohl to join the party and have champagne with the rest of the guests.

The story diverts from the day of the party to other points in the lives of the main characters. It explains Marta's mysterious illness, which she never discusses with Kohl, as the result of a self-induced abortion. It also explains that Kohl once meets the narrator outside of her school to walk her home and describes the shame she feels at being seen with this strange older man. He shows up several more times to walk her home, but she avoids him when she can. When she tells Marta about her embarrassment over his attentions, she looks up to see him standing there, having heard every word.

When the narrator starts spending time with Marta and her friends, Kohl warns the narrator's aunt to beware, telling her stories about how wild Marta was when they met, when he was forty and she was sixteen. When the narrator sits in his studio to be sketched by him, Marta makes a point of coming in to intrude, which angers Kohl. They each are interested in her—Kohl is interested in teenaged girls in general, and Marta sees herself in the narrator—and they compete for her attention, each putting the other down in the process.

The narrative jumps to the future, to what happens to the various refugees and others who come to the house in 1946 and 1947. Mann moves away, ending up back in East Germany, the area now run by communists, and becomes a political activist like he was before the Nazis made him leave. The lawyer, who thinks of himself as a sophisticated art critic, brings some people connected to the art world to the house to see Kohl's works. This leads to a successful art show in London, then one in Paris, starting him on the path to international fame. Kohl moves to Zurich, but Marta refuses to go with him. They have a fight as he is leaving, in which she tears up the sketch he gave her for her birthday, though the narrator says that the pieces were eventually put back together and sold to an art collector and that the sketch is famous and often reproduced in books of Kohl's work.

Marta ends up falling further and further into poverty. She moves from one boardinghouse to another, keeping sporadic contact with the narrator and her aunt. She asks the narrator to take her to the movies so she can see Mann, now an important politician, in a newsreel. Kohl's fame grows, though he seldom associates with anyone but his housemaid, a sixteen-year-old girl he is rumored to be sleeping with. When he dies in 1955 at the age of sixty-four, he leaves most of his money to this girl.

The narrator goes on to Cambridge on a scholarship and eventually moves to New York. One of the first things she does upon arriving there is to go to a museum that has a room dedicated to Kohl's works. She admires his sketches, which are almost exclusively of girls—Marta, then herself, then his housemaid—but she finds his landscape paintings to be savage and oppressive. She ends the story amazed that this artist who showed so much gloom in his paintings could also find such sweetness in the girls that he admired.

CHARACTERS

Elsa
SeeLa Plume

Kohl

Kohl is one of the main characters in the story. He has come to London with his wife, Marta, from Germany, where he has had some limited fame as an artist. They rent two rooms at the top of the boardinghouse the narrator's aunt manages, but they live there separately. Kohl focuses every day on his art. He is bothered that Marta has relationships with other men, but he does nothing to stop her.

Kohl met Marta when he was forty and she was sixteen. He says that she pursued him, though she says he pursued her. At the time of the story, around 1946, he is about fifty-five years old, a short, fat man with an unsightly mustache. As a refugee, he is cut off from his fame as an artist, and he is not in good physical shape. Everyone treats him as a foolish figure. The narrator likes Kohl because he is interested in her. She can see the concentration that he puts into his artwork, and she respects it. His interest in her becomes a bit too much, though: her aunt and his wife hang around his studio protectively when he has her sitting for drawings. In public, when Kohl takes her arm, the narrator is embarrassed. When he comes to meet her as she gets out of school, she makes up a story about his being her uncle so that the other students will not mock her for having an old man for a boyfriend.

Although Kohl and Marta bicker constantly and she has affairs with other men, it is clear that they still have affection for each other. His memories of how she was when they met cause him to become sentimental.

After his art gains widespread recognition, Kohl moves to Zurich. There he has a housemaid who is about sixteen years old: Marta's age when he meets her and the narrator's age when he spends so much time with her. When Kohl dies in 1955, the newspapers give his age as sixty-four. He leaves a substantial amount to his young housemaid, which is evidence that she probably was his lover. He also leaves sketches of her along with his sketches of young Marta and the narrator.

Marta Kohl

Marta is one of the story's main characters. She is just a teenager when she becomes involved with Kohl, an artist, in Germany. She goes on to be an actress and dancer, though she never becomes successful at it. Throughout the story, Marta and Kohl, are talked about as husband and wife, though in the end, after his death, Marta is not certain whether they were ever actually married.

The uncertainty about their marriage matches the vagueness with which Marta lives her life. She has been with Kohl since she was sixteen. In the time of the story, she is in her early thirties and still lives with him in the boardinghouse the narrator's aunt runs. Despite living near her husband, they have separate rooms, and she has affairs with other men in hers. She and Kohl argue often and mock each other, but they also have a strong bond. When Marta is surrounded with male admirers at her birthday party, her interest is drawn to where Kohl is and what present he has for her. As they recall their early days together, she makes sure to remind him of what a beautiful girl she was, a fact that he remembers well. She is so vain that when she is given a picture that Kohl drew of her when she was young, she focuses more on how she looks than on this acclaimed artist's work.

In the end, Marta's vanity turns out to be pathological. She spurns both Kohl and Mann, another boarder in the house, who offers to take her with him when he returns to Germany. Both men go on to successful careers and could provide Marta with a comfortable life, but she is proud about mocking them and sending them away. She ends up moving from room to room in boardinghouses, from man to man, falling into obscurity and becoming increasingly mentally unstable. She cannot apply for a government grant because she does not know where she lost her birth certificate and cannot prove that she was married to Kohl, rendering her unable to make a claim on his estate. Centering her life on her good looks and the fun times she has with admirers who are willing to pay her way leaves Marta alone and destitute as she ages.

The Lawyer

The character known only as the lawyer does not appear until late in the story, when Marta's birthday party is described, but he plays an important part in the story after he arrives. He is one of Marta Kohl's male friends and is therefore presumably one of her lovers.

The lawyer considers himself to be knowledgeable about art. He looks over Kohl's works and finds them unimpressive. Later, though, he is the one who brings some people active in the London art world to Kohl's studio. They are impressed with the work and arrange an art show for Kohl, which leads eventually to his rise from obscurity to international fame.

After the people in the story have gone their separate ways, the lawyer is the one who keeps in touch with them all. He arranges payments for the narrator's aunt through a government trust for refugees and tries to make similar arrangements for Marta, but she cannot find her birth certificate. He visits Kohl at his studio in Zurich and reports that the artist has a young housemaid who is probably his mistress. When Kohl dies, the lawyer offers to help Marta sue for part of his estate, but she cannot find her marriage certificate.

Dr. Levicus

Dr. Levicus does not appear in the story but is mentioned early as the sort of person who lives in the boardinghouse for refugees. He moves into the house with his wife of thirty years but soon takes up with a twenty-year-old girl who lives there. Though the narrator's aunt, who runs the boardinghouse, is prudish about sex between boarders, she did not bother about Dr. Levicus, possibly because he was a doctor.

Gustav Mann

Mann is one of the boarders in the rooming house for refugees at the center of this story. He is apparently one of several men having an affair with Marta Kohl. There is no specific evidence of this, but everyone in the house assumes it. Kohl is particularly bitter whenever he has to interact with Mann.

Before the rise of Hitler and the Nazi Party in Germany, Mann was a trained engineer and a union leader. At the end of the story, he returns to East Germany and becomes influential in the Communist Party. He is a big, cheerful man, a backslapper who jokes with men and flirts with women. The narrator's aunt pretends to be unimpressed, even annoyed, by Mann, but she jokes with him and genuinely likes him. The narrator, on the other hand, agrees with Kohl in being unimpressed by him.

Long after Mann has returned to Germany, Marta goes to the movie theater, even though she cannot afford it, to see a newsreel that she claims shows Mann, among other people. That the narrator does not believe it really is him indicates that Marta may be straining to imagine him. If she has tender feelings for him, though, she does not admit it. She mocks him for the way she rejected him when he asked her to go back to Germany with him. Mann, the dejected lover, ends up famous and successful.

The Narrator
The narrator of this story may be like Jhabvala, whose parents moved from Germany to London to escape the World War II. One of the few details revealed about the narrator's life is that she grows up to be a writer. At the time most of this story takes place, the narrator is about sixteen years old. She is living in a house her aunt runs, with boarders from different countries moving in and out. She is not good looking and has no friends among her schoolmates.

In the course of the story the narrator draws the attention of Kohl, a once-famous artist who works in obscurity. He uses her as a subject in his drawings, as he does other boarders in the house, because he cannot afford to hire models. Over time, however, he starts showing an uncomfortable amount of interest in the narrator. He goes for walks with her and takes her hand. He shows up after school to walk her home. Though she is repulsed by the attentions of an older, homely man, she is also interested in the way he derives pleasure from the world through his art.

Kohl's wife, Marta, is highly competitive: she often interrupts when the narrator and Kohl are alone together. She does not seem jealous, since she freely has affairs with other men, and instead seems to want the attention the narrator is giving Kohl. She takes the narrator out to restaurants and parties. The narrator likes this life more than she likes the old man's attention.

Late in the story, after Kohl has become famous and Marta has moved off to one house after another, the narrator goes on to a successful life. She attends Cambridge on a scholarship and moves to New York. When she sells one of the sketches that Kohl made of her, she is surprised to find that it provides her a way to pay her debts and also affords her several years of income.

Because she is an orphan, having been sent away by her parents at age two to live in London with her aunt, the narrator is looking for role models. Marta offers her a look at how a young woman can have fun with wealthy friends. Kohl seems intense and humorless. He has a romantic side that makes him a great artist but also makes him a bit threatening to an inexperienced girl. In the end, she learns how to appreciate his worldview, to see beyond his personal flaws and look at things the way an artist does.

La Plume
The narrator's aunt is named Elsa, but the narrator refers to her as La Plume, because of a famous phrase that is almost always taught in rudimentary French language books, *la Plume de ma Tante* (which translates to the mostly useless phrase "the pen of my aunt"). She takes in the narrator when the girl is only two years old, promising to eventually reunite her with her parents.

La Plume is a refugee who is the manager of a boardinghouse for refugees. Though she is in charge of the house and has the power to evict tenants that she feels are not behaving properly, like Miss Wundt, she does not actually own the house and has to move out later in the story when the owner decides to sell it.

As she looks over the narrator, La Plume recognizes the kinds of mistakes a girl can make. When she sees the narrator, a girl of sixteen, spending too much time with Kohl, a middle-aged man, she relates her own story about when she was young and interested in an opera singer. She realized before it was too late that she could end up in danger if she let herself be seduced by the older man. She does, however, encourage the narrator to spend time with the friends who take Marta out to restaurants. When Kohl warns her that people like that can lead a girl into trouble, La Plume laughs him off. Like Marta's friends, she looks at Kohl as a sort of prude who does not enjoy fun, though La Plume's relationship with the narrator requires her to make sure that not too much fun is involved.

Miss Wundt
Miss Wundt is mentioned briefly early in the story as the sort of person the narrator's aunt evicts from the boardinghouse. The aunt knows about and accepts some of the sexual activity in

the house, but she believes Miss Wundt is too openly sexual and sets a bad example. Later, Miss Wundt is mentioned when the narrator speculates about why, after moving from her aunt's house, Marta Kohl frequently has to move from one rented room to another. She assumes that other building managers have found Marta to be promiscuous in the way her aunt finds Miss Wundt to be.

THEMES

Community

The title "Refuge in London" prepares readers for the sort of characters they will meet in the story. These are refugees, people who have been driven from their homelands by hostile circumstances (as opposed to émigrés, who move across borders by choice). The people who end up living in the boardinghouse the narrator's aunt runs come from different countries and end up in different countries by the end of the story, but for about two years they create a community with one another.

The sense of community is best shown in the way La Plume, the house manager, fusses over birthday parties. Birthday parties in the boarding house are generally festive gatherings in which all of the boarders do what they can to contribute. The party for Marta Kohl is exceptional because so many of her guests are from outside the house and because she excludes the female boarders. But the point is made in the story: these refugees celebrate birthdays together to make up for the families they have left behind in their homelands.

Coming of Age

At sixteen years old, the narrator of this story is a little older than characters in most contemporary coming-of-age stories. Still, she is learning who she is and is defining where adulthood will take her.

The narrator is torn between two potential paths for her life, each path being represented by one of the Kohls. Marta offers the most appealing path for a young woman: she has men admiring her beauty, bringing her presents, and taking her to restaurants that she could never afford on her own. The people that she goes out with are described as witty and fun. The narrator's aunt tells her to beware of them

because they lack morals. La Plume tells the narrator a cautionary tale about when she herself went around with a crowd of interesting intellectuals; she quit before she could end up in trouble. Although her aunt's story is meant as a warning, the aunt's coy flirtation with Marta's big, boisterous suitor Mann shows how much La Plume still finds that sort of person interesting. It would be very easy for a sixteen-year-old girl to devote her life to partying and sex, as Marta apparently has done.

Kohl, on the other hand, is not appealing. He is old, in the narrator's eyes, and short and balding, and he wears an ugly mustache. He has a weird interest in the narrator that may be inappropriately sexual. Still, she admires his serenity, the happiness that comes over him when he blocks the world out of his mind to engage in his artwork. Kohl gives her a window into the way art can lead to self-satisfaction.

The narrator follows Kohl and becomes an artist herself, a writer. She turns away from the simple childish pleasures that hold Marta in a state of suspended adolescence until she is too old to be attractive and has faded into obscurity.

Art and Life

One of the central themes of this story concerns how a great artist like Kohl can be left to such a meager existence. He toils in a boardinghouse in a city far from his home. His neighbors are not familiar with the little fame he has gained in Germany, and they know him only as an ugly little man with poor social skills. His wife remembers his fame, but she is more concerned with her own popularity than with Kohl's artistic career. Still, he ignores his sad social situation because he is focused on his art. It is fulfilling to him.

If a different man were paying the attention to a teenage girl that Kohl does—taking her arm when they walk, meeting her after school, and continually asking her up to his room, where they will be alone—it would seem that he plans to seduce her. The narrator is not that certain about Kohl's intentions. He seems too focused on her as an artistic subject to view her romantically. He shows the same interest in other sixteen-year-old girls, but only girls that he draws. As the narrator explains, his drawings of Marta, the narrator, and his housemaid later in life are his best works, much more artistically engaging than his landscapes.

TOPICS FOR FURTHER STUDY

- The issue of refugees who are forced to leave hostile war zones for safer countries continues to be as relevant as it was during World War II. Contact a center for refugees and interview one of the counselors, in person or online, to determine what services would be available today that were not available to the characters in this story. Using a computer program, create a graph showing how the two worlds (yours and the story's) compare in the treatment of refugees.

- Choose a sketch of a person done by an artist whom you admire but do not know much about. Write a short story about the person in the picture, including such facts as how the artist knew the person and what they felt about the artist while posing. Try to copy Jhabvala's dry, matter-of-fact style in your narrative.

- Lois Lowry's novel *The Giver* is a modern classic for young adults. First published in 1993, it tells a story that is almost the reverse of the story told in "Refuge in London": instead of trying to cope with the chaos of an all-too-real war zone, a young man is struggling against a futuristic world where everyone's life is controlled and made the same. After reading *The Giver*, establish the rules that would control three different societies in the way Lowry describes her controlled society: one guided by Kohl's worldview, one guided by Marta's worldview, and one that the narrator of "Refuge in London" would design if she were in control. Share your lists with your class and lead a discussion about the rules.

- An important element in "Refuge in London" is that the people of London do not know about Kohl's former fame. People who have to leave their homes behind often leave behind the prestige they have built in their chosen professions. Is it possible in this age of electronic reproduction, of web pages and Pinterest, for an artist's identity to be lost? To answer that question in an essay, look online for someone who is living in the United States and who is famous in the country he or she came from. In a well-structured essay, explain whether you think the person's fame made the move with him or her and why you think that way.

- Jhabvala became famous for writing screenplays well before this story was published. Choose one scene from the story—the narrator and Kohl in the park, Kohl's having his pants mended, Marta's tearing up the drawing, or Marta's going to see Mann in a newsreel—and write a script to bring that scene to life on the screen. Before you present a table reading of the script to your class, write out a brief explanation of the techniques you used to convey the emotions of Jhabvala's story.

- In the story, the narrator describes being moved by Kohl's sketches while being unimpressed by his landscapes. Study the work of an artist who did both types of artwork. Establish criteria to support your claim that this artist was better at depicting either humans or nature. Using a program like PowerPoint, present your findings and opinions to your class, including images of your chosen artist's work.

- In the end, Marta can find neither her marriage certificate nor her birth certificate. There are many ways to trace family trees online these days. If you suspected that she was a distant relation of yours, how would you go about confirming who she was? Write a brief guide for tracing the heritage of someone who lived around World War II and left no clear document trail.

The story takes place in a London boarding house after World War II. (© *Ron Ellis | Shutterstock*)

Narcissism

One of the most telling actions from Marta is opening her birthday present from Kohl. She is faced with a masterpiece, a work that will come to be reproduced in art books, that an art collector will find worth acquiring even after it has been torn apart and reassembled. She does not see the sketch's artistic quality, though. All she focuses on is how pretty she was when she was young.

For most of the story, Marta's interest in herself—her narcissism—makes life in the boarding house interesting to the narrator and, by extension, to the reader. It attracts interesting outsiders, like the lawyer and a Russian count, who bring gifts such as champagne. It drives Marta to take a series of lovers, and the immorality of her sexuality offers a fresh look at life. The narrator and her aunt are used to people working in silence and trying to be inconspicuous in their new land.

Marta's obsession with herself causes her downfall, however. She rejects Kohl because he is not sufficiently willing to drop everything, even his art, for her. She rejects an invitation from Mann to move to Germany with him, feeling that she is more important than he is. In the end, both men become internationally famous while Marta, her looks fading with age, sinks further and further into obscurity. She still mocks them for wanting her and not getting her, but her fascination with herself starts to unravel at the end. She sees Mann in a film, even though the narrator is not so sure that it actually is Mann, indicating that Marta has self-doubt and a vague, belated interest in someone other than herself.

STYLE

Varying Time Frames

Most of "Refuge in London" takes place in the same span of time, around 1946 and 1947, the narrator's last two years in school. Near the end, however, Jhabvala accelerates the passage of time. This acceleration is handled with a section of general information about where the boarders move to after leaving her aunt's house. The whereabouts of Kohl, Marta, the lawyer, and Mann become vaguer as these people move away from the narrator's social circle.

The narrator does not detail the trajectory of her life either. She does not talk about her new friends or even about what her new life in New York is like. At the end of the story, however, she does briefly reflect on what brings her to New York. Kohl is dead and is by that time legendary, and her connections to the others are severed. The final scene takes place after her arrival in New York, where she says she has lived "ever since," implying that this story is being told many years after her departure from

London. Using a device many writers do, Jhabvala does not tell readers how long it has been between the telling of the tale and the events in it, but readers can see by her narrative that the protagonist has matured and gained a philosophical perspective about the events that occurred.

Character Names

Jhabvala is particular about the names she does and does not give to characters in this story. In an early paragraph, she mentions Dr. Levicus by name, even though he is only mentioned once. By contrast, the character known as the lawyer is never given a name, even though he plays an important part in the story. He gets Kohl's artwork recognition in London, and he arranges for the narrator's aunt to draw a comfortable stipend so that she can leave the boardinghouse business. The story mentions that the narrator knows Mann's first name, Gustav, though no one ever uses it, but never acknowledges the first name of one of its most important characters, Kohl. It mentions the aunt's name, Elsa, just once and usually refers to her by the nickname the narrator makes up for her, La Plume—a name that she almost certainly would not call her to her face.

The most interesting use of names in this story is that the narrator's name is not given. It would have been easy for Jhabvala to work it into the tale by having another character say it while talking to her. Leaving the character without a name puts readers closer to her mind. She goes through life without thinking of herself by name, and that experience is extended to readers, who view her world as if they are seeing it from within her mind. This technique does not make her a mystery—the story gives many details about her life—but it does help readers feel what it is like to be this narrator.

HISTORICAL CONTEXT

Prewar Germany

As World War II approached, many people, particularly those of backgrounds that were endangered by the ascending Nazi regime, found it in their interest to leave Germany. Those of Jewish descent found increasing pressure from the Nazis to leave the country, being encouraged, in the 1930s, to move to nearby nations. According to the *Holocaust Encyclopedia*, approximately 37,000

COMPARE
&
CONTRAST

- **Late 1940s:** The populations of Europe are on the move. World War II has made it necessary for many people from countries invaded by the Axis powers to relocate to new countries where they can be safe.

- **2003:** The Iraq War pits the United States and Europe against the countries of the Middle East. Many people find it in their best interests to leave the countries around Iraq for safer homes.

  Today: Jordan, Lebanon, and Turkey are overwhelmed with the number of people fleeing civil strife in Syria as tens of thousands of refugees are absorbed into countries that can accommodate them.

- **Late 1940s:** An artist who is famous in one country can fall into obscurity by moving to another country.

- **2003:** It is easy to find the works of a famous artist on the Internet, particularly on websites that are interested in selling their works.

  Today: Social media sites for artists make it possible to follow the works of any artist at any level of achievement, even if the artist moves from place to place around the globe.

- **Late 1940s:** Boardinghouses, which rent rooms in a large private house to individuals, are common.

- **2003:** The real estate bubble is about to burst. Companies are doing what they can to sell mortgages, even to people who are unqualified to meet their responsibilities. More low-income people than ever before buy houses or condominiums, making inexpensive housing less necessary.

  Today: Mortgage lenders are more careful about whom they lend to, making it more difficult to buy. Short-term single-family housing is available, however, as large international chains such as Marriott and Fairmount establish extended-stay chains to cater to people who once may have rented rooms in unlicensed boardinghouses.

- **Late 1940s:** A woman like Marta stays with her husband, a famous artist, because there are not many prospects for her alone, given that she seems to have no clear talent in the arts.

- **2003:** The rock-and-roll culture has produced the groupie, who can make a life's work out of being associated with famous people.

  Today: In the parlance of reality television, someone like Marta can be considered a celebrity because of her close association with people who are famous.

---

to 38,000 of Germany's estimated 523,000 Jews left the country before the war broke out. Those who did not waited to see if conditions would stabilize, often believing that the country would never end up following the policies of genocide against an entire population that did in fact become official policy during the war.

Many of the refugees moved to nearby European countries, such as France, Belgium, the Netherlands, and Czechoslovakia. Because these countries were eventually taken over by the Nazis, the refugees fell under the net of the oppressive

regime they had sought to escape. In the end, about two-thirds of the Jews who lived in countries that were under Nazi control died.

In addition to the ethnic and social groups targeted by the Nazi Party—not only Jewish people but also Gypsies, homosexuals, Christians, people of color, and people with disabilities, among others—artists were given particular attention. According to Stephanie Barron in *"Degenerate Art": The Fate of the Avant-Garde in Nazi Germany*, the July 19, 1937, attack on the Entartete Kunst exhibition in Munich was the worst attack against modern art in history. The Nazis followed a program of incorporating art into politics to help maintain control of populations by controlling their beliefs. To this end, they censored practically any works that had been part of the modern art scene in Germany before their rise in 1933, whether those works had a political message or not. Artists who did not join official government-sanctioned groups lost teaching positions and found it hard to gain employment in other jobs. Like the other groups targeted by the Nazi regime, artists were forced to flee the country or to wait and see to what extent their lives were in danger.

Postwar London

The war left millions of Europeans without homes. Many of the Germans who had been moved into territories conquered by the Axis powers during the war were forced to leave those territories once the Germans lost, and the people who had fled from the Nazis often stayed in their adopted countries. The United Nations Relief and Rehabilitation Administration was founded in 1943 to help people in war zones or fleeing from war zones to establish new lives for themselves; it became the International Refugee Organisation in 1946, and that became the office of the United Nations High Commissioner for Refugees in 1950. In all of its different versions, the focus of the organization was to cope with the need for massive resettlement of people from their homelands caused by World War II—a disruption on a scale never before seen.

London was a focal point for refugees because of its status as one of the largest cities in Europe that, unlike Paris and Rome and other large cities, had not been under the control of the Axis powers. It was also, however, a city that suffered much destruction. The Blitzkrieg was an intense series of bombing attacks starting early in the war to terrorize the British into surrender. Almost thirty thousand bombs were dropped on London in a few months, causing massive destruction, damaging about one-third of the city. Though the Blitz was concentrated in those few months of 1940, German planes continued to attack London sporadically well into the following year until, in May of 1941, Hitler's Luftwaffe (air force) was redeployed to participate in the invasion of Russia.

The destructive bombing, combined with the influx of refugees from across Europe, made London of the late 1940s a place with strained social resources. Food was scarce, and housing was

The narrator lives in the basement apartment with her aunt, who runs the boarding house.
(© Everett Collection / Shutterstock)

expensive. People had to resort to communal situations such as the large boardinghouse in "Refugee in London" when they would have preferred to live independently. Massive rebuilding projects were begun as soon as the war ended, but the country was almost bankrupt. A socialized medicine program, the National Health Service, begun in 1948, offered free health care to all citizens for their entire lives. It was the start of ambitious government service projects aimed at rewarding the citizenry for their patience during the austere days of the war. Though these projects extended some of country's wartime financial troubles, continuing the sense of poverty Londoners felt while fighting the Germans, they eventually helped London become a place worthy of being a world capital once more.

CRITICAL OVERVIEW

Jhabvala was an acclaimed fiction writer. She was most frequently recognized as focused on what it was like being a European living in India, which was her own circumstance after her marriage to the Indian architect Cyrus Jhabvala in 1951. She lived in India for twenty-five years and wrote about the experience. As Shernaz Mehta Mollinger notes in a review of Jhabvala's novel *Heat and Dust* for *Library Journal* in 1976, "Ruth Jhabvala is probably the best Anglo-Indian novelist writing today." To explain why the setting was so significant in Jhabvala's work, Mollinger continues, "Jhabvala uses India as a catalyst, as an outrageous force that elicits unexpected, frequently frightening reactions from its visitors." *Heat and Dust* was the novel for which she won the Booker Prize, Britain's highest honor for writing.

Though she was known in the literary world, Jhabvala was best known as the screenwriter who created the scripts for films by the producing and directing team of Ishmael Merchant and James Ivory. Her first film with them was *The House-holder*, in 1963, which she adapted from her novel of the same title. In 1983, she wrote the adaptation of *Heat and Dust*, which fared well everywhere except the United States. From the 1960s through the 2000s, she wrote the screenplays for twenty-three of the company's forty-four films, winning Academy Awards for her scripts for *A Room with a View* in 1987 and *Howard's End* in 1993. She was the only writer to win both the Booker Prize and an Oscar. Reviewing *Howard's End* in the *New Republic*, the critic Stanley Kauffmann explained that the novel's author, E. M. Forster, had a style that was impossible to film but notes that Jhabvala

> has done as well as we can imagine. . . . Jhabvala has fashioned a screenplay that is very usable by actors. Thus, for me, she supports the prime reason why this film had to be made—why it would have been a sin not to make it—the acting.

Often, critics focused on the acting in Merchant-Ivory productions, taking the technical excellence of Jhabvala's writing for granted.

Jhabvala remained a critical favorite in fiction, even as she was an internationally known screenwriter. As a review of her short-story collection *East into Upper East: Plain Tales from New York and New Delhi*, published in the *Virginia Quarterly Review*, puts it,

> Jhabvala has a knack for the quirks of human relationships, especially the spiritual kind. . . . Her stories are well paced and well put, serving as an entertaining and thoughtful imposition into the lives of rather human people in strangely human predicaments.

> MARTA HAS SOME SORT OF AUTHENTICITY THE NARRATOR'S AUNT CAN SEE. DESPITE HER TAWDRY LIFESTYLE, THE STORY SHOWS A CHILDLIKE INNOCENCE IN MARTA, AN EXUBERANCE ABOUT AT LEAST ONE SUBJECT, HER OWN BEAUTY, THAT MAKES HER APPEALING."

The review concludes that the book is "a good read from an excellent fiction writer."

CRITICISM

David Kelly

Kelly is an instructor of creative writing and literature at a college in Illinois. In the following essay, he discusses how Jhabvala uses the characters of Kohl and Marta in "Refuge in London" to represent symbolic elements of the narrator's life at that place and time but also renders them as individuals with specific mysteries.

Much about Jhabvala's story "Refuge in London" seems familiar. It is not in and of itself an ancient tale, an archetype or a legend that has been told at different times in different cultures, but it is a story constructed of eternal elements. In it, a once famous artist loses his pretty younger wife when he loses his fame; a girl is uncertain whether the artist's interest in her is aesthetic or romantic; a party girl who uses men and taunts her hapless husband finds her power over them all fading as she ages; the artist finds himself gaining a second chance for fame at a time when he just does not care anymore. Individually, each of these pieces of the story's puzzle makes sense. Together, though, they are all bound by some vague paste that readers cannot clearly explain. It is human emotion that gives such a familiar-feeling story its air of unpredictability.

The story belongs to the narrator, but it tells her story by focusing on the relationship between an artist, Kohl, and his wife, Marta. They each represent a different life path available to the young narrator, who is a sixteen-

WHAT DO I READ NEXT?

- Sitting in the park with the narrator, Kohl recites poetry by the French poet Charles Baudelaire, and the narrator realizes that the scene would be romantic if Kohl were not such an unappealing man. Baudelaire is considered one of the greatest poets to ever write poetry. The book often considered his best, *The Flowers of Evil* (originally published in 1857 as *Les Fleurs du mal*) is available in a dual English and French edition, translated by James N. McGowan, from Oxford World Classics, published in 2008.

- Jhabvala did not write an autobiography, but she does give readers glimpses of her life throughout her 2005 short-story collection *My Nine Lives: Chapters of a Possible Past*, published by Counterpoint. The protagonists of each of the nine stories have circumstances that Jhabvala lived through, with different characters living in London, New York, and India, though details have been omitted and added to fit the story point.

- One of the few studies of Jhabvala's works—Ralph J. Crane's book *Ruth Prawer Jhabvala*—came out in 1992, before "Refuge in London" was published. The book provides useful information about the author's early life and works. It is part of Twayne's English Authors series.

- Linda Sue Park's novel for young adults, *A Long Walk to Water*, tells of a modern-day refugee, Salva, who leaves his village in war-torn Sudan in 1985 and, after a long adventure that covers most of the country, does not return home until years later, having become one of the famous lost boys of the Sudan. When he returns home, he is grown and is one of the people responsible for making water available to his village. This view of population displacement has a happier ending than most modern refugee stories. It was published in 2010 by Clarion Books.

- Celeste Ng's 2014 novel *Everything I Never Told You* weaves together a family tragedy and a look at what life is like for a Chinese American family living in a small Ohio town. Unlike the narrator of "Refuge in London," who lives in a houseful of people who share the refugee experience, the main character, a teen girl, does not have a community of other Asian Americans to fit in with.

- One short story that captures the rage that young people felt in London after the devastation of World War II and the poverty that rebuilding required is Graham Greene's "The Destructors," about a gang of boys left to play in bombed-out streets each day while their parents work. They decide to destroy the one sound, architecturally significant house in their neighborhood that survived the German bombs. This story is available in many anthologies and in Greene's *Twenty-One Stories*, published in 1954 with a Penguin Twentieth-Century Classics softcover release in 1993.

---

year-old girl when most of this story takes place. The narrator is young and, although not pretty, vibrant enough to be welcomed into a social world of free-spending men that welcomes young girls simply because of their youth. Because she is not pretty and not popular with people her own age, the social high life holds great appeal for her. Marta ignores her husband and sleeps around with men who treat her to a good time. The narrator could grow up to be another Marta, and Marta has fun.

On the other hand, the narrator's time with Kohl, posing for him (she is his favorite portrait subject), presents her with a view of the serenity true artists find in their work. Kohl is not famous when the narrator knows him. He has been famous before, back in prewar Germany, a world impossibly geographically and culturally distant from the narrator's imagination. She does not know his reputation, but when he draws, she sees that unlike the people of Marta's crowd, he simply does not need the company of others. His life could be the future for her to follow, except that he is physically unappealing and she is young and unsophisticated enough to overrate physical appeal. Another thing hindering her is that there is always the sneaking suspicion that Kohl is interested in her sexually, using his artistry to mask his lust for a sixteen-year-old girl. He just may be a spiritual fraud.

It comes down to a question of authenticity. Marta does not claim to be authentic; she claims to be popular, and for the most part she is. She cannot hold a job—the story indicates that her place with the British Broadcast Corporation was lost to incompetence and unreliability—but men flock to her.

There are strong reasons to believe that Marta's appeal goes no deeper than her willingness to have sex with men. The story does indeed make her sexual promiscuity clear, but there is more to her than that. The narrator's aunt, who runs the boardinghouse they all live in, likes Marta. Early on, though, the story mentions a Miss Wundt, whom the aunt evicted for exactly the kind of sexual activity she lets Marta get away with. One could say that the teen girl idolizes Marta for superficial reasons—for the popularity that a teen might value—and that the men around her are only interested in sex. But the aunt is a woman of the world and is actually a bit of a prude about Miss Wundt. Marta has some sort of authenticity the narrator's aunt can see. Despite her tawdry lifestyle, the story shows a childlike innocence in Marta, an exuberance about at least one subject, her own beauty, that makes her appealing.

Kohl wins points for authenticity for his inability to waste his life in bars and restaurants, as his wife does. He is socially awkward, but he does know the value of a tiny stream running through a small city park. When he draws, the narrator can see that Kohl needs nothing else in this world, and this kind of self-sufficiency appeals to her. It does not hurt his image that he is an artist, though he is an artist who works in obscurity, with no verification of his greatness except his and Marta's memories of their former life in Germany. Living among refugees, the narrator is fairly immune to stories about how great someone else's former life was.

Kohl loses respect in the eyes of the narrator, and the world around him, by being cuckolded—his wife sleeps with other men openly, and he does nothing about it. In itself, that would be a private matter between the two of them. If he does not mind her behavior, then why should it be the business of anybody else? The problem is, though, that he does mind—sometimes. She has many suitors, according to the story, but Kohl minds only one of them, Mann.

That Kohl's anger is specific to Mann implies that he is not particularly jealous about losing Marta's affection. Marta has other suitors that Kohl does not mind, but there is something about Mann that irritates him. Mann is his opposite: cheerful, outgoing, humorous, and popular. Kohl's hatred toward him helps readers define Kohl's personality. It is safe to deduce that he hates humans who are social creatures. If that is true, though, then his relationship with Marta must be particularly hurtful to Kohl, because he loves her enough to hold on to her despite the way she taunts him, and being a social creature is what Marta is all about.

If Kohl disdains Marta's social side, then what does he love about her? That much is obvious: her looks. It would be superficial of him to hold that position if he were merely a man. For instance, the lovers who abandon Marta as she ages in this story are boring to the reader and, in general, not interesting enough to the narrator to deserve individual names. The only notable one among them, Mann, is only marginally interesting, earning him just a passing role in the story. But Kohl is not a mere man. He is an artist. If his interest in Marta's beauty is artistic, then he deserves the respect the narrator gives him, but if he is responding to her only sexually, he does not.

If the narrator is trying to determine whether Kohl is an authentic artist or just a sexually motivated person using his talent as an artist to get himself close to teenage girls—if she is wavering between the beliefs that he is interested in her artistically or sexually—she is not helped as much as one would expect she would be by the fact that the story multiplies her situation by three. Throughout the story, Kohl has relationships with three sixteen-year-old girls: Marta in her youth, the narrator, and then, late in his life, his housemaid in Zurich. Each one poses for him, making their relationships with him primarily artistic, but there is also an implied sexual element to each. Any or all could be a manifestation of the concept of beauty to Kohl, but any of them could also be a sex object to him.

Kohl's relationship with Marta back in Germany before the war is the relationship that defines his life. He was younger then, and gaining fame as an artist. An even younger and beautiful actress-dancer paid him the kind of attention a nonfamous artist with his looks and disposition could not hope to gain. They may have been using each other, but if they were, they were also building an emotional bond. Later, in London, they reminisce about their old drunken escapades, but they are both equally nostalgic about the beauty Marta had at sixteen. It could be that Kohl found her the physical manifestation of his artistic vision. It could just be that he had an appetite for young girls, driving him, as Marta ages, toward the story's narrator.

The introduction of the housemaid at the end of "Refuge in London" complicates the reader's view of Kohl. His relationship with her takes place offstage, in another country, out of the narrator's presence. The narrator never meets her or finds out her name. It is clear that Kohl's relationship with her has some depth. He is reported to have spent his last years with no companionship except hers. He drew her often. He left his estate to her. It is said that they had a sexual relationship, though Jhabvala cleverly hides the truth of that through word of mouth from an unreliable, minor character. It is also possible that he views the housemaid as a person-ification of youthful beauty—the "youth with a capital Y" that is mentioned three times in the story. All of these possibilities are left floating in the air, leaving the narrator in the end no closer than ever to understanding Kohl's motivations.

By the time the housemaid comes into the story, the narrator has already chosen her life path. She is a writer, having followed the artistic lifestyle of Kohl rather than the live-for-the-moment posture Marta exemplifies. By that point, the narrator is curious about what made Kohl tick, but nothing she finds out is bound to change her.

The story leaves its meaning ambiguous. It presents a sixteen-year-old girl at a time in her life when going out to taverns and restaurants is a glamorous life and art seems like alienating drudgery. She observes Marta and Kohl, the representatives of two possible paths available to her, and she chooses one. She does not grow

up to be another Kohl, just as, had she chosen to spend her talents partying, she does not become a Marta. They both are left familiar but also personal characters that fit their distinct roles in the story while having enough individuality to leave the reader wondering.

Source: David Kelly, Critical Essay on "Refuge in London," in *Short Stories for Students*, Gale, Cengage Learning, 2016.

Clare Colvin

In the following review, Colvin points out that My Nine Lives *is autobiographical to the point of almost being a memoir rather than fiction.*

. . . The subtitle, "chapters of a possible past," hints that this book is a memoir rather than a series of short stories. It is, according to Ruth Prawer Jhabvala, "potentially autobio-graphical": even when something didn't actually happen to her, it might have done. The novelist explores nine possible lives against the background of her past, ranging from the London and New York of German Jewish refugees to the India of Westerners in search of a guru.

It is enticing to try and glimpse the real author through the fiction woven around the facts of her life. In all the stories there is a narrator: a young woman who may be a poet, writer or translator, whom Prawer Jhabvala admits is herself. She often has estranged parents. The woman sometimes has an affair—in one story, with an egocentric pianist, in another, with a young Indian politician. It usually ends in tears.

Several characters could have stepped out of an old Merchant Ivory film, like the flamboyant adventuress in "Springlake," who infiltrates a rich, dysfunctional family with the idea of setting up a performing arts centre in their Hudson River house. Or the fat, crooked Indian businessman in "Gopis," who is likened to Krishna, the god of love.

The nine variations follow a theme or life for a number of years rather than concentrating on one point of change. The most haunting are the first, "Life," and the eighth, "Refuge in London." In "Life," a woman leaves New York for India in old age, as the only place she can afford to live after the death of a stepmother who had exploited her goodwill. As a young woman she had lived there and written an unfinished thesis on an Indian poetess-saint. Now, nearly penniless, she spends her days among tombs in a ruined pavilion. Gradually, people

The narrator feels truly happy when Kohl is sketching her, but his paintings make her uneasy.
(© bepsy / Shutterstock)

are drawn to her; and in the closing years of her failed life, she begins to assume the dimensions of a saint.

In "Refuge in London," the teenage narrator lives in her aunt's boarding house among European émigré lodgers. An ageing artist falls in love with her and she becomes the innocent catalyst of a crisis with his fiery wife. It's a raw depiction of a marriage where passion has been soured, but the memory of happier days still exerts its stranglehold.

All the central narrators have in common a sense of loss of early promise, or elusive love. In "Life," songs betray anguish for "the Friend who will not come, not even now at the end of our lives of unrequited longing." It's a theme that Prawer Jhabvala echoes in her introduction—her sense of wanting to feel exiled in order to go back in search of another place, or rather, always of "a person . . . Someone better, stronger, wiser, altogether other . . . Does such a person exist, and if so does one ever find him?" It seems a strange question from an author whose life has

been successful and surrounded by loved ones, and it makes one wish she would write a memoir, rather than what is almost a dance of the nine veils. In the meantime, we will have to be content with these tantalising clues.

Source: Clare Colvin, Review of *My Nine Lives*, in *Independent*, July 9, 2004.

Philip Horne and Ruth Prawer Jhabvala
In the following interview excerpt, Jhabvala talks about her writing and about adapting literature for screenplays.

Philip Horne: Am I right in saying that after escaping from Nazi Germany you came to London in 1939, and later studied English at London University? Does English literature, or Anglo-American literature, have a special meaning for you?

Ruth Prawer Jhabvala: Well, I was very lucky to come here when I did, I was also very lucky to have the years of doing nothing but reading, mostly English literature. So my whole background is that. It was extremely fortunate for me. Also English became my first language.

"NOTHING REALLY—USUALLY I FIND THAT I LOOK FOR SOME POIGNANCY OR SOME SCENE THAT MIGHT CONTRIBUTE MORE, THAT MIGHT POINT SOMETHING OUT THAT SHOULD BE THERE IN THE SCREENPLAY. I TRY AND FIND THAT. OR EVEN JUST HALF A LINE OF DIALOGUE CAN BE A GOD-SEND TO ME AT THAT POINT."

PH: Do you think studying literature is a better preparation for writing screenplays, or at any rate adapting classics for the screen, than going to film school would be?

RPJ: Well, I started off and still am primarily a novelist, and not a screen writer. Studying English literature is really not studying—to have all those years to read is a gift. Particularly as I wasn't really very good at anything . . . It was wonderful to have all those years to read. But I will say that while I was preparing for my degree I never wrote. I wrote before and after, but during those years I just read. I even wrote a thesis on the short story in England from 1700–1750. There weren't any of course but that was my thesis!

PH: Do you think that studying literature at university is why you were interested in adapting classics?

RPJ: I was never interested in adapting classics at all. I've written four novels. I was never interested in film. Never. I never even thought of it. I wasn't even a film buff, I didn't see many films ever. I never thought of it until Merchant Ivory came to India and filmed one of my books—they said "Why don't you write the screenplay?" and I said, "Well, I've never written a screenplay and I haven't seen many films," because I was in India by that time and hadn't really had any opportunity to see new films or art films or classic films or anything. So they said, "Well try. We haven't made a feature film before." So that was really my introduction into film.

PH: Is there a main purpose in adapting classics for film?

RPJ: The main purpose is, well, you have to, well the main purpose is that I have such a

good time—I mean think of all that marvellous material. Just think of spending all that time in *The Golden Bowl* and other James and Forster books we have done. But especially Henry James because, not so much in *Golden Bowl*, but the other two [*The Europeans*, *The Bostonians*]— he has such marvellous characters and he has such strong dramatic scenes. You just put your hand in and pull them out.

PH: There isn't an educational impulse?

RPJ: I'm afraid not! Maybe there should be, but I'm afraid I only think of myself.

PH: I suppose you are trying to communicate your enjoyment?

RPJ: Yes, yes. I suppose, yes. And in a way it's a homage to a great author. You know I never write any critical articles or critical reviews, never write anything except fiction and screenplays, so it is a kind of homage. But I never think I'm doing a public service or anything . . .

PH: Do you have any idea why American literary classics from the turn of the century seem to be so fashionable at the moment?

RPJ: Is Henry James particularly fashionable? Well let me think. Well yes, I think so.

PH: Over the last few years . . .

RPJ: Yes. Well, it is such grand material, wonderful scenes, great characters, such wonderful relationships between the characters— well the material is there.

PH: The French director Jacques Rivette said in 1974 that James is one of the "unfilmable" authors, who "can be filmed diagonally, taking up their themes, but never literally." You obviously don't agree . . .

RPJ: No, I do agree! Any adaptation you do it diagonally. You can take up the theme but you can never, never, never do it literally. You'd come up with a kind of travesty, if you tried to interpret anything literally.

PH: But fidelity, is that important?

RPJ: Fidelity is not the first [thing] No I don't think so. Like I said, the theme and the feel of the characters the ambience and their relationships that is what you try and but never, never literally.

PH: So it's a separate work, really?

RPJ: In a way. I'll tell you what I usually do. I read the book several times, usually it's a book I know very well anyway, but I read it several times and make some notes and make a kind of plan that I think I would want to follow—usually I don't, it breaks down at some point—and then I put the book away and really don't look at it again until I've filled out my own thing. And then I look at it again and see what I have missed. But there is a period when the book and I are two separate entities.

PH: How much changing do you do when you go back to the book at that stage? Or what kinds of things do you change?

RPJ: Nothing really—usually I find that I look for some poignancy or some scene that might contribute more, that might point something out that should be there in the screenplay. I try and find that. Or even just half a line of dialogue can be a God-send to me at that point.

PH: How well do you find Henry James' dialogue works?

RPJ: Well, again, it works diagonally. You really have to transcribe it. He's not the only person—all the others—you can never just take it off the page. However colloquial the language might sound, this is not how actors can speak.

PH: Could I ask what you liked or what you didn't like about any of the recent James adaptations?

RPJ: Well, I like *Portrait of a Lady* very much, and that was a book we had wanted to do over 20 years ago, but we never had the money for it. We did two other Jameses, it was easier, we started with *The Europeans* because that was all in America so it was much easier and a much smaller film so it was much easier to raise the money. And then again with *The Bostonians*, that was all in America, easier for us to shoot. Then other things came in-between and *Portrait of a Lady* went I'm afraid.

PH: Did you ever get as far as a script?

RPJ: No.

PH: I really should congratulate you on making a film, and on getting a film made, of The Golden Bowl *at all. Was it hard work getting it made?*

RPJ: To get it made? Um, well, no, we got, well people said "This is not a good novel" or "This is not one of Henry James' really good novels." They didn't want to go ahead with it. But we did get money for the screenplay, money for the development, and once we had that we didn't have too much difficulty.

PH: How did you pitch the story?

RPJ: I wrote a sort of outline of the book—how we were going to see it and a background of the characters—and that's what we sent out. Because I didn't really expect anyone to have read the book.

PH: Was there an emphasis that you thought was central to that?

RPJ: Well, yes, I think that we said that this was a passionate encounter between four people, and we thought that might sound good to them. So if this had been our first second film or our third film we may have had more difficulty, but we did have a good [track] record, so people came forward and said, "Well, it may not look like much, but, you know" [laughs] But certainly if we had started out and it had been an early film, we might have had real difficulties.

PH: How different is The Golden Bowl *to how you would have done it, say, straight after* The Europeans?

RPJ: I don't think it would have worked so well for me. No, I think I needed a lot more practice, because this was a very difficult script. This was the hardest. This was the nicest and the hardest. The only other one that has been equally difficult and equally rewarding was *Mr and Mrs Bridge*—I don't know if you know that one, by Evan S. Connell. Well it was two books actually, which we adapted into one. And that was one of my favourite films. But those two were the hardest.

PH: When Jack Pulman adapted The Golden Bowl *for the BBC in 1972, in the famous version directed by James Cellan Jones, with Cyril Cusack, Daniel Massey and Gayle Hunnicutt, they had six 45-minute episodes—a total of four-and-a-half hours. At 130 minutes, your version is only half that length. Are you at all envious?*

RPJ: Oh no, no, no. Not at all. That's the difference between television and film, television rests so much on dialogue, not as visual as a film is. You can develop things much more slowly and carefully. But in a film, I mean you just couldn't do it. I wouldn't want to.

PH: But were there sections you would have liked to have taken longer on?

RPJ: No, not really. We were in a two-hour format. Since we did not have time for four or six hours, I thought, well we might as well adapt ourselves to what we have, and just take the essence of the situation and each incident and turn in the story. We couldn't dwell on it.

PH: You obviously have a wonderful working relationship with James Ivory. But late Henry James is notoriously ambiguous and difficult, and no two readers of The Golden Bowl *read it quite the same way—in fact, a single reader often sees different things in it at each reading. Did you always see it the same way?*

RPJ: Yeah. I think we must have done. I mean the screenplay—he read it, and he had some objections, but there was nothing fundamental. I don't think we ever had a fundamental difference of opinion.

PH: Could you talk about how your process of collaboration with James Ivory works?

RPJ: Well, when I lived in India and he lived in New York, or wherever he was, we did a lot through correspondence. But now we all live in New York . . . I am still so used to working on my own that I do several drafts for myself first and then send them to him to make marks in the margin. And then I rewrite, and this goes on over a few months. And then finally, before he really starts to get it all together, we sit together and see where we still might have disagreements. Then he goes and shoots the film—I have nothing to do with that—I only go along to see some rushes. But I will see the rough cut, which is usually twice the length of the final version, then I see it again, and we sit in the editing room for some time and, you know, fiddle about.

PH: So you are involved in the editing?

RPJ: Yes, I am involved in the editing but not in the actual production, or in the casting. . . .

Source: Philip Horne and Ruth Prawer Jhabvala, "Philip Horne in Conversation with Ruth Prawer Jhabvala," in *Guardian*, October 27, 2000.

SOURCES

Barron, Stephanie, "1937: Modern Art and Politics in Prewar Germany," in *"Degenerate Art": The Fate of the Avant-Garde in Nazi Germany*, edited by Stephanie Barron, Harry N. Abrams, 1991, pp. 9–24.

Gates, Anita, "Ruth Prawer Jhabvala, Screenwriter, Dies at 85," in *New York Times*, April 3, 2013, http://www.nytimes.com/2013/04/04/movies/ruth-prawer-jhabvala-writer-dies-at-85.html (accessed August 21, 2015).

"German-Jewish Refugees, 1933–1939," in *Holocaust Encyclopedia*, United States Holocaust Memorial Museum website, http://www.ushmm.org/wlc/en/article.php?ModuleId = 10005468 (accessed August 23, 2015).

Jhabvala, Ruth Prawer, "Refuge in London," in *The O. Henry Prize Stories 2005*, edited by Laura Furman, Anchor Books, 2005, pp. 276–99.

Kauffmann, Stanley, "Forster—Again and Better," in *New Republic*, March 23, 1992, pp. 26–27.

Mollinger, Shernaz Mehta, Review of *Heat and Dust*, in *Library Journal*, January 15, 1976, p. 361.

Review of *East into Upper East: Plain Tales from New York and New Delhi*, in *Virginia Quarterly Review*, Spring 1999, p. 59.

"Ruth Prawer Jhabvala," in *New York Times*, 2010, http://www.nytimes.com/movies/person/96051/Ruth-Prawer-Jhabvala/biography (accessed August 21, 2015).

"Victims of the Nazi Era: Racial Ideology—The Holocaust," in *Holocaust Encyclopedia*, United States Holocaust Memorial Museum website, http://www.ushmm.org/wlc/en/article.php?ModuleId = 10007457 (accessed August 23, 2015).

Wasserstein, Bernard, "European Refugee Movements after World War Two," BBC website, updated February 17, 2014, http://www.bbc.co.uk/history/worldwars/wwtwo/refugees_01.shtml (accessed August 23, 2015).

"WW2—The Blitz Hits London," History website, http://www.history.co.uk/study-topics/history-of-london/ww2-the-blitz-hits-london (accessed August 23, 2015).

FURTHER READING

Gooneratne, Yasmine, *Silence, Exile and Cunning: Fiction of Ruth Prawer Jhabvala*, Sangam Books, 1991.
    Published before Jhabvala became primarily known as a screenwriter, this book gives modern readers insight by focusing on her themes and technique, which stayed consistent throughout the writer's life.

Horne, Philip, "Philip Horne in Conversation with Ruth Prawer Jhabvala," in *Guardian*, October 27, 2000, http://www.theguardian.com/film/2000/oct/27/2.
    Although the focus of this interview is Jhabvala's work as a screenwriter, her reminiscence on how her training as a fiction writer affected her screenplays is insightful to fans of her fiction.

London, Louise, *Whitehall and the Jews, 1933–1948: British Immigration Policy, Jewish Refugees and the Holocaust*, Cambridge University Press, 2000.
    Though the story never clearly states that the characters are Jews who moved to London to avoid persecution by the Nazis, the characters' surnames and Jhabvala's life story indicate that probably to be the case. (Her father

moved her family to London, where she grew up, because they were Jewish.) This book gives a detailed account of the political situation for Jewish refugees who fled to England, offering readers a look at the situation that the narrator of "Refuge in London" does not explain.

Rank, Otto, *Art and Artist: Creative Urge and Personality Development*, W. W. Norton, 1989.

Rank, who was one of Sigmund Freud's most trusted followers, wrote a series of studies into the minds of artists, covering from a psychological perspective the issues, such as esteem and the struggle against worldly values, that Jhabvala covers in the Kohls' marriage.

SUGGESTED SEARCH TERMS

Ruth Prawer Jhabvala

Jhabvala AND "Refuge in London"

Jhabvala AND biographical fiction

Jhabvala AND refugees

World War II AND refugees

London AND postwar AND art

Hitler AND artists

Jhabvala AND biographical fiction

Jhabvala AND art AND exile

Jhabvala AND London AND New York

The Secret of Cartwheels

PATRICIA HENLEY

1990

Patricia Henley's short story "The Secret of Cart-wheels" was first published in *Atlantic Monthly* in 1990, followed by its selection for inclusion in *The Best American Short Stories of 1990*. It was later featured in Henley's second short-story col-lection, *The Secret of Cartwheels* (1992). The story of an eldest daughter's helplessness in the face of her family's dissolution following the hos-pitalization of their unstable mother, "The Secret of Cartwheels" portrays Midwestern adolescence and rural poverty at its bleakest. Coming of age within the confines of an orphanage rather than the family farm, Roxanne learns that when no one is there to catch you when you fall, you have no choice but to catch yourself.

AUTHOR BIOGRAPHY

Henley was born in 1947 in Terre Haute, Indiana. The oldest of eight siblings, Henley attended high school in Rising Sun, Maryland, before going on to St. Mary's College, which was a two-year col-lege at the time. Unable to complete her under-graduate degree there, Henley enrolled in Johns Hopkins University without a bachelor's in 1974, earning her master's of fine arts in writing.

After graduation, Henley joined Tolstoy Farm, an anarchist commune in Davenport, Washington, where she lived from 1975 to 1978 without running water or plumbing, growing her own food and

In her childhood, the narrator notices that nothing in the house matches, perhaps a sign of her mother's illness. (© *Lori Werhane / Shutterstock*)

tending a dairy cow. After Tolstoy Farm, Henley traveled the United States, Mexico, and Central America. She taught English in a school in British Columbia from 1982 to 1984 before settling in Bozeman, Montana.

Her first collection of short stories, *Friday Nights at the Silver Star* (1986), won the Montana Arts Council First Book Award in 1985. As a result, Henley was offered a position teaching the creative writing master's degree program at Purdue University in West Lafayette, Indiana, which she accepted. Her second collection of short stories, *The Secret of Cartwheels*, was published in 1992. The titular story, "The Secret of Cartwheels," had been published in *Atlantic Monthly* before being anthologized in *The Best American Short Stories of 1990*. Henley's short stories have appeared in a variety of literary magazines and anthologies, including a Pushcart Prize anthology, *Ploughshares*, *Glimmer Train*, *Missouri Review*, *Northwest Review*, and the *Boston Globe Sunday Magazine*. Her first novel, *Hummingbird House* (1999), was a finalist for the National Book Award as well as the *New Yorker* Best Fiction Book Award.

Additionally, Henley has published two chapbooks of poetry, *Learning to Die* (1977) and *Back Roads* (1996); two other collections of short stories, *Worship of the Common Heart: New and Selected Stories* (2000) and *Other Heartbreaks* (2011); and a young-adult novel co-written with Elizabeth Stuckey-French, *Where Wicked Starts* (2014). As of 2015, she lives in Cincinnati, Ohio.

PLOT SUMMARY

"The Secret of Cartwheels" begins with the narrator gazing out of the school bus window, excited to tell her mother that she has chosen a confirmation name for her confirmation into the Catholic Church. She absently answers her younger sister's question about her math homework as she thinks about her confirmation name—Joan—the same as her mother's. Her mother had explained that the name Joan is strong and battle hardened.

The bus driver sings as the bus gradually empties. Frost curls at the corners of the windows. The narrator and her siblings get off at the final stop on the route. As they walk toward the house, the narrator notices her Aunt Opal's Cadillac parked strangely in the yard. Fearing bad weather, Aunt Opal never visits in the winter, and her presence, coupled with the rushed parking job, alerts the narrator that something is wrong. The night before, when she was lined up with her siblings to receive a good night kiss, her mother told her to look for the signs in life that will guide her. The narrator was frightened by the timbre of her mother's voice.

The narrator's younger sister, Jan Mary, does not understand the significance of Aunt Opal's hastily parked car, but Christopher, who is closer to the narrator's age, shares her unspoken dread. When they enter the house, their mother is gone. Their four-year-old sister, Suzanne, Aunt Opal, and the baby, Laura Jean, are waiting for them. Aunt Opal looks uncomfortable, her eyes full of pity. The narrator asks where their mother is, as Christopher and Jan Mary hang back in the doorway. Aunt Opal explains that their mother is at the veterans hospital because she is sick and needs a rest. She has left them.

At this news, Christopher and Jan Mary skulk into the living room to watch television. The narrator begins to peel potatoes for dinner.

She tries to convince herself that if they continue on with their daily chores, it will seem as if their mother is not missing.

Aunt Opal tells them they will be separated: Christopher will stay with their grandparents, while the baby will go to their cousin Janice. The narrator says that they will stay in their house, together. Aunt Opal chides her, calling her Roxanne and explaining that she cannot take care of all of her siblings alone.

Suddenly, Roxanne feels childish, desperately wanting someone to take care of her, but she cynically knows that no one will. Not until many years later does she wonder where her father was during her mother's hospitalization. She asks Aunt Opal how long they will be separated, but her aunt does not know.

Roxanne is thirteen, Christopher is twelve, and Jan Mary is eight. They attend Catholic school, St. Martin's, but ride the public school bus home. Roxanne's mother kept her home from school twice in the week leading up to her disappearance, to do household chores and help with the younger children. They have very little money to spare. Roxanne's father works in a different state, and their nearest neighbors live a mile away. Roxanne loves summer on their isolated property but finds the winters to be unforgiving. They must share bathwater and heat the house with wood. Her mother's hands crack from feeding the fire all through winter. Seeing the state of them makes Roxanne want to cry. The loneliness of the house in the winder is overwhelming, like a strong smell.

After dinner, while the others would watch television, Roxanne's mother would tell her secrets, cursing their father and speaking of her true love—a woman she met working in the motor pool during World War II. Roxanne feels weighed down by her mother's confessions and wishes for a life without her.

Suzanne, Jan Mary, and Roxanne are taken to Entiat Home, a place where children whose parents cannot care for them live. On the drive there, Suzanne asks after their baby sister. Aunt Opal assures her the baby will be fine with Janice. Earlier, when they dropped Christopher off at their grandparents' house, Roxanne resisted the urge to beg to stay with them, too. She and Christopher were close, listening to high school basketball games on the radio together as they imagined life as high school students.

Aunt Opal pulls up to Entiat Home, where Mr. and Mrs. Thompson usher the children inside. Opal departs quickly afterwards. Left alone for a moment, the girls realize they will have to go to a different school now. Mrs. Thompson, a thin woman wearing pearls, sees that they are bathed, checked for lice, and put to bed on cots. To Roxanne, Mrs. Thompson seems like the ideal mother. Roxanne sees their stay at Entiat as an affront to their mother, feeling the shame of failure as if she were the mother rather than the abandoned child. She stays up very late, worrying. She dreams of getting a second chance at home to try harder, to check her siblings' homework and clean the house more thoroughly than before: "Keeping domestic order was, inexplicably, bound up with being good, blessed."

When Roxanne wakes up the next morning, she has wet the bed. She thinks of Mary, the protagonist of the classic children's novel *The Secret Garden*, and how Mary's anger kept her safe. Roxanne's anger cannot help her. She once confessed to a priest that she wished on her birthday for her mother to leave, but the priest did not take her sin as seriously as she felt was appropriate.

Mrs. Thompson arrives to wake the girls. Roxanne tells her she wet the bed. She insists on cleaning the sheets herself, silencing Jan Mary's taunts with a stern look. During her six-month stay at Entiat Home, Roxanne wets the bed on all but four nights, no matter what precautions she takes to prevent it.

Though she is of a borderline age and could be placed in the Big Girls' House, Roxanne lives in the Little Girls' House along with her siblings. The dorm mother, Mrs. Hayes, owns two enormous, indoor cats. Roxanne is impressed by the organization of the chores performed in the dorm, writing to her mother about changes they could make at home to improve efficiency. With twenty-three dorm mates in the Little Girls' House, the siblings drift away from each other into their own age groups.

Roxanne is horrified by the close proximity in the locker rooms at her first gym class at her new school. The P.E. teacher, Georgia Cowley, tells her they are learning how to tumble. Roxanne has never tumbled before, so she is instructed to sit on the sidelines, watching the other girls turn cartwheels and make forward rolls. Nadine Jefferson, another girl from Entiat, is sitting out, too, and she tells Roxanne the secret of cartwheels:

"Catch yourself before you kill yourself. . . . Catch yo-*self*."

For Christmas, the siblings are further separated. Mr. and Mrs. Thompson take Suzanne, Aunt Opal takes Jan Mary, and Roxanne goes to a neighbor's house, where her former friend, Darla Reamer, lives. Roxanne and Darla, who is two years older, were best friends until Darla found a girl she liked better named Julia. Roxanne was heartbroken to be ignored. She finds enduring the hospitality of Darla's family painful. Darla spends hours on the phone with Julia. She is relieved to return to Entiat.

The girls take to revealing secrets to each other in whispers after lights out in the dorm. Rather than participate, Roxanne dreams of running away to strike out alone. One night, she tells the girls that she once saw her mother hit her father with a belt. Nadine says no wonder her mother is in the hospital, making the other girls giggle. Roxanne hates Nadine in that moment.

On Valentine's Day, Roxanne receives a valentine from her mother informing her that she is home with Christopher and Laura Jean. She says she will see Roxanne soon. Roxanne imagines her mother caring for her siblings without her help and feels invisible and utterly worthless. Despondent, Roxanne forces it out of her mind.

In April, the girls are allowed to go home for the weekend. Roxanne crackles with excitement at the chance to see her mother and Christopher. Mr. Reamer picks them up at Entiat Home. The car ride is silent. Roxanne wonders if her mother knew that morning in December that she would not see her children again for months.

The girls approach the house shyly, wearing their second-best dresses. They find their mother sitting on the lawn with Darla, who is painting her nails bright red. Roxanne does not know how to act with Darla there. Song lyrics drift from inside the house: "*you made me love you.*"

Roxanne, who imagined a more impressive homecoming, stands disappointed as Suzanne run forward to kiss their mother. Jan Mary asks Darla if she will do her nails next. Laura Jean begins to cry somewhere inside the house. Her mother starts to rise, before remembering her wet nails. She looks to Darla for help. Darla goes inside to tend to the baby.

Her mother embraces Roxanne before lighting a cigarette. She tells Roxanne that Darla has been helping her around the house. Roxanne

holds her breath, close to tears. She feels exhausted by the knowledge that her life has changed, but not in the way she had dreamt. She wants to resent her mother but knows she must forgive her instead. Her mother searches her eyes for their old connection, but Roxanne looks away. Jan Mary bites her cuticles. Christopher walks around the side of the house swinging his baseball bat. The green spring leaves hurt Roxanne's eyes.

CHARACTERS

Georgia Cowley
Georgia Cowley is the gym teacher at Roxanne's new school. She is a strict and gruff instructor.

Father
Roxanne's father lives and works in another state. She does not know what he is doing during the events of the story. She writes him a letter after Christmas but receives no response. Once, Roxanne saw her mother beat him with a belt. Roxanne's mother curses Roxanne's father, claiming to have found her true love with a woman during World War II.

Mrs. Hayes
Mrs. Hayes is the dorm mother of the Little Girls' House at Entiat Home. The girls call her Gabby Hayes behind her back. She owns two pampered cats, Springer and Beau, who live inside the dorm. She wears her makeup too thick and smells of cigarette smoke but keeps firm control of the dorm with polite but firm instruction of what is and is not allowed.

Janice
Janice is Roxanne's cousin. She takes the baby, Laura Jean, after the family is separated, because she has a baby of her own close to Laura Jean's age.

Nadine Jefferson
Nadine Jefferson is a gregarious African American girl who lives at Entiat Home and attends school with Roxanne. She teaches Roxanne the secret of cartwheels but later makes a joke at Roxanne's mother's expense, earning Roxanne's ire.

Julia

Julia replaces Roxanne as Darla's best friend. Over Christmas, Darla spends hours on the phone with Julia.

Christopher Miller

Christopher is twelve years old and the only son of the family. He is closest to Roxanne, with whom he listens to high school basketball games on the radio before they are separated. Christopher goes to live with his grandma and grandpa and returns home well before his sisters are able to leave Entiat Home.

Jan Mary Miller

Jan Mary is a precocious eight-year-old. She is sent with Roxanne and Suzanne to Entiat Home to live. She is not quite old enough to understand the complexity of the situation, which causes her to make unintentionally insensitive remarks.

Laura Jean Miller

Laura Jean is the youngest of Roxanne's siblings, still a baby during the events of the story.

Roxanne Miller

Roxanne is thirteen, the oldest of her siblings. She considers the care of the house and children her responsibility, taking pride in her successes. When her family is forced to separate after her mother is hospitalized, she considers it a failure on her part, wishing for a chance to prove that she could run the house better than before so that the family can stay together without their mother there. She wishes sometimes for her mother to disappear, but is wracked with guilt afterwards. At Entiat Home, she wets the bed all but four days during a six-month stay. She dreams of running away from Entiat Home but does not attempt it.

When Roxanne returns home after months of wondering about her mother to find her with Darla, who spurned Roxanne's friendship, she almost cries. The thought of not being useful to her mother makes Roxanne feel as if she has no purpose on Earth. Though her impulse is to resent her mother's selfishness, she has been taught to forgive by her Catholic upbringing. At the story's end she feels disconnected completely from the family she so desperately wanted to unite.

Suzanne Miller

Suzanne is four years old and is the first to embrace their mother after the sisters' long stay at Entiat.

Mother

Roxanne's mother leaves her children to go to the VA Hospital. She leaves most of the household duties, including child rearing, to others—first Roxanne, then Darla. Roxanne's mother smokes, drinks, and stays in bed often. An unhappy wife, she tells Roxanne that she fell in love with a woman while working in the motor pool during World War II. She once beat her husband with a belt, an event that Roxanne witnessed. Roxanne frequently wishes her mother would disappear but is crushed when she actually vanishes without a word.

Aunt Opal

Aunt Opal is waiting at the house for the children the day that their mother goes to the hospital. Her green Cadillac is parked haphazardly, as if she came to the house in response to an emergency. She tells Roxanne and her siblings that their mother is sick and that they will be split up. She is not a naturally gentle woman and seems uncomfortable interacting with the children, her face frequently overcome with pity. She is quick to leave Entiat Home after dropping the girls off, giving Roxanne the impression of a passive delivery driver.

Priest

When Roxanne confesses that she wants her mother to disappear, the priest at her church gives her only five Hail Marys. Roxanne does not feel this is a harsh enough penance for her crime.

Darla Reamer

Darla Reamer is Roxanne's former best friend. Although Darla is two years older than Roxanne, they were very close before Darla met Julia and abandoned her friendship with Roxanne. When Roxanne returns home in April, she finds Darla has been helping her mother, usurping Roxanne's role as her mother's helper. She is painting Roxanne's mother's nails in the front yard when Roxanne returns home.

Mr. Reamer

Mr. Reamer is Darla's father. He shows Roxanne his apiary during Christmas vacation. He picks the girls up from Entiat Home to drive them home for the weekend in April. He drives a pickup truck and his clothes are splattered with paint from painting beehives.

Mrs. Reamer
Mrs. Reamer is Darla's mother and a neighbor of the Miller family. She and her husband take Roxanne in for the Christmas holiday, giving her a sweater and hand cream as Christmas presents.

Grandma Swanson
Grandma Swanson, Roxanne's maternal grandmother, takes Christopher in when the children are separated.

Grandpa Swanson
Grandpa Swanson, along with his wife, takes Christopher in after his mother's hospitalization.

Mr. Thompson
Mr. Thompson is Mrs. Thompson's husband. He has black hair and a cheerful voice. He works at Entiat Home alongside his wife.

Mrs. Thompson
Mrs. Thompson works at Entiat Home with her husband, Mr. Thompson. She has a quietly commanding presence, wears pearls, and smells of floral perfume. Roxanne thinks she must be a perfect mother. She respects Roxanne's role as the leader of her siblings.

THEMES

Abandonment
Roxanne reflects early in the story that she does not know where her father is during her stay at Entiat Home. However, his prolonged absence from her life does not rankle in the same was as her mother's sudden disappearance. Kept home from school in order to help with her younger siblings and told secrets while the TV distracts them, Roxanne feels a partnership with her mother that is at once upsetting and exciting. When her mother disappears, Roxanne feels twice abandoned: both by her mother and by a partner in looking after her large family, though she acts as if she is prepared to carry on alone. First her father, then her mother, and then all but two of her siblings are swept out of Roxanne's sight. Even Suzanne and Jan Mary

TOPICS FOR FURTHER STUDY

- Read *Where Wicked Starts* (2014), a young-adult novel cowritten by Henley and Elizabeth Stuckey-French. What differences in writing style can you find between the young-adult novel and "The Secret of Cartwheels," a short story about adolescence written for adult readers? What do you think is the purpose of the adult perspective provided in "The Secret of Cartwheels," and what information do we learn from Roxanne's adult voice? Organize your comparison between the works and your answers to these questions into an essay.

- Create a time line infographic to demonstrate the shifting relationships that occur within the family during Roxanne's stay at Entiat Home, from her arrival in December to her visit home in April. Choose four to six important events during that time to serve as examples of the separation between Roxanne and her siblings. Free infographic templates can be found at easel.ly.

- Write a short story based on an event from your childhood in which you felt caught between the world of adults and that of children. Your short story should be fictionalized—using literary elements like symbolism, figurative language, themes, and so on—rather than a strictly nonfiction account of the event you choose.

- Choose one of Roxanne's younger siblings to study further. What is his or her role within the Miller family? How would you describe the sibling's personality? When the family is separated, where is that child taken and why? When does the child come home and how has life has changed because of the time the family's mother spent at the hospital? Finally, how is his or her experience different from Roxanne's? Organize your thoughts into bullet points in preparation for a class discussion.

drift away at Entiat Home, more comfortable socializing among their own age groups.

Stripped of her illusions of taking on the motherly duties herself, left out of the decision-making process for dividing the children among relatives and friends during the Christmas holiday, last to know about her mother's return from the hospital, and teased by the other girls over her family's collapse, Roxanne is utterly alone by the time she arrives home to find her role as her mother's helper usurped by the neighbor girl, Darla, who once spurned Roxanne's friendship for that of another girl. Roxanne experiences a loss of place: her place in the world at her mother's side. It is as if everyone else—including her closest sibling, Christopher—has moved forward while she remained stuck in place.

However, in reality, her mother's abandonment has triggered Roxanne's maturation. What she perceives as a betrayal by everyone—from Darla to little Jan Mary to her mother—is in fact the first bloom of adolescent resentment. To find her adult independence, Roxanne must loose her childish insistence that the family is somehow dependent on her. The crisis of her mother's abandonment allows Roxanne to realize it is not the grave sin she once thought it was to wish for your mother to disappear. Instead, it is a natural part of growing up and out of the childhood home.

Adolescence

Dreaming of their futures as teenagers, Roxanne and her twelve-year-old brother, Christopher, listen to the radio broadcasts of the high school basketball games. Roxanne wets the bed at Entiat Home, fights her shame in order to admit it to Mrs. Thompson, and then insists that she will clean the sheets herself. Roxanne wishes for her mother to vanish and then, consumed by guilt, confesses to a priest. These are all moments that mark Roxanne's unsteady entry into the adult world.

Between childhood and adulthood, adolescence brings turbulence, confusing emotions, and startling realizations about a world that once seemed simple. Roxanne battles her need to be held, comforted, and indulged as if she were a child with her need to be respected, listened to, and acknowledged as responsible for her family. When she receives neither loving care nor the respect of adults, Roxanne realizes she must rely on herself and feels the first sting

of her new independence when she faces her mother after months away. Life without her was not what Roxanne expected. Where she thought she would step seamlessly into the role of caregiver, she finds herself powerless.

Despite her resentment of her mother's absence and the truths she learned as a result, Roxanne still feels a childlike impulse to be her mother's good helper. Returning to their home after months away to find their mother has chosen a new helper in Darla robs Roxanne of her contribution. She is reduced to the role of just another child at the exact moment when she feels more adult than ever before. This tug of war between childish ideals and adult realities defines Roxanne's adolescence.

Motherhood

Roxanne's mother is overwhelmed by the burden of her children. Living a mile from the nearest neighbor with a husband working in another state and a sister who rarely makes the drive during the long, harsh winters, Roxanne's mother turns to Roxanne for company in her isolation, spilling her secrets to a thirteen-year-old daughter who does not want to hear about her mother's resentment of her father or the woman she loves in Detroit. Roxanne goes so far as to wish her mother away, believing she could steer the family better on her own than with the help of this frequently drunk and generally unstable woman.

When her wish comes true, however, Roxanne is placed under the care of a new mother figure: Mrs. Thompson, who runs Entiat Home alongside her husband. Well-coiffed, sober-mannered, and kind, Mrs. Thompson appears to Roxanne as a vision of the perfect mother. Yet Mrs. Thompson remains aloof from Roxanne during her stay, and Roxanne must acknowledge how thoroughly alone she is at Entiat Home despite her first impression of the woman. She is someone else's perfect mother, not Roxanne's.

Roxanne considers her and her sisters' stay at Entiat Home to be an embarrassing symbol of her mother's failure—one that could have been avoided if Roxanne had been given free rein over the house. However, Roxanne believes that motherhood is about control: a well-planned chore regiment and keeping the messy secrets of the past secret. She does not understand the emotional toll, the loneliness, and the sacrifices necessary for a woman to become a mother.

Riding the bus home from school, the daughter is looking forward to talking to her mother.
(© Kris Yeager / Shutterstock)

STYLE

Coming-of-Age Story

A coming-of-age story, also known as a *bildungs-roman* when it takes novel form, traces a protagonist's transition from a child to an adult, often brought on by a cataclysmic event in the character's life. Examples of coming-of-age stories include J. D. Salinger's *Catcher in the Rye*, Sandra Cisneros's *The House on Mango Street*, and Nick Hornby's *About a Boy*. "The Secret of Cartwheels" is Roxanne's coming-of-age story.

Introduced as a daughter eager to please her mother in the first scene, the final scene finds Roxanne filled with an adult's sense of resentment toward the woman who abandoned her, as well as a sense of displacement from the world she once knew. The catalyst for her change is her mother's hospitalization, the first time in Roxanne's life in which she is separated from her mother for a long period of time. During her mother's absence, Roxanne's delusions of anchoring the large family herself are punctured as the siblings are separated. Roxanne matures paradoxically by recognizing her own immaturity. As she avoids her mother's searching gaze in the story's final scene, she realizes how much her life will change as a result of her new perspective.

Literary Realism

"The Secret of Cartwheels" is written in the style of literary realism, meaning that the events of the story are portrayed without exaggeration or fantasy. Realism, as a movement in art, began in the eighteenth century with the aim of producing work representative of everyday life as lived by everyday people. Roxanne and her family are neither idealized nor particularly

COMPARE & CONTRAST

- **1960:** Without access to the Internet, Roxanne's primary method of communication with her family outside Entiat is through letters to her mother.

  1990: Though the Internet has been invented, it is used for military purposes and is not yet available to the public.

  Today: Separated family members and friends communicate easily via cell phones, e-mail, and social media.

- **1960:** As she contemplates running away from Entiat, Roxanne worries that boys who run away can return to their families without consequence, but girls who do so ruin their good reputations among the community.

  1990: Runaways of any gender face extreme danger, but no longer is there a double standard in which female runaways are considered morally lacking.

  Today: Many resources are available for girls who flee their situation at home, including homeless shelters for women and children exclusively. One of the top reasons teens run away is discomfort during the transition to foster care homes or shelters.

- **1960:** Women are expected to wear nylons in public to cover their bare legs. Roxanne considers the nylons newly added to her wardrobe to be a sign of her maturity.

  1990: Nylons remain a fashion staple for women and are included in school and workplace dress codes but are not socially required in every situation.

  Today: Women are no longer expected to wear nylons as bare legs are considered inoffensive.

---

remarkable in their troubles; rather the issue they face—poverty, absent parents, growing pains—are common problems in society. Likewise, the conclusion of the story does not offer an absolute resolution but indicates a new trajectory in Roxanne's life as relationships have been reestablished at home. Tidy endings, as one might find in a fairy tale, are rare in real life—as rare as a person who is entirely good or evil. Reflecting this, realist works feature characters with human motivations (an overwhelmed mother, a loyal daughter who craves recognition), as well as conclusions based on subtle shifts rather than momentous change.

HISTORICAL CONTEXT

Second-Wave Feminism

In Robert Boucheron's interview of Henley for *Construction Literary Magazine*, he asks if she identifies as a feminist. Henley answers: "Yes, I am a feminist. I'm not an academic feminist, but an over-the-back-fence feminist. I have lived my life breaking free over and over again of our culture's expectations of me as a woman." The first wave of feminism in the United States focused on women's suffrage—the right to vote—a goal they achieved in 1920 with the passage of the Nineteenth Amendment to the Constitution. In the 1960s, the second wave of feminism, characterized by a push towards reproductive rights, workplace equality, and addressing the issues of domestic violence and rape, spread through the United States, changing the way society perceived, treated, and regulated women's lives.

Second-wave feminism, while not directly addressed in "The Secret of Cartwheels," is subtly referenced throughout the story, foremost through the proliferation of female characters and the marginalization of males in the story. Henley writes a woman's story about the relationships between mothers, daughters, sisters, and aunts and friendships forged between girls. Radical feminism has not reached the small, rural

The mother is mentally ill and goes to a mental hospital. (© *Oleg Golovnev / Shutterstock*)

town of the story, where girls who run away from home are considered ruined, but certainly Roxanne's mother is a scandalous, if miserable, woman. She drinks, smokes, falls in love with another woman, and once beat her husband with a belt. She fits neither the image of a docile homemaker nor a good Catholic wife, but—isolated in the country with her children—cannot reconcile her need to live colorfully with the sacrifices required of a mother of five.

Women's Army Corps

Roxanne states that her mother worked in the WAC motor pool in Dayton, Ohio. *WAC* stands for "Women's Army Corps" (originally known as WAAC: Women's Army Auxiliary Corps), a branch of the United States Army that existed from 1942 to 1978. Women in the WAC served as switchboard operators, mechanics, seamstresses, and bakers and in other auxiliary military roles. Opposition to the program was strong, despite the desperate need for personnel during the long years of World War II, because many believed that enrollment in the military would undermine traditional gender roles. A smear campaign was launched against the program immediately after it went into effect in 1943, accusing enlisted women of moral corruption and playing on male fears of emasculation at the hands of liberated women.

However, the 150,000 women who enlisted in the WAC were lauded for their contributions by the war's end, with a select few working on the Manhattan Project, in combat zones abroad, and on General Dwight D. Eisenhower's staff. The women of the WAC, along with the millions of Women Ordnance Workers (WOWs) who left home to join the industrial workforce, gave rise to the well-known figure of Rosie the Riveter, an American folk heroine of the war effort. Recognition of women's abilities to serve in the military and work outside the home brought about changing ideas about women's roles in society.

CRITICAL OVERVIEW

Henley has been embraced by the literary community of critics and readers alike for her allegiance to rural settings and humble characters and her realistic, no-nonsense personal style. In his interview with Henley for *Identity Theory*, Robert Birnbaum praises Henley's depiction of life in the Midwest rather than focusing her work on big cities or coasts: "This is a big, beautiful country and frequently that is forgotten." Throughout her career, Henley has not forgotten her rural roots, inspiring others to follow in her footsteps of writing from the heart. Natalie Lund writes in her interview of Henley and Elizabeth Stuckey-French for *Sycamore Review* of Henley's advice for young writers: "I was fortunate enough to have her for a semester of workshop, and I remember her encouraging us to write the story only we could write."

Christy Porter, writing for the *Los Angeles Times* in her article "Bright Lights, No City: Montana's the Literary Capital of the Country and Its Authors Have a Best Seller to Prove It," lists Henley among the artists who make up the proud literary tradition of the state of Montana, where Henley briefly made her home:

> How Montana came to harbor the literary likes of A. B. Guthrie Jr., Ivan Doig, Wallace Stegner, Norman Maclean, Thomas McGuane, Richard Ford, Patricia Henley . . . to name only a few, is a question not easily answered.

Boucheron notes that Henley's characters "are sometimes poor, sometimes down on their luck, but they behave responsibly. They make ends meet, and they hold middle-class values of thrift and self-improvement." On the strength of such characters, coupled with the striking emotional precision of the story, "The Secret of Cartwheels" was anthologized in the *Best American Short Stories of 1990*.

CRITICISM

Amy L. Miller

Miller is a graduate of the University of Cincinnati, and she currently resides in New Orleans, Louisiana. In the following essay, she examines how Roxanne's time living at Entiat Home effects her perception of her mother in Henley's "The Secret of Cartwheels."

In Henley's "The Secret of Cartwheels," Roxanne's idealistic view of her role within her family is shattered when her overwhelmed mother commits herself to the VA Hospital. Though she is enthusiastic to prove her competence by running the household in her mother's

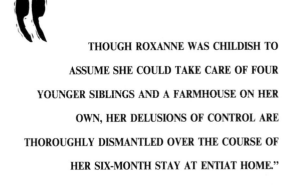

THOUGH ROXANNE WAS CHILDISH TO ASSUME SHE COULD TAKE CARE OF FOUR YOUNGER SIBLINGS AND A FARMHOUSE ON HER OWN, HER DELUSIONS OF CONTROL ARE THOROUGHLY DISMANTLED OVER THE COURSE OF HER SIX-MONTH STAY AT ENTIAT HOME."

absence, Roxanne—too young to be left in charge—is committed as well, to a home for children whose parents cannot care for them. With her mother in the hospital and Roxanne a ward of Entiat Home, the house that Roxanne briefly dreamt of controlling sits empty. Separated from her mother for the first time, Roxanne's experiences at Entiat provide her with a new perception of the self-absorbed woman she meets again four months later.

Paulette Bates Alden writes in "Capturing Childhood/Engaging the Adult Reader": "The challenge for the writer of childhood stories is to capture the non-verbal felt experience of children while still appealing to the adult verbally sophisticated reader." Through balancing a child's perspective with adult complexities, Henley creates in Roxanne an example of the greatest terror of adolescence: the realization that parents can be as petty, vulnerable, and thoughtless as any child. By recognizing her mother's fallibility, Roxanne joins the adult world.

"Without our mother there, I was suddenly older," Roxanne thinks, as she demands answers from her Aunt Opal at the story's start. For a moment, she acts on this sudden sense of maturity by distracting herself from the emotional blow by settling the baby in her high chair and starting dinner for the family. Her identity is wrapped up in household chores as well as her perceptions of goodness and value. By helping her mother keep their home clean, Roxanne contributed to the spiritual and symbolic health of the family. If she can continue to do so in her mother's absence, then "we might feel as though she'd just gone through the orchard to visit a neighbor, and that she might return at any moment." Then reality comes

WHAT DO I READ NEXT?

- Frances Hodgson Burnett's classic young-adult novel *The Secret Garden* (1911) tells the story of Mary, a lonely orphan whose life is changed by her discovery of a secret garden. Roxanne turns to *The Secret Garden* in "The Secret of Cartwheels" to help escape from her own grim reality at Entiat Home.

- Mary Karr's memoir, *The Liar's Club* (1995), details the adventures of her colorful family growing up in a Texas oil town. With a drunken, yarn-spinning father, a scandalous mother, and a fast-talking sister, Mary comes of age with a sharp eye for truth, lies, and trouble.

- Henley's short-story collection *Friday Night at Silver Star* (1986) won the 1985 Montana Arts Council First Book Award. Inspired by her time in a Washington commune, Henley's stories feature characters living close to the land, aptly contrasting human drama with the serenity of nature.

- *Dubliners*, by James Joyce (1914), describes life among the poor in Dublin, Ireland, in a series of concise and unflinchingly realistic short stories that expose humanity at its worst. The collection's final story, "The Dead," is considered a flawless example of the short-story form.

- *Winesburg, Ohio*, by Sherwood Anderson (1919), is a classic collection of interrelated short stories describing small-town life in the Midwest. Surrounded by family and neighbors, yet isolated in his dreams of something more, young reporter George Willard witnesses the small community's dark secrets as well as its public lies.

- Robert Stone's *Bear and His Daughter* (1997) collects stories set from 1969 to the late 1990s about the darker side of human relationships forged in the criminal underbelly of American life. A finalist for the Pulitzer Prize, *Bear and His Daughter* is written in sparse, uncompromising narration that reveals the depth of the characters' pain.

- The tragicomic stories of Flannery O'Conner's legendary collection *A Good Man Is Hard to Find* (1955) illustrate just how bad things can get in the land of opportunity. Macabre, cruel, and unquestioningly beautiful, O'Conner's voice is as original as her unforgettably hopeless characters.

- Steve Almond's *My Life in Heavy Metal* (2002) collects twelve modern coming-of-age stories in which hearts and eardrums are shattered. At once funny and poignant, Almond depicts the chaos of American youth and the harsh realities faced in the morning after.

- *Knockemstiff*, by Donald Ray Pollock (2008), tells the story of a rough-and-tumble valley in the middle of nowhere where the residents live lives defined by loss, lack, and stagnation. Madness, poverty, violence, and dark humor flourish in this collection of short stories based on the author's hometown.

- Alice Munro's short-story collection *Dear Life* (2013) won the 2013 Pulitzer Prize for its portrayal of the impact of coincidences and chance meetings in the lives of the characters—all ordinary people in an extraordinary world.

---

crashing down. Aunt Opal explains that a thirteen-year-old cannot take charge, and Roxanne crumbles: "I remember feeling small and powerless then, and I saw that I still needed to be taken care of—in fact, wanted to be taken care of—but I did not think I would be." Her childish impulse for control is dwarfed by what she already knows of the chaos of the adult world. What is worse: Roxanne's prediction comes true.

Though she is taken under the care of Entiat Home, Roxanne is never truly nurtured, and no new mother figure appears to save her from her sadness, though she at first carries high hopes for Mrs. Thompson. Instead of love and care, she receives a series of brutal humiliations that bring about her change of heart at home. First, Roxanne wakes up every morning to wet sheets and shame during her mother's absence. She wets the bed all but four days of her six-month stay at Entiat, which is both a child's problem and a symbol for the loss of control. Second, she is kept in the Little Girls' House, though she is of age to be admitted to the Big Girls' House. To add insult to an already injured ego, her mother greets her as "my big girl," upon their reunion. Used to life as a big girl, Roxanne's sense of maturity is bruised again and again. Finally, her P.E. teacher embarrasses Roxanne in front of the class at her new school. Forced to attempt to tumble without adequate instruction, Roxanne fails and is made to sit out.

After surviving these initial humiliations with stoic determination, Roxanne is taught the secret of cartwheels: "Catch yourself before you kill yourself." However, she will not put this lesson into practice until she is even further demoralized. After a Christmas spent being ignored by her former best friend, after hearing her family's instability mocked by the other girls in her dorm, and after learning that her mother, Christopher, and the baby are all living happily at home again while she remains at Entiat, Roxanne is faced with the worst humiliation of all. She arrives home to find Darla, the older girl who spurned her friendship, acting as her mother's right hand. "I held my breath to keep from crying," Roxanne says.

Only two years older than Roxanne, Darla seems steeped in maturity. The difference between the girls is shown through their nylons. Roxanne, hoping to still be seen as her mother's little girl, leaves them off the day of their reunion. Darla, used to wearing nylons and moving with the cool grace of an older teen, seems like a member of Roxanne's mother's glamorous adult world. A focal point for Roxanne's adolescent insecurities, the sight of Darla and the knowledge that her place has been taken by a girl who has broken Roxanne's heart before exhausts Roxanne's supply of hope that things will return to normal. Alden writes: "Children are not 'lesser' humans; they're just at a different stage of the life

experience. They have the same ability to feel things (sometimes more intensely)." At this watershed moment of her young life, Roxanne feels the disconnection between herself and her mother acutely, more so than she ever felt during their physical separation. When her mother, oblivious to the change in her oldest, tries to reestablish their connection, Roxanne does not allow herself to be humiliated again. She wears her spite and anger like a cloak, though she once thought herself incapable of such an act, and enters the adult world wrapped in resentment. The bright spring leaves that hurt her eyes represent her own rebirth into a harsher world.

In "From Aspiring Nun to Fiction Writer," Boucheron writes, "In [Henley's] work, which weaves together motives and outcomes, women's issues frequently come into play. In particular, female characters look for and achieve independence." Roxanne's emotional independence is won from a woman who rarely acts like a mother. A heavy drinker and smoker who struggles with mental illness, Roxanne's mother is shown early in the story telling her daughter her secrets, much to Roxanne's distress: "You can learn too much too soon about your mother's past." After her stay at the VA Hospital, she is shown failing to answer to the cry of her baby: "Mother, startled, rose partway from her chair and then sank back, waving her wet fingernails and looking helplessly at Darla." Thus, from her oldest to her youngest child, she has failed in her role.

Roxanne, a devotee of cleanliness and efficiency, found purpose in picking up her mother's slack around the house but never felt truly unrepentant anger towards her until her return from Entiat. She has emerged from their separation hardened by the humiliations of a luckless, loveless life, while her mother emerged from her own exile as selfish as before. Roxanne finds her tiresome and, with a newfound, weary wisdom, admits: "I didn't want to forgive her for being the way she was, but you have to forgive your mother." This adult sense of resignation is a startling change from the young girl of the story's beginning, who felt the priest did not understand the gravity of her sin when she wished her mother would disappear.

Roxanne's father is absent throughout the episode. He works in another state, Roxanne explains, but also mentions that her mother once beat him with a belt. After she has been drinking, she curses his name and speaks instead of a

Without warning, the mother wanders off. (© *Thomas Zsebok / Shutterstock*)

woman she loves. Roxanne is more aware of these marital strains than she is of her mother's struggle as a parent, just as her mother seems unaware of the damage she causes her child through such revelations. Only when her mother's problems shift from her husband to her children does Roxanne begin to find real fault with her. She finds the strength to place blame on her mother rather than assume it is she herself who is in the wrong, as she has done previously. Though Roxanne was childish to assume she could take care of four younger siblings and a farmhouse on her own, her delusions of control are thoroughly dismantled over the course of her six-month stay at Entiat Home. From the depths of humiliation, she rises to maturity, and with an adult's perspective, she recognizes that her days of childhood devotion to her mother are at an end: "She searched my eyes and tried to make some long-ago connection, sweet scrutiny, perhaps the way she'd looked at me when I was a new baby, her first baby. I looked away."

Boucheron neatly summarizes Roxanne's inauspicious six-month journey to maturity: "A mentally ill mother, an absent father, family conflict, an orphanage episode, a girl emerging as an adult." With so much on her shoulders and an assertive tendency to take responsibility for her actions, Roxanne is strengthened by adversity. Recognizing her mother's faults, she successfully adopts the secret of cartwheels, catching herself before it is too late. By allowing herself to feel genuine adult resentment toward her mother, Roxanne overcomes her childhood sense of loyalty to her. A life devoted to such a mother would be a life wasted. Roxanne's life, like the bright spring leaves newly unfurled, is just beginning.

Source: Amy L. Miller, Critical Essay on "The Secret of Cartwheels," in *Short Stories for Students*, Gale, Cengage Learning, 2016.

Barbara Shoup, Margaret-Love Denman, and Patricia Henley

In the following interview excerpt, Henley talks about her writing process.

You published three collections of short stories before publishing your first novel, Hummingbird House. *How did you make the transition from short fiction to the novel?*

"

ANOTHER TRANSITION COMES TO MIND:
PLOTTING, OF COURSE. I CAME TO REALIZE
THAT SHORT STORIES ARE MUCH MORE LIKE
POEMS THAN THEY ARE LIKE NOVELS. PLOTTING
PERPLEXED ME FOR A LONG TIME."

When I first started writing fiction in 1979, I started a novel. Some of the characters that were in my early short stories were in that novel. That was my first effort at fiction writing. It wasn't working. I didn't have a sense of what I was doing. So I turned that novel into stories. Then I wrote the second collection. I didn't really have the idea of a novel in my mind at all until I went to Guatemala.

So the trip to Guatemala came first, before the idea that you would like to write about that place.

I went with a friend in 1989. I had always been interested in indigenous people, the fate of indigenous people, and I followed what was going on there from afar. I had no idea how it would affect my writing, but I was willing to find out. When I went down there, it just seemed like material that begged to be a novel. So I took it on.

Was there anything in particular that struck you that way, or just the general experience?

I felt that somebody reading a short story about that could ignore the historical context, but if you write a novel, hundreds of pages, no one could ignore it. It seemed like really big issues kept coming up. The lives of women and children in wartime, religion. I thought, "This has to be a novel," though I still had no idea what I was doing. One of the hardest technical things I dealt with was switching from writing a tidy, ten-to-twenty-page piece that's finished, to writing chapters, where you want just the opposite. You want a book. You want something that's going to keep the reader reading. Short story writers are used to exposition, conflict, closure, and I found myself doing that a lot with the chapters. I think that's one of the hardest things for short story writers to get over.

Yes, there's a seamlessness to a good novel. It's an alternate reality in a way a short story

can't be. You live in it for a while. You want it to feel that way.

I think that's the naive, childlike reader in us. We like to be deeply engaged. We want to have that feeling that we can't put it down. It's kind of old fashioned, I guess. But I wanted that sustained tension throughout. So that's one of the difficulties—and then just sustaining the energy for the project, the mental and emotional and physical energy. My life as a short story writer went like this: I would write a draft in maybe a week or ten days, let it sit maybe for a week or ten days, revise it for a couple of weeks. In a month or six weeks, I would have a story. Maybe I would go back to it in another month or so, but I could have a sense of completion and take some time off. Live my life. Writing a novel requires so much more letting go of the rest of your life.

Another transition comes to mind: plotting, of course. I came to realize that short stories are much more like poems than they are like novels. Plotting perplexed me for a long time. Now that I feel I've learned a little bit about my own way of plotting, at least, I enjoy it very much. It's problem solving, and I've always enjoyed problem solving.

How did you go about learning your own way of plotting?

My son and husband helped me a lot. They were more analytical about [the book] and they helped me see that I needed to arrange the events in a way that continued to raise questions. I looked at what I had and thought, "Okay, where do I want those questions to be raised? How can I keep the reader wondering? How many balls can I get in the air?" I approached it that way, kind of by the seat of my pants.

How did you look at the whole thing?

I would read it over and over again and look at the way one thing inevitably led to the next thing. Screenplay books were helpful to me. It also helped me to look at films and to see how structured they were. The writers who write screenplays have that moment very early on, that instigating event that changes everything, and complications spin out from that moment.

Plot is like a skeleton. I tell my students that our structures can be the same, just like our skeletons can be the same. But nobody would ever look at us and think we're the same, because it's the way we're fleshed out that matters. You can start with that basic structure, that skeleton, but that's the wonderful thing about the novel—it can go off on this cul-de-sac or that cul-de-sac. And every time, it's so different.

Philip Roth said in an interview, years ago, that no matter how long you've been writing, it's not like a dentist doing a root canal. The dentist goes in every day, he does a root canal. But you sit down and you have to face that blank page and start all over again. One thing that helped was that I had these different elements, people, and situations that were dangerous. So lots of different things could happen. I had Sunny with that newspaper and Vida Luz with her husband in jail. I had all these people who had potential danger in their lives, and so I had a lot to work with. I came across these stories or I invented stories that seemed to be a really rich broth.

There's a difference between an emotional plot and an action plot. I think if you write stories with emotional plots, it's really hard to get the other. But you've got to have both. The reader gets attached to all the characters, so there's emotional growth and inner turmoil. But it's triggered by something with such great dramatic possibilities. You have to have that outer tension of some kind. It doesn't have to be something cliché, like a car chase. But you need to have something on the outside. You can't just have inner tension.

So it's translating the inner tension into something you can see and follow and track.

When it comes to plotting, you have to be willing to spend the time in solitude playing out different scenarios in your mind, working it through, daydreaming about it, thinking about whether that's really the way you want it to go, whether that feels authentic enough, whether that's provocative enough. You play these things out and then maybe you back up and think, no that's not it, and try another one. I think oftentimes when we're writing, we think that the first thing we write down is going to be the great thing. It usually isn't. You have to be willing to backtrack and try another path.

When you started the book, what did you know for sure?

I knew that I had Kate. I knew she was a midwife. I've always had an attraction to midwifery. I helped a friend deliver her baby years ago—one of my short stories came out of that, "The Birthing." I wanted a central character

who was bringing life into the world. There was so much death and destruction around her, and I wanted that to be part of the conflict and the tension.

I started the material in first person, and I was just writing endlessly Kate's point of view. Then I realized that I wanted a narrator who was more knowledgeable than Kate, who saw a bigger picture than Kate was able to see. So I started writing some third person passages which I was quite happy with. But I didn't want to give up Kate's voice. I wanted her voice to have that ring of the friend who's sitting down with you over a cup of coffee or a beer, telling you, "This is what happened and this is how I'm making sense of it now." I really liked that.

The choice to make her a midwife was interesting because it is such an essentially unpolitical thing to be. This is in so many ways a political novel, yet you avoided any sense of having an agenda behind it. How did you do that?

First of all, I didn't want to come down on the side of any one political group or military group. I just kept reminding myself, "Don't let yourself get bogged down in those things. Pull back and ask the biggest questions you can possibly ask." I kept bringing myself back to, "What happens to women and children when there's war?" That just kept informing my movement through the project.

So I knew Kate, I knew she was going to be a midwife, and I knew that she had had a troubled love life. That's all I knew at the beginning. It didn't take long for me to start thinking about Dixie. I met and talked with and read about men and women of the church who've done a lot of work down there. There's no one exactly like Dixie. But there was a priest in Guatemala in the '80s who was killed, and the people of the village asked if they could have his heart to bury in the churchyard. That stuck with me. Someone told me that story when I'd been in Guatemala for two weeks, and I thought, "I'm going to write about a priest." So I always knew that Dixie was going to die.

And you knew that his heart would be buried in the churchyard.

Yes. I knew I had to put that in the book. You go around like a vulture, stealing these things.

What about the time of the novel? How did you decide when it would take place?

I knew I couldn't set the novel in an era when I hadn't been there. I felt incapable of doing that. So I decided to set it in 1989, the summer when I was there for the first time. I took five trips, researching the book. But that summer was a very intense summer for me, emotionally. I wanted to write what I knew, and I knew the mood in Guatemala that summer because I was there. So that's what I knew. I knew these two people. I knew their lives intersected the summer of 1989 in Antigua, Guatemala, and I just started writing.

When did you start the book?

I started it in 1989, when I came back. I worked on it off and on for a couple of years, but I was also working on *The Secret of Cartwheels* at that time. I completed two hundred pages, abandoned them, wrote a short story about Marta and Eduardo, the orphans. I put that away, didn't do anything with it. Then in 1993, after the publication of *The Secret of Cartwheels*, I got back to the book. I didn't complete it until the spring of 1996, when I was on sabbatical in New Mexico.

So the book was in your mind for a long time.

Yes. And then the book wasn't accepted for two more years. So it was ten years between having that idea and holding the book in my hands. It was a very long time. I changed so much.

Yes. That's another thing that happens with a novel that doesn't happen with a short story. You start out writing the novel as a certain person, but you may very well be a different person by the time you get it finished.

I had to allow myself to be transformed by the material and the experience. I had to just let go. My life was so ruled by that book. The second time I went to Guatemala, in 1990, I went by myself for six weeks. I was a little scared of going because nobody knew what I was doing. It was a dangerous place, where artists and writers, especially, had been killed. I went, and I can remember lying awake—I can picture the place where I was when this happened—thinking, "What am I doing here? Do I really have to do this?" I was really questioning the wisdom of the path I was on. I was just so convinced that I had to write about this in a way that would make the oppression of the Guatemalan people accessible to more people.

Do you find that you write, generally, because there's something you feel you want the

world to know? Or is it because there's something you need to know for yourself?

The things I want to figure out for myself are usually the emotional things—thorny issues in my own life and the lives of my friends. But right now I'm in a phase of my life of writing about things that will be provocative. So many people will come to a story. So many people have come to *Hummingbird House* who never would have picked up a book of nonfiction about Guatemala. So that's how I'm approaching my work now. I can pick an issue, any issue, and pursue it in fiction and so many more people will come to it. I'm a very political person.

Passion, really caring about what you write, seems crucial in the mix of talents novelists bring to the page. So does a willingness to embrace the kind of ambiguity of process you describe. What else makes a good novelist?

A compassionate heart seems to me to be very, very important. A willingness to really look closely at human beings and their motivations and their foibles without judging them is really important. To be a novelist you have to be willing to sit there all those hours, just endure. I advise my students to get involved in an endurance sport. It's helped me a lot. I work out. I walk, run. I used to do long-distance skiing and mountain climbing. Anything that pushes you, that makes you push yourself will help you push yourself to get a project like a novel done. That's so much of it, the willingness to be there, to meet with it every day. There's a great essay by Ted Solaratoff called "Going Through the Pain."

What do you do when you're really stuck?

I don't usually get really stuck for more than a few days. I get stuck between sections or chapters, and I'll know that something's cooking in me. I'll get glimmers of it once in a while as I'm going about my day. But it's not ready to spring forth on the page yet. No matter how many times I go through those things, I always find them a little bit frustrating. But I try to have faith. I always say to myself, "You've done this before, you can do it again." I wait it out, and usually when I least expect it the first sentence of that next section will come to me. So I go on about my business and maybe use the time to get a lot of grading done. Or cook. I love to cook.

What surprised you in the process of writing Hummingbird House? Were there things in the story that you didn't know were going to happen?

Oh, so much of it. Marta and Eduardo came into the story rather late in the process. I had written this story about them, "Orphans."

So you wrote the story not thinking it was a part of the novel.

Right. My husband said to me several times, "You need to get those kids in the story." Finally, I listened to him, and probably they came into it in the second-to-last draft, when I was really pulling it together. Or maybe third to last. Late in the process. A big question throughout the novel was, would Dixie and Kate sleep together? That was an enormous question for me, almost to the very end. I finally decided that it wasn't consistent with Dixie's character and I didn't want this to be a book about a priest who breaks his vow.

When did you know how the book would end?

I remember the day that the ending came to me. It was probably two or three months before I finished the whole manuscript. I had this wonderful situation. I was in New Mexico, living in an adobe house, and I was set up in the dining room where there were two windows and I could see the mountains, and I could see the sun coming up. . . .

Source: Barbara Shoup, Margaret-Love Denman, and Patricia Henley, "The Interviews: Patricia Henley," in *Novel Ideas: Contemporary Authors Share the Creative Process*, University of Georgia Press, 2009, pp. 183–89.

Publishers Weekly

In the following review, an anonymous reviewer praises Henley's ability to write "from both the heart and the head."

Post-hippie attitudes—disdain for conventional mores, a preference for relationships with like-minded free spirits and an appreciation of nature—inform this impressive third story collection by Henley, whose first novel, *Hummingbird House*, was a finalist for both the National Book Award and the *New Yorker* Best Fiction Book Award. Set across the U.S. wherever loose communities of family and friends settle down, from hardscrabble rural Indiana to the Pacific Northwest, the 19 stories capture defining moments in otherwise ordinary lives. "The Secret of Cartwheels" is one of two tales about a large Catholic family, no doubt inspired by Henley's own experience as the eldest of eight children. At age 13, narrator Roxanne and two of her younger sisters are sent off to a children's home because their mother, an alcoholic, can't

cope with her many offspring. Roxanne, plagued by her inability to turn cartwheels and her habit of wetting the bed, dreams despite herself of the life she used to know. In "Cargo," Roxanne reappears as an adult, settled in Montana. Her sister has called to say their mother is dying and the family is gathering. In attempting to decide whether she'll go home, Roxie acknowledges that she's left many places hoping for a new beginning, forgetting every time "that the things you hate the most are the things that travel with you." Many of Henley's characters live transient lives, work at menial jobs—mechanic, fruit picker, waitress—identify with the lyrics of country music and look to dope, booze and casual sex as palliatives. They recognize their weaknesses, but they don't give up the game. The author's sense of humor shines often. In "Slinkers," Joanne, whose "laughter always made you feel good" is an "intuitive shopper" who proclaims, "If you find a pair of jeans that really fit, buy two pair." These stories, by a marvelous writer who speaks from both the heart and the head, are as comfortable as wellworn denim.

Source: Review of *Worship of the Common Heart*, in *Publishers Weekly*, Vol. 247, No. 33, August 14, 2000, p. 328.

Publishers Weekly

In the following review, an anonymous reviewer asserts that Henley's story "rings true."

To be strong enough for the path she's chosen, 42-year-old American midwife Kate Banner, the protagonist of this moving novel, must "cut off pieces of her heart." Her three-week visit to Mexico during the 1980s becomes an eight-year Central American sojourn once she witnesses the poverty and war-torn devastation of the people she encounters and decides to help. She delivers babies and administers basic medicine at a makeshift clinic, and travels, passionately but somewhat aimlessly, from Mexico to Nicaragua to Guatemala. She moves through the countrysides both with and without her compadres, a group of mostly North American activists, including the lover who soon leaves her and a priest whose love for Kate makes him question his vows. After experiencing many tragic losses, Kate occasionally wrestles with the notion of returning home to Indiana, but her heart (however assaulted) lies with the native peoples and their struggles. Her sacrifices achieve meaning when a collectively imagined school/clinic for destitute Guatemalan children becomes a very real possibility. And when Hummingbird House is established, Kate is satisfied she has helped make one lasting contribution to a community despite all she has lost, including, she laments, her youth. This first novel by short story writer (*The Secret of Cartwheels*) and poet (*Back Roads*) Henley is darkly atmospheric, with fluent dialogue and an assured prose style. Numerous subplots, though clearly heartfelt and informative, sometimes detract from Kate's centrality. The prismatic trajectory of the tale may be deliberate, for the author's message is double-edged: that trying for a better world is necessary, demanding work, but no one can save herself through saving the world. Kate's tale rings true in her realistic conclusion that gross injustice calls for more than merely sorrow, but also rage, sacrifice and the ability to simultaneously love and lose.

Source: Review of *Hummingbird House*, in *Publishers Weekly*, Vol. 246, No. 6, February 8, 1999, p. 195.

Charlotte M. Wright

In the following review, Wright praises Henley's writing but believes she ought to broaden her range of characters.

Patricia Henley made waves with her first book of stories, *Friday Night at Silver Star* (Graywolf, 1986). It was chosen as a Notable Book of the year by the American Library Association and featured as an Editor's Choice for both the *New York Times Book Review* and *Publishers Weekly*. At the same time *Esquire* called Henley an "up-and-coming" author, and *Western American Literature*'s reviewer found the book a "quiet but forceful" evocation of characters "who came of age in the sixties and early seventies [and are] trying to bring the past and present into perspective." Henley has a professional flair to her writing that will continue to attract kudos from critics.

Yet I have some reservation. Yes, a *Booklist*'s reviewer notes, Henley is capable of "convincing us utterly of the flesh and the feelings of her characters." What bothers me is the sameness of those characters, who seem recycled from story to story. Nearly all are wanderers, with "sixties" attitudes towards drugs, sex, and health foods. I am of the right age to appreciate such attributes, but I found that after a few stories, I wanted to see the author's lively, polished, and accessible style applied to different types of characters.

Another complaint I have is less a problem with Henley's writing than with how it is billed. Graywolf Press, her publisher, seems determined to cash in on the current interest in the western "sense of place." Their press release states that she "vividly captures the lives and landscapes of the American West," and that her stories contain a "brilliant evocation of place." The cover copy reiterates this theme: "Patricia Henley's new stories are set in the American West [where] we meet marginal westerners . . . whose lives lead them to a certain type of longing." I read a lot of fiction by western authors, and much of it does depend on setting, on details of landscape, on western dialect and lore. Such is not the case with these stories, which seem less dependent on a sense of place than a sense of time. The characters could just as easily be living in rural New England, in a southern college town, or in a cabin in the Appalachians—but they could only be products of the 1960s.

Ironically, the best stories in the collection are the two which depend the least on setting. In the title story and in "Labrador," Henley achieves a startling level of emotional verity. Both stories center on the experiences of a young girl forced too early from childhood by the mental breakdown of her mother and the simultaneous disappearance of her father. In each case, the child tries in vain to find in the language and signals of the adults who surround her a clue to interpreting the threatening events. Roxanne's mother in "The Secret of Cartwheels" is committed to a mental institution right after telling her "there are signs in life . . . that tell you what you have to do." Her Aunt Opal, in explaining her mother's absence, adds to Roxanne's sense of guilt for not "reading the signs" by telling her: "She's sick. Surely you must have known?" In fact, the only "truth" Roxanne hears throughout the whole ordeal is from another girl at the Orphan's Home, who tells her that "the secret of cartwheels . . . [is to] catch yourself before you kill yourself." It is this that Roxanne applies to her life thereafter.

In "Labrador," adolescent Kate has a similar problem. Her mother, too, slips into an early madness, forcing Kate "out of childhood" and into an adult sense of guilt and responsibility for family tragedies. She says, "I thought by the weight of . . . my energy, I could make it all better . . . that if I worked hard enough and loved her enough she would change." And she does work hard to keep her own sanity and to keep you her younger siblings happy, but when her mother comes home, Kate sees that nothing she has done has made a difference:

But I felt none of what I'd expected to feel when she returned home. The welcome; the affection; the relief; the praise. The praise. More than anything, I'd expected her to tell me what a fine job I'd done, how selfless I'd been. . . . [But] she treated me like any other child.

Patricia Henley's writing explores her characters' search for connections between themselves and others. Occasionally, they find a link; more often than not, they lose what few connections they already have. I admire her writing, and can only hope that she will expand her considerable skills by experimenting with a variety of character types.

Source: Charlotte M. Wright, Review of *The Secret of Cartwheels*, in *Studies in Short Fiction*, Vol. 31, No. 2, Spring 1994, pp. 263–65.

SOURCES

Alden, Paulette Bates, "Capturing Childhood/Engaging the Adult Reader," in *paulettealden.com*, October 18, 2010, http://paulettealden.com/articles/capturing-childhood engaging-the-adult-reader (accessed August 5, 2015).

Bellafaire, Judith A., "The Women's Army Corps: A Commemoration of World War II Service," CMH Publication, February 17, 2005, http://www.history.army. mil/brochures/wac/wac.htm (accessed August 6, 2015).

"Bio," in *patriciahenley.org*, http://www.patriciahenley. org/?page_id = 7 (accessed August 4, 2015).

Birnbaum, Robert, "Author Interview: Patricia Henley," in *Identity Theory*, December 18, 2002, http://www .identitytheory.com/patricia-henley (accessed August 4, 2015).

Boucheron, Robert, "From Aspiring Nun to Fiction Writer," in *Construction Literary*, http://construction litmag.com/interview/aspiring-nun-fiction-writer (accessed August 5, 2015).

Finzel, Rochelle, "Homeless and Runaway Youth," National Conference of State Legislatures website, October 1, 2013, http://www.ncsl.org/research/human-services/homeless-and-runaway-youth.aspx (accessed August 4, 2015).

Henley, Patricia, "The Secret of Cartwheels," in *The Secret of Cartwheels*, Graywolf Press, 1992, pp. 1–18.

Lund, Natalie, "Writing YA: An Interview with Patricia Henley & Elizabeth Stuckey-French," in *Sycamore Review*, November 3, 2014, http://sycamorereview.com/ 2014/11/03/writing-ya-an-interview-with-patricia-henley-elizabeth-stuckey-french (accessed August 4, 2015).

Porter, Christy, "Bright Lights, No City: Montana's the Literary Capital of the Country and Its Authors Have a Best Seller to Prove It," in *Los Angeles Times*, March 19, 1989, http://articles.latimes.com/1989-03-19/news/ vw-225_1_montana-writers (accessed August 6, 2015).

Rampton, Martha, "The Three Waves of Feminism," Pacific University website, October 23, 2014, http://www. pacificu.edu/about-us/news-events/three-waves-feminism (accessed August 6, 2015).

Roorbach, Bill, "Table for Two: An Interview with Patricia Henley," in *Bill and Dave's Cocktail Hour*, October 10, 2011, http://billanddavescocktailhour.com/table-for-two-an-interview-with-patricia-henley (accessed August 4, 2015).

Spivak, Emily, "Stocking Series, Part 1: Wartime Rationing and Nylon Riots," Smithsonian website, September 4, 2012, http://www.smithsonianmag.com/arts-culture/stocking-series-part-1-wartime-rationing-and-nylon-riots-25391066/?no-ist (accessed August 6, 2015).

"Supporting the Nation: The Women's Army Auxiliary Corps & Women's Army Corps," Army Heritage Center Foundation website, https://www.armyheritage.org/ education-and-programs/educational-resources/education-materials-index/50-information/soldier-stories/297-wacwwii (accessed August 6, 2015).

Walsh, Kenneth T., "The 1960s: A Decade of Change for Women," in *U.S. News and World Report*, March 12, 2010, http://www.usnews.com/news/articles/2010/ 03/12/the-1960s-a-decade-of-change-for-women (accessed August 6, 2015).

FURTHER READING

Barrish, Phillip J., *The Cambridge Introduction to American Literary Realism*, Cambridge University Press, 2011.

Barrish explores realism from its conception in the nineteenth century as a reaction to the Industrial Revolution to its incorporation of feminism and racial equality to keep pace with a changing country. Authors featured include Mark Twain, Charlotte Perkins Gilman, Edith Wharton, and Theodore Dreiser.

Henley, Patricia, *Hummingbird House*, MacMurray & Beck, 1999.

A finalist for the National Book Award, *Hummingbird House* tells the story of an American midwife's travels in Mexico, Nicaragua, and Guatemala, where she falls in love with a lapsed priest named Dixie Ryan.

Smiley, Jane, *A Thousand Acres*, Ballantine, 1999.

A retelling of William Shakespeare's *King Lear* set on a farm in Iowa, *A Thousand Acres* explores the depths of betrayal, responsibility, and madness in the Cook family: owners of a successful thousand-acre farm. Winner of the Pulitzer Prize, the novel's moral ambiguities and complex characters recreate a timeless human drama in the present day.

Wolff, Tobias, *The Vintage Book of Contemporary American Short Stories*, Vintage Contemporaries, 1994. This collection of thirty-three short stories exemplifies the ability of the short-story form to express American life at its most personal and powerful. Authors include Tim O'Brien, Jamaica Kincaid, Robert Stone, Joy Williams, Amy Tan, Ralph Lombreglia, Raymond Carver, Joyce Carol Oates, and many more.

SUGGESTED SEARCH TERMS

Patricia Henley

"The Secret of Cartwheels"

"The Secret of Cartwheels" AND 1993

Henley AND "The Secret of Cartwheels"

"The Secret of Cartwheels" AND short story

"The Secret of Cartwheels" AND abandonment

"The Secret of Cartwheels" AND family

"The Secret of Cartwheels" AND coming of age

"The Secret of Cartwheels" AND motherhood

Sinking House

T. CORAGHESSAN BOYLE

1988

At the start of T. Coraghessan Boyle's story "Sinking House," an old man dies. His wife responds by turning on all of the faucets in the house and then the garden faucets in the yard. As readers learn about the fifty-year marriage of Monty and Muriel, her motives become increasingly unclear. Is the running water meant to soothe her in the terrible silence after his loss, or is it meant to symbolically cleanse her life of a cruel violent man who dominated her? The story gives no definitive answer as the water flows for weeks, saturating the lawn of the young couple next door and creeping into their house, compelling them to call the police to investigate. The young husband and wife are in their twenties and dismiss Muriel's behavior as a problem of age and grief. Observing Muriel, however, twenty-three-year-old Meg, who thought she was living a peaceful and stable life with her husband and daughter, realizes how much her life is like Muriel's.

Boyle, who now goes by the name *T. C. Boyle*, has been considered one of America's great fiction writers since his first collection of stories was published in the 1970s. This story's strange conceit of a woman letting her house fill up with water is common for his imaginative style: readers count on Boyle's stories to be rich with details that boldly make the most improbable circumstances seem perfectly natural, which is something he achieves with "Sinking House."

"Sinking House" was first published in *Atlantic Monthly* in February 1988. The version

T. Coraghessan Boyle (© *ZUMA Press, Inc. | Alamy*)

used in preparing this entry is from *T. C. Boyle Stories*, published in 1998 by Penguin Books.

AUTHOR BIOGRAPHY

Thomas John Boyle was born on December 2, 1948, in Peekskill, New York. His father worked as a janitor, and his mother was a secretary. He attended Lakeland High School in Shrub Oak, New York, where he developed his sharp eye for detail and his rich imagination. At the age of seventeen, he officially changed his middle name to "Coraghessan," a name that he made up because it sounded vaguely Irish. Early in his career, he published under the name "T. Coraghessan Boyle," though he formally started using "T. C. Boyle" in the 1990s—his acclaimed 1998 collection *T. C. Boyle Stories* uses the subtitle *The Collected Stories of T. Coraghessan Boyle* to accommodate readers who knew him by either name.

Boyle graduated from high school in 1964 and then attended State University of New York, Potsdam, earning degrees in both English and history in 1968. He taught at Lakeland High School for four years. In 1972, he entered the writers workshop program at the University of Iowa, earning his master of fine arts degree in creative writing in 1975. Then he stayed on at Iowa for further graduate work, earning a PhD in nineteenth-century British literature in 1977. After graduating with his doctorate, Boyle went to teach at the University of Southern California at Los Angeles, where he helped design the school's creative writing program. He is still affiliated with USC to this day as a distinguished professor of English.

Boyle is the author of twenty-four books of fiction, starting with his collection *Descent of Man and Other Stories* (1979) on up through the novel *The Harder They Come* (2015). His works have been published in many of the world's prestigious magazines, such as the *New Yorker*, *Atlantic Monthly*, *Harper's*, *Granta*, and *McSweeney's*, and have been translated into over two dozen languages. He has been the recipient of the National Endowment for the Arts award; the PEN/Faulkner Award (in 1988, for the novel *World's End*); the 1989 Prix Passion publishers' prize in France, for the novel *Water Music*; the Henry David Thoreau Award for excellence in nature writing (2013); and multiple inclusions in the O. Henry Awards and the annual Best Short Stories of the year collections. Boyle lives near Santa Barbara, California, with his wife, Karen Kvashay, and their children.

PLOT SUMMARY

In the very first sentence of "Sinking House," an old man, Monty Burgess, dies. The rest of the story is about his widow's coming to grips with his death and the next door neighbors' coping with the strange way she expresses her feelings of loss.

As soon as her husband dies, Muriel goes to the kitchen and turns on the water in the sink. She then goes to the bathroom in the guest bedroom and turns on the water in the sink and tub. The sound of water running calms her. After a while, she goes outside and turns on the sprinklers in the yard. To turn on the water in the master bathroom, she has to pass the bed where Monty lies dead. She avoids looking at him. She flushes the toilet and then props the mechanism open so that it will keep running.

The story moves ahead two weeks and changes perspective to Muriel's next-door neighbor, Meg Terwilliger. Meg is a young housewife, twenty-three years old, with a four-year-old daughter, Tiffany. Meg is concerned about her chores, such as taking the dog to the veterinarian and taking her husband's shirts to the dry cleaners and buying groceries. As she does her morning stretching exercises, Meg notices that the rug under her in the sunroom is wet. She pulls it back and sees that the floor under it is wet. This is something that does happen sometimes in winter, but it is summer now. There has not even been any rain in Los Angeles in months.

She goes to the backyard to see where the water is coming from. The yard is wet. The hose is rolled up and turned off. As she wanders around the yard, she looks into the yard next door and sees that the sprinklers are going at their fullest. Meg knows that Muriel recently lost her husband, and she thinks of how distraught she herself would be if her husband, Sonny, died. She empathizes with Muriel, but still, she has to stop the flow of water that is soaking her yard and affecting her house. She decides that she will tell Sonny about it when he comes home and let him decide how to handle it.

The perspective changes back to Muriel. She is sitting in the house, its rugs soaked with water. She has a stack of sympathy cards that she has not opened. She imagines the house as a boat that is sinking.

When the doorbell rings, Muriel goes to answer. It is Meg. Muriel thinks that she looks familiar, but she thinks of a prostitute on a television show she once saw who murdered the pimp who took advantage of her. When Meg introduces herself as the neighbor and asks if Muriel is aware that her lawn sprinklers have been running, she reminds Muriel of a college student who once came to the house to interview her about her past, to record her memories for an oral history project.

While Meg is telling Muriel that she can have her husband come over and fix the hose if there is some problem with it, Muriel wanders away from the door, muttering vaguely that there is no problem, that everything is all right.

The next scene takes place in the Terwilliger house, while Meg is preparing dinner. She

tells Sonny about the situation with Muriel's house. Sonny, who works in real estate, has come home after a hard day and is having a drink to unwind. He has trouble following Meg's story. When she shows him the soaked rug in the sunroom, Sonny is infuriated. She does not accompany him outside because all of the earthworms in the yard have gathered on the stone steps to get out of the water-soaked soil, but Sonny walks around to investigate. Seeing that the flood in the yard is forcing the fence to collapse drives him into a rage. Meg has seen his rages before.

Sonny, with Meg following him, goes to knock on Muriel's front door. When there is no answer, he bangs on it with his fist. Meg's attempt to calm him only makes Sonny angrier. As his rage reaches a high point, Muriel opens the door. The couple looks past her and sees that the house is filled with water. The carpets are soaked, and the plaster walls are absorbing the water from the floor. Sonny tells her that she has to stop this flow of water, and Muriel says that she does not know anything about any water.

Looking at Sonny, whom she does not recognize, Muriel is reminded of the violent way that Monty used to abuse her. He was verbally and physically abusive for the fifty years of their marriage. She feels vindicated now that he is dead.

A uniformed police officer comes to the house. Sonny's violent anger reminded Muriel of Monty, and now the officer's bearing, his swagger, reminds her of him too. The policeman comes into the house, which is dark because the water has caused the electricity to short out, and he goes from room to room, turning off the water. When he asks her why she has all of this water running, she does not answer, even though she can see that he believes she is mentally incompetent. He talks patronizingly to her, telling her to leave the water off, or he will come back and arrest her. Having been married to a domineering man like Monty, Muriel knows how to answer in a subservient way. She agrees to what the policeman asks, and he leaves. When he leaves, though, Muriel finds the silence in the house to be oppressive.

The story skips ahead to the next morning and shifts to Meg's perspective again. She has watched the policeman come to the house, noting that he came because Sonny called him there. She knows that the policeman shut off all of the water when he came that night, but the next morning it was all turned on again. Sonny called the police three times again in the morning, to complain.

This time there are two officers: the one with the moustache who came the night before and a woman. Meg is home alone. The policeman is gruff and rude and reminds her of Sonny as he pounds on Muriel's door, getting no answer.

Meg sees Muriel through the window and points her out to the police. When she still will not answer the door, the policeman breaks it in. The officers go into the house, and Meg watches, waiting for a long time until Muriel comes out, led by the policewoman. The policeman follows them with a suitcase of Muriel's clothes. Just before she is put into the police car, Muriel turns around and looks Meg right in the eyes.

In the final segment of the story, Meg returns to her household chores and tries to forget about the story of Muriel. She does not think that Muriel's look at her was an accusation: it just seemed sad.

In the backyard, Meg sinks into the mud, indicating that she is as stuck in her domestic situation as Muriel was stuck for fifty years with her abusive spouse. The fence between the two houses has fallen down, further indicating a connection between her life and Muriel's. She thinks of what life would be like for her if Sonny died, and she sees herself reflected in the water on the ground. At the end of the story, she decides to turn on her own sprinklers. She will not leave them on for long, though, because she knows that if she does, the foundation of her house, the thing that holds it up and makes it strong, might be damaged, and her happy domestic life might collapse.

CHARACTERS

Monty Burgess

The story begins with the death of Monty Burgess. When his widow, Muriel, immediately responds in the emotionally strange way of turning on all the water taps she can find, it seems at first as if she is beside herself with grief. As the story develops, however, readers gain more insight into Muriel's feelings about Monty. He had been her lover at first, back when they were dating in a Model A Ford (a car that was manufactured only up until 1931). Later on, though, he was a bully who abused her both physically (the story says that he "cuffed" her, using an

old-fashioned expression for hitting), mentally (the story lists derogatory words he called her), and probably sexually (as implied by the way he pinned her down). Monty's mistreatment of his wife is tied to the fact that he was an alcoholic, and alcoholism is a disease that often becomes progressively worse with the passage of years. The story also indicates that, as Monty's health declined, he was left at Muriel's mercy. She watched over him and even spoon-fed him, remaining dutiful to her abuser until his death.

Muriel Burgess

Muriel is the first character featured in the story. She is an old lady who is trying to find a way to react when the man she was married to for fifty years dies. Almost immediately after watching Monty die, she starts turning on faucets in the house. Not long after, she moves outside to turn on the garden faucets as well.

The fact that she leaves the water running day and night for weeks, as it destroys her house and the ground around it, indicates that Muriel is not mentally capable of coping with her husband's death. She is not as crazy as the people in the story think she is, though. It is true that she responds to their concerns as if she does not even know that the faucets are running, and she does not even recognize her own neighbors. However, she shows a silent lucidity that they do not recognize. She knows the water is running; she is aware of what she has done.

Her lack of clarity about the people in her neighborhood is understandable when one realizes that Muriel has just, as the story begins, come out of fifty years of being bullied and insulted. She is defensive and guarded, but she is also celebrating the death of the man who shredded her self-esteem. As a random act, turning on the faucets seems simply irrational. As an act of defiance, however, it represents a carefully planned rebellion against Monty when he is finally no longer capable of making her suffer any more. She is destroying the house he built and tended with his own hands, showing him that she is now in charge.

Muriel's last act in the story is to look at Meg Terwilliger with sad eyes. This is her acknowledgement of what the story had earlier only hinted at. Meg is also married to a loud, rough man, Sonny. He is not abusive in the way that Muriel's husband, Monty, was, but he does have a short temper and, like Monty, he drinks.

Muriel does not know her neighborhood, but she does know what things were like between her and Monty back before the abuse began. With that one sad look, she seems to be admitting that she can easily imagine how Sonny could end up like Monty and how Meg could end up like Muriel herself.

In the end, the police take Muriel away, presumably because she is in need of mental counseling. The fact that one of the officers leaves her home with a suitcase indicates that Muriel is cooperating with them and that they think that she needs professional, in-patient mental care for an extended length of time.

The Policeman

The policeman, identified by his moustache, shows up in two scenes. When he first comes to Muriel Burgess's house, he is hostile and patronizing. He tells her that she must behave better, talking to this much-older woman as if she were a child. As he is talking to her, he touches the weapons on his belt, which sends a subconscious message of having power over her, though Muriel is well aware of it as a power play. He reminds Muriel of Monty. The policeman does not know that Muriel has just finished an abusive relationship that lasted a half a century and that she therefore cannot be intimidated easily.

In his second scene, the policeman returns to Muriel's house with a policewoman. Though the story does not say what they talk about in the house, it implies that the policeman is more subdued on this visit. When they leave, Muriel is walking with the policewoman, while the policeman walks behind them carrying Muriel's suitcase, as if he is their employee.

The Policewoman

The policewoman is only in one scene of the story. She comes to Muriel Burgess's house at the end to persuade her to surrender quietly and check herself into a program for mental evaluation. It is clear that she accomplished her goal, because Muriel leaves the house holding on to the policewoman's arm, as if they are friends after their one half-hour encounter. Whatever she has said to Muriel inside the house, it has earned her trust.

Meg Terwilliger

Meg is a young housewife and mother who lives with her husband and four-year-old daughter next door to Muriel Burgess's house. Meg is only twenty-three, having had her daughter while she was still a teenager. At the start of the story, she has simple concerns: she has to take the dog, Queenie, to the vet and to make sure her daughter, Tiffany, gets to and from day care. She has to plan her menu and shop for the food she will need. She has time in the morning to exercise.

Meg is a passive character. When Meg discovers that the water from the Burgess house is affecting her own house, she tries to talk to Muriel, but when that does not work she leaves the matter for her husband, Sonny, to handle when he comes home. When Sonny raises his voice, Meg is quick to agree with him to try to calm him down. The story does not say that Sonny ever abused Meg, but her passive demeanor implies that if or when he ever did become abusive, Meg would make excuses for his behavior. At one point, she even imagines what it would be like for her if Sonny were dead.

At the end of the story, in its last section, Meg is left alone. Sonny is off at work, Tiffany is off at school, and Muriel has been taken away by the police. With time to think, Meg reflects on how much her life is like the life of Muriel Burgess, who has just been taken into custody for mental observation. Meg never really admits, even to herself, that her situation is very much like Muriel's when her marriage was just starting out. Though Meg does not explicitly acknowledge the similarities, she does find herself drawn to running the water in her yard, as Muriel did in hers, just to see what it feels like. She identifies with Muriel, whether she knows that she does or not.

Sonny Terwilliger

Sonny is the last of the major characters to appear in the story. He is twenty-eight years old, with a twenty-three-year-old wife and a four-year-old daughter, Tiffany. He works hard in the competitive real estate business. When he comes home, he just wants to unwind with a drink.

His wife, Meg, is hesitant to tell him about the water that is flowing onto their property from the neighbors' house because she knows how upset Sonny can get. She remembers unexplained instances in the past when he became excessively emotional about high long-distance phone bills or changes in business arrangements. She attributes his anger in these situations to his need for a stable environment. This, she feels, is why Sonny is so infuriated with the damage the water is doing to his fence and the rest of his property.

Whatever the reason is for Sonny's rage, its eventual result is implied in the story. Sonny drinks to unwind, and he becomes angry when there is a change in his expectations. He is not abusive in the way that Monty Burgess was, but he has certainly started down that path. He calls the police to take away Muriel, the neighbor, because his sense of entitlement tells him that her water creeping onto his property is not to be tolerated, implying that his perspective is similar to that of the abusive Monty Burgess.

Tiffany Terwilliger

Tiffany is the four-year-old daughter of Meg and Sonny. She does not appear in the story.

THEMES

Grief

"Sinking House" begins with the death of a man, and it follows from there with the life of his widowed wife, who was married to him for fifty years. After his death, she behaves unusually. Because of this, there is a temptation to read this as a story about grief. It may be a story about grief, but only in a limited sense of the word.

Muriel does not know what to do with her emotions once Monty is dead. She does not express any feelings in words, but the flowing of the water, as she opens every faucet in the house, represents her outpouring of emotions in a nonverbal way. She is reacting to her husband's death, and she is reacting in an extreme way, so it seems reasonable to assume that the death caused that extreme reaction.

However, grief is usually thought of as being based in sorrow, and Muriel does not seem at all sorrowful when she remembers Monty. His death does move her strongly, but the way she reacts is not the way a person saddened by news would react. Her behavior might just be highly specific to her and her alone, which would be a sign of just how devastated she is. On the other hand, there is a very good possibility that she does not behave like a standard grieving widow because she does not feel the emotions that most people in her situation would feel.

Eccentricities

At the beginning of the story, Meg views Muriel's behavior as irrational. Many other characters in the story see Muriel as eccentric because they do not recognize the flow of water as a symbolic gesture, expressing the feelings that Muriel has bottled up for decades. They are feelings that she still cannot freely admit to herself even after Monty has died.

Meg thinks that Muriel is devastated by the loss of her husband and is acting irrationally because of that. Meg imagines what she herself would do if her husband died, even though she and Sonny have been married only a fraction of the time that Muriel and Monty were together. The policeman, on the other hand, treats Muriel as if she suffers from dementia brought on by old age. He asks her the kind of direct, clear questions that one would ask someone who does not have complete control of their mental faculties. This is actually a reasonable assumption on his part—when she talks to him, Muriel does not seem to understand that water is destroying her house and yard and that she herself caused it. She seems to have trouble remembering what she did just a few days earlier.

Still, what Muriel does with her own house and yard could be viewed as nobody's business but her own. If it were just a matter of something that damaged her property, her actions would be forgotten, waved away as the eccentricities of an old, grief-stricken woman. When the water damages the property of her neighbors, however, Muriel is viewed not just as an eccentric but as a threat to herself and to others as well.

Middle-Class Values

This story pits Muriel Burgess's powerful emotions against the materialistic concerns of her neighbors, the Terwilligers. Meg Terwilliger is introduced into the story with a list of things that she does to keep her household running smoothly, such as buying groceries and taking her husband's shirts to the dry cleaner and even doing her stretching exercises, to keep in the kind of shape that is expected of a young wife in her social situation in Los Angeles. When she discovers the water seeping into the cement slab their house is built on, her first reaction is to blame her husband, Sonny, for not putting the tile she wanted in the sunroom. When Sonny comes home later on, he follows a clichéd

TOPICS FOR FURTHER STUDY

- Graham Greene's classic short story "The Destructors" is about a group of boys in postwar London who decide to amuse themselves by destroying the one house on their block that survived the wartime bombings, a famous house that was designed by a legendary architect. Read Greene's story (it is available in his *Complete Stories*, published by Penguin in 2005), and compare the destructive attitudes of the boys with the reasons Muriel has for willfully destroying her own home. Write the letter that Muriel would write to the London boys, if she could, either encouraging them or discouraging them from their action, listing explanations for your position.

- In this story, the Terwilligers do not suspect any problem in Muriel's life until her water starts affecting their lives. Watch several episodes of the TV program *Hoarders*, which features people with obsessive hoarding disorder syndrome. Create a chart to show the signs that would indicate how you would know if somebody in your own neighborhood was a hoarder and then include information about what you could do to get help for the person while intruding as little as possible.

- In the story, Muriel is taken off by the police with a suitcase. Research the mental health system in your community, preferably with interviews with the people who work at such facilities, and write the next chapter of Muriel's story: Will she return to her house? When? Will she be likely to do something as drastic as flooding her house again, or will she likely have found a way to cope with her anger and grief? Your story must include an index to show what sources gave you the ideas that were the basis for your fiction.

- Many home owners fear water damage because it can weaken structures and cause mold to grow in unreachable places. Research what building professionals do to rehabilitate houses that have water damage and how they apply their methods to a house as severely damaged as Muriel and Monty's house. Then create a plan to fix the damage. To explain your plan, you will have to make a model of the Burgess house, either an actual structure or a three-dimensional computer graphic, drawing from facts mentioned in the story and what you can find about typical Los Angeles bungalows.

- Boyle implies that Sonny's temper—for instance, his banging on the neighbor's door in a way that makes his wife think of the Gestapo—is building toward the temper that made the late Monty Burgess an abusive husband. Research spousal abuse to determine if this similarity between the two men is just a literary parallel or if Meg really should expect him to become worse. If you think Sonny really is destined to become physically abusive, write out a plan of action that you think Meg should take to protect herself.

- Most laws are written after unexpected circumstances come up. As a group project, write a local ordinance that you think would prevent the sort of damage that takes place in the story. Of course you would start with forbidding people to do anything to harm their neighbors' property, but you also have to anticipate ways a law like that might inhibit one's freedom to use one's own property in the way one wishes. If you can have a local lawmaker review your draft, do so, to help iron out ways that you tilt too far in the direction of personal freedom or interfering with the rights of others.

pattern of trying to find peace in drinking alcohol and separating himself from his wife and daughter. He feels that he has worked hard all day and deserves to relax and that quietness from his family is a part of his middle-class sense of entitlement.

After Monty dies, Muriel turns on all the taps in the house. (© *Joe Gough / Shutterstock*)

The water seeping into the yard bothers Sonny at first, but his annoyance grows to anger when he realizes that it might cause permanent damage to his fence. His concern about the fence works in the story psychologically, because it shows that Sonny's biggest concern in life is for things that might cost him more money, while he feels that his life is already nothing but working to pay for things. Symbolically, it makes sense that it would be a fence that drives Sonny into a rage: the fence is a not-too-subtle symbol of the way he has separated himself from his neighbors, hoping to build his own perfectly orderly world on his own property, a middle-class dream.

Anger

The two characters this story focuses on most are Muriel and Meg. Their emotions are not very clearly expressed, however. There is more attention given to how the two women react to things, particularly how they react to the anger around them.

Monty's anger is not revealed immediately in the story. Muriel is introduced to readers as an old woman who has a strong, irrational reaction to the death of her husband, implying that it was a long, loving marriage. After a while, though, Muriel dwells on the abuse that Monty directed at her: the insults that he shouted at her and the way he hit her, which she likens to the way a person would hit a dog. Anger is so much of Muriel's memory of her husband that she thinks of him as she watches the policeman take a threatening posture, trying to assert his control over the scene he is investigating. When he touches his gun or his nightstick as he is talking to her, Muriel thinks of the ways Monty used his powerful physical presence to intimidate her.

The policeman also reminds Meg of her own husband. When the policeman bangs on Muriel's door, Meg's mind goes to Sonny. When Sonny knocks on Muriel's door, Meg thinks of the Gestapo. Sonny is not shown being violent toward Meg, though the end of the story strongly implies that Monty-style violence might be where Sonny is headed. For now, he is a man who drinks and is prone to anger, which is probably where Monty was when he was, like Sonny, in his twenties.

STYLE

Shifting Point of View

Most writers are careful to keep a consistent point of view while they are telling a story. Hopping from one character's perspective to another character's perspective throughout the story is unsettling, and it feels unnatural. Of course, it would make the writer's job easier to change perspectives constantly, because all of the information that is known by different characters could be revealed in just one scene. Fiction theorists, however, generally agree that going from one perspective to another is so different from the way that people experience the real world that it makes the writing feel false.

In "Sinking House," Boyle does change perspectives, but he does so scene by scene. He does not jump quickly from one character's consciousness to another's. Instead, he devotes a whole scene to one character and then devotes the next scene to another. Readers might start the story thinking that it will be about Muriel, only to quickly find themselves in the Terwilliger sunroom with Meg; when Meg goes to Muriel's house, she is viewed through Muriel's eyes; when Sonny comes home, the developing situation, and what Meg has to say about it, are seen through his eyes and processed through his emotions.

Boyle avoids the problems of having a shifting narrator by staying consistently with one character at a time. Changing the point of view allows him to show the larger scope of the story, not just Meg's or Muriel's limited knowledge.

Ambiguity

Ambiguous describes a symbol that has different meanings for different readers. It is different from *vague* because each interpretation of an ambiguous symbol can create a whole, clear interpretation, while an ambiguous symbol yields no clear interpretations at all. Writers like T. C. Boyle use ambiguity to open up their work to as many different interpretations as possible.

There is no one clear meaning to the water that flows throughout "Sinking House." Muriel never explains why she has turned on the taps. Readers can read it as an act of mourning, an act of revenge, an unstated message to Meg, or a sign of the onset of dementia, and each interpretation works for the story. By finding a symbol that works in many different ways, Boyle invites readers to participate in the storytelling process as they use their skills of interpretation to judge which possible meaning works the best.

HISTORICAL CONTEXT

Los Angeles and Water

This story takes place in Los Angeles, a city that has always had a complicated relationship to water. At the start of the twentieth century, San Francisco was the biggest town in California, while Los Angeles was a dusty pueblo. The area showed promise, though: the land in the nearby San Fernando Valley had soil that was good for agriculture, and oil had been discovered in the region. In the early 1900s, the movie industry began to take advantage of the area's reliable weather and ample sunlight, and studios relocated from New York and Chicago to make their home base there. In the first decade of the century, the population of Los Angeles more than tripled, from approximately one hundred thousand to over three hundred thousand. Still, the lack of water hindered the growth of the city.

A former city mayor, Fred Eaton, came up with a plan to move water to the valley from the Owens River. Eaton then bought up water rights from the area, eventually selling them to Los Angeles. To this day, there is question about whether Eaton's move was a scandalous back-door deal to cut a profit for himself or a civic-minded move to get the rights in place to irrigate Los Angeles. At any rate, a group of local investors with an interest in seeing the city grow, such as the publisher of the *Los Angeles Times* and the man whose company provided the city's streetcars, were on a board that approved the Los Angeles Aqueduct.

Engineer William Mulholland, head of the city's Department of Water and Power, oversaw the project. Building the aqueduct took nearly four thousand workers, often building in the desert in one-hundred-plus-degree heat. The finished aqueduct went through nine canyons, across more than sixty miles of open canals and through two hundred tunnels. The engineering logistics involved were massive, but in the end, the project, completed in 1913, was a success. It brought water to the San Fernando

COMPARE
&
CONTRAST

- **1988:** People know that there is such a thing as "dementia" affecting older people, but they are inclined to find erratic behavior to be a character flaw or a personality problem rather than looking to biological explanations.

  Today: Since the 1980s, organizations such as the Alzheimer's Society (founded in 1989) have been instrumental in advocating for more realistic expectations for people who suffer from mental deterioration.

- **1988:** If a neighbor calls with a complaint, an older person living alone might be contacted by a police officer, who is likely to leave the person alone if no evidence of a crime is found.

  Today: Police forces in most municipalities have links to social workers and psychiatric professionals whom they can contact if they find someone whose odd behavior might create a danger to their well-being.

- **1988:** Excessive water use is not noticed by the Department of Water and Power until the next monthly meter reading, conducted by an individual walking house to house.

  Today: "Smart meters," which report water usage on a regular basis, have been installed in many California locations to help control water waste during the recent record-breaking drought. Even when smart meters are not monitoring usage, neighbors are asked to report water wasters to the city government.

- **1988:** Muriel Burgess talks about being interviewed by a girl from the local community college for an oral history about what the area was like when she was young.

  Today: The Internet has led to a proliferation of such oral history projects. Instead of being transcribed into a book or a scholarly paper, these interviews can be posted online and experienced by people all over the world.

Valley and Los Angeles, but it was at the expense of the farmers who had settled near the Owens River, who saw their livelihoods shrivel. With the newfound water source, Los Angeles was able to grow, over the course of the twentieth century, from a moderate town to the second-largest urban area in the country.

Because the city imports mountain runoff from hundreds of miles away, its water supply has always been vulnerable. A hundred years after the Los Angeles Aqueduct was completed, a drought of epic proportions hit California, affecting the entire state and Los Angeles in particular. A lack of rain in the West provided no humidity for snow in the mountains, and without mountain snow, the rivers and streams that feed cities and farms dried up in the 2010s. By 2015, after encouraging voluntary cuts in water usage, the government used its power to push consumers to cut water usage by 25 percent, first for gardening and then for commercial agriculture. In a climate emergency such as this, the behavior of Muriel in the story would be viewed not only as a personal idiosyncrasy but also as a public menace, stealing limited public resources from others who need them.

Magic Realism

Although nothing in "Sinking House" is impossible, it does present events that are improbable. Even if a woman like Muriel were to open up all of the faucets in her house, for whatever reason, she would probably draw more attention than that of just her next-door neighbors over the course of a few weeks. The story makes readers accept this as reality, though, by filling in so many details that it feels realistic, even at its most fantastic.

Meg notices the water seeping into the concrete under her house and finds that her neighbor has left all of her garden sprinklers on. (© connel / Shutterstock)

In writing this way, Boyle is following the literary style referred to as *magic realism*. The term was first used in art criticism in 1925. In 1955, critic Angel Flores used it in literary criticism to describe a style of writing that was flourishing in Central and South American literature. In such works, unrealistic elements appear in the middle of otherwise realistic stories. The "magic" elements could run the range of things that simply could not occur in the real world that we know to things that one would not really expect, like Muriel's running all of her faucets for weeks. Writers in this mode gave their works the tone of folktales, but they followed the magic elements to their logical conclusions, treating them as if it actually could have happened.

The most commonly referred-to writer of magical realism is Colombian Nobel Prize winner Gabriel García Márquez. In one of his stories, a man with wings lands in a village, and the locals are divided about whether or not he is an angel. In another story, "The Handsomest Drowned Man in the World," the body of a giant washes up on the shore of an island community, and the citizens, in preparing him for a proper burial at sea, find him so attractive that they name him, accept him as one of their own, and dedicate their lives to making their village a place worthy of having been home to such a fine gentleman. In the book considered Márquez's great masterpiece, *One Hundred Years of Solitude*, ghosts interact with the living frequently with no outstanding notice, a rainstorm lasts for five years, and a flying carpet is given the same attention as such scientific marvels as a magnet or a telescope.

Though Márquez is perhaps the most familiar writer in this genre, there are others, such as Jorge Amado from Brazil and Isabel Allende from Chile. This style of writing is frequently associated with late-twentieth-century writers from Latin America, though it is not necessarily bound to that part of the world or that time; for instance, *The Metamorphosis*, published by Franz Kafka of Prague in 1915, examines how a man might react to waking one morning to find that he has been transformed to a cockroach. Writers throughout history have pushed the bounds of "reality" when writing fiction, but the recognition of magic realism as a literary genre would have been at its apex when Boyle was writing "Sinking House."

CRITICAL OVERVIEW

Boyle has been a celebrated author throughout his entire career, though critics seem to agree that he has grown as an artist over the years. He has published fourteen novels, which are usually positively reviewed, but his short fiction is almost universally acclaimed as his significant contribution to the world of literature. His first book, the short-story collection *Descent of Man*, was rich with imaginativeness. In those stories, people cope with a sudden rainfall of blood, a scientist loses his girlfriend to the chimp she is studying, a jungle plane crash causes civility to devolve among the surviving passengers, and so on. When the book was reviewed in the *New York Times Book Review*, which is itself an impressive achievement for a writer's first book, Max Apple was quick to note the author's "energy." He explains that the "circumstances in these stories are always surprising," though he determined that the energy was too often used in the service of cleverness for its own sake. "The failures are the honest failures of an energetic writer who is willing to try anything," Apple judges, before concluding that "an adventurous new bird, T. Coraghessan Boyle, has come to roost in the literary jungle."

Twenty years later, in 1998, Boyle already had enough publications to warrant a collection that would gather his short stories into a "greatest hits"–style collection (and he would continue to accumulate enough stories to fill the almost one thousand pages of *T. C. Boyle Stories II* fifteen years later). *T. C. Boyle Stories* was hailed as a major literary accomplishment in 1998 and won the Bernard Malamud Award that year. Critics see the progression of Boyle's stories and acknowledge that while he is always entertaining and sometimes more focused on being amusing than being insightful, Boyle is indeed a major artist in the field.

In *World Literature Today*, for example, James Knudson starts his review of *T. C. Boyle Stories* by noting that "T. Coraghessan Boyle is undeniably a talented writer." He makes note of Boyle's verbal skills and his talent for crafting engaging sentences, before making a distinction between the stories that lean more toward fun for its own sake and the true literary works. Knudson feels that "the reader who looks deeper into *T. C. Boyle Stories* will find that Boyle, at his best, 'makes art' of the highest order and that even his less interesting stories 'weave a web of mystery'" (referring to a line from the story "We Are Norsemen," quoted earlier in Knudson's review).

CRITICISM

David Kelly

Kelly is an instructor of literature and creative writing at a college in Illinois. In the following essay, he examines the many details in Boyle's "Sinking House" that make it a feminist story about women who, consciously or not, work to subvert their situations.

Boyle's 1987 story "Sinking House" starts with an interesting, surreal concept: a woman's husband of fifty years dies, and in response she turns on all of the faucets inside and outside the house. The response is unique and illogical. It seems like the kind of emotional outburst that grief can cause. As the story progresses, however, it becomes abundantly clear that the old widow's behavior, far from being random, is actually clear and logical. This is a feminist cautionary tale. She is transmitting a warning to the young housewife who lives next door, letting her know—through destruction and through one direct look that passes between them in the end—that the young woman needs to take control of her life now, while she is twenty-three, or spend the rest of her days hopelessly trying to please someone who will never appreciate what she sacrifices for him.

What makes it fair to call this a feminist tale is the way the characters are divided up along gender lines. The single worst character is without

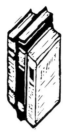

WHAT DO I READ NEXT?

- A young person who wonders about the histories of the older neighbors is portrayed in a fanciful way in the young-adult novel *Al Capone Does My Shirts* (2004), by Gennifer Choldenko. Like the younger couple in Boyle's story, Choldenko's protagonist, twelve-year-old Moose Flannigan, is suspicious of his neighbors, but in his case he has good reason: it is 1935, his father has taken a job at Alcatraz, and his neighbors are convicts.

- Kate Chopin's classic 1894 short story "Story of an Hour" has a character similar to Meg. Chopin's protagonist, Louise, hears that her husband has died, and faced with that news she realizes that she is not horrified—that she is in fact relieved at the idea of being free. This story is in many anthologies and at online sites and in Chopin's Penguin Classics collection *The Awakening and Selected Stories*, published in 2003.

- Boyle edited the 2015 edition of the long-running annual book series *The Best American Short Stories*; as such, all of the stories in that volume reflect his own worldview to some extent. One of his selections, "Thunderstruck," by Elizabeth McCracken, concerns parents who take their two daughters to Paris to distract them from a troubled lifestyle at home, only to be faced with a whole new view of life when the younger daughter is seriously injured, requiring a lifetime of continuous care. This tale is also the title story in the McCracken collection *Thunderstruck*.

- In "Sinking House," Boyle barely touches on the tension between wealthy Anglo Californians and the Mexican migrants who live among them, though it is a subject that is central in his novels, particularly *The Tortilla Curtain* (1995), and many of his short stories.

This subject is the focus *of Under the Feet of Jesus* (1996), by Helena Maria Viramontes, a novel that looks at the balance from the perspective of the migrants.

- Russian writer Anton Chekhov (1860–1904) is well known for his dramas, but he is also considered one of the best short-story writers to ever live. In Chekhov's story "Misery," a taxi driver copes with the death of his son by carrying on with his work, hoping to find someone to talk to but finding that, as with the relationship between Muriel and her neighbors, the rich people he drives are too concerned with their own status to care about his problems. Chekhov's story can be found in numerous anthologies and online sources as well as in *Anton Chekhov's Short Stories*, published by W. W. Norton in 1979.

- While "Sinking House" concerns an old woman dealing with the loss of her husband of half a century, Boyle's story "Greasy Lake" deals with the other end of the spectrum: a group of teens are faced with the dead body of a man they hardly knew. It is one of Boyle's most often anthologized and studied stories, and it is included with "Sinking House" in the "Death" section of *T. C. Boyle Stories*, the acclaimed collection published in 1998.

- Catherine Tidd, whose husband died in their eleventh year of marriage, wrote about the experience in *Confessions of a Mediocre Widow*, published by Sourcebooks in 2014. Tidd's sense of humor helped her get through the experience, and it helped many of her readers find perspective in their own grief, showing one way that people in real life cope with the situation that starts Boyle's story.

a doubt Monty Burgess, the old man who dies in the story's first sentence. The subsequent narrative reveals that he beat his wife and shouted crude, demeaning names in her face. The man in the house next door, Sonny Terwilliger, is not as awful, but still, he is a man with anger issues. He

> THE WATER IS A DESTRUCTIVE FORCE, BUT
> IT IS A DOMESTICATED DESTRUCTIVE FORCE, HELD
> CAPTIVE IN THE PIPES IN THE SAME WAY THAT
> MURIEL'S TRUE NATURE IS HELD CAPTIVE UNTIL
> SHE RELEASES IT ONCE MONTY IS DEAD."

leaves for work early, and when he comes home in the evening, all he wants is to relax in peace, which to him means silence from his wife and daughter while he reads the newspaper and drinks. He might be Monty in training, which could account for the author's giving him the name Sonny. There is one more male character, a policeman with a moustache who fingers the weapons hanging from his belt while asserting his control of the unpredictable situation he is called to handle: a woman flooding her own property and that of her neighbors.

The female characters, on the other hand, are the ones responsible for coping with the males' aggression. Muriel Burgess never does cope with it—she has put up with Monty's abuse for fifty years, even caring for him while he is an invalid in his final days, spoon-feeding him as if he were an infant. She only lashes out against the way Monty treated her after he is dead. Similarly, her neighbor Meg does not stand up to her husband's less aggressive bullying, though it is clear that it annoys her at best and intimidates her at worst. This is why she needs to learn from the older woman's experiences, before it is too late for her.

Even the minor female characters, mentioned only once or twice in the story, confirm this pattern of social order that is based on female domesticity. The Terwilligers' daughter has the fairy-princess name Tiffany, inspired by a high-end store: she is either shuttled off to preschool or is in her room playing with expensive dolls. The Terwilliger family dog is named Queenie, indicating that she is rare and valued and pampered, but the only information given about her in the story is that she is sickly, going to and from the veterinarian. The female police officer who shows up at the end takes a nurturing approach to Muriel, in contrast to the male officer's threatening stance. She leads Muriel tenderly from her house,

having apparently persuaded her to give herself over to psychiatric care.

With the gender distinctions drawn as they are in "Sinking House," the female characters are at a clear disadvantage. The men are violent and aggressive or at least prepared to be so, but their interests are not so different from the women's. Muriel wanted to be a good wife almost as much as Monty wanted her to be one. Meg obviously thinks that her life with Sonny is a rich one—she exercises and cooks and gardens and cares for their daughter and their dog, presumably because that is the life she has chosen. Both women are attracted to a domestic lifestyle, but the story goes out of its way to show how, consciously or not, each woman is working to subvert her domesticity.

The many subversive acts reach their peak, of course, with Muriel's destruction of her own house with a cleansing tide of water, but there are smaller examples scattered throughout the story. Most of these examples come from Meg's life, for the obvious reason that the story is structured around the way that Muriel's domestic stability can be disrupted only once she is freed of Monty by death.

Meg has surrounded herself with a beautiful, apparently harmoniously existence, but there are plenty of signs of discontent, starting with her looks: she is described when she first enters the story as having "fine bones," implying fragile beauty, but also as having "haunted eyes," indicating repressed fear. She is slim, a fact that she takes pride in—comparing herself to Muriel, she quickly notes that, at Muriel's age, she expects to be skinnier than Muriel is now. She maintains her figure by exercising in her sunroom in the morning, which indicates a commitment to life, but as she exercises she smokes, which indicates a callous disregard for her own health, almost inviting death to hurry along.

Meg's constant challenge of her simple domestic life is conveyed symbolically throughout the story. For dinner, she prepares tacos, a sign of her open-minded, multicultural worldview, a willingness to include the culinary styles that surround her in Los Angeles. Those tacos, though, are filled with thresher shark: a scary, predatory animal. Meg compares the wet spot hidden beneath her rug to a Rorschach test, the famed inkblot test to reveal people's psychological dispositions by examining what they think a random splatter of ink looks like. Her first interpretation is of a butterfly, matching the beautiful domestic life Meg has built around herself, but she immediately revises that to a dark, ugly, scavenging crow and then a bat. In a sense, Meg's watering the cane plant in the living room—a wild plant that has been domesticated and brought indoors to live—is just a tiny hint of the desperation that makes Muriel flood everything around her.

Meg makes use of her traditional feminine role, turning a "pleading" look, with "pouty lips" and "tousled hair," on Sonny when she wants him to do something, just as the policeman uses his physical presence to assert his masculine control. *Swagger* is a word repeated in Muriel's mind several times. For example, Muriel notices the way he "he swaggered and puffed out his chest." Muriel may have once been at the mercy of her abusive husband, but since his death she has nothing to fear but that some supernatural form of Monty will reach out from the grave to get her. If she is delusional at all, her delusion is in thinking that the neighbors and the police—people she herself brought to her house through her conspicuous behavior—are all working to bring Monty back to life, an actual fear that she expresses in the story. She is that afraid of him.

If Monty could be brought back, physically or even just symbolically, flooding the house is actually a reasonable thing to do. After the first time the policeman walks through and shuts off all the faucets Muriel has opened, she finds the silence unbearable. The house is sick, she decides, "sick as the grave." It is unclean, still contaminated by Monty's continual post-death influence. From this perspective, flooding the house and yard with water, in fact, makes good sense. The water is a destructive force, but it is a domesticated destructive force, held captive in the pipes in the same way that Muriel's true nature is held captive until she releases it once Monty is dead. Of course she would think that freeing herself of Marty is a kind of cleansing because, after fifty years as a housewife, cleaning is one of her main points of reference.

If Muriel and Meg cannot see how similar their lives are, it is because there are so many things obscuring their view. There is age, of course. And there is a general sense of self-worth: being as healthy as she is, as active and committed to her lifestyle, makes it hard for Meg to recognize herself in the older woman. Also, she seems to know nothing about Muriel and Monty,

to have never given them a thought at all before their water leaked into her yard.

What Meg does recognize in the end, though, is that her own marriage is unhappy. She has been fighting her marriage to Sonny without even knowing that she was fighting it, subverting and resisting while at the same time imagining herself happy enough. It is Muriel's house that is filling up with water, but in the end, Meg's house is the "sinking house." A glance between them makes Meg acknowledge her connection to the neighbor, and a reflection in a puddle makes her see herself. She turns on her own faucet, not wanting to flood her house but just to feel what open subversion is like, after so much of her behavior throughout the story has stopped short of open rebellion.

Source: David Kelly, Critical Essay on "Sinking House," in *Short Stories for Students*, Gale, Cengage Learning, 2016.

Paul Gleason

In the following essay, Gleason explores how Boyle mixes the bizarre and the realistic in his stories and novels.

Thomas John Boyle was born on 2 December 1948 in Peekskill, New York. When he was seventeen years old, he changed his middle name to Coraghessan (pronounced kuh-RAGG-issun), which came from his mother's side of the family and was his attempt to distance himself from his lower-middle-class upbringing and parents, both of whom died of alcoholism-related illnesses before he was thirty. Boyle, who earned poor grades in high school, wanted to major in music and become a jazz saxophone player when he left Peekskill and entered the State University of New York at Potsdam in the fall of 1965. He failed his audition with the music department and instead chose history as a major. "Why history?" he asks in his important autobiographical essay of 1999, "This Monkey, My Back." "I didn't know at the time," he answers, "or I couldn't have defined it, but it had to do with writing. I didn't yet realize it, but I could write, and in history—unlike, say, biology or math—what you did was write essays."

As a college student, Boyle did not attend classes regularly, choosing instead to drum, sing, and play saxophone in a rock-and-roll band. One of the courses that he did attend, however, immediately caught his attention: his sophomore literature class. It was in this course that he discovered the American short-story

Meg is sympathetic to Muriel's situation, but Sonny is furious, pounding on Muriel's door.
(© Photographee.eu | Shutterstock)

writer and novelist Flannery O'Connor and "felt a blast of recognition" in her dark comic vision and moral seriousness. Boyle became an enthusiastic reader and independently read the works of some of the twentieth century's greatest writers, including John Updike, Saul Bellow, Albert Camus, and Samuel Beckett. The works of Beckett and other absurdist writers, which he eventually read as a student in a creative writing workshop offered by Professor Krishna Vaid, particularly affected him "because it was readily apparent that their authors were wise guys just like [him]—albeit very sophisticated, very nasty, and very funny wise guys." Inspired by these writers, Boyle wrote his first creative piece for Professor Vaid's class, a comic one-act play called *The Foot*, in which a husband and wife mourn the death of their child, whom an alligator has devoured. When Boyle read the play aloud in class, he experienced his first public triumph as a writer. After hearing the play, Professor Vaid "began to smile and then to grin and chuckle and finally to laugh without constraint." Professor Vaid and Boyle's fellow

students applauded after the reading was finished, and Boyle experienced "the sort of exhilaration that only comes from driving the ball over the net and directly into your opponent's face." Boyle eventually graduated from SUNY Potsdam in 1968 with degrees in English and history and shortly thereafter took a job as a high-school English teacher in Peekskill, a position he held to avoid the Vietnam draft until he entered graduate school at the University of Iowa in 1972.

Boyle's college experience and first reading encapsulate what would eventually become the central aesthetic of his fiction, as well as his understanding of the social role of the fiction writer. Fiction, according to Boyle, should be cynical and funny, performative and strange, but, above all, entertaining and fun. In addition, as his famous public readings and the regularly updated blog at his official Web site demonstrate, Boyle thinks that the fiction writer should be a performer and an entertainer who regularly interacts with his audience in public. As a former history major, Boyle also

BOYLE'S STORIES AND NOVELS TAKE THE
BEST ELEMENTS OF CARVER'S MINIMALISM,
BARTH'S POSTMODERN EXTRAVAGANZAS, GARCÍA
MÁRQUEZ'S MAGICAL REALISM, O'CONNOR'S DARK
COMEDY AND MORAL SERIOUSNESS, AND DICKENS'S
ENTERTAINING AND STRANGE PLOTS AND BRING
THEM TO BEAR ON AMERICAN LIFE IN AN
ACCESSIBLE, SUBVERSIVE, AND INVENTIVE WAY."

posits that the fiction writer's texts should contextualize his characters in specific eras of
American history and use satire as a moral
force for the improvement of society. But as
Boyle writes in "This Monkey, My Back," his
central identity as a fiction writer, the one that
informs every word that he writes, is that of the
wise guy—that is, the intelligent, funny, and,
perhaps even, arrogant and disrespectful smart
aleck who makes readers laugh even as he or
she teaches them a lesson.

This concept of the fiction writer as wise guy
derives in part from Boyle's reading of absurdist
writers such as Beckett but also from his formative
engagement with great American postmodernist
novelists, particularly John Barth, Thomas Pynchon, and Robert Coover. When Boyle was an
undergraduate in the late 1960s and a graduate
student in the 1970s, Barth, Pynchon, and Coover
were publishing their most experimental, influential, encyclopedic, erudite, and, many readers
would argue, difficult works. In particular, four
of their novels—Barth's *The Sot-Weed Factor*
(1960), Pynchon's *V.* (1963) and *Gravity's Rainbow*
(1973), and Coover's *The Public Burning* (1977)—
inventively combine historical fact and fiction to
satirize specific events in American history.

Barth, Pynchon, and Coover are famous
wise guys who poke fun at American mythology, politics, and institutions in their long, difficult, and ambitious historical novels. In his
fiction Boyle retains their comic spirit and interest in history but makes his work more accessible and entertaining to his readers. Unlike the
difficult canonical modernist writers of the first

half of the twentieth century—for example,
James Joyce, Marcel Proust, William Faulkner,
and Virginia Woolf—and the equally difficult
postmodernist writers who followed them in the
second half of the twentieth century—Barth,
Pynchon, and Coover, of course, but also William Gaddis, William H. Gass, William S. Bur-
roughs, and Joseph McElroy—Boyle constructs
plots and characters that are weird but accessible, thought provoking but immediate. In addition, unlike some of the major works of
twentieth-century modernist and postmodernist
fiction, Boyle's fiction is earnest, using its comedy to provide clear moral messages at the
expense of modernist ironic detachment and
postmodernist nihilistic humor.

Boyle's interest in writing funny, entertaining, and moral fiction also derives from his
reading of another group of writers when he
was in the graduate program at the University
of Iowa. Deciding to pursue a Ph.D. in English
literature, Boyle specialized in British literature
of the Victorian period. This meant that just as
he was reading the novels of Barth, Pynchon,
and Coover, he was also reading the didactic,
popular, and moralizing novels of George Eliot,
Thomas Hardy, Charlotte and Emily Brontë,
Anthony Trollope, William Makepeace Thack-
eray, and, above all, Charles Dickens.

Dickens influences Boyle's conception of
himself as a socially engaged, entertaining, popular, and prolific writer of fiction. In an interview
conducted in 1988 (but not published until 1991),
Boyle told Elizabeth Adams that he admires
Dickens for being "a quintessential artist, one
who was a very popular author, and who also
wrote brilliantly and well and originally." In a
2000 interview with Judith Handschuh, Boyle
acknowledged the Dickens connection to his
own work: "Critics and reviewers have compared
me with Dickens, and I take that as a compli-
ment . . . I look to writers like Dickens . . . for
inspiration." Boyle learned from Dickens to
entertain his readers with dark humor, strange
plots, and even stranger characters. Dickens also
taught Boyle to use comedy to provide readers
with a moral education. The reader's laughter
and anger at the ineffective legal and government
systems of *Bleak House* and *Little Dorrit* result in
a feeling of compassion for the downtrodden and
poor, whose happiness and well-being are
harmed by those systems. In addition Dickens,
who was an actor and spent his last years giving

public readings of his most famous works, exemplifies for Boyle the importance of the writer's role as a public figure, as well as his willingness to reach his readers through public appearances. In the Adams interview, Boyle said, "You have to envy [Dickens] his readings, his famous readings. He was the Mick Jagger and all entertainment of his day wrapped up in one." Finally Boyle and Dickens are both highly prolific writers. By the time he turned fifty-eight at the end of 2006, Boyle had published eleven novels and more than one hundred and fifty short stories.

When Boyle was reading postmodern and Victorian fiction at the University of Iowa, he was also attending the university's Writers' Workshop, where he studied with the important American writers John Irving, Raymond Carver, and John Cheever. Carver and Cheever had a particular—and surprising—impact on Boyle. One of the most important practitioners of literary minimalism, a movement that is characterized by an economic deployment of words and a focus on surface description, Carver inspired Boyle as a graduate student to abandon temporarily the encyclopedic aesthetic of Barth and Pynchon to concentrate on short fiction, a decision that eventually led to the publication of Boyle's first collection of stories, *Descent of Man*, in 1979. This collection disciplined Boyle to condense his dark comic vision and verbal pyrotechnics to the space of individual short stories. Cheever, on the other hand, provided Boyle with necessary advice. In "This Monkey, My Back," Boyle remembers that Cheever "couldn't make any sense out of *The Sot-Weed Factor* and didn't see that it was worth the effort trying." Cheever taught Boyle that "all good fiction is experimental . . . and don't get caught up in fads." Boyle learned from Cheever to harness his experimental impulses and love of postmodern fiction and write texts that appeal to a large audience through an emphasis on plot and character.

After submitting the *Descent of Man* collection as his creative dissertation in 1977, Boyle graduated from the University of Iowa with a Ph.D. in Victorian literature. In 1978 he accepted an assistant professorship in the English department of the University of Southern California, where he has taught ever since.

The best way to read the work of this self-professed wise guy is to remember its origins in the mind of a man who came of age in the tumultuous decade of the 1960s. Like many members of his generation, T. C. Boyle (he stopped using Coraghessan on his book covers when he published an omnibus collection of his short stories, *T. C. Boyle Stories*, in 1998) as a young man resisted the authority of the establishment, experimented with drugs, rock music, avantgarde literature, and radical ideas, and avoided the Vietnam draft. Some of Boyle's best and best-known fiction—the short story "Greasy Lake" (1981) and the novels *World's End* (1987), *The Tortilla Curtain* (1995), and *Drop City* (2003)—explore his generation from many perspectives, always searching for the motivations for idealism in individual lives and the results of this idealism on American society and history.

Elsewhere in his fiction, Boyle extends his analysis of idealism to other eras of American history. *The Road to Wellville* (1993) and *The Inner Circle* (2004) combine fact and fiction in their explorations of the lives of historical American reformers who have a passionate commitment to changing society for the better and who obsessively and irrationally pursue their quests. *The Road to Wellville* examines Dr. John Harvey Kellogg's attempts at the beginning of the twentieth century to change the eating and exercising habits of Americans in an effort to extend their life spans, presenting the megalomania and fanaticism that existed alongside Kellogg's idealism. *The Inner Circle*, Boyle's novel on the activities of the sex researcher Dr. Alfred Kinsey in the 1930s through the 1950s, works the same thematic territory as *The Road to Wellville*, simultaneously admiring Kinsey for the openness that he brought to American sexuality and deploring him for the harm that his sexual theories caused his family and the members of his research team. In these two historical novels, Boyle concludes that hypocrisy and autocratic authoritarianism reside at the heart of much idealism and many reformist movements. As Boyle himself said in an interview with David L. Ulin, "As an iconoclast and punk who never really grew up . . . I can't stand the idea of authority, and I think it's detrimental to the character of people to give themselves over blindly to authority."

In addition to considering the ramifications of idealism, Boyle's fiction also takes up specific social and political issues. Many of Boyle's novels and short stories consider the relationship between humanity and nature. The marijuana farmers of Boyle's second novel, *Budding Prospects* (1984), get injured when they fight a forest fire that threatens to destroy their illegal crop. A similar fire threatens to destroy the residents of Arroyo Blanco Estates, a fictional community just outside of Los Angeles, in *The Tortilla Curtain*. The unforgiving cold of an Alaskan winter endangers the lives of the residents of a hippie commune in *Drop City*. In *A Friend of the Earth* (2000), an aging environmentalist and hippie experiences the devastating effects of global warming on the earth's biosphere in the year 2025. And Boyle's most recent short-story collections, *After the Plague* (2001) and *Tooth and Claw* (2005), present nature as a violent force that menaces humanity.

Illegal immigration and racism are other key issues that inform Boyle's fiction, especially the novels *East Is East* (1990) and *The Tortilla Curtain*. Both novels discuss the ways in which political theory and personal actions intersect in the lives of characters. *East Is East* considers the interactions of a primarily liberal contingent of authors living in Georgia and the local police and government authorities who apprehend an illegal alien from Japan hiding in the local swamps and cottages. Boyle's text exposes the hypocrisies of both the writers and the authorities. Boyle employs this same method of exposure in *The Tortilla Curtain*, showing how formerly idealistic characters surrender their beliefs in equal human rights as they construct a wall around their wealthy community to deter the entrance of illegal Mexican immigrants. The hypocrisies of the Americans in both texts emphasize underlying racist attitudes that lead to suffering and, ultimately, death.

A final theme that characterizes much of Boyle's fiction concerns the ways in which popular culture helps construct the identities of characters. Boyle's characters are very concerned with their book and record collections, especially the hippies of *Drop City*, who listen to such musicians as Hank Williams, Sonny Rollins, and Jimi Hendrix, read such writers as Julio Cortázar and Hermann Hesse, and name one of their dogs after a character from J. R. R. Tolkien's *The Lord of the Rings*. For Boyle these musicians and writers define the zeitgeist of late-1960s and early-1970s America, so he refers to their works to create his characters in *Drop City*. His other novels use music, literature, and other elements of pop culture in the same way, with even the eighteenth-century characters of *Water Music* (1981) humming catchy songs and attending public concerts.

Two other defining characteristics of Boyle's fiction are his prose style and comic sensibility. Ever since the publication of *Descent of Man* in 1979, critics have remarked on the energy, verve, and highly stylized quality of his prose. In an interview with Patricia Lamberti, Boyle claimed that "language is the key to stories that are purely comic. They are serious because they have underpinnings in extraordinary language." The first sentence of Boyle's first novel, *Water Music*, illustrates the salient features of his prose style: "At an age when most young Scotsmen were lifting skirts, plowing furrows and spreading seed, Mungo Park was displaying his bare buttocks to the al-haj' Ali Ibn Fatoudi, Emir of Ludamar." By presenting his characters in this way, Boyle intensifies the feeling that they exist primarily as linguistic creations and not as real people. Boyle's prose, then, enhances the effect of his characters as vehicles for his satire, social commentaries, and comedy.

Boyle is a great comic writer in his short stories and novels, not just in his style, but also in his outlandish plots. Many of Boyle's detractors have accused him of not constructing plots in his short stories at all but rather comic routines that function primarily as jokes. These detractors emphasize Boyle's comic tales and ignore his morally serious stories, such as "Greasy Lake," "If the River Was Whiskey," "The Fog Man," "Sinking House," and "Rara Avis." Yet there is something of the showman about Boyle in his comic stories. He experiences such public adulation and enjoys a strong base of devoted readers because many of his stories *are* funny. The paranoid hero of "Modern Love" has a lover who wears a full-body condom to prevent the spread of sexually transmitted diseases. A character named T. C. Boyle in "I Dated Jane Austen" takes the author of *Pride and Prejudice* and *Emma* out on the town. The disaffected young narrator of "Beat" goes on a pilgrimage to visit Jack Kerouac at his home, only to find out that the rebel-hero of the Beat Generation lives with his mother. And the hero of "56–0" plays outfield in a seemingly endless—and pointless—baseball game. The origins of these fantastic plots can be found in Boyle's reading of Latin American magical realist writers, such as Julio Cortázar, Jorge Luis Borges, and Gabriel García Márquez, as well as in his engagement with Dickens, Barth, and Pynchon.

But, for the most part Boyle's novels embed their bizarre occurrences in more conventionally realistic plots. *Budding Prospects* provides a good example of how this embedding process works. The main, realistic plot of the novel concerns a group of aging hippies and their attempt to grow marijuana for profit on an illegal farm. The novel, however, occasionally loses touch with realism when strange events happen to the characters.

Boyle's stories and novels take the best elements of Carver's minimalism, Barth's postmodern extravaganzas, García Márquez's magical realism, O'Connor's dark comedy and moral seriousness, and Dickens's entertaining and strange plots and bring them to bear on American life in an accessible, subversive, and inventive way. There is no one quite like Boyle writing in America today. But even as Boyle takes a cynical attitude toward institutions and the men who lead them, even as he thunders for racial tolerance, environmental awareness, and gender equality, he cannot help but convey his love for his characters and, above all, for his audience. Love, then, is the overriding emotion that prevails in Boyle's work—love for language, love for all forms of artistic expression, love for sex and food, love for laughter, and, most important, love for an America that could be so much better.

Source: Paul Gleason, "Understanding T.C. Boyle," in *Understanding T.C. Boyle*, University of South Carolina Press, 2009, pp. 1–11.

Ian Sansom

In the following review, Sansom praises Boyle's attention to detail in his work, such as finely drawn minor characters.

Capitalism, it might be argued, can be reduced to a simple equation: $x + 1 = y$ (where x = what you have, and y = what you wish you had). If you substitute the soul, or wisdom, or meaning for mere capitalistic stuff, then the same equation can be applied also to literature, from the story of Adam and Eve to *The Da Vinci Code*. Dr Johnson once remarked on "how small a quantity of REAL FICTION there is the in the world"; it's possible that $x + 1 = y$ is in fact the only real fiction there is.

T. C. Boyle's up-to-the-minute new novel copies out in full the old equation. The book's wonderfully vivid villain, Peck—a.k.a. William a.k.a. Will a.k.a. Billy a.k.a. Frank ("Sex M, Race W, Age 33, Ht 6-0, Wt 180, Hair BRO, Eyes BRO, SS# ?, D/L 820 626 5757, State NY") wants the best that money can buy. Unfortunately, he doesn't have a lot of money himself, so he just steals the identities of those who do, and is busy living the good life on their behalf and to the full extent of their credit-card limits: the cars, the clothes, the fine wines, the condo overlooking the ocean, the attractive young Russian girlfriend, and plenty of state-of-the-art pots and pans, because like any sociopathic pussy-hound ex-jailbird worth his salt Peck loves to cook ("he thought he might make Wiener schnitzel, with pickled red cabbage, spatzle and butter beans, just for a change, though on second thoughts. . . he might just go with potato salad and bratwurst on the grill").

Someone, of course, has to pay the price for Peck's living the American Dream and that someone is Dana Halter, a deaf woman and one among the many whose identity Peck has stolen. Dana lives a quiet life as a teacher with her boyfriend Bridger in San Roque, the sort of small, sweet, juicy American coastal city that everyone dreams of living in—nice restaurants, plenty of culture, plus sunshine—but when Dana's identity is stolen and she finds herself in jail, falsely accused of crimes she did not commit, she soon discovers her inner bitch and sets out to hunt down the man who has ruined her life. Can Dana and Bridger find the dastardly Peck?

And will their coast-to-coast chase strengthen or destroy their troubled relationship?

This may sound like the plot of a made-for-tv movie, but the book is in fact far superior to your average genre fiction.

Boyle is the author of numerous fine, super-crafted novels (most famously *The Road to Wellville*, 1993, which was made into a film starring Anthony Hopkins) and perhaps even finer and certainly more numerous short stories. He specialises in high-toned but broad-sweeping historical fiction—*World's End* (1987), *Drop City* (2003) and *The Inner Circle* (2004), hefty but readable books which cover the 17th century, the 1940s, and the 1970s respectively. So, he is a writer accustomed to dealing with grand narratives and themes; and Talk Talk, clearly, is all about identity.

Peck has learnt everything he knows about identity theft from a shady character called the Sandman whom he met in prison, and who is basically Uncle Sam in reverse: "He was talking about the Internet . . . He was talking about Photoshop and color copiers, government seals, icons, base identifiers. The whole smorgasbord. Be anybody you can be." This is perhaps not what Ralph Waldo Emerson had in mind when he wrote his essay "Self-Reliance."

Boyle has a firm grasp of his major themes, and his books are typically thick and sticky with detail. Even minor characters are sketched with a kind of gooey brilliance: "Radko Goric, a 38-year-old entrepreneur wrapped in 200-dollar designer shades, off-color Pierro Quarto jackets and clunky vinyl shoes out of the bargain bin." Everything is so flavoursome, everything painted in such vivid colours, there's such richness and zest—like one of Peck's sauces—that it's a disappointment when the inevitable confrontation occurs and there is, suddenly, satisfaction; no more suspense; no more curiosity; no more more. The problem with $x + 1 = y$ is that sometimes you do get what you want.

And it's not enough.

Source: Ian Sansom, "The Good Life Lived for Others," in *Spectator*, July 8, 2006.

Grace Fill

In the following review, Fill points out Boyle's "verbal athleticism and comedic insight."

Boyle fans will be delighted by the release of this collection of 68 short stories, spanning a period of more than 20 years and including all stories published in previous collections as well as 4 stories not previously published in book form and 3 stories not previously published at all. For those not yet introduced to Boyle, or readers whose interest has been piqued by the recent success of *The Road to Wellville* (1993) and *Riven Rock*, there is plenty of variety in this collection, showcasing the wide range of Boyle's imaginative dexterity. Always entertaining, often provocative, Boyle's work combines verbal athleticism and comedic insight to illuminate the darkest corners of the human psyche. The stories are arranged in three broad sections: "Love," "Death," and "Everything in Between," with much unavoidable overlap among the categories. Of the three previously unpublished stories, "Little Fur People" pits an old woman's caring for sick and injured squirrels against the long arm of the same body that sanctions "no bag limit" killing of the creatures—in season with a valid license, of course; mutinous culinary frustration, as only the French could feel it, erupts among the crew aboard the Calypso in response to Jacques Cousteau's unceasing compulsion to dive deeper in "The Rapture of the Deep"; and the awkward romantic adventures of an American tourist are set in the vacation backdrop of "Mexico." Terrific storytelling and amazing artistry throughout.

Source: Grace Fill, Review of *T.C. Boyle Stories*, in *Booklist*, Vol. 94, No. 22, August 1998, p. 1920.

SOURCES

"About the Author," T. C. Boyle website, http://www.tcboyle.com/page2.html?4 (accessed September 11, 2015).

Apple, Max, "Characters in Search of a Difference," in *New York Times Book Review*, April 1, 1979, https://www.nytimes.com/books/98/02/08/home/boyle-descent.html (accessed September 12, 2015).

Bartholomew, Dana, "100 Years of Water: Los Angeles Aqueduct, William Mulholland Helped Create Modern L.A.," in *Los Angeles Daily News*, November 1, 2013, http://www.dailynews.com/environment-and-nature/20131101/100-years-of-water-los-angeles-aqueduct-william-mulholland-helped-create-modern-la (accessed September 12, 2015).

Boyle, T. Coraghessan, "Sinking House," in *T. C. Boyle Stories*, Penguin, 1998, pp. 292–301.

Janes, Regina, "Magic Realism: Does He or Doesn't He?," in *One Hundred Years of Solitude: Modes of Reading*, Twayne Publishers, 1991, pp. 98, 100.

Knudson, James, Review of *T. C. Boyle Stories*, in *World Literature Today*, Summer 2000, pp. 591–92.

"Magic Realism," in *Encyclopædia Britannica*, 2015, http://www.britannica.com/art/magic-realism (accessed September 12, 2015).

Nagourney, Adam, "California Imposes First Mandatory Water Restrictions to Deal with Drought," in *New York Times*, April 1, 2015, http://www.nytimes.com/2015/04/02/us/california-imposes-first-ever-water-restrictions-to-deal-with-drought.html (accessed September 12, 2015).

FURTHER READING

Adams, Elizabeth E., "T. Coraghessan Boyle, The Art of Fiction No. 161," in *Paris Review*, Summer 2000.

> The "Art of Fiction" interviews in the *Paris Review* are the standard for insightful interviews with the most important literary figures of the day. In this interview, Boyle talks candidly about his surprising success in his youth and how he has managed to keep his career developing over the years.

Friend, Tad, "Rolling Boyle," in *New York Times*, December 9, 1990, https://www.nytimes.com/books/98/02/08/home/boyle-rolling.html.

> This profile of the author, published on the occasion of an early novel, shows the kind of casual, rock-star persona that he has cultivated over his years in the literary spotlight.

Gleason, Paul William, *Understanding T. C. Boyle*, University of South Carolina Press, 2009.

This study is the first full book dedicated to Boyle's works. Though his stories and novels are mostly self-explanatory, the background this book gives about his life can help readers provide some context to his fiction.

Sanford, Jason, "T. Coraghessan Boyle and Surviving the Baby Boom," in *Story South*, 2005, http://www.storysouth.com/nonfiction/2006/08/t_coraghessan_boyle_and_surviv.html.

Boyle's writing is known for its cultural references that mark him squarely as a member of the baby boom generation, but he has, throughout his career, been able to avoid the cultural quirks that are often associated with members of that group. In this article, published only in an online journal, the author examines the ways that Boyle is a baby boomer but is also a unique entity very different from others in his age bracket.

SUGGESTED SEARCH TERMS

T. C. Boyle

T. Coraghessan Boyle

T. C. Boyle AND "Sinking House"

T. C. Boyle AND old age

T. C. Boyle AND grief

T. C. Boyle AND Los Angeles AND aging

T. C. Boyle AND short fiction

T. C. Boyle AND imaginative fiction

T. C. Boyle AND extended metaphor

T. C. Boyle AND middle class

Sweetheart of the Song Tra Bong

TIM O'BRIEN

1990

Tim O'Brien has made a career of weaving his personal experiences as a soldier in the Vietnam War into fictional accounts of that war. Among his many writings on the subject is the short story "Sweetheart of the Song Tra Bong" (first published in *Esquire* in July 1989), which appears in his 1990 collection, *The Things They Carried*. The book includes twenty-two short stories, all tied together by the characters and events of Alpha Company. Together, they tell a bigger story about the men who served in the company and how some of them adjust to life back home. The narrator is a character named Tim O'Brien who happens to be a Vietnam War veteran and an author. O'Brien is known for his intentional blurring of the lines between memoir and fiction, so the reader can assume that the narrator O'Brien is not exactly the same person as the author O'Brien.

In "Sweetheart of the Song Tra Bong," it is this narrator who introduces the story and gives the reader some context about Rat Kiley, who will tell the chilling story of Mary Anne. She is the girlfriend of a medic who flies her into the medical detachment where he is stationed. She is sweet and all-American, but within a short period of time she begins to change. This transformation goes much further than anyone could have predicted, until she has become a primal creature, with no trace of her former humanity. "Sweetheart of the Song Tra Bong" moves back and forth between the story Kiley tells and the

Tim O'Brien (© Peter Power | Getty)

discussions Kiley has with one of the other men to whom he is telling the story. O'Brien explores complicated themes of storytelling, loss of innocence, and the mental ravages of war. It is a disturbing story, but it is also intended to be a cautionary tale.

AUTHOR BIOGRAPHY

William Timothy O'Brien Jr. was born in Austin, Minnesota, on October 1, 1946, to an insurance salesman and an elementary school teacher who met in the navy during World War II. O'Brien is the eldest of three children. The O'Brien family settled in a typical 1950s small town, Worthington, Minnesota. O'Brien loved to read and do magic tricks.

As a "baby boomer" (a man or woman of the generation born right after World War II), O'Brien's teenage and early adult years were influenced by the activism and youth culture

of the 1960s. O'Brien attended Macalester College, where he studied government and politics. He was a serious student who became an opponent of the Vietnam War. While working on Eugene McCarthy's 1968 presidential campaign, O'Brien set his sights on working in the State Department someday. He was such an outstanding student that when he graduated, he was admitted to a doctoral program at Harvard, where he planned to study political science. However, a few weeks after graduating from Macalester, he received his draft notice for military service.

That summer, O'Brien worked in a meatpacking plant while privately expressing in writing his fears and anger about his forced participation in the war. As much as he hated the fact that he was going to have to fight in a war he opposed, he could not consider escaping by running to Canada. Added pressure came from his patriotic small-town community and his parents, who had been in the navy.

On August 14, 1968, O'Brien reported for duty in the army and went to Fort Lewis, Washington, for basic training. After his individual training, he started his thirteen-month tour in Vietnam (1969–1970). There, he served with the Alpha Company, Fifth Battalion of the Forty-sixth Infantry, 198th Infantry Brigade, Americal Division. He was a foot soldier who worked as a rifleman and also as a telephone operator. He received a Purple Heart for being wounded twice, and he advanced to the rank of sergeant.

In March 1970, O'Brien returned home with plans to resume graduate school. He studied at Harvard for five years but did not complete his dissertation. After a short stint in 1974 with the *Washington Post* covering national affairs, O'Brien realized he wanted to pursue writing fiction. His books explore the complexities of war as he draws from his own experiences and insights. He uses his own life extensively in his work, but he intentionally blurs the line between fiction autobiography and war memoir.

After completing three books, O'Brien published "The Things They Carried" in *Esquire* magazine in 1987. It caught the attention of a lot of readers and critics and earned awards and honors. He took that short story and combined it with others to create *The Things They Carried* (1990), in which "Sweetheart of the Song Tra Bong" appears. Again, O'Brien found himself receiving numerous honors and awards, including having the novel selected as a finalist for the Pulitzer Prize in Fiction. O'Brien has continued writing since then, publishing two more novels to date. He lives in central Texas and is married with two sons.

PLOT SUMMARY

The narrator begins by telling the reader that the Vietnam War has generated a lot of wild stories, and this is one that he never forgets. It was told by the medic Rat Kiley, a man known for his extravagant embellishments of stories. Several times, however, the narrator emphasizes that this was a story from which Kiley never wavered. He insisted that it was true. He claimed to be an eyewitness to it and actually became upset when one of the other men did not believe it.

Before being assigned to Alpha Company, Kiley was sent to a small medical detachment in the mountains near the village of Tra Bong and a river called the Song Tra Bong. He and eight other men worked at an aid station for emergency cases that were flown in by helicopter. They would treat patients and stabilize them enough to go to a hospital. Kiley liked it because they were not on the move, carrying everything around all the time, and there were no officers. Security was very minimal. It had originally been a Special Forces outpost, and when Kiley got there, a squad of six Green Berets still had their base of operations there. They had their own supplies and kept to themselves most of the time. Kiley said that sometimes they would disappear for days or weeks at a time before mysteriously reappearing in the night.

Kiley said that the base felt safe, despite being in a war zone. They were exposed, but they never took any fire, and the war felt as if it was at a safe distance. Except for occasional flurries of activity when a helicopter arrived, the men spent their days resting and playing games. During a late-night drinking session, Eddie Diamond (the drug-addicted highest-ranking man of the detachment) made a joke about pooling their money to bring some women in from Saigon. They continued to talk about how easy it would be to do, but nobody was serious about it. One medic, Mark Fossie, however, kept bringing up the subject. He claimed that if you were bold enough, it really would not be that difficult to do. He left to write a letter, and six weeks later, his girlfriend arrived in a helicopter with a

MEDIA ADAPTATIONS

- Audible produced an audiobook of *The Things They Carried* in 2013. Narrated by Bryan Cranston, it has a run time of seven hours and forty-seven minutes.

shipment of supplies. Kiley described her as a tall blonde with long legs, wide shoulders, blue eyes, and a creamy complexion. Fossie greeted her and introduced her to the other men before taking her to put away her luggage. That night, Fossie explained the logistics of how he did it.

Fossie and Mary Anne had been sweethearts for many years and always knew they would get married and live out the American dream. They were in love and full of hope for their future. Kiley said that under ordinary circumstances, that is likely what would have happened. For the next two weeks, the couple was always together, laughing and holding hands. The other men were envious because Mary Anne was a pretty, friendly girl who liked to have fun.

Mary Anne was very interested in everything about military life and the country that surrounded them. She asked a lot of questions and listened intently as the men answered about weapons, the mountains, how to cook over a Sterno and anything else relevant to their unique situation. She even started to learn a little bit of Vietnamese. When she persuaded Fossie to take her into the village so she could see how the people lived, she delighted in it and seemed wholly oblivious of the danger around her. On the way back, she swam in the river despite warnings about snipers. The men were impressed with her nerve even as they called her naive. When someone suggested that she would learn, Diamond said ominously, "There's the scary part. I promise you, this girl will most definitely learn."

The narrator says that even though there were parts of the story that were funny, Kiley would just wait for the listeners to finish laughing. There was always something troubling him when he told it. He reminded his listeners that Mary Anne was not dumb when she came to Vietnam; she was just young and innocent, just as they were when they came to Vietnam. And like the soldiers, she learned quickly when she got there.

As Mary Anne continued to immerse herself in life at the outpost, she started helping with bloody surgeries, and Fossie was amazed and proud of her composure and intelligence. Still, he was not sure what to think about the changes he was seeing in her. Within a short period of time, she was no longer worried about keeping herself pretty, but she was very interested in using and disassembling an M16. When Fossie suggested it was time to think about going home, she responded that she had everything she wanted right there. Fossie noticed that her demeanor had changed and that where she once was bubbly, she had become brooding and dark.

Mary Anne started to come in later at night, and then she did not come home at all. Fossie was convinced that she was sleeping with someone else, and he enlisted Kiley's help in finding her. After an exhaustive search of the bunks, the mess hall, and the entire perimeter, Kiley became extremely concerned that Mary Anne was nowhere to be found. As it turned out, Mary Anne was out on an ambush with the Green Berets.

Upon her return, Mary Anne was in full fatigues, with blackened face, and carrying an M16. She told Fossie she did not want to talk about it, but he insisted. Kiley said that the men never knew exactly what was said, but when Mary Anne showed up in the mess hall for dinner, she had fixed herself up to look as she had looked when she first arrived. She was also very quiet and careful not to do what Fossie did not want her to do. Fossie told Kiley that they had made compromises and were officially engaged. Over the next few weeks, they behaved like a couple in love, but they were both obviously tense and cautious. On the third week, Fossie started making arrangements for her to go back home, and she became very solemn and withdrawn. Then one morning, she and the Green Berets were gone. Fossie was devastated.

By chance, Kiley saw the group return late at night three weeks later. Mary Anne did not, however, go to Fossie's bunker. She continued on to the Green Berets' housing. Kiley recalled how she did not look like the same person anymore.

After hearing that Mary Anne had returned, Fossie waited all day outside the Green Berets'

area. Kiley brought him something to eat and cautioned him against being too pushy with the Green Berets. After midnight, Kiley and Diamond went back to check on Fossie. They heard strange music coming from the dark, and there was a woman's voice singing or chanting along with it. Diamond tried to convince Fossie that it was a radio, but Fossie insisted that it was Mary Anne. Finally, Fossie forced himself into the one hutch that had a light. Kiley and Diamond followed him.

The scene inside the hutch was bizarre and assaulted the senses. There were candles, tribal music coming from a tape deck, Mary Anne's high chanting, incense, and another smell like death that was overpowering and unsettling. On a post was a decaying black leopard head; above were strips of animal skin hanging from the rafters; and there were piles of bones. Fossie called to Mary Anne, and she appeared barefoot, wearing a pink and white outfit. As she stared at Fossie, he realized that even though she looked peaceful, her eyes had gone flat and emotionless. She wore a necklace made of human tongues laced together on copper wire. She told Fossie that she knew he thought it was bad, but it was not, and he did not belong there. She then blankly explained to him that she had an insatiable appetite for the place and being out in it at night. She felt that only there could she really feel like herself. Kiley took Fossie back outside, and Fossie said he could not just leave her there. Kiley told Fossie that it was too late because she was already gone.

Sanders asked what happened next because Kiley paused at this point in the story. Kiley shrugged and said that it was hard to say what happened to her. He flew out to join Alpha Company a few days later, and that was the last he ever heard or saw of the place. Sanders became angry because Kiley was not following the rules of storytelling; Kiley was telling a story without an ending. Kiley reminded him that up to this point, everything in his story was firsthand, so the rest was just what he heard from others.

Kiley said that he heard from Diamond that Mary Anne continued with the Green Berets, especially liking night patrol. She was skilled and could move silently wherever she pleased. Over time, she stopped wearing shoes and then stopped carrying her weapon. She took risks that even the Green Berets thought were too much. When they were under fire, she just smiled as she watched rounds go by her. Sometimes, she disappeared on her own for hours or days. One morning, she left for the mountains and never returned, and no sign of her was ever found. A search was made, but the military failed to find any clues at all. According to the Green Berets, she was still out there somewhere. They felt watched sometimes when they were out in the jungles. The story ends with the statement that she had become part of the land, wearing her culottes, sweater, and tongue necklace. The narrator states that she was dangerous and ready for the kill.

CHARACTERS

Mary Anne Bell

Mary Anne is Mark Fossie's girlfriend, seventeen and just out of high school, who flies into Vietnam to see him. When she arrives, she is a cute blonde with a suitcase and a cosmetic bag, and she is wearing white culottes and a pink sweater. She is bright, curious, and very likable. She is accepted easily as one of the group, and the men are happy to answer her questions about the country, military life, and everything else.

Mary Anne's transformation is gradual, but steady. She changes her appearance, then her demeanor, then her activities, and then eventually turns from real relationships with people. Ultimately, the transformation cannot be slowed or stopped, and she becomes primal. The best reports about her fate indicate that she left to go into the jungles of the mountains and stayed there.

Eddie Diamond

Eddie Diamond is the highest-ranking man at the medical detachment. His main interest is in drugs, so he by no means brings a strong sense of military discipline to the outpost. He takes pity on Fossie when he is distraught about Mary Anne, and he has a level of insight Fossie lacks.

Mark Fossie

Mark Fossie is a tall, blond, eighteen-year-old medic stationed at the medical detachment with Kiley. When a late night discussion jokingly turns to the idea of flying women into the outpost, Fossie gives it serious thought. He arranges a series of flights to get his girlfriend, Mary Anne, to see him. At first, Fossie is thrilled to have her there and proud of how curious and capable she is, but as she starts to transform, he becomes troubled. When she starts to go out for long periods of time with the Green Berets, he tries to take control of the situation, but it is too late.

Fossie clearly loves Mary Anne and is desperate to save her from what the war is doing to her. He reluctantly realizes, however, that his best efforts cannot change anything, and he is devastated. He knows he has lost her for good.

Rat Kiley

Rat Kiley is the medic of Alpha Company. He is prone to telling wildly embellished stories, to the point that the other men know to believe about a quarter of what he says in his stories. Still, with this story, he steadfastly maintains that it is absolutely true and that he saw it with his own eyes. He has an emotional attachment to the story and especially to the character Mary Anne. He clearly feels sorrow about what happened to her, but he defends her as being a sort of victim of the war.

Kiley is very defensive when Sanders challenges him on anything. He stands by his statements about the veracity of the story, and he does not change the way he tells the story just because Sanders objects. When he finishes all of the story he personally witnessed, he makes it clear that everything else in the story is second-hand and, therefore, less reliable.

Narrator

The narrator, Tim O'Brien, is a member of Alpha Company and records Rat Kiley's story, but not without adding his own introductory statements about the questionable reliability of Kiley's storytelling. Beyond that, the narrator interjects nothing but his observations about the interactions between Kiley and Sanders. He does not make any judgments about the story or its characters, and he does not advance any themes.

Mitchell Sanders

Mitchell Sanders is one of the men in Alpha Company with Rat Kiley and the narrator. He rejects the premise of the story, that a soldier could fly his girlfriend into Vietnam in the first place. When Kiley gets upset, swearing it is true, Sanders simply crosses his arms and gives the narrator an amused look.

Sanders also challenges Kiley's storytelling periodically as Kiley tells it. He chastises Kiley for interrupting the story with commentary, and he gets very angry when Kiley attempts to finish the story without providing an ending. Sanders' role in "Sweetheart of the Song Tra Bong" is to act as a foil to Kiley, while keeping the subject of storytelling alive. The art of storytelling frames

TOPICS FOR FURTHER STUDY

- From its muddled beginning, the Vietnam War was a complex and layered war and one that met with consistent opposition in virtually every public forum. Research the war, looking to compile as objective a history as possible that includes a time line, major events, and differing points of view. Using Adobe Voice, create a video complete with visuals, such as photographs and headlines.

- The Vietnam War was the subject of much debate, songwriting, protest, impassioned defense, and flag waving. It was a dominant subject in the public square. Imagine if social media had been available at the time. Choose a Twitter handle and write at least twenty tweets you might have sent out at the time. It may help to listen to popular music of the time, read speeches, or watch video interviews to help you develop your voice.

- The cost of any war includes such factors as lives, money, and patriotic unity. Research some of the measurable costs of the Vietnam War and consider the outcomes of the war. Write an article for a special edition of a magazine remembering the war, and make a case for why the war was or was not worth the cost.

- Read back through "Sweetheart of the Song Tra Bong" and look for references to speech, tongues, words, and language. What point do you think O'Brien is making? Write a poem about the insight you gain.

- It is important to remember that the people of Vietnam during the war were going through their own experiences. Take on the persona of one of them (for example, a Viet Cong soldier, a Vietnamese farmer, or a spy), and write a one-week diary.

- Go back and read the descriptions of the country and its landscape. Using paint, chalk, pencils, or any other flat medium, create a piece of artwork showing Vietnam as Rat Kiley describes it.

- In her wildly popular *Hunger Games* trilogy, author Suzanne Collins offers an extraordinary heroine in Katniss Everdeen. Katniss is forced into an unimaginable situation in which she must use her giftedness as an archer, her survival instinct, and her sharp mind to survive and stand up for what is right. However, brutal situations require brutality to survive, and Katniss finds herself doing things that are not in her nature. Read at least the first book of the trilogy and compare Katniss to Mary Anne. In what ways are the two young women similar, and in what ways are they different? How do you account for their differences? Prepare a speech for teenage girls that inspires them to be more like Katniss in unpredictable situations and warns them against losing their moral center, as does Mary Anne.

---

the content of the story itself, and Sanders is the one who makes that happen.

THEMES

Wars

Taking place during the Vietnam War, "Sweetheart of the Song Tra Bong" offers a vivid setting for the events of the story. O'Brien introduces the

reader to life in a medical detachment, where the gut-wrenching work of field surgeons is described alongside descriptions of their lengthy periods of rest between patients. The presence of the Green Berets shows the separateness of Special Forces from regular troops. They are independent, cocky, and closed off to the other men. The dangers of being in a foreign country at war are depicted in Mary Anne's insistence on going to the village to see how the people live, and in swimming in the river despite the danger of snipers.

The story takes place in the mountains of Vietnam. (© *Galyna Andrushko | Shutterstock*)

Most of all, the story portrays the many ways war changes people and their aspirations. Mary Anne goes from an all-American teenager to a primal killer who has no place in society. Eddie Diamond becomes a drug addict. The Green Berets are all-business, lacking warmth or compassion. Fossie desperately clings to his childhood hopes and dreams but has his heart broken by what becomes of the woman he loves. Nobody leaves the war the same as they came into it.

Storytelling

Throughout *The Things They Carried*, O'Brien explores the interrelatedness of fiction and nonfiction. He also explores memory and remembrance. All of this is tied together in the theme of storytelling that is dominant across the twenty-two stories that make up the book, including this story, "Sweetheart of the Song Tra Bong." The story opens with a profound statement about the stories of the Vietnam War:

> Vietnam was full of strange stories, some improbable, some well beyond that, but the stories that will last forever are those that swirl back and forth across the border between trivia

and bedlam, the mad and the mundane. This one keeps returning to me.

This opening lets the reader know that what will follow will be an incredible story with elements that may be hard to believe. When the narrator says that the story came from Rat Kiley, a man whose stories could only minimally be believed, he is letting us know that the process of telling a story is central to the story itself. The reader is put on alert that not everything in the story is reliable because Kiley intentionally embellished to make stories bigger. However, the narrator adds that this is a story on which Kiley stood steadfast.

Later in the story, Sanders guesses that Mary Anne was with the Green Berets when she went missing. His reasoning is that the Green Berets were mentioned, so they had to be part of the story because that is how stories work. He also criticizes Kiley for interrupting the story with his own commentary because it "breaks the spell. It destroys the magic." He adds, "What you have to do . . . is trust your own story." He also claims that it interferes with the story's tone,

Innocence

The horror of the story is how the war transforms an all-American innocent into a brutal killer who seems to revert to a primal state. Mary Anne is not the only one who is affected by the war this way. The story is never meant to suggest that what happens to her is isolated. Although her story is darker and more intense, becoming harsher and colder is typical of the soldiers' experience. Other stories in the collection bear this out, but O'Brien makes the point clear within "Sweetheart of the Song Tra Bong." Kiley tells his listeners that Mary Anne was not dumb when she first arrived, and he never intended to portray her that way. He reminds them that she was just young and innocent, like all of them, and that she learned quickly, just as they did. He seems adamant that they not think of Mary Anne as being completely different from themselves.

When Kiley is telling the ending of the story he heard from Diamond, he says that what happened to Mary Anne was the same thing that happened to all of them. It is just a matter of degree, he says. They come to the war innocent, clean, and pure, and they leave changed. They become tainted, cynical, and dark. For Mary Anne, he speculates that the combination of unknown terror and unknown pleasure was irresistible. It took her to places and situations and a mindset that she never could have predicted for herself.

STYLE

Verisimilitude

Verisimilitude is the appearance of truth and realism in a work. It is at the heart of O'Brien's mixture of fiction and nonfiction. He uses non-fictional details, for example, to bring verisimilitude to fictional accounts. In "Sweetheart of the Song Tra Bong," this is the ironic reason the narrator gives for Kiley's wild embellishments of his stories. He says that Kiley "wanted to heat up the truth, to make it burn so hot that you would feel exactly what he felt."

O'Brien incorporates a lot of realistic detail in the story and is so effective at developing characters (even those with minor roles) that the story has a very realistic feel. Details about the landscape and daily life in the detachment make the reader feel what it must have been like to be there. Even scenes as unfamiliar to the reader as the visit to Tra Bong have enough detail to make

the strange setting accessible. The dramatic transformation of Mary Anne is portrayed so methodically that her gradual descent into madness does not seem sudden, yet it is disturbing as each step gets progressively darker.

Story within a Story

"Sweetheart of the Song Tra Bong" is not just the story of Fossie and Mary Anne. The narrator sets it up as the telling of the story by Kiley. The effect is that there is the narrative of Kiley telling the story, and there is the narrative of the story itself. The narration goes back and forth, reminding the reader that Kiley's role is an important one. The debates between Kiley and Sanders are significant, and the narrator intends for the reader to be just as pulled into the action going on there as he is into the action going on in the story of Mary Anne.

Imagery

O'Brien draws on quite a bit of sense imagery to bring the reader deeper into the story. He paints a verbal picture of the landscape, describes what it looks and feels like to do battlefield surgery, and includes the fog and weather in eerie nighttime scenes. The pink-and-white outfit Mary Anne wears when she arrives at the outpost is a very different picture from the dark green fatigues and black face paint she wears when she goes out with the Green Berets. Most notably, he brings sight, sound, and smell into his description of Mary Anne in the hutch toward the end of the story. It makes the reader feel that his own senses are being assaulted as he takes in the horror of the whole scene.

HISTORICAL CONTEXT

Vietnam War

The history of the Vietnam War is long and complicated, but it had its origins around the end of World War II and the onset of the Cold War. The Cold War's main players were the United States and the Soviet Union, and the division was ideological in nature; it was over democracy versus communism. The possibility of communism's spread was considered quite threatening by the United States. Consequently, when France's colonial holdings in Vietnam led to the French Indochina War, America stepped in to help the French. Vietnam's position, although it was not major in global politics,

COMPARE
&
CONTRAST

- **1969:** Americans are sharply divided over the Vietnam War and whether or not America should be fighting the war at all. Selective Service requires young men to register for possible draft duty, which is very unpopular with opponents of the war. Between 1965 and 1973, 1,728,344 young men are drafted into military service to fight the war.

  1990: In August 1990, the United States leads thirty other nations to defend Kuwait against Saddam Hussein's Iraqi invasion, an initiative called Operation Desert Shield. By January 1991, the situation escalates, thus launching Operation Desert Storm. Public opinion is largely in favor of this military move. Since the draft was abolished in 1973, the American forces are all volunteers.

  Today: Americans are divided over America's military presence in the Middle East and what should be done to pursue peace in that part of the world. After being in Afghanistan for over a decade and Iraq for almost a decade, American troops recently started returning home for good. There is still no draft.

- **1969:** Most Americans see the spread of communism as a serious ideological threat that should be contained globally.

  1990: Emerging from the relative security and comfort of the 1980s, America is not faced with any particular ideological threat.

  Today: Many Americans see radical Islam as a serious ideological threat that must be contained in the Middle East and around the world.

- **1969:** During the Vietnam War, the role of women in the military is limited to nursing, clerical, intelligence, and transportation work. Women do not fight in combat roles.

  1990: The role of women in military operations has expanded to include roles like flying aircraft and refueling planes. A total of forty-one thousand women are deployed during Operations Desert Shield and Desert Storm.

  Today: As of 2013, the ban on women serving in combat roles is lifted.

---

represented to many the first domino that could fall, leading to the establishment of communism in Asia. Ultimately, France could not win its war, so America took over, trying to crush the spread of communism.

A turning point came in August 1964 with the Gulf of Tonkin incident that led Congress to grant President Lyndon B. Johnson authority to use military force in Vietnam. Motivated by the urgent need to stop communism from gaining a stronghold in Asia, the United States took action. There are volumes written about the Vietnam War, and there is a great deal of controversy in many areas. However, most authors and commentators agree that a huge problem with waging war in Vietnam was the absence of an exit strategy.

The Vietnam War was a defining issue of its generation. Debates, writings, songs, and protests of all kinds were impassioned. Those who supported the war regarded themselves as patriotic, but so did the war's opponents. The reasons for the war, the events of the war, the casualties of the war, and government secrecy all helped to create a deep tension in the country. During the war, there was a draft in place, meaning that young men of eligible age were required to register with the Selective Service and could be drafted into military service. As a result, many young men were shipped off to fight whether or not they liked it, which only made resentment worse.

The war officially ended in January 1973, and it took two years to remove American resources from Vietnam. Considering that most

When Mary Ann arrives, she is cheerful and naïve, but then she starts to change. (© Piotr Marcinski / Shutterstock)

historians put the start of the war in 1954, it is little wonder that a twenty-year war would take a toll on the nation.

Period of Confession and Postmodernism in American Literature

The period of confession and postmodernism in American literature began in 1960 and lasted until 1989. "Sweetheart of the Song Tra Bong" was first published in a magazine in 1989 and then in *The Things They Carried* in 1990. Besides the time line placing the work in this literary period, the characteristics of the period are relevant to O'Brien and his work. The period of confession and postmodernism embodied the cynicism and rebellion of the 1960s and saw many American authors become more introspective and philosophical. Writers sought meaning more within themselves than in society or politics. As American moved into the 1970s and survived an energy crisis and the ongoing civil rights struggle, people questioned the systems and leaders making the decisions. Cynicism toward capitalism deepened as the 1980s brought in the "yuppie" generation and the mantra "Greed is good."

Among the dominant novelists of the time were William Styron, Saul Bellow, John Updike, and Norman Mailer. Other fiction writers, such as Thomas Pynchon, produced work that found freedom in experimentation. That spirit of throwing off the rules and embracing imagination and possibility was typical of the youth culture of the time. O'Brien's unique point of view as an author is anchored in the violence and unrest of the Vietnam War era, and his voice is one that tells stories the way he wants to tell them. Rules of storytelling are not as important to him as the results of the storytelling. His content, style, and purposes put him right at home among the writers of this period.

CRITICAL OVERVIEW

Critical reception of O'Brien's *The Things They Carried* has been overwhelmingly positive; critics have found the book to be an important addition to Vietnam War literature and war literature in general. In the *New York Times Book Review*, Robert R. Harris places the book "high up on the list of best fiction about any war." Harris explains that O'Brien "not only crystallizes the Vietnam experience for us, he exposes the nature of all war stories." He calls the collection "a stunning performance" and says that "the overall effect of these original tales is devastating." D. J. R. Bruckner of the *New York Times* is also drawn to the storytelling importance of O'Brien's collection, as he notes: "For Mr. O'Brien the stories are larger than the war, and considerably more important," adding that they are "at least as much about storytelling as about men at war." In *Harper's Magazine*, reviewer Vince Passaro connects this storytelling with memory. He writes, "In *The Things They Carried*," O'Brien plays with the embattled terrain of a soldier's memory, with his embellishments of memories in conscious reconstructions—stories told, then corrected—to startling and intriguing effects in narrative and language."

In her list of books she recommends most often, Jennifer Epolito of *Bookmarks* includes *The Things They Carried* because it is a "magnificent tale or loss, grief, guilt, and love." Sybil Steinberg of *Publishers Weekly* describes the book as "beautifully honest," and she concludes that the stories "are rooted in a need to rekindle an innocence— of buddies, of victims, of himself—snuffed out by war and history." Richard Eder of *Los Angeles Times Book Review* takes a longer view of *The Things They Carried*, commenting, "But the best of these stories—and none is written with less than the sharp edge of a honed vision—are memory as prophecy. They tell us not where we were but where we are; and perhaps where we will be." He goes on to end his review, "It is an ultimate, indelible image of war in our time, and in time to come."

Many critics have taken special note of "Sweetheart of the Song Tra Bong" as an exceptional story in an excellent collection. In *Contemporary Literature*, Tina Chen deems the story "one of the most powerful . . . in the collection." Chen takes a special interest in Mary Anne as a character study, noting, "Mary Anne becomes *other* than Mary Anne, turning instead into some new, unidentifiable entity who simultaneously registers displacement and substitution through her physical transubstantiation into the imaginative landscape of Vietnam." She adds, "It becomes impossible to distinguish between Mary Anne and Vietnam. As woman and land merge, their fusion complicates easy categorical distinctions. Both are alive with possibilities and imbued with the capacity to signify beyond themselves."

The story has garnered special attention for its depiction of gender roles and the implications of O'Brien's handling of them. For example, Lorrie N. Smith of *Critique* described "Sweetheart of the Song Tra Bong" as "an elaborately far-fetched 'what-if,'" saying that "the story unsettles and stretches our ability to suspend disbelief precisely *because* it is calculated to overturn gender roles." Smith also makes note of how Mary Anne's increased autonomy and transformation effectively rob her boyfriend of his initiation into manhood. In *Massachusetts Review*, critic Pamela Smiley asks, "Are women less warlike than men because they have breasts and give birth? Mary Anne is O'Brien's argument that the kinder, gentler world of the feminine is nothing but an illusion." She takes it a step further and asserts, "Mary Anne illustrates not just the release the war brings, but also how women (and this *is* gender-specific) are 'freed' when they travel outside of their culture and its definitions of what it means to be a woman." Susan Farrell in *CEA Critic* observes the differences between gender expectations as portrayed in Mary Anne's character, going so far as to claim that Mary Anne's descent makes the male soldiers look perfectly normal. She writes, "A woman who defies traditional notions of gender, Mary Anne becomes more horrific, more savage, than any of the male soldiers, thus validating the normalcy

of the regular soldiers." Farrell also notes the many boundaries brought into question in the story. She observes, "'Sweetheart' is a story about transgressing boundaries: narrative boundaries, gender boundaries, racial and national boundaries, as well as ethical boundaries."

CRITICISM

Jennifer Bussey

Bussey is an independent writer specializing in literature. In the following essay, she examines the short story "Sweetheart of the Song Tra Bong" in light of how author O'Brien uses contrast not to designate "other," but rather to show difference and possibility.

"Sweetheart of the Song Tra Bong" is one of twenty-two short, interrelated stories that make up O'Brien's *The Things They Carried*. The book is about the men of Alpha Company, a platoon of young men serving in the Vietnam War. "Sweetheart of the Song Tra Bong" is a complex and chilling story, and O'Brien demonstrates great skill in his telling of it. His use of contrast in the story is subtle, but very effective. Through contrast, O'Brien shows the differences among groups of men in the army and between the Americans and the Vietnamese and, most important, the changes that overcome a single person. A basic rule of fiction writing is to show, not tell. O'Brien uses contrast to show the reader how people are different and why those differences matter. The contrasts are not meant to portray an "us" and a "them" or a "we" and a "she," but instead portray the contrasts and capacity for change within each of us. These differences, whether between groups of people or within a person, destroy unity and continuity.

The first major contrast in the story is between the Green Berets and the medical team stationed to the detachment. Even though they are

> O'BRIEN IS INTENTIONAL IN MAKING SURE THAT THE STORY IS NOT MEANT TO JUDGE HER FOR HER TRANSFORMATION BUT TO SHOW A LITTLE UNDERSTANDING AND EVEN COMPASSION FOR HER."

WHAT DO I READ NEXT?

- Joseph Conrad's *Heart of Darkness* (1899) is the story of a sailor named Marlow, who tells a haunting story of his journey into the African continent. What he sees is disturbing and devastating, but he is fascinated by a man named Kurtz who has somehow ascended to power over the natives. What Marlow discovers challenges everything he believes about human nature and civilization.

- Joseph Heller's 1961 classic, *Catch-22*, is a satire featuring bombardier Yossarian, who is bent on getting relieved of his wartime duty. He is constantly frustrated by the changing requirements of his position and by the nonsensical insanity standard for dismissal. *Catch-22* is among the best war fiction for its irreverent tone, memorable protagonist, and treatment of the theme of madness in war.

- *Band of Sisters: American Women at War in Iraq* (2007), by Kirsten Holmstedt, addresses the often overlooked but very real stories of women in combat. Comprising various real-life tales of women serving in Iraq, the stories' content ranges from frontline battles to personal ones, including the experiences of the first African American female pilot, a nurse, a gunner, and others.

- Robert McMahon's *Major Problems in the History of the Vietnam War* (1990) is a collection of multiple primary sources and scholarly essays covering the issues and dividing points of what is widely regarded as the most controversial war in America's history.

- Written by a former North Vietnamese soldier, *The Sorrow of War* (1990, published in English in 1994), by Bao Ninh, opens just after the Vietnam War. The main character, Kien, is a soldier who is helping with the job of recovering corpses, and his return to battlegrounds forces him to face his painful memories. The book is known for its disjointed structure as Kien's thoughts and feelings go back and forth from the past to the present to the more distant past and back to the present. The overall effect is a sense of the chaos of war on a person's psyche, and the story offers a perspective most Americans miss.

- O'Brien's *Going after Cacciato* (1978) won the 1979 National Book Award. It tells the intriguing story of a young soldier who leaves his post in Indochina and journeys to Paris for the peace talks, but it is told from the perspective of one of the members of his squad as they search for him. The story is a strange mix of realism and something akin to surrealism. It is a favorite of readers of war fiction because of its unusual story and its treatment of typical war themes like fear and heroism.

- Harry Mazer's and Peter Lerangis's 2012 *Somebody, Please Tell Me Who I Am* is about Ben, a popular senior in high school who decides to enlist instead of going to college. When his convoy is attacked, Ben suffers a brain injury that puts him in a coma. When he comes out of it, he suffers amnesia and has to find the inner strength to struggle and persevere through a situation more difficult than he imagined.

---

living together, they are not really living as a community. The medics are there because they have been sent there to tend to emergency cases coming in by helicopter. They live a pretty relaxing, undisciplined life most of the time. When a helicopter arrives, there is a flurry of activity while they give critical care to wounded men from the field. Most of their surgeries are amputations, but all of the surgeries are urgent and bloody. Once their patients are stabilized enough for travel, they are sent to a proper hospital. Then the men return to their leisure. The highest-ranking man among them, Eddie Diamond, is a heavy drug user who places no priority on bringing much military discipline to the medical team.

In contrast, the Green Berets seem to be at the outpost not so much because they have been sent there but because they never left. Before the detachment became a field emergency room, it had been a Green Beret station. The Green Berets live in their own area, have their own supplies, keep to themselves, and are on constant watch. Like the medical team, they have flurries of activity, but they are carefully planned and carried out in secret. O'Brien does not even give them names, even though there are only six of them. They are such a secretive group, and so unified, that they function as a single character in the story, whereas the men in the medical team have distinct personalities. The only character in the story who moves easily between the two groups is Mary Anne, and she eventually folds herself into the Green Beret group before disappearing altogether.

In setting up this contrast, O'Brien does not make the medical team out to be more important because they save lives or more personable, nor does he make the Green Berets seem more important for their discipline and their carrying out of secret missions. Instead, O'Brien places these two very different groups side by side to show how, surprisingly, both groups are part of the same army and how both perform vital tasks. It seems there is a place for every kind of person and skill in the army.

Another contrast O'Brien depicts is between the Americans and the Vietnamese. Mary Anne is anxious to go see the neighboring village of Tra Bong, despite Fossie's objections. Mary Anne brushes off his concerns by looking for similarities instead of differences. She says, "Listen, it can't be that bad. They're human beings, aren't they? Like everybody else?" Her failure to recognize differences makes her unable to respect the very real danger of leaving the military compound. Once she and the medics who accompany her get to the village, O'Brien points out the ways in which the village is different from the outpost. He notes the hostile atmosphere, the thatched roofs, and the naked children. Interestingly, Mary Anne does not recognize any of these things as anything but quaint and charming. When she wants to stop to swim in the river on the way back, she fails to recognize the danger in that. Swimming in the river is not like going for a swim

back home in America, where it is safe, but she disregards warnings of snipers and ambushes. Again, she fails to recognize the differences between what is familiar and appealing to her and where she actually is. Everyone else, however, from Fossie and Kiley to the narrator, is acutely aware of the contrast between being outside the military outpost and being safely within it.

The last example of contrast is the most significant one to the plot. There is a sharp contrast in Mary Anne before and after her transformation. When she arrives to see her boyfriend, Fossie, at his medical post, she is an all-American teenager. She is innocent, fresh-faced, and wearing pink and white. She is friendly and carefree, playing volleyball with the guys and excited to be with her boyfriend. The change is gradual but easy to track as she stops tending to her appearance and becomes increasingly inquisitive about everything from the country around them to using an M16. Outwardly, her appearance changes along with her activities, and eventually her entire demeanor changes. Fossie has known her for many years, as they have been small-town sweethearts for a long time. He knows her very well, and they plan to get married and have a typical American life together. He is troubled by her change. She becomes more introspective and mysterious, and the fun-loving part of her vanishes completely. It is more than being obsessed with war or with Vietnam; her transformation is not merely mental. She actually becomes a different person.

Mary Anne after her transformation is almost monstrous. After she disappears with the Green Berets yet again, Fossie goes looking for her upon their return. What he finds is startling and disturbing. The girl who once arrived holding a cosmetic bag and wearing culottes is now surrounded by the stench of death, chanting among piles of bones and a decaying leopard head. As horrifying as all of that is, the worst of it is that she is wearing a necklace made of overlapping human tongues. Her demeanor is distant but calm, and she tells Fossie that it is not that bad and that he does not belong there. O'Brien emphasizes the contrast in who Mary Anne used to be and who she is now by portraying her in this scene wearing pink and white. The reader would expect her to be in fatigues and with black face paint, but her outfit is a chilling reminder that this is still Mary Anne and that her starting point was as a typical teenage girl.

The last we hear of her is that she left for the mountains and was never seen again. She became part of the jungle.

The use of contrast in Mary Anne's character is the heart of "Sweetheart of the Song Tra Bong." O'Brien's use of it is brilliant in that he is not setting up a distinction between monster Mary Anne and the saner men of the outpost. She is not meant to be altogether "other." Kiley's speech about how everyone who comes to the war changes from clean to dirty is O'Brien's way of reminding the reader that war changes people in profound ways. Kiley says it is just a matter of degree. It is impossible for anyone to go into that situation and come out innocent and optimistic. What Mary Anne became is just the extreme of what everyone else experiences. It is a cautionary tale in that Mary Anne never intended to go see her boyfriend and become a savage woman comfortable going on missions with Special Forces and eventually turning herself completely over to the setting. But nobody gets to choose how far they are willing to go. Perhaps that is why Kiley seems to have a sense of compassion for her.

While many authors use contrast to demonstrate that one person or one way is better than another, O'Brien does not do that in "Sweetheart of the Song Tra Bong." The contrasts he sets up in the story only inform and give insight, showing how differences create misunderstanding and distrust. The Green Berets and the medics have almost nothing in common, but O'Brien never gives the sense that one group is superior to the other in any way. The Americans and the Vietnamese are very different from each other culturally and in their present experience at this point in the war, but O'Brien does not castigate either group. He merely shows how the war is bringing together very different groups of people and how it is affecting them differently. Even in the case of Mary Anne, it certainly seems that the original Mary Anne, the innocent one, is much better than the animalistic one she becomes. Yet even here, O'Brien is intentional in making sure that the story is not meant to judge her for her transformation but to show a little understanding and even compassion for her. Kiley makes it very clear that what happened to her was just a more extreme version of what happens to them all.

Source: Jennifer Bussey, Critical Essay on "Sweetheart of the Song Tra Bong," in *Short Stories for Students,* Gale, Cengage Learning, 2016.

> AS O'BRIEN DOES IN MUCH OF HIS WORK, HE THWARTS READERS' DESIRES TO TAME THE NARRATIVE, TO FIND THE MORAL OF THE STORY OF MARY ANNE AND HER DISAPPEARANCE INTO THE JUNGLES OF VIETNAM."

Elisabeth H. Piedmont-Marton
In the following essay, Piedmont-Marton offers a close reading of the story.

Like many stories in *The Things They Carried,* "Sweetheart of the Song Tra Bong" folds back on itself, at once asserting and challenging its own veracity, telling a story and at the same time commenting on how to tell a story. Because the stories are interrelated, "Sweetheart of the Song Tra Bong" invites readers to read it against its companion stories. It is the central story of the book, and it's a particularly rich one to teach, because it reaches beyond its own textual boundaries and refers to images and narratives of the Vietnam War in film, literature, and popular imagination. Students respond powerfully to it, and their reading can be deepened and complicated by encouraging them to unpack the layers of narrative and metanarrative. This essay offers a close reading of "Sweetheart of the Song Tra Bong," focusing on the theme of crossing over, or transgression, and illuminates sites in the text that invite opportunities for students to engage in complex, nuanced responses.

Technically a story within a story, "The Sweetheart of the Song Tra Bong" is an account of what happens when Mark Fossie, a foot soldier—an ordinary grunt—imports his girlfriend, Mary Anne Bell, from Cleveland Heights to Vietnam. The story is related to Tim O'Brien the character by Rat Kiley, who claims to have witnessed at least some of the events. (It's useful to call students' attention to the differences among the three instantiations of Tim O'Brien at work in the text: author, narrator, and character.) The point of the story is not, as Rat's interlocutors and readers alike may suspect, the logistics of Fossie's daring feat of bringing Mary Anne and her pink sweater and white culottes to their outpost. Instead, the narrative's power inheres in

By the end of the story, Mary Ann is accompanying the soldiers on patrol at night, and then she disappears altogether. (© *Przemek Tokar | Shutterstock*)

what happens to her once she arrives in Vietnam and how her transformation from American suburban schoolgirl to nascent guerrilla affects Mark, Rat, and the others in their sense of who and where they are.

The story takes place near the village of Tra Bong, "in the mountains west of Chu Lai," in the early 1970s. O'Brien isn't specific about the date, but he indicates that "in the early 1960s, the place had been set up as a Special Forces outpost" and that "Rat Kiley [had] arrived nearly a decade later." The critic Benjamin Goluboff explains that this story, as well as others in O'Brien's work, takes place in Quang Ngai Province, the tactical area of operations for the United States Army's Americal Division in 1968 and 1969. A likely source for O'Brien's Quang Ngai was the work of the journalist Jonathan Schell in the *New Yorker* in 1967 and 1968, which later became a book, *The Military Half: An Account of the Destruction in Quang Ngai and Quang Tin*. Chu Lai is located south of Danang, at the point where Vietnam narrows between the South China Sea and the wild

Annamite Mountains to the west and the border with Laos. The medical post where Rat and Mark are stationed is "clearly indefensible," but Rat claims that "he always felt a curious sense of safety there" because "[n]othing much ever happened" and "the war seemed to be somewhere far away." In fact, according to the historian Marilyn Young, the war, at least as far as American forces were concerned, was changing course and winding down beginning in 1970. (Although there were still 334,000 American military personnel in Vietnam at the end of 1970, the number would drop to 23,000 by early 1973.) The year 1970 marked the beginning of the "Vietnamization" of the war, in which the United States decreased its participation in ground combat and handed over the responsibilities of defending border areas to the South Vietnamese Army. During the first half of 1971, awareness of and resistance to the war in the United States was escalating; the Pentagon Papers were published in the *New York Times*, and the Winter Soldier Investigation, a protest organized by the Vietnam Veterans against the

War, took place in Detroit. That year also brought a pause from the bombing of North Vietnam and a reduction of the United States forces to 156,800 by December.

The haunting story of what happens when Mark Fossie imports his Ohio girlfriend to Vietnam is arguably one of the most powerful and memorable American literary responses to the Vietnam War. Ultimately, it is a story about transgression, about the costs and consequences of crossing over boundaries and perimeters on whose impermeability a great deal depends. It is also a story that transgresses the normal boundaries of storytelling.

If students have read some or all of the stories in *The Things They Carried*, they will be familiar with O'Brien's metanarrative strategies and his deliberate blurring of the boundaries between truth and fiction. But even if "Sweetheart of the Song Tra Bong" is the only piece they read, it's worthwhile here to refer briefly to a passage in "How to Tell a True War Story." In that story, which functions as a kind of gloss for the book and a deliberately obtuse explanation of his technique, O'Brien deconstructs simple claims and offers instead a pluralistic and even contradictory model for evaluating the veracity of war stories. As Catherine Calloway explains:

> O'Brien draws the reader into the text, calling the reader's attention to the process of invention and challenging him to determine which, if any, of the stories are true. As a result, the stories become epistemological tools, multidimensional windows thorough which the war, the world, and the ways of telling a war story can be viewed from many different angles and visions. ("How to Tell")

In a passage in "How to Tell a True War Story" that has particular resonance with "Sweetheart of the Song Tra Bong," O'Brien explains that "[f]or the common soldier, at least, war has the feel—the spiritual texture—of a great ghostly fog, thick and permanent." Referring both to the war itself and to the acts of telling and reading war stories, O'Brien elaborates:

> There is no clarity. Everything swirls. The old rules are no longer binding, the old truths no longer true. Right spills over into wrong. Order blends into chaos, love into hate, ugliness into beauty, law into anarchy, civility into savagery. The vapors suck you in. You can't tell where you are, or why you're there, and the only certainty is overwhelming ambiguity.

For readers of "Sweetheart of the Song Tra Bong," the significance of this passage is its emphasis on the anxiety that surrounds fluidity and the breaching of boundaries thought to be fixed and impenetrable. At this point, it's useful to ask students to map the topography of the story and identify some of the boundaries and perimeters that O'Brien and his narrator describe and then to ask students to discuss or write about the metaphorical boundaries or the ways in which the story offers a critique of the idea of the boundary itself. Some of the boundaries they may find productive to discuss are those between the world and the war, the domestic and the military spheres, women and men, (Western) soldier and (Asian) enemy, and civilization and nature. Students will soon see that their mapping of boundaries won't hold, that O'Brien sets up expectations and then undermines them. The breach of perimeters, confusion of categories, and inversion of hierarchies cause tremendous anxiety among the men of O'Brien's company because their already tenuous and contingent position is revealed to be completely unanchored. Readers are in an analogous position: They don't know whom to believe or what to trust. The words in "How to Tell a True War Story" take on new meaning, as the sense of disorientation they describe becomes as intimately psychological as it is geographical: "You can't tell where you are, or why you're there." Readers might also add, "You don't know who you are."

Students should be encouraged to push their analysis of the text and interrogate O'Brien's use of perimeter imagery. In what ways are these boundaries both literal methods of organizing the social world and metaphors for the metaphysical borders that are breached when Mary Anne Bell arrives in Vietnam? How do the boundaries get crossed and the positions inverted? Rat describes the outpost as being both "clearly indefensible" and "isolated and vulnerable." And yet, as he says, "he always felt a curious sense of safety there." As he goes on to describe the post in more detail, it appears that the sense of security is derived, at least in part, from its high level of organization: people stay where they are supposed to stay and do what they are expected to do. This is analogous to the highly structured and segmented nature of the military in general. Rat's duties are gory but predictable: casualties are flown in, have legs and feet amputated, then are flown back out. There's "[n]o humping at all. No officers, either." And yet this organization, which appears natural and organic, is, in fact, highly artificial and unstable. The entire compound is surrounded by rolls of concertina wire and abutted on two sides by jungle, mountains, and gorges. At the outermost of the concentric circles are the Greenies (Green Berets, or Special Forces), with their own "hootch . . . fortified with sandbags and a metal fence." It may appear that the Greenies are the defenders of the perimeter, but as the story unfolds, they are the boundary itself: porous, shifting, and illusory. They are liminal creatures, Rat suggests, whom it is best to avoid, as if whatever they have or know is contagious. Not only do they inhabit a space on the perimeter, they also instantiate a figurative perimeter, the last outpost of "civilized" behavior and values. All these boundaries and perimeters are threatened when Mark Fossie succeeds in flying Mary Anne Bell in from Cleveland Heights. What seems at first blush a story about a girl who comes to a remote part of Vietnam, takes up with a renegade band of Greenies, is last seen wearing a necklace of human tongues, and eventually disappears into the hills and the mists is, on closer reading, really a story about what happens to the men themselves—the men who witness, and are dislocated by, her transgression. As Alex Vernon argues, "Sweetheart of the Song Tra Bong" is "a story of the male imagination" in which Mary Anne is an "abstraction" among O'Brien's other fully drawn characters, on whom the men project their anxieties about the masculine enterprise of war making and about the women for whom they fight (*Soldiers*). Mark Fossie thought he could import Mary Anne into his world as if she were a care package or a personal USO tour. He regards her as an object, a prized possession, and his greatest fear is that she'll be unfaithful to him with one of the other Americans inside the concertina wire, that he will lose possession of her. This kind of infidelity would be a threat to his masculinity, and he does his best to prevent it. Neither he nor apparently any of the other witnesses anticipates that Mary Anne's actions are a threat to their very concept of masculinity. Insofar as American stories of the Vietnam War take up larger cultural narratives, the story of Mary Anne is about generalized anxiety regarding gender roles (both at the time the story is set, in the 1960s, and at the time of its publication). But the power of the story derives from more than its threat to gender roles. Because the concepts of masculine and feminine are integral to the entire chain of reasoning that justifies war. Mary Anne's dangerous transformation threatens to unravel the already strained fabric of rationalization that

makes the men's missions in Vietnam appear worthwhile and purposeful. The taboo that's violated is the one that contains the feminine in the domestic sphere and the masculine in the martial sphere. In Vernon's words:

> Mary Anne paradoxically represents Vietnam and the enemy, and the United States and that social bond that sends men to suffer the horrors of war and thereby earns their hostility. As the fresh-faced sweetie and bride and mother-to-be, she clearly represents the culture and values men are willing to fight to preserve. (*Soldiers*)

As many military historians and war theorists (John Keegan and Elaine Scarry chief among them) have pointed out, men do not fight in wars for the sake of the larger geopolitical reasons that leaders offer for the war. Instead, they fight for more intimate and immediate reasons, such as loyalty to fellow soldiers, and for an entire constellations of reasons back home. Like ancient knights, men fight for women—and for what women represent. The qualities embodied in women are those most conspicuously absent from the experience of war: purity, goodness, cleanliness, civilization, pink culottes. Like Lieutenant Cross's beloved and remote Martha in the title story and the perpetually virginal child Linda in "The Lives of the Dead," Mary Anne is, from Mark Fossie's point of view, an object, a prized possession, a totem. Mary Anne's transformation not only challenges Mark Fossie's proprietary claim on her but, more important, exposes as a fiction or a lie the entire chain of reasons underpinning the idea "that men without women trip," to borrow Michael Herr's memorable phrase from *Dispatches*.

In the masculinist world of Mark Fossie and the others, Mary Anne's body, which has been the object of each man's gaze since she arrived, becomes the text on which her transgressions are inscribed. The pink sweater and culottes she wears when she arrives are an emblem of girlish American suburban innocence, and she looks to the men "like a cheerleader visiting the opposing team's locker room" when she visits the hamlet with Mark, Rat, and the other medics. Soon, however, her outward appearance begins to change, and to Mark "[h]er body seemed foreign somehow." With her hair cut short and "wrapped . . . in a dark green bandanna," wearing "no cosmetics" and no jewelry, Mary Anne sheds her midwestern femininity, and she seems to move out of Mark's reach. Eventually, she moves so far beyond his tether that she stays out all night; she moves beyond the perimeter of war stories that would cloister her safely in Cleveland Heights. By the end of the story she has "moved through femininity and through masculinity to a place beyond gender" (Vernon, *Soldiers*).

Focused on her appearance and obsessed with her potential for sexual exploitation and his own cuckolding, Fossie concludes that Mary Anne has run off with one of the other men; or to put it more accurately, he thinks another man has taken her, since he views her as an object on which others act rather than an agent in her own right. Once Mark and Rat have searched the compound without finding her, Rat says, in a sentence that foreshadows the rest of the story, "Okay. . . . We got a problem." The immediate problem—and the only one that Mark seems concerned about—is the mystery of Mary Anne's whereabouts. Why has she disappeared? The bigger and thornier problem is that though she's with the Greenies, it isn't for "sex or anything." She's been out all night "on . . . *ambush*." When she walks back into the hootch she shares with Fossie, she's wearing "a bush hat and filthy green fatigues." As Rat tells the story, Fossie hesitates, "as though he had trouble recognizing her." Students should consider the significance of the conditional in this sentence: he doesn't actually have trouble recognizing her—she's the only civilian American woman for miles around—but he is unable to see her without her familiar outer attributes. In fact, when Mary Anne and Mark appear in the mess hall later that evening, it's her traditional suburban girlish appearance that's been reconstituted, as if she could be brought back under Fossie's control as long as he can keep her in "a white blouse, a navy blue skirt, [and] a pair of plain black flats." But no matter what she wears, Mary Anne has already moved beyond the perimeter, to shadowy places Rat and Mark haven't been to, and she's undergone an inner transformation that no schoolgirl outfit can disguise. In Vernon's words, "[S]he is either a body in front of them or a mystery beyond them, either way teasing them in their desire to penetrate her" (*Soldiers*).

The truce that Mark Fossie achieves with Mary Anne is short-lived. After a few weeks, during which she appeared "as if she had come up on the edge of something, as if she were caught in that no-man's land between Cleveland Heights

and deep jungle," she disappears with the Greenies. Three weeks later, Rat happens to be awake the night she and the ghostly column slip back through the wire and into the Greenies' hootch. With Mary Anne inside the hootch, Mark Fossie begins a vigil outside that dramatizes a version of the male gaze in which the object is not only hidden from sight but has wrested the power from the gazer. When he finally stumbles through the door of the hootch, he finds himself in terra incognita, a shadowy hut filled with "a weird deep-wilderness sound," a miasma of smoke, and a smell "like an animal's den, a mix of blood and scorched hair and excrement and the sweet-sour odor of moldering flesh—the stink of the kill." Fossie's first glimpse of Mary Anne as she emerges from the shadows suggests for a moment that she's "the same pretty young girl who had arrived a few weeks earlier." But her clothing—a "pink sweater and a white blouse and a simple cotton skirt"—which had in the past functioned as a sign of her reliably domesticated femininity, are now appropriated into a new and strange semiotics that discards the expected strand of pearls or girlish locket in favor of "a necklace of human tongues . . . one overlapping the next, the tips curled upward as if caught in a final shrill syllable." Mary Anne's appearance in the bizarre setting of the hootch, a chilling retelling of the final spectacle of Kurtz in Joseph Conrad's *Heart of Darkness*, certainly signifies her crossing over from Cleveland Heights to a Vietnam that is beyond the bounds of even Fossie's experience. As if her physical attributes weren't sufficient evidence of her transgression and transformation, her explanation, framed in the language of desire, proves to Fossie that she's escaped his gaze and his possession. As Terry Martin and Margaret Stiner point out, Mark Fossie, like Conrad's Intended, "desperately clings to the romanticized image of his beloved." Chiding him that "[y]ou're in a place where . . . you don't belong," Mary Anne says, "Sometimes I want to *eat* this place. Vietnam. I want to swallow the whole country—the dirt, the death—I just want to eat it and have it there inside me." Her assertion reorganizes the economy of desire on which Fossie's masculine identity depends: the object of desire has become the agent of desire, and the landscape of fear has been transformed into one of empowerment. Mark, whose daring act set in motion Mary Anne's transformation, is reduced to a feminized passivity; he is rendered powerless and almost speechless and has to be physically supported by Rat Kiley.

Rat tells Mark, "She's already gone," suggesting not only that Mary Anne is lost to Mark but also that the version of American femininity and the social world it represents is lost forever in the jungles of Vietnam. But Rat, who has been the proprietor of the story since the beginning, offers a coda that suggests the possibility of a reaction to the final vision of Mary Anne different from Mark's paralysis and collapse. Conceding that the final chapter in the story is, in Mitchell Sanders's words, "speculation," Rat confesses that he "loved her." He loved her, he says, because "[t]he way she looked, Mary Anne made you think about all those girls back home, how clean and innocent they all are, how they'll never understand any of this, not in a billion years." While this declaration suggests that Rat loved Mary Anne in her Cleveland Heights, culottes-wearing incarnation, his further explanation hints instead that it's the Mary Anne with the necklace of human tongues that he loves: "She was *there*. She was up to her eyeballs in it. After the war, man, I promise you, you won't find nobody like her."

For Mark, the story of Mary Anne is a story of loss: of a world of innocence and purity that she represents, of masculine authority that licensed him to regard her as a possession, and of faith that the savagery of war exists only in the arena of war rather than in the human psyche. Rat's telling of the story suggests that Mary Anne's disappearance into the jungle is at least as much a story of liberation as it is one of loss. His final words turn mythic and wistful, as if Rat envies Mary Anne her escape. Despite his claim to love her, he expresses no desire to rescue or possess her. Rather, he seems to simply want to be her: "She had crossed to the other side. She was part of the land. She was wearing her culottes, her pink sweater, and a necklace of human tongues. She was dangerous. She was ready for the kill."

As O'Brien does in much of his work, he thwarts readers' desires to tame the narrative, to find the moral of the story of Mary Anne and her disappearance into the jungles of Vietnam. "A true war story is never moral," he tells us in "How to Tell a True War Story." "It does not instruct, nor encourage virtue, nor suggest models of proper human behavior, nor restrain men from doing the things men have always done."

Students should ask if O'Brien's warning in "How to Tell a True War Story" applies to their own readings: "[I]f you feel that some small bit of rectitude has been salvaged from the larger waste, then you have been made the victim of a very old and terrible lie." Many students will be troubled by the difficulty of reading "Sweetheart of the Song Tra Bong" as a feminist text because Mary Anne is less a real person than an abstraction or a device and because her moral position at the end is highly ambiguous. Other students may want to explore how the narrative register of the story moves further and further away from Rat's "truth" to a fourth-hand account and is taken over by the unnamed narrator, who finally posits Mary Anne as a kind of mythic and allegorical creature:

> Late at night, when the Greenies were out on ambush, the whole rain forest seemed to stare in at them—a watched feeling—and a couple of times they almost saw her sliding through the shadows. Not quite, but almost. She had crossed to the other side.

Like Mary Anne herself, the story slides through the shadows of our understanding, barely discernible, hauntingly familiar, yet strange, always eluding our interpretive grasp and continuing to seduce us into its dangerous enclosure.

Source: Elisabeth H. Piedmont-Marton, "Doing Gender and Going Native in 'Sweetheart of the Song Tra Bong,'" in *Approaches to Teaching the Works of Tim O'Brien*, edited by Alex Vernon and Catherine Calloway, Modern Language Association of America, 2010, pp. 163–70.

Tobey C. Herzog

In the following excerpt, Herzog defends O'Brien's work against charges of racism and sexism.

. . . O'Brien also unifies this novel of stories, as he does with the nonfictional *If I Die*, through the limited center of consciousness and observation of a first-person narrator, who carries with him guilt and disturbing memories from distant and recent events in his life: "The bad stuff never stops happening: it lives in its own dimension, replaying itself over and over" (*Things*). As O'Brien has noted on several occasions, *Things* is intended to be read as a memoir, a writer's memoir. Therefore, everything in the book (stories, interpolated stories, confession, commentary, fragments, and sketches) is filtered through the eyes, memory, and imagination of Tim O'Brien, a fictional 43-year-old narrator recalling people, events, and stories

"

> SIGNIFICANTLY, ALL OF THESE FEMALE
> CHARACTERS, ALONG WITH THE WAR ITSELF, ARE
> PRESENTED THROUGH THE WORDS OF MALE
> STORYTELLERS, AND ONLY KATHLEEN AND LINDA
> ARE GIVEN A VOICE OF THEIR OWN IN THE STORIES."

from his life and Vietnam War experience. This fictional O'Brien also creates new stories and comments on his career as an author.

Since *The Things They Carried* exhibits some of the same content, structure, narrative strategies, and themes of O'Brien's previous books, the work receives similar criticism: charges of perceived racism (absence of the fully developed Vietnamese perspective) and sexism (objectifying, excluding, or silencing women). It should also be noted that such criticism is certainly not targeted at O'Brien alone but has been directed generally at many modern war authors, particularly male American authors writing about the Vietnam War. As in *If I Die* and *Going After Cacciato*, O'Brien devotes minimal space in *The Things They Carried* to developing Vietnamese characters, examining war experiences from the Vietnamese perspective, or exploring the larger political issues involved in this war. Granted, in this novel and in his two previous war narratives, the land of Viet Nam plays a prominent role, becoming a character—threatening, ever changing, mysterious: "'The whole country, Vietnam. The place talks. It talks. Understand? Nam—it truly talks'" (*Things*). Only a few native inhabitants of this land, however, appear in *The Things They Carried*: a poppa san who leads American troops through a dangerous minefield, two Buddhist monks living near an abandoned pagoda, a dancing Vietnamese girl traumatized by the burning of her hamlet and the killing of her family, a corpse of an old Vietnamese man, and a Vietnamese farmer described in the narrator's story about his return to Viet Nam 20 years after his tour of duty. Yet, as is particularly true in *If I Die*, the roles of these individuals in the book are insignificant, either as victims of the war or background figures in the war stories.

Perhaps narrator Tim O'Brien's most noticeable attempt to humanize and understand these mysterious others occurs in his description of a young Vietcong draftee killed in an ambush. This death-recognition story, told in "The Man I Killed" and repeated with variations in two other sections, seems a prose version of Thomas Hardy's famous World War I poem "The Man He Killed." It connects with a tradition in war literature of a protagonist engaging in a sympathetic identification with the enemy, but an experience always presented from the protagonist's point of view. In O'Brien's story, narrator Tim O'Brien imagines his enemy—a Vietnamese citizen-soldier—being the same age as the narrator (born in 1946), beginning college in the same year (1964), and responding to the war in a similar fashion: "The young man would not have wanted to be a soldier and in his heart would have feared performing badly in battle" (*Things*). Although linking the two soldiers, such a self-centered perspective of this other soldier suggests an effort at projecting the narrator's own traits onto this unknown Vietnamese rather than imagining a separate person. As noted earlier, author O'Brien responds to criticism about his excluding the Vietnamese voice in *Things* and other books by arguing that he is neither capable of presenting a Vietnamese perspective he is unfamiliar with nor required to speak for people who can speak for themselves.

If, for the most part, O'Brien excludes the Vietnamese from meaningful roles in this novel, he does include more women in this book when compared with their presence in the earlier war narratives. Specifically, females figure prominently in several of the stories: Kathleen, narrator Tim O'Brien's nine-year-old daughter; Linda, the narrator's nine-year-old girlfriend from his childhood in Worthington, Minnesota; Martha, Lieutenant Jimmy Cross's girlfriend; and Mary Anne Bell, a 17-year-old who has a "heart-of-darkness" experience at a fire base in Vietnam. In addition, the narrator briefly refers to Curt Lemon's sister, a woman in an audience listening to one of the narrator's war stories, a dancing Vietnamese girl, and Norman Bowker's girlfriend and his mother.

But such inclusions do not diminish some feminist criticism of this book. Significantly, all of these female characters, along with the war itself, are presented through the words of male storytellers, and only Kathleen and Linda are given a voice of their own in the stories. For these and other reasons, a few critics view O'Brien's portrayal of the female characters in *Things* as antifeminist, in particular because they lack an "agency and sensibility of their own" and instead are "projections of a narrator trying to resolve the trauma of war" (Smith 1994, 19). Specifically, Lorrie Smith in examining *The Things They Carried* notes the verbal and emotional hostility directed toward women in the story "How To Tell A True War Story" and their exclusion from the war throughout O'Brien's book because of their supposed inability to understand the male war experience. She comments that the story "Sweetheart of the Song Tra Bong," which becomes O'Brien's attempt at deconstructing gender differences within the context of war by describing a woman's violent battlefield experiences, simply "portrays the woman as *more* masculine than the men, hence monstrous and unnatural" (Smith 1994, 32).

O'Brien's response to such criticism is a cryptic "I think I often am much more a feminist than the so-called feminists criticizing me" (McNerney, Interview, 17). In a 1994 interview he characterizes some of the objectionable language and comments directed toward women in his stories as a realistic "recording" of details rather than an "endorsing" of such language and views. Furthermore, O'Brien disagrees that "Sweetheart" is an antifeminist story; in fact, he sees it as just the opposite, an "utterly feminist" story promoting gender equality. He argues that the story promotes the notion that American women, who are currently excluded from serving in ground combat, would have the same experiences and feelings on the battlefield as their male counterparts, given the chance: "They would be going to the same dark side of the human hemisphere, the dark side of the moon, the dark side of their own psyches" (McNerney, Interview, 21).

Within this context of critical debate and this novel's place within O'Brien's efforts at interconnecting his books, we will examine the specific form and content of *The Things They Carried*. Because of the diverse content and structure within the 22 sections, finding a workable approach to synthesizing the whole book may appear problematic. But as noted previously, the numerous thematic and character links among the chapters, as well as the first-person point of view, create an integrated novel based on

an interdependence Philip Beidler characterizes as "each story needing another or others for completion" (Beidler, 33).

Also linking the different stories is a loose tripartite structure somewhat paralleling the form of O'Brien's other two war narratives. For example, drawing upon the relationships of past, present, and future time so artfully manipulated and intertwined in *Going After Cacciato*, the author establishes roughly equivalent time relationships in this novel. Similar to the present time in the observation-post chapters of *Cacciato*, the narrator's commentary, constituting separate chapters or appearing within other chapters, represents the present time in *Things*. Yet unlike the fixed present time in the observation-post chapters, which is restricted to a six-hour period, the sections and passages in *Things* devoted to present-time commentary range over an imprecise period during the fictional narrator's 43rd year of life. During this time, Tim O'Brien assesses his life up to this point; he considers his current state of mind ("I feel guilty sometimes. Forty-three years old and I'm still writing war stories": *Things*). He comments on the stories he is about to tell ("This is one story I've never told before": *Things*) and analyzes the purposes and nature of stories ("By telling stories, you objectify your own experience. You separate it from yourself. You pin down certain truths": *Things*). . . .

Source: Tobey C. Herzog, "A Soldier's Heart and Mind: *Going after Cacciato* and *The Things They Carried*," in *Tim O'Brien*, Twayne, 1997, pp. 109–12.

Steven Kaplan

In the following excerpt, Kaplan examines O'Brien's narrative strategy.

. . . However, when Rat Kiley tells a story in another chapter the reader is warned that he "swore up and down to its truth, although in the end, I'll admit, that doesn't amount to much of a warranty. Among the men in Alpha Company, Rat had a reputation for exaggeration and overstatement, a compulsion to rev up the facts, and for most of us it was normal procedure to discount sixty or seventy percent of anything he had to say."

Rat Kiley is an unreliable narrator, and his facts are always distorted, but this does not affect storytelling truth as far as O'Brien is concerned. The above passage on Rat Kiley's credibility as a storyteller concludes with the statement that "It wasn't a question of deceit. Just the opposite: he

FOLLOWING THE NARRATIVE TECHNIQUE OF THIS BOOK, A STORY'S TRUTH IS CLEARLY NOT SOMETHING THAT CAN BE DISTINGUISHED OR SEPARATED FROM A STORY, AND THE VERACITY OR FALSENESS OF A STORY CANNOT BE DETERMINED FROM A PERSPECTIVE OUTSIDE THE STORY."

wanted to heat up the truth, to make it burn so hot that you would feel exactly what he felt." This summarizes O'Brien's often confusing narrative strategy in *The Things They Carried*: the facts about what actually happened, or whether anything happened at all, are not important. They cannot be important because they themselves are too uncertain, too lost in a world in which certainty has vanished somewhere between the "crazy and almost crazy." The important thing is that any story about the war, any "true war story," must "burn so hot" when it is told that it becomes alive for the listener/reader in the act of its telling.

In Rat Kiley's story about how he wrote to Curt Lemon's sister, for example, the details the reader is initially given are exaggerated to the point where, in keeping with O'Brien's fire metaphor, they begin to heat up. Curt Lemon, according to O'Brien, "would always volunteer for stuff nobody else would volunteer for in a million years." And once Lemon went fishing with a crate of hand grenades, "the funniest thing in world history . . . about twenty zillion dead gook fish." But the story does not get so hot that it burns, it does not become so "incredibly sad and true," as O'Brien puts it, until Rat tells the reader at the story's close that "I write this beautiful . . . letter, I slave over it, and what happens? The dumb cooze never writes back." It is these words and not the facts that come before them that make the story true for O'Brien. These words make a reader *feel* Rat's loss and his anger.

At the beginning of this chapter, O'Brien asks his readers several times to "Listen to Rat," to listen more to how he says things than to what he is saying. And of all of the words that stand out in his story, it is the word "cooze" that

makes his story come alive. "You can tell a true war story by its absolute and uncompromising allegiance to obscenity and evil." This is just one of the many ways O'Brien gives for determining what constitutes a true war story in an unending list of possibilities that includes reacting to a story with the ambiguous words "Oh" and "There it is." Like these two phrases, Rat Kiley's word "cooze" is an attempt in an unending sequence of attempts to utter some truth about the Vietnam experience and, by extension, about war in general. There is no simplistic moral to be derived from this word, such as that war is obscene or corrupt. "A true war story is never moral. It does not instruct." There is simply the very real and true fact that the closest thing to certainty and truth in a war story as in life is a vague utterance, a punch at the darkness, an attempt to momentarily rip through the veil that repeatedly returns and covers the reality and truth of what actually happened.

It is thus no coincidence that right in the middle of this chapter on writing a true war story, O'Brien says that the main thing he can remember from the short time encompassing Lemon's death, "Even now, at this instant," is Mitchell Sanders's "yo-yo." This toy can be seen as a metaphor for the playful act of narration that O'Brien practices in this book, a game that he plays by necessity. The only real way to tell a true war story, according to O'Brien, is to keep telling it "one more time, patiently, adding and subtracting, making up a few things to get at the real truth," which is ultimately impossible because the real truth, the full truth, as the events themselves, are lost forever in "a great ghostly fog, thick and permanent." The only way to "tell a true war story" is "if you just keep on telling it" because "Absolute occurrence is irrelevant."

"How to Tell a True War Story" ends with the narrator's finally telling how he and Dave Jensen were ordered to climb up into a tree and remove the parts of Curt Lemon's body: "I remember the white bone of an arm. I remember pieces of skin and something wet and yellow that must've been the intestines." He makes six attempts to tell this story before he can finally confront the "truth" as opposed to the mere facts of this story, and the "truth" of the story is that which speaks to a person's heart and stomach: "But what wakes me up twenty years later is Dave Jensen singing 'Lemon Tree' as we threw down the parts." Important in this story, as in all of the stories in the book, is not *what* happened, but what *might have happened.*

Following the narrative technique of this book, a story's truth is clearly not something that can be distinguished or separated from a story, and the veracity or falseness of a story cannot be determined from a perspective outside the story. As Geoffrey Hartman says regarding poetry, "To keep a poem in mind is to keep it there, not to resolve it into available meanings." Similarly, for O'Brien it is not the fact that a story actually happened that makes it true and worth remembering, any more than the story itself can be said to contain a final truth. The important thing is that a story becomes so much a part of the present that "there is nothing to remember except the story." This is why O'Brien's narrator feels compelled to tell and then retell many variations of the same story over and over and over again. This is also why he introduces each new version of a story with such prefatory comments as "This one does it for me. I have told it before many times, many versions but here is what actually happened." What actually happened, the story's truth, is contained in the way the story is told and in how it makes a reader feel—it must take a person beyond the mere facts. A story is true when it entertains, "but entertain in the highest way, entertain your brain and your stomach, and your heart, and your erotic zones, and make you laugh."

There is nothing new in what O'Brien demonstrates here about trying to tell war stories— that the "truths" they contain "are contradictory," elusive, and thus indeterminate. Two hundred years ago, Goethe also reflected on the same inevitable contradictions that arise when one speaks of what happened or might have happened in battle, when he tried to depict the senseless bloodshed during the allied invasion of revolutionary France in his autobiographical book *Campaign in France*; and, of course, Homer's *Iliad* is the primal statement on the contradictions inherent in war. However, what is new in O'Brien's approach to depicting war in *The Things They Carried* is that he makes the axiom that in war "Almost everything is true. Almost nothing is true" the basis for the act of telling a war story.

The narrative strategy that O'Brien uses in this book to portray the uncertainty of what happened in Vietnam is not restricted to depicting war, and O'Brien does not limit it to the war alone. *The Things They Carried* opens, as it closes, with a love story. The book also ends as it begins: with a man thinking of someone he loved in the past. Besides these two women, the reader is also introduced to the Sweetheart of the Song Tra Bong, who is idealized and worshiped as are Martha in the first chapter and Linda in the last. There is also Henry Dobbin's girlfriend, whose nylon stocking continues to protect him even after he learns she has dumped him. In each of these instances, the reader is shown someone conjuring up memories of a person from the past and then telling themselves stories about that person. Moreover, the stories remembered and told in the chapters just mentioned are remembered and told *precisely* to make the present and future bearable and even possible. Storytelling, in short, becomes a means for survival in this book, much as it is in *Going After Cacciato*. When O'Brien tells the story of the death of Curt Lemon, for example, he informs his readers that this story "wasn't a war story. It was a love story." As I said above, there are several other love stories in this book, and I would even argue that this entire book can be seen as a love story. It is O'Brien's expression of his love of storytelling as an act that can wrestle tolerable and meaningful truths from even the most horrible events.

O'Brien concludes his book with a chapter titled "The Lives of the Dead," in which he moves from Vietnam back to when he was nine years old. On the surface, the book's last chapter describes O'Brien's first date, with his first love, a girl named Linda who died of a brain tumor a few months after he had taken her to see the movie "The Man Who Never Was." What this chapter is really about, however, as its title suggests, is how the dead (which can also include people who may never have actually existed) can be given life in a work of fiction. In a story, O'Brien says, "memory and imagination and language combine to make spirits in the head. There is the illusion of aliveness." Like the man who never was in the film of that title, the people that never were except in memories and the imagination can become real or alive, if only for a moment, through the act of storytelling.

When you tell a story, according to O'Brien, "you objectify your own experience. You separate it from yourself." And by doing this, you can externalize "a swirl of memories that might otherwise have ended in paralysis or worse." The storyteller does not, however, just escape from the events and people in a story by placing them on paper. The act of telling a given story is an ongoing and never-ending process. By constantly involving and then reinvolving the reader in the task of determining what "actually" happened in a given situation, in a story, and by forcing the reader to experience the impossibility of ever really knowing with any certainty what actually happened, O'Brien liberates himself from the lonesome responsibility of remembering and trying to understand events. He creates instead a community of individuals immersed in the act of experiencing the uncertainty of all events, regardless of whether these events occurred in Vietnam, in a small town in Minnesota, or somewhere in the leader's own life.

O'Brien thus saves himself, as he says in the last sentence of his book, from the fate of his character, Norman Bowker, who eventually kills himself in a chapter called "Speaking of Courage," because he cannot find some lasting meaning in the horrible things he experienced in Vietnam. O'Brien saves himself in that he demonstrates through the narrative strategy of this book that the most important thing is to be able to recognize and accept the fact that events have no fixed or final meaning and that the only meaning events can have at all is one which momentarily emerges, then shifts and changes each new time they come alive when they are being remembered and portrayed in stories. . . .

Source: Steven Kaplan, "*The Things They Carried*," in *Understanding Tim O'Brien*, University of South Carolina Press, 1995, pp. 181–88.

"The Iraq War (Timeline)," Council on Foreign Relations, http://www.cfr.org/iraq/timeline-iraq-war/p18876 (accessed September 3, 2015).

O'Brien, Tim, "Sweetheart of the Song Tra Bong," in *The Things They Carried*, Houghton Mifflin, 1990 pp. 85–110.

Passaro, Vince, "Book Review: *The Things They Carried*," in *Harper's Magazine*, Vol. 299, No. 1791, August 1999, p. 80.

"Persian Gulf War," in *UXL Encyclopedia of U.S. History*, edited by Sonia Benson, Daniel E. Brannen Jr., and Rebecca Valentine, UXL, 2009, pp. 1217–22.

Smiley, Pamela, "The Role of the Ideal (Female) Reader in Tim O'Brien's *The Things They Carried*: Why Should Real Women Play?," in *Massachusetts Review*, Vol. 43, No. 4, Winter 2002, pp. 602–13.

Smith, Lorrie N., "'The Things Men Do': The Gendered Subtext in Tim O'Brien's *Esquire* Stories," in *Critique*, Vol. 36, No. 1, Fall 1994, pp. 16–40.

Steinberg, Sybil, "Book Review: *The Things They Carried*," in *Publishers Weekly*, Vol. 237, No. 4, January 26, 1990, p. 404.

"The United States and Its Allies Prepare for War," in *War in the Persian Gulf Reference Library*, edited by Laurie Collier Hillstrom and Julie Carnagie, UXL, 2004, pp. 37–51.

"Vietnam War Statistics and Exclusive Photos," Veteran's Hour website, http://www.veteranshour.com/vietnam_war_statistics.htm (accessed September 3, 2015).

Villahermosa, Gilberto, "Women in Military Service," in *Dictionary of American History*, edited by Stanley I. Kutler, Scribner's, 2003, pp. 502–505.

SOURCES

Bruckner, D. J. R., "Storyteller for a War That Won't End," in *New York Times*, April 3, 1990, p. C15.

Chen, Tina, "'Unraveling the Deeper Meaning': Exile and the Embodied Poetics of Displacement in Tim O'Brien's *The Things They Carried*," in *Contemporary Literature*, Vol. 39, No. 1, Spring 1998, pp. 77–97.

Eder, Richard, "Has He Forgotten Anything?," in *Los Angeles Times Book Review*, April 1, 1990, p. 3.

Epolito, Jennifer, "Have You Read?," in *Bookmarks*, July–August 2011, p. 8.

Farrell, Susan, "Tim O'Brien and Gender: A Defense of *The Things They Carried*," in *CEA Critic*, Vol. 66, No. 1, Fall 2003, pp. 1–21.

Harris, Robert, "Too Embarrassed Not to Kill," in *New York Times Book Review*, March 11, 1990, p. 8.

FURTHER READING

Bennett, William, *America: The Last Best Hope*, Vol. 3, *From the Collapse of Communism to the Rise of Radical Islam*, Thomas Nelson, 2011.

Conservative author Bennett reviews American history from the decline of communism in the late 1980s to the present threat of radical Islam. Bennett considers how these major ideologies have factored into American history and politics.

Downs, Frederick, *The Killing Zone: My Life in the Vietnam War*, W. W. Norton, 1978.

Regarded by many as one of the best accounts of combat life in the Vietnam War, *The Killing Zone* recounts Downs's personal experiences during the war. In addition to describing the intensity of fear and hope, he includes postwar accounts of what happened to the men in his platoon.

Grossman, Dave, and Loren W. Christensen, *On Combat: The Psychology and Physiology of Deadly Conflict in War and in Peace*, Warrior Science Publications, 2004.
Grossman and Christensen review the history and evolution of war as they present research about the impact of wartime experiences on people's bodies and minds. It is at times practical, discussing specific breathing techniques, the importance of debriefing, and the latest information on posttraumatic stress disorder. However, the authors also consider issues like guilt, religion, and justice.

The Vietnam Wars: 50 Years Ago—Two Countries Torn Apart, LIFE, 2014.
LIFE's collection of photographs represents the first time a war was documented in color photography, many of which became famous and even iconic of the war. Here, the magazine compiles photos of the war years, both abroad and at home. The book also includes veteran interviews, a look at Vietnam today, and an essay about the Vietnam Memorial.

SUGGESTED SEARCH TERMS

Vietnam War

Tim O'Brien

Tim O'Brien AND The Things They Carried

Tim O'Brien AND "Sweetheart of the Song Tra Bong"

gender expectations

women in military

stress AND insanity

soldiers becoming savage

PTSD

traditional gender roles

gender roles in America

psychotic break

The Zahir

JORGE LUIS BORGES

1947

The Argentinian poet, short-story writer, and essayist Jorge Luis Borges was one of the greatest writers of the twentieth century and, with perhaps the exception of Cervantes, is acknowledged as the greatest writer in Spanish. "The Zahir" (1947) is among his best stories. It tells the story of a man (also named "Borges") who finds the Zahir, a magical apparition out of the traditional world of Islamic folklore. The man's imagination is being consumed by the Zahir, or by the terrible power of lost and unrequited love, or by the destructive force of modernity sweeping away everything that is dear to a learned bookish scholar, or by all of these or none of these. Just as the "Borges" who labors inside the story as a character can never fully comprehend the enormity of what is happening to him, the reader is carried through a labyrinth of obscure, incomprehensible literature and philosophy that he can never know to be real or fiction, if that distinction does not lose all meaning. "The Zahir" was published in *Collected Fictions* (Viking, 1998).

AUTHOR BIOGRAPHY

Jorge Francisco Isidoro Luis Borges was born in Bueno Aires, the capital of Argentina, on August 24, 1899. His father was a successful lawyer. His maternal grandfather, Isidoro Acevedo, had been

Jose Luis Borges (© *Clement | Getty*)

a military hero of the Argentine War of Independence. His maternal grandmother was English, and by tradition the family was fully bilingual in English and Spanish. (Borges was known to his intimates as *Georgie*.) At the age of nine, Borges translated and published Oscar Wilde's fairy tale *The Happy Prince*. Severely myopic, the young Borges immersed himself in his father's huge library of Spanish and English books.

The family stayed in Switzerland during World War I, in part because of civil unrest in Argentina. Borges attended the Collège de Genève, where the language of instruction was French. He never attended university but taught himself many additional languages, including Old English and Old Norse. In the 1920s, Borges began publishing poetry, at first in surrealist journals, but he never made formal ties to that movement. Throughout the 1920s, he published poetry, essays, and eventually short stories in the leading Argentinian literary journals and moved in the main literary and intellectual circles of the country. He published his first story collection, *A Universal History of Infamy*, in 1935. Borges never attempted a novel or epic poem because his worsening eyesight made shorter forms more convenient for him. Only in 1938 did he take an actual job, as an assistant librarian at a branch library in the Buenos Aires suburbs. He genuinely loved cataloging new books and had several free hours each day at work to write.

At a Christmas Eve party in 1938, Borges suffered a severe head injury that would become the basis of "The South," his favorite among his own stories with its fantasy of a librarian thrust into a

world of macho gaucho heroism. The story was included in his 1941 collection, *The Garden of Forking Paths*, whose title story describes what is now known as a hypertext novel, one whose text can be read in any order to create different narratives.

In 1946, the fascist Juan Perón became the dictator of Argentina. Borges had outspokenly criticized fascism during the war, so he was removed from his government library job. In fact, Perón made a point of publicly humiliating Borges by offering to let him transfer to a job at a higher pay grade inspecting chicken and rabbit carcasses in the Buenos Aires meat market. In 1949, Borges published *The Aleph*, whose title story and its companion, "The Zahir," are often thought by critics to be among his best work. Perón was deposed by a military coup in 1955, and Borges was immediately made director of the National Library. He was also made a professor at the University of Buenos Aires. It was widely expected that Borges would win the Nobel Prize in Literature, but he never did. He used to joke that not giving him the Nobel Prize was the national pastime of Sweden.

As his eyesight failed and his international fame grew, Borges devoted the last decades of his life to lecturing in Europe and North America. Borges lived with his mother until she died at age ninety-nine, largely because he increasingly needed her to read to him. He was infamous for the number of affairs he had; however, his mother pushed him into a marriage because she wanted him to have a caretaker, but this quickly failed. After his mother's death, his assistant, María Kodama, came to cover his mother's role, and they were married eight weeks before Borges's death from liver cancer on June 14, 1986, in Geneva, controversially giving her control over Borges's literary estate.

PLOT SUMMARY

At the time the story is set, the Zahir exists in the form of a twenty-centavo coin. The Zahir is something that has existed in many times and places, always in a different form. Here, as he will in several places in the story, Borges gives a list of brief references. The narrator gives the current date and explains how the Zahir came into his possession. He says, "I am not the man I was then, but I am still able to recall, and perhaps recount, what happened. I am still, albeit only partially, Borges."

"Borges" the narrator turns to the story of Teodelina Villar. She died the day before the character "Borges" saw the Zahir. She was a Buenos Aires socialite and sometime fashion model. Against all expectation, following his unflattering portrayal of her as vain and superficial, "Borges" confesses he was in love with her and naturally attended her funeral. It is in a bar after the funeral that "Borges" receives the Zahir in change after buying a drink. Wandering through the streets drunk after seeing the Zahir, "Borges" is reminded of dozens of different famous coins from history, folklore, and literature. Though he does not realize it at the time, the coin is already started to take over his mind. The first sign of the falseness of the Zahir is the wild idea that money is freedom. When he finally gets home, he dreams he "was a pile of gold coins guarded by a gryphon," a strange mixture of Norse and Greek mythology.

The next day, still feeling obsessed by the coin, he decides he had simply been drunk the night before, so rather than bury the Zahir in his garden or hide it someplace at work, he wanders through the city's subway and eventually goes into another bar and spends the coin on another drink. That night, he sleeps soundly. For a few weeks, he distracts himself by writing a story that adapts the *Nibelungenlied* (the story from Norse myth that provided the basis of both Wagner's Ring operas and Tolkien's *Lord of the Rings*), transformed by retelling it from the point of view of the dragon Fafnir. However, he cannot stop thinking of the coin. He goes to a psychiatrist, complaining to him of insomnia and certain unspecified fixations, but he gets no help.

Finally, from a used bookstore, "Borges" "exhumes a copy of Julius Barlach's *Urkunden zur Geschichte der Zahirsage* (Breslau, 1899)." While just before, "Borges" boasted of the scholarly manner in which he had interpolated different Norse sagas, here Borges invents a book that an unsuspecting reader might take as real and as a source for the present story. The title means "Materials towards a History of the Zahir Legend." The fictional book describes precisely the syndrome from which Borges is suffering, producing a narrative based on a combination of real and fabricated sources (though even the real ones say nothing directly about the Zahir).

Zahir is an Arabic name of God, meaning the "visible" or the "manifest": "in Muslim countries, the masses use the word for 'beings or things which have the terrible power to be unforgettable,

and whose image eventually drives people mad.'" This sentence most fully encapsulates Borges's invention of the Zahir (as opposed to the genuine theological term *zahir*). Borges repeats with greater elaboration the list of the Zahir's manifestations with which the story began: in medieval Shiraz, it was an astrolabe; in the Sind (Pakistan) in the 1830s, it was a tiger; in Java, it was a blind beggar in a mosque; during the Mahdi uprising in Sudan, it was a compass; in the synagogue of Cordoba, it was a vein in a marble pillar; and in Morocco, it was the bottom of a well.

According to the fictional tradition, there is nothing that exists that does not tend to become a Zahir. The mercy of God does not allow more than one to exist at a time, yet there is never a time when there is not a Zahir. Borges adds to the list of Zahirs the idol Yahuk, whose worship the Qur'an (71:23) mentions as having prevented men from boarding the ark in the time of Noah, and al-Moqanna, the veiled prophet. "Borges" reads without comprehension the further prophecy that whoever sees the Zahir will soon see the rose (that is, have a mystical vision of divinity). At least now "Borges" knows that, doomed as he is, he is not at fault for his condition. He is uneasy to find that there is a cryptic Sufi teaching that "the Zahir is the shadow of the Rose and the rending of the Veil."

"Borges" thought it was odd that Teodelina's sister, Julia, was not at her funeral. Now he hears that she is in a mental institution in a state of near catatonia, raving about a coin, just like the chauffeur of Morena Sackmann (another socialite presumably). The narrative does not need to add that these people, too, are victims of the Zahir. Finally, "Borges" resigns himself to the fact that he will meet the same fate and go mad: "I will have to be fed and dressed, I will not know whether it's morning or night, I will not know who the man Borges was." "Borges" reconsiders the Sufi mystical teaching about the Zahir. Perhaps just as the Sufi repeats the names of god to quiet his mind and enter a trance, once his mind has been eaten away from his body by the Zahir, he will find God behind it.

CHARACTERS

Julia Villar Abascal

Julia is Teodelina's sister. She is known to her intimates by the diminutive form of her name, Julita. "Borges" wonders why she is not at her sister's funeral. A few weeks later, he runs into a friend of hers who tells him Julia is in Bosch, a rest home for wealthy neurotics. However, she has become catatonic, unable to do anything except sit in a chair, eat the food nurses spoon-feed her, and gibber about a coin. Clearly she is under the spell of the Zahir, and "Borges" accepts her condition as a vision of his own future.

"Borges"

The character "Borges" is different from the author Borges. The difference is both obvious and impenetrable. In his short story, "Borges and I" (which is often considered more of an essay than a fictional story), the author talks about himself as someone dedicated to investigating the world of obscure literature. He also discusses the other Borges, who has a career traveling around the world writing and lecturing. What the one man says and writes does not seem to have that much to do with what the other one reads. At the same time, the story ends with the confession that the author cannot tell which of them wrote the aforementioned note. So there seem to be at least two Borgeses. Really, however, the "Borges" that can be clipped out of the text of "The Zahir" and several other stories with quotation marks—the "Borges" who is a character—is someone else yet again.

The character "Borges" shares with the author Borges his broad erudition, but "Borges" has loved and lost only one woman, whereas Borges had the same experience with several. "Borges" is destined to be dead or mad by the end of 1948, whereas Borges lived until 1986. One could find many such differences between the real and the fictional. One that is often overlooked is that "Borges" is not going blind; at least he does not mention it. Still, if one wishes to be supplied with the details that Borges the author conspicuously leaves out, such as the age, appearance, general circumstances of life, or anything else of that kind about "Borges" the character, one might reasonably try to supply them from the life of Borges.

"Borges" becomes all too aware that his soul is being eaten alive by the Zahir as it grows to fill his consciousness. He recounts a similar experience that he had, though he does not see the parallel, namely falling in love with Teodelina Villar. "Borges" is a man who will go to any length to get to the bottom of things, to discover their true and hidden nature. Who,

other than such a man, could have found and understood a work like *Urkunden zur Geschichte der Zahirsage*? Teodelina, however, was nothing but surface, nothing but the obvious, so what could have attracted such a man to fall in love with her? "Borges" claims it was obvious and inevitable that he should do so, rather cryptically attributing it to Argentine "snobbery." If Teodelina was not herself the Zahir and his love for her the beginning of his fascination, then his love for her at least shows that he is prone to fall into such a fascination.

Before he realizes what is happening to him, the only way "Borges" can distract himself even a little from the Zahir is through work, suggesting that this is another kind of obsession for him. Once he learns the truth, however, he becomes resigned to his fate. This perhaps is what "Borges" has learned from his research. Resignation and submission (the very meaning of the word *Islam*) is not a modern reaction to a crisis. Modern man would fight until the end, even if the fight is hopeless, but the acceptance of fate is as much a part of Islam as it is of Christianity or even stoicism (an ancient Greek philosophy which taught the control of one's reactions in the face of fortune). "Borges," at least, is able to act authentically as a man of the past. Borges, in contrast, struggles against his growing blindness every step of the way, even when he must have known that he was long past any hope.

Morena Sackmann's Chauffeur

When "Borges" learns of Julia's condition from her anonymous friend, the same informant mentions offhandedly that the chauffeur of Morena Sackmann (who must be another socialite) had been driven mad in precisely the same way, unable to stop talking about a coin. He too is a victim of the Zahir, and from his case "Borges" deduces that he is part of the beginning of an epidemic of those who will lose their minds to the Zahir.

Morena Sackmann

Morena Sackmann does not appear in the story. Her chauffeur is one of the people driven mad by the Zahir's power.

Teodelina Villar

The name *Teodelina* is not an ordinary one. Its roots are certainly Greek, with its first half meaning "god" (*theos*). The second half would seem to derive from *delos*, which means "clear" or "manifest." Therefore, the name is a translation of the Arabic *zahir* as a name of God: God the manifest. Borges was interested in *gematria*, the practice of manufacturing significance by manipulating numbers and letters, so it is probably not a coincidence that the Zahir is a twenty-centavo coin. Also, with a little calculation, one can find that Teodelina was twenty years old when "Borges" fell in love with her. This event took place in 1929, the same year the coin was minted. The letters *N* and *T* and the numeral *2* scratched on the coin doubtless have a similar significance, but their meaning has not so far been penetrated. These parallels would support the suggestion that the fascination of the Zahir has something to do with the love "Borges" feels for Teodelina.

If, as her name suggests, Teodelina is herself the Zahir, the coin is her transformation into a new form. This relates to the pseudo-folklore that all things tend to become the Zahir, but God allows only one thing at a time to do so: once Teodelina dies, the coin is free to become the Zahir. In that case, Borges had merely imagined he loved Teodelina; in fact, he was enchanted by the Zahir in the form of a young woman. It is clear from his description of her that he holds her in contempt, so it seems odd (though by no means impossible) that he would be in love with her in the ordinary way.

In other respects, however, Teodelina seems as if she might be the true first victim of the Zahir. Any young woman might follow fashion, particularly a middle-class young woman with plenty of money and no responsibilities. However, Teodelina followed fashion the same way a rabbi follows the Talmud or the same way a Buddhist monk follows the rules of his temple, except even more precisely and exactingly. For her, the tragedy of World War II had cut her off from *Paris Vogue*. Even when her father's medical practice declines for some reason and she must earn her own money, Teodelina becomes a fashion model, the subject of advertising photography herself (another way, perhaps, in which she can be construed as a Zahir). This kind of behavior—irrational and extravagant in "Borges's" view (in part because of her age, in part because of what he considered its vulgarity)—although it is presented as the ideal in a universe of advertising and marketing, could be explained within the logic of the narrative if her will were already fascinated by the Zahir, as if fashion, meaning the commercial

nature of the coin, possessed her. However, the diminution of the money available to her to waste on extravagance was finally too much for her and so she died, unable to bear living without the ability to buy haute couture. "Borges" allows that Teodelina was very beautiful, but only from certain angles or in a certain light. At her funeral,

> Teodelina Villar magically became what she had been twenty years before; her features recovered the authority that arrogance, money, youth, the awareness of being the *crème de la crème*, restrictions, a lack of imagination, and stolidity can give.

She was restored to the beauty, such as it was, that she had at the time "Borges" fell in love with her, or perhaps before "Borges" fell in love with her; she was restored to the beauty she had before the Zahir came into existence (it bore the date 1929). One way to read this passage is that, finally freed from the Zahir by death, her body reverted to its natural state from the time before her fascination.

<hr>

THEMES

Fantasy Fiction

In the afterword to *The Aleph*, Borges tells his readers that the stories in the collection, including "The Zahir," belong to the genre of fantasy. He does not, for many reasons, mean modern genre fantasy. A reading of what "The Zahir" would be if it were modern genre fantasy is offered by Gene H. Bell-Villada in his 1999 work *Borges and His Fiction: A Guide to His Mind and Art*, and it bears little resemblance to what the story means. Bell-Villada points out how Borges "dreams up an elusive Islamic icon, a bit of underground popular necromancy that serves to infuse this narrative of mental derangement—hardly a new subject—with a freshly magical, oriental aura." He thinks "The Zahir" is interesting to the public because Borges included some pseudointellectual occultism. Borges is proudly claimed for this kind of fantasy literature by *The Encyclopedia of Fantasy*, a reference work devoted to the genre.

However, Borges's statement that "The Zahir" is a fantasy story is far more complicated. In the 1940s, the phrase *fantasy literature* had two meanings. One was indeed the kind of literature being published in the American pulp magazines by authors like H. P. Lovecraft or Robert E. Howard. The other usage, however, refers to

TOPICS FOR FURTHER STUDY

- Much of Borges's work, including "The Zahir," was originally translated into English by Norman Thomas di Giovanni, working closely with Borges himself, who was fully fluent in English. After his death, Borges's wife, María Kodama, refused to allow these translations to be republished but commissioned an entirely new translation of Borges's fiction by Andrew Hurley. Some suggest her reasons were cynical, because di Giovanni's contracts with Borges allowed him an unusually high royalty on sales. Make a presentation to your class comparing the two translations on points of style and aesthetics. If you can read Spanish yourself, you can also offer comparisons with Borges's original texts.

- Imagine that the Zahir is a real object. In the 1940s in Argentina, the Zahir took the form of a twenty-centavo coin. In earlier times in other places, it was a tiger or an astrolabe or a vein of marble in a column in a mosque; it could be a person as well. There is no rational principle linking those items together. Use the Internet to research what form the Zahir takes today. "Zahir" will be useless as a search term. Instead, your imagination and chance must guide you to the Zahir (as they did Borges). Use a combination of text searches, image searches, book searches, and paths through hyperlinks. Your goal in looking for something that does not exist is to let the random create meaning. Create a PowerPoint presentation outlining your findings and share it with your class.

- Select one of Borges's lists of literary and historical references from "The Zahir." For example, you could use the list of past forms of the Zahir, the list of coins or the list of sources that discuss the Zahir. Fully annotate the list, giving the literary source to which Borges is referring and explaining the context or information about the original. Also, suggest the reason Borges might have included it. For instance, the alms begged for by Belisarius refers to an actual historical person, the Byzantine general Belisarius, who reconquered much of Italy for the Byzantine Empire in the sixth century. According to legend, he eventually fell into disfavor with the emperor Justinian, who had him blinded and forced to stand on the streets of Rome as a beggar. Although the story has older sources, Borges is probably thinking of Jean-François Marmontel's influential 1767 *Bélisaire*, which incorporates the episode and inspired several paintings on the theme. Philosophers took up the story as a symbol of the tyrants of the despotic monarchies of their own day. Borges may well have been attracted to the story because of the theme of blindness and also as a symbol for the tyranny of Perón in Argentina. Consider this an outline, and go into as much detail as possible for each item in your actual paper.

- *Kalilah and Dimnah Stories for Young Adults* (2000), by Muhammad Nur Abdus Salam, is a collection of stories from the *Mathnawi* of the Sufi poet Rumi, adapted for younger readers. Write a report of some of these stories that compares their use of allegory with Borges's in "The Zahir."

---

literature derived from mythological folk traditions, such as collections of fairy tales, for example the colored fairy books of Andrew Lang, of which Borges was a known devotee. It is undoubtedly his engagement with mythology to which Borges refers. In "The Zahir" itself,

"Borges" says: "Until the end of June I distracted myself by composing a tale of fantasy." What he wrote was a retelling of the *Niebelungenlied* (the Norse myth in which Sigurd slays the dragon Fafnir) from the point of view of Fafnir (compare Borges's "The House of Asterion" in *The Aleph*,

The Zahir is a coin that has been enchanted or cursed. (© Sementer / Shutterstock)

which retells the myth of Theseus from the viewpoint of the Minotaur). Therefore we can conclude that what Borges has in mind when he refers to fantasy is the revisiting and transformation of myth.

Sufism

Borges says, "In Arabic, 'zahir' means visible, manifest, evident; in that sense, it is one of the ninety-nine names of God." This is true, as far as it goes. In the work of ninth-century Sufi theologian Sahl At-Tustari (whose work is accessible in the monograph of Gerhard Böwering, *The Mystical Vision of Existence in Classical Islam*), the term *zahir* (which most literally means "back," "outside," or "surface") is used in interpretation of the Qur'an. Islamic philosophy incorporated many elements of Greek Neoplatonic theology, including its framework for interpreting texts.

In Neoplatonic thought, a sacred text (which for Islam means principally the Qur'an), has three levels of meaning. The first is the simple meaning to be derived from the text without interpretation. In Arabic, this is called the *zahir*; it is one of the names of God because it is one of the means through which God reveals himself. However, a text also has a moral meaning, which can found by interpreting the text allegorically, as a metaphor or some other way of reading the words of the text in a nonliteral fashion; Islam usually divides this into separate moral and legal senses. The third sense is also found by allegory and reveals a secret meaning relating to philosophy or mysticism that cannot be fully understood by the human mind and that can be known only to the adept and is called *batin* ("the hidden") in distinction to the *zahir*. Judaism and Christianity also adopted this kind of Neoplatonic allegorical interpretation of their own sacred texts. In addition, in Islam, the term *zahir* can be used to describe a hypocrite, someone who puts on an outward show of being a Muslim but does not truly embrace Islam in his heart.

Luce López-Baralt, in her article in *The Cambridge Companion to Jorge Luis Borges*, places Borges's Zahir in its Sufi context. Even for the mystic, the *zahir* or literal meaning of the text is not to be discounted. *Zahir* is the ninety-ninth name of God, whereas the hundredth name cannot be comprehended by the conscious mind. When the last name (the *batin*) is finally grasped in some more subtle way, the mystic receives the vision of God. In order to cultivate the vision, the mystic chants the ninety-nine names over and over until he discovers the one hundredth, so although the *zahir* is the opposite of the *batin*, it is the *zahir* that leads to the *batin*.

It is not a coincidence that "Borges" receives the Zahir in change after buying a drink, when he is drunk, because intoxication is a frequent Sufi metaphor for mystical ecstasy. This was well known from the Sufi poetry that Borges had read extensively and that he quotes in "The Zahir," citing: "Attar's *Asrar Nama* ('The Book of Things Unknown'): 'the Zahir is the shadow of the Rose and the rending of the Veil.'" The rose is a Sufi symbol for the presence of god, and the veil is the thing that separates the *zahir* from the *batin* and that must be torn to enable perception of the mystical vision. The two sides of the veil are separate like the faces of a coin, but they must be joined into a single perception to fully perceive God and the universe.

Although there is no Islamic folklore of a magical object that drives mad everyone who sees it, filling their imaginations with its own image, Borges is creating his fantasy within a well-informed Sufi context. Borges's work often describes a metamorphosis, and he transforms the theological *zahir* into his fictional Zahir.

STYLE

Metafiction

Metafiction is an emerging category of postmodern literary criticism whose scope and definition are far from clear. Metafictional characteristics present in "The Zahir" include the story's structure as a conversational confession and its frequent references to real historical sources to supply its background, as if to imply the work itself is part of reality. Another metafictional trait is Borges's creation of false historical sources, as if the historical world and the fictive world of the narrative were indistinguishable. In other words, one tendency of the story is to promote the willing suspension of disbelief, to make the story seem real, but another is to suggest that the reader is reading something other than a story (a memoir or a letter) whose form breaks down the boundary between narrative and reality. The overall effect is to make the reader conscious of disentangling the text woven by Borges. That consciousness of reading fiction, the disbelief that cannot be suspended, is at least one effect that metafiction aims to provoke.

All throughout the story, there are dozens of examples of Borges playing with his sources, but two instances stand out. In his survey of sources of the Zahir, "Borges" mentions Philip Meadows Taylor's 1839 novel *Confessions of a Thug*. Although Borges admits Taylor's work is a novel, he uses it as if it were a historical document. Borges lends realism to his account with a pseudoscholarly footnote in which he mentions that Taylor spells the word as *Zaheer* (which he

would have done, given the spelling conventions of the time). Taylor supposedly heard of a whole population in Gujarat (in modern-day Pakistan) that had seen the Zahir in the form of a tiger and years later tracked down the prison cell where one of them had died after covering the floor and walls of his cell with a map of the world in the form of

> a drawing . . . of an infinite tiger. It was a tiger composed of many tigers, in the most dizzying of ways; it was crisscrossed with tigers, striped with tigers, and contained seas and Himalayas and armies that resembled other tigers.

This, of course, plays on Borges's well-known fascination with tigers. However, scholars have found that Taylor's novel mentions no Zahir and has no such description of a tiger-covered cell. It is easy to dismiss the reference, then, merely as Borges's attempt to add orientalist color to his narrative, but Taylor does describe a scene in which a suspected thug (a murderous highway bandit) is being interrogated by an official in the courtyard of a palace before a crowd. The magistrate tells the thug that unless he confesses, he will die when a shadow on the ground reaches a certain spot: "There was not an eye in the crowd that was not fixed on the advancing shadow, barely a hand's breadth of light remained, and the Thug gazed on it as though he were fascinated by the eye of a tiger." Could Borges be telling the reader that his imagination transformed what he read in Taylor into what he wrote in "The Zahir"?

A source that Borges, in the postscript to *The Aleph* volume, cites as a source for the Zahir, as well as the Aleph, is H. G. Wells's 1897 short story "The Crystal Egg." In this text, an antique dealer comes into possession of an egg-shaped crystal with strange properties. If a viewer with the right temperament looks into the crystal, he can see a strange landscape and at times even strange animals moving in it. It soon becomes apparent that the viewer is seeing a live transmission from the planet Mars. This egg and many more like it were scattered over the earth by the Martians, and just as the antique dealer can see Mars in the egg, a Martian looking at a connected egg on Mars could see the earth. It was a form of intelligence gathering before the invasion. An imperceptive reader could read this text and think that Borges was pulling his leg, because the egg does not provide any kind of mystical vision like a Zahir or an Aleph but is instead a technological device more like a drone-mounted television camera. Yet Borges must have read the story as a boy and in the intervening decades found inspiration in it for both the Aleph and the Zahir. In both cases, someone, either the reader or the author, cannot tell the difference between the real and fictional.

Magic Realism

Seymour Menton, writing in *Hispanic Review* in 1982, offers a standard definition of magic realism: "The Magic Realist painting or short story or novel is predominantly realistic and deals with the object of our daily life, but contains an unexpected or improbable element that creates a strange effect leaving the viewer or reader somewhat bewildered or amazed." Under this definition, he classifies Borges's works (and he makes mention specifically of "The Zahir") as magic realism, a not uncommon judgment among scholars. However, Menton adds this specification: "Magic Realism, involved as it is with the improbable rather than the impossible, never deals with the supernatural." This is problematic from a number of viewpoints. In the first instance, the Zahir as Borges describes it is an undeniably supernatural object. One can interpret the Zahir allegorically, but that cannot alter the fact that in its own terms the Zahir is part of a magical existence removed from everyday life: its power erupts into reality.

Menton's denial of magic in Borges's fictions may be related to another comment: "Indian and African cultures have made Latin America a continent or world of magic." Menton may be implying that magic is somehow intrinsically not Spanish and therefore not worth considering in the case of Borges. While it is undeniable that indigenous and African traditions played an important role in shaping the tradition of magic in the Americas, Borges does not specifically refer to them, instead drawing the magical elements in his fictions from the ancient traditions of magic, religion, and philosophy expressed variously in Christianity, Judaism, and Islam. Also, the superstructure of Latin American magic was decidedly European in character. Spain participated in the international magical culture of the Renaissance and exported this form of magic into its colonial empire, where it combined with other magical traditions. This phenomenon of combination was recognized by the inquisitors, whose task it was to police such deviant magical practices.

Borges is perfectly capable of speaking about the role he sees for magic in his own work. In his essay "Narrative Art and Magic," which is a criticism of the novel as a genre, Borges suggests that the difference between the real world of daily experience and the fictional world of the novel is that in the fictional world, magic is operative. He means magic in the sense of everything in nature having a cause based on the occult sympathies that connect together a certain root, a constellation, and an organ of the human body, sympathies that the magician can manipulate to cure disease or to curse. In a work of fiction, everything happens for a reason: nothing comes to be by chance, and nothing comes into being without a purpose. However tenuous and unlikely, there is a clear though invisible chain connecting the characters and events of the story. These occult networks are manipulated and controlled by the author as the magician—or even the god—of the fictional world.

HISTORICAL CONTEXT

Philip Meadows Taylor

In "The Zahir," Borges alludes to a wide range of historical persons and circumstances, real as well as invented. Any of these references would repay further study, because Borges had their full symbolic resonance in mind when he invoked them. One of the authors he cites most extensively is Meadows Taylor. Borges says that he drew on Taylor's novel *Confessions of a Thug* for the account of the Zahir in the form of a tiger, although the text in question contains at most the embryo of that idea and does not mention the "Zaheer" at all. Although Borges was obviously familiar directly with Taylor's work, "Borges" knows it only at secondhand, through the report in the *Urkunden zur Geschichte der Zahirsage*. This source calls Taylor's book a "report" or an "account" as if it were not a fictional work (and why should it be in another fictional work?).

In addition to *Confessions of a Thug*, Taylor also wrote an autobiography, *The Story of My Life*, which his daughter published posthumously in 1882. Raised in poverty in the slums of Manchester, Taylor sailed to India when he was fifteen years old. On the single qualification of being English, he was hired by the Nizam of Hyderabad, the ruler of a princely state (meaning that he had accepted British colonial rule peacefully in exchange for being allowed to keep his lands). Taylor proved adept at learning the languages spoken in the area and soon was given more and

COMPARE & CONTRAST

- **1940s:** Argentina is governed a fascist dictatorship under Juan Péron.

  Today: Argentina is governed by a constitution closely modeled on that of the United States.

- **1940s:** The only way that Borges can accomplish his remarkably wide range of reading is through learning the incredible number of languages that he mastered.

  Today: A major achievement of scholarship over the past fifty years has been to translate many obscure works of religious or esoteric literature out of little-known languages, especially into English. There are still many works awaiting translation (including, Farid al-din Attar's *Asrar Nama*), but texts are far more widely available than in Borges's day.

- **1940s:** The new interconnections of language and ideas that are possible with globally networked computing as yet only exist as a hypothesis.

  Today: The Internet, connected by hyperlinks, is an indispensable tool of work and research.

more important posts. He also began to write a series of successful novels, of which *Confessions of a Thug* was the first. He eventually became the governor of the so-called Ceded Districts, an area in Southern India with a population of five million people at the time. The Thugs, the subject of Taylor's novel, were a secret society of highwaymen operating in India, with a system of occult practices in combination with swift recourse to bloody violence, exactly the kind of institution that would attract Borges's interest.

The Veiled Prophet

The veiled prophet was a favorite figure of Borges and appears in several of his stories (especially "Hakim, the Masked Dyer of Merv"). Borges spells his name "al-Moqanna"; today, it is more regularly spelled "al-Muqanna." The story of the veiled prophet really begins with Abu Muslim, who was the military commander for the Abbasid dynasty when they overthrew the Umayyad Caliphate. Al-Muqanna went from an early life as a tailor to become a soldier for Abu Muslim and eventually one of his generals. Both men came from Khorasan, an area today split between northeastern Iran and southern Turkmenistan. After Abu Muslim had installed As-Saffah as Caliph, the new ruler, who was not a military man himself, felt Abu Muslim was a threat to his own position and had him assassinated in 755. In response, al-Muqanna led a revolt in Khorasan.

Prior to this, Islamic armies had quickly conquered the whole of the Iranian cultural world, but many Iranian populations still had not converted by the eighth century, and many Zoroastrian religious beliefs had been incorporated into sectarian Islam. For example, Shia Islam transformed a Persian myth about the return of the Prophet Zoroaster into a new conception of the Mahdi. For Shias, the Mahdi is alive somewhere in the world and will reveal himself at the end of time. The Mahdi will cooperate with Jesus, who will return from heaven, to defeat the Antichrist before the last judgment.

Al-Muqanna let it be known that Abu Muslim was the Mahdi and would soon return to overthrow the corrupt Abbasid Caliphate. Al-Muqanna dressed his troops in white uniforms to make them distinct from the Abbasids in their black clothing and inspired his troops with displays of miracles. He also incorporated many more explicitly Iranian religious elements into his version of Islam. He began to wear a veil, saying that his face had to be covered to hide the light that shone from it as it had shone from the face of Moses, while Abbasid propaganda claimed he wore the veil because he was one-eyed

The protagonist manages to get rid of the coin by going to an unfamiliar neighborhood and using it to pay for a drink, but he still cannot put it out of his mind. (© Edler von Rabenstein / Shutterstock)

and badly scarred. Al-Muqanna was eventually defeated and supposedly killed himself rather than be captured, but his sect persisted for five hundred years, with his followers expecting that he and Abu Muslim would finally return.

CRITICAL OVERVIEW

Scholarship on Borges and on "The Zahir" in particular is remarkably extensive, even more so in Spanish than English. However, thanks to the

complexity of the text, very little consensus has been reached. There is not one major or generally accepted interpretation of the story. In looking, then, at a few recent, interesting studies, Gene H. Bell-Villada's *Borges and His Fiction: A Guide to His Mind and Art* is a useful place to start for both his positive and his negative conclusions. Bell-Villada naturally pairs "The Zahir" with "The Aleph" but takes the minority view that the former is aesthetically superior on account of the tightly interwoven density of its prose. He also offers a good case for a Freudian reading of the story (although Borges was anti-Freudian) that the Zahir that eats up the imagination of "Borges" is only a symbol for guilt; unexplained guilt that "Borges" feels about his relationship with Teodelina.

About the main idea of "The Zahir" Bell-Villada says:

> After much library sleuthing and personal interviewing . . . I have concluded that the mystical entity "Zahir" is an invention for Borges. Although the Arabic word does signify "visible" (as he indicates in the story), there appears to be no such occult phenomenon by that name in Islamic lore.

What Bell-Villada says is literally true, but he may not have been asking the most useful questions. He went to the effort of looking up all of the references Borges cites in "The Zahir" and seems surprised that many of them are fictitious. When he does find a source and it makes no mention of the Zahir, Bell-Villada is even more surprised. He does not seem curious as to why Borges cited the text in that case, instead explaining it away as a method of building oriental color.

The Cambridge Companion to Jorge Luis Borges has two substantial discussions of "The Zahir." The first, by Luce López-Baralt, discusses the Zahir in the context of Islam. The article is, if anything, too informative. An expert on the influence of Islam on Spanish mystical literature, she knows even more on that subject than Borges could have, making it difficult to see in her work where Borges ends and she herself begins. The second, by Robert González Echevarría, treats "The Zahir" in the context of its original publication in *The Aleph*. Echevarría considers that the Zahir, like the Aleph, is merely a delusion of the character "Borges" and sees the stories simply as a chronicle of insanity induced in both cases by the death of the beloved. He does not consider that his reading of the texts as if they obeyed the laws of the real world limits their aesthetic or philosophical interest.

Echevarría rightly sees that the list of forms that the Zahir took in the past (like the things seen in the Aleph) is essentially random, like a free association exercise in psychoanalysis. Its lack of meaning compels the reader to search for a meaning to assign to it. Echevarría makes this shrewd observation:

> It could be imagined that with Borges being such a systematic writer, one could construct a story that is a synthesis of all his stories by using his well-known topics, stock characters, settings, objects, and even words, and that such an exercise would be very much in keeping with his poetics.

Edwin Williamson, in his *Borges: A Life*, suggests several women with whom Borges had affairs that might have been the model for Teodelina (as well as her counterpart in "The Aleph"). He points out that many of the symptoms caused by the Zahir are part of the depression that follows romantic loss: sleeplessness, obsessive memories, and anxiety.

CRITICISM

Bradley A. Skeen

Skeen is a classicist. In the following essay, he examines the significance of the Zahir, considered as an ordinary literary symbol, in Borges's "The Zahir."

Borges's story "The Library of Babel" takes place in a universe that consists of an endless library. It is divided into rooms connected to each other by walkways and ladders and inhabited by a race of librarians. They can wander the library their whole lives and never enter the same chamber twice. The number of books is infinite. They contain every possible combination of letters in all languages and every possible combination of signs that are not letters. The librarians, at least some of them, are convinced that all the books have meaning, if only it could be discovered. This could be a prophecy of the Internet. Borges knew instinctively that the human impulse for knowledge is unlimited and knew the form it would take, if it was not impossible. Borges was extremely well read, and his literary art consisted of joining together the different threads of his reading into new combinations. He assigns new meaning to each verse, each idea, and each passage by juxtaposing it in a new context. It is as if he surfed the web and found meaning in the string of sites visited. The idea of hyperlinking was originally invented to let new meanings be created in just this way, allowing ordinary people to do what Borges could accomplish in his imagination.

One of the threads followed in the research for this article was to look at the *The Life and Death of Jason*, by pre-Raphaelite artist William Morris. Borges mentions this work in one of his essays in a way that suggests it may belong to what he considered the genre of

WHAT DO I READ NEXT?

- Although he does not seem to have been a favorite of Borges, the Sufi mystical poet whose works are the most accessible in English is Jalal al-Din Rumi. Four hundred of his ghazals (out of a corpus of more than three thousand) were translated by A. J. Arberry and published by the University of Chicago Press in 1969 as *Mystical Poems of Rumi*. They were reissued in 2009 with a new commentary by Hasan Javadi.

- *The Book of Imaginary Beings* is a bestiary by Borges, illustrated by Peter Sis. Andrew Hurley's translation was published in 2006. The book is a collection of descriptions of imaginary creatures, including familiar ones such as the dragon (Western and Chinese); more obscure animals such as Buraq, the beast on which Muhammed flew in one night from Mecca to Jerusalem; and the truly esoteric, such as the animal dreamed by Franz Kafka.

- Rumi's great mystical epic poem *Mathnawi* incorporates Persian folklore in a philosophic presentation of Sufism. Several collections adapting selections of these stories for young adults have been made, including *Tales from Rumi*, by Ali Fuat Bilkan (2008), and *Rumi Stories for Young Adults from the Mathnawi* (2000), translated by Muhammad Nur Abdus Salsm.

- *Professor Borges: A Course on English Literature* (translated by Katherine Silver and published in 2014) is a series of lectures surveying English literature in academic fashion from Old English through the close of the nineteenth century, with an emphasis on the first generation of romanticism.

- The Brazilian novelist Paulo Coelho's 2005 novel *The Zahir* concerns a famous novelist's search for his wife after she disappears from their Paris apartment. He realizes that in order to understand why she might have left or where she might be, he must reassess his whole way of life, which has alienated her. He is told, by a friend of his wife's who is schizophrenic, that in order to find her, he must search for his own Zahir. Although the work is admittedly indebted to Borges, the concept of the Zahir has been reinterpreted again.

- *The Book of Fantasy* (1988) is an anthology of fantasy stories collected by Borges, including works by authors such as Oscar Wilde and James Joyce and also genre authors like Ray Bradbury.

---

fantasy. To get to the text of this obscure work, an Internet search was executed using the following search term: William Morris Jason. At first, the terms might seem poorly chosen, because these three common first names might occur in many volumes unrelated to the poem.

However, half of the search results were, in fact, various editions of the poem, and the other half were not random noise: they were mostly individual issues of software and video-game development magazines from the late 1970s: *Softside* or *Transactor*; a small third category were articles from astronomy journals relating to the recent discovery of exo-planets. What could this result possibly mean? It does not mean anything, but the human imagination evolved to see connections and read signs everywhere, to impose meaning and pattern on the world revealed to it by the senses. It is easier to imagine that this simple search unearthed some strange connection between the unconnected results than it is to accept that they have no meaning. Such lists evoke, according to Borges, a "vast, inexplicable importance." In his essay "A Defense of the Kabbalah," Borges concedes that Kabbalistic *gematria* (the practice of making new meaning out of biblical verses by

---

WHY IS THE ZAHIR NOT A DESCRIPTION OF BORGES'S PHYSICAL BLINDNESS?"

rearranging the letters into different words) is nonsense, but he nevertheless finds it important because it allows an infinite expression of human meaning. Creating something new by recombining the old is a common theme for Borges. The various images that the Zahir takes during history, all beloved icons from Borges's world of books, are not linked together in any way in the text: the reader's imagination makes the connections all by itself.

Borges's works have been extensively studied, but their very character had directed research along certain channels. The variety of sources that Borges cites—real as well as fabricated ones—reflect his own vast and unique reading. Simply to get some kind of control over Borges's library is a monumental task to which many articles are devoted. Another approach is to apply expertise in one field, such as Sufi mysticism, to the study of a story like "The Zahir." That can be fruitful, and an expert in a given field may have knowledge and understanding that exceeds Borges's, but that does not necessarily get him any closer to what Borges is doing with Sufism. Precisely because the difficulties in figuring out what Borges is saying are so great, very few critics get as far as asking what Borges means; that is, few critics ask what Borges is using Sufi legends and mysticism to say, the way that one would interrogate any other author.

It is no easy task to understand what the Zahir in the story is and how it fits into the history of philosophy and religion from which Borges fabricates its background. However, Borges came to create it; whatever the obscure references one must track down to understand its history, it is still a literary symbol, something that Borges is using to try to communicate with the reader—even the reader who has not done extensive research. What does the Zahir mean as a literary symbol? What is Borges trying to convey through the Zahir? Some attempts along these lines have been made to interpret the Zahir in a Freudian manner, although Borges was not

a Freudian. According to this kind of reading, the Zahir represents guilt that grows and fills up "Borges's" consciousness. Another similar suggestion makes the Zahir the anguish of lost love.

However, the Zahir seems to have a much more obvious significance than that. Borges always suffered from extreme myopia, leaving the world a few inches beyond his face in a haze. In 1928, he had his first cataract surgery to try to save his deteriorating vision (there would be eventually be seven more) from the same condition that had robbed his father of his sight. By 1955, he would be totally blind. Before that, however, the intermediary effects of the condition would have made his vision still more blurry and produced effects like halos around light sources. If he developed glaucoma, this could result in loss of the periphery of the visual field, allowing him to see only what he looked at directly. In 1947, this is how Borges describes the Zahir coming to dominate "Borges's" visual field:

> First I could see the face of it, then the reverse; now I can see both sides at once. It is not as though the Zahir were made of glass, since one side is not superimposed upon the other— rather, it is as though the vision were itself spherical, with the Zahir rampant in the center. Anything that is not the Zahir comes to me as though through a filter, and from a distance.

Within the year, "Borges" predicts, "I will no longer perceive the universe, I will perceive the Zahir."

Why is the Zahir not a description of Borges's physical blindness? Might it not be that the Zahir, which inexorably fills and removes "Borges's" vision, is a symbol for the literal blindness that is inexorably swallowing up Borges's sight? Might it not be that Borges is simply describing his own inevitable loss of sight, blowing the prospect of his own blindness up to cosmic proportions, which would hardly seem an exaggeration to the one facing it?

If the Zahir might be a reference to Borges's own blindness, what more general meaning does he intend for the reader to understand from it? "Borges" expects that before the end of the year he will be in the same position as Julia, with the Zahir filling his mind as a catatonic in an insane asylum. The Zahir replaces everything else that exists in the mind of its victims, as seen in the artist who saw the Zahir in the form of a tiger and created an image of the world in the form of a tiger, which was itself composed of tigers. Although Borges does not say so outright, he gives clear evidence of what the modern Zahir is composed. It is a coin, of course, but what that entails can be seen from the particular form of insanity it inspired in its first victim (Teodelina), just as in the past it inspired tiger mania. "Borges" does not say that Teodelina was a victim of the Zahir, but then, he does not say directly that Julia was either. She certainly had some mysterious connection to the Zahir, whether she might have seen it, or if she was the Zahir herself. Teodelina

> sought to make every action irreproachably correct, but her task was even more admirable and difficult . . . for the laws of her creed were not eternal, but sensitive to the whims of Paris and Hollywood. . . . She sought the absolute . . . but the absolute in the ephemeral.

As the tigers were painted on the walls of a jail cell for their canvas, Teodelina's canvas was her own body: "She passed through endless metamorphoses, as though fleeing from herself; her coiffure and the color of her hair were famously unstable, as were her smile, her skin, and the slant of her eyes." If these aspects of her life were manifestations of what she saw in the Zahir, then the modern Zahir is composed of mass-produced commercial culture, the kind manufactured by marketing firms and advertising, the kind propagated by Paris and Hollywood. The modern Zahir is the literal, least meaningful, most superficial understanding of the world, the one that is obliterating the profound meaning of moral and mystical truth. Forgetting the meaningful and recalling only the meaningless is the madness of the Zahir, a madness that one can see spreading all too rapidly if one looks at mass culture. When he is first affected by the demonic temptation of the Zahir, "Borges" reflects:

> There is nothing less material than money, since any coin (a twenty-centavo piece, for instance) is, in all truth, a panoply of possible futures. *Money is abstract*, I said over and over, *money is future time*. It can be an evening just outside the city, or a Brahms melody, or maps, or chess, or coffee, or the words of Epictetus, which teach contempt for gold; it is a Proteus more changeable than the Proteus of the isle of Pharos.

"Borges" thinks at first that money, with its infinite possibilities, must be free will. But this is a deceptive trap. It is exactly this limitlessness that will entrance and destroy his mind. Commercial, international culture is coming to supplant the Buenos Aires that Borges knew in his childhood and the old city he knew through his father's memories and through tradition.

This is an experience that everyone has as they age and an experience that civilization has as it drifts further and further from its source into something unpredictable and unrecognizable from what went before. Of course the future is balance. It is also new life, new growth, and new salvation. Borges, for whom tradition is everything, whose life was devoted to old books, can be indulged in looking for a moment on the past's destruction by the future as a catastrophe, as the Zahir.

Source: Bradley A. Skeen, Critical Essay on "The Zahir," in *Short Stories for Students*, Gale, Cengage Learning, 2016.

Jaime Alazraki

In the following essay, Alazraki asserts that Borges has not received his share of critical and popular attention in the United States.

Although he has been writing poems, stories, and critical essays of the highest quality since 1923, the Argentinian writer Jorge Luis Borges is still much better known in Latin America than in the U.S. For the translator of John Peale Bishop, Hart Crane, E. E. Cummings, William Faulkner, Edgar Lee Masters, Robert Penn Warren, and Wallace Stevens, this neglect is somewhat unfair. There are signs, however, that he is being discovered in this country with some of the same enthusiasm that greeted him in France, where he received major critical attention, and has been very well translated. Several volumes of translations in English have recently appeared, including a fine edition of his most recent book *El hacedor* (*Dreamtigers*) and a new edition of *Labryinths*, which first appeared in 1962. American and English critics have called him one of the greatest writers alive today, but have not as yet (so far as I know) made substantial contributions to the interpretation of his work. There are good reasons for this delay. Borges is a complex writer, particularly difficult to place. Commentators cast around in vain for suitable points of comparison and his own avowed literary admirations add to the confusion. Like Kafka and contemporary French existential writers, he is often seen as a moralist, in rebellion against the times. But such an approach is misleading.

It is true that, especially in his earlier works, Borges writes about villains: The collection *History of Infamy* (*Historia universal de la infamia*, 1935) contains an engaging gallery of scoundrels.

The story takes place in Buenos Aires, Argentina. (© *javarman* / *Shutterstock*)

But Borges does not consider infamy primarily as a moral theme; the stories in no way suggest an indictment of society or of human nature or of destiny. Nor do they suggest the lighthearted view of Gide's Nietzschean hero Lafcadio. Instead, infamy functions here as an aesthetic, formal principle. The fictions literally could not have taken shape but for the presence of villainy at their very heart. Many different worlds are conjured up—cotton plantations along the Mississippi, pirate-infested South seas, the Wild West, the slums of New York, Japanese courts, the Arabian desert, etc.—all of which would be shapeless without the ordering presence of a villain at the center.

A good illustration can be taken from the imaginary essays on literary subjects that Borges was writing at the same time as the *History of Infamy*. Borrowing the stylistic conventions of scholarly critical writing, the essays read like a combination of Empson, Paulhan, and PMLA, except that they are a great deal more succinct and devious. In an essay on the translations of *The Thousand and One Nights*, Borges quotes an impressive list of examples showing how translator

after translator mercilessly cut, expanded, distorted, and falsified the original in order to make it conform to his own and his audience's artistic and moral standards. The list, which amounts in fact to a full catalogue of human sins, culminates in the sterling character of Enna Littmann, whose 1923–1928 edition is scrupulously exact: "Incapable, like George Washington, of telling a lie, his work reveals nothing but German candor." This translation is vastly inferior, in Borges's eyes, to all others. It lacks the wealth of literary associations that allows the other, villainous translators to give their language depth, suggestiveness, ambiguity—in a word, style. The artist has to wear the mask of the villain or order to create a style.

So far, so good. All of us know that the poet is of the devil's party and that sin makes for better stories than virtue. It takes some effort to prefer *La nouvelle Héloise* to *Les liaisons dangereuses* or, for that matter, to prefer the second part of the *Nouvelle Héloise* to the first. Borges's theme of infamy could be just another form of *fin-de-siècle* aestheticism, a late gasp of romantic agony. Or, perhaps worse, he might be writing out of moral despair as an escape from the trappings of style.

ONE DOES NOT EXPECT THE SAME KIND OF

PSYCHOLOGICAL INSIGHT OR THE SAME

IMMEDIACY OF PERSONAL EXPERIENCE FROM

CANDIDE AS FROM *MADAME BOVARY*, AND BORGES

SHOULD BE READ WITH EXPECTATIONS CLOSER TO

THOSE ONE BRINGS TO VOLTAIRE'S TALE THAN TO

A NINETEENTH-CENTURY NOVEL."

But such assumptions go against the grain of a writer whose commitment to style remains unshakable; whatever Borges's existential anxieties may be, they have little in common with Sartre's robustly prosaic view of literature, with the earnestness of Camus's moralism, or with the weighty profundity of German existential thought. Rather, they are the consistent expansion of a purely poetic consciousness to its furthest limits.

The stories that make up the bulk of Borges's literary work are not moral fables or parables like Kafka's, to which they are often misleadingly compared, even less attempts at psychological analysis. The least inadequate literary analogy would be with the eighteenth-century *conte philosophique*: their world is the representation, not of an actual experience, but of an intellectual proposition. One does not expect the same kind of psychological insight or the same immediacy of personal experience from *Candide* as from *Madame Bovary*, and Borges should be read with expectations closer to those one brings to Voltaire's tale than to a nineteenth-century novel. He differs, however, from his eighteenth-century antecedents in that the subject of the stories is the creation of style itself; in this Borges is very definitely post-romantic and even post-symbolist. His main characters are prototypes for the writer, and his worlds are prototypes for a highly stylized kind of poetry or fiction. For all their variety of tone and setting, the different stories all have a similar point of departure, a similar structure, a similar climax, and a similar outcome; the inner cogency that links these four moments together constitutes Borges's distinctive style, as well as his comment upon this style. His stories are about the style in which they are written.

At their center, as I have said, always stands an act of infamy. The first story in *Labyrinths*, "Tlön, Uqbar, Orbis Tertius," describes the totally imaginary world of a fictitious planet; this world is first glimpsed in an encyclopedia which is itself a delinquent reprint of the *Britannica*. In "The Shape of the Sword," an ignominious Irishman who, as it turns out, betrayed the man who saved his life, passes himself off for his own victim in order to tell his story in a more interesting way. In "The Garden of the Forking Paths" the hero is a Chinese who, during World War I, spies on the British mostly for the satisfaction of refined labyrinthine dissimulation. All these crimes are misdeeds like plagiarism, impersonation, espionage, in which someone pretends to be what he is not, substitutes a misleading appearance for his actual being. One of the best of his early stories describes the exploits of the religious imposter Hakim, who hides his face behind a mask of gold. Here the symbolic function of the villainous acts stands out very clearly: Hakim was at first a dyer, that is, someone who presents in bright and beautiful colors what was originally drab and gray. In this, he resembles the artist who confers irresistably attractive qualities upon something that does not necessarily possess them.

The creation of beauty thus begins as an act of duplicity. The writer engenders another self that is his mirror-like reversal. In this anti-self, the virtues and the vices of the original are curiously distorted and reversed. Borges describes the process poignantly in a later text called "Borges and I" (it appears in *Labyrinths* and also, in a somewhat better translation, in *Dreamtigers*). Although he is aware of the other Borges's "perverse habit of falsifying and exaggerating," he yields more and more to this poetic mask "who shares [his] preferences, but in a vain way that converts them into the attributes of an actor." This act, by which a man loses himself in the image he has created, is to Borges inseparable from poetic greatness. Cervantes achieved it when he invented and became Don Quixote; Valéry achieved it when he conceived and became Monsieur Teste. The duplicity of the artist, the grandeur as well as the misery of his calling, is a recurrent theme closely linked with the theme of infamy. Perhaps its fullest treatment appears in the story "Pierre Ménard, Author of the Quixote" in *Labyrinths*. The work and life of an imaginary writer is described by a devoted biographer. As the story unfolds, some of the details begin to have a familiar ring: even the phony, mercantile, snobbish Mediterranean atmosphere seems to recall to us an actual person, and when we are told that Ménard published an early sonnet in a magazine called *La conque*, a reader of Valéry will identify the model without fail. (Several of Valéry's early poems in fact appeared in *La conque*, which was edited by Pierre Louys, though at a somewhat earlier date than the one given by Borges for Ménard's first publication.) When, a litter later, we find out that Ménard is the author of an invective against Paul Valéry, as well as the perpetrator of the shocking stylistic crime of transposing "*Le cimetière marin*" into alexandrines (Valéry has always insisted that the very essence of this famous poem resides in the decasyllabic meter), we can no longer doubt that we are dealing with Valéry's anti-self, in other words, Monsieur Teste. Things get a lot more complicated a few paragraphs later, when Ménard embarks on the curious project of re-inventing Don Quixote word for word, and by the time Borges treats us to a "close reading" of two identical passages from Don Quixote, one written by Cervantes, the other by Pierre Ménard (who is also Monsieur Teste, who is also Valéry) such a complex set of ironies, parodies, reflections, and issues are at play that no brief commentary can begin to do them justice.

Poetic invention begins in duplicity, but it does not stop there. For the writer's particular duplicity (the dyer's image in "Hakim") stems from the fact that he presents the invented form as if it possessed the attributes of reality, thus allowing it to be mimetically reproduced, in its turn, in another mirror-image that takes the preceding pseudo-reality for its starting-point. He is prompted "by the blasphemous intention of attributing the divine category of *being* to some mere [entities]." Consequently, the duplication grows into a proliferation of successive mirror-images. In "Tlön, Uqbar Orbis Tertius," for example, the plagiarized encyclopedia is itself falsified by someone who adds an entry on the imaginary region Uqbar, presenting it as if it were part of an imaginary country as *his* starting point, another falsifier (who, by the way, is a Southern segregationist millionaire) conjures up, with the assistance of a team of shady experts, a complete encyclopedia of a fictional planet called Tlön—a pseudo-reality equal in size to our own real world. This edition will be followed in turn by a revised and even more detailed edition written not in English but in one of the languages of Tlön and entitled *Orbis Tertius*.

All the stories have a similar mirror-like structure, although the devices vary with diabolical ingenuity. Sometimes, there is only one mirror-effect, as when at the end of "The Shape of the Sword" Vincent Moon reveals his true identity as the villain, not the hero, of his own story. But in most of Borges's stories, there are several layers of reflection. In "Theme of the Traitor and the Hero" from *Labyrinths* we have: (1) an actual historic event—a revolutionary leader betrays his confederates and has to be executed; (2) a fictional story about such an occurrence (though in reversed form)—Shakespeare's *Julius Caesar*; (3) an actual historic event which copies the fiction: the execution is carried out according to Shakespeare's plot, to make sure that it will be a good show; (4) the puzzled historian reflecting on the odd alternation of identical fictional and historical events, and deriving a false theory of historical archetypes from them; (5) the smarter historian Borges (or, rather, his duplicitous anti-self) reflecting on the credulous historian and reconstructing the true course of events. In other stories from *Labyrinths*, "The Immortal," "The Zahir," or "Death and the Compass," the complication is pushed so far that it is virtually impossible to describe.

This mirror-like proliferation constitutes, for Borges, an indication of poetic success. The works of literature he most admires contain this element; he is fascinated by such mirror-effects in literature as the Elizabethan play within the play, the character Don Quixote reading *Don Quixote*, Scheherazade beginning one night to retell *verbatim* the story of *The Thousand and One Nights*. For each mirrored image is stylistically superior to the preceding one, as the dyed cloth is more beautiful than the plain, the distorted translation richer than the original, Ménard's Quixote aesthetically more complex than Cervantes's. By carrying this process to its limits, the poet can achieve ultimate success—an ordered picture of reality that contains the totality of all things, subtly transformed and enriched by the imaginative process that engendered them. The imaginary world of Tlön is only one example of this poetic achievement; it recurs throughout Borges's work and constitutes, in fact, the central, climactic image around which each of the stories is organized. It can be the philosophically coherent set of laws that makes up the mental universe of Tlön, or it can be the fantastic world of a man blessed (as well as doomed) with the frightening gift of total recall, a man "who knows by heart the forms of the southern clouds at dawn on the 30th of April 1882" as well as "the stormy mane of a pony, the changing fire and its innumerable ashes" ("Funes the Memorious," in *Labyrinths*). It can be vastly expanded, like the infinitely complex labyrinth that is also an endless book in "The Garden of the Forking Paths," or highly compressed, like a certain spot in a certain house from which one can observe the entire universe ("The Aleph"), or a single coin which, however insignificant by itself, contains "universal history and the infinite concatenation of cause and effect" ("The Zahir"). All these points or domains of total vision symbolize the entirely successful and deceiving outcome of the poets irrepressible urge for order.

The success of these poetic worlds is expressed by their all-inclusive and ordered wholeness. Their deceitful nature is harder to define, but essential to an understanding of Borges. Mirror images are indeed duplications of reality, but they change the temporal nature of this reality in an insidious fashion, even—one might say especially—when the imitation is altogether successful (as in Ménard's Quixote). In actual experience, time appears to us as continuous but infinite; this continuity may seem reassuring, since it gives us some feeling of identity, but it is also terrifying, since it drags us irrevocably towards an unknowable future. Our "real" universe is like space: stable but chaotic. If, by an act of the mind comparable to Borges's will to style, we order this chaos, we may well succeed in achieving an order of sorts, but we dissolve the binding, spatial substance that held our chaotic universe together. Instead of an infinite mass of substance, we have a finite number of isolated events incapable of establishing relations among one another. The inhabitants of Borges's totally poetic world of Uqbar "do not conceive that the spatial persists in time. The perception of a cloud of smoke on the horizon and then of the burning field and then of the half-extinguished cigarette that produced the blaze is considered an example of association of ideas." This style in Borges becomes the ordering but dissolving act that transforms the unity of experience into the enumeration of its discontinuous parts. Hence his rejection of *style lié* and his preference for what grammarians call parataxis, the mere placing of events side by side, without conjunctions; hence also his definition of his own style as baroque, "the style that deliberately exhausts (or tries to exhaust) all its possibilities." The style is a mirror, but unlike the mirror of the realists that never lets us forget for a moment it creates what it mimics.

Probably because Borges is such a brilliant writer, his mirror-world is also profoundly, though always ironically, sinister. The shades of terror vary from the criminal gusto of the *History of Infamy* to the darker and shabbier world of the later *Ficciones*, and in *Dreamtigers* the violence is even starker and more somber, closer, I suppose, to the atmosphere of Borges's native Argentina. In the 1935 story, Hakim the impostor proclaimed: "The earth we live on is a mistake, a parody devoid of authority. Mirrors and paternity are abominable things, for they multiply this earth." This statement keeps recurring throughout the later work, but it becomes much more comprehensible there. Without ceasing to be the main metaphor for style, the mirror acquires deadly powers—a motif that runs throughout Western literature but of which Borges's version is particularly rich and complex. In his early work, the mirror of art represented the intention to keep the flow of time from losing itself forever in the shapeless void of infinity. Like the speculations of philosophers, style is an attempt at immortality. But this attempt is bound to fail. To quote one of Borges's favorite books, Sir Thomas Browne's *Hydrothapia, Urne-Buriall* (1658): "There is no antidote against the *Opium* of time, which temporarily considereth all things. . . ." This is not, as has been said, because Borges's God plays the same trick on the poet that the poet plays on reality; God does not turn out to be the archvillain set to deceive man into an illusion of eternity. The poetic impulse in all its perverse duplicity, belongs to man alone, marks him as essentially human. But God appears on the scene as the power of reality itself, in the form of a death that demonstrates the failure of poetry. This is the deeper reason for the violence that pervades all Borges's stories. God is on the side of chaotic reality and style is powerless to conquer him. His appearance is like the hideous face of Hakim when he loses the shining mask he has been wearing and reveals a face worn away by leprosy. The proliferation of mirrors is all the more terrifying because each new image brings us a step closer to this face.

As Borges grows older and his eye-sight gets steadily weaker, this final confrontation throws its darkening shadow over his entire work, without however extinguishing the lucidity of his language. For although the last reflection may be the face of God himself, with his appearance the life of poetry comes to an end. The situation is very similar to that of Kierkegaard's aesthetic man, with the difference that Borges refuses to give up his poetic predicament for a leap into faith. This confers a somber glory on the pages of *Dreamtigers*, so different from the shining brilliance of the stories in *Labyrinths*. To understand the full complexity of this later mood, one must have followed Borges's enterprise from the start and see it as the unfolding of a poetic destiny. This would not only require the translation into English of Borges's earlier work, but also serious critical studies worthy of this great writer.

Source: Jaime Alazraki, "A Modern Master," in *Critical Essays on Jorge Luis Borges*, G. K. Hall, 1987, pp. 55–61.

SOURCES

Bell-Villada, Gene H., *Borges and His Fiction: A Guide to His Mind and Art*, rev. ed., University of Texas Press, 1999, pp. 219–26.

Borges, Jorge Luis, "The Aleph," in *Collected Fictions*, translated by Andrew Hurley, Viking, 1998, pp. 274–86.

———, "Borges and I," in *Collected Fictions*, translated by Andrew Hurley, Viking, 1998, p. 324.

———, "A Defense of the Kabbalah," in *Selected Non-Fictions*, edited by Eliot Weinberger, translated by Suzanne Jill Levine, Viking, 1999, pp. 83–86.

———, "Narrative Art and Magic," in *Selected Non-Fictions*, edited by Eliot Weinberger, translated by Suzanne Jill Levine, Viking, 1999, pp. 75–82.

———, "The Zahir," in *Collected Fictions*, translated by Andrew Hurley, Viking, 1998, pp. 242–49.

Böwering, Gerhard, *The Mystical Vision of Existence in Classical Islam: Quranic Hermeneutics of the Sufi Sahl At-Tustari (d. 283/896)*, Walter de Gruyter, 1980, pp. 138–42, 198.

Chuchiak, John F., *The Inquisition in New Spain, 1536–1820: A Documentary History*, Johns Hopkins University Press, 2012, pp. 292–307.

Chute, John, "Borges, Jorge Luis," in *The Encyclopedia of Fantasy*, edited by John Chute and John Grant, St. Martin's, 1998, pp. 128–29.

Crone, Patricia, *The Nativist Prophets of Early Islamic Iran: Rural Revolt and Local Zoroastrianism*, Cambridge University Press, 2014, pp. 106–43.

Echevarría, Robert González, "The Aleph," in *The Cambridge Companion to Jorge Luis Borges*, Cambridge University Press, 2013, pp. 123–36.

López-Baralt, Luce, "Islamic Themes," in *The Cambridge Companion to Jorge Luis Borges*, Cambridge University Press, 2013, pp. 68–80.

Menton, Seymour, "Jorge Luis Borges, Magic Realist," in *Hispanic Review*, Vol. 50, No. 4, 1982, pp. 411–26.

Tausiet, María, *Urban Magic in Early Modern Spain: Abracadabra Omnipotens*, Palgrave Macmillian, 2014, pp. 1–8

Taylor, Philip Meadows, *Confessions of a Thug*, Richard Bentley, Vol. 3, 1839, p. 316.

———, *The Story of My Life*, William Blackwood, 1882, pp. 85–86.

Wells, H. G., "The Crystal Egg," in *Tales of Space and Time*, Macmillan, 1903, pp. 1–34.

Williamson, Edwin, *Borges: A Life*, Viking, 2004, pp. 167–68, 297–98.

FURTHER READING

Attar, Farid ud-Din, *The Conference of the Birds*, translated by Afkham Darbandi and Dick Davis, Penguin, 1984.
> Attar was a medieval Persian Sufi whose mystical theology is referenced in "The Zahir." His *Conference of the Birds* is a long allegorical poem about a quest by birds to find their ideal king. The poem reflects Sufi doctrine.

Borges, Jorge Luis, *Selected Poems*, edited by Alexander Coleman, Viking, 1999.
> Borges originally made his reputation as a poet, and this is the most extensive single collection of his work available in English. The poems are presented in a simultaneous edition, with the original Spanish facing the English version, prepared by a large number of translators.

Di Giovanni, Norman Thomas, *The Lesson of the Master*, Continuum, 2003.
> Norman Thomas Di Giovanni was Borges's chosen translator, with whom he worked closely to render his fiction into English. This is a collection of eight essays that are mainly recollections of his experiences working with Borges.

Sells, Michael Anthony, *Early Islamic Mysticism*, Classics of Western Spirituality, Paulist Press, 1994.
> This anthology of early Islamic mystical writings provides a survey of the mystical tradition in Islam that is the underlying basis of "The Zahir."

SUGGESTED SEARCH TERMS

Jorge Luis Borges

"The Zahir" AND Borges

The Aleph AND Borges

magic realism

surrealism

symbolism

allegory

Sufism

mysticism

Glossary of Literary Terms

A

Aestheticism: A literary and artistic movement of the nineteenth century. Followers of the movement believed that art should not be mixed with social, political, or moral teaching. The statement "art for art's sake" is a good summary of aestheticism. The movement had its roots in France, but it gained widespread importance in England in the last half of the nineteenth century, where it helped change the Victorian practice of including moral lessons in literature. Oscar Wilde and Edgar Allan Poe are two of the best-known "aesthetes" of the late nineteenth century.

Allegory: A narrative technique in which characters representing things or abstract ideas are used to convey a message or teach a lesson. Allegory is typically used to teach moral, ethical, or religious lessons but is sometimes used for satiric or political purposes. Many fairy tales are allegories.

Allusion: A reference to a familiar literary or historical person or event, used to make an idea more easily understood. Joyce Carol Oates's story "Where Are You Going, Where Have You Been?" exhibits several allusions to popular music.

Analogy: A comparison of two things made to explain something unfamiliar through its similarities to something familiar, or to prove one point based on the acceptance of another. Similes and metaphors are types of analogies.

Antagonist: The major character in a narrative or drama who works against the hero or protagonist. The Misfit in Flannery O'Connor's story "A Good Man Is Hard to Find" serves as the antagonist for the Grandmother.

Anthology: A collection of similar works of literature, art, or music. Zora Neale Hurston's "The Eatonville Anthology" is a collection of stories that take place in the same town.

Anthropomorphism: The presentation of animals or objects in human shape or with human characteristics. The term is derived from the Greek word for "human form." The fur necklet in Katherine Mansfield's story "Miss Brill" has anthropomorphic characteristics.

Anti-hero: A central character in a work of literature who lacks traditional heroic qualities such as courage, physical prowess, and fortitude. Anti-heroes typically distrust conventional values and are unable to commit themselves to any ideals. They generally feel helpless in a world over which they have no control. Anti-heroes usually accept, and often celebrate, their positions as social outcasts. A well-known anti-hero is Walter Mitty in James Thurber's story "The Secret Life of Walter Mitty."

Archetype: The word archetype is commonly used to describe an original pattern or model from which all other things of the same kind are made. Archetypes are the literary images that grow out of the "collective unconscious," a theory proposed by psychologist Carl Jung. They appear in literature as incidents and plots that repeat basic patterns of life. They may also appear as stereotyped characters. The "schlemiel" of Yiddish literature is an archetype.

Autobiography: A narrative in which an individual tells his or her life story. Examples include Benjamin Franklin's *Autobiography* and Amy Hempel's story "In the Cemetery Where Al Jolson Is Buried," which has autobiographical characteristics even though it is a work of fiction.

Avant-garde: A literary term that describes new writing that rejects traditional approaches to literature in favor of innovations in style or content. Twentieth-century examples of the literary avant-garde include the modernists and the minimalists.

B

Belles-lettres: A French term meaning "fine letters" or "beautiful writing." It is often used as a synonym for literature, typically referring to imaginative and artistic rather than scientific or expository writing. Current usage sometimes restricts the meaning to light or humorous writing and appreciative essays about literature. Lewis Carroll's *Alice in Wonderland* epitomizes the realm of belles-lettres.

Bildungsroman: A German word meaning "novel of development." The *bildungsroman* is a study of the maturation of a youthful character, typically brought about through a series of social or sexual encounters that lead to self-awareness. J. D. Salinger's *Catcher in the Rye* is a *bildungsroman*, and Doris Lessing's story "Through the Tunnel" exhibits characteristics of a *bildungsroman* as well.

Black Aesthetic Movement: A period of artistic and literary development among African Americans in the 1960s and early 1970s. This was the first major African-American artistic movement since the Harlem Renaissance and was closely paralleled by the civil rights and black power movements. The black aesthetic writers attempted to produce works of art that would be meaningful to the black masses. Key figures in black aesthetics included one of its founders, poet and playwright Amiri

Baraka, formerly known as Le Roi Jones; poet and essayist Haki R. Madhubuti, formerly Don L. Lee; poet and playwright Sonia Sanchez; and dramatist Ed Bullins. Works representative of the Black Aesthetic Movement include Amiri Baraka's play *Dutchman,* a 1964 Obie award-winner.

Black Humor: Writing that places grotesque elements side by side with humorous ones in an attempt to shock the reader, forcing him or her to laugh at the horrifying reality of a disordered world. "Lamb to the Slaughter," by Roald Dahl, in which a placid housewife murders her husband and serves the murder weapon to the investigating policemen, is an example of black humor.

C

Catharsis: The release or purging of unwanted emotions—specifically fear and pity—brought about by exposure to art. The term was first used by the Greek philosopher Aristotle in his *Poetics* to refer to the desired effect of tragedy on spectators.

Character: Broadly speaking, a person in a literary work. The actions of characters are what constitute the plot of a story, novel, or poem. There are numerous types of characters, ranging from simple, stereotypical figures to intricate, multifaceted ones. "Characterization" is the process by which an author creates vivid, believable characters in a work of art. This may be done in a variety of ways, including (1) direct description of the character by the narrator; (2) the direct presentation of the speech, thoughts, or actions of the character; and (3) the responses of other characters to the character. The term "character" also refers to a form originated by the ancient Greek writer Theophrastus that later became popular in the seventeenth and eighteenth centuries. It is a short essay or sketch of a person who prominently displays a specific attribute or quality, such as miserliness or ambition. "Miss Brill," a story by Katherine Mansfield, is an example of a character sketch.

Classical: In its strictest definition in literary criticism, classicism refers to works of ancient Greek or Roman literature. The term may also be used to describe a literary work of recognized importance (a "classic") from any time period or literature that exhibits the traits of classicism. Examples of later works and authors now described as classical include French literature of the seventeenth century, Western novels of the nineteenth century, and American fiction of the mid-nineteenth century such as that written by James Fenimore Cooper and Mark Twain.

Climax: The turning point in a narrative, the moment when the conflict is at its most intense. Typically, the structure of stories, novels, and plays is one of rising action, in which tension builds to the climax, followed by falling action, in which tension lessens as the story moves to its conclusion.

Comedy: One of two major types of drama, the other being tragedy. Its aim is to amuse, and it typically ends happily. Comedy assumes many forms, such as farce and burlesque, and uses a variety of techniques, from parody to satire. In a restricted sense the term comedy refers only to dramatic presentations, but in general usage it is commonly applied to nondramatic works as well.

Comic Relief: The use of humor to lighten the mood of a serious or tragic story, especially in plays. The technique is very common in Elizabethan works, and can be an integral part of the plot or simply a brief event designed to break the tension of the scene.

Conflict: The conflict in a work of fiction is the issue to be resolved in the story. It usually occurs between two characters, the protagonist and the antagonist, or between the protagonist and society or the protagonist and himself or herself. The conflict in Washington Irving's story "The Devil and Tom Walker" is that the Devil wants Tom Walker's soul but Tom does not want to go to hell.

Criticism: The systematic study and evaluation of literary works, usually based on a specific method or set of principles. An important part of literary studies since ancient times, the practice of criticism has given rise to numerous theories, methods, and "schools," sometimes producing conflicting, even contradictory, interpretations of literature in general as well as of individual works. Even such basic issues as what constitutes a poem or a novel have been the subject of much criticism over the centuries. Seminal texts of literary criticism include Plato's *Republic,* Aristotle's *Poetics,* Sir Philip Sidney's *The Defence of Poesie,* and John Dryden's *Of Dramatic Poesie.* Contemporary schools of criticism include deconstruction, feminist, psychoanalytic, poststructuralist, new historicist, postcolonialist, and reader-response.

D

Deconstruction: A method of literary criticism characterized by multiple conflicting interpretations of a given work. Deconstructionists consider the impact of the language of a work and suggest that the true meaning of the work is not necessarily the meaning that the author intended.

Deduction: The process of reaching a conclusion through reasoning from general premises to a specific premise. Arthur Conan Doyle's character Sherlock Holmes often used deductive reasoning to solve mysteries.

Denotation: The definition of a word, apart from the impressions or feelings it creates in the reader. The word "apartheid" denotes a political and economic policy of segregation by race, but its connotations—oppression, slavery, inequality—are numerous.

Denouement: A French word meaning "the unknotting." In literature, it denotes the resolution of conflict in fiction or drama. The *denouement* follows the climax and provides an outcome to the primary plot situation as well as an explanation of secondary plot complications. A well-known example of *denouement* is the last scene of the play *As You Like It* by William Shakespeare, in which couples are married, an evildoer repents, the identities of two disguised characters are revealed, and a ruler is restored to power. Also known as "falling action."

Detective Story: A narrative about the solution of a mystery or the identification of a criminal. The conventions of the detective story include the detective's scrupulous use of logic in solving the mystery; incompetent or ineffectual police; a suspect who appears guilty at first but is later proved innocent; and the detective's friend or confidant—often the narrator—whose slowness in interpreting clues emphasizes by contrast the detective's brilliance. Edgar Allan Poe's "Murders in the Rue Morgue" is commonly regarded as the earliest example of this type of story. Other practitioners are Arthur Conan Doyle, Dashiell Hammett, and Agatha Christie.

Dialogue: Dialogue is conversation between people in a literary work. In its most restricted sense, it refers specifically to the speech of characters in a drama. As a specific literary genre, a "dialogue" is a composition in which characters debate an issue or idea.

Didactic: A term used to describe works of literature that aim to teach a moral, religious, political, or practical lesson. Although didactic elements are often found inartistically pleasing works, the term "didactic" usually refers to literature in which the message is more important than the form. The term may also be used to criticize a work that the critic finds "overly didactic," that is, heavy-handed in its delivery of a lesson. An example of didactic literature is John Bunyan's *Pilgrim's Progress.*

Dramatic Irony: Occurs when the reader of a work of literature knows something that a character in the work itself does not know. The irony is in the contrast between the intended meaning of the statements or actions of a character and the additional information understood by the audience.

Dystopia: An imaginary place in a work of fiction where the characters lead dehumanized, fearful lives. George Orwell's *Nineteen Eighty-four,* and Margaret Atwood's *Handmaid's Tale* portray versions of dystopia.

E

Edwardian: Describes cultural conventions identified with the period of the reign of Edward VII of England (1901–1910). Writers of the Edwardian Age typically displayed a strong reaction against the propriety and conservatism of the Victorian Age. Their work often exhibits distrust of authority in religion, politics, and art and expresses strong doubts about the soundness of conventional values. Writers of this era include E. M. Forster, H. G. Wells, and Joseph Conrad.

Empathy: A sense of shared experience, including emotional and physical feelings, with someone or something other than oneself. Empathy is often used to describe the response of a reader to a literary character.

Epilogue: A concluding statement or section of a literary work. In dramas, particularly those of the seventeenth and eighteenth centuries, the epilogue is a closing speech, often in verse, delivered by an actor at the end of a play and spoken directly to the audience.

Epiphany: A sudden revelation of truth inspired by a seemingly trivial incident. The term was widely used by James Joyce in his critical writings, and the stories in Joyce's *Dubliners* are commonly called "epiphanies."

Epistolary Novel: A novel in the form of letters. The form was particularly popular in the eighteenth century. The form can also be applied to short stories, as in Edwidge Danticat's "Children of the Sea."

Epithet: A word or phrase, often disparaging or abusive, that expresses a character trait of someone or something. "The Napoleon of crime" is an epithet applied to Professor Moriarty, arch-rival of Sherlock Holmes in Arthur Conan Doyle's series of detective stories.

Existentialism: A predominantly twentieth-century philosophy concerned with the nature and perception of human existence. There are two major strains of existentialist thought: atheistic and Christian. Followers of atheistic existentialism believe that the individual is alone in a godless universe and that the basic human condition is one of suffering and loneliness. Nevertheless, because there are no fixed values, individuals can create their own characters—indeed, they can shape themselves—through the exercise of free will. The atheistic strain culminates in and is popularly associated with the works of Jean-Paul Sartre. The Christian existentialists, on the other hand, believe that only in God may people find freedom from life's anguish. The two strains hold certain beliefs in common: that existence cannot be fully understood or described through empirical effort; that anguish is a universal element of life; that individuals must bear responsibility for their actions; and that there is no common standard of behavior or perception for religious and ethical matters. Existentialist thought figures prominently in the works of such authors as Franz Kafka, Fyodor Dostoyevsky, and Albert Camus.

Expatriatism: The practice of leaving one's country to live for an extended period in another country. Literary expatriates include Irish author James Joyce who moved to Italy and France, American writers James Baldwin, Ernest Hemingway, Gertrude Stein, and F. Scott Fitzgerald who lived and wrote in

Paris, and Polish novelist Joseph Conrad in England.

Exposition: Writing intended to explain the nature of an idea, thing, or theme. Expository writing is often combined with description, narration, or argument.

Expressionism: An indistinct literary term, originally used to describe an early twentieth-century school of German painting. The term applies to almost any mode of unconventional, highly subjective writing that distorts reality in some way. Advocates of Expressionism include Federico Garcia Lorca, Eugene O'Neill, Franz Kafka, and James Joyce.

F

Fable: A prose or verse narrative intended to convey amoral. Animals or inanimate objects with human characteristics often serve as characters in fables. A famous fable is Aesop's "The Tortoise and the Hare."

Fantasy: A literary form related to mythology and folklore. Fantasy literature is typically set in non-existent realms and features supernatural beings. Notable examples of literature with elements of fantasy are Gabriel García Márquez's story "The Handsomest Drowned Man in the World" and Ursula K. Le Guin's "The Ones Who Walk Away from Omelas."

Farce: A type of comedy characterized by broad humor, outlandish incidents, and often vulgar subject matter. Much of the comedy in film and television could more accurately be described as farce.

Fiction: Any story that is the product of imagination rather than a documentation of fact. Characters and events in such narratives may be based in real life but their ultimate form and configuration is a creation of the author.

Figurative Language: A technique in which an author uses figures of speech such as hyperbole, irony, metaphor, or simile for a particular effect. Figurative language is the opposite of literal language, in which every word is truthful, accurate, and free of exaggeration or embellishment.

Flashback: A device used in literature to present action that occurred before the beginning of the story. Flashbacks are often introduced as the dreams or recollections of one or more characters.

Foil: A character in a work of literature whose physical or psychological qualities contrast strongly with, and therefore highlight, the corresponding qualities of another character. In his Sherlock Holmes stories, Arthur Conan Doyle portrayed Dr. Watson as a man of normal habits and intelligence, making him a foil for the eccentric and unusually perceptive Sherlock Holmes.

Folklore: Traditions and myths preserved in a culture or group of people. Typically, these are passed on by word of mouth in various forms—such as legends, songs, and proverbs—or preserved in customs and ceremonies. Washington Irving, in "The Devil and Tom Walker" and many of his other stories, incorporates many elements of the folklore of New England and Germany.

Folktale: A story originating in oral tradition. Folk tales fall into a variety of categories, including legends, ghost stories, fairy tales, fables, and anecdotes based on historical figures and events.

Foreshadowing: A device used in literature to create expectation or to set up an explanation of later developments. Edgar Allan Poe uses foreshadowing to create suspense in "The Fall of the House of Usher" when the narrator comments on the crumbling state of disrepair in which he finds the house.

G

Genre: A category of literary work. Genre may refer to both the content of a given work—tragedy, comedy, horror, science fiction—and to its form, such as poetry, novel, or drama.

Gilded Age: A period in American history during the 1870s and after characterized by political corruption and materialism. A number of important novels of social and political criticism were written during this time. Henry James and Kate Chopin are two writers who were prominent during the Gilded Age.

Gothicism: In literature, works characterized by a taste for medieval or morbid characters and situations. A gothic novel prominently features elements of horror, the supernatural, gloom, and violence: clanking chains, terror, ghosts, medieval castles, and unexplained phenomena. The term "gothic novel" is also applied to novels that lack elements of the traditional Gothic setting but that create a similar atmosphere of terror or dread. The term can also be applied to stories, plays, and poems. Mary Shelley's *Frankenstein* and Joyce Carol Oates's *Bellefleur* are both gothic novels.

Grotesque: In literature, a work that is characterized by exaggeration, deformity, freakishness, and disorder. The grotesque often includes an element of comic absurdity. Examples of the grotesque can be found in the works of Edgar Allan Poe, Flannery O'Connor, Joseph Heller, and Shirley Jackson.

H

Harlem Renaissance: The Harlem Renaissance of the 1920s is generally considered the first significant movement of black writers and artists in the United States. During this period, new and established black writers, many of whom lived in the region of New York City known as Harlem, published more fiction and poetry than ever before, the first influential black literary journals were established, and black authors and artists received their first widespread recognition and serious critical appraisal. Among the major writers associated with this period are Countee Cullen, Langston Hughes, Arna Bontemps, and Zora Neale Hurston.

Hero/Heroine: The principal sympathetic character in a literary work. Heroes and heroines typically exhibit admirable traits: idealism, courage, and integrity, for example. Famous heroes and heroines of literature include Charles Dickens's Oliver Twist, Margaret Mitchell's Scarlett O'Hara, and the anonymous narrator in Ralph Ellison's *Invisible Man*.

Hyperbole: Deliberate exaggeration used to achieve an effect. In William Shakespeare's *Macbeth,* Lady Macbeth hyperbolizes when she says, "All the perfumes of Arabia could not sweeten this little hand."

I

Image: A concrete representation of an object or sensory experience. Typically, such a representation helps evoke the feelings associated with the object or experience itself. Images are either "literal" or "figurative." Literal images are especially concrete and involve little or no extension of the obvious meaning of the words used to express them. Figurative images do not follow the literal meaning of the words exactly. Images in literature are usually visual, but the term "image" can also refer to the representation of any sensory experience.

Imagery: The array of images in a literary work. Also used to convey the author's overall use of figurative language in a work.

In medias res: A Latin term meaning "in the middle of things." It refers to the technique of beginning a story at its midpoint and then using various flashback devices to reveal previous action. This technique originated in such epics as Virgil's *Aeneid*.

Interior Monologue: A narrative technique in which characters' thoughts are revealed in a way that appears to be uncontrolled by the author. The interior monologue typically aims to reveal the inner self of a character. It portrays emotional experiences as they occur at both a conscious and unconscious level. One of the best-known interior monologues in English is the Molly Bloom section at the close of James Joyce's *Ulysses*. Katherine Anne Porter's "The Jilting of Granny Weatherall" is also told in the form of an interior monologue.

Irony: In literary criticism, the effect of language in which the intended meaning is the opposite of what is stated. The title of Jonathan Swift's "A Modest Proposal" is ironic because what Swift proposes in this essay is cannibalism—hardly "modest."

J

Jargon: Language that is used or understood only by a select group of people. Jargon may refer to terminology used in a certain profession, such as computer jargon, or it may refer to any nonsensical language that is not understood by most people. Anthony Burgess's *A Clockwork Orange* and James Thurber's "The Secret Life of Walter Mitty" both use jargon.

K

Knickerbocker Group: An indistinct group of New York writers of the first half of the nineteenth century. Members of the group were linked only by location and a common theme: New York life. Two famous members of the Knickerbocker Group were Washington Irving and William Cullen Bryant. The group's name derives from Irving's *Knickerbocker's History of New York*.

L

Literal Language: An author uses literal language when he or she writes without exaggerating or embellishing the subject matter and without any tools of figurative language. To say "He ran very quickly down the street" is to use literal language, whereas to say "He ran like a hare down the street" would be using figurative language.

Literature: Literature is broadly defined as any written or spoken material, but the term most often refers to creative works. Literature includes poetry, drama, fiction, and many kinds of nonfiction writing, as well as oral, dramatic, and broadcast compositions not necessarily preserved in a written format, such as films and television programs.

Lost Generation: A term first used by Gertrude Stein to describe the post–World War I generation of American writers: men and women haunted by a sense of betrayal and emptiness brought about by the destructiveness of the war. The term is commonly applied to Hart Crane, Ernest Hemingway, F. Scott Fitzgerald, and others.

M

Magic Realism: A form of literature that incorporates fantasy elements or supernatural occurrences into the narrative and accepts them as truth. Gabriel Gárcia Márquez and Laura Esquivel are two writers known for their works of magic realism.

Metaphor: A figure of speech that expresses an idea through the image of another object. Metaphors suggest the essence of the first object by identifying it with certain qualities of the second object. An example is "But soft, what light through yonder window breaks? / It is the east, and Juliet is the sun" in William Shakespeare's *Romeo and Juliet*. Here, Juliet, the first object, is identified with qualities of the second object, the sun.

Minimalism: A literary style characterized by spare, simple prose with few elaborations. In minimalism, the main theme of the work is often never discussed directly. Amy

Hempel and Ernest Hemingway are two writers known for their works of minimalism.

Modernism: Modern literary practices. Also, the principles of a literary school that lasted from roughly the beginning of the twentieth century until the end of World War II. Modernism is defined by its rejection of the literary conventions of the nineteenth century and by its opposition to conventional morality, taste, traditions, and economic values. Many writers are associated with the concepts of modernism, including Albert Camus, D. H. Lawrence, Ernest Hemingway, William Faulkner, Eugene O'Neill, and James Joyce.

Monologue: A composition, written or oral, by a single individual. More specifically, a speech given by a single individual in a drama or other public entertainment. It has no set length, although it is usually several or more lines long. "I Stand Here Ironing" by Tillie Olsen is an example of a story written in the form of a monologue.

Mood: The prevailing emotions of a work or of the author in his or her creation of the work. The mood of a work is not always what might be expected based on its subject matter.

Motif: A theme, character type, image, metaphor, or other verbal element that recurs throughout a single work of literature or occurs in a number of different works over a period of time. For example, the color white in Herman Melville's *Moby Dick* is a "specific" motif, while the trials of star-crossed lovers is a "conventional" motif from the literature of all periods.

N

Narration: The telling of a series of events, real or invented. A narration may be either a simple narrative, in which the events are recounted chronologically, or a narrative with a plot, in which the account is given in a style reflecting the author's artistic concept of the story. Narration is sometimes used as a synonym for "storyline."

Narrative: A verse or prose accounting of an event or sequence of events, real or invented. The term is also used as an adjective in the sense "method of narration." For example, in literary criticism, the expression "narrative technique" usually refers to the way the author structures and presents his or her story. Different narrative forms include diaries, travelogues, novels, ballads, epics, short stories, and other fictional forms.

Narrator: The teller of a story. The narrator may be the author or a character in the story through whom the author speaks. Huckleberry Finn is the narrator of Mark Twain's *The Adventures of Huckleberry Finn.*

Novella: An Italian term meaning "story." This term has been especially used to describe fourteenth-century Italian tales, but it also refers to modern short novels. Modern novellas include Leo Tolstoy's *The Death of Ivan Ilich,* Fyodor Dostoyevsky's *Notes from the Underground,* and Joseph Conrad's *Heart of Darkness.*

O

Oedipus Complex: A son's romantic obsession with his mother. The phrase is derived from the story of the ancient Theban hero Oedipus, who unknowingly killed his father and married his mother, and was popularized by Sigmund Freud's theory of psychoanalysis. Literary occurrences of the Oedipus complex include Sophocles' *Oedipus Rex* and D. H. Lawrence's "The Rocking-Horse Winner."

Onomatopoeia: The use of words whose sounds express or suggest their meaning. In its simplest sense, onomatopoeia may be represented by words that mimic the sounds they denote such as "hiss" or "meow." At a more subtle level, the pattern and rhythm of sounds and rhymes of a line or poem may be onomatopoeic.

Oral Tradition: A process by which songs, ballads, folklore, and other material are transmitted by word of mouth. The tradition of oral transmission predates the written record systems of literate society. Oral transmission preserves material sometimes over generations, although often with variations. Memory plays a large part in the recitation and preservation of orally transmitted material. Native American myths and legends, and African folktales told by plantation slaves are examples of orally transmitted literature.

P

Parable: A story intended to teach a moral lesson or answer an ethical question. Examples of parables are the stories told by Jesus Christ in the New Testament, notably "The Prodigal Son," but parables also are used in Sufism, rabbinic literature, Hasidism, and Zen Buddhism. Isaac Bashevis Singer's story "Gimpel the Fool" exhibits characteristics of a parable.

Paradox: A statement that appears illogical or contradictory at first, but may actually point to an underlying truth. A literary example of a paradox is George Orwell's statement "All animals are equal, but some animals are more equal than others" in *Animal Farm.*

Parody: In literature, this term refers to an imitation of a serious literary work or the signature style of a particular author in a ridiculous manner. Atypical parody adopts the style of the original and applies it to an inappropriate subject for humorous effect. Parody is a form of satire and could be considered the literary equivalent of a caricature or cartoon. Henry Fielding's *Shamela* is a parody of Samuel Richardson's *Pamela.*

Persona: A Latin term meaning "mask." Personae are the characters in a fictional work of literature. The persona generally functions as a mask through which the author tells a story in a voice other than his or her own. A persona is usually either a character in a story who acts as a narrator or an "implied author," a voice created by the author to act as the narrator for himself or herself. The persona in Charlotte Perkins Gilman's story "The Yellow Wallpaper" is the unnamed young mother experiencing a mental breakdown.

Personification: A figure of speech that gives human qualities to abstract ideas, animals, and inanimate objects. To say that "the sun is smiling" is to personify the sun.

Plot: The pattern of events in a narrative or drama. In its simplest sense, the plot guides the author in composing the work and helps the reader follow the work. Typically, plots exhibit causality and unity and have a beginning, a middle, and an end. Sometimes, however, a plot may consist of a series of disconnected events, in which case it is known as an "episodic plot."

Poetic Justice: An outcome in a literary work, not necessarily a poem, in which the good are rewarded and the evil are punished, especially in ways that particularly fit their virtues or crimes. For example, a murderer may himself be murdered, or a thief will find himself penniless.

Poetic License: Distortions of fact and literary convention made by a writer—not always a poet—for the sake of the effect gained. Poetic license is closely related to the concept of "artistic freedom." An author exercises poetic license by saying that a pile of money "reaches as high as a mountain" when the pile is actually only a foot or two high.

Point of View: The narrative perspective from which a literary work is presented to the reader. There are four traditional points of view. The "third person omniscient" gives the reader a "godlike" perspective, unrestricted by time or place, from which to see actions and look into the minds of characters. This allows the author to comment openly on characters and events in the work. The "third person" point of view presents the events of the story from outside of any single character's perception, much like the omniscient point of view, but the reader must understand the action as it takes place and without any special insight into characters' minds or motivations. The "first person" or "personal" point of view relates events as they are perceived by a single character. The main character "tells" the story and may offer opinions about the action and characters which differ from those of the author. Much less common than omniscient, third person, and first person is the "second person" point of view, wherein the author tells the story as if it is happening to the reader. James Thurber employs the omniscient point of view in his short story "The Secret Life of Walter Mitty." Ernest Hemingway's "A Clean, Well-Lighted Place" is a short story told from the third person point of view. Mark Twain's novel *Huckleberry Finn* is presented from the first person viewpoint. Jay McInerney's *Bright Lights, Big City* is an example of a novel which uses the second person point of view.

Pornography: Writing intended to provoke feelings of lust in the reader. Such works are often condemned by critics and teachers, but those which can be shown to have literary value are viewed less harshly. Literary works that have been described as pornographic include D. H. Lawrence's *Lady Chatterley's Lover* and James Joyce's *Ulysses*.

Post-Aesthetic Movement: An artistic response made by African Americans to the black aesthetic movement of the 1960s and early 1970s. Writers since that time have adopted a somewhat different tone in their work, with less emphasis placed on the disparity between black and white in the United States. In the words of post-aesthetic authors such as Toni Morrison, John Edgar Wideman, and Kristin Hunter, African Americans are portrayed as looking inward for answers to their own questions, rather than always looking to the outside world. Two well-known examples of works produced as part of the post-aesthetic movement are the Pulitzer Prize–winning novels *The Color Purple* by Alice Walker and *Beloved* by Toni Morrison.

Postmodernism: Writing from the 1960s forward characterized by experimentation and application of modernist elements, which include existentialism and alienation. Postmodernists have gone a step further in the rejection of tradition begun with the modernists by also rejecting traditional forms, preferring the anti-novel over the novel and the anti-hero over the hero. Postmodern writers include Thomas Pynchon, Margaret Drabble, and Gabriel García Márquez.

Prologue: An introductory section of a literary work. It often contains information establishing the situation of the characters or presents information about the setting, time period, or action. In drama, the prologue is spoken by a chorus or by one of the principal characters.

Prose: A literary medium that attempts to mirror the language of everyday speech. It is distinguished from poetry by its use of unmetered, unrhymed language consisting of logically related sentences. Prose is usually grouped into paragraphs that form a cohesive whole such as an essay or a novel. The term is sometimes used to mean an author's general writing.

Protagonist: The central character of a story who serves as a focus for its themes and incidents and as the principal rationale for its development. The protagonist is sometimes referred to in discussions of modern literature as the hero or anti-hero. Well-known protagonists are Hamlet in William Shakespeare's *Hamlet* and Jay Gatsby in F. Scott Fitzgerald's *The Great Gatsby*.

R

Realism: A nineteenth-century European literary movement that sought to portray familiar characters, situations, and settings in a realistic manner. This was done primarily by using an objective narrative point of view and through the buildup of accurate detail. The standard for success of any realistic work depends on how faithfully it transfers common experience into fictional forms. The realistic method may be altered or extended, as in stream of consciousness writing, to record highly subjective experience. Contemporary authors who often write in a realistic way include Nadine Gordimer and Grace Paley.

Resolution: The portion of a story following the climax, in which the conflict is resolved. The resolution of Jane Austen's *Northanger Abbey* is neatly summed up in the following sentence: "Henry and Catherine were married, the bells rang and every body smiled."

Rising Action: The part of a drama where the plot becomes increasingly complicated. Rising action leads up to the climax, or turning point, of a drama. The final "chase scene" of an action film is generally the rising action which culminates in the film's climax.

Roman a clef: A French phrase meaning "novel with a key." It refers to a narrative in which real persons are portrayed under fictitious names. Jack Kerouac, for example, portrayed various friends under fictitious names in the novel *On the Road*. D. H. Lawrence based "The Rocking-Horse Winner" on a family he knew.

Romanticism: This term has two widely accepted meanings. In historical criticism, it refers to a European intellectual and artistic movement of the late eighteenth and early nineteenth centuries that sought greater freedom of personal expression than that allowed by the strict rules of literary form and logic of the eighteenth-century neoclassicists. The Romantics preferred emotional and imaginative expression to rational analysis. They considered the individual to be at the center of all experience and so placed him or her at the center of their art. The Romantics believed that the creative imagination reveals nobler truths—unique feelings and attitudes—than those that could be discovered by logic or by scientific examination. "Romanticism" is also used as a general term to refer to a type of sensibility found in all periods of literary history and usually considered to be in opposition to the principles of classicism. In this sense, Romanticism signifies any work or philosophy in which the exotic or dreamlike figure strongly, or that is devoted to individualistic expression, self-analysis, or a pursuit of a higher realm of knowledge than can be discovered by human reason. Prominent Romantics include Jean-Jacques Rousseau, William Wordsworth, John Keats, Lord Byron, and Johann Wolfgang von Goethe.

S

Satire: A work that uses ridicule, humor, and wit to criticize and provoke change in human nature and institutions. Voltaire's novella *Candide* and Jonathan Swift's essay "A Modest Proposal" are both satires. Flannery O'Connor's portrayal of the family in "A Good Man Is Hard to Find" is a satire of a modern, Southern, American family.

Science Fiction: A type of narrative based upon real or imagined scientific theories and technology. Science fiction is often peopled with alien creatures and set on other planets or in different dimensions. Popular writers of science fiction are Isaac Asimov, Karel Capek, Ray Bradbury, and Ursula K. Le Guin.

Setting: The time, place, and culture in which the action of a narrative takes place. The elements of setting may include geographic location, characters's physical and mental environments, prevailing cultural attitudes, or the historical time in which the action takes place.

Short Story: A fictional prose narrative shorter and more focused than a novella. The short story usually deals with a single episode and often a single character. The "tone," the author's attitude toward his or her subject and audience, is uniform throughout. The short story frequently also lacks *denouement*, ending instead at its climax.

Signifying Monkey: A popular trickster figure in black folklore, with hundreds of tales about this character documented since the 19th century. Henry Louis Gates Jr. examines the history of the signifying monkey in *The Signifying Monkey: Towards a Theory of Afro-American Literary Criticism,* published in 1988.

Simile: A comparison, usually using "like" or "as," of two essentially dissimilar things, as in "coffee as cold as ice" or "He sounded like a broken record." The title of Ernest Hemingway's "Hills Like White Elephants" contains a simile.

Socialist Realism: The Socialist Realism school of literary theory was proposed by Maxim Gorky and established as a dogma by the first Soviet Congress of Writers. It demanded adherence to a communist worldview in works of literature. Its doctrines required an objective viewpoint comprehensible to the working classes and themes of social struggle featuring strong proletarian heroes. Gabriel Gárcia Márquez's stories exhibit some characteristics of Socialist Realism.

Stereotype: A stereotype was originally the name for a duplication made during the printing process; this led to its modern definition as a person or thing that is (or is assumed to be) the same as all others of its type. Common stereotypical characters include the absent-minded professor, the nagging wife, the troublemaking teenager, and the kindhearted grandmother.

Stream of Consciousness: A narrative technique for rendering the inward experience of a character. This technique is designed to give the impression of an ever-changing series of thoughts, emotions, images, and memories in the spontaneous and seemingly illogical order that they occur in life. The textbook example of stream of consciousness is the last section of James Joyce's *Ulysses*.

Structure: The form taken by a piece of literature. The structure may be made obvious for ease of understanding, as in nonfiction works, or may obscured for artistic purposes, as in some poetry or seemingly "unstructured" prose.

Style: A writer's distinctive manner of arranging words to suit his or her ideas and purpose in writing. The unique imprint of the author's personality upon his or her writing, style is the product of an author's way of arranging ideas and his or her use of diction, different sentence structures, rhythm, figures of speech, rhetorical principles, and other elements of composition.

Suspense: A literary device in which the author maintains the audience's attention through the buildup of events, the outcome of which will soon be revealed. Suspense in William Shakespeare's *Hamlet* is sustained throughout by the question of whether or not the Prince will achieve what he has been instructed to do and of what he intends to do.

Symbol: Something that suggests or stands for something else without losing its original identity. In literature, symbols combine their literal meaning with the suggestion of an abstract concept. Literary symbols are of two types: those that carry complex associations of meaning no matter what their contexts, and those that derive their suggestive meaning from their functions in specific literary works. Examples of symbols are sunshine suggesting happiness, rain suggesting sorrow, and storm clouds suggesting despair.

T

Tale: A story told by a narrator with a simple plot and little character development. Tales are usually relatively short and often carry a simple message. Examples of tales can be found in the works of Saki, Anton Chekhov, Guy de Maupassant, and O. Henry.

Tall Tale: A humorous tale told in a straightforward, credible tone but relating absolutely impossible events or feats of the characters. Such tales were commonly told of frontier adventures during the settlement of the west in the United States. Literary use of tall tales can be found in Washington Irving's *History of New York*, Mark Twain's *Life on the Mississippi*, and in the German R. F. Raspe's *Baron Munchausen's Narratives of His Marvellous Travels and Campaigns in Russia*.

Theme: The main point of a work of literature. The term is used interchangeably with thesis. Many works have multiple themes. One of the themes of Nathaniel Hawthorne's "Young Goodman Brown" is loss of faith.

Tone: The author's attitude toward his or her audience maybe deduced from the tone of the work. A formal tone may create distance or convey politeness, while an informal tone may encourage a friendly, intimate, or intrusive feeling in the reader. The author's attitude toward his or her subject matter may also be deduced from the tone of the words he or she uses in discussing it. The tone of John F. Kennedy's speech which included the appeal to "ask not what your country can do for you" was intended to instill feelings of camaraderie and national pride in listeners.

Tragedy: A drama in prose or poetry about a noble, courageous hero of excellent character who, because of some tragic character flaw, brings ruin upon him- or herself. Tragedy treats its subjects in a dignified and serious manner, using poetic language to help evoke pity and fear and bring about catharsis, a purging of these emotions. The tragic form was practiced extensively by the ancient Greeks. The classical form of tragedy was revived in the sixteenth century; it flourished especially on the Elizabethan stage. In modern times, dramatists have attempted to adapt the form to the needs of modern society by drawing their heroes from the ranks of ordinary men and women and defining the nobility of these heroes in terms of spirit rather than exalted social standing. Some contemporary works that are thought of as tragedies include *The Great Gatsby* by F. Scott Fitzgerald, and *The Sound and the Fury* by William Faulkner.

Tragic Flaw: In a tragedy, the quality within the hero or heroine which leads to his or her downfall. Examples of the tragic flaw include Othello's jealousy and Hamlet's indecisiveness, although most great tragedies defy such simple interpretation.

U

Utopia: A fictional perfect place, such as "paradise" or "heaven." An early literary utopia was described in Plato's *Republic,* and in modern literature, Ursula K. Le Guin depicts a utopia in "The Ones Who Walk Away from Omelas."

V

Victorian: Refers broadly to the reign of Queen Victoria of England (1837–1901) and to anything with qualities typical of that era. For example, the qualities of smug narrow-mindedness, bourgeois materialism, faith in social progress, and priggish morality are often considered Victorian. In literature, the Victorian Period was the great age of the English novel, and the latter part of the era saw the rise of movements such as decadence and symbolism.

Cumulative Author/Title Index

Cumulative Nationality/Ethnicity Index

Subject/Theme Index

Poetry
Blackness: 6, 8
Point of view (Literature)
Diary of a Madman: 34–35
Fat of the Land: 86
The Moonlit Road: 126–127
Sinking House: 237
Politics
Diary of a Madman: 51
Popular culture
Railroad Standard Time: 178–181
Sinking House: 247
Possessiveness
Sweetheart of the Song Tra Bong: 268, 269
Postcolonialism
Blackness: 11, 15, 16
Postmodernism
Blackness: 6
Railroad Standard Time: 170–171, 173
Sinking House: 245, 248
Sweetheart of the Song Tra Bong: 260
Poverty
Fat of the Land: 88, 90, 91
The Secret of Cartwheels: 208
Power (Philosophy)
Blackness: 10
Open Secrets: 144, 157
Powerlessness. *See* Impotence
Progressive era
Fat of the Land: 94
Psychoanalysis
Diary of a Madman: 29, 31
The Zahir: 286–287, 289

R

Race relations
Emmy: 65–66, 75–77
Racial identity
Blackness: 8, 10–13, 15
Emmy: 62, 65–66
Racism
Emmy: 72, 74
Railroad Standard Time: 183
Sinking House: 247
Sweetheart of the Song Tra Bong: 270
Rationality
Emmy: 71–74
Realism
Fat of the Land: 84, 89
The Fly: 111–112, 115
The Moonlit Road: 138
The Secret of Cartwheels: 215–216
Sinking House: 248
Reality
Diary of a Madman: 34–37
Open Secrets: 157, 158
Rebellion
Blackness: 15
Refugees
Refuge in London: 187, 198

Reliability
The Moonlit Road: 130–132
Open Secrets: 156, 161
Religion
Blackness: 7
Diary of a Madman: 51, 53
The Moonlit Road: 135
The Zahir: 285–286, 289
Repetition
Blackness: 14
Diary of a Madman: 32–34
Resentment
Blackness: 11
Fat of the Land: 89
Railroad Standard Time: 177
The Secret Life of Cartwheels: 221
The Secret of Cartwheels: 214
Rhythm
Fat of the Land: 79
Right and wrong
Railroad Standard Time: 180
Rituals
Railroad Standard Time: 167
Romantic love
Emmy: 73
Rumor
Open Secrets: 144, 146, 149–150, 156
Russian history
Diary of a Madman: 27, 46–48

S

Sadism
The Fly: 101, 115, 117, 118
Sadness
The Secret of Cartwheels: 220
Sinking House: 232
Satire
Diary of a Madman: 18, 24, 28, 49
Sinking House: 245
Secrets
Open Secrets: 146, 159
Self
Blackness: 5, 14
Self deception
The Fly: 105
Self hatred
Railroad Standard Time: 179
Self identity
Blackness: 14
Railroad Standard Time: 181
Self reliance
The Secret of Cartwheels: 214
Selfishness
The Secret of Cartwheels: 220
Sentimentality
Emmy: 71–74
The Moonlit Road: 129
Separation
Blackness: 11
Sinking House: 236

Setting (Literature)
The Fly: 115
The Moonlit Road: 127
Sex roles
Sinking House: 243
Sweetheart of the Song Tra Bong: 261, 267
Sexism
Railroad Standard Time: 183
Sweetheart of the Song Tra Bong: 270–271
Sexual politics
Railroad Standard Time: 184
Sexuality
Refuge in London: 201, 202
Shame
The Secret of Cartwheels: 220
Silence
Blackness: 12
Sinking House: 231
Sin
The Moonlit Road: 135
Small town life
Open Secrets: 146, 151
Social change
Sinking House: 246
Social class
Diary of a Madman: 33
The Dream of a Ridiculous Man: 40
Open Secrets: 150–151
Social commentary
Fat of the Land: 88
Sinking House: 244
Social conventions
Emmy: 77
Social criticism
Fat of the Land: 94
Social satire
Diary of a Madman: 19
Sinking House: 245
Socialism
Diary of a Madman: 49
Spanish history
Diary of a Madman: 26
Spirits
The Moonlit Road: 124, 132
Spirituality
Blackness: 5, 7, 8
Diary of a Madman: 51–52
The Moonlit Road: 129, 135
Spouse abuse. *See* Domestic violence
Stereotypes
Railroad Standard Time: 177, 184, 185
Storytelling
Railroad Standard Time: 173
Sweetheart of the Song Tra Bong: 252, 253, 257–258, 264, 266, 271–274
Struggle
The Fly: 108